Different Minds

of related interest

Asperger's Syndrome
A Guide for Parents and Professionals
Tony Attwood
Foreword by Lorna Wing
ISBN 1 85302 577 1

Freaks, Geeks and Asperger Syndrome
A User Guide to Adolescence
Luke Jackson
Foreword by Tony Attwood
ISBN 1 84310 098 3

Pretending to be Normal
Living with Asperger's Syndrome
Liane Holliday Willey
Foreword by Tony Attwood
ISBN 1 85302 749 9

The ADHD Handbook
A Guide for Parents and Professionals
Alison Munden and Jon Arcelus
ISBN 1 85302 756 1

Bright Splinters of the Mind
A Personal Story of Research with Autistic Savants
Beate Hermelin
Foreword by Sir Michael Rutter
ISBN 1 85302 932 7 pb
ISBN 1 85302 931 9 hb

Different Minds

Gifted Children with AD/HD, Asperger Syndrome, and Other Learning Deficits

Deirdre V. Lovecky

Jessica Kingsley Publishers
London and New York

First published in the United Kingdom in 2004
by Jessica Kingsley Publishers
116 Pentonville Road
London N1 9JB, UK
and
400 Market Street, Suite 400
Philadelphia, PA 19106, USA

www.jkp.com

Library of Congress Cataloging in Publication Data
Lovecky, Deirdre V., 1945-
    Different minds : gifted children with AD/HD, Asperger syndrome, and other learning deficits
/ Deirdre V. Lovecky.— 1st American pbk. ed.
        p. cm.
    ISBN 1-85302-964-5
    1. Gifted children—Mental health. 2. Attention-deficit hyperactivity
disorder. 3. Asperger's syndrome. I. Title.
    RJ507.G55L68 2004
    618.92'8589—dc22

                                                    2003026799

British Library Cataloguing in Publication Data
A CIP catalogue record for this book is available from the British Library

ISBN-13: 978 1 85302 964 6
ISBN-10: 1 85302 964 5

Printed and Bound in Great Britain by
Athenaeum Press, Gateshead, Tyne and Wear

Contents

Acknowledgments

It is always hard to acknowledge everyone who helped in the making of a book, especially when the book has been long in the writing. I would first, and foremost, thank all those parents who allowed me to know their lives with their children, and who graciously allowed me to use little pieces of who they are in the anecdotes. Without you, there would not be a book.

I would like to thank my professional colleagues who encouraged the writing of this book, especially Linda Silverman and Julia Osborn. Both contributed much of their long experience with gifted children and learning differences to help me formulate my initial ideas. I would also thank Ellen Winner for helping me to understand how Theory of Mind might function in gifted children.

John Ratey and Tony Attwood helped me in formulating some ideas about giftedness and Attention Deficit/Hyperactivity Disorder (AD/HD) and Asperger Syndrome (AS), especially on what causes AD/HD and AS, and on the topic of creativity. I value both their friendship and their thoughtful replies immensely.

My readers deserve special thanks. Julia Osborn read the first draft of this book and offered many helpful comments about point of view. She also gave me her professional opinion about the strengths and weaknesses of the newest Wechsler and Stanford-Binet IQ tests. Ruth Breindel and Mary Codd read the whole book in the final draft and helped with organization and wording, never my strong points. Both of them, along with Joan Hornsby and Stephanie Machell, have given friendship and support throughout.

I could not have written this book without the help of the special Librarians at Rhode Island College Adams Library and Province Public Library Fox Point Branch who helped me get references as well as learn to access and utilize online services.

I certainly want to thank Jessica Kingsley and her staff for their help in putting this book together, and for their patience as I rewrote it, and then changed it again.

Finally, of course, I thank Honey, my dog, for her sweet help with my patients, her excellent guarding of the house, and her wonderful companionship.

In memory of the Reverend Thomas E. Ahlburn
who allowed me to share part of his wondrous journey.
I will never forget.

May all beings be happy. Or something like that.

Introduction

The idea for writing this book arose from the frustration of parents discussing their gifted children's attention problems. Being parents of gifted children, and usually gifted themselves, these parents had an insatiable curiosity about giftedness, Attention Deficit/Hyperactivity Disorder (AD/HD), Asperger Syndrome (AS), Nonverbal Learning Disability (NVLD), and all the other parenting and educational issues they brought to discuss. What they wanted was a book that would give them information about their child's problems, and also would have helpful suggestions about what to do, far beyond what I was able to tell them in a report or feedback session. There were no such books.

"Why don't you write a book?" they would ask. So eventually, I decided I would, because there is a need for a book that discusses not only the disorders, but also the issue of giftedness and how being gifted amplifies problems or ameliorates them.

The central themes of this book

Giftedness

This book focuses on gifted children with a particular emphasis on the special needs and strengths of those with attention deficits. This is a book about giftedness because a person cannot be viewed separate from his or her giftedness. Giftedness isn't a part of a person, like hair color, but all of a person, more like personality. Thus, in each chapter, differing aspects of giftedness are explored, and certain themes followed. This is not a book specifically about parenting gifted children, or teaching or counseling them. Though each chapter has some suggestions for parenting, teaching, and/or counseling, this book hopes to show a bigger picture: how being gifted brings to each person special strengths and weaknesses.

This book is not just about AD/HD. There are many wonderful books about parenting, teaching, and counseling children with AD/HD. In fact, what this book hopes to show is that one cannot separate giftedness from AD/HD either. They are both part and parcel of a person, and being both gifted and AD/HD brings a special share of blessings and curses.

This book is not just about AS either. There are many books that are more comprehensive. There are also books that focus specifically on one important aspect of AS such as social skill issues in school, or dealing with parenting issues. In this book, the focus is on both the giftedness and the AS symptoms because they are so intertwined.

Attention deficits

Attention deficits mean many different things to different people. Attention deficits can encompass strengths, as well as weaknesses. For example, sticking with something and not shifting attention at every distraction is an asset. Some people are exceptionally good at sticking to what they are doing, but they may have trouble stopping themselves from continuing with the task when it is necessary to stop. Some of these people have one-track minds. They need to stay with one aspect of something, and can be rigid and inflexible about how they solve a problem or perform a task. Thus, sustaining attention and hyperfocusing are related.

Shifting attention when a new stimulus occurs is really important as a survival tool. Imagine if our ancestors had not shifted attention when a bear approached! Or if we do not shift attention as the house burns down. Thus, shifting attention is a good trait, and if a person has trouble shifting attention, they can be eaten. On the other hand, people who shift attention too quickly and easily – for example, at every distraction – have trouble getting anything done. They might see the bear, but they also might starve to death because they never finish the job of gathering food or preparing it for dinner. Thus, the ability to shift attention and distractibility are related.

Being able to divide attention is important. Some people are exceptionally good at this skill and can work on two problems at the same time. Others are more apt to be conscious of several aspects of a task at once: for example, holding a math problem in mind while solving it, or listening to the teacher's or boss's instructions while making a mental list of supplies that will be needed to do the task. These people see the bear and think of how to evade it or capture it, while also thinking of all the other things they need to do. These are positive aspects of divided attention. People who are very creative divide their attention between what is going on, and what their own thought processes generate: an inner picture or dialogue. This can result in a creative product, or it can be a distractor from what needs to be done.

Multitasking and creativity are important skills. Some people, though, have difficulty holding material in mind. Their working memory is small, and they cannot focus on more than one aspect at once. Also, they are easily distracted by inner thoughts, including divergent and creative thoughts. These are the people who spend time imagining how they would hunt the bear, only to miss it because it leaves meanwhile. Or they might get interested in making cave paintings of bear hunts and forget the danger of the immediate bear.

Focusing on the right aspect of material is important. It is valuable to be able to pick out the underlying thesis or design, to see how the material falls into a pattern or develops a point. Some people have the ability to hone right in on the most important aspect of any material. They see to the core instantly. They are also good at generating a big picture, and at seeing how all the parts add up. They can support an argument because they understand what went into making that argument. Others have much more trouble attending to the central point. They lose the forest for the trees because they are focused more on details. This can be fruitful when the detail leads them in a new direction, and to a new way of seeing something, but it is less productive when they misinterpret material because they assume they know the whole from just this interesting part. These are the people who see a brown patch of fur caught on a tree and think it is a bear, so they go bear hunting and miss the huge mammoth they might have had for dinner.

People with AD/HD and AS have attention deficits; however, they also have attention strengths. It all depends on the purpose of the task, and their ability to produce when needed. Thus, people with AD/HD and AS fail miserably under conditions where others are able to mobilize appropriate attention. On the other hand, those with AD/HD and AS can be exceptionally creative and productive by mobilizing attention under conditions that allow them freedom to engage in the material in their own way.

This book is about both the problems and the strengths of those with AD/HD and AS. In each chapter a different aspect of how gifted children with these problems show strengths and weaknesses will be explored.

Asynchrony

This book is about asynchrony. Every gifted child shows asynchrony in at least some ways. Leta Hollingworth (1931, 1942) was perhaps the first to make the point that gifted children are not miniature adults, but rather a mixture of ages because development in all areas is not equal. What asynchrony means is that all areas of functioning within the gifted individual do not develop equally or simultaneously. Asynchrony in gifted children covers all areas of functioning: intellectual, emotional, social, creative, and moral.

What asynchrony means is that what gifted children can conceptualize is not what they can emotionally or socially manage. A good example of asynchrony in a young gifted child is the girl who wants to write a story, can hear the story in her mind, but cannot yet use a pencil well enough to write for very long, so the story cannot be written. Another example would be the boy who asks sophisticated questions about such subjects as the end of the universe and death at an age when emotionally he still needs to feel that parents can keep him safe from all dangers.

Asynchrony also describes the aspects of gifted children that depart from developmental norms and age-peer expectations. Thus, gifted children will be cognitively asynchronous from age-peers in abstract reasoning, but more like age peers in size or physical development.

It is important that parents understand the concept of asynchrony. It can be all too easy to think that because a gifted child can ask questions about an abstract concept, he or she really can deal with that concept. Often gifted children cannot. On the other hand, gifted children are not quite like more average children in how they express emotional or social needs either. Thus, parents need to think about asynchrony when children's thinking and feeling, or thinking and behaving, do not match.

Teachers of gifted children need to understand the concept of asynchrony in terms of differing strengths and weaknesses even within a subject area. A child may have sophisticated concepts, yet not be able to express them at the level of older children who are studying these concepts. For example, a child may be more like age peers in the amount of homework he or she can do at night, or the amount of material that can be handwritten, even when the child is ready to study material several grade levels ahead. Neither holding the child to the expectations of the older children, nor making him or her do grade-level work, is appropriate. Teachers need to think about asynchrony whenever gifted children show a variety of cognitive, social, and emotional strengths and weaknesses within a classroom setting.

Therapists (school counselors, school psychologists, school social workers, marriage and family counselors, clinical social workers, psychiatric nurses, clinical psychologists, and psychiatrists) who work with gifted children should consider asynchrony when they think about developmental issues, and how these interplay with cognitive advancement. Not only do many gifted children go through stages of emotional, social, moral, and spiritual development at earlier ages than more average children, but also they experience crises within each stage in a qualitatively different way because of their exceptional intensity and sensitivity. Hollingworth (1931) noted that psychologists who have knowledge about gifted children will be able to observe the special problems of adjustment that arise specifically because the child is gifted. The more gifted the child, the more issues he or she has due to uneven development.

It is not just that gifted children know more things; they know more things at a more sophisticated level of understanding than age peers. They also have higher standards for achievement, and more sophisticated reasoning about rules, fairness, and justice than age peers. Many are also quite sensitive and intense in their emotions. This leaves many gifted children feeling different from others without understanding why. It leaves them vulnerable to feeling isolated and alienated. Without understanding the difference that being gifted brings to a person's experience of the world and other people, mental health professionals miss the essential aspect of their clients' issues.

Asynchronous development is even greater in children with AD/HD. Even among average children with AD/HD, cognitive skills of some types (especially skills that help regulate behavior and make learning efficient – that is, executive function and self-regulatory and organizational skills) may lag behind chronological age expectation. When these skills lag, so also may social and emotional development. Overall, the biggest discrepancies are found between knowledge of what to do and ability to do it.

Gifted children with AD/HD show much more asynchrony than do other gifted children. Consequently, gifted children with AD/HD may appear more like other gifted children on some occasions, and more like more average peers with AD/HD on others. This will be explored further in each chapter.

Another group of gifted children with attention deficits who show asynchrony are those with AS. As with AD/HD, those with AS show much more asynchrony than either other gifted children or more average children, particularly in communication skills, social functioning, emotional functioning, and some areas of cognitive functioning.

The children of this study

This book is based on work at the Gifted Resource Center of New England with more than 250 gifted children with AD/HD. About one-third were girls. Also included in the study group were 30 children with AS, about half of whom also had AD/HD. An additional 50 gifted children without AD/HD or AS were studied. Gifted children in this study (including those with AD/HD and/or AS) ranged in intellectual potential from IQ 120 to IQ 230, and from ages 3 to 22.

Many of the children in this study were assessed using standardized intellectual, educational, neuropsychological, and personality instruments. Assessment usually took place over the course of two to five sessions and included extensive history-taking and examination of a portfolio of a child's work and projects.

In order to try to keep perspective and not think that every gifted child had some deficit, this author has also worked with teachers of gifted children by offering consultation on specific issues related to giftedness at local schools and at a school for gifted children. Finally, observations and anecdotes from friends and church acquaintances about their own gifted children, and others they know, have provided some balance.

Many examples used in this book involve incidents from actual children. In all cases where a specific child is described, permission was obtained from the parents for the description. However, most examples are composites, especially when similar anecdotes were offered by several parents. Both actual incidents and composites are written so as to disguise actual identity and to protect client confidentiality. Nevertheless, experience has shown, from past publications, that any time an incident has seemed unique to one child, invariably other parents reading about it will volunteer similar information about their own child. Thus, using composites will allow many parents to find themselves, and their own children, within this book.

The anecdotes in this book describe different children at different ages. In succeeding chapters, a child with the same name is meant to be the same child, though he or she may be a different age; some children have been known to the author for several years. Also, it is important to show the same person at different times in his or her life, even if the child described is a composite of several people.

Most of the children assessed and treated for problems wrought by the dual exceptionality of attention deficits and giftedness are boys. This is related to a common problem for gifted girls: they blend in all too well, so their giftedness is never noticed. Gifted girls with AD/HD also suffer from neglect. Unless they are disruptive, they fade into the woodwork, daydreaming their time away in unchallenging classrooms. In the literature, there are many debates about the statistical prevalence of AD/HD among girls in the general population. Generally, boys outnumber girls by about 3:1. In the AS population, there are usually four boys to every girl, with some authors finding more girls than expected. Although in the gifted population, boys and girls are about equal in number at every IQ level, more boys than girls are assessed for giftedness alone. It is not uncommon for parents to come for an assessment of their gifted sons and not also test their gifted daughters.

In the highest IQ group assessed, those children over IQ 195, 7 of 25 assessed were girls. This was slightly less than one-third. All of these girls had issues similar to those of such highly gifted boys, though the girls showed them in somewhat different ways. Because there are many hidden girls with high IQs, including those who are also hiding AD/HD, this book will explore some of the needs of gifted girls.

This book grew out observations of the gifted children I assessed and saw in therapy. It grew from the frustration expressed by parents that no one really understood their children, from either a gifted or AD/HD perspective. Often what was offered to children was inappropriate. Academic programs focused on remediating weaknesses for some children with AD/HD, but did little to challenge or stimulate them. For the children with AS, focus was overwhelmingly on their weaknesses. Gifted children with AS were rarely given work commensurate with their cognitive and academic strengths unless the AS was so mild that they did not come to the attention of school personnel at all. Thus, those gifted children with AS who were in special education programs usually had little done to accentuate their areas of strength even though these strengths were what will be most useful in adult life.

This book is not a diagnostic manual. Long experience in assessing gifted children with and without attention deficits convinces me that diagnosis of AD/HD or AS in gifted children is not always easy. Many of the commonly used criteria simply do not work. Thus, unless the professional doing the assessment knows something about both giftedness and attention deficits, mistakes may be made. Diagnosis cannot be based on one meeting or on a few criteria. A full evaluation is often needed. The chapter on assessment makes this point in more detail.

This book is intended to explore both giftedness and attention deficits from a broad perspective. To that end, separate chapters will deal with each developmental aspect. Also, chapters on what gifted children are like, what constitutes the diagnosis of AD/HD, the diagnosis of AS, and how to assess children are included. Within each chapter, strategies for parents, teachers, and other adults who work with these gifted children are included. It is the hope of this author that by reading this book, parents, teachers, and mental health therapists who work with gifted children will understand more completely their unique needs.

Mighty things from small beginnings grow.

John Dryden
Annus Mirabilis, CLV

Chapter 1

The Gifted Child

Bobby

Bobby spoke his first word at six months of age. He also loved listening to music and giggled at the playful passages in Tubby the Tuba. He seemed to understand the musical joke involved. Even earlier, at age three months, Bobby had shown a long attention span for his Humpty Dumpty. He would place this toy behind him, and then would reach back to the same spot with his hand and get the toy without ever looking at the spot. He never missed.

Bobby's language skills were quite precocious. He spoke in short phrases by 12 months and full sentences by 16 months. Before age two he could identify shapes and colors by name. He could also identify six musical instruments by sound. Between ages two and three, Bobby began to ask questions and make observations that showed his unique perspective on the world. Bobby was especially interested in why things happen, the place of animals and people in the world, why people have to die and what happens to them after death, who God is, and what God is like. One of his interesting perspectives had to do with aging. His idea was that first people grow up, then – when they get old and die – they grow down again to babyhood. Bobby's philosophical interests continued through early childhood. By age four, he was commenting on the nature of his good self and his bad self, thinking there would be a battle between these two sides of himself until he finally died in 20 million years.

Bobby had a great imagination. He loved to think up interesting questions: "Mom, if I ate too much calcium, would I turn white?" When his mother asked him why he wondered this he replied, "Well, if I ate too much carotene I'd turn orange." Bobby also used his imagination to create imaginary playmates. He included his entire Beanie Baby collection, all of whom had distinctive personalities. He also made up fantasy games to play with his brother and friends. Though only four years old, his ideas were so exciting that everyone wanted to follow his lead. While Bobby preferred older children because he had more in common with them, he got along well with age mates. His imagination served him in good stead here because he could always introduce an imaginary game or scene for everyone to play out.

Bobby loved puzzles from an early age. He was able to put together complex 500 or more piece puzzles by age four. Math also came easily and was a delight. By three years of age he had figured out addition and subtraction, by age four, multiplication. In fact, he got into some trouble in his preschool class at age four when his teacher would not accept "a googol" as a real number.

Bobby loved school on the first day of kindergarten. By the second day, he felt bored. At the end of the third day, he announced that he was going to stay home until after college. School was such a disaster after this that his parents had him tested. At age six, he scored an IQ of 190 on the Stanford-Binet Intelligence Scale Form LM. With a mental age of about 11 years, it is little wonder he felt bored with kindergarten. Only when his school arranged both a grade skip and an advanced curriculum in math and reading was he again happy.

Elizabeth

Elizabeth, at age four, had "wonderments," as her family called them. She mused about whether it hurt leaves to fall to the ground, or if the crescent moon was God's cut big toe nail. Once, when passing a cemetery when she was age four Elizabeth asked her mother, "Mommy, when you die, do your bones show?" When her mother answered that they did, Elizabeth then replied, "So your soul goes up to heaven, but your bones stay here?"

Music and art both brought her pleasure and she would muse about the feelings evoked by the music she heard or the colors she painted. In preschool, she painted a pillow, which she called the "Color of Dusk."

Elizabeth loved stories and art, so she wrote books about everything, even before she could actually write. Her early books, about colors, were fantasies of color in swirls and splashes. Later books, written from age four on, included a cookbook, a dictionary, a coloring book with pictures and captions, a summer book of various summer activities, a gymnastics book, and a book of mazes. Elizabeth could amuse herself for hours using her imagination or making things. She loved to create things from paper and odds and ends around the house. She also loved to sew and made her own Beanie Babies. Her pretend play included dance shows, opera, and scenes from *Madeline* and other books that she loved.

Elizabeth played well alone or with others. Often she involved them in her fantasy games, but she also enjoyed jump-rope play with other girls, and other sports activities. Elizabeth was well known for her kindness to other children at school. She was sympathetic and caring about feelings. Also, she liked to do things for others, especially small favors, and she liked to make and give tokens of affection. Elizabeth was very aware of social dynamics and commented often on how the other children seemed to view things, how they thought and felt, and what seemed to be the rules they followed. Elizabeth thought that some of the ways that others behaved were unfair, and she commented to her mother on how different situations could be made more fair, especially at school. Situations at home also underwent their share of Elizabeth's scrutiny and comment.

Elizabeth was an early talker and an early reader. She was talking in full sentences by 16 months, and she read her first words soon afterwards. Currently, at age seven, she prefers mysteries, *Wishbone*, the series in which the little dog annotates classics for children, and *Little House On the Prairie* books. Writing, spelling, and vocabulary have continued to advance prodigiously for her age.

Elizabeth was adept at science. On television she liked *Kratts' Creatures*, *Blue's Clues*, and *Figure It Out*. Usually, she could solve the puzzles presented. In school she was advanced in math, and already knew how to multiply and solve some problems with fractions in 2nd grade, but she needed to be taught math to do well. She loved to do math puzzles at home, especially logic puzzles that use clues to find the answers.

When she grows up, Elizabeth wants to be a veterinarian, dancer, writer, and clothes designer all at once. A highly gifted child, she has the potential to do any or all of these well. For Elizabeth, with an IQ in the 150 range, deciding what to be will be her problem. How can she settle on one thing when so many seem so interesting?

Commonalities

Bobby and Elizabeth are both gifted children. Both have a variety of traits and characteristics that make them quite different from other children of the same chronological ages. Their early development was quite advanced when compared to the guidelines for average children. They showed evidence of precocity in one or more areas of accomplishment. Bobby and Elizabeth showed exceptionally early language development. While the average child says first words at about a year of age, they were both far in advance of this. In fact, when most average children are still saying single words, Bobby and Elizabeth were using full sentences. Both also showed very early curiosity. Early language development allowed them the chance to ask questions about areas of interest. Also, these early questions showed particular interests in life, death, God, how the world works, and the wonders of nature. Besides questions, both children, from an early age, startled parents with their observations and theorizing about issues.

Bobby and Elizabeth showed early aesthetic appreciation for the arts, both music and color. Elizabeth also enjoyed opera and dance. They were early readers and enjoyed using stories in play. Both composed their own stories and also played out those they had read or listened to. Imaginary play was important to both. Also, imagination was revealed through humor and imaginary friends.

Fairness, and its relationship to social situations, was also shown to be a concern for each child, though in slightly different ways. Bobby thought school was unfair because he was not allowed to advance as fast as he could. He thought his teacher unfair for not listening to him when he was scolded for making up what she thought was an imaginary number, the googol. Elizabeth focused her judgments about unfairness on situations she saw develop at school and at home, based on the underlying social dynamics she perceived.

Both children showed early academic development in reading, story telling and writing, math, and science. They also had a wide variety of interests and a vast fund of knowledge about them.

In addition to the traits both had in common, each child also had specific traits that were different from the average. These included, for Bobby, an unusually early long-attention span, spatial ability, and musical ability. For Elizabeth, these included an unusual adeptness at art and craft work, inventiveness in making things from useless household trash items, and social awareness, empathy, and compassion for others.

The traits common to Bobby and Elizabeth have also been noted by others who work with and observe gifted children.

The focus of this chapter

This chapter focuses on giftedness. To understand how giftedness interacts with attention deficit, it is important to look at giftedness and attention deficits separately, as well as together. Thus, this chapter examines:

- The development of gifted children
- The traits of giftedness and how they are manifested in the children seen at the Gifted Resource Center of New England
- The special needs of the different levels of giftedness, as well as of particular groups of gifted children
- Theories of giftedness
- A definition of giftedness.

Early development

Indications of giftedness are often seen early, even in infancy. It is not unusual for parents to report early language development, early memory, or early reading. One parent reported that her son could, before the age of one, point out the way to various places in the car. This was before he could even talk. One parent showed pictures of her eight-day-old child pulling herself across the crib. Other parents report babies' unusual alertness and interest in faces, toys, and objects in the room, as Bobby's mother did.

When exploring early development of gifted children, it is important to recognize which characteristics are those most likely to be noted by parents. A child who says first words at a few months old is sure to be identified as unusual, but the reflective child who thinks deeply, but does not speak until a more average age, may not be so easily recognized. For those gifted children who eventually score above IQ 160, early talking, walking, and reading may be early indicators of precocity. However, many very highly gifted children do not differ from average in age at which first abilities appear, and they may even be delayed. McGuffog, Feiring and Lewis (1987), in their study of gifted and extremely gifted children (IQs over 160), found that extremely gifted children generally were ahead of age peers in preschool years in developmental milestones, especially language and memory. Most also had areas of special knowledge, great curiosity, rapidity of learning, and advanced motor skills. However, delays were also noted with some children showing large discrepancies between areas of strength in language and weakness in motor skills. Gross (1993) also noted such advanced early development coupled with areas of weakness in several of her very highly gifted children, one with an IQ over 200. Thus, while early precocity usually indicates giftedness, more average development is not necessarily an indicator of a lack of exceptional ability. Some gifted children simply do not blossom until later.

Preschool years

In the preschool years, ages three to five, gifted children often show a boundless curiosity and exuberant joy in living. Many parents report these as years of delighted discovery for their child. There is a special internal spark as if the child were totally enraptured by the tasks of life. Children love learning, being, doing. During these years, children spend every waking hour learning things. They are eager to go to school, having visions of teachers who will delight in their explorations too. Many of these children learn basic academic skills before going to school. They may be advanced in reading, math, vocabulary, science, spatial perception, reasoning ability, story telling, spelling, and/or writing.

Gifted preschool children continue to ask many questions or make unusually perceptive comments about observations they have made. They show a more sophisticated grasp of material at an earlier age, and are more persistent about getting adequate answers. This can mean they demand a great deal of attention from parents and teachers. To the child, these adults are there to help them figure out all the many amazing things there are to know. Though preschool gifted children can share materials and activities with other children, they are too young yet to have much sense of needing to share adult attention, or class time, especially when they recognize that other children don't ask very interesting questions. It can seem to the gifted child that the teacher is spending time answering easy questions that everyone already knows and, therefore, needs more difficult things introduced. Other gifted children are so exuberant and joyful about their discoveries they cannot conceive that others might not also be interested or might not understand (the googol, for example).

Many preschool gifted children are very imaginative and curious. Imaginary playmates are frequent for both boys and girls. These gifted children are often more advanced in play skills than age peers. For one thing, their expectations for complex play are more like those of older children, as are their ideas about rules and fairness. Gifted children may have imaginary companions as do more average children, but also may develop imaginary families, countries or sports teams. Some then have complex games in their minds in which they remember every move by every player over many games, or they have complex languages they invent for their imaginary lands that they remember even as they add more words and complex grammars. They may hold entire conversations in the made-up language.

Childhood

Gottfried *et al.* (1994) followed a group of children from birth through middle childhood. They found that children who scored in the gifted range at age eight had shown superior intrinsic motivation (motivation from within) from their earliest years. They were superior in attention, persistence, curiosity, enjoyment of learning, and tendency to desire mastery and challenge.

In the years of childhood, from ages six through twelve, gifted children continue to show curiosity and passion about those things that most interest them. Many start collections of various types. These can include objects (such as sports cards or coins), facts (all there is to know about dinosaurs, black holes, or languages), or strategies (such as how best to win at chess or beat favorite computer and Nintendo games). Some seem to collect people – that is, they have an amazing variety of relationships.

Gifted children also continue their academic advancement by accelerating past age peers in both basic skills and applications of those skills. That means many elementary-age gifted children can solve sophisticated analytical problems, derive a general principle from a collection of facts, find symbolic meaning in written material that goes beyond the superficial, and find general themes and patterns in data. These are skills not usually taught until late middle school and high school. It is little wonder that many, before age 13, are able to score on the Scholastic Aptitude Tests (SATs) above the mean for high-school seniors. Such high scores at an early age qualify many gifted children for talent development programs such as Johns Hopkins' Center for Talented Youth (CTY) program.

Elementary-age gifted children generally reason to a much higher abstract level than age peers. This means they are able to make more sophisticated analyses of common problems, social interactions, and moral dilemmas. It does not mean, however, that they are able to act on their knowledge. Many times, actual behavior is driven by emotional needs, so gifted children may know what one ought to do, but not think about doing it in the heat of the moment.

Social awareness is very high, especially in young gifted girls. Many are especially adept at analyzing social dynamics of peers from an early age, as Elizabeth was. In the elementary years, imaginary friends frequently disappear, and many gifted children instead find, or long for, one best friend with whom to share interests and ideas. While many are able to find some peers to share common interests, such as computer games or sports activities, fewer are able to find peers who really understand who they are. Many gifted children of this age feel as if they are in hiding, going to school and presenting one aspect of themselves to teachers and peers, and at home being their real selves. The stress of this takes a tremendous toll in self-esteem and feelings of acceptance.

The biggest change of the elementary years, reported by parent and children alike, is the loss of passion and joy. Many parents report the loss of the exuberant child full of the spark of discovery and passion for learning they knew in preschool years. For the majority of gifted children, learning becomes something expected from school, not something one does on one's own anymore. As children reach middle-school years, learning and activities become more and more circumscribed to what is required by teachers and acceptable to peers. It is only those who are willing, in at least some ways, to march to a different drummer who continue to pursue independent studies outside of school. When school is less than stimulating, the gifted child risks losing a major piece of identity. Inundated with mediocrity all around, these gifted children may give up entirely any independent work. They may get all "A"s, but will underachieve right through high school and even college.

Adolescence

Early adolescence can be a turning point for gifted children. In the early adolescent years, many are ready and able to accelerate in academics. This can allow much faster progress in high-school subjects, with the chance to learn more in depth. Advanced placement courses and CLEP examinations (College Level Examination Program) allow many to enter college with requirements fulfilled and college credit earned. Some are fortunate enough to be in school systems which have provisions for dual enrollment in high school and college.

Many gifted adolescents hunger for more content in high-school courses, even in the advanced and honors courses. The pace still seems much too slow, and the mind-numbing pace of work in progress can seem extremely stressful. Quinn O'Leary (2001) wrote a poignant essay on being in high school as a highly gifted student. He felt his intelligence was regarded as a nuisance by his school administration.

Some gifted adolescents solve the problem of boredom by devising their own secret curriculum. Thus, while the class reads one Greek play by Aristophanes, they read all his plays, as well as all the other Greek plays they can find. Other gifted adolescents do the minimum of work to get excellent grades, but spend their time on other endeavors of their own choosing. These endeavors can range from finding a mentor in a special field such as drama, music, science, or art, to dedicating themselves to a sport, to hanging round the mall with friends. Still others tune out, give up, or join in with peers in disrupting classes and making trouble.

Adolescents are developmentally engaged in the tasks of learning to be independent, finding their own unique identity, and developing intimacy. These tasks are more difficult for gifted adolescents. Young people who are academically advanced may be ready for college at an early age, and that may mean they spend fewer years with their families than expected. Some are exceptionally mature and able to fit in well with college life, even at a younger age. In fact, no one knows their true age; they seem just like the older students. Nevertheless, some gifted teens who are ready for a college curriculum from an academic point of view are not emotionally ready to live away at college. They simply have not yet had the life experience to feel or be safe enough to live away from home, nor to make the choices that young adults commonly have to make in college. Some are happy to live at home if that can be arranged; others are chafing at the structure of home. They want nothing more than to leave and be their own persons at an age when they are really not prepared to meet the challenges of self-directed work, or the personal responsibility of day-to-day living needs. They also are not yet ready for the challenges of intimacy, sexual relationships, and social expectations of older college students. Finding a solution that meets both the academic requirements and emotional and developmental needs of these adolescents can be quite challenging.

Solutions that have at least partially worked for these adolescents have included participation in the Talent Searches developed by several major universities around the country, such as Johns Hopkins, Duke, and the University of Washington among others. Also, some universities have allowed young students to participate in early college through combined high-school/college programs. Simon's Rock of Bard College, Boston University Academy, Mary Baldwin College and the University of Washington are examples of these types of programs. They allow younger students to accelerate in the company of other gifted people of their own age, slowly integrating them into the college program. Just as the Talent Search programs allow younger gifted students to take advanced courses with others of their own age over the summer, these full-time programs try to meet both the academic and developmental needs of gifted students.

Helping adolescents and young adults find the sources of work and love that rekindle the passions of the preschool years are the tasks educators, parents, therapists, and young people themselves are faced with. Only through finding satisfying life's work and satisfying relationships can the gifted young person grow into adulthood.

Traits of giftedness

Most parents do not have access to information about early development of the characteristics associated with giftedness. Because they usually do not have a great deal of experience with more average children against whom to compare their child's early development, many parents are likely to think all children are like theirs. However, by preschool years, astonished responses from other people about the child's early unusual abilities, complaints from the child about the limits of activities available in preschool, or teacher observations convince most of these parents that their child is unusual.

Other parents know there is something different about their children from the earliest months. Gogel, McCumsey, and Hewett (1985), in a study of 1039 parents of gifted children, found that 87% recognized giftedness in their children by age five. However, many of these had recognized signs of giftedness much earlier. Seven percent recognized giftedness by six months of age. Thirty-eight percent did so by age two.

There have been a number of lists of traits that best exemplify giftedness. When the lists from seven researchers (Gross 1993; Powell and Hayden 1984; Roedell 1984; Silverman 1993a; Webb, Meckstroth, and Tolan 1982; Whitmore

1980; Winner 1996) were compared, a number of traits were found in common. Early talking, early physical development, having a large and advanced vocabulary for one's age, facility with abstraction, analytical thinking, complexity in thinking, having a longer attention span, ability to concentrate, and persistence were mentioned. Also, gifted children were found to show curiosity and to put ideas together in unusual and creative ways. They showed a passion for learning so they learned easily and quickly without needing much practice to learn basic skills. They showed a wide variety of interests and knew a lot of information in areas of interest. Along with that went unusually early development of long-term memory, and well-developed memory for facts and events.

Most researchers mentioned gifted children's sense of humor, vivid imagination, and sensitivity. Also, emotional intensity and early concerns about issues of fairness and justice were observed. In studying gifted children over IQ 160, Gross (1993) and Winner (1996) mentioned traits such as early movement and physical development, early speech, and early recognition memory.

Other traits mentioned by at least one researcher included interest in experimenting and doing things differently or preference for novelty (Webb, Meckstroth, and Tolan 1982; Winner 1996), perfectionism (Roedell 1984; Silverman 1993a; Whitmore 1980) capacity for reflection (Silverman 1993a), metacognitive awareness, obsessive interests, and experiences of awe (Winner 1996).

Whitmore (1980) found that gifted children placed in stimulating environments, even if not achieving academically, showed characteristics that included learning quickly and easily when interested, having exceptional power to learn, retain and apply knowledge, curiosity, initiative, creativity and inventiveness, perfectionism, independence and nonconformity, supersensitivity of the central nervous system, and acute perceptiveness. Even beneath "lazy" behavior, children were found to be self-critical and motivated to meet high standards of personal achievement.

While many of the traits mentioned by researchers are positive, Roedell (1984) described characteristics of gifted children that led to increased vulnerability. These included perfectionism, difficulty with too high adult expectations, intense sensitivity, multipotentiality (can do too many things well), difficulty finding appropriate peers, development of alienation, high need for intellectual stimulation, and difficulty with societal role expectations, especially for girls. The increased vulnerability created could lead to social maladjustment, unhappiness or underachievement.

When parents examine lists of characteristics of gifted children, it is common to think that a child is not gifted unless he or she has almost all the traits. This is a fallacy; no child exhibits all the traits. Furthermore, some traits are more evident at some ages than others. Finally, a child may exhibit few of the early signs and still be quite gifted. We have only to think of Einstein to find an example of such a child. Children who exhibit few traits of early precocity may be those who are more reflective than average, and have more difficulty expressing their ideas. Some are learning disabled, or have attention deficits such as Attention Deficit Hyperactivity Disorder, so they appear more average on the surface. People who know them well, however, see the moments of deep comprehension, sudden insight and original thinking that blooms like a flower and then is gone. It is important that parents of such children recognize their child's unique giftedness and build on the sometimes not so obvious strengths.

Traits of gifted children at the Gifted Resource Center of New England

Gifted children seen at the Gifted Resource Center of New England showed many of the traits listed by Gottfried *et al.* (1994), Roedell (1984), Silverman (1993a), Webb, Meckstroth, and Tolan (1982), Whitmore (1980), and Winner (1996). Most showed early development of some type: physical dexterity, language, early academics, unusual alertness, or concentration. All of them were curious and asked complex questions, especially in preschool years. All learned rapidly at least those things in which they were most interested, and they appeared to feel a drive to master skills that allowed them to progress in some chosen realm. All showed exceptional ability to abstract and think with complexity about at least some topics or areas of interest. All needed mental stimulation, and without it behavior tended to deteriorate so the child became less able to perform adequately. Most had unusual play interests that age mates did not share. For example, Cameron, age seven, was the only boy in his primary school who was interested in the game "Magic." His attempts to explain the complexities of the cards to other boys was met with disinterest. His classmates preferred discussing Pokémon instead.

Most, but not all, of the gifted children in the study also showed complex use of language, had large vocabularies, were academically advanced, had a complex imagination, a wide range of interests, or a deep and abiding interest in one area. Nate, for example, was a collector of Beatles memorabilia. His interest in the Beatles helped him complete difficult school tasks because he could turn many of the more open-ended tasks in his high school towards a further pursuit of knowledge about them. This intense interest and avid determination paid off for Nate. It was the subject of his college admissions essay. In his first semester of college, he found to his delight that a course on the culture of the Beatles was offered. He found a whole roomful of other fans, and eventually a number of friends. In this way, his entry into college was much eased.

Most of the gifted children in this study also showed perseverance, as well as a need for precision, on difficult tasks. Most also showed some area of creativity, thought about things in unusual ways, and questioned accepted ways of doing things. They needed reasons for why things were so, and why they had to be done in certain ways. Most also had a keen sense of justice that went along with this and showed especial concern for their own rights. Most also had exceptional memories for facts, wrongs done to them, or lists of things they wanted. Some were also less conforming and argued often with parents and sometimes with teachers.

A high percentage of children in this study, especially the boys, were interested in computers and computer games. These gifted boys loved the strategy, challenge and fast action inherent in these games. Many also loved the violence and found it stimulating. A number of these children went on to develop computer skills, planning a life that would allow use of these skills in adulthood. At age 13, Ted already designed websites for a fee for adults who could not do this themselves. Others, on their own, started to learn, and later to invent, computer languages so they could program their own games. Some of these boys could do almost anything with a computer – except their homework!

Both boys and girls were also Star Trek and Star Wars fans. A large percentage spent their time learning about minutiae associated with all the television series, movies, books, and computer sites. Children who couldn't seem to retain material for a school test nevertheless knew large amounts of material and could pass any test of Star Wars trivia. Josh, a devoted Star Trek fan, knew Spock's blood type – T negative – and he and other boys spent hours trying to learn Klingon. The power of challenge and interest as forces in driving motivation is compelling once one studies phenomena like these. Nevertheless, because of lack of appropriate mental stimulation and challenge, as well as learning disabilities for some, many of these gifted children found school difficult.

Many of these boys and girls were not at the top of their classes in upper grades. They struggled with academics and only when they got to college, or even later, did they fully develop their abilities. It is important to note that many of the current theories about gifted education, and what giftedness is, leave these students out of the discussion. The definitions for inclusion in gifted programs require task commitment, and are based on performance and development of products. Some programs require overall high ability in both math and English. Learning how to explore the Internet and build websites, beat others at computer games, or acquire the most possible knowledge about Star Trek including how to speak Klingon with one's far-flung friends over the Internet usually doesn't count.

Of special interest was the way some of the children could use their areas of giftedness to solve problems that beset them. For example, Dan, an eight-year-old with Asperger Syndrome (AS), was able to use his unusual ability to recall dialogue. He made up scenarios using dialogue from famous movies and stories, and then had peers help him act them out. His Star Wars scenes were particularly compelling to peers. By using this skill and his ability to mimic, he had peers eager to join him in playground games. Other children liked Dan and protected him. Some coached him on appropriate social interactions when he did not know. In this way, Dan overcame some social skill deficits and learned how to interact with some peers. Later, he found another boy who also liked the same science explorations that he did, and he developed other skills of friendship.

Mary-Louise used her writing ability and her unique sense of humor to weather a setback she experienced when her behavior problems caused her to be asked to leave a school for gifted children. She spent her 6th-grade year in the local public school, where she was found to have AD/HD. Medication helped her control her inappropriate disruptions of the class, and she became a model student. After 6th grade, she reapplied to the school for gifted children and was readmitted. Part of her application was an essay she entitled, "What I Learned During My Time in Exile." In 7th grade, Mary-Louise was calmer, less argumentative, but more able to question in appropriate and meaningful ways. Her interesting comments about topics in literature and history won her much praise from peers and teachers alike.

Some of the gifted children in this study showed a high degree of moral concern. Some showed empathy and compassion for others, and were interested in social causes. Tiffany became interested in the plight of children in homeless shelters after she and her family visited one. When Tiffany learned that the children often had left home with no possessions, and that there were few toys available at the homeless shelter, she sponsored a toy drive at school to collect good, but used, toys for the shelter. Then she learned that art supplies were desperately needed as art therapy was used to help children deal with the tragedies in their lives. She and her friends were given permission to hold a talent show at school. They charged admission by asking people to bring in markers, crayons, paint, art pads, clay, etc., as the price of both performing in and attending the show. It was so successful, Tiffany repeated the idea for several years afterwards until she went off to college.

While many gifted children seem no more compassionately aware of others' needs than more average children, there were a significant number of children like Tiffany who had a clear vision and determination to do what was right for others. Many were able to respond to structured efforts to help. These included collecting toys, food, and clothes for needy families, collecting money for the children in India, Pakistan, and Nepal who are forced into child labor in rug factories and soccer-ball plants, thinking about ways to save endangered species and the rain forest, sponsoring children in foreign countries through international organizations, and doing good deeds around their homes and neighborhoods.

Special needs of gifted children

Gifted children can range in intelligence from an IQ of 120 to an IQ of more than 200. Such a range suggests diversity, as much at least as among people from IQ 40 to 120. Yet gifted children are usually thought of as one group with similar needs. Consequently, they are given the same type of program, even when it may not fit very well due to both individual strengths and weaknesses of the child, and the level of intelligence. Also, being from a minority racial, ethnic, or cultural group, being a gifted girl, being creatively gifted, or having an attention deficit or learning disability can all interact with level of intelligence and add to the need for specific programming.

Levels of giftedness

THE MILDLY GIFTED CHILD (IQ 120 TO 139)

Children who range between IQ 120 and 139 tend to be more like age peers in many respects. Often they are children who achieve good grades in school, respond to enrichment and challenge in assignments, and are just far enough advanced from age peers that they can serve as models and leaders. In fact, these are often the children who are popular with peers. They are good at many things and are able to excel with some effort. If these children put a lot of effort into something they can become experts. Peers appreciate this because they are able to identify with the achieving child by thinking that more effort on their own part would result in similar achievement.

These gifted children are often fact collectors, whose general knowledge is great. They are the typical smart children in most classrooms. They are also the leaders in student government, class activities, and often in sports. Also, many children with creative ability, especially in the arts, fall into this range of intellectual potential.

At this level of giftedness, most school work is easily learned. Many children already know much of the material, but there are still areas in which they still may need to struggle. Barry, age nine, with an IQ of 133, usually received excellent grades in reading, spelling, and mathematics and science. He did less well in writing, mainly because he did not like to write and often avoided doing so until he was forced. Then, he did adequate but not very creative work. Barry loved to sing and had outstanding talent. He spent much of his time out of school engaged in practicing for shows, choirs, and his individual voice lessons. He was able to learn songs in a foreign language he did not know within two sessions of hearing the song. Barry's wish was to be discovered like Billy Gilman, the young country and western star, who had a top selling song at age 12.

THE MODERATELY GIFTED CHILD (IQ 140 TO 159)

Children who score in the 140 to 159 range of intellectual potential are moderately gifted. These children tend to be good problem solvers, quick to learn, motivated, and energetic. They are often popular and can serve as school leaders because, while more discrepant from average than the children scoring 120 to 139, they still are not so far advanced that peers find them extremely different. This group may have different play interests from age peers, and may develop expertise in areas of interest outside of school. Also, these are usually very busy children with many activities scheduled. They want to do it all, have the capability of doing so, and also can achieve good grades without too much effort, so they have the time to expend on interests. Often these are the high scorers on national competitions in a typical school, and they are the ones who are likely to become valedictorians. Many of these children are also creative and, if they choose a career that allows for creative production, often produce prodigiously in art, music, literature, and science.

For these children, academic work is often repetitive. They frequently know most of what they are being taught and, if they do the work required, easily earn top grades. In order to receive some academic challenge, this group needs more in-depth work, some acceleration of content, and work with mentors on special projects.

Kate, with an IQ of 150, in junior high school developed a science-fair project that examined attitudes of students in several local high schools towards math and science ability in boys and girls. Despite many obstacles, she was interested enough in this work to continue it through the next year, and expand to more schools and more topics. Kate later presented her project to the School Board to express her concern about the attitudes she had found expressed by both pupils and teachers about girls' abilities.

THE EXCEPTIONALLY GIFTED CHILD (IQ 160 TO 179)

Children in the 160 to 179 range of intellectual potential tend to notice that they are different from age peers. They may share enough in common with peers that socially and emotionally they may still fit in on the surface, but many will feel internally out of synch. Children at this IQ level are far ahead of age peers. For example, a chronological six-year-old will be four years ahead intellectually, and a ten-year-old, seven years ahead. Thus, while not so far ahead socially or emotionally, intellectually these gifted children require very different programs than age peers. This means that they may be working with peers years older than themselves, or working on their own on special projects. They will likely be the only one at this level in their school. It will be harder for them to fit in with age peers because interests, other than sports, will be different. In fact, even if children in this range of intellect have similar interests with age peers (collecting sports cards, or playing board or computer games) the way they develop and discuss the activities will be more complex. Most age peers will not fully comprehend the rules or systems used by these gifted children. In addition, some of these gifted children have social difficulties because they want to do things their own way. The problem for them is that they see how something ought best to be done, and they may have little patience with, or understanding of, age peers who do not see as clearly as they do.

School work is so easy that these gifted children are not challenged at all, unless they are fortunate enough to attend academically rigorous schools where they have the opportunity to take advanced work and subjects not usually offered such as Greek. If not challenged, many give up. Some never do school work, relying on their memories and what they have already learned to do well. Instead, they may spend time on their own special interests. This is the group that will usually score at the top on national competitions, easily qualify for the Johns Hopkins Talent Search, and will be able to accelerate several grades before entering college. Many are very creative and, starting in elementary years, develop problems for themselves to solve. These may be actual experiments or thought problems. "What would happen if..." is a favorite question. These children can grow up to be successful at whatever profession they choose. If they choose to work on creative problems, especially in science or math, they may make original discoveries and win prestigious awards.

Caitlin, age ten, with an IQ of 178, asked to be home-schooled so that she could spend time on activities of interest. Though she had already skipped two grades, she was still bored by the curriculum and its slow pace. She was allowed to take the year off and spent her time learning about young children's acquisition of language. This project involved library research, attending class at a local college, and making her own videotapes of several young children that she then analyzed for linguistic structure.

THE PROFOUNDLY GIFTED CHILD (IQ 180 AND ABOVE)

Children who score above 180 in intellectual potential are most different from age peers. At this level they are exceptionally discrepant in almost all ways. A child of six, at this level, is five-and-a-half years ahead of age peers intellectually, and a child of ten is nine years ahead. Social and emotional development are also advanced, and the child may not find anyone like him or herself at all. These children can radically accelerate, often in every academic subject. Some of these children learn so fast, it seems that they are born knowing all there is to learn, and then they only need to be reminded of something to recall it to current status in their minds. They learn instantaneously, as soon as they hear of a topic (Dahlberg 1992). This spontaneous knowing (Morelock 1996) is especially prevalent with children over IQ 200. At a level of sufficient challenge (which may be difficult to reach as the child masters material so quickly), the profoundly gifted child will have to struggle to learn. The problem is that they are ready for complexity long before there are appropriate materials that are at the levels needed. Thus, children above IQ 180 also start to learn about adult topics much sooner than peers, and they may develop adult concerns much earlier as well.

Age peers may seem a mystery to them, in fact, because they are so different in interests, speed of learning, ability to understand complex material, and desire to learn. These profoundly gifted children spend much more of their time than other gifted children in intellectual pursuits, or in perfecting abilities in sports or music. They also are ready to work with adult mentors from an early age.

These children can be very inventive. Not only do they ask interesting "What if…" questions, but they also create whole systems of thought: for example, reasoning out mathematics, learning foreign languages, or exploring science concepts. They develop interesting problems for themselves to solve from their preschool years on (Morelock 1997). Others are less original in developing systems of thought, but are able to take what they have been taught, elaborate on it, and develop new ideas based on further analysis of material. One girl, Lydia (Lovecky 1992a, 1994a), with an IQ over 200, took the material from her 7th-grade English class, analyzed it, and gained insights into it far above the level of the other students. She also read all the other books the author had written in order to see what themes emerged from an overall analysis of the author's work. This gave her difficulties in class because she then could not write a simple paper on the theme the teacher thought was important in the assigned book. Not only did Lydia not agree with the teacher's analysis, but she had developed new insight into the work of the author as a whole, and she did not know how to develop this into something her teacher could understand. What Lydia was doing with her analyses was what college students are able to do in analyzing material. Lydia did not fit into this class or school at all, and had many problems before she was finally accelerated by starting college at age 15.

Profoundly gifted children differ from more moderately gifted children. In an earlier study (Lovecky 1994a), I described the differences found in two groups of gifted children. The higher IQ group (170+) differed from the more moderate IQ group (140 to 159) in a number of traits and characteristics. The children with IQs over 170 most often had more difficulty with easier than with more complex material. They had a higher need for precision, and used complex thinking processes to grasp and then integrate material. They were able to reason abstractly from an early age, and the essence of this reasoning was the ability to grasp the essential element of an issue. Often they gave themselves problems to solve. They showed exceptionally early memory for facts and personal experiences. Finally, they showed a tendency to want to learn as much as possible about a subject. These traits were found to a lesser degree in the more moderately gifted children; however, there were both qualitative and quantitative differences between the two groups. Similar evidence of such cognitive differences was found by J. Osborn (1995).

Special populations of gifted children

GIFTED CHILDREN FROM MINORITY GROUPS

Gifted children who belong to minority groups are a unique population because of their special needs. Poverty is not equally a problem for all ethnic groups, but prejudice is, and it can affect aspirations and achievement (Ford 1994/5; Kitano 1994/5). The availability of necessary resources is also important. For example, in New York City in the 1920s and 1930s many gifted children of immigrants were well served by the public schools of the times. Hollingworth (Harris 1992) set up her gifted programs in Public Schools 165, 500, and 208. Many of the children selected for her program were immigrants, or children of immigrants. Children of immigrants also took advantage of the free tuition at City College of New York; some of them developed into the top scientists in the United States, the Nobel Prize winners. Still, opportunities were very limited for people of color. Opportunities today are different, but there is a scarcity of resources, and there is less opportunity for a young person to find his or her own way into education than there was at the turn of the 20th century. Thus, finding and serving children of minority populations who have limited access to resources is necessary. There is just as large a reservoir of gifted children among immigrant populations and people of color today as there has always been, and some of them fall into the highest ranges of intelligence. Programs such as Project Synergy in New York City (Borland, Schnur, and Wright 2000; Wright and Borland 1993) are models for intervention.

GIFTED GIRLS

Gifted girls are also a special needs group. When Linda Silverman (1994/5) wrote about the plight of gifted girls, she took note of the forced choice dilemma in which many gifted girls still find themselves. They can either develop in academic areas (and look "smart") or hide academic achievement in order to be socially accepted by other girls and by boys. Girls who are sure of their academic talents and intelligence in elementary school, no longer view themselves as having ability by high school. This has been borne out in a number of national studies on female students in general (AAUW Education Foundation 1992 Sadker and Sadker 1994).

Gifted girls are no less affected than other girls by the national view that women's achievement still matters less than that of men's, that girls need to be socialized rather than intellectually challenged, and that to be socially accepted girls must sacrifice achievement (Callahan 1991; Cramer 1989; Kerr 1985, 1991; Roeper 1995c; Siegle and Reis 1994/5; Silverman 1986, 1991, 1993c, 1994/5).

Some gifted girls do not sacrifice achievement, but are more independent thinkers who may pay a price in loneliness and peer disapproval for their continued academic competition. Others survive by finding accepting peers, becoming social loners, or relating to adults (Kerr 1985; Lovecky 1994/5; Silverman 1994/5). Gifted girls who have special opportunity and encouragement for continued achievement may give up neither social acceptance nor future accomplishment. Home-schooling has helped many very gifted girls to continue to achieve because they are not so subject to peer approval. Others who experience a special relationship with an adult mentor or who are placed in special advanced programs continue to achieve (Reilly and Welch 1994/5; Subotnik and Strauss 1994/5).

Gifted girls are identified less often than are gifted boys, especially at the higher levels of ability. This appears to be due to parents having less interest in identifying girls. Often when boys have been identified, sisters who appear equally gifted are not tested. Parents state that they know the boy's IQ score, and the girl seems happy enough, so it is not necessary to have to make special plans for her education. Often, gifted girls are ignored, unless they are unhappy enough to complain as loudly as young boys do when their educational needs are not met.

Another reason that girls are identified less often as gifted is that girls are socialized to fit in with more average peers so they look average too. These gifted girls are adaptable and will put up with a lot of boring work to fit in with peers. It is not uncommon to note that quite gifted girls mysteriously lose their abilities in average classrooms (Gross 1999; Silverman 1993c). Thus, girls who at home read several grade levels above age mates appear to be struggling to learn to read at school, just as are best friends and other female classmates (Silverman 1993c).

Girls also may be more socially aware and more mature than boys at every age and IQ level. Consequently, they may show less discrepancy among areas of development (asynchrony) than do gifted boys at every level of potential: that is, cognitive, social, emotional, moral, and physical areas of development may be more similar than for boys. Gifted girls may also experience more social maturity than age peers. Because they are more adaptable and emotionally mature, they are able to get along by using advanced skills to do so. Advanced social and emotional ability is approved by adults, and the gifted girl maintains this superiority by not challenging others intellectually. Thus, gifted girls, and especially those who are highly gifted, of minority groups, with AD/HD, or any combination of these, may be even more at risk than are gifted boys.

CREATIVELY GIFTED CHILDREN

Creatively gifted children have special needs. They may be noticed as very differ-ent from age peers because of their nonconformity. Creatively gifted children often need to do things in their own way and on their own schedule. They also tend to be less involved with peers in activities that peers think important. They may be accepted by peers who recognize them as trendsetters or unique souls, or they may be loners. These are often children working on their own on creative projects, who tend to be absorbed in their own imaginations. They have unique learning styles, and may need school work to be relevant to their interests before they can become engaged. They function as if the process of doing something were the most important aspect.

Completing a project may be less important than the process of engagement in it. In many ways, these students are experimenting with "What if…" and once the question is answered to their satisfaction, they see little reason to go on and show anyone else. Many of these children appear then to jump from thing to thing, idea to idea. Novelty is what excites them; discovery engages them; passion holds their interest. These older creatively gifted children keep their passion by total immersion in one project, and then jump to the next interesting project.

Some of the traits of creativity overlap with those of AD/HD. Further exploration of this topic is found in Chapter 5 on creativity.

GIFTED CHILDREN WITH AD/HD, AS AND LEARNING DISABILITIES

These twice-exceptional children, who are the focus of this book, share many qualities in common with other gifted children, but also show differences that may hinder the development of their giftedness. Children with attention deficits may show deficits in cognitive, creative, emotional, social, and moral areas that affect how they are able to use their abilities. On the other hand, these children also show special strengths that may be responsible for much of the new, innovative work in the world. These aspects will be explored further in subsequent chapters.

Theories of giftedness

Developing a definition of giftedness is not easy; there are so many conflicting views and divergent opinions. Morelock (1996) described the problem from a historical perspective by following two main threads of argument through time.

One thread starts with adult genius and attempts to find correlates of prodigious achievement both in adulthood and in the childhood of the accomplished adult. This group focuses on what constitutes genius, and what is its relationship to eminence. The underlying assumption of this group is that extraordinary achievements can be traced to childhood behaviors that can then be fostered in today's children to develop future accomplished adults. This model is product-oriented – that is, it focuses on what was done. Thus, development of talents would, therefore, result in tangible products. Since this model focuses on specific achievement within a particular realm or domain of talent, such as music or spatial ability, this group can be referred to as the talent development model.

The second thread focuses more on the developmental needs of current gifted children. Gifted children are seen as having high cognitive ability and various social and emotional traits that require adjustments in schooling and parenting in order to meet their special needs. The underlying assumptions of this group are that the needs of gifted children require accommodation whether or not the child produces tangible accomplishments. The child may, or may not, grow up to produce something noteworthy. In fact, future accomplishment is not important. What matters are the needs of the child now. Nurturing the whole child is necessary, and worth doing for its own sake to meet the specific current needs of the child. Because of the specific focus on the needs of gifted children, this group can be referred to as the gifted child model. Neither model is totally clear-cut because there is considerable overlap in how the two models delineate what is needed by gifted children.

Which model of giftedness?

Both models have features that by high school can support the developmental needs of gifted children. The talent development model is useful with many gifted children who are ready to explore an area in depth. A child like Caitlin, age ten, who wanted to spend her time studying language acquisition in young children, could be accommodated under this model. Caitlin videotaped young children, and then analyzed the tapes for certain criteria with the help of an adult mentor in the field of linguistics. Her videotapes and linguistic analysis are products worth accomplishing. On the other hand, the lock-step academics of Caitlin's school meant that her needs for intellectual stimulation were not met on a day-to-day basis. In this regard, the gifted child model would allow acceleration and more in-depth work in regular academic subjects as well as the chance to study with a mentor on a special project. Caitlin's emotional sensitivity would also be important in the gifted child model. As a small child, Caitlin showed unusual empathy towards others. Her language acquisition project grew from her wish to see the world from another's eyes: that is, as language was acquired, how did the young child begin to formulate ideas about the world, and did these change as words were acquired? Focusing with Caitlin on this empathic projection allowed a more in-depth analysis of what she wanted to accomplish from her project. Thus, using emotional sensitivity was important in accomplishing her goal.

In terms of gifted children with attention problems, AD/HD, or learning disabilities, both models have something to offer. Programs using the talent development model offer children who may not be able to achieve to a high level academically a chance to develop particular talents in areas of interest. Thus, a boy like Mark, age 11, who was several years behind in reading and writing, nevertheless could develop his special talent in art. In fact, lessons with a mentor around his art interests, coupled with using those interests with a resource teacher, would likely improve Mark's reading and writing as well. On the other hand, those gifted children with AD/HD who are fast learners, and need mental stimulation, challenge, and both advanced and in-depth work, benefit more from a model that places emphasis on acceleration, in-depth projects, and enrichment.

Different Minds

A definition of giftedness

There have been a number of definitions of giftedness. Giftedness has meant genius, or a high IQ on an intelligence test. It has meant prodigious accomplishment in a particular field of endeavor. Winner (1996) defined giftedness as precocity, an insistence on marching to one's own drummer, and a rage to learn. The Columbus Group (1991) defined giftedness as asynchronous development in which advanced cognitive ability and intensity combine to create quantitatively different inner experiences and awareness. These, then, require modifications in parenting, teaching, and counseling to meet the needs of the gifted. Both Winner's and the Columbus Group's definitions have particular application to the gifted and exceptionally gifted.

In defining giftedness, the philosopher Immanuel Kant's (as cited in Thorndike and Lohman 1990) idea about mental faculties seems appropriate. Kant described three: cognition (thought), conation (will or motivation to do), and emotion (feeling).

Giftedness, as a construct, needs to include all three of these. Giftedness can be defined then as *cognition* (precocious development, high cognitive ability, reasoning ability, creative ability); *conation* (high motivation, a passion to master), and *emotion* (intense emotional experiences, sensitivity, compassion and empathy). These aspects of cognition, conation and emotion are not really independent of each other. Creativity, for example, requires ability, a problem to work on, an intense desire to know the answer to the problem, and a passion to overcome obstacles in order to find out the answer.

GIFTEDNESS AS COGNITION

Giftedness is manifested by precocious development in general, though the specific areas of advancement, and the combinations of strengths and weaknesses, are unique to each child. Precocious development, as used in this book, means advanced development of childhood milestones, advanced academic abilities, and advanced overall speed of learning new material. Thus, the traits described in this chapter as indicators of giftedness are markers because they describe precocious development or unusual abilities. Early talking, reading, and development of mathematical ability are examples of precocity. An ability to compose original music is an example of unusual ability.

High cognitive ability includes a component of ability to learn abstract concepts in advance of age peers, and to learn them with more complexity. This means the gifted child relates concepts to other concepts in advance of the expectation of the child's chronological age. Also, high cognitive ability involves unusual insight about the essence of something. There are both quantitative and qualitative differences from average age peers in speed and complexity of learning. Thus, cognition means early learning of complexity and abstraction. This is often, although not always, measured as intelligence.

Some children may not score high on an IQ test and yet may be quite gifted. This can occur with reflective thinkers, those with handicaps or AD/HD, learning disabilities, or because children are raised in poverty, or are recently from other cultures. For example, when people came to Rhode Island from Southeast Asian countries, in the 1970s and 1980s, the culture they had fled was so different from the USA that the cognitive abilities of these children could not be assessed; yet some of these children were likely quite gifted. One boy was high-school valedictorian even though he had only been in the United States a few years.

Creative ability means engaging in the process of discovery, either of things new to the child, or original thought. A child discovering something new, on his or her own, is engaging in a creative process. Gifted children ask more interesting and original questions of others and of themselves.

Creativity means both finding a pattern in observations or data that one did not see previously (recombination), or thinking of something entirely new (originality). An example of recombination might be the gifted child's discovery, at age five, of how multiplication tables form a pattern. An example of originality would be Gareth Matthews, at age six (Matthews 1994), as he struggled to understand the question he posed for himself: "Supposing that God created the world at some particular time – how is it that the world looks as if it had been going on forever?" (p.13). When his mother could not help him answer the question, he developed an analogy that satisfied him. He decided that the creation of the world was like looking at a completed circle. If one saw the circle being drawn, one knew the beginning, but the completed circle gave no clue as to its beginning; the end connected up with the beginning in a perfect way.

GIFTEDNESS AS CONATION

Conation describes the aspect of motivation, striving, effort, and will that drives all productive work. Without conation, cognition cannot come to fruition. Thus, giftedness has to do with a will to do. This will can include the drive of curiosity to find out something, or the desire to master. The drive of curiosity means that gifted children have what Winner (1996) calls "a rage to learn." These latter children love learning for its own sake. They have an intense desire to solve the problem in their minds, find out about things, or complete the pattern observed. This is an intrinsic motivation. The only reward is the satisfaction of the learning itself.

A passion to master means that the gifted child continues on a project despite obstacles, wanting to do more. A passion to master means the child loves to engage in the activity, and does so because of the joy engendered. These gifted children have the ability to focus sharply and experience states of "flow" during engagement on self-selected interests. Flow is a state of absorption in which the person is hyperfocused and the outside world does not intrude. In a state of flow, the level of challenge and the skills needed to do a task are exactly balanced (Csikszentmihalyi 1996). Learning a musical instrument, completing a project, and solving a problem are examples of a desire for mastery. These gifted children will persist in the face of obstacles, feel determination to prove something, and need to reach closure. The work meets the child's needs for stimulation, interest, and challenge.

GIFTEDNESS AS EMOTION

Intense emotional experiences are part of the definition of giftedness. The intensity and sensitivity of gifted children causes them to feel strongly about things, show great earnestness about life problems, have a clear vision about how things ought to be, and experience a need to interact with others at a deeper level.

Sensitivity has both emotional and cognitive aspects (Mendaglio 1995). Sensitivity refers to awareness of feelings, sensibility to the sound and meaning of language, to sensory input, and to how things work. Affective experience is an important part of creative production. Without it, projective identification, that putting of oneself directly into one's work, is impossible. Sensitivity also means aesthetic experience of sensory input, an attunement with subtle sensory perception. Creative work cannot take place without this type of sensitivity.

Empathy is part of giftedness – that is, sensitivity to the feelings of others and to the underlying dynamics of interactions. Empathy includes understanding and using feelings to comprehend people, aesthetics, and even nature.

Intensity is also a part of giftedness. While sensitivity speaks to the range of feeling possible, intensity speaks to the depth. Gifted children experience life more deeply. There is a richer nuance of meaning, more texture and color to everyday experiences, especially for young gifted children. It is the joy with which young gifted children experience each moment of life that brings a richness.

All three aspects (cognition, conation, and emotion) are important in the definition of giftedness. High intellectual ability is necessary, but so is a strong drive to do and be. A gifted child does not need to accomplish concrete tasks to be gifted. Wanting to know, a desire to find out, and a will to be all that one can be are aspects of giftedness that have little to do with whether the child will ever be eminent. A strong sensitivity that drives perception, insight, and interrelations among different things bring affective and cognitive aspects together. It is not possible to really be involved in learning without using emotion or desire. Thus, all three aspects – cognition, conation, and emotion – are part of all creative and exploratory endeavors of gifted children. Furthermore, the unique way in which gifted children experience the world, and the joy this brings, cannot be separated from the endeavors themselves.

I have seen
A curious child, who dwelt upon a tract
Of inland ground, applying to his ear
The convolutions of a smooth-lipped shell,
To which, in silence hushed, his very soul
Listened intensely; and his countenance soon
Brightened with joy, for from within was heard
Murmurings, whereby the monitor expressed
Mysterious union with its native sea.

William Wordsworth
The Excursion, Book IV, l.1132

Chapter 2

Attention Deficits: Attention Deficit/Hyperactivity Disorder

Phillip

Phillip was an engaging boy. Charming and cute, with big brown eyes and dark hair, he had a mischievous grin. At age six, Phillip loved school. He enjoyed knowing things, and especially sharing them with his classmates and teacher.

Phillip was an expert on methods of transportation, implements of war, outer space, and black holes. Phillip also loved to draw, designing elaborate scenes of battles with accompanying stories he would dictate to an adult. In class Phillip was exceptionally advanced in math. In 1st grade he already had the concepts of a 5th-grade student. Nevertheless, he was struggling to learn to read and spell. What concerned his teacher most, though, was his behavior.

Phillip had a hard time sitting in his seat, letting other children alone, not interrupting lessons, and letting the teacher help other children. He acted like the teacher was there for him alone. In fact it was not only the teacher; he acted like all the activities were for him too. Thus, when a visitor came to class to talk about handicaps, he dominated the conversation and attention, letting few of his classmates say anything. Another problem occurred when Phillip became frustrated. He would refuse to do the lesson and, if pressured, would throw the paper on the floor or rip it up. He sometimes would refuse tasks and argue with his teacher about what he was willing to do. He acted as if he had a say in what assignments the teacher was supposed to give him. The biggest problem, though, occurred with his leaving the school grounds at recess or when he felt stressed or upset. An episode of this "running away" precipitated a conference with his parents, and further evaluation was required in order for him to continue at that school.

At home things were somewhat better. Phillip was generally a good-natured boy who was highly creative. He loved to draw and spent hours doing so. He also played extensively with construction toys like Lego. Nevertheless, he was not asked to help very much because he would have tantrums and refuse. Getting him to do a task he did not like was a nightmare. Phillip was excellent at arguing his parents into letting him do what he wanted when he wanted. Arguments also arose over clothing and food because Phillip was fussy about what he wore and ate. He only liked soft clothes washed many times, and he ate a limited number of foods. His parents made many accommodations for him; these avoided much of the trouble he experienced at school.

Phillip's parents took him to be evaluated at the Gifted Resource Center of New England. He had an initial diagnostic session and then, as his school required, further psychological, neuropsychological, and academic testing to assess both his behavior and his learning issues.

Phillip was found to be a moderately gifted boy, with an IQ in the 150+ range on the *Stanford-Binet Intelligence Scale – Fourth Edition*. He was quite advanced in mathematics reasoning and computation, but slightly below grade level in reading, spelling, and writing. When asked to dictate a story, Phillip was able to do so and produced a complex action story about a space battle. Neuro-psychological evaluation showed him to have difficulty with organization and planning, listening to directions and instructions, inhibiting responding, selecting targets, scanning for symbols, and rapidly and efficiently shifting attention. He also showed poor short-term memory, and had trouble with efficiently starting and stopping himself on tasks. Phillip worked best for an immediate reward that he could select as soon as testing was over for the session. He also needed a point system in which he earned points for cooperative behavior and for "trying" in order to maintain control and do tasks.

This evaluation of Phillip showed him to be a highly gifted and creative child with AD/HD Combined Type and dyslexia. In addition, Phillip had some symptoms of sensory integration problems and Oppositional Defiant Disorder (ODD).

A boy like Phillip is disturbing in a regular classroom – that is, a class of 18 to 25 children with one teacher. Yet what part of Phillip is most disturbing? Is it his AD/HD, that part of him that never stops talking, wants instant attention, and doesn't complete tasks? Or is it his giftedness, that part of him that wants to suck in learning as if he were a sponge child, and needs all those facts and ideas to feed his insatiable curiosity? This part of Phillip wants to know everything, wants to share what he knows, and wants to drain the last drop from any encounter to make sure he has it all.

The truth is, both parts of Phillip are disturbing, and both his AD/HD and his high degree of giftedness feed on each other, so he is in need of stimulation, novelty, and complex new ideas that will engage his mind and keep him thinking, interacting, and developing new creative connections. Needless to say, this is hard for one teacher to do. Phillip has the perfect solution. He wants (and acts as if he has) a one-on-one tutor there for him alone, able to move at his own pace and with his interests.

The focus of this chapter

In order to answer the question of what part of Phillip's behavior is due to AD/HD and what to giftedness, it is necessary to have some knowledge of both areas. Giftedness was explored in Chapter 1. This chapter is more focused on what constitutes AD/HD. This is a long chapter and it will help to have an outline. This chapter is divided into six major sections.

- Development and types of AD/HD.
- Symptoms of AD/HD.
- Understanding AD/HD.
- Gifted children with AD/HD.
- Executive functions affected by AD/HD in gifted children.
- Positive aspects of AD/HD.

Each chapter section is further divided into subsections and these will be summarized at the start of each section.

Attention deficit disorders: Development and types

AD/HD is currently thought of as an executive function disorder: that is, it is seen as a dysfunction of that part of the brain that attends to, organizes, processes, and outputs information. The particular symptoms that comprise the core of AD/HD – attention, impulsivity, and hyperactivity – describe a disorder that impacts life in several settings. However, the symptoms displayed may differ from setting to setting, so subtle symptoms may be missed in some settings, especially in milder cases.

In this section of the chapter, the development of AD/HD, the types of AD/HD, prevalence and genetics of AD/HD, and other conditions that can coexist with AD/HD will be discussed.

AD/HD as a developmental disorder

AD/HD appears to be a developmental disorder: that is, symptoms start in youth and can continue into adulthood. Symptoms predominating at each stage of development will be somewhat different. Thus, young children may show less inattention and more hyperactivity.

Symptoms of AD/HD can change over time, and with them, the specific diagnosis. Hart *et al.* (1995) found the predominantly Hyperactive/Impulsive Type of AD/HD primarily in preschoolers and young children. Later on, many of these children appeared to show the Combined Type of AD/HD. This may mean that the predominantly Hyperactive/Impulsive Type is a developmental stage of the Combined Type, with attention deficits appearing later (Barkley 1998). Also, it is well known that symptoms of hyperactivity and impulsivity decrease substantially in many boys with AD/HD as they grow through adolescence. In adulthood, it is not hyperactivity or impulsivity that is a problem but underlying deficits in attention. Because symptoms vary with age, a set of symptoms for diagnosis at each developmental stage is needed, but not currently available (National Institutes of Health 1998).

Age of onset of symptoms also varies with severity of symptoms. Though the *Diagnostic and Statistical Manual* of the American Psychiatric Association (the DSM-IV-TR, American Psychiatric Association 2000) – the "Bible" that codifies each of the mental health disorders in the United States – describes AD/HD as a disorder with symptoms recognizable prior to age seven, in practice many people are not diagnosed until much later in life. Their earlier symptoms were less noticeable. Consequently, there is more controversy currently about the age criterion for symptom onset.

In making a diagnosis of AD/HD, one of the current criteria from the DSM-IV is that the disorder be present before age seven. However, Barkley (1998) suggested that this requirement, as specified by DSM-IV, may be unrealistic. Hartmann (1996) suggested that for some gifted children, AD/HD is not identified until 4th through 9th grade, because they are able to get by with minimum effort in primary years.

Research has suggested that girls have somewhat different brain structure than boys, and this may mean that AD/HD does not reveal itself in girls until adolescence when girls' brains change with puberty (Ratey and Johnson 1997).

Nadeau *et al.* (1999) suggested that differences in development of the dopamine neurotransmitter system in the brain (which is related to the symptoms of AD/HD), increased sensitivity of the female brain to estrogen levels, and differences in actual brain structure may account for the differences between boys and girls with AD/HD. For example, with puberty, many boys seem to decrease symptoms of hyperactivity, and their AD/HD looks less severe, while for girls with AD/HD, ability to self-monitor and self-regulate behavior and learning decreases with the onset of puberty. In addition, mood swings and irritability may become more problematic.

This accords with this author's clinical experience with gifted children. Many do quite well through elementary school, only to fall apart when the more complex academic demands of middle school are placed on them. For some, the crash may not occur until much later, even as late as graduate or professional school. Consequently, a more flexible age of onset is needed, with recognition that compensation can occur at earlier ages due to high intellectual capacity. This is especially true of AD/HD Inattentive Type.

Types of AD/HD

The American Psychiatric Association's (2000) *Diagnostic and Statistical Manual* (DSM-IV-TR) describes criteria needed to make the diagnosis of AD/HD. The reader is referred to Appendix A for a full description. The DSM-IV describes different types of AD/HD:

- *AD/HD Inattentive Type* (symptoms of inattention)

- *AD/HD Combined Type* (aspects of inattention, impulsivity, and hyperactivity)

- *AD/HD Hyperactive/Impulsive Type* (few symptoms of inattention; impulsivity and hyperactivity predominate).

In addition to DSM-IV, the coding system of the World Health Organization's *International Classification of Diseases – Tenth Edition* (ICD-10) (WHO 1993) criteria is often used, especially in Europe. Behaviors from the diagnostic criteria from DSM-IV and/or ICD-10 have been codified into checklists, structured interviews and history forms to help in the diagnosis of AD/HD.

Prevalence and genetics of AD/HD

AD/HD Combined Type is the most prevalent type found in childhood. Estimates of prevalence of the Combined Type range from 2 to 10% or even higher (Barkley 1990; Ross and Ross 1982) for the United States. An interesting study by Szatmari *et al.* (1989) in Ontario, Canada, found that the rate of AD/HD peaks at some ages for boys with a high at 6 to 9 years, and a low at 14 to 15 years; however the overall incidence of AD/HD for boys was 9%. In contrast, for girls, the prevalence was about 3.3%.

AD/HD Combined Type has also been found in other countries than the United States. However, depending on how it is diagnosed, prevalence rates can be much lower than in the United States. For example, in Great Britain, until very recently, the prevalence rate was about 1%, the most severely affected children being diagnosed with "hyperkinesis" (Blakemore-Brown 2002).

At the National Institute of Health's Consensus Conference on AD/HD (1998), the prevalence rate was hotly debated. The consensus statement issued at the end of the conference suggested that a prevalence rate of 1 to 3% was likely using the strictest guidelines for AD/HD Combined Type. This would pick out only the most severe cases. Using more liberal guidelines, allowing for other types of AD/HD and other accompanying conditions such as ODD, the prevalence could rise to 5 to 15% of the population. AD/HD was also found across cultures, but the prevalence depended on cultural norms. This means that behaviors that are seen as problematic within one culture are seen as normal within another (Bird 1998).

Children with AD/HD Inattentive Type tend to be diagnosed much later, in mid-elementary school years. Girls are more prevalent in the sample, and the ratio of girls to boys is almost equal (1.4% boys to 1.3% girls, Szatmari *et al.* 1989). These ratios do not change over time. What does appear to change is the prevalence. That is, the prevalence of AD/HD Inattentive Type increases through adolescence into adulthood.

Goldstein and Goldstein (1998) reported that children with AD/HD tend to fall to a greater than expected degree at the high end of intellectual potential. They point out that there has been no well-controlled research to demonstrate the validity of this anecdotal evidence. This is certainly true. No one can say for sure what the prevalence of AD/HD is among gifted children. In Korea, Chae, Kim and Noh (2003) found that 9.4% of gifted children in their study had AD/HD. In this office, more than 200 gifted children have been diagnosed with AD/HD. At the Gifted Development Center in Denver, over 3000 gifted children have been assessed since 1974 and about 10% have positive diagnoses of AD/HD. A great many more exhibit some AD/HD symptoms (Chae *et al.* 2003; Lovecky and Silverman 1998). Thus, while an accurate prevalence figure is not known, there are a significant number of gifted children with AD/HD.

AD/HD appears to run in families. There is a strong hereditary component found in studies of families (Biederman, Faraone, and Lapey 1992a; Smalley 1997), and identical and fraternal twins (Hewitt *et al.* 1997; Levy *et al.* 1997). Thus, in an Australian study, Levy *et al.* (1997) found that in 1938 families with twins, if one twin had AD/HD, 82% of their identical and 38% of fraternal twins' siblings also had AD/HD.

The heritability of intelligence is well known. In fact, high intelligence also can be seen in some studies to have a genetic component (Thompson, Detterman, and Plomin 1993, cited in Winner 1996; Thompson and Plomin 1993). It would be interesting to know the concordance of heritability for high intelligence and AD/HD, but such studies have not yet been done.

Coexisting conditions with AD/HD

AD/HD is very commonly associated with other psychiatric conditions. It is quite common for gifted children with AD/HD at the Gifted Resource Center of New England to have more than AD/HD. Anxiety, depression, and oppositional defiant behavior are the most common coexisting complaints. This is similar to results found in more general populations.

Biederman *et al.* (1992a) found that among children with AD/HD, 51% had at least one other diagnosis; among adults 77% had AD/HD and at least one other diagnosis.

Recently, Jensen, Martin, and Cantwell (1997) reviewed all the literature on conditions coexisting with AD/HD – what are called "comorbid" conditions. They concluded that the largest body of literature was on AD/HD and conduct disorders (Conduct Disorder, ODD, Disruptive Disorder). They also postulated that there was enough evidence to postulate two new types of AD/HD: AD/HD aggressive subtype, characterized by an earlier onset, greater male to female ratio, and decreased chance of later amelioration; and AD/HD anxious subtype, characterized by decreased impulsivity, and decreased acting-out behaviors. Faraone, Biederman, and Monuteaux (2000) suggested that, even in girls, AD/HD with Conduct Disorder appears to be a distinct familial subtype: that is, relatives were also at risk for the development of conduct disorders.

OPPOSITIONAL DEFIANT DISORDER (ODD)

Oppositional Defiant Disorder is quite prevalent in children with AD/HD Combined Type. Barkley (1995) estimated that up to two-thirds of children with AD/HD Combined Type will have ODD. Of these, 45% may progress on to a more serious conduct disorder. A high percentage of children referred in clinic samples with AD/HD also have ODD, up to 80%. ODD includes behaviors that are aggressive, hostile, argumentative, and negativistic. They occur at home, school, and in social settings. These children lose their tempers, argue with adults, defy or refuse to comply with reasonable requests or rules, deliberately annoy or tease others, blame others for mistakes or misbehavior, are easily annoyed by others, are angry and resentful, spiteful, and often vindictive. A child needs four out of these eight characteristics to be given the diagnosis (American Psychiatric Association, DSM-IV-TR 2000). Boys are found at a higher ratio than girls by three to one (Barkley 1998).

ANXIETY DISORDERS

AD/HD is also associated with anxiety disorders such as Overanxious Disorder, Obsessive Compulsive Disorder (OCD), and Separation Anxiety Disorder. About 30 to 40 % of children with AD/HD have one or more anxiety disorders, while 15 to 30% of children with anxiety disorders have AD/HD as well (Tannock 2000). Tannock further suggested that the rate of association of anxiety disorders and AD/HD is greater that would be expected given base rates of each disorder. Thus, anxiety disorders are likely to occur in children with AD/HD. Children with OCD and AD/HD overlapped by 6 to 33% (summarized in Brown 2000a).

Differentiating between anxiety disorders and AD/HD is not so easy. However, as both disorders can coexist, it is important to treat both. Thus, if treatment for AD/HD does not decrease anxiety symptoms, children need to be further assessed for anxiety disorders. On the other hand, children presenting with symptoms of anxiety need to be assessed for AD/HD if treatment for anxiety symptoms does not decrease significantly symptoms of poor attention, poor concentration, excessive worrying, and jitteriness. A word of caution with coexisting anxiety and AD/HD: stimulant medication, especially methyl-phenidate, can increase feelings of jitteriness.

TOURETTE SYNDROME

Tourette Syndrome has a high rate of coexistence with AD/HD. Comings (2000) suggested that most studies have found that between 25 and 85% of children with Tourette Syndrome also have AD/HD. Furthermore, there is a high rate of tics in relatives (25 to 50%). Often the first symptom of Tourette Syndrome is the appearance of AD/HD. Because the prevalence of AD/HD is so high, it is impor-tant to carefully assess if a child with symptoms of Tourette Syndrome also has AD/HD. If tics appear to be present in children with AD/HD, they also need to be assessed for Tourette Syndrome.

It has been thought that stimulant medication was responsible for producing Tourette Syndrome in children with AD/HD. However, Barkley (1998) suggested that while it was less likely that stimulant medication caused Tourette Syndrome, it was still necessary to screen children with AD/HD for a familial history of tic disorders since these might be brought out in susceptible children by stimulant medication.

OCD is also commonly found with Tourette Syndrome. Finally, a large percentage of people with AS also have coexisting Tourette Syndrome, and benefit from medication to alleviate symptoms of tics.

MOOD DISORDERS

Mood disorders coexist with AD/HD to a high degree. Major Depression, Dysthymia (mild chronic depression), and Bipolar Disorder are found at rates far beyond expectancy in the AD/HD population. Biederman, Newcorn, and Sprich (1991a) found 15 to 75% rates of coexistence for all types of depression with AD/HD in their review of studies. Biederman *et al.* (1995) found that in samples of children with depression, about 74% also had AD/HD. The association between AD/HD and mood disorders was likely due to common familiar etiological factors. That is, both could have a genetic basis, but the basis is due to related, not identical genes (Biederman *et al.* 1991b)

Children with symptoms of AD/HD who also have symptoms of Major Depression need assessment of both disorders, and treatment of both disorders if warranted. If symptoms of Major Depression are alleviated, but poor concentration and difficulty with arousal continue, AD/HD may be a part of the picture. Also, sometimes people, especially adolescents with both depression and AD/HD, abuse alcohol and drugs as a means of self-medicating. Children with substance abuse need to be evaluated for both depression and AD/HD.

There is a high correlation between Juvenile Onset Bipolar Disorder and AD/HD. Biederman *et al.* (1992b, 1996) and Spencer *et al.* (2000) found that 91% of children with Bipolar Disorder also met the criteria for diagnosis of AD/HD. Faraone *et al.* (1997) investigated families with and without Bipolar Disorder and AD/HD; they found that there may be a subtype of AD/HD in which AD/HD is comorbid with Bipolar Disorder and this type is different from other types of AD/HD.

Those children with Juvenile Onset Bipolar Disorder appear to have AD/HD and also a cyclic mood disorder. The cycle can be very rapid, several within a day. Thus, children with extreme behavior problems, irritability, and hyperactivity need assessment of both mood disorder and AD/HD. It should be noted that children and young adolescents with Juvenile Onset Bipolar Disorder do not fit within the DSM-IV criteria for adult Bipolar Disorder. There are currently several checklists available for clinicians that detail the symptoms of Bipolar Disorder in children (Papolos and Papolos 1999).

PERVASIVE DEVELOPMENTAL DISORDER (PDD)

Frazier *et al.* (2001) assessed the overlapping symptoms of AD/HD and PDD. Part of the diagnostic criteria for PDD is that AD/HD cannot be a coexisting condition: that is, the symptoms of AD/HD are subsumed under the PDD criteria. However, Frazier *et al.* argued that children with clear-cut symptoms of AD/HD should be diagnosed with AD/HD in addition to a PDD diagnosis so that their symptoms can have adequate treatment, including stimulant medication.

ASPERGER SYNDROME (AS)

Asperger Syndrome can coexist with AD/HD. Some clinicians have found that 60 to 70% of children with AS also have AD/HD. Rosenn (2002) distinguished two groups of children with AS and AD/HD symptoms. In one group, symptoms may have more relation to anxiety. These children do not respond well to stimulant medication, but do respond to anti-anxiety medication which decreases problems with attention and tic-like movements. A second group appears to have more typical AD/HD and responds quite well to stimulant medication in alleviating symptoms.

Distinguishing whether a child has AD/HD or AS can be difficult. Children with AS have more pervasive developmental delays in gross and fine motor skills, affective modulation, neurocognition, sensory integration, pragmatic speech, and socialization skills (Rosenn 2002). The most distinguishing feature is the lack of appreciation of children with AS for social reciprocity. Children with AD/HD may have difficulty acting in the moment, but they do recognize what another's thoughts, feelings, and perspective will be; children with AS do not. This is discussed further in Chapter 3.

LEARNING DISABILITIES

Learning disabilities, reading disorders, and language deficits are also well known to coexist with AD/HD. About 20 to 25% of all children with AD/HD have some type of learning disability (Tannock and Brown 2000). Tirosh and Cohen (1998) found a 45% rate of language problems in children identified with AD/HD. Central Auditory Processing Disorder (CAPD) can co-occur with AD/HD with a high rate of overlap (45 to 75%), though the high level may be the result of difficulty in making a diagnosis since language problems can occur in both CAPD and AD/HD (Tannock and Brown 2000). See Chapter 4, under the section on visual-spatial learning styles, for more information.

NONVERBAL LEARNING DISABILITY

Nonverbal Learning Disability (NVLD) can occur with AD/HD. Children with NVLD have right-brain deficits that affect many areas including: visual-spatial-organizational skills; motor coordination deficits; language deficits in metaphoric language; academic skills deficits such as math, reading comprehension, and written expression, and often deficits in social awareness and social judgment (Denckla 1991; Rourke and Tsatsanis 2000; Thompson 1997). In evaluating NVLD in gifted children with AD/HD, it is important to discriminate whether weaknesses in visual-perceptual-motor tasks are the result of attention problems, or if they truly constitute an NVLD. Evaluation needs to based on more than the Performance section of the Wechsler Intelligence Scale because the timed aspect of the Performance section can be affected by slow processing speed and poor attention. A fuller description of the problems of children with AD/HD and NVLD is presented in Chapter 4.

Diagnosing AD/HD

Diagnosing AD/HD can be difficult when other disorders are present. Sometimes, AD/HD is missed because the person presents predominantly as having depression or substance abuse, and no one looks further. Sometimes, everything is attributed to the person's AD/HD, and other disorders, like depression, are overlooked.

Kaplan *et al.* (2001) took a different perspective. They evaluated children for seven disorders: AD/HD, ODD, Conduct Disorder, Developmental Coordination Disorder (delayed motor milestones, motor clumsiness, poor coordination, poor handwriting that interferes with performance), reading disability, depression, and anxiety. Only 20% of those with AD/HD had only that one disorder. Forty percent had one additional disorder; 28% had two additional disorders, and 12% had three or more additional disorders. Based on these percentages, Kaplan *et al.* disputed the idea of separate disorders. They think of these conditions as one underlying condition of brain dysfunction with different manifestations.

Biederman *et al.* (1992a) suggested that the high rate of coexisting conditions with AD/HD may be the result of AD/HD being not a single entity, but a group of conditions with different etiologies, risk factors and outcomes. T.E. Brown (2000b) attempted to modify this idea by offering this compromise: AD/HD is the name for a spectrum of deficits of cognitive executive functions that often manifest together and respond to similar treatments. They may have differing etiologies, risk factors and outcomes, and may also coexist with other psychiatric disorders. Thus, Brown sees AD/HD as a cluster of attentional and executive dysfunctions that may occur together, persist, and may occur with other psychiatric conditions.

Major symptoms of AD/HD

Symptoms that describe AD/HD appear to cluster into a number of main areas that reflect the underlying deficits in executive function and behavioral disinhibition. Major symptoms include inattention, hyperactivity, and impulsivity. This section of the chapter will focus on these symptoms.

AD/HD Combined Type has been extensively studied. For the Combined Type, Barkley (1995) described characteristics such as difficulty sustaining attention, distractibility, difficulties with delayed gratification, difficulty controlling impulses, hyperactivity and hyperresponsive behaviors, difficulty following directions, and difficulty working consistently.

Goldstein and Goldstein (1990, 1998) listed inattention and distractibility, hyperactivity and overarousal, impulsivity, difficulty with delaying gratification, and problems with emotions and locus of control.

In general, deficits of attention, difficulty with distractibility, impulse control, delayed gratification, hyperactivity, and hyperarousal are traits agreed on by the majority of researchers to describe AD/HD Combined Type.

AD/HD Inattentive Type has been less well studied. In general, symptoms of poorer attention, difficulty shifting attention, slower processing and arousal, distractibility, memory deficits, and emotional overarousal predominate. Hallowell and Ratey (1994b) described children with the Inattentive Type as more daydreamy, motorically slow, but more imaginative. They saw distractibility as the core symptom. Barkley (1990, 1998) described the problem more as one of difficulty with focused or selective attention and slower processing speed rather than of disinhibition.

Goldstein and Goldstein (1998) summarized research in the differences between AD/HD Inattentive Type and AD/HD Combined Type children. Symptoms described by various writers for AD/HD Inattentive Type included increased anxiety and worry, increased social withdrawal, sluggish tempo and drowsiness, increased frequency of learning disabilities, older age of referral, and fewer who responded to stimulant medication in the AD/HD Inattentive Type samples studied.

The core symptoms of AD/HD – that is, difficulty with attention, including distractibility and arousal – appear common to both types. In addition, those with AD/HD Combined Type have difficulty with hyperactivity and impulsivity.

Difficulties with attention

Arousing, focusing, and sustaining attention have long been viewed as main symptoms of AD/HD. These difficulties are related to deficits in underlying executive functions. T.E. Brown (2000b) described five executive functions that impact attention: organizing and activating for work or arousal; sustaining attention and concentration and avoiding distraction; sustaining effort and energy for work (or motivation/reward); managing emotions (dealing with frustration); and utilizing working memory. These difficulties affect those with both types of AD/HD.

Children with AD/HD can have trouble with certain types of attention, but not others. In fact, they can focus on some types of material very well and for long periods of time (Wender 1987). This confuses parents, and sometimes physicians, who see a child able to focus on things he or she likes to do for a long time, or who can focus well in a one-to-one situation such as a doctor's office. In the latter case, the novelty of the situation, as well as the adult interaction, tends to help the child to focus. In this case it is the motivation system that appears affected since the novel or self-selected activity is rewarding, and thus the child is able to pay attention.

There are several types of attention; recall the discussion in the Introduction to this book. Goldstein and Goldstein (1990, 1998) suggested that some children may have more trouble with divided attention: that is, the ability to do two different things at once such as listen to the teacher and take notes (working memory). Others do less well at focused attention; they have difficulty getting going on what they are asked to do (arousal).

Selective attention (motivation) can be another area of difficulty. Children cannot easily select what to pay attention to; they cannot prioritize among competing things to see which is the most important. Instead, they select the most important to them. Sustained attention and persistence is another source of difficulty for some children. They cannot stick with tasks long enough to complete them. Finally, vigilance and readiness to respond (arousal) can be affected. Here, the child is not ready to respond when a series of responses is required. He or she is supposed to wait for a target item to occur, and then respond or not according to a cue (such as hitting a button whenever an "X" is seen, or continuing to hit a button for "X" but not "Y").

Barkley (1997) suggested that children with AD/HD Combined Type are distinctly different from those with AD/HD Inattentive Type in the difficulties they have with attention. Those with Combined Type AD/HD have more trouble with sustained attention and persistence, with resisting distraction and inhibiting responding. They therefore have difficulty with selecting what to pay attention to, and when to respond or stop responding, as well as with sticking to something. Phillip exhibited all of these types of attention problems. He had trouble doing school work unless he was interested. He was willing to discuss topics but refused to attempt to write anything. Phillip was also easily distracted. If he was doing a task, and a noise occurred outside, he had to run to the window to see what it was. Sometimes, he just stopped working and started drawing his own battle scenes because he had started thinking about them. It was also difficult if Phillip was involved in drawing for him to stop, put his work away, and go to lunch. Paying attention was a big problem for Phillip.

Children with the Inattentive Type of AD/HD appear to have difficulty with arousing attention so they are slower to start things. They have more trouble shifting attention, and may become stuck on irrelevant parts. They also may hyperfocus when they do focus attention. Getting them to stop focusing can be as difficult as getting them to start. Since these children tend to daydream a lot, both their own thoughts and outside stimuli disrupt focusing. Sometimes, the daydreaming of these children is without thought, almost a meditative state. Grace, age nine, was an exceptionally slow worker. It took her a long time to do any written school work, and she often had to take the work home and complete it for homework. This made her homework take several hours each night. Grace daydreamed extensively. She would be working hard on a project and the next thing she knew the bell was ringing. Grace was usually surprised at how little work she had done. She didn't remember not working, or anything else that she had been doing. She was such a quiet girl her teachers never caught on to her difficulties with attention, but just thought she worked slowly.

DEVELOPMENT OF ATTENTION

Attention deficits can be studied early in life even though they are not usually recognized as problems until children reach school age. Parents usually don't note problems with sustained attention because young children don't sustain attention very long in adult terms, especially on things that are not of interest. Differences in ability to sustain attention, on something of less interest, might be small but significant (say the difference between three and seven minutes at age two). The gap gets larger as the child gets older so that by school age, when peers are able to sustain attention much longer, the child with AD/HD stands out more.

DeGangi (1991; DeGangi *et al.* 1993) studied sustained attention in infants and young children from 7 months to 30 months of age. Sustained attention was defined as the ability to initiate and sustain attention to novel events, persistence on a given task over time, self-initiation of organized responses, and ability to shift attention between stimuli and maintain focus despite competing stimuli. DeGangi was able to differentiate young children with normal attention from those with attention deficits at an early age.

Ability to stick with an activity for a period of time increases with age. A child at age two can sustain attention for an independent activity that is not constantly changing (as television, for example, changes) for about seven minutes, at age four for 13 minutes, at age six for closer to an hour (Call 1985, cited in Goldstein and Goldstein 1990). Children with AD/HD typically act like much younger children in the length of time they can sustain attention. Barkley (1995) estimates they are generally about two years behind age peers.

Difficulties with hyperactivity and impulsivity

The ability to both start and stop behavior is important in being able to regulate one's own responses. Thus, the child who has trouble with inhibiting responses has trouble with four clusters of impulsive behaviors (Goldstein and Goldstein 1998): ability to stop and suppress action (inhibition); ability to use reflection in acting (internalized speech); ability to think of consequences (rule-governed behavior); and ability to act spontaneously (working memory).

Children with AD/HD Combined Type can't organize their behavior. They have difficulty with starting and stopping. It is difficult for them to wait or follow rules easily. They interrupt and disrupt others, are less mature in controlling motor activity, and they need to do things quickly so they are not very accurate.

They also have trouble with timing, following directions, delaying gratification, and working for a longer-term goal rather than one that's promised immediately. Children with AD/HD-Combined Type do know what to do, and they do learn from experience. Their difficulty is more performance based: they can't connect knowing with doing, and so they are inefficient in performing. The example of Phillip at the start of this chapter is a description of a boy who has difficulties with disinhibition. For example, Phillip's interrupting his teacher to get attention when she was working with other children, his running to the window to see what was making that noise outside, or his running away when he was upset all showed poor ability to stop and think, and to inhibit impulsive responding.

Boys with AD/HD Combined Type tend to show more externalizing behaviors: that is, they tend to act more impulsively and aggressively. Externalizers see consequences due to forces outside themselves, such as luck. These boys think their mistakes and misbehavior just happened, or are someone else's fault. In social situations, boys with AD/HD, compared to boys without AD/HD, tend to misread their own social mistakes, thinking they are successful when they are not. Boys with AD/HD often don't see the social problems they are having or causing either (Hoza *et al.* 2000). Phillip never thought that he was disruptive or intruding on other children's games. He thought they were just being mean to him if they didn't want him to play or yelled at him for intruding. He never saw how he contributed to the problem.

DEVELOPMENT OF INHIBITORY MECHANISMS

Problems with disinhibition arise early in life. DeGangi (1991) studied infants he recognized as being "regulatory disordered." These children were fussy, irritable, had trouble with self-soothing, were intolerant of change, had a difficult temperament, were hypersensitive to environmental stimulation, and had trouble with sleep, mood regulation, arousal, feeding, and transitions. Many were also hyperactive and showed disorders of sustained attention. A high incidence of these same symptoms were still present at age four (DeGangi *et al.* 1993). Problems in self-regulation that occur after the first six months of life are a common early presentation of symptoms that later may represent developmental delays in impulse control (Quinn 1997).

Another aspect of the disinhibition of children with AD/HD Combined Type is their variability of behavior. They do much better in some situations, particularly those in which few demands are placed on them. They do much less well when specific demands are placed on them, when behavioral restraint is required, when tired, upset, hungry, when they have too much to do at once, when the level of stimulation within a task is low, when consequences are not immediate, or they have to wait too long for something to happen, when there is a lack of adult supervision during a task, or if the task is something they do not like doing. Many children do best one on one with adults and peers, and least well in a large group. Some do well in novel situations with peers (as on a field trip to a place they find especially interesting), but do not do well when time is unstructured and the purpose of the activity is less well defined (as at a birthday party).

Phillip did better at home than at school because the demands placed on him were different in both places. At home, he had more choice of his own activities, and his parents had learned not to ask too much of him. They adjusted the environment to fit his needs. At school, though, he had to fit into the structure already there, and he could not.

AD/HD in girls

When people think of AD/HD, they think of boys. Partly, this is because much of the focus on AD/HD has been on the hyperactive/impulsive component, which is more predominant in boys, and less on the inattentive component, which is more predominant in girls. Also, much of the research on symptoms, developmental course, and outcome has been done with boys. Nevertheless, much of what is reported about symptoms, diagnostic criteria, and development appears to be true for girls, but there are some differences. The rest of this section of the chapter will focus on the internalizing behaviors, symptoms of hyperactivity and impulsivity, cognitive differences, and difficulties with peer relationships seen in girls with AD/HD.

Nadeau, Littman, and Quinn (1999) have reviewed much of what is known about girls with AD/HD in their book, *Understanding Girls with AD/HD*. These authors suggested that girls with AD/HD struggle with different issues than boys because girls are neurologically different from boys. They socialize and verbalize differently and are raised according to different social expectations. An analysis of the literature of gender differences in AD/HD (Gershon 2002) showed that, compared to boys with AD/HD, girls had lower ratings on hyperactivity, inattention, impulsivity, and externalizing behaviors. Girls had more intellectual impairments on Full Scale and Verbal IQ in intelligence tests than boys but were equivalent on measures of achievement and neuropsychological functioning.

INTERNALIZING BEHAVIORS

Internalizing behaviors refer to how a girl sees the responsibility for what happens. Is it due to fate or to her own failures? People who see consequences as the result of their own failures tend to be internalizers; those who see consequences due to forces outside themselves (fate or the other person's fault) are externalizers. Internalizers tend to feel more anxious and depressed, to have more psychosomatic symptoms, and to withdraw more. Externalizers tend to be more aggressive and attention seeking.

One of the biggest differences between boys and girls is in referral patterns. Girls tend to cluster more in the Inattentive Type; yet most of the parent and teaher scales used to assess AD/HD emphasize externalizing behaviors, behaviors much more prevalent in boys. There are some exceptions including the new scales developed by T.E. Brown (2001) and the newest revision of Conners (2001). Related to this is the likelihood that when teachers fill out checklists on girls, they compare them to boys. Thus, boys stand out as having problems, and girls slip through the cracks. At home, parents are more likely to compare their daughters to other girls they know, and thus are more able to see the subtle differences (Nadeau *et al.* 1999).

Girls who have symptoms which would place them in the AD/HD Inattentive Type show many internalizing behaviors. They are daydreamy, slow to start work, slow to accomplish work, and anxious about the result of their work. Because of this they can be perfectionistic. Some also show anxiety with worries, fears, and excessive concern about consequences. These gifted girls, even when they do well, constantly worry that they will fail the next test, forget to study, or make some terrible mistake in their assignments. Perfectionism is a means of trying to ward off these concerns by obsessively working to avoid errors.

These girls are never free of worry. Due to their attention problems, they can never depend on getting all the directions the first time, or on knowing when they have done enough. Their attention and organizational problems mean that they have real difficulty paying attention to the content of messages, seeing errors, and knowing that they are doing a good job. This can lead to depression because these girls can feel that nothing they do is enough. Even when they are getting straight "A"'s, and are on the honor roll, these gifted girls feel as if they are impostors, only getting their grades by the sheerest of luck, by the skin of their teeth.

These girls manage their AD/HD symptoms by being hyperfocused and working extremely hard. They are driven, anxious, and have little energy to do things other than school work. In fact, they are afraid that if they stop studying so intensely they will not do as well. These are often bright girls who want to succeed, but they cannot do it all, so they sacrifice social and recreational pursuits for academics. High-achieving gifted girls who show excessive anxiety and perfectionism should be evaluated to see if they have underlying AD/HD.

Alissa, age ten, actually was a high achiever in class, though she had some trouble with writing. However, she managed her inattention by asking other girls what the teacher meant, by asking for feedback from her mother on her written homework, and by being slow and extra careful in doing her work. Still, Alissa was excessively worried about school work.

She studied hard for each test, yet was so anxious she would vomit just before taking it. Her anxiety was so intense she made errors, then was devastated when she had not gotten 100%. Nevertheless, she usually scored in the 90s. Alissa was also overly concerned about doing assignments exactly the way the teacher wanted. To this end, she asked the teacher too many questions about exactly what was required. She was not good at intuiting what requirements were. She never knew whether she had done a satisfactory job until she obtained her grade. Alissa had no ability to sense for herself whether or not she had learned something. Alissa's anxiety and AD/HD made it difficult for her to feel good about her accomplishments or to learn from her failures. Because she made errors no matter how hard she tried, she never felt in control.

SYMPTOMS OF HYPERACTIVITY AND IMPULSIVITY

Nadeau *et al.* (1999) described severe cases of hyperactivity/impulsivity in girls as similar to that of boys. However, girls are also likely to show hyperactivity in behaviors such as talking too much, being silly or showing off, being a "tomboy," or showing emotional overreactivity, as opposed to the more acting-out behaviors that boys exhibit. Consequently, while these girls are less apt to be labeled "oppositional" by teachers, they are apt to be seen as exhibiting negative or immature behavior.

Sydney, a gifted 3rd-grade girl with AD/HD, was excessively talkative in school. It didn't matter where her teacher moved her desk; Sydney would talk to whoever was next to her. The other children complained that she disrupted their work because she talked even when she was working. When working, however, Sydney wasn't talking to her classmates, but guiding herself through the tasks by talking aloud.

Sydney was too enthusiastic, too exuberant, and intensely involved in everything. She had to know what was going on with everyone else, at every minute. She loved to try new things and had trouble waiting for directions, or for the teacher to choose, in a fair way, who should go first. Sydney popped her hand up, volunteered, and jumped up to do things. In gym, art, music, and science class she played the hardest, painted the most colorful pictures, blew her recorder the loudest, and jumped up and down with enthusiasm at every new science assignment. While her teachers appreciated her humor, and her great knowledge, they admitted that after a day with Sydney they felt exhausted.

COGNITIVE DIFFERENCES

A number of studies of girls with AD/HD show slower work speed and slower mental processing. Some studies have shown girls with AD/HD less impaired in executive functions (skills that help us learn efficiently) than boys with AD/HD (Seidman *et al.* 1997), while others have shown no differences between girls and boys. Biederman *et al.* (1999) found girls with AD/HD, when compared to girls without AD/HD, to have lower IQ and achievement scores and more impairments on social, school, and family functioning. Girls, however, showed fewer conduct and disruptive behaviors. In adolescence, girls with AD/HD were found to have lower achievement on all cognitive and achievement measures compared to girls without AD/HD. When compared to boys with AD/HD, girls with AD/HD were found to have more problems with vocabulary (Rucklidge and Tannock 2001).

The gifted girls with AD/HD at the Gifted Resource Center of New England showed the slower work speed and slower processing reported in the literature, and they showed problems with executive function skills including organization and planning. Unlike gifted boys with AD/HD, more girls tended to do and hand in homework, even while they complained it was boring and useless. They were more able to organize work compared to gifted boys with AD/HD. For example, they did know when projects were due and had plans about how to do the projects. However, they needed as much help breaking projects down into smaller parts, and in getting these parts done by the deadline, as did boys with AD/HD. On the whole, gifted girls with AD/HD seemed to have less difficulty with writing on creative topics than did boys, but they had as much trouble with writing to a specific topic using supporting evidence. Gifted girls with AD/HD did not show lower IQ or achievement scores. Their scores were similar to those of gifted boys with AD/HD. However, both boys and girls with AD/HD did show lower scores on some subtests of IQ tests (Digit Span, Coding) and in some areas of achievement, especially basic skills like math facts and spelling.

PEER RELATIONSHIPS

Studies of girls with AD/HD suggest that peer relationships are more difficult than for other girls. Girls with AD/HD suffer more peer rejection (Berry, Shaywitz and Shaywitz 1985; Blachman and Hinshaw 2002; Gaub and Carlson 1997) and as they get older they are rated as less popular (Brown, Madau-Swain, and Baldwin 1991). Greene *et al.* (2001) found girls with AD/HD to have significant impairments in social relationships when compared to other girls. They show as significant a degree of impairment as boys with AD/HD. These authors emphasized that the deficits appeared to stem from behaviors associated with AD/HD and from coexisting conditions.

Girls with the Inattentive Type of AD/HD tended to be quieter and more introverted. Nadeau *et al.* (1999) suggested that these girls have more problems with shyness, timidity, and expressive language difficulties. Wheeler and Carlson

(1994) found that these girls were less likely to be socially rejected by peers, but more apt to be ignored.

Nadeau *et al.* (1999) considered that social impairments in girls with AD/HD appeared more negative to others because of the expectations of other girls for friendships. Thus, most girls are more verbal, cooperative, and sensitive to the feelings of others, and girls with AD/HD have more trouble with these skills, as do boys with AD/HD. However, boys with AD/HD act more like other boys in relating around shared activities rather than verbal interaction.

Sydney had significant difficulty with her peers. The other girls really didn't like her. They thought she was too pushy in getting her own way all the time, and also too bossy in telling them what to do. Sydney thought they were doing the wrong thing, so she needed to correct them. Though most of the boys in her class ignored Sydney, some liked her, and would accept invitations to her house for play dates. Sydney liked physical activities, and she and these boys would build tree houses in the yard, and play fort, cops and robbers, or spacemen. Because Sydney read a lot of adventure books, she always had new ideas for a drama to act out with the boys. The only problem occurred when she wanted to be the main character, like Harry Potter, and the boys thought a boy should get to be Harry.

Gifted girls with AD/HD may have even more difficulty than other girls in some areas. Since gifted girls in general have more trouble finding acceptance for their achievement, especially as they reach middle-school and high-school years, gifted girls with AD/HD may have a double handicap. Not only are they different in the same ways other gifted girls are different, but they are also different because of their AD/HD symptoms. Thus, gifted girls with AD/HD may be even more at risk than gifted boys for underachievement, alienation and depression.

Understanding AD/HD

To understand how gifted children are the same and different from other children with AD/HD and from gifted peers, it will be helpful to explore some of the mechanisms proposed to underlie the core symptoms of attention, hyperactivity, and impulsivity. This section of the chapter will focus on an overview of what the executive functions are and how they give us symptoms of inattention and disinhibition.

The executive functions

In general, AD/HD is recognized as a disorder that involves the executive functions of the brain. It is this system located in the front of the brain, the frontal and prefrontal regions and their interconnections, that organizes, plans, modulates, and integrates function. T.E. Brown (2000b) offered the metaphor of a conductor of an orchestra to describe what executive functions really do. The conductor does not play an instrument, but instead enables the orchestra to play the music.

Brown suggested that this conductor organises, focuses, integrates, sets into action, and gives direction to the musicians as they play. With actions and directions, the conductor interweaves the sounds of the different instruments, both controlling the musicians' pace and signing them to bring in or fade out their particular sounds to bring the musical score to life. The brain's executive functions act like those of the conductor to organize, focus, activate, integrate, and direct the brain to perform both everyday and original work.

Martha Denckla (1991, 1994, 1996, 2000) described executive dysfunction as a neuropsychological weakness. Executive dysfunction results in impairments in abilities that have academic, emotional, and interpersonal consequences. These impairments involve selective, focused and sustained attention, efficient memorization and problem solving, inhibition of verbal and nonverbal responses, organization, planning, self-monitoring and self-instruction, sequencing of complex behaviors, and management of space and time. Denckla emphasized that the executive function system is a central management system, and is crucial to the organization and integration of cognitive processes over time. This system plays an increasingly complex role as the child matures and does more complex tasks and works more independently. Executive functions thus become more necessary and complex as the child matures. Denckla (1996) has suggested that growing up is essentially the development of competence in executive function.

AD/HD can be viewed as an underlying deficit in executive functions: that is, these are the higher-level cognitive skills that allow us to learn how to learn. They help us figure out what we are going to do, how we are going to do it, and then help us to do it. In addition, executive functions help us deal with new information by thinking of ways to incorporate it into what we already know, or by problem solving our way through an obstacle. Finally, executive functions allow us to create new ways of looking at material by manipulating it in our mind and using different sets of parameters. These skills of organizing, planning, problem solving, mental flexibility, connection, prioritizing, integration, strategizing, focusing, monitoring, and modifying all help us with the assimilation, memory and recall, and output of tasks.

Executive functions are not an either/or thing. It is not that a child with AD/HD does not have the necessary parts, but rather that the overall smooth and efficient use of executive functions is faulty. Other children can choose to focus attention on many types of tasks. Children with AD/HD are less able to function when work is less interesting. In fact, they may not be able to function at all.

As children grow older, the necessity for using more complex and efficient executive functions increases. Thus, children who were able in primary years to do quite well because tasks placed minimal demands on executive functions find it much more difficult as time goes on, and task demands require more sophisticated and integrated executive functions. Gifted children with AD/HD are particularly likely to have difficulty with the complexity of executive functions as they get older. As they get into higher-level work, the pressure on executive systems increases. It doesn't help, though, to give these students easier work. In fact, it makes things worse. What they need is work tailored to their needs: short, stimulating tasks that call for more higher-level reasoning skills and creativity than for step-by-step learning.

In envisioning what the executive functions do it can be helpful to think about how they are related to some of the symptoms of AD/HD.

AD/HD AS ATTENTION DYSFUNCTION

T. E. Brown (2000b) described defects in attention as the underlying mechanism for the symptoms of AD/HD, and his model encompassed both AD/HD Combined Type and AD/HD Inattentive Type. In forming his model of how AD/HD affects attention, T.E. Brown (1995, 1996) studied adolescents and adults with AD/HD and derived from their self-reports five aspects of attention deficits: organizing and activating for work; sustaining attention and concentration; sustaining energy and effort for work; managing affective interference; and utilizing working memory and recall.

Simply put, Brown sees inattention as an impairment of efficient use of executive function. Brown's hypothesis attends to the attention aspects of AD/HD, and less so to the hyperactive or impulsive parts. However, his model does incorporate working memory, affective control, motivation, and arousal, as well as attention, as aspects of the symptoms of AD/HD.

Brown hypothesized that young children who show hyperactivity and impulsivity may not show attention deficits because the demands on them to organize their environment and manage their lives are minimal. Only those who are hyperactive and impulsive to a high degree are noticed before school age. Once children go to school though, those with difficulties in attention will have an increasingly difficult time performing.

AD/HD AS DISINHIBITION

Russell Barkley's (1997) model of AD/HD regards the main deficits as problems with regulating inhibitory functions. That is, the AD/HD child has difficulty modulating and monitoring behavior. This *disinhibition* is the hallmark for Barkley of what causes problems in behavior and attention functions. Barkley's model applies only to the Hyperactive/Impulsive and Combined Types of AD/HD. The Inattentive Type is not accounted for by this model.

Barkley's model considers that inhibition is both primary and essential in regulating, organizing, and controlling four other aspects of executive functions. Inhibition serves as a central manager. The behavioral inhibition system allows an individual to initiate a response, inhibit a response, interrupt an ongoing response, or deal with interference from the outside. The four other aspects of executive function, regulated by the inhibitory function, include:

- verbal working memory – internalized self-speech, generalization of rules, and moral reasoning

- nonverbal working memory – rule-governed behavior, delay of gratification, and sense of time

- self-regulation of affect, motivation, and arousal – motivation, perspective taking, and arousal

- reconstitution (taking apart and putting together stored information) – fluency, creativity, and prospective role playing.

Barkley's model is useful for giving us insight into the deficits that result in impulsive and hyperactive behaviors.

INTEGRATION OF MODELS OF AD/HD

T.E. Brown (2000b) attempted to integrate his ideas with those of Barkley (1997). Barkley sees the impairment of behavioral inhibition, the master control-ler of the executive function system in his model, as the core problem for those with AD/HD Combined Type. Brown sees other executive functions (working memory, arousal, self-regulation of affect, motivation) as impaired in the inatten-tion aspect of both AD/HD Combined Type and AD/HD Inattentive Type. Thus, Brown thinks of AD/HD as having a common core of attention problems, with those who suffer from impulsivity and hyperactivity also having additional impairments in inhibition.

Thus AD/HD Combined Type is seen by Brown (2000b) as impairment in a number of executive functions: both those that regulate behavioral inhibition and those that regulate the other cognitive impairments of inattention (short-term memory, activation/arousal, affective/emotional). AD/HD Inattentive Type is seen as an impairment in aspects of executive function related to inattention.

Certainly both behavioral inhibition and attention appear to be vital aspects of managing executive functions. However, understanding the deficits in particular executive functions allows a fuller picture of individual strengths and weaknesses to be delineated. No two people with AD/HD are exactly alike and it is the nuances of how executive functions are shown as strengths and weaknesses that cause some of the individual differences.

In discussing problems of gifted children with AD/HD it is useful to explore deficit areas more closely in relation to the various types of AD/HD. Since only the Combined Type and Inattentive Type have been at all well studied, the focus in this chapter will be on these two types, and how they relate to gifted children.

Gifted children with AD/HD

Gifted children with AD/HD are both the same as and different from other gifted children. In order to explore some of these similarities and differences, this section of the chapter will focus on AD/HD and giftedness in the literature, and comparisons of gifted children with the Combined Type and the Inattentive Type with both average children with AD/HD, and with other gifted children who do not have AD/HD. Comparisons are based both on the literature and on assessment data and anecdotal information collected at the Gifted Resource Center of New England.

AD/HD and giftedness in the literature

A number of writers in recent years in the field of gifted education have suggested that AD/HD is overdiagnosed in gifted children (Baum, Olenchak, and Owen 1998; Cramond 1994; Freed and Parsons 1997; Webb and Latimer 1993). These writers tend to see the problems exhibited by the gifted children in question as related to an unstimulating school environment. Thus, though they recognize AD/HD in some gifted children, many more who are identified as AD/HD are seen as misidentified and mainly in need of more stimulating school work. Creative children, with some of the symptoms of AD/HD, are especially likely to be seen as misidentified, pushed to the extremes of behavior by too rigid and constrictive an environment.

These authors do make some valid points. An unstimulating environment is a problem for many gifted children, and such an environment can contribute to behavior problems which can be mistaken for AD/HD. In fact, the *Diagnostic and Statistical Manual of Mental Disorders, Fourth Edition, Text Revision* (American

Psychiatric Association 2000) makes the point that in the diagnosis of AD/HD, "Inattention in the classroom may also occur when children with high intelligence are placed in academically unstimulating environments" (p.91).

Gifted children with high energy levels and a need for stimulation can resemble children with AD/HD when their needs for stimulation and expenditure of energy are not met. So these researchers are not wrong about this. What they are wrong about is the extent of the problem. That is, AD/HD may be *underdiagnosed* in gifted children, especially with younger children when the need for self-monitoring and adaptation to rule-based norms is not yet so pervasive. Gifted children with mild to moderate AD/HD may be able to get by with some adaptation of curriculum until higher grades. Thus, the phenomena of gifted children being referred for underachievement in upper elementary school and middle school can be explained by previously undetected AD/HD.

In earlier years, a stimulating school environment, coupled with small classes, will significantly decrease symptoms of AD/HD in many gifted children with mild AD/HD (Freed and Parsons 1997; Hartmann 1996). In fact, for some children with very mild AD/HD, the stimulation of a specialized class may help them organize their energy significantly. These children can utilize the stimulation of the class with their own abilities to hyperfocus well enough that they can achieve good results.

Another aspect of the problem is that researchers in the field of giftedness have very little clinical experience in diagnosing AD/HD. Many are not clinicians at all. They have not evaluated hundreds of children, and so have little idea of how the symptoms of AD/HD can manifest. Many people, including many clinicians, still think that if a child can concentrate at all, he or she could not possibly have AD/HD. The truth is that many children with AD/HD can concentrate quite well on something that interests them, or on material that is novel, fast paced or highly rewarded (Barkley 1995, 1998; Goldstein and Goldstein 1990, 1998; Hallowell and Ratey 1994b; Quinn 1997), but they cannot focus well on material that is less stimulating even when it is to their advantage to do so. This, of course, is the nature of AD/HD: difficulty sustaining focus on less stimulating, less interesting material that is needed to learn a skill or produce a specific product.

Gifted children with AD/HD, with many more interests and greater ability to move faster than age peers through material of interest, may show amazing powers of concentration at times (Lovecky 1994b). Also the range of activities that are easy for them is greater than average. Thus, gifted children with AD/HD can appear focused on easier tasks because they do not have to expend any energy in struggling to learn them. This "effortless" performance may hide the AD/HD underneath (Kaufmann *et al.* 2000). For most gifted children with AD/HD, it's the things that they cannot concentrate on that tell the story: repetitive work, work that requires sustained effort, work that requires breaking bigger things into smaller parts and following a procedure to reach an endpoint, work that is only moderately interesting, and work that has little intrinsic reward or in which the reward is delayed for a long time.

There have been several small studies of gifted children with AD/HD. One study compared gifted boys with Hyperactive/Impulsive AD/HD (Combined Type) with a group of nongifted boys with AD/HD, and a group of gifted boys without AD/HD on a variety of measures. Moon *et al.* (2001) reported that the gifted boys with AD/HD in their study were less mature than either other gifted boys or average boys with AD/HD of their age. They showed poor regulation of emotion and were easily frustrated. They tended to overrespond to situations. They described themselves in extremes: with exceedingly positive or exceedingly negative characteristics. Socially, they were impulsive, and made inappropriate physical contact with other children. They engaged in irresponsible, irritating, and annoying social behaviors.

Zentall *et al.* (2001b) explored learning and achievement with the same small group of students. Gifted boys with AD/HD were more like other boys with AD/HD in underachievement, difficulties with homework and long-term projects, attending to and following directions, completing worksheets, difficulty with handwriting, and getting started with assigned reading. They also expressed a clear preference for high-interest content, learning novel things, and free reading. Gifted boys without AD/HD did not have these difficulties. On the other hand, gifted boys with and without AD/HD were good readers, had special talents in science, math or social studies, were high in spatial and mechanical skills, preferred challenge, competition and use of memory skills, as well as cognitive stimulation, and tended to be creative.

Kalbfleisch (2000, cited in Kaufmann *et al.* 2000) suggested that gifted boys with AD/HD are more prone to hyperfocusing, especially on material of interest. As a result they have a difficult time shifting attention from task to task. The effect was especially pronounced for gifted boys with AD/HD-Inattentive Type.

Chae *et al.* (2003) studied gifted children with and without AD/HD on a number of measures that included behavior checklists, teacher observations, IQ testing and performance on the T.O.V.A. Continuous Performance Test. They found that gifted children in general scored better on the T.O.V.A. than age peers who were not gifted; they made fewer errors of omission and commission and were more consistent in performance. In addition, gifted children with AD/HD did better on the T.O.V.A. than more average children with AD/HD prompting researchers to suggest the need for higher norms to avoid false negatives. Finally, based on only the parent and teacher information an additional 13% of children were found to have symptoms of AD/HD; nevertheless, these children performed above the cutoff on the T.O.V.A. The authors suggested that these children might not have AD/HD; on the other hand, the T.O.V.A. norms may be inadequate to assess the performance of these children.

Leroux and Levitt-Perlman (2000) suggested behavioral, curricular, and instructional strategies to improve functioning in gifted students with AD/HD. They particularly focused on some of the particular needs of gifted students for appropriate challenge and motivation.

Silverman (2002) reviewed all the test protocols from children at the Gifted Development Center in Denver, Colorado, as part of her study of children who had visual-spatial learning styles. She found that there was a high overlap of characteristics of AD/HD and visual-spatial learning style.

In reviewing the research on AD/HD, therefore, it is important to consider how giftedness may play a role in the symptoms of AD/HD. However, most researchers who work with children with AD/HD have little understanding about giftedness. Their samples either do not include gifted children or do not control for level of IQ. An exception to this was Shaw and Brown (1990) who evaluated boys in 6th and 7th grade with above-average intelligence and AD/HD. The boys were found to use more diverse and nonverbal information in problem solving, and they obtained higher scores on a test of creativity than did high-aptitude boys without AD/HD. Also, T.E. Brown (1998) studied AD/HD in adults with superior IQs, and found unique risks due to intelligence.

Because of the lack of knowledge about giftedness, what may hold true for more average children may not be true for gifted children with AD/HD. Thus, it is important to understand how giftedness and AD/HD interweave. In what ways do the advanced cognitive skills of giftedness serve to mitigate difficulties and even serve as strengths? In what ways do the problems of AD/HD interfere with developing potential and hinder achievement in all areas of life? In what ways are gifted children with AD/HD the same and different from other AD/HD children, and how do they compare to their gifted peers without AD/HD?

Gifted children with AD/HD Combined Type
COMPARISONS TO AVERAGE CHILDREN WITH AD/HD

How do gifted children with the Combined Type of AD/HD compare to more average children? It is important to know similarities and differences because most of the literature on AD/HD is based on the average child. Therefore, differences of gifted children from average children with AD/HD are overlooked, and inappropriate recommendations can be made: for example, for repetitious skill-building work. Gifted children with AD/HD may actually do worse with this type of work because it is so unstimulating. What then distinguishes gifted children and average children with AD/HD Combined Type?

Variability. Gifted children with AD/HD have a much greater degree of variability on intellectual assessments. Scores for untimed items tend to be among their highest scores, and are often in the high superior to very superior range. A child who, on the Wechsler Intelligence Scales, has subtest scores of 14+ on Similarities, Vocabulary, Comprehension, General Information, Block Design, or Digit Span (average is 9 to 11) is likely to be gifted no matter what the Full Scale Intelligence Score.

Scaled scores on the Wechsler Scales are also likely to show much greater variability for gifted children. For example, scores can vary from below average to very superior (4 to 19) on the same test. Spencer, a boy with motor coordination problems as well as AD/HD, scored Scale Score 4 on Coding and SS 19 on Vocabulary, Similarities, Comprehension, and Information on the Wechsler. Average children with AD/HD do not show this amount of variability. They may score below average on some subtests, but their highest scores are close to average (8 to 12).

On standardized tests, gifted children with AD/HD may show greater variability with some scores quite high, at 95% or more, while other scores can be average or below. Sometimes these students surprise teachers with their exceptionally high standardized test scores because class work seems so average. Average children with AD/HD may score below average on some tests and more average on others, but they do not score very high on any test. Thus, though both gifted and average students with AD/HD show a profile of academic strengths and weaknesses on standardized testing, gifted children with AD/HD show a wider range of scores, and more likelihood of at least some scores being at the high end of the range. Some gifted children are so bright that despite AD/HD they score exceptionally well on standardized academic tests: at 99%, for example.

The class work of the gifted child with AD/HD is more variable than that of average children with AD/HD. While both groups are less efficient in producing written work on demand, and less able to consistently complete tasks, their range of grades can vary. That is, in the same subject, grades for the gifted child with AD/HD can range from failing to 100%. Also, gifted children with AD/HD can score quite high grades on tests but do poorly on written class work and homework, resulting in a range of grades within a subject. Both gifted children and average children with AD/HD do better in subjects they find interesting.

Both groups are likely to have trouble with homework, and both groups have difficulty with basic skills.

The gifted child with AD/HD is also likely to have higher-level functioning, well above average, in at least one academic subject. Thus, while the child may read or write at about grade level, math may be well above. Or the child may show an unusual grasp of a particular topic within a subject, such as science or social studies, but not necessarily do well in that subject all the time, especially when he or she has to write down answers rapidly. These students may be funds of knowledge and show excellent skills for class discussion but may be unable to show their level of thinking on tests or in written work. In general, average students, while having academic strengths, do not show this exceptionally high level of functioning some of the time. They do not have the same breadth of knowledge and ability to discuss topics in depth as do gifted children with AD/HD. Gifted children with AD/HD, while deficient in many of the supporting work skills needed to succeed in school (note taking, outlining, organization of ideas, writing skills), are often more proficient at learning things rapidly than average children with AD/HD. They also have more knowledge of strategies to use in learning things. What gifted children with AD/HD have trouble doing is using these strategies efficiently. Sometimes they use them and sometimes they don't. Strategies are used readily in one subject area but not at all in another. More average children with AD/HD have less knowledge of strategies than age peers without AD/HD, and they forget to use the strategies they do know.

Big-picture thinking. Gifted children with AD/HD tend to be big-picture thinkers. That is, they quickly grasp the concept, the endpoint, and the implications. While average children with AD/HD need material broken down into small steps and the big picture built up slowly, these gifted children, like most gifted children, see the whole and chafe under the necessity of going through all the parts. In fact, it can be difficult for many of them to do so. On the other hand, gifted children with AD/HD have as much trouble as average children with AD/HD in breaking big tasks down into component parts and completing each part. Thus, they grasp the whole, but have trouble showing the steps. They have the concept but find it hard to demonstrate it.

Because they have trouble with attention and with doing small sequential steps, these children do not complete rote work. It is hard for them to focus on it. Like other children with AD/HD, gifted children with AD/HD need more stimulating and interesting work. Unlike average students with AD/HD, gifted children with AD/HD need higher-level work that points to a goal and that incorporates thinking and abstract reasoning.

Asynchrony. Gifted children with AD/HD Combined Type may also differ from more average children with AD/HD in the greater degree of uneven development or asynchrony they show in cognitive, social, and emotional areas. They may behave less maturely than average peers some of the time, but more maturely at other times. Andrew, at age eight, behaved much less maturely than age peers. As he ran down the corridor at school, he pretended he was flying an airplane. His arms were stretched wide and he made loud motor noises. On the other hand, Andrew would never tell a lie. He either would keep silent or admit he had done something. His ability to take responsibility for his actions was much more mature than most age peers and other children with AD/HD.

Gifted children with AD/HD Combined Type may show differences in social functioning as well. They often have more specialized interests than average children with AD/HD, and perform similar activities in more complex ways. For example, they know more ways to organize card collections, have more knowledge about the cards, and more ability to think about the future benefit of collecting unique cards. Gifted children with AD/HD need and like more complexity than average children with AD/HD, and seek it out in activities and interests. They often like to play with older children, to play complex games using strategy that age peers cannot yet understand, and they know all the rules. Often their friends are other gifted children or older children with whom they can play the more complex versions of games. They may be rejected by other gifted children, though, because of their irritating, annoying, and intrusive behavior. Average children with AD/HD often play with younger children and in less mature ways. They have fewer interests and less ability to develop hobbies. Like gifted children with AD/HD, they tend to like activities that are stimulating: video games, television, activities like skateboarding and go-carting, and using the computer to play games, send instant messages, or enter chat rooms on the Internet.

COMPARISONS TO GIFTED CHILDREN

How do gifted children with the Combined Type of AD/HD compare to other gifted children? This can be an issue because gifted children with AD/HD need the same sort of stimulation and engagement of their intellect as do other gifted children, yet they also show difficulty in performing. Thus, they may be missed when school personnel select students for the typical gifted program.

What distinguishes the gifted children with AD/HD Combined Type from other gifted children?

Variability. Gifted children with AD/HD have much more difficulty than other gifted children completing assignments. When in a class with other gifted children, those children with AD/HD do not do as much homework, or finish as many assignments, as the other gifted children do. They rush through their work, do less written work on the whole, and have more behavior problems. They are also less organized, have less sense of how long something will take, tend to procrastinate, and resist following structure or direction. They often want to do things their own way, will not correct errors when asked to do so, and argue about how much they have to do. Usually they are satisfied to do the fastest, least accurate job possible in any subject area, except for work that is novel, highly stimulating, or their own choice. When engaged in tasks they like or find stimulating, however, their work quality and productivity is as high as that of other gifted children. Thus, in any subject, the quality and quantity of work done will vary across days depending on the ability of the gifted child with AD/HD Combined Type to feel engaged by the topic.

It was noted that, for many of the gifted children with AD/HD, getting the task done is not particularly rewarding. Gifted children without AD/HD find rewards in finishing complex work. They enjoy the challenge and like immersing themselves in material. Finding out the answer to a question is intriguing. Some of the gifted children with AD/HD feel rewarded completing complex work too, but many do not.

Gifted children with AD/HD are less efficient in their use of executive function skills than other gifted children. Though they can often verbalize a strategy, they do not as often use it in learning, for example, a list of words. Also noted is the tendency of gifted children with AD/HD Combined Type to make initial use of a strategy, but then quickly to revert to more reliance on pure memory. Thus, in learning a list of words, the gifted children with AD/HD might use a strategy to group words sometimes, but other times would just depend on recalling them all. Gifted children without AD/HD tend to use strategies more consistently.

Big-picture thinking. Gifted children without AD/HD are much more able to think sequentially and to solve problems using both part-to-whole, and whole-to-part methods. They get the big picture, and can also see what comprises it, much more easily than gifted children with AD/HD. They can take a big project and break it down into smaller steps, and they can build up an argument using logical steps, one at a time. While both groups are good at deductive reasoning, the gifted children with AD/HD, assessed at the Gifted Resource Center of New England, tended to have much more trouble with inductive reasoning because they had trouble finding the main idea and then drawing conclusions from material. Extracting the essence was really much more difficult for them than for other gifted children.

Asynchrony. Gifted children with AD/HD Combined Type differ from other gifted children in the greater degree of asynchrony shown. While gifted children without AD/HD show discrepancies in cognitive, social, emotional, and physical maturity, those with AD/HD show greater variability in their ability to act maturely. They are likely to show more areas of cognitive asynchrony as well. For example, while able to grasp concepts easily, communicating these concepts via writing or step-by-step delineation is more difficult.

Gifted children, with and without AD/HD, like work that is more abstract and more intellectually stimulating. The gifted children without AD/HD are more able to endure the less stimulating aspects of their work. Many are able to find ways to make less interesting work more challenging for themselves. The gifted children with AD/HD have much more trouble doing this. They often can not work for very long on unstimulating work and are unable to make it more challenging or interesting for themselves. They do best if the work is presented in smaller, highly stimulating chunks that can be finished fairly readily and with less need from them to organize or structure it.

Gifted children with AD/HD Inattentive Type

COMPARISONS WITH AVERAGE CHILDREN WITH AD/HD

Gifted children with AD/HD Inattentive Type are more apt to be seen as "absent-minded professors" or daydreamers than as children with attention deficits. The blank stare or the "I forgot" that characterizes this type of child tends to make adults exasperated after a while, because they feel the child could remember if he or she only tried. More average children with AD/HD Inattentive Type tend to slip through the cracks. Unless they really stand out as learning disabled, they are more apt to be seen as lazy or unmotivated.

Variability. Compared to more average children with AD/HD, gifted children with AD/HD Inattentive Type show more variability in subtest patterns on the Wechsler Intelligence Scales. The range of scores is greater than for average children with more higher scores (above 15) but some below average. For many gifted children with AD/HD Inattentive Type, recalling digits in reverse is an area of average or below-average performance, though number of digits forward is often quite high. The score for processing speed is often much lower than other scores. Processing speed reflects one of the problems for gifted children with AD/HD Inattentive Type: slower performance speed in general.

For a proportion of gifted children with AD/HD Inattentive Type all the performance subtests on the Wechsler Scales are lowered due to the necessity to work quickly to gain bonus points for speed. The slower processing of these children results in slower starts and slower work speed. The resulting discrepancy between verbal and performance areas can then lead examiners to think the child has an NVLD. More average children with AD/HD Inattentive Type also show some test scatter with lowest scores on items that require processing speed. However, while the lowest scores of both groups can be similar, the highest scores of average children with AD/HD Inattentive Type are in the average range.

On standardized tests, gifted students with AD/HD Inattentive Type may do exceptionally well or have difficulty with the timed aspect of the test. Partly, it depends on both the length of the test and the interest of the gifted child with AD/HD Inattentive Type. Interest can increase ability to focus and so the child may do well. On the other hand, dislike of the task, boredom, fatigue, or anxiety can all decrease scores.

On standardized tests, average children with AD/HD Inattentive Type also have difficulty showing what they know due to the timed aspect of the test. Thus, they may score much lower than expectancy. If they also have learning disabilities they can score well below grade level.

Executive functions. Both average and gifted children with AD/HD Inattentive Type work much more slowly in the classroom. These children do not finish tasks that other children do easily because it takes them longer to start and longer to finish. Many are perfectionists and will insist on completing work perfectly, which further decreases work speed.

Gifted children with AD/HD Inattentive Type have more difficulty with writing skills than average children with AD/HD. That is, there is a bigger discrepancy between what they know and what they can produce in written form. They are inefficient both in translating thoughts to writing and in the physical act of writing.

Disorganization is a particular problem for gifted children with AD/HD Inattentive Type. Because they are so bright it is much more disconcerting when they have trouble organizing their belongings, books, materials, homework, and even their thoughts, writing, and projects. Not only do they lose and forget things, but they seem to lack an internal sense of how to order things. Thus, they have less ability in performing sequential tasks and in developing work that requires an internal structure. More average students with AD/HD are also disorganized but because they are not expected to do better than age peers, their organization appears less problematic. Nevertheless, these children do need help in learning to organize belongings, projects, written work, books, and homework.

Gifted children with AD/HD Inattentive Type are recognized as gifted, but also as daydreamy and unproductive. In school, these children are reflective, show a depth of knowledge, and contribute thoughtful comments to discussions.

They have brilliant ideas and are able to make many interconnections to other material they know. More average children with AD/HD are seen as less competent, less reflective, and they make less thoughtful comments. They are more often off the topic. They also need help in making connections among aspects of material because it is more difficult for them to get the big picture.

Gifted children with AD/HD Inattentive Type, unlike more average children with AD/HD, are more likely to experience problems with both underfocusing and hyperfocusing. Thus, while looking rather sluggish on the outside, they actually are experiencing hyperactivity inside with their thoughts and feelings, so they are distracted and pay less attention to the task at hand. Their tendency to space out, or drift off, can mean they are hyperfocused on an internal idea. They also can get locked onto one idea, immerse themselves into it, and contemplate it for hours, unaware of the passage of time or outside requirements. In fact, gifted children with AD/HD Inattentive Type appear to be more prone to hyper-focusing than even gifted children with AD/HD Combined Type (Kalbfleisch 2000, cited in Kaufmann *et al.* 2000). Average children with AD/HD Inattentive Type are likely to hyperfocus on activities such as television or video games, not on ideas. When they are daydreaming, they typically are not really thinking of much of anything at all.

Asynchrony. Gifted children with AD/HD Inattentive Type show more uneven development (asynchrony) than average children with AD/HD. They are far more emotional and anxious. Because they are more anxious, they can dwell on the negative, foresee dire consequences for far more possibilities than anyone else, and have trouble weighing the actual likelihood that bad things will happen. Things that never would occur to more average children, with and without AD/HD, will give these children nightmares. Also, they can become easily upset about minor issues: for example, if required to move quickly, or finish things on someone else's schedule.

Gifted children with AD/HD Inattentive Type tend to be more introverted than most other children. Since descriptions of children with AD/HD Inattentive Type in general suggest shyness, reticence, and withdrawn social behavior, it may be likely that introversion is characteristic of AD/HD Inattentive Type. Introversion is also somewhat more characteristic of gifted children in general (Silverman 1993a). Average children with AD/HD Inattentive Type also may be introverted and some of these traits can be characteristic of their AD/HD.

Gifted children with AD/HD Inattentive Type tend to have many more interests than average children with AD/HD, and they tend to pursue these interests for long periods of time, both in a time interval (hours) and over years. These children readily develop long-term interests in which they immerse themselves. Ian, for example, loved dinosaurs and knew every dinosaur that ever existed. Later, when he ran out of dinosaurs he learned all the mammals, then all the insects. Lonnie loved to draw cartoons. He spent a lot of his spare time drawing comic strips that made rather wry commentary on the state of the world, adult fallibility, and the need for superheroes. On the whole, average children with AD/HD Inattentive Type have fewer interests than gifted children. They are more likely to be interested in age-level activities (dolls, building toys, sports, video games) and television.

COMPARISONS WITH OTHER GIFTED CHILDREN

Variability. Compared to other gifted children, those with AD/HD Inattentive Type have more trouble with completing work because they can be so distracted by inner thoughts and associations that they forget what they are doing. They also have more trouble recalling the directions and getting started on tasks.

Compared to other gifted children, those with AD/HD Inattentive Type are less attentive to detail, less able to complete tasks, and more likely to forget things and not to have heard them. They often don't know what to do even if they have been given directions. They are more apt to go off on tangents, miss the main point, and forget part of the assignment. They are apt to produce work they think fits the requirements, only to find out they missed the point. This results in very uneven performance. Even when the task is enjoyable and stimulating, gifted children with AD/HD Inattentive Type can have difficulty with attention and show variable performance.

Executive functions. Some types of tasks are more difficult for gifted children with AD/HD Inattentive Type. They have more trouble with memorizing lists of things, recalling what was said to them in lectures, and organizing their thoughts in essays and compositions. They often have wonderful ideas and are original in their analyses, but have trouble assessing the validity of their ideas or if the idea really fits the intent of the question. Holding two things in mind at once is more difficult for them (working memory). Some have difficulty with reading comprehension because they drift off so much as ideas occur to them. Some have trouble with math because they skip steps without realizing it. Handwriting can also be much slower than it is for other gifted children.

These students also are very disorganized. They have trouble keeping track of things, dates, time, and plans. Even their thinking seems disorganized and it can be harder for them to follow logical reasoning. Many are creative and find their tendency to see things differently means they also make unusual assumptions but have difficulty assessing the validity of them. Thus, these gifted students have creative ideas that they find difficult to communicate effectively due to their difficulties with output and organization.

Asynchrony. Gifted children with AD/HD Inattentive Type can accomplish significant achievements due to their especially good imagination and hyper-focusing abilities. Whether they actually do so is dependent on the support and stimulation they receive. In order to function well, they need to feel emotionally safe and in control of the environment around them. They need to receive the right amount of stimulation and challenge to inspire them without overwhelming them. Since they have trouble breaking things up into smaller parts, projects often seem overwhelming to them. Unlike gifted children with AD/HD Combined Type, who presume the project will get somehow magically get done, those with AD/HD Inattentive Type have trouble conceiving of themselves being able to manage doing it all. The feeling of being overloaded and overwhelmed reduces effort and performance.

Compared to other gifted students, those with AD/HD Inattentive Type have more difficulty with emotional control. Because they are easily over-whelmed, they feel more worried and anxious. They are likely to lose control when upset and are more easily upset by more lower-level stimuli than other gifted children. They also tend to be more perfectionistic and hyperfocused in unproductive ways.

Executive functions affected by AD/HD in gifted children

Underlying the difficulties of gifted children with AD/HD are executive function deficits that have a specific impact on learning, emotional functioning and interpersonal relationships. In fact, deficits in executive functions decrease the ability of gifted children with AD/HD to show what they know, to learn effi-ciently, and to deal effectively with frustration and challenge. Executive functions affected by AD/HD include problems with working memory; internalization of speech; arousal, activation, and effort; holistic/sequential performance; emo-tional control; and delaying gratification. These six areas of dysfunction are sum-marized below and further explored in subsequent chapters.

Working memory

Working memory is the ability to hold facts and concepts in mind while doing something with them. For example, a student may have to manipulate informa-tion by rearranging it, adding to it, connecting it to other information, looking for a pattern, or grouping it. Consequently, working memory includes holding material in mind while also imitating complex sequences of behavior, thinking about consequences, and using rules to govern behavior (Barkley 1997). Working memory is short-term memory, similar to computer RAM. It lets us organize and put things together for the short term. For example, thinking of the steps to solve a math problem, recalling the multiplication table needed while organizing the problem on paper, and remembering how to form numbers with a pencil at the same time are aspects of working memory (Ratey 2001).

Problems with working memory mean that children with AD/HD show poor memory for facts. They are forgetful because they can't keep several things in mind. Distraction also decreases working memory as the new things take over attention. Working memory includes aspects of the following.

- *Short-term memory capacity.* Children with AD/HD, including gifted students, can have difficulty with hearing and remembering directions, recalling facts on demand, memorizing math facts and spelling words, and forgetting to do parts of math problems or parts of questions.

- *Prioritizing.* Because they can't hold material in mind, students with AD/HD have trouble holding two ideas and comparing or contrasting them. They cannot follow through on tasks that require summarizing or paraphrasing. They have difficulty picking out the main point and in deciding which is the most important idea among several. This makes outlining difficult. Difficulties with prioritizing are especially a problem for gifted children who are in higher-level courses.

- *Sense of time.* Because students with AD/HD have trouble with holding events in mind, they have trouble with recalling the past and learning from their mistakes; they don't prepare for future events. They have trouble judging how much time has passed, or how much time will be required to do something, so they wait too long. They have more trouble planning for the future. Because they can't hold time in mind, it is hard to think about consequences of what might happen, or make a plan for how to change something. Foreseeing obstacles and making plans for overcoming them is difficult, and leads to inefficient problem solving.

- *Using rules to govern behavior.* Because of poorer capacity to hold two things in mind at once, children with AD/HD may know the rules, but thinking of how to apply them in the moment is difficult. Thus, noting social nuances or expressions that indicate a need for change of behavior, recognizing the change needed, and executing the change are all difficult for children with AD/HD.

Gifted children with AD/HD have particular difficulty because, while academically advanced in reasoning ability and abstract thinking, they are less advanced in using working memory. Thus, they will have wonderful ideas but will be unable to execute them. They may be able to dictate a terrific piece of written work but are unable to write it down. They know a lot of information but have trouble organizing that information for presentation. They have high reading comprehension but cannot write a book report. They may be exceptionally advanced at math reasoning but have trouble with math computation because they cannot do all the steps accurately.

Thinking ahead to plan a project involves knowing what is required, attending to the deadline, and doing the work. This kind of planning is just as difficult for gifted children with AD/HD as for average children with AD/HD. In fact, it can be more difficult for gifted children because there is much more of a gap between what they can think about and what they can accomplish.

A lack of focus on the future means that many gifted children with AD/HD cannot take advantage of opportunities offered them because they cannot plan well enough to make the event happen. Gifted children with AD/HD have trouble with getting work in on time; they always plan to do better but have trouble organizing the actual steps needed to make a change. Because they have trouble with recalling past consequences, they get into trouble for the same problems again and again.

For example, Shawn, age 15, could not get the idea that if he didn't do his Spanish homework he would fail the term. His teacher counted homework for 40% of the grade. Shawn would say he knew he had to do his homework, but that he had only missed a few assignments. In fact, Shawn had missed nearly half the assignments. When confronted with this, Shawn was surprised. He could have sworn it was only one or two. The next term Shawn didn't improve any. He resisted any attempts to help him keep track of assignments, saying he felt humiliated to have to do that, and that he would work it out. Pointing out to Shawn that good students wrote down assignments made no difference. Shawn could not organize his behavior enough to plan and execute a way to get his homework done. Trying to make a change in how he did things was too much effort and felt too alien to him. He opted for the familiar, safe, and failing method each time. Consequently, he had to repeat Spanish.

Internalization of speech

From infancy onwards, children learn to use language to regulate behavior. Initially, young children use language to regulate the behavior of others towards themselves, and then increasingly they internalize language to regulate themselves. Self-regulatory speech starts to develop in preschool years when children start to talk out loud to themselves as they play. Over time, this speech becomes less external and more internal. Completely internal speech occurs by the mid-elementary years. Barkley (1997) presented research evidence that showed that children with AD/HD Combined Type were delayed, compared to age peers, in acquisition of the various stages of internalization of speech. Thus, they were more like younger children in using internalized speech to guide behavior. Because of this they had less ability to follow rules.

Barkley (1997) described internalized speech as a form of verbal working memory. In his schema, internalization of speech included the ability to describe and reflect on experience, self-questioning and problem solving, giving oneself instructions in the process of doing a task, making self-corrections, generalizing rules to many situations, and making meta rules (rules that are more general such as expectations for indoor as opposed to outdoor behavior) to serve as guidelines for living. Barkley also included reading comprehension and moral reasoning as part of internalized speech.

Internalized speech allows people to hold rules in mind over time and helps to organize and guide behavior. Also, self-directed speech plays a role in planning and executing strategy in problem solving. Children with AD/HD are much less able to talk to themselves to plan an approach to a difficult task, or to try a different strategy if the first results in failure. In essence, the person using internalized speech is mentally rehearsing plans, strategies, and formulation of rules. Children with AD/HD who are less able to use internalized speech also have more difficulty with this type of planning.

Internalized speech includes aspects of the following.

- *Planning and goal setting.* Children with AD/HD have trouble planning ahead and setting appropriate goals. They are more focused on the short term. When they can set longer-term goals, it is difficult for them to conceive of how they will reach them.

- *Self-direction and instruction.* As most children do tasks, they give themselves verbal directions. These directions are audible in very young children, but become more internalized as the child matures. Children with AD/HD have trouble internalizing this private speech. Either they don't use it at all or they vocalize aloud long after peers have turned to internalized speech.

- *Course correction and problem solving.* Children with AD/HD have trouble with correcting mistakes. They often don't notice the errors, or make no plans to go back and check work. Also, since they live more in the present, once the task is perceived to be finished, it is over so far as these children are concerned. Children with AD/HD have difficulty with problem solving because they don't talk to themselves about alternative plans. They choose their first option.

- *Generalizing from one specific to a whole class of items.* Because they don't internalize speech, children with AD/HD have trouble thinking about how a particular instance fits into a bigger whole of related actions. Instead, they focus on the one item or situation. This means they have trouble learning to generalize rules. They also then have trouble with thinking of meta rules: for example, we don't litter because we have a civic responsibility to each other regarding the proper disposal of trash.

Gifted children with AD/HD have trouble with internalizing speech. When asked what they are thinking as they try to solve a problem, they often respond, "Nothing." While younger gifted children with AD/HD talk aloud to themselves, many older children have stopped this behavior but have substituted nothing else in its place. Sometimes, though, older children evolve a strategy of whispering instructions to themselves or talking as they go along to remind themselves what to do. Ned used this strategy all the way through college.

Deficits in arousal, activation, and effort

Children with AD/HD have a difficult time starting tasks, maintaining attention and effort, and completing tasks. Procrastination, lack of motivation, slow work speed, easy distractibility, and loss of energy partway through a task are typical. T.E. Brown (2000b) noted that attention has aspects of arousal, activation, and effort that may vary considerably in intensity across tasks. With a slower arousal, it takes time to start paying attention, and with less effort attention is not sustained. Distractibility is another aspect. Children who are easily distractible have trouble with sustaining activation and effort. To them, each part of the task seems separate – what they do in between distractions. Without a sense of continuity, it is difficult for these children to gain a sense of the meaning of the task. T.E. Brown (2001) has codified the particular behaviors that involve activation/arousal.

Deficits in arousal include the following:

- *Difficulty being aroused and activated.* Children with AD/HD have difficulty with getting aroused in the morning, shifting to a new task, and getting started on tasks. They feel easily overwhelmed and have difficulty getting organized to start. They procrastinate: put off tasks and wait until the last minute.

- *Problems with sleep.* Children with AD/HD can have difficulty falling asleep at night, as well as in staying asleep and in getting up the next morning. Sleep problems arise from difficulties in arousal; that is, arousal fluctuates so the child feels wide awake at bedtime. Often such children become more hyperactive the more tired they become. Gruber, Sadeh, and Raviv (2000), using a sleep-monitoring system and sleep diaries, found that children with AD/HD had more difficulty with sleep onset, sleep duration, and amount of true sleep. These authors concluded that instability of the sleep–wake cycle is likely to be found with children with AD/HD.

  Some gifted children with AD/HD, who are exceptionally creative, have particular trouble turning off their minds. They have tired bodies, but minds that think 24 hours a day. Children who do not fall asleep easily have trouble maintaining daytime alertness. Contrary to what it may seem, they do need sleep as much as peers without AD/HD but are often sleep deprived, which results in less alertness, more irritability, and less ability to focus attention. Stimulant medication also may exacerbate the problem for some children, although for others, sleep problems occur because the medication is wearing off. Some children actually do better if they fall asleep before medication wears off. Newer medications for AD/HD may be less problematic.

  Gifted adolescents with AD/HD may have an especially difficult time with sleep. Not only do they have an increased amount of school work, but they also need more sleep than when they were children. It can be harder to maintain a regular sleep schedule when the adolescent sleeps very late on weekends or takes a nap after school in the afternoon.

  Jim, a 17-year-old gifted adolescent with AD/HD, took a nap each evening until eight, did his school work until four a.m., and then went to bed. He could not get up for school and his parents usually had to drive him at the last minute. Finally they refused to do so anymore and told him he'd just have to walk the five miles to school if he was late, or pay for a cab himself. When he then refused to go to school, his mother would not write an excuse note. One Saturday detention later, Jim decided to go to bed earlier and get up on time.

- *Sensory overarousal.* Many children with AD/HD have a hyperaroused central nervous system. This results in oversensitivity to sensory stimulation such as touch, taste, and sound. Children with difficulties in sensory integration have trouble tolerating stimulation that others find neutral or even pleasant. On the other hand, they may seek out specific types of stimulation. Thus, some children with AD/HD have difficulty tolerating certain fabrics, seams of clothing, textures, and even wrinkles in cloth. They like old, well-washed, and soft clothing. Taste and smell can be another problem for these children, who may refuse specific textures and tastes in foods. They can eliminate so many foods that there is only a small number of preferred foods that they will eat. Sound can affect children with AD/HD who have auditory sensitivities. They dislike sudden loud noise such as the fire-drill bell, or steady but low-level sounds like buzzing clocks or hissing heat vents. On the other hand, these same children can seek out stimulating sound and may prefer loud music or masking sound when they do tasks. Avoiding or seeking out certain types of sensory stimulation is the way children with AD/HD may try to adapt to fluctuations in arousal and sensory system sensitivities.

  Sensory overarousal in mild form is known in gifted children without AD/HD. These "overexcitabilities" (Piechowski 1991; Silverman 1993d) lead to imagination, creativity, emotional awareness, and empathy and compassion. However, more severe sensory overarousal leads to discomfort in the child and behavioral problems, as the child tries to cope with the negative aspects of too intense stimulation. Severe sensory overarousal can be a sign of other deficits including AD/HD.

- *Sustaining effort on tasks.* Children with AD/HD have trouble sustaining effort. They may start a task full of enthusiasm but soon lose the energy needed to complete it. Sometimes this occurs because the child has become frustrated. However, often the arousal system of the child is not stimulated enough by the task, and so ability to sustain attention and effort lags. It is also difficult to get children with AD/HD motivated to do nonpreferred tasks.

- *Slow work speed.* Children with AD/HD often work quite slowly and need more time on tasks than others. This is especially the case for the Inattentive Type of AD/HD. Even when focused and working, these children work very slowly. Slow work speed can reflect slow processing speed or slowness in organizing the parts of the task. It can be the result of slow handwriting. Slow work speed keeps children with AD/HD from completing as many tasks as other children. Also, the slowness is fatiguing, so children with AD/HD have less energy to spend on doing tasks.

- *Quality of work.* Children with AD/HD are variable in the quality and quantity of work they are able to produce. Children can appear not to know something, yet a day later score 100% on a more difficult test. Variability also can be seen in discrepancies among subjects, between homework and test grades, and between grades and standardized tests.

Gifted children with AD/HD have as much trouble as other children with AD/HD in activating effort, sustaining attention, and completing work. Gifted children with AD/HD work less consistently than other gifted children. Some, especially those with AD/HD Inattentive Type, can be exceptionally slow, so they have immense difficulty completing work within the allotted time. If they are in advanced classes, the workload can seem overwhelming, yet they need the stimulation of the advanced work to perform at all. On the other hand, it is much harder for them to arouse attention and effort to perform tasks they already know. Unlike others with AD/HD, gifted children with AD/HD have more difficulty doing repetitious, well-learned tasks.

Variability of quality and quantity of work is an exceptionally difficult problem for these gifted children. What seems so easy one day is impenetrable the next. Often these students leave tests thinking they scored 100%, only to find out they barely passed. On the other hand, if really interested, they can produce complex projects with intriguing ideas. It is interest that arouses them and allows them to get through the task.

Holistic / sequential performance

Barkley (1997) postulated that an important executive function is the ability to break information apart and then to recombine it into new wholes (reconstitution). This analysis and synthesis allows for problem solving, imagination, and creativity. When children with AD/HD cannot wait, but respond impulsively, the chance that this analysis and synthesis will happen decreases. Children with AD/HD do not seem to take things apart into as many pieces as they might. They also appear to have a decreased capacity for verbal and nonverbal fluency (producing many possibilities as alternatives) and less ability to be mentally flexible and to problem solve.

Nadeau *et al.* (1999) described the sequencing difficulties present in many of the girls they assessed who had AD/HD. The skill of sequencing something means breaking a larger goal into steps, then prioritizing among steps and placing them in some sort of time order. Due to impulsivity, sequencing can be difficult for children with AD/HD even when they can do the step-by-step ordering necessary. Also, sequencing by itself can be difficult because many boys and girls with AD/HD do not experience life as sequential, but as momentary. Each moment is separate from the one before and not really connected.

Aspects of holistic/sequential performance include the following.

- *Being a big-picture thinker.* Hallowell and Ratey (1994a) suggested that people with AD/HD are more right than left brain in learning and thinking preferences. They have a distaste for logic and linear reasoning, but do recognize patterns quickly, get the whole from little information, use the visual and emotional to construct ideas, and think in patterns and rhythms rather than words. This means that they are exceptionally good at intuition. However, it is difficult for these right-brained people to articulate the ideas and insights that come to them. Hallowell and Ratey see people with AD/HD as actually "trapped" in their right hemispheres so they can't articulate the holistic ideas they have. To do so would involve a transfer to more left-brain thinking in which logic, detail, and analysis is involved. In effect, they are blocked from producing the ideas they have and cannot easily share them fully with others.

  Not all people with AD/HD are holistic thinkers. Some lack both holistic thinking and sequential processing, especially if they also have an NVLD (see the first section of this chapter, and also Chapter 4). Gifted children with NVLD and AD/HD have trouble both putting together a whole from parts, and breaking a whole into component parts.

- *Difficulty with part-to-whole relationships.* Children with AD/HD have difficulty breaking bigger tasks down into smaller ones, and also going step by step to build to a conclusion. This means they have trouble with planning, organizing, and performing. The deficits in part-to-whole relationships mean they have trouble with projects, completing work, and generalizing from specific instances to a more general whole. Because of this, children with AD/HD also have trouble finding the main point, getting to the essence, analyzing material to find a theme or metaphor or, conversely, developing a theme in reading or writing.

- *Prediction.* Children with AD/HD have difficulty making the connection between now and the future. Because of problems with analysis and synthesis of material, they cannot easily use "if...then" structures. Thus, they have trouble understanding how consequences follow from actions; they have trouble saying to themselves, "If I do this, then...will happen." Prediction in emotional and social situations is also similarly affected.

Because of problems with sequential reasoning, part-to-whole performance, and prediction, children with AD/HD have trouble with organizing narratives about themselves: that is, thinking about how they ought to act or what to do. This means they don't have very clear pictures of who they are. In adolescence, many of these children have more trouble developing identity than do other teens because of these deficits.

- *Difficulty with demand performance.* When life appears to be a series of disconnected moments, and students have trouble with part-to-whole relationships, they can have trouble with demand performance. That is, children with AD/HD cannot organize their thoughts into categories or easily find material; when asked to perform, they do not know what to say, but instead blurt out answers. In part, if thoughts are disorganized, there is no clear starting place, so children with AD/HD do not how to get going, find the material they have learned, and produce it efficiently.

  With younger children, the need for attention and stimulation can be so great that this is all they can focus on. An example is the child with AD/HD who raises her hand when the teacher asks a question but has no idea what to answer if she is called upon. To this little girl, the act of raising her hand is what she associates with the asking of a question. She does not know that she is supposed to have thought of an answer first before raising her hand. She also has no idea that what she answered was wrong. For her, the sequence is that the teacher asks a question and children raise their hands. To other children, the sequence is the teacher asks a question and, if they know the answer, they raise their hands.

Gifted children with AD/HD tend to be big-picture learners who do less well on basic skills and other tasks requiring sequential processing. While other gifted children may dislike sequential tasks, they can perform them. Gifted children with AD/HD have a great deal of difficulty doing so. In academic tasks this is reflected in difficulties with phonics skills, spelling, math computation, and written expression, including handwriting.

Gifted children with AD/HD may do quite well in earlier grades because they are able to recall fact-based information. What they have increasing difficulty with is integrating material; so, in upper grades, they have more trouble with analysis and synthesis of material, generating material, and organizing material into coherent theses. These difficulties affect projects and papers that require research, analysis of results, and conclusions drawn from the data. Thus, gifted students with AD/HD find themselves struggling to do work that other gifted students find time-consuming but not difficult. Gifted students with AD/HD also have trouble using the logical, sequential methods of outlining and data collection that are usually taught: for example, writing material on index cards which are sorted into categories. They find it impossible to build up a thesis using supporting data in this way because they cannot juggle all the material at once. What they do better is to write a paper and then make an outline. Using this outline, they then reorganize the paper, and fill in missing aspects.

Gifted students with AD/HD have trouble with prediction in academic as well as in social contexts. Though they are better than age peers at predicting in hypothetical situations, in real life they cannot juggle all the details, nor easily break a complex situation up as it is happening in order to say and do the best thing. Another aspect of this is demand performance. Demand performance means that a person has to think of a specific answer on the spot: for example, in class in response to a specific question. Gifted children with AD/HD have difficulty with thinking on the spot. Some can get around their difficulty thinking of an answer by talking until it comes to mind. On the other hand, when these gifted children are in control of the conversation topic, words often flow, and they can present material with good organization and detail. Despite some trouble with demand performance, many gifted children with AD/HD actually do better giving verbal answers and making speeches. Alissa had trouble thinking of the answer when the teacher called on her. Because she was so anxious, her difficulty with demand performance increased. To circumvent the problem, Alissa started to talk about everything she knew on the topic and, eventually, the right answer popped into mind.

Emotional control

Impaired regulation of emotional arousal also affects many other areas including motivation. Barkley (1997) suggested that people with AD/HD have difficulty with managing emotion and arousal states. Therefore, they also have difficulties with emotional self-control. This means children with AD/HD tend to be more emotional than age peers, and react more emotionally to small events that others would brush off. There is also a decreased objectivity in responses to events. Children with AD/HD cannot so easily set aside their immediate feelings to deal with an event. They also may have trouble stepping back to see another's perspective or to consider another's feelings. Other aspects of emotional regulation such as ability to self-soothe and use self-directed comments to decrease emotional states are also affected.

T.E. Brown (2000b) described emotional control as necessary in order to pay attention. When memory is activated, it can arouse emotion and that arousal can derail or enhance attention. Feelings of frustration, worries about failure, being overwhelmed, and disliking the work are all emotions that affect attention negatively. Conversely, great interest or liking for a topic can produce hyperfocusing and good performance.

Aspects of emotional control related to AD/HD include the following.

- *Separating feelings from content.* Children with AD/HD react first, think second. They often hear the emotional aspect, the tone, and miss the message. This leads to a focus on how they are feeling rather than what they are doing. Negative affect then can derail effort. Also, when the child has made a mistake or misbehaved, his or her own emotional response may delete the message of what he or she did wrong. When Phillip's two-year-old brother touched his Lego spaceship and broke it, Phillip was enraged. He was so angry that he could not stop to think of what he was doing. He started to beat his brother with his fists. Later, when he had calmed down, he was told he was punished by being deprived of his Lego for the week. Phillip had great difficulty thinking of what he had done to deserve this punishment. All he could think of was his broken toy, and why it wasn't fair that his brother wasn't the one in trouble.

- *Sensitivity and intensity of emotion.* Children with AD/HD tend to be much more emotional than age peers and to react emotionally in more intense ways at ages when peers have learned to modulate emotional responding. This means children with AD/HD act less emotionally mature. They have tantrums at a later age and feel upset over things other children can let pass. Also, children with AD/HD can feel emotional upset for a longer time. For example, making a mistake can lead some children with AD/HD into a downward spiral of self-blame and self-recrimination. On the other hand, the very same child may have a huge tantrum, and once it is over feel fine and act as if nothing happened even as family members still try to recover.

- *Tolerating frustration.* Children with AD/HD are well known for their difficulty tolerating frustration. This occurs because they need to have immediate reward, or high stimulation, and cannot perform well on the material that is frustrating. However, children with AD/HD also give themselves negative emotional messages that increase frustration. At the first sign of difficulty they tell themselves the task is impossible, and then they feel angry they have to do it. Struggling to do something difficult is a skill many never learn. Kutner (1999) described gifted adults with AD/HD who seemed to think their ability to do any task was related to how likable it was. When frustrated, the task was not liked, and not doable.

- *Acting without thinking.* Children with AD/HD have trouble with impulsivity. Part of the problem is the emotional price tag that comes with stopping oneself. To be able to stop, a child has to know what to do next. Children with AD/HD do not know what to do next and feel overwhelmed if they have to try to think of alternatives. While they often regret impulsive acting, stopping themselves also has an emotional price, such as less stimulation. Also, impulsivity can be driven by emotion. Once the emotion overtakes the child, thinking of alternatives is not possible or even desirable. For example, a child with AD/HD who is teased may feel so angry all he can do is think of revenge. At that moment, he cannot stop himself, and even if he is stopped, he may not see an alternative as desirable.

- *Recognition of feelings and how they contribute to events.* Children with AD/HD have trouble knowing what they are feeling, and how that feeling contributes to what happens next. The child who is angry is bent on revenge, but will not be able to see what he did that led to the teasing: for example, he was teasing first.

  Children with AD/HD may also have difficulty with empathic responding. Braaten and Rosen (2000) found that boys with AD/HD were less empathic than other boys. They also had more difficulty matching emotions of story characters with their own. These boys also showed more sadness, anger, and guilt than other boys.

- *Timing of behaviors.* Children with AD/HD have trouble with emotional timing: that is, they miss the subtle sequence of low-level emotion that is ongoing in an interpersonal interaction. Then, they do not respond appropriately. For example, a friend is quiet and sad, but the AD/HD child does not notice and continues to talk about a movie recently seen. Conversational turn-taking is hard for some of these children because they have trouble noticing when they can talk, waiting their turn, and not monopolizing the conversation themselves.

Gifted children with AD/HD show the same difficulties with emotional control as age peers with AD/HD. They have trouble with separating emotion and content, and instead let their feelings get in the way of their judgment. They have trouble with emotional reactivity. In fact, since gifted children in general are more sensitive and intense than more average children, those with AD/HD can be even further along the spectrum of increased proclivity for emotional reactivity, sensitivity, and intensity. On the other hand, gifted children with AD/HD can be more passionate as well, and this passion can guide them into more positive emotional interactions.

While some gifted children with AD/HD are like those reported by Braaten and Rosen (2000) in showing less empathy, others are quite empathic. Some gifted children with AD/HD are responsive to others much of the time. They can be exceptionally empathic, more so even than most other gifted children, because they are so intuitive. Others have trouble being empathic when they feel their own needs are not being met.

Gifted children with AD/HD may have more trouble tolerating frustration than average peers with AD/HD because the gap between what they want to do and what they can do is so much greater. The gifted child with AD/HD can see the whole picture in her head, wants to hurry and get there, and is impatient with details, mistakes, and obstacles. Since the projects conceived may be more complex and require more work than that of the average project, these gifted children with AD/HD may not be able to accomplish them. Their dreams may be too big for their skills.

Timing of behaviors can be a problem for gifted children with AD/HD when they are invested in doing something and feel thwarted. For example, those children who are ready to do more complex and advanced math, or who already know all the spelling words, feel frustrated when forced to complete this work again. They may not be able to wait to express their feelings. Also, many of these children know a great deal about particular topics of interest, but have no one to talk to about them. When they get an audience, they are unwilling to relinquish their turn in conversation. Instead, they take all the turns and develop a monologue.

Many gifted children with AD/HD have an exquisite sense of timing for humor. They can play the role of the class clown and know the exact moment to act up, say something funny, or do an imitation. This intuition is coupled with positive feelings for the esteem received by making everyone laugh.

Ability to delay gratification

Children with AD/HD have trouble waiting for rewards. Research has shown that given a choice of a small, immediate reward and less work, or more work and a much larger but more distant reward, the children with AD/HD will opt for the immediate satisfaction while children of the same age, without AD/HD, will opt for the larger but delayed reward (Barkley 1995). In effect, children with AD/HD are acting like children of a much younger age. The underlying problem is not that they are distracted by the immediate reward so much as that they have trouble seeing far enough into the future to see the benefits of waiting. They also can't work for very long without a reward. If no reward is offered, work soon stops because something in the environment that offers more reward will occur. Ratey (2001) described how disinhibition adds to the problem: that is, the inability of people with AD/HD to stop themselves from responding to the immediate novel or pleasurable stimuli instead of the longer-term reward. The person can't abstain from ineffective, but rewarding, activity.

Children with AD/HD have little patience for boring work and rush to get through the unpleasant parts as soon as possible, if they do them at all. More aspects appear unpleasant to these children than to children who do not have AD/HD. Children with AD/HD don't finish the work, and so do not experience the rewards that children without AD/HD receive. Because they do complete their work, children without AD/HD experience satisfaction from the work itself (it's fun to do it; it's fun to see how fast they can do it), from getting the work done (a job well done is satisfying), and from praise received from adults for doing the work. Children with AD/HD miss all of these rewards.

Motivation is also a source of difficulty because children with AD/HD cannot easily induce the arousal state that would lead to getting going. Since they have trouble seeing the future, the current emotional response is the most predominant and that is what is more easily responded to. Sydney wanted to learn to play the piano but found it difficult to stop playing and go to a lesson or practice. She had initially been enthusiastic, but over time, she began to fuss and complain. Then, it was hard for her to change from her negative emotional state to a positive mode for piano playing. Sydney's parents found it easier to motivate her if they broke piano playing into a series of small parts that required little commitment. Piano lessons were twice weekly for 15 minutes, and practice sessions, 15 minutes a day. Since Sydney was enthusiastic but easily frustrated, her parents set a timer, and for each of the five-minute intervals in her 15-minute block, she received a token if she could continue without getting up or talking. At the end of each week, the tokens were counted and she received a small reward (an ice-cream cone, a video rental, parents reading her favorite book or playing a game with her) depending on how many chips she had earned over the week. In this way, Sydney's parents slowly built motivation.

Aspects of difficulty delaying gratification that cause problems for children with AD/HD include the following.

- *Sustaining attention without immediate rewards.* Children with AD/HD have difficulty with longer-term rewards, even those that will occur in the near future. For younger children, rewards need to be immediate or they simply are not seen as rewards. There is no connection between what was done in the past and the reward obtained now. Thus, children with AD/HD cannot wait for the end of the week to be rewarded for behaving well or completing work. They do better with immediate feedback. Even older children benefit from shorter-term rewards that are artificially introduced so they acquire some of the skills they will need in the future. Therefore, even an older child may need homework collected and given a check mark though age peers have long been independent about homework. For older students, a weekly reward can work but something longer term, such as grades on their report card, is not rewarding. For many children with AD/HD, increasing the stimulation of the work by adding color, novelty, interest or one-on-one personal interaction, by breaking work down into smaller units that require less effort, and by offering more immediate rewards for finishing each part is more successful in increasing productivity.

- *Inability to feel rewarded by ordinary rewards.* Some children with AD/HD do not respond to ordinary rewards like check marks or verbal approval. It is as if they don't even notice these are supposed to be rewards. To them, rewards are material, or high-stimulation activities. Some children with AD/HD also satiate easily on a reward and need types of rewards changed frequently. These children have particular difficulty with motivation. They only can do highly stimulating or rewarding activities of their own choosing. Many of them resist reward programs, and seem unmotivated about almost everything. To them, though, very little feels rewarding. They aren't trying to be difficult. Instead, they really have a severe problem with recognizing and feeling rewards. For some, the only things that feel rewarding on a regular basis are intense video games.

- *Marching to their own drummer.* Some children with AD/HD are less motivated to do routine activities because their own interests are so much more compelling. Rewarding them for doing work that is routine is less than successful because they are always thinking about their own ideas, interests, and activities. These children with AD/HD cannot perform tasks unless they do them their own way, on their own terms. They are highly resistant to pressure or threats. Even failure makes little impression. The reward in their own minds and in performing their own activities far outweighs any other reward offered. Some of these children are highly creative and spend their time in their own imaginations. That is their internal reward. Others are less imaginative but equally strong willed and independent. They accept nothing unless they want to do it. Unfortunately, some will go so far as to refuse to do enough work to pass so they may graduate from high school.

Gifted children with AD/HD can have motivation problems like those of their more average AD/HD age peers. However, many gifted children with AD/HD are not motivated because they are offered work that is not challenging or rewarding to perform. When bored by the level and repetition of the work, and the slow pace of the class, some of these gifted children give up trying, or only do what they are interested in. Gifted children with AD/HD who are creative may not respond to the usual rewards but may be more responsive to rewards based on novelty, the chance to explore interests, and the time to create.

Positive aspects of gifted children with AD/HD

All too often the focus is on the deficits of children with AD/HD. Gifted children with AD/HD have particular strenghs and weaknesses that need attention. Only through using their strengths will these children overcome weaker areas. Accommodation and compensation both depend on recognizing and incorporating strengths. Thus, it is important to describe areas of particular strength for gifted children with AD/HD.

Gifted children with AD/HD Combined Type

Gifted children with AD/HD Combined Type have a number of particular strengths. When motivated with interesting and stimulating work, these children can perform very quickly and produce work of outstanding quality. Among gifted children who came to the Gifted Resource Center of New England, many with AD/HD Combined Type were found to have creative ideas, and used these in thinking, talking, writing, and in the visual and performing arts. Because they tended to notice things no one else does, they saw new connections and developed different ways of looking at things. Sometimes these were inventing games. However, stories and play were also quite creative.

Spontaneity is a positive trait. Being spontaneous allowed these gifted children to move past mistakes. They rarely felt overwhelmed by having made errors. They also could be very happy and spread that joy to others, especially when they were enthusiastic about a self-chosen venture. Frequently, they invited others to join in their pursuits, even if they had been rejected before. They often had a sweet temperament and a trust of people that was somewhat naive, but quite endearing; thus, they were readily forgiven for their mistakes. Also, they tended to forgive quickly. Perhaps because they had such short attention spans, and poorer sense of the past, they had a harder time recalling their anger. Or perhaps their poorer awareness of social cues made them less aware of social rejection. In either case, they rarely held grudges.

These gifted children did not worry a great deal about how they appeared to others. This allowed many to be disinhibited in the service of entertaining others. They were performers such as musicians, actors, comedians, and athletes. Most of these gifted children also had a wonderful sense of humor, and could recall and even make up funny jokes. Eric, for example, when told by his mother that they had to eat and run, quipped, "Oh, like carnivorous panty hose!" (Lovecky 1994a).

Thom Hartmann (1993, 1996) developed a very positive view of AD/HD behaviors with his books on the hunter and farmer types of people. The AD/HD Combined Type is more like the hunter/gatherer mode of existence. These people are "hunters in a farmer's world" (Hartmann 1993). In fact, Hartmann's research on indigenous tribes around the world has suggested that in peoples whose traditions are still in a hunter/gatherer mode of living, AD/HD-like behaviors predominate (as in many Native American tribes). AD/HD behaviors also predominate in cultures with people who were pioneers or who emigrated for political reasons, such as people on Taiwan (Hartmann 1996). Thus, AD/HD behaviors may have had, and still have, especially in their milder forms, significant evolutionary advantage in certain environments.

Hallowell and Ratey (1994a) also described a number of positives related to having AD/HD including high energy, creativity, intuitiveness, resourcefulness, sensitivity, tenacity, being hardworking and having a never-say-die-approach, warmheartedness, trusting attitude, forgiving attitude, ability to take risks, flexibility, good sense of humor, and loyalty.

Gifted children with AD/HD Inattentive Type

Gifted children with AD/HD Inattentive Type showed strengths in creativity and humor. They often appreciate more subtle types of jokes, especially sophisticated puns. Much of their humor is offbeat, quirky, and can have a dark side.

When motivated, these gifted children produce a great deal of work in areas in which they immerse themselves, and they can have startling insights into a subject area or into people, because they are often quiet observers. While they seem not to be paying attention, off in their own little worlds, they are taking it all in for later processing.

Luke, with AD/HD Inattentive Type, was a prodigious writer for his age. At age 13, he liked to write novels and poetry, which he also illustrated. While he finished few complete works, his strength was his feel for characters. His insight into the foibles of humanity was wise beyond his years. Luke's one wish in life right now is to write. School work and other expected duties feel to him like an intrusion on his valuable creative process. When performing tasks other than writing, he is disorganized, careless, and shows poor completion of work. He likes to learn things, but finds he loses energy partway through longer tasks and so doesn't complete them. Often he is tired and irritable. What Luke requires is an alternate school program in which he can have time to write, as well as somewhat different expectations than the traditional college preparatory program.

Another particular strength of gifted children with AD/HD Inattentive Type is their ability to reflect carefully about the subject at hand. Thus, they are not quick to answer. Answers require thinking about many aspects that the child considers carefully before responding. Thus, there is often a long pause after a question is asked. Also, this type of child splits hairs frequently, saying "yes, but" because he or she can see all the alternatives and exceptions quite well. This is sometimes crippling but also means that they consider ramifications that others never see.

Gifted children with AD/HD Inattentive Type, despite their tendency to be emotionally overwhelmed easily, also care deeply about things. They are passionate and need to know why bad things happen in the world. Many of these children ask disturbing moral and spiritual questions, and may not suffer fools too gladly.

Conclusion

Gifted children with AD/HD show both great strengths and weaknesses. Both of these need to be addressed in order for the child to reach potential and develop a satisfying adult life. Strengths in cognitive, social, emotional, and creative areas and moral reasoning need to be developed both to enhance the child and to help the child to compensate for weaker areas. Weaknesses need to be addressed by remediation and use of compensatory mechanisms so the child can learn to work efficiently and with less frustration. Because of this, gifted children with AD/HD need a differentiated educational program to meet needs in both the gifted area and the area of weakness. Gifted children with AD/HD need to be educated with gifted peers. However, in accelerating them or giving them extra work, one needs to be sure they have the support skills to manage the tasks. Thus, they may need to go ahead in a subject, but they also need to be taught how to structure their approach to the learning of the subject. Content area needs are often out of sync with ability to use executive functions. This should not come as a surprise.

Finally, many gifted children with AD/HD do need medication. Specific evaluation of what type, dose, and possible side effect needs to be carefully considered. Medication alone, though, is not a total answer. Gifted children with AD/HD also need a multipronged program that works to change the academic curriculum and to teach them specific skills in areas of deficits such as basic skills, skills related to executive functions, interpersonal skills, emotional control, etc.

Throughout this book each of these suggestions will be amplified within the various chapters to give a better idea of how to deal with these wonderful but challenging children.

A foolish consistency is the hobgoblin of little minds.

Ralph Waldo Emerson
Essays First Series: Self-Reliance

Chapter 3

Attention Deficits:
Asperger Syndrome

Harry

Four-year-old Harry brought all his numbers to show on his first visit to the psychologist. Harry loved numbers and shapes. He wrote numbers constantly, counting higher and higher on paper, wanting to know the highest number. He also liked to know things that had numbers in them. For over an hour he regaled all the adults with accounts of the exact routes near his house and all the ways home from various places. He knew the numbers of all the major roads in the USA and Canada. He knew house and phone numbers of friends. In his house he numbered all the rooms. "I'm going into room number six," he would tell his parents as he went into his bedroom. Harry was also advanced at adding numbers together and subtracting them. He had just turned four, but was able to solve problems from the end of the 2nd-grade math curriculum. He was reading simple primers and spelling many words which he loved to write on lined paper hour after hour. Harry also knew all the states by shape, name, and capital. He loved to quiz adults on these and took delight in showing up their errors.

Harry was a delightful little boy, obviously bright and interested in learning. Nevertheless he was difficult to teach. He only wanted to do what was on his own agenda. Consequently, he ignored his preschool teacher, did not participate in group activities such as circle time, and could only be persuaded to try some of the preschool tasks if his teacher made them into geography or math games. He acted as if the teacher were there only for him, when he wanted her, and the other children were more or less part of the furniture.

Harry ignored the other children at school. He was not interested in being with them unless they were doing something he was interested in. Then, he often moved over to them to tell them how to do it. The other children accepted Harry because his ideas were often interesting. At the preschool level, friendship exists because another child asks one to play. Thus, while Harry never asked anyone to play, he was not socially rejected and, in fact, at times was sought out by others.

As Harry entered elementary school, his problems became more evident. He did little of the work asked of him and spent his time inventing math problems for himself to solve. He also wrote up geography quizzes and studied the atlas and dictionary. Because of all this self-imposed independent work, Harry's reading, vocabulary, spelling, and math were far above grade level. His handwriting was poor despite all the hours he spent writing words and facts on paper. He refused to write any stories, or even to dictate any. Participation in art, music, and physical education was poor because Harry rarely did any of the tasks assigned.

Harry's social skills were undeveloped. In elementary years, play and friendship become reciprocal. Each child expects the other to act in return. Thus, they take turns, care about each other's interests and feelings, and try to adapt in order to play together. Harry could not do any of this. He still acted as he had in preschool. However, the other children were no longer preschoolers. They slowly became less tolerant of Harry's intrusiveness and bossiness. They did not like his monologues on geography, and they did not like the fact that he would not play games as they wanted to do. He also reacted badly to teasing, screaming and carrying on in a way that the others thought was babyish.

Harry started to stand out as immature. He had tantrums and was rigid about changes. To other children, it seemed as if Harry was being purposely annoying by talking too much and interrupting, and wanting everything his own way when working on a project. Others didn't see the context he operated from – that is, that all things are related to his own inner interests and fixations. Because Harry was thinking of his interests all the time, when he started to talk to others, it seemed to him that he was just continuing a narrative started long ago, one that others were supposed to remember. Harry did not have much idea that others had lives and thoughts of their own. It was almost as if they were animated objects that he could return to, left in exactly the same state he'd left them in, and therefore they should know exactly what he meant. After all, he'd already told them.

At home, Harry's rigid expectations caused problems with his parents and siblings. For instance, he insisted that he had to finish what he was doing before he came to dinner. If his parents tried to insist he stop, he needed to start all over again at the beginning and still would not come. He had trouble getting off the computer to do anything else. In fact, by 5th grade, the only thing Harry wanted to do was play computer games. Now, he talked constantly at home and at school about his favorite game, how he knew all the cheat codes, and how high he had scored. He did not do anything he was told; he dawdled and disobeyed. He also was quite mean to his baby sister. His parents had caught him poking and pinching her, and he seemed to enjoy the reaction he got. He also played mean tricks on the baby-sitter. After reading a cartoon book of Calvin and Hobbes one day, when he was ten, he put a pail filled with water balanced over the top of a door, and then he called the baby-sitter to come in. He was gleeful about how he'd fooled her, just like cartoon Calvin had fooled his baby-sitter. Harry was not at all concerned about the fact he'd hurt her when the pail hit her on the head. Needless to say, that was the last time that sitter came.

Harry was brought for evaluation to the Gifted Resource Center of New England following a recommendation by his school for a comprehensive assessment of his cognitive, social, and emotional functioning. When assessed on the *Wechsler Intelligence Scale for Children* (WISC), Harry was found to have an IQ in the 130s (gifted range). He did especially well on most verbal tasks including knowledge of words, general knowledge, mental arithmetic, short-term memory for digits, noting missing details in pictures, sequencing pictures, and putting blocks together to make a design. He was weaker at rapidly copying shapes, at social knowledge, and at putting together puzzles, a task that required putting parts together to make a whole.

Harry was exceptionally skilled academically at reading words, reading comprehension, mathematics, spelling, general knowledge, vocabulary, and knowledge of punctuation and grammar. Academically he was weak on written expression and handwriting. He wouldn't write a story but did consent to write sentences. Even so, his ability to write according to directions and to elaborate the content beyond the barest description was poor.

Social and emotional assessment showed him to have difficulty knowing the most common expected thing to say in social situations. Given a test of telling a story about different social situations using pictures, he had trouble under-standing others' perspectives, and he didn't know what someone else might feel. After all, he wasn't them and, no, he couldn't imagine himself in the picture. He'd never had that happen to him.

Harry's parents filled out extensive questionnaires and history forms. Several of Harry's relatives had had mental health problems with depression and anxiety, and there was a cousin who had autism.

Children like Harry have AS. They are also gifted children. Like Harry, gifted children with AS have many difficulties with communication and social development. Some of these gifted children act like "little professors." Unlike gifted children with AD/HD Inattentive Type who may also be known for their professorial tendencies, gifted children with AS show less concern about the other people who are part of their world. Many have little interest in other children, though some want very much to have friends and do try to interact, albeit inappropriately. What interests gifted children with AS are their own ideas, fascinations, and activities. So far as they are concerned this is what matters. They also have trouble seeing adults as anything but there for their convenience. On the other hand, they also have wonderful gifts and talents that need development in order for them to have productive lives.

The focus of this chapter

In order to answer the question of what part of Harry's behavior is due to AS and what to giftedness, it is necessary to have some knowledge of both areas. Giftedness was explored in Chapter 1. This chapter is more focused on what constitutes AS. This chapter is divided into five major sections.

- Development and types of AS.

- Symptoms of AS.

- Understanding AS.

- Gifted children with AS.

- Positive aspects of AS.

Each chapter section is further divided into subsections, and these will be summarized at the start of each section.

Development and types of AS

Asperger Syndrome (AS) is a developmental disorder in which children have pronounced and pervasive difficulty with social relationships. They also show stereotyped behaviors and have restricted interests. Poor communication skills, difficulties with motor coordination and sensory integration, and problems with some aspects of cognition are common. These core symptoms describe people who have difficulty understanding how and why others think and act in certain ways, and who have trouble understanding how to know what to do themselves in any situation. AS is a mild form of autism.

In this section of this chapter, the development of AS, the types of AS, prevalence and genetics of AS, and other conditions that can coexist with AS will be discussed.

AS as a developmental disorder

AS starts in early childhood, and is likely present from birth; however, the main difficulties may not be evident until the child has to face more formal settings such as school. For many children with AS, early development does not appear to be very unusual. Thus, many (but not all) children with AS learn to walk and talk on time and learn self-help skills and early academics.

The earliest descriptions of AS did not focus much on early development. Asperger (1991) thought that early development was essentially normal. However, Lorna Wing (1981) reviewed Asperger's original work and discussed modifications based on 30 cases she had observed. Wing suggested that differences were apparent in children with AS in the first two years of life. These differences included little interest in others, limited babbling, and poor joint attention (that is, if the child saw a toy he or she would not point it out to the parent; if the parent tried to show a toy to the child, he or she would not pay attention). Also, these children lacked imaginative play. They might play out scenes from books in a repetitive way, but added little to them. If other children were involved, they were assigned roles by the child with AS, and could not add anything to the play.

Wing modified Asperger's ideas about precocious language. She found that many of the children with AS that she observed had good grammar and vocabulary but lacked flexibility in content. Much was copied from what was heard or read. In addition, nonverbal communication was impaired. Wing noted that walking and talking were not generally advanced in her subjects, and were delayed in many.

Wing discussed the imagination and intelligence seen by Asperger in his subjects. She noted, instead, more restrictive interests and less meaningful application of content. She thought interests and skills were more based on rote memory than innovation.

More recent descriptions of AS have emphasized the lack of early diagnostic symptoms. For example, Fred Volkmar and Ami Klin's (2000) review suggested that in early years children with AS were not seen as having problems with social interest or language by their families. They did not show the same type of problems with emotionally and socially connecting to their parents (early attachment) as children with autism do. The children with AS for the most part wanted social interaction with others, but were inappropriate in how they tried to elicit it. Thus, they stood out as "little professors" in peer groupings, but were not oblivious to the presence of others.

In language areas, the development of language was normal in grammar and vocabulary. However, these children were likely to be deficient in pragmatics: that is, knowing what to say in social situations, and when to say it (apologizing or using polite language are examples of pragmatics). Motor clumsiness was also noted to be a frequent symptom.

Diagnostic criteria according to DSM-IV

The American Psychiatric Association's (2000) *Diagnostic and Statistical Manual* (DSM-IV-TR) and the ICD-10 (WHO 1993) are very similar in their descriptions of autism and AS. In each system, social impairment, communication deficits, and stereotypy/restricted interests are delineated as a means of diagnosing and distinguishing the two disorders. Both autism and AS have diagnostic criteria that are similar for social deficits and stereotypy/restricted interests, but children with AS do not have the degree of impaired communication that those with autism show. The DSM-IV-TR criteria are reprinted in Appendix A.

There are other diagnostic systems and each describes AS somewhat differently, including different features and exclusions. Thus, in one system a child might be diagnosed as autistic, and in another as AS.

One disorder or different types?

AS is defined as an autism spectrum disorder. It is seen as a mild disorder compared to autism; however, where it falls on the spectrum of autism spectrum disorders is also disputed. Some see AS as the same thing as High Functioning Autism (HFA); others see two different disorders with differentiating symptoms.

One of the problems in deciding if a child has AS or autism comes from the diagnostic criteria. For example, the criteria for both DSM-IV and ICD-10, the two major assessment systems, specify that children with AS cannot have had clinically significant language delays, nor can they have had clinically significant delays in adaptive functioning except for social interactions. That is, self-help and communication skills should be closer to age level. Nevertheless, many researchers and clinicians dispute these restrictions and classify some children as AS even with language delays or adaptive functioning lower than average, because the children do not have some of the more severe features that are associated with autism.

Some children are classified differently because they are diagnosed according to a different classification system such as that of Gillberg and Gillberg (1989), reprinted in Appendix A. In this system, social impairment, narrow range of interests, repetitive routines, speech and language peculiarities, nonverbal communication problems, and motor clumsiness are evaluated as part of the diagnosis. Recently, Gillberg *et al.* (2001) have developed a rating procedure, the Asperger Syndrome Diagnostic Interview, based on these criteria.

Mildness of symptoms is often a reason for diagnosing AS rather than autism, even in children who had delays in language or adaptive functioning. Improvement of symptoms over time also may result in a reclassification. In fact, some children classified as autistic in childhood are classified as AS in adolescence or adulthood. Temple Grandin is an example of this. She suggests that were she age two now, she would be seen as a child who has autism; as an adult, were she to be diagnosed now, she'd be seen as having AS (Grandin 1995).

HFA OR AS?

From the time of Hans Asperger's original paper, first published in the 1940s (Asperger 1991), researchers have been asking if there really is a difference between AS and autism. Are they really two different disorders or are they on the same spectrum with AS at the mild end? Is there a difference then between AS and HFA? Perhaps they are two slightly different types of the same disorder? It depends on what criteria are used.

Eisenmajer *et al.* (1996) compared diagnoses given by a variety of professionals in England and Australia, and found that clinicians appear to diagnose AS or autism on the basis of published research and case-study accounts rather than by strict DSM-IV or ICD-10 criteria. Their findings questioned whether DSM-IV and ICD-10 criteria adequately describe the individual with AS, particularly in the communication domain.

Not only do clinicians vary in the criteria used to diagnose AS or autism, but also researchers use different criteria in studies that attempt to differentiate AS from HFA. Gillberg and Gillberg in Sweden, Szatmari in Canada, Wing in the United Kingdom, and Klin, Volkmar, and Sparrow in the USA all use different criteria. In addition, it is difficult to match subjects exactly on chronological age, mental age, verbal skills, and early history in order to find exact comparisons in experimental studies. Thus, many studies are inconclusive and different studies contradict each other.

In deciding whether there are differences between people with AS and HFA, researchers have studied motor development and functioning, visual-spatial functions, theory of mind, and executive functions. Ozonoff and Griffith (2000) reviewed all the available literature and concluded that, on the whole, there was no clear evidence for a distinction between the two groups. There were some hints that for some subjects, in some studies, differences in motor clumsiness, theory of mind, right-brain functioning, and executive dysfunction did exist, but until studies are conducted using set selection criteria and more careful matching of subjects, it is difficult to say that AS is not really HFA.

Researchers who think that AS is a distinct disorder, different from HFA, have mostly focused on right-brain functioning. These researchers, especially Klin *et al.* (1995), find that there is strong evidence that the major deficit in AS is right-hemisphere dysfunction. In HFA, the main deficit is left-hemisphere dysfunction. Thus, children with AS are seen as more like children with NVLDs, and children with HFA as more like children with language disabilities. Nevertheless, both groups share many similarities and overlaps in deficits. It may be that there are several different types of mild autism based on intellectual functioning, right-brain dysfunction, degree of language delay, or degree of mildness of symptoms.

The difference in diagnostic criteria used, particularly by clinicians, makes it impossible to determine if a child has mild autism or AS. This is particularly the case if checklists or surveys are used. Many checklists include criteria drawn from DSM-IV and ICD-10 but also extend the symptoms list further. Because of the wide variation in diagnosis, and the disagreement by many with some of the DSM-IV criteria (especially language development, adaptive functioning, and imaginative play), many clinicians have their own criteria. Thus, children with somewhat differing profiles of strengths and weaknesses all may be diagnosed as having AS. This means they all share the characteristics listed in DSM-IV and ICD-10 for social deficits and stereotyped behaviors/restricted interests but may differ significantly on other deficits and strengths.

WHY DOES THE LABEL MATTER?

For many, a label of autism often brings to mind a severe disability with a poor prognosis. Many children with autism are mentally retarded as well as autistic. Their needs are different from those of higher-functioning children. Labeling a child with HFA brings puzzlement. People don't see how a child can be high functioning and autistic too. Of course, it's a matter of degree. To be labeled high functioning, one needs an IQ in excess of 70. The more typical IQ of a child with an AS label is above average.

What label a child has is important in terms of research about interventions. If the two groups of children are really different, it may be that different interventions are needed for each. Thus, it might be important to determine if there really are two distinct groups.

There does seem to be some validity for defining a group of people with right-hemisphere dysfunction. These children and adolescents have NVLDs that extend into more severe dysfunction. Thus, one group of people with mild autism may be those with severe NVLDs. Another group appear to be more visual, and more like the descriptions of typical autism. Both of these could be labeled HFA, or AS.

For the purpose of this book, children were diagnosed as having AS if they had developed fluent language skills by age five, and otherwise met the criteria for AS from DSM-IV.

Prevalence and genetics of AS

More boys than girls are diagnosed with AS by about a ratio of four boys to every one girl. More recent research, using also suspected and possible cases of AS, suggested a lower ratio of two boys to each girl (Ehlers and Gillberg 1993).

Fewer girls may be diagnosed for several reasons. There may be a sex-linked heredity of AS so more boys are actually affected. On the other hand, like children with AD/HD, it may be that girls on the whole can compensate more in childhood and may be protected by other girls in ways that boys are not (Attwood 1998). Hans Asperger, in his original studies, found no girls, but puzzled how it was that the mothers of some of the boys he studied had mild AS symptoms (Asperger 1991). Likely, these mothers grew up not being noticed as significantly different, either because the structure of society at the time supported them, or symptoms were milder and not noticed in a time when differences had to be extreme to be noticed. Even today, girls are less likely to be noticed and diagnosed with any disorder. Of the seven girls with AS in the sample used in this book, two were home-schooled, and three were in regular classes with no special attention given their symptoms at all. In fact, their schools did not see any issues with them. Only two girls had problems at school significant enough to warrant special education services. In contrast, 12 of the 23 boys received special education services, and three were home-schooled.

AS is quite rare. Depending on what criteria are used to diagnose AS, prevalence estimates range from about 3 to 7 per 1000 (Ehlers and Gillberg 1993). Compare this to the estimates of prevalence for AD/HD of 1 to 15 per 100.

AS, along with other autism spectrum disorders, appears to run in families. There are fewer studies than there have been for AD/HD because it is more difficult to agree on diagnosis of disorder in different family members (HFA versus AS), and because autism is so rare. Those studies that do exist have attempted to study genetics by seeing if family members had traits similar to, or a diagnosis of, an autistic spectrum disorder to a greater degree than would be expected based on the frequency in the general population. That is, were there more family members affected with autism-like traits than would be expected if they were randomly selected people?

Folstein and Santangelo (2000) reviewed several studies to see if autism, AS, and a broad autism phenotype (milder symptoms than AS) co-occurred in families. They concluded that these disorders did appear to cluster in families and also appeared to be genetically related conditions. Gillberg (1989) reported on data from 23 families with AS. In these families, autism was present in one sibling of a child with AS (4%). On the other hand, 2% of the parents had AS, and 21% of parents had some symptoms. In a study of 99 families with AS, Volkmar *et al.* (1998) found a rate of autism of 3.5% in siblings, 11% AS in parents, and 46% of families showed at least one first-degree relative with some autistic traits. Since the expected rate of autism is 4 in 10,000, of AS, 4 in 1000, and of broader traits, 4 in 100 (Folstein and Santangelo 2000), the actual prevalence is far beyond expectancy.

Coexisting conditions with AS

AS can coexist with a number of other conditions. These include AD/HD, Tourette Syndrome, OCD, anxiety, depression, ODD, NVLD and Developmental Coordination Disorder.

AD/HD

AD/HD can commonly occur with AS. In one Swedish study reported by Gillberg (2002) the great majority of all children with AS also had AD/HD and Developmental Coordination Disorder. In one clinician's report in the United States, 60 to 70% of children in his practice with AS also had AD/HD (Rosenn 2002). At the Gifted Resource Center of New England, 22 of 30 children diagnosed with AS also had diagnoses of AD/HD. Thus, the association of AS and AD/HD is quite high. Rosenn (2002) also mentions that children with AS who have symptoms of AD/HD appeared to fall into two groups: those who responded well to stimulant medication, and those who did better with anti-anxiety medications. This second group may have had AD/HD symptoms generated by anxiety.

Differentiating AD/HD and AS

The differential diagnosis of AD/HD and AS is not easy. Some children have both diagnoses, and benefit from strategies and treatments that benefit others with each diagnosis. However, children with AD/HD can have social impairments and not have AS, and those with AS can have attention deficits and not have AD/HD. There is a point where some symptoms overlap and appear similar but have different underlying causes in the two different diagnoses. Therefore, it is important to differentiate between children who fit best into one or the other.

Rosenn (2002) described some of the differences between AD/HD and AS. These can be broken down into four categories.

- *Developmental delays.* Children with AS have more developmental delays than those with AD/HD in gross motor, fine motor, sensory integration, attention regulation, pragmatic language, social skills, play interests, emotional regulation, and executive function disorders. Not only are there more areas of delay for children with AS, but also they are more extreme in the delays. For example, children with AD/HD appear two to four years less mature than age peers, but those with AS are much more immature (play skills at age two to four level while chronologically an adolescent).

- *Social reciprocity.* Children with AS show severe impairments of social reciprocity, while those with AD/HD have more difficulty with consistent application of social skills. Children with AD/HD know what to do but forget to do it, while those with AS have difficulty seeing that relationships are two-sided. This also applies to conversation skills. Children with AS have great difficulty learning to engage in a two-sided conversation. Those with AD/HD also have trouble learning to do so initially, but once they have the skill, they can use it if they are reminded or if it is important to them that they do so. Social failure occurs for different reasons in each group. Those with AS fail because their behavior is so idiosyncratic that it makes little sense to others. Children with AS like rules and obey those they understand. Rule violations occur when the child does not understand the rule. Those with AS are more likely to be oppositional when they want to avoid something that makes them feel anxious or when they feel disinterested in a topic. Children with AD/HD fail socially because they cannot modulate their behavior. They break rules if they disagree with them or if it would be fun to do so. They are impulsive and act without thinking. Those with AD/HD can be more oppositional to seek attention or to avoid something they don't like.

- *Emotional functioning.* Both groups have difficulty with anxiety and depression but those with AS have more anxiety related to small changes. They crave order and dislike deviations from routine or expectancy. Anxiety about change can lead to tantrums. Those with AD/HD are more flexible in their thinking and more fluid in reasoning. Anxiety comes more from a sense of incompetence and inability to reach the goals set, as well as from frustration with having to deal with details that appear unrelated to current desires.

- *Cognitive aspects.* Children with AS have much more trouble seeing the big picture. They like details and love to accumulate them but cannot organize or prioritize them. Children with AS tend to have more trouble telling a coherent story, more trouble with seeing the whole, and more splinter skills than those with AD/HD. Those with AD/HD tend to be more big-picture thinkers, have more mental flexibility, and can group or categorize different facts according to different aspects. They can also think of alternate plans and solve novel problems with novel solutions.

- *Both groups* may have trouble with social skills, perspective-taking skills, conversation skills, sensory integration, be obsessed by video games and computers, talk constantly and too loudly, be teased, have tantrums, and have no friends. Both groups can be uncoordinated and impulsive, have difficulty with a lack of structure, and have difficulty modulating behavior.

TOURETTE SYNDROME

Tourette Syndrome and other tic disorders are relatively common in children with AS. Gillberg (2002) described a Swedish study of children with AS or suspected AS who had tic disorders: about 60 to 80% had definite tics. In addition, 10 to 20% of all children with AS have full-blown Tourette Syndrome.

OBSESSIVE-COMPULSIVE DISORDER (OCD)

OCD symptoms are fairly common in AS. However, it is likely not a separate disorder but rather part of AS. After all, the AS person's life is filled with attempts to keep things the same, and obsessions about special interests as well as about disliked things (foods, clothing, sounds, and the like). Also, people with AS tend to make rituals. Thus, once they have done something a particular way or experienced something happening one way, they expect it to be that way all the time. That's one of the reasons social scripts work so well for these children: they learn the words to say and say them each time. If a child with AS develops a ritual of carrying a book a certain way, is that the same or different from someone without AS but with OCD who needs to do the same? And what about counting? Many children with AS delight in counting and labeling things with numbers, as Harry did in the vignette at the start of this chapter. While similar to OCD, such behavior is more likely part of AS. OCD may be diagnosed as a separate disorder when it appears that rituals and obsessions not common to AS are involved, such as compulsive hand washing.

OTHER ANXIETY DISORDERS

Anxiety is common in people with AS, and may be part of AS as well. Specific anxiety disorders such as panic attacks, generalized anxiety, and phobias all can occur in children with AS. Also, more free-floating anxiety, less attached to specific fears and worries, can be present. The level of anxiety seems to depend on how much the child is aware of his or her difference, and how easily frustrated he or she becomes. Thus, anxiety increases as children with AS reach adolescence. Younger children may show anxiety around specific negative situations. For example, Harry was quite anxious about lunch because eating in the school lunch room was a negative experience for him: it felt overwhelming with the noise, smells of food, and numbers of children running around. Harry was also quite anxious about going to new places. He liked to know exactly what would happen next, and in a new place he did not know. Other children with AS may not show much anxiety because they are unaware of their differences or don't care. To them, they are fine and if people would just leave them alone, they could be really happy.

Those children with AS who worry a lot may do so because they can foresee negative consequences. Thus, bright children with AS who begin to become socially aware, or who have high standards for their own performance, may start to worry and become anxious. On the other hand, things that would worry most other children without AS may not be disturbing at all.

DEPRESSIVE DISORDERS

Depression can coexist with AS. However, it is important not to mistake the rather solemn, low-key demeanor and blank look of many children with AS for depression. This blankness is part of the difficulty people with AS have in showing facial expression. They also may feel a sort of blankness, but it is not usually described as unpleasant. True depression does occur, though, and when it does, these children are more likely to be irritable, cry, whine a lot, act hopeless and gloomy about the future, and be pessimistic. They may also make suicide threats, or talk frequently about gore and blood. Talking about gore and blood is not, in itself, a sign of depression in children with AS – it might be part of an obsession; however, it needs to be carefully evaluated in the context of other symptoms.

Children and adolescents with AS can also have Juvenile Onset Bipolar Disorder with its symptoms of cyclic mood disorder and mania. Mania in particular can be seen in a sudden decreased need for sleep, silliness and giddiness, greater irritability, increased talkativeness, reckless behaviors, and even a sense of grandiosity or inflated self-esteem. Children who seem to become manic at times may need evaluation for Bipolar Disorder.

OPPOSITIONAL AND CONDUCT DISORDERS

Oppositional Defiant Disorder (ODD) can appear to be present in some children with AS. However, while they argue, lose their tempers, refuse to comply with requests, are easily annoyed by others, are angry and resentful, can blame others for mistakes, and can be spiteful and revengeful, people with AS are not manipulative in the same way that children with ODD and conduct disorders are. Thus, though they may meet criteria for ODD, children with AS are showing the symptoms of AS in their behavior. Their argumentativeness and failure to comply come from their rigidity and inability to do things another way. Thus, a diagnosis of ODD is not generally useful in describing or planning for children with AS.

LEARNING DISABILITIES

Nonverbal Learning Disability (NVLD) occurs in a high percentage of children with AS. Some, like Klin *et al.* (1995), hypothesize that NVLD is a part of AS. Certainly, a large proportion of children with AS do have symptoms commensurate with NVLD: visual-spatial organizational deficits, problems with tactile perception, poor time perception, difficulty adapting to new situations, deficits in mental flexibility, motor coordination deficits, difficulty with the metaphoric aspects of language, great verbosity without substance, deficits in social judgment, social perception, and interaction, and difficulty with sensory integration (Denckla 1991; Rourke and Tsatsanis 2000; Thompson 1997).

Developmental Coordination Disorder is present in many children with AS. Gillberg mentions that in a normal population of people without AS, up to 10% may have at last mild coordination deficits, including handwriting deficits. In the AS population, motor coordination deficits are quite frequent. Gillberg (1989), Klin *et al.* (1995), and Asperger himself (1991) considered motor clumsiness and coordination deficits to be part of AS. Manjiviona and Prior (1995) found that 50% of individuals they classified as HFA, and 67% of those they classified as AS showed significant motor impairment.

In addition, specific deficits in written expression (composition), reading comprehension, and mathematics reasoning and computation often occur.

Major symptoms of AS

Children and adolescents with AS show significant deficits in social functioning, emotional functioning, language, executive functioning, motor functioning, restricted interests, and often sensory defensiveness and sensitivity. In this section of this chapter each of these areas of deficit will be discussed. Differences of gifted children with AS from other children with AS will be described where applicable.

Social functioning

Both DSM-IV and ICD-10 indicate that deficits in social functioning are crucial for the diagnosis of AS. Both of these diagnostic systems include qualitative impairments in social interactions such as impairment in nonverbal behaviors, failure to develop peer relationships to an appropriate degree, lack of spontaneous seeking to share enjoyment, interests or achievements with others, and lack of social and emotional reciprocity. In addition, diagnostic criteria developed by Christopher and Carina Gillberg (1989) describe social impairment as inability to interact with peers, lack of desire to interact with peers, lack of appreciation for social cues, and socially and emotionally inappropriate behavior. Not all aspects of each criteria nor all criteria need to be met to have a diagnosis of AS. Nevertheless, a certain number of criteria must be met in each category for the diagnosis to be given.

In this section, the focus will be on the problems with interpersonal relationships, in understanding others, in making and keeping friends, and in understanding reciprocity.

- *Failure to develop appropriate peer relationships* includes difficulty developing relationships at an age-appropriate level that depend on reciprocity and mutual sharing of activities, interests, and emotions. The key is age appropriate. Children with AS do not act like their peers. They stick out as different either because they are inappropriate or because they do not seek out others. Most children with AS want friends but do not have the skills to make them. Some have little idea about what friendship really is. They think that casual contact is friendship. For example, Harry, the boy described at the start of this chapter, thought that anyone he met was a friend. Will, age 16, thought that saying "Hi," to a girl made her a girlfriend. Thus, the desire for friendship translates to the child with AS as the actual thing.

  Gifted children with AS show the same difficulties as more average children with AS. However, they can be more intense about their one-sided relationships. Will felt so deeply hurt by the girl he had thought of as his girlfriend when she told him to leave her alone that he would not leave the house and threatened to kill himself. He couldn't understand why his girlfriend would treat him so badly. In fact, Will had barely spoken to this girl, but had started to follow her around the school.

Children with AS are very immature for their ages in what they expect from friendship. As age peers mature, more give and take in friendships is expected, and those with AS have no idea how to be reciprocal. Because their interactions with others are on their terms, they have little idea how to share ideas, interests, or activities. They may offer their own ideas, but they expect everyone else to follow them. Children with AS do not know how to join in with others or how to participate in mutual activities. Thus, while they know people take turns in games, they may not know what constitutes a turn. Stuart, age nine, thought that a turn meant the other person watched as he threw the dice for them and moved their piece on the game board. This can be a particular problem for gifted children with AS who want to play more sophisticated games of strategy than age peers but still act as if they were much younger, not only with turn-taking but in getting upset if they lose.

Difficulty with turn-taking also extends to choosing activities. It is the negotiation of activity, what will we do together, that they have great difficulty in understanding. Attwood (1998) described the many difficulties playing with others: sharing, joining in, melding oneself to the rhythm of the group norm, and using social cues – who does what and when.

Attwood described difficulty with use of social rules: social politeness, conversational skills, ability to generalize, and understanding rules, as well as adherence to extreme honesty and exact rules. Not understanding how to be flexible about rules, and when to allow exceptions, causes social difficulty. Children with AS attempt to keep rules and want others to keep them too. Thus, in games, it can be hard for them to understand the idea of handicapping or allowing someone younger or less experienced to have more freedom about the rules. They also don't get the idea of teaching a game to new players. Most children allow mistakes, retakes of turns, and suggest strategies and ways to win when they are teaching another how to play a game. Children with AS explain the rules and then expect others to know how to play as if they were experienced. They allow for no coaching or leeway.

Gifted children with AS find rules and flexibly dealing with younger and less experienced players especially difficult. They act like very young gifted children who cannot understand why age peers don't adhere to rules. Young gifted children, however, soon learn about the differences between themselves and age peers, and want to play with older children. Gifted children with AS may not be able to be flexible in allowing leeway in rules even when they are adolescents.

Teasing and being teased are a problem for many children with AS. Their inappropriate social skills and poor ability to read others may mean they misinterpret and think they are being teased when they are not. On the other hand, their very difference and inappropriateness opens many to being tormented and bullied by others. Tantam (2000) reported that 64% of people with AS had been bullied and teased at school. Bullying involved being aggressive, tearing clothes, opening boys' pants, spitting on someone. Teasing included name calling and saying mean things about the victim's family. Adolescents with AS often made things worse because they responded by being aggressive themselves. The early years of secondary school (ages 11 to 15) were reported to be the worst. Tantam hypothesized that many peers attributed the unusual and insensitive reactions of those with AS to malice instead of disability, and so retaliated.

Gifted children with AS have as much difficulty with understanding and dealing with teasing as other children with AS. However, they may also be teased because of their academic skills just as many other gifted children are. A gifted child with AS who talks like a walking dictionary in his or her use of sophisticated vocabulary is even more likely to be teased than a more average child with AS.

- *A lack of a spontaneous seeking to share enjoyment, pleasure, interests, and achievements with others* includes a lack of pointing out, showing, or bringing objects of interest to show others. This describes what has been called "lack of shared joint attention." From as early as six months of age, children look in the direction parents point. They also point out objects of interest to parents. They pay attention to what is important to parents, usually objects and people. They respond to reciprocal gaze and affective exchanges with parents (Stern 1974). Even as early as three months of age, children engage with parents in turn-taking, including verbal turn-taking. Young children do this by playing babbling games, looking games, movement games, and smiling games with parents.

Joint attention skills and turn-taking are important precursors to conversational and social joining skills later on (Landa 2000). People with AS have difficulty using joint attention skills, even in later life. They do not follow gaze, or use gaze to determine if another person is engaged with them. They have more trouble with using signals to indicate whose social turn it is, such as using eye contact to understand when someone is about to change topics or finish a turn of talking. People with AS do not note the signals of others and send unclear signals themselves (Landa 2000). Gifted children with AS often do want to share interests and achievements with others, especially adults. What they find more difficult is staying in the moment with the adult and discussing the interest or achievement. It is more one-sided and not really a sharing. That is, once the achievement is shown, the child wants to move on. Christopher, age 13, brought in his favorite music to show his counselor at school. However, he just wanted to show the CDs and not actually to play any. Christopher liked to listen to music but he didn't know how to listen to it with anyone else. Christopher needed to learn what to do and say when he listened to music with another person.

- *Lack of social and emotional reciprocity* includes a lack of or deviant response to others' emotions, lack of modulation of behavior according to social context, and weak or absent give and take in relationships in children with AS. Reciprocity occurs as children start to learn both how to respond to and to initiate interpersonal interactions with others. Children with AS have great difficulty with reciprocity because they have trouble understanding how others think and feel. They assume whatever they are thinking is what others think and, therefore, whatever they want must be what others want also. This makes learning simple social skills such as turn-taking, sharing, helping, giving to others, initiating contact, and responding to a contact all difficult for the children with AS. It's the mutuality they don't get.

  In addition to physical reciprocity (turn-taking), relationships require emotional reciprocity. People with AS have difficulty with empathy because they don't understand the feelings of others and have difficulty reading them. Mutual empathy builds closeness and intimacy from middle childhood on; so, as these children mature, they lack one of the many building blocks of relationships, and their relationships do not have an emotional basis. Instead, relationships center around meeting the needs of the person with AS.

Gifted children with AS lack the idea of reciprocity as much as do other children with AS. They look a lot more immature though because they can reason at a much higher level. Thus, gifted children with mild AS can be seen as purposely selfish. People think that because they are so smart, they ought to act more maturely, and thus less selfishly. Patrick, age eight, still had trouble with the idea of sharing. If something was important to him, he saw no reason to allow someone else to have any or to share the item. This behavior puzzled his teacher who thought that because Patrick was so bright he ought to know what was fair, and be able to act upon it without making such a babyish fuss.

Because they lack empathy, emotional and social responses can be inappropriate. People with AS seem rude, insensitive, and self-centered because they have little idea of what the emotional needs of others are. This is not to say that they do not care about others; in fact, they do. It is more that in the immediate situation they have no idea what to feel, or what someone else may feel, and so their response is more from their needs than from the others. This is why young children with AS have been noted to ask irrelevant questions or want their own needs met in the face of news of a family tragedy. Attwood (1998) and Ratey and Johnson (1997) mentioned examples of people who related to catastrophic events as if they had no emotional meaning.

Different types of people have different ways of showing social deficits. Children with AS who are more extroverted will seek out people and want to be with them. They are gregarious and interactive. Thus, an extroverted child with AS will act like Jacob, who on first seeing me in the waiting room immediately approached me, stared into my face, opened his mouth, and began to discuss his favorite topic, outer space. Jacob continued talking for the next 25 minutes without even seeming to pause for breath. He knew a lot of material and wanted to tell me about it. He showed no reciprocity in that he could not listen to my comments or even my questions.

In contrast, an introverted AS child acts more like Jack. He did not look up, would barely talk at all, and usually answered, "I don't know" to any question. Jack was just as obsessive about his special interest, dinosaurs, as Jacob was about outer space, but he was only willing to share that interest when he knew the person and felt comfortable. Mostly what Jack wanted to do in the initial session was to continue reading a cartoon book. When it was removed from his visual field, he then spent all his time reading everything else in the office: the posters on the wall, the names of the assessment kits, the names of the board games piled on the floor.

While Jacob was willing to approach peers and try to make friends, Jack stayed on the sidelines reading a book. Jack acted as if the other children were invisible, and he had little interest in approaching anyone. Jacob was able to name three other boys and say they were his friends. Jack did not know the names of any boys, and stated that he had no friends and did not need any.

Restricted interests/stereotyped behaviors

Both DSM-IV and ICD-10 list restricted interests and stereotyped behaviors as an essential part of the diagnosis of AS. These diagnostic systems suggest an encompassing preoccupation with interests that are narrow in scope or abnormally intense. Inflexible adherence to nonfunctional routines is a second criteria, as well as stereotyped and repetitive motor mannerisms and movements. Finally, preoccupation with parts of objects or nonfunctional elements of materials is important. Gillberg and Gillberg (1989) also listed both narrow interests (to the exclusion of other activities, repetitive, more rote than meaningful) and repetitive routines (on self and in aspects of life, on others).

- *An all-encompassing preoccupation with an interest.* The interest is stereotyped or restricted in breadth or application: that is, it is repeated unchanged, or it has limited usefulness, such as collecting bus tickets. The interest is also abnormal in intensity or focus. This means it is done to the exclusion of other interests, is repetitive, and more rote than meaningful (Gillberg and Gillberg 1989). Often people with AS are interested in collecting things that others would regard as unusual such as bottle caps, colored lids, or ticket stubs. Interests can include sport statistics, makes of cars, transport, highway routes, weather maps and such.

    Some people with AS appear to collect facts and are eager to talk about these as if they were reading them off a page. Some interests are similar to those of peers, but are much more intense. Thus, many boys collect baseball cards and know sports statistics, but the boy or girl with AS spends all of his or her time pursuing this interest, only talks about this interest, and knows minutiae that others do not care about. During the Pokémon craze, several boys with AS collected cards and played their Game Boys, but unlike other children, Pokémon was their only topic of conversation. The other children talked about Pokémon, and played it intensely too, but also had other things they liked to do. Except briefly at the introduction of a new game, Pokémon was not their whole life. The only exceptions to this were some children with AD/HD who played computer games obsessively. However, they tended to brag about their scores rather than about the details of the Pokémon characters. Finally, the Pokémon interest lasted much longer for children with AS than for other children. Some gifted teens with AS were still collecting cards and playing Game Boy long after age peers had moved onto other activities.

Sometimes the obsessive activity of the special interest resembles that of children who are prodigies. For example, one boy played the piano for hours each day. Another girl endlessly wrote poetry. However, the piano musician was not interested in lessons, but only wanted to play his own music. The poet also wrote endless amounts of material, but had little substance to her writing. When these children were at the age when others could perform publicly or produce a complete and polished piece, the children with AS had remained at the same level of development of their skill. That is not to say that all talented people with AS lose their gifts. In fact, that is not the case. Some go on to develop further and make their special interest into a career or a successful adult hobby. Aaron, for example, at age 12, was an excellent composer. He loved piano and not only played quite well, but also composed sophisticated pieces with complex themes. He loved learning new approaches to composition and continued to study it throughout high school and college. On the other hand, once he was an adolescent, Aaron's area of obsessive interest became computer games. Consequently, though his area of expertise was piano, his area of narrow interest had become computer games.

Attwood (1998) described several developmental stages that people with AS might follow with their interests. The first level involved collecting things. Like Harry, described at the start of this chapter, children with AS collect all sorts of things. In Harry's case it was numbers. Some people with AS never go beyond this stage.

The second stage is development of a topic of interest such as transport, dinosaurs, or science. The idea here is the person has a topic they can learn about and impose order on. They learn the statistics, make charts, and categorize. Sometimes the passionate interest is in a person, animal, or historical period. Then the person with AS spends time enacting scenes involving the target person or animal. One little girl, Abby, age five, became interested in Pilgrims and made her family eat from trenchers. She would only eat foods the Pilgrims would have eaten. She wore to school a costume she had made, and she acted out being a Pilgrim all day long for several months. Children who engage in being a person or animal often bring creativity and a great deal of imagination to their activity. The problem, of course, is that they can't be creative or imaginative about anything else.

The third stage Attwood (1998) described is a romantic stage in which the person with AS, often an adolescent, becomes enamored of a particular person. This may be a real person or a media star. One girl devoted herself to Elvis. While other girls swooned over the most recent pop star, she listened to Elvis, imagined conversations with him, and talked endlessly about him. Will also acted somewhat like this when he decided a girl at school was his girlfriend based on little real contact.

Attwood (1998) described several reasons why people with AS devote so much time to their special interests. These included using the special topic or interest to facilitate conversation, to indicate intelligence, to provide order and consistency, as a means of relaxation, and as an enjoyable activity. Gifted children with AS showed a variety of special interests at the Gifted Resource Center of New England. These included computer games and Nintendo, Pokémon cards, trains, maps, geography, dinosaurs, mythical beasts and legends, roadways and routes, mathematics, computer programming, music playing and composition, reading, animals, chess, Scrabble, acting out scenes from books and movies, acting and drama, and making up stories and poems.

- *Inflexible adherence to specific but inflexible routines or rituals.* People with AS need to know what to expect and adherence to a routine allows them not to have to make decisions. If they fixate on only one choice done each time in the same way, they decrease their level of anxiety and stress. Unfortunately, they also cannot let go of the routine when it would be helpful to do so. Just as Harry needed to go through a certain routine before he would come to dinner, others need to read to the end of the book, listen to the end of the music, and follow a certain schedule or their world is upset and they cannot function. Gifted children with AS can need to follow routines they have imposed on themselves and others: for example, eating their lunch in a certain order.

- *Repetitive and stereotyped motor mannerisms.* Some, but not all, people with AS engage in repetitive motor acts. Some of these are typical of younger autistic children such as rocking and hand flapping, but repetitive motor acts also may include other body movements. One boy shook a stick in a repetitive manner. Sometimes these motor movements are actually tics and can be part of Tourette Syndrome or other tic disorders. Whether the movements are tics or not depends on what is done and how.

- *Preoccupation with parts of objects,* or with the nonfunctional aspects of objects such as color, texture, or noise. Some young children with AS like vacuum cleaners because of their noise. Others become fascinated with minutiae; they spend all their time describing all the aspects of an object of interest. For example, one boy described exactly how one version of a favorite computer game differed from the next version in the details of one particular character. The problem, of course, is that while such details may matter somewhat to a fellow game fan, as a repeating topic of conversation, they are boring to another person.

Communication and language

While deficits in nonverbal communication are listed in DSM-IV and ICD-10, neither lists particular deficits in language skills as part of the diagnosis of AS. In fact, both DSM-IV and ICD-10 specifically limit the diagnosis of AS to those who have had normal language development in early childhood. Many disagree with this criterion and many children with delayed speech are classified as having AS. DSM-IV and ICD-10 also do not address the deficits that are seen in language and communication even with those children who do meet the criterion for normal acquisition of speech and language. Gillberg and Gillberg (1989) list speech and language peculiarities in their criteria. These include: delayed development, superficially perfect expressive language, formal or pedantic speech, odd prosody or peculiar voice quality, and impairment of comprehension including misinterpretations of literal and implied meanings. Gillberg and Gillberg also list nonverbal communication problems including limited use of gestures, clumsy/gauche body language, limited facial expression, inappropriate expression, and peculiar stiff gaze.

- *Nonverbal communication* is particularly problematic for those with AS. Limited eye contact and limited use of eye gaze in communication are issues. Also, people with AS show limited and inappropriate use of body gestures in social interactions. They have stiff body postures and inexpressive faces; it is difficult for another person to know what they are feeling from their facial expression. Such physical aspects of social interaction as proper distance to maintain, use of touch, smiling to acknowledge someone, and use of eye gaze to discern intent are all difficult for people with AS. This means that they miss social cues, and misinterpret the body language of others. Nonverbal communication is deficient in gifted children with AS. Their lack of ability to read body language is a particular deficit when they try to take advanced courses where they are supposedly mature enough to read more subtle body language between teacher and students, as well as among students. A lack of ability to efficiently read body language is a detriment in a job as well; there are many gifted people with AS who cannot hold a job despite many talents and advanced degrees due to deficits in reading subtle cues.

- *Verbal functioning is also an issue.* Though people with AS have good verbal skills insofar as verbal expression, use of grammar, and vocabulary, they have much more trouble with the social use of language, its pragmatics. Thus, they don't modulate language for the audience, know how to use polite language, or know what to do when someone is using sarcasm. Understanding metaphoric speech is another language difficulty. People with AS are too literal and don't comprehend idiomatic and figurative language. On the other hand, people with AS use language idiosyncratically. Thus, they may use terms in only one way and either not understand or argue about alternate uses. One boy refused to use the word "icebox" at home and insisted that only the word "refrigerator" was proper. If asked to get something from the icebox, or fridge, he would not do it until the proper word (to him) was used. This pedantic, overly literal, and overly precise speech is a problem for many with AS. In fact, it is this very characteristic that makes gifted children with AS sound as if they were "little professors." Some also sound as if they were speaking English with an accent despite being native English speakers. One boy spoke with a mild British-sounding accent though he was actually American, and had spoken both English and Spanish at home since birth. He also always sounded as if he were giving a lecture whether he was talking about his favorite subject (computer games) or about his homework.

- *Prosody* refers to the rhythm and sound of speech. The speech of people with AS tends to be flat and somewhat less inflected with emotion than that of most people. In addition, many children with AS repetitively use lines they have heard or read; lines from television, videos, and books are part of their speech. They also give monologues on favorite topics, often using the same words as memorized speech. They talk too much and too long, having little sense of their effect on others. They are unaware that they are not making a point. Conversely, because they have trouble understanding how others think and feel, they assume the other person is thinking about the same thing that they are. So, they answer questions with one word, thinking that is all they need to say. If the other person does not understand, they may not be able to explain further because they have trouble elaborating.

- *Conversational skills* are a challenge and need to be specifically taught. Because giving a monologue on a favorite interest is so enjoyable, and so much a part of communicating, the idea of reciprocity is hard to understand. In fact, the idea of listening and then responding to what someone else has just said is a foreign concept. People with AS don't know how to listen. They interrupt and talk about their own interest. They change the subject and discuss their own topic. They find it hard to listen to the content of other's messages and respond appropriately. Thus, even when a sympathetic comment or offer of support would be warranted, people with AS cannot make these appropriate expressions. Instead, they are more apt to start talking about their interest.

  Another problem is irrelevant comments. People with AS interrupt with whatever they are thinking – that is, they find it difficult to stop themselves and stick to a topic even when they are talking. Answering questions is another difficult task. Unless the answer pops into mind quickly, people with AS are apt to say they don't know. This is especially the case if asked to make a decision or a choice or if they have to initiate anything. This may be because prioritizing among possibilities is hard or generating ideas themselves proves difficult.

  People with AS have trouble with cohesion (Landa 2000). That is, they have trouble tying together and organizing information. In normal conversations, material relates to what just came before, or the speaker provides a bridge to a new topic. Cohesion helps to maintain a topic. For example, a speaker might repeat part of what the other person just said, or make a connection between old and new. By kindergarten most children know how to do this ("Speaking of video games, I got a new one today. Have you seen the new Sims yet? That's what I just got.") Children with AS have great difficulty using cohesive statements. Fine *et al.* (1994) found that children with HFA referred more to the physical environment and less to the previous statement. Children with AS used more unclear references; that is, their references could have been to any of a number of previous statements, or may not have been related to the previous statement at all.

- *The memory of people with AS for other people's personal events is deficient.* This makes conversation difficult. While they recall small details about the aspects of another that interest them, people with AS do not recall emotional information. Thus, they won't ask how your vacation was, or if you are feeling better after your operation, or if your sales presentation went well. This emotional glue that holds social relationships together over time is missing for those with AS. On the other hand, children with AS may know the details of their trip to your house and would be able to relate in detail each event of the journey.

- *Humor is another type of emotional glue that people with AS lack.* Children and adolescents with AS are good at puns and like to tell jokes. This sort of humor appeals to them. They also enjoy and can share humorous cartoons. What they have trouble with is humor based on irony or sarcasm. They also miss the point of witty comments, double entendres, and jokes told on the self. They don't get the point of funny stories people tell about their own lives, or see how something that could be terrible today could seem humorous later on. Other people laugh in camaraderie about the foibles of everyday life; people with AS miss this shared enjoyment in the same way they missed sharing the joy of showing a toy or flower to a parent when they were younger.

  The gifted children with AS at the Gifted Resource Center of New England usually liked humor, especially puns. Sometimes, though, they laughed but didn't necessarily get the joke. What they were laughing at often had nothing to do with the point of the joke. For example, political cartoons were often taken literally. Sometimes, they enjoyed the story aspect of a joke even if they didn't get the point. A few of the brightest children had quite good senses of humor, and got the idea of irony and incongruence. However, they enjoyed both verbal and visual puns the most.

Cognition and executive function

None of the current diagnostic systems require evidence of deficits in cognition or executive function. Beyond requiring normal intelligence as part of the diagnostic criterion, there is no discussion of specific deficits that also may occur. This does not mean there are no such deficits; however, they may be difficult to pinpoint and may differ from person to person. Thus, though there is evidence of deficits in executive functions, for example, none of these deficits are specifically diagnostic of AS. Nevertheless, a picture of some of deficits found in groups of people with AS can be helpful.

- *Intelligence test profiles.* There has been extensive research on the Wechsler Intelligence Scales profiles in autism and AS. On the whole, there is some evidence that children with AS tend to have higher Verbal IQs than Performance IQs, while those with autism have higher Performance IQs than Verbal IQs (Klin *et al.* 1995; Volkmar and Klin 2000). Lincoln *et al.* (1998) performed a meta analysis (this means they used statistics to look for trends across studies) and found similar results to Klin's and Volkmar's across studies that had slightly different criteria for the selection of people with autism versus AS. There are a number of studies that give opposite or inconclusive results as well (Ozonoff, Rogers, and Pennington 1991; Szatmari *et al.* 1990, 1995).

  In addition to Verbal and Performance IQ differences, some studies have found particular subtest score strengths or weaknesses. Szatmari *et al.* (1990) found higher Similarities scores for those with AS. In autism, higher visual-perceptual skills are the rule with Block Design and Object Assembly scores among the highest (Lincoln *et al.* 1998; Shah and Frith 1993). Ehlers *et al.* (1997) found children with AS to be higher on Information, Similarities, Vocabulary, and Comprehension with lower scores on Arithmetic, Coding, and Object Assembly. Those with autism scored highest on Block Design.

  At the Gifted Resource Center of New England, children were diagnosed based on meeting DSM-IV criteria with the exception of speech delays. Thus, some had clear WISC-III profiles that showed Verbal scores higher than Performance, but a number showed the opposite. Some showed no clear patterns, especially if they scored over IQ 180 on the Stanford-Binet LM. Of the total number of children (55) scoring over IQ 180, 11 had AS. However, some of the highest scorers – that is, five children with scores over 200 – had AS. This suggests that very bright children need further assessment in order to adequately plan for them.

The mean Binet LM score of this group was IQ 194 and the mean WISC-III FSIQ (Full Scale IQ) was 142. This 52-point difference becomes important not only in planning for the child's education, but also in other aspects of assessing the child. Scores nearer average on some tasks then suggest much more difficulty than for children who have smaller discrepancies.

On individual subtests of the WISC-III, many showed profiles with verbal skills high for Information, Similarities, Vocabulary, and Arithmetic. Digit Span was often also high. Comprehension scores were often slightly lower. On the Performance side of the WISC, the score most frequently affected was Object Assembly with Coding second. Picture Arrangement varied from being the lowest score to being the highest Performance score. On the Stanford-Binet IV, those children who scored lower on the Performance part of the WISC-III did not always score lower on the Stanford-Binet Abstract/Visual Subarea because the Binet does not award points for speed. For further information on test scores see Chapter 9.

- *Executive function deficits* have been found in a number of disorders and are especially prominent in AD/HD. However, executive function deficits are also common in autism and in AS. Using standard neuropsychological tests (Wisconsin Card Sorting Test, Tower of Hanoi, Trail Making Test, Rey-Osterrieth Complex Figure), a number of researchers have found evidence of difficulty with organization, planning, and mental flexibility in both autism and AS (Ozonoff, Pennington, and Rogers 1991; Szatmari *et al.* 1990).

    Harris and Leevers (2000) reviewed the literature and suggested that those with autism have particular difficulty on tasks calling for sustained planning of a novel action. In contrast, they are well able to visualize material and even to make a new visual composite from well-known parts. Klin *et al.* (1995) noted visual-spatial deficits in those with AS. Deficits included poor fine and gross motor skills, visual-motor integration problems (how well they could copy what they saw), visual-spatial perception deficits, difficulty with nonverbal concept formation, and poor visual memory. Those with HFA performed less well on tests of language functioning.

Gifted children with AS were found to show a number of deficits in executive functions especially in mental flexibility in problem solving, in quick and accurate performance, in organization and planning, and in getting the big picture. These deficits will be further explored in Chapters 4 and 9.

- *AS as NVLD.* A number of researchers have noted the similarities between NVLD and AS (Klin *et al.* 1995; Molina, Ruata, and Soler 1986; Rourke and Tsatsanis 2000). Based on their results and on extensive reviews of the literature, they hypothesized that AS is a form of severe NVLD. Also, some propose that autism is a form of left-hemisphere dysfunction (Chiron *et al.* 1995; Dawson, Warrenberg, and Fuller 1982). Ozonoff and Griffith (2000), in a review of the literature, noted that people with AS and people with autism both have some deficits in both right- and left-hemisphere functions.

In general, children with NVLD and AS have difficulties in three areas of executive function – organization, integration, and expression – as well as in visual-spatial and sensory motor integration. Stewart (2002) described these as follows:

Organization: Difficulty with novel situations, slow processing speed, rigid thinking, concrete interpretation, perfectionism, focus on the wrong detail, difficulty with "if...then" thinking.

Integration. Poor frustration tolerance, work production limited, overloaded easily, difficulty creating written documents, rigid and perfectionistic about work, emotional shutdown occurs when overwhelmed.

Expression. Misses the main idea, sees all details as equally important, poor ability to use metaphor and analogy, difficulty reading between the lines, relies on pattern learning and misses concept, prefers step-by-step, sequential mode of learning, but misses whole concept.

Visual-spatial and sensory-motor deficits. Slow processing of visual material, poor eye–hand coordination, difficulty with facial recognition; difficulty with handwriting, directional confusion, poor attention and arousal.

Many children with NVLD have good visual-perceptual skills. It is not that they have no skills, but rather that the integration of skills coupled with weak skills in some areas makes it much more difficult to use visual-perceptual information efficiently. Thus, children with NVLD and AS can have even above-average skills in some areas of visual-perception but function at a much lower level when skills require integration. They can do quite well with visual reasoning, visual memory of simple geometric figures, visual discrimination (seeing similarities and differences), visual closure (given a partial drawing, visually completing it), and visual sequencing. They have more subtle difficulty with material that requires holding part in mind and doing something with it (such as reversing digits), with motor organization and planning, complex visual memory, and with part-to-whole relationships. Thus, these children may do less well with rotated figures, with multiple variables, and with estimating qualities such as length and time. Neuropsychological assessment measures how well children do on each of these skills.

Of the 30 children with AS seen at the Gifted Resource Center of New England, 20 had clear signs of NVLD. Two children were too young to test. Two children who were not diagnosed as AS but as NVLD had some symptoms of AS; however, they were not sufficiently impaired to be given the diagnosis. In all, of the testable children, 71% had a test profile indicating NVLD. Thus, symptoms of an NVLD are prominent features of AS for more than five in seven of the gifted children in this study.

Emotional functioning

Emotional functioning is only addressed in DSM-IV and ICD-10 as lack of social and emotional reciprocity. ICD-10 describes this as impaired or deviant responses to others' emotions, lack of modulation of behavior for the social context involved, or a weak integration of social, emotional, and communicative aspects of an interaction.

- *Impaired empathy* is a problem for children and adolescents with AS. A lack of empathy, resulting in self-centeredness has been noted. Asperger (1991) reported that some children made quite perceptive comments about others but could not act on any of them. At the same time, he noted, there can be a total disregard for the feelings of others, as if others had no feelings. However, people with AS are not devoid of empathy in the sense of caring about others. Many have compassion for suffering; it's the day-to-day understanding of feelings that is problematic.

Gifted children with AS can be quite compassionate about suffering as a larger issue. Patrick cared about world hunger, and participated in a food drive at his school and church. Using his computer, he made posters to encourage people to donate to the food drive. On the other hand, Patrick ignored feelings expressed to him. When a friend's mother was injured in a car accident, Patrick continued to discuss a computer game he had played. When Patrick was asked about this later, he said that he didn't like to discuss bad news, and so he had continued to discuss the game since it was good news.

- *Understanding, labeling, and attending to their own feelings* is problematic for those with AS because they have no language of feelings. It is difficult for them to know what they are feeling and to explain complex feelings. While they may learn how to identify and label their own feelings, talking about the feeling and sharing feelings with others remain difficult throughout life. Gifted children with AS do learn to readily label feelings, and can even distinguish some subtleties of feelings when describing an incident later. Using these feeling labels with people in everyday situations is much more difficult. George, age 13, could say he felt sad about something that had happened, but he could go no further in talking about his sadness. To him, saying he was sad summed it up. This meant he also had less means of receiving comfort because he did not know what would be comforting to him either.

- *Emotional control and modulation of emotions* are difficult for those with AS. People with AS resemble younger children in their expression of emotions so they look immature. Many still have tantrums well past the age when others have outgrown such extreme expressions of emotion. Also, because of their preoccupations with their own interests, these children and adolescents appear more self-centered. Gifted children with AS can have great difficulty modulating emotion, much more so than gifted children with AD/HD. Tantrums can be more intense and continue for a much longer time, and these gifted children are not easily soothed. For example, they cannot be distracted, or given a substitute, as children with AD/HD often can.

Olivia, age ten, loved to pet my dog when she came to the Gifted Resource Center of New England. Her mother said that Olivia loved animals, and indeed she did. However, she tended to hold the dog too tightly, and tried to insist the dog bend and move exactly as she wanted. Olivia had no ability to predict that her behavior would have

consequences, and that these would make her feel bad. She
disregarded warnings. When the dog was removed from Olivia, and
Olivia was barred from seeing the dog for one week, she had a
massive tantrum. She raged and screamed for several hours. In fact,
Olivia really only calmed down after she went to sleep that night.

Olivia couldn't see what she had done wrong. It took a great
deal of work with Olivia to get her to see that she had to allow the
dog to have some choice in being held, and that she could not
disregard warnings that she was hurting the dog. If the dog didn't
want to sit on Olivia's lap, Olivia had to let her alone. A list of rules
for being with the dog and consequences for disregarding the rules
was drawn up, and after her week's deprivation of the dog's presence,
Olivia was allowed once again to pet her. Olivia now behaved more
appropriately.

- *Emotional obsessions* can be a particular problem and can be difficult to
  treat. These obsessions occur when the child with AS mentally
  repeats an emotional situation and then, feeling it again intensely, is
  convinced it will reoccur. Because these obsessions can be part of a
  person's particular interest, talking about the interest can also trigger
  the emotional obsession.

  Another kind of emotional obsession is triggered by anxiety
  when the child's sense of order is disturbed. Thus, one gifted girl
  with AS obsessed about skipping a grade and being a year younger
  than classmates. This offended her sense of how things were
  supposed to be, and she could not stop thinking or talking about the
  topic. Some adolescents have been obsessed with fitting in to the
  usual norm to an extreme degree. Another child was obsessed about
  blood and gore. The key to dealing with these can be finding the
  trigger, often a sense of frustration or anxiety about something else.
  Anxiety and mood disorders can occur as the child becomes more
  aware of rejection by others, of not fitting in, or of always doing the
  wrong thing.

Motor functioning

DSM-IV and ICD-10 do not list motor clumsiness as an aspect of diagnosis of AS.
However, in the prelude to the Diagnostic Criteria, DSM-IV notes that motor
clumsiness and motor delays are common. Gillberg and Gillberg (1989) listed
motor clumsiness as one of the criteria for diagnosis of AS. Other researchers have
recently added motor clumsiness as part of their criteria, particularly Klin *et al.*

(1995). They, and others, think that motor clumsiness differentiates AS from HFA. This is an area of controversy; however, several studies have shown that children with AS are likely to show deficits in motor skills. For example, Ehlers and Gillberg (1993) found 50 to 90% of children with AS to have motor deficits. Manjiviona and Prior (1995) found 50% or more. Smith (2000) reviewed a number of studies in this area and concluded that the designation of clumsy/not clumsy was too crude and did not reveal meaningful results. Thus, she divided motor functioning into a number of categories: manual dexterity, gait and balance, and dyspraxia.

- *Manual dexterity* was impaired in some studies of children with AS, for example, speed to complete a complex pegboard and motor tapping (Smith and Bryson 1998). In real life, manual dexterity has to do with a variety of skills including self-help skills such as tying laces, fine motor coordination, and even handwriting. Deficits in these areas produce difficulty in family, academic, and social situations. For example, deficits in eye–hand coordination mean deficits in learning to play games, to engage in sports, and participate in arts and crafts activities. Gifted children with AS can have difficulty with manual dexterity in areas of self-help skills such as dressing themselves, and tying laces, long after gifted children with AD/HD have mastered them. Also, gifted children with AS who have handwriting deficits will find it difficult to engage in large amounts of written work. It is one of the reasons for refusing to do class work and homework.

- *Gait and balance* were found to be unusual for people with HFA and AS. Vilensky, Damasio, and Maurer (1981) noted abnormalities in gait for children with autism. Hallett *et al.* (1993) found gait atypical in adults with HFA, while postural control was atypical in children (Kohen-Raz, Volkmar, and Cohen 1992). These deficits were thought to be related to problems with cerebellar functioning. Deficits in these areas mean that people with AS may walk in an odd way: they may have difficulty walking in a straight path and so bang into others. They may have trouble judging distance from others. They also may have balance problems which prevent them from learning to ride a bicycle or skate. They may have trouble with kicking a ball, and in doing any sort of tandem walking: for example, walking a narrow line.

- *Dyspraxia* refers to the ability to plan and organize movement patterns. Smith and Bryson (1994) found evidence for deficits in these abilities. They ascertained that people with autism spectrum disorders have specific deficits in pantomiming use of objects. Smith (1996, cited in Smith 2000) and Smith and Bryson (1998) found that there was a specific deficit in ability to combine visual and kinesthetic information. For example, children with autism made errors by imitating what they saw, not the actual hand they were supposed to imitate (a mirror-image type of error). Thus, asking them to point to my right hand would result in them pointing to my left hand since that was where their right hand was. These authors suggested that deficits in imitation have to do with underlying information-processing errors in these children. Deficits in imitating others means that people with AS have trouble planning movements, so it is difficult to fit into the flow of an activity. They may have trouble with coordinated walking: for example, walking in line or as a group on parade.

Attwood (1998) described difficulties with following and imitating rhythm. People with AS have trouble with synchronized walking rhythm when with another person. Those with AS either forge ahead or lag behind. They may have trouble with keeping rhythm in a group: for example, some can play a musical instrument well as a solo, but not as a part of an orchestra.

In conversation and in relating to others, people tend to synchronize movements. One can do this very consciously to change the level of activity or emotion in an interaction by first matching the expression, posture, and activity of the other person and then changing aspects of it. Usually the other will follow. This does not happen as well for people with AS.

Gifted children with AS can show great asynchrony of motor functioning. Compared to their abstract reasoning ability, motor ability is often well below average. Consequently, there is a much larger gap between what the child knows and what the child can do. It also makes these children seem even less mature. A ten-year-old boy who can read at high-school level, knows extensive amounts of information about world cultures, geography and maps, and wants to go to college early, but who can't dress himself yet or tie his shoes, is operating with a huge handicap. Also, his deficits in understanding and keeping rhythm mean he doesn't understand the rhythm of conversation or the flow of social events. All of this will present problems to him as he tries to navigate the higher expectations of college life.

Sensory function

None of the diagnostic criteria lists difficulties with sensory defensiveness, sensory sensitivity, or sensory integration. However, anecdotal evidence suggests that such difficulties are prominent in people with autism spectrum disorders including AS. However, they are not limited to these disorders. Children might have sensory integration deficits as a primary disorder or in combination with another nonautistic spectrum disorder such as NVLD or AD/HD. Kimball (2000) noted deficits in sensory defensiveness and sensory integration that could cause difficulty for a range of children. Those with the most difficulty with sensory defensiveness and sensory integration often have autism spectrum disorders.

- *Sensory defensiveness* refers to difficulties with being touched, needing pressure or deep touch, and disliking sensations others find pleasurable. Temple Grandin (1995) is an example of someone so sensitive to touch and so in need of deep touch that she invented her own machine to provide the exact pressure she craved. Children with problems in sensory defensiveness do not like being hugged or tickled and feel pain at touches others might not even notice. For this reason some will get upset or strike out at someone who barely touches them. Adults then punish them for striking out at "nothing," when to them the light touch felt painful. Some siblings and classmates capitalize on this aspect and tease by light touch, knowing they will get their AS sibling or classmate into trouble.

  Another aspect of sensory defensiveness has to do with overarousal. Children who have sensory defensiveness have difficulty letting go after they are emotionally or physically aroused. The feelings of overarousal stay much longer than for other children. For this reason many dislike getting upset and try to avoid emotional situations such as books, movies, or information that may be emotionally arousing. Physical arousal can occur in crowded places and these children have trouble with school lunchrooms, malls, and other big, noisy, and visually bright places.

  Sensory sensitivity is a form of sensory defensiveness that refers to difficulty with sensory input from any or all senses. Children with this problem have trouble tolerating textures, flavors, smells, sounds, intensity of light, and color. They reject sensory input that is overarousing. Conversely, at other times, some appear to crave certain types of input and may seek it out. Like Temple Grandin (1995), they may find ways to give themselves exactly what they need. Attwood (1998) described difficulties with sound sensitivity. People with AS had trouble with sharp noises, sudden noise, high pitched, continuous noise, or confusing multiple noise as from a shopping center. Attwood indicated that many children could hear sounds that parents could not, such as a hand dryer located in a bathroom down the hall or an arriving train or truck. One of the problems with such sounds is that the person with AS not only feels them intensely but does not know if they will soon shut off.

Tactile sensitivity is another aspect of sensory sensitivity. Being touched, and touching certain types of materials and textures, can be unpleasant to the person. Thus, many children with AS do not like to have their hair washed or cut or their teeth brushed. They only like old, well-worn clothing, and dislike textures like paint or mud (Attwood 1998).

Sensitivity to the taste and texture of food and to smells is another area of difficulty for people with AS . Foods touching each other on a plate is a problem for some, as are slimy or mixed foods. Smells, especially aromatic smells, including perfumes, and cleaning fluids, can be disturbing to people with AS (Attwood 1998).

Visual sensitivity includes discomfort with levels of illumination, colors, or distortions of visual perception (Attwood 1998). Thus, some children cannot stand bright light or intense glare. They dislike certain colors or see colors in an unusual way. Some show distortions of visual perception so things look bigger or smaller than they are.

Attwood (1998) described sensitivity and insensitivity to pain and temperature. Thus, some people with AS are less able to rely on their body sense to tell them to wear a coat or change to summer clothing. They also might not notice injury and be somewhat insensitive to pain. This means that certain illnesses or injuries may be overlooked such as chronic ear infections or appendicitis. Thus, parents need to be alert to small changes in behavior that may clue them that something is different.

Synaesthesia, mentioned by Attwood (1998), refers to mixed sensory sensations. People with this rare condition can hear colors and see sounds. One man was able to taste shapes (Cytowic 1993). This interesting phenomenon is not limited to those with autism spectrum disorders but occurs in other people too. Cytowic pointed out that there are 30 possible combinations of sensory mixes since the mixes do not usually go both ways. (One person may hear colors but not have colored hearing and vice versa. The man who tasted shapes experienced various tastes as shapes. He did not taste shapes and have the sensation of flavors.) "Hearing" musical notes as colors is the most frequent of these synaesthesias. Some people have several types of synaesthesias. This makes it difficult for these individuals to depend on the information they receive from their senses.

• *Sensory integration* refers to difficulties in the vestibular system, proprioception, tactile discrimination, and motor planning (praxis). Balance, postural stability, and muscle tone are parts of the vestibular system. Proprioception refers to our sense of position in space, and the monitoring of how lax or toned muscles and joints are. Tactile discrimination deals with tactile sensations over all our body. Praxis is motor planning, and involves the ability to sequence activity to do a whole action. For example, zipping a coat requires a sequence of acts in order.

  Sensory integration deals with different sensory systems working together as in visual-motor planning. Thus, a visual task that needs to be translated to a motor action is integrated across both sensory systems. Handwriting is a common example of a visual-motor task. It requires motor coordination, visual perception, visual and kinesthetic memory, visual and kinesthetic sequencing, and monitoring of speed and space, as well as many other things all at once. Children with AS often have trouble with handwriting: that is, speed, letter formation, and legibility. A frequent recommendation for these children is use of computer or dictation services instead of an emphasis on handwriting.

Understanding AS

Children with AS have a number of interesting cognitive differences from other children. The social, communication, and learning deficits of these children appear to have common underlying features which are apparent from earliest years. These cognitive differences are subsumed under the larger constructs of Theory of Mind, central coherence, and executive function. These three theories are interrelated: that is, deficits may arise because of difficulties in any or all of them. Researchers tend to focus on one of these constructs as a means of illuminating the underlying problems of autism spectrum disorders. However, none of these three theories answers all the questions or covers all the symptoms. Therefore, it is likely that the deficits seen in AS are the result of differences in several different parts of the brain corresponding to the systems described by these three theories.

Different Minds

Theory of Mind

Theory of Mind (ToM) is the name given to the ability to understand the thoughts, beliefs, feelings, intentions, and point of view of others. Children with deficits in ToM have difficulty inferring what others think because they have difficulty recognizing that others have minds of their own.

From about age three to four, average children begin to understand that other people have thoughts, feelings, beliefs, and desires different from the child's own, and that they use these to guide actions. People with disorders on the autistic spectrum have trouble with understanding and using this knowledge. ToM is important because the ability to understand another's point of view is the basis for empathy, and thus for understanding most human interactions.

ToM is measured by using a number of ingenious scenarios that require children to put themselves into another's place and make a decision about what that other will think about a scene. One of the most famous of these is the False Belief Test. In this test, the child is shown a tube of candy and asked what is inside. When he or she answers with a candy name, the tube is opened and the child sees that pencils are inside instead. He or she then has to decide what a person outside the room will think is inside the tube when shown it. A child who is at the level of beginning to understand others' minds will know that the person will answer, "Candy." A child who cannot understand others' minds yet will answer "Pencils" because the knowledge he or she has seems to be the only knowledge there is. That is, little children can only think of what they know to be true, not what someone else might think. About age four, most children can pass this test, but not young children with autism. Children with AS pass this test, but somewhat later than most children.

There are more sophisticated tests of ToM which involve thinking of what Mary will think John will think. This second-order type of thinking requires holding two people's thinking in mind. Most children of about age six can pass this type of test, but children with autism generally do not pass. More high-functioning people with autism or AS (that is, those who have higher verbal intelligence) will pass such tests by age ten. This may be because there is a relationship between verbal intelligence and ability to pass ToM tests at least to a certain level (Ozonoff, Pennington, and Rogers 1991). Still more sophisticated tests require thinking about a double bluff or understanding the purpose of a lie. Even more high-functioning people with autism or AS may fail these tests, which are at about an age eight mental level (Happé 1994). They also fail at decoding complex mental states from the expression in the eye region of the face (Baron-Cohen *et al.* 1997a, 1997b). In all, there are about 20 different types of ToM tests (Baron-Cohen 2000).

ToM studies are important because they suggest why children with autism and AS may make certain types of social mistakes. Baron-Cohen (1995) described the several aspects of "mindreading" that must occur in order for a person to be able to interpret social messages and respond appropriately.

One important aspect of being able to understand other people involves understanding intention. Baron-Cohen described an Intentionality Detector that people use to make interpretations of the meaning of actions in self and others. People with AS have a great deal of difficulty with this. In a study by Heider and Simmel (1944, cited in Baron-Cohen 1995), subjects were shown a silent film of geometric shapes moving around, and were asked to describe what was happening. All but one of the subjects described these actions in human terms. That is, they attributed human intentions to the actions of geometric shapes.

In a more recent study, Klin, Schultz, and Cohen (2000a) used a similar film to develop the Social Attribution Task. They measured the responses of a group of people with AS, and found that they had difficulty describing the movement of shapes as others did. Instead, they described the movement solely in geometric terms. They did not make attributions of social intention. Also, their comments about social aspects tended to be irrelevant. Klin *et al.* (2000a) suggested that about one-third of the utterances of people with AS were not relevant or pertinent to the constraints of the social situation.

Only about 25% of the salient social features were detected in the Social Attribution Task video, even when the people with AS were specifically instructed to make the story into a social one. In contrast, 90% of the statements by people without AS were salient. Thus, in real life, Klin *et al.* (2000a) suggested that a large amount of pertinent social information is not detected by individuals with AS. Their reasoning about the social situation is often irrelevant to a social understanding of it; even when present, social attributions rarely involve a consideration of others' mental states, and an understanding of people may be limited to their physical appearance.

The Eye Direction Detector is a second part of mindreading. This function allows people to detect when eyes are present, whether eyes are directed to something, and what another person might be seeing based on what the first person would see if looking that way. For example, most people know that when someone is thinking, he or she tends to look up. Most young children can point to a picture of someone thinking, by knowing this type of eye direction detection. Baron-Cohen *et al.* (1997a, 1997b) found that those with AS and autism have difficulty with reading eye directions and noting the meaning of aspects of gaze.

The Shared Attention Mechanism is the third part of mindreading. This mechanism allows the child to learn to note what others see as important, by following their gaze or pointing finger, and later by following their voice. This skill arises in early childhood as parents and children share enjoyment of objects together. In the long run, shared joint attention allows infants to learn how to respond in reciprocal social interactions, first with their parents and later with others. The lack of shared attention is hypothesized to be one of the main deficits in the developing child with autism and AS.

All three of these aspects must be present and working together to have an adequate ToM and thus to comprehend social information. However, these aspects must not only be present, but the person must be able to utilize them coherently in action. It is known that people with AS can have knowledge of other people's minds, but are unable to apply this knowledge in real life (Asperger 1991; Bowler 1992).

The weak central coherence theory

Weak central coherence refers to the inability of people with AS to see the whole. Instead of understanding that there is a larger picture, these children and adults focus on the details. Thus, they miss the relevance of certain types of knowledge to themselves or to a particular problem. In normal information processing, a person draws together different types of information to construct a concept at a higher level of meaning, the big picture. For example, in recalling the gist of a story we are using central coherence: that is, we pick out the important parts and recall these, not all the details. In reading a story we quickly discern the meaning of two words that look alike and pick out the correct one (she had a tear in her dress versus she had a tear in her eye). This also occurs with nonverbal material when we pick out salient features or make sense of a whole.

Frith (1989) proposed that in autism people have trouble with integration of material at different levels. They have more trouble with the gist of a story, and with picking out ambiguous meaning. On the other hand, they have little trouble with tasks like copying a design with blocks (Block Design) because they see the patterns as parts (as the individual blocks) versus how others see them (as whole patterns). Shah and Frith (1993) showed that this was why people with autism were very good at tasks like Block Design (and Tangrams). Happé (2000) and Hermelin (2001) suggested that weak central coherence not only produced deficits for people with autism, but was also responsible for some of their savant characteristics. Skills such as perfect pitch, savant drawing skills, upside-down recognition of face and patterns, finding smaller shapes within bigger ones (embedded figures), and detecting patterns in numbers and music all formed the initial building blocks upon which savant skills depend.

Deficits in people with autism and AS that reflected weaker integration of parts to a whole, or of recognizing a whole given component parts, included picking out what should go together or what was incongruous about a picture. Ambiguous meanings were also problematic in verbal areas with difficulty noted in interpreting incongruous sentences, arranging sentences to tell a coherent story, or using context to infer reasons for a character's behavior (Jolliffe 1997, cited in Happé 2000).

Central coherence is not independent of ToM. Though each aspect may come from separate systems of brain functioning, they work together to produce social functioning, so social understanding is not independent of coherence. In order to appreciate others' thoughts and feelings in real life, people must be able to take into account context, as well as to integrate diverse information. Consequently, people with weaker central coherence and detail-focused processing have more difficulty putting together information to make appropriate social inferences (Happé 2000). They are more likely to focus on an aspect of the situation that is salient to them but may not be important in understanding what is going on.

People with AS make errors in judgment because they do not get the whole, but base what they do on the part they see. It is difficult to hold in mind all the aspects of the situation at once, even if they can be brought to mind. Thus, individuals with AS may be able to pass tests of each part of understanding a social situation but be unable to put it together in real life. For example, Roselyn, at age 12, decided she wanted to read a book from my office shelf. She helped herself to the book and was leaving with it, when I saw it and questioned her. In her mind, she was borrowing it. She had not asked my permission, and when I pointed this out, she did not see why she had to do so. After all, I knew she was taking it, she intended to return it, and why shouldn't she be able to take it? The following week, she tried to take another book. When told that she had to return the first one before I'd allow her to take any others, she called me "selfish." It seemed hard for Roselyn to put together the parts of the social script she needed: when it is someone else's possession, one needs to ask permission, and then one has to return the other person's possessions. Given a hypothetical situation, Roselyn was well able to explain the idea of individual property rights and what the concept of borrowing meant; she had trouble applying it in her interactions.

This type of taking without permission has occurred with several other adolescents with AS. In each case, they thought only of the moment, of their immediate desire, and could not put together the parts of the situation: what is the social expectation; what are the consequences of doing it this way; what will the other person likely say or do?

Another example of problems with social referencing that appears related to both central coherence and ToM occurred with a social skills class. Nigel, a boy with AS, was supposed to get a small gift for a holiday party for Fred, whose name he'd drawn from a box. Directions about the gift getting were specific in terms of trying to think about what the other person might like (and how to get clues about that), how much could be spent, how to ask for help with the task etc. Nigel brought in a shoe box for Fred, with no wrapping or holiday decoration on it. When Fred opened it, he found a clay lump. Of course the other boys immediately started to tease Fred. Fred burst into tears. Nigel had no clue about why Fred was upset. In his mind, he'd made Fred a gift, a clay horse (Nigel loved horses), and he didn't see why everyone didn't like it. Nigel, who was about age nine, had made similar gifts at school for his parents who'd loved them, so he assumed Fred would too. Nigel never did see that his gift was inappropriate, and he never understood the difference between making a gift for a parent and getting a gift for an acquaintance. Fred, who did not have AS and was a very empathic boy, calmed down, and thanked Nigel for his thoughtfulness.

Executive function disorder

Some researchers see autism and AS as an executive function disorder. Organizing, recalling, mentally shifting from one context to another, problem solving, shifting attention, inhibiting inappropriate behaviors, planning and organizing alternate goals or ideas, and translating plans to actions are all types of executive function with which people with AS have difficulty.

Executive function deficits in people with AS involve problems with attention including: overfocused attention, difficulty shifting attention, and difficulty with shared attention. That is, the child has difficulty letting go of what he or she is already focused on to do something else. Shifting attention is especially problematic when going from a preferred activity to a nonpreferred one, like stopping playing a video game to eat dinner; however, difficulty shifting can occur even between preferred activities. It's the stopping and starting that's the problem.

Children with AS hyperfocus: that is, they focus for a prolonged period on something of interest to them. On the other hand, attention problems may occur when they do not have an investment in what they are asked to do. If it is not interesting to them, they do not focus on it. It may be they cannot focus well because the disliked activity has no meaning to them, and they can only focus on things that are meaningful. This may go along with weak central coherence; that is, because people with AS cannot easily find relevance in complex material, or relate material together to make meaning, they may be unable to focus.

Planning and organizing actions is an area of difficulty. Often people with AS do not know what to do. The directions that have been given may make little sense. They overfocus on the details and lose the sense of the overall plan or goal. Irrelevant aspects capture their attention and they are easily distracted by aspects of the task important to them, but not necessarily relevant to the goal. Internal distractions impede progress, so organizing a plan of action is difficult.

People with AS do not organize material as do others. Their responses are a mixture of facts, personal experience, and interesting associations. Thus, they appear to organize in units that are mixtures of factual and personal material. These pieces are put together to make a whole, but they do not necessarily fit well together. Judgments and conclusions are then made based on a partial picture of material relevant only to the person with AS. This difficulty with part-to-whole relationships impedes forming realistic judgments and makes for some of the emotional and social deficits noted with AS.

People with AS have difficulty with being mentally flexible. They make plans based on mental structures that are rigid. Often these are learned as scripts and rituals. The person with AS cannot tell when these are meaningful in a particular context. They apply the same strategy or use the same solution even if the situation is different because they cannot change their approach. They have no new ideas about what to do. They have no way of taking the new aspect and integrating in into the whole. Thus, they cannot compare the new aspect with a previous solution and see how to change the response so it will fit better. This inability to compare aspects of proposed actions to situations, and to come up with a different response based on situation demands, is a primary aspect of the social problems of people with AS.

People with AS also are slow to integrate material together. Even when they are able to make comparisons, or think of the big picture, they do so at a much slower speed than other people. Thus, in most situations, the aspects they note are the most outstanding, and by the time they integrate these, the situation already has changed. Most people can note the subtle nuances rapidly and adjust their behavior because they have a sense about what is likely to happen. People with AS not only integrate slowly, but they have more trouble making the prediction of what will most likely occur next. Very gifted people with AS can, in the abstract, relate what should happen in story scenarios. They can make predictions and think about consequences because they can do this at their own pace. In real life, they cannot and so cannot act in the moment.

People with AD/HD who have executive function problems that affect social relationships often know what to do, but have trouble doing it because of slower processing. However, many of these people can catch themselves and know what they ought to have to done, even if they did not do it at the time. They have some measure of prospective and retrospective ability to look at the bigger picture and see themselves, and how they actually acted, versus what the situation demanded. People with AS have more trouble with all of these aspects of executive functions.

Gifted children with AS

There has been some interest recently in gifted children with AS from both a gifted perspective and from the AS perspective. Nevertheless, most experts in the field of gifted education have had little experience in recognizing the import of the social, cognitive, and emotional deficits that are part of AS. Experts who deal with AS usually have had little experience in working with gifted children; therefore they have little recognition of the special needs of gifted children with AS. However, there have been some recent articles describing autism and AS in gifted children, as well as anecdotal material about bright children in the AS literature.

Literature about gifted children with AS

Donnelly and Altman (1994) focused on high-functioning children with autism with savant skills and suggested the need for awareness of the unique needs of this population for both advancement of their particular gifted abilities, as well as remediation of their deficits.

Cash (1999) studied gifted children with autism and discussed the idea that their giftedness allowed the development of talents that could be nurtured into hobbies and vocations that are satisfying to the person, and positive in the view of society. On the more negative side, the deficits still caused problems when the gifted person with autism was stressed or in a situation that could not be rehearsed or prepared for.

Neihart (2000) studied gifted children with AS, emphasizing ways to distinguish between giftedness and AS. Neihart emphasized differentiating characteristics in speech patterns, response to routine, awareness of difference, disturbances of attention, sense of humor, motor clumsiness, inappropriate affect, poor insight, and presence of stereotypies.

Literature about children with autism/AS

Hans Asperger (1991), in his original study, described a number of children who were intellectually gifted. He pointed out that autism could occur at different levels of ability from highly original creative genius, through eccentrics who lived in worlds of their own and achieved little, down to severely delayed individuals.

In his studies he described children with high levels of intelligence and originality who coined unusual words and made unusual associations to material. One
boy of age six to seven described the difference between stairs and a ladder as "the
ladder goes up pointedly and the stairs go up snakedly" (p.71). Another boy, Fritz
V., showed mathematical giftedness, with an ability to solve complex problems
before even attending school. On the other hand, Fritz had severe difficulty in
school and was considered uneducable by his local school. In fact, he could not
do any of the math presented there. Another man followed from young boyhood
to adulthood was exceptional at math, able to work out cube roots before attending school. By adulthood, he was an assistant professor in the Department of
Astronomy. Other children described by Asperger had talents in chemistry, art,
music, and technology of different types.

Gillberg (1991) described six families with children with AS. Three of the six
had intelligence in the gifted range. Two of the others also showed unusual ability
in an area of interest, much like as is described for a prodigy. One boy with an
unusual interest in battles grew up to become a lawyer. Another boy was an actor.
A third, at age seven, had the mathematical skills of first-year university students.
The fourth had an IQ of 150 and was interested in chemistry. By age 11, he was
judged by a professor of chemistry at a polytechnic institute to have fulfilled the
requirements for a university degree in chemistry. The fifth child, a girl, was
interested in preventing research on animals. All of these children also showed
major social and cognitive deficits in other areas of functioning.

In their book, *Asperger Syndrome*, the editors Klin, Volkmar and Sparrow
(2000b) end with a number of parent essays. Wallace (2000) described her son,
Walter, who was identified as gifted in 4th grade, and in 5th grade qualified for
the Johns Hopkins CTY program, but could not write a report in class. His mother
was determined he would grow up able to negotiate life. To this end, she limited
video-game time, and persuaded him to write essays at home, take flute lessons,
play board games, converse with her, and swim. This all took immense coaxing.
Later, Walter was placed in a small private school that allowed him to progress
intellectually via computer and distance learning that was accelerated to meet
academic needs while his social and emotional needs were the focus of much of
the school day. Other parents (Rietschel 2000; Shery 2000) also described
similar stories with their very gifted children.

Hermelin (2001) described the talents of autistic savants and how they
compared to gifted children with similar areas of talent. The productions of the
gifted children and the savants were often similar. For example, one girl, Kate, a
poetry savant, was compared to a very gifted child, Emily, who also wrote poetry
at an advanced level. Much of their writing of poetry was similar though there

were differences noted in some areas. Emily, for example, was better at using a poetic voice that spoke to an audience rather than just for her own expression; Kate focused much more on her own expression. Hermelin discussed the need for self-expression in the creative work of people with AS, since they rarely produce work for an audience.

Comparisons of gifted children with AS to average children with AS

Special interests. Compared to other children with AS, gifted children with AS have a greater passion to learn. While they are also stubborn about not doing things they consider trivial or uninteresting, they also have many more things they want to know about. Some have several areas of passionate interest. Also, the passionate interest is more likely to have substance and depth. Rather than merely collecting and arranging things, some gifted children with AS, especially those with very high IQ scores, are more likely to classify material, and to integrate it with other areas of knowledge. Stuart, a gifted 13-year-old boy with AS, knew a great deal about maps and geography. He also liked to study historical battles and plot them on maps. Over time, he began to think about how the changing of maps through the ages represented major historical events. He began to study these events and to draw his own ideas about how the maps had looked at different points in history. This led to theorizing about how different forces change maps over time.

Gifted children with AS have a greater chance that their area of special interest will result in a productive career or hobby. For example, the children described by Gillberg (1991) who had advanced levels of achievement in mathematics and chemistry had a greater chance of becoming productive in these fields than do more typical children with AS. Because of this, the gifted child with AS also has a greater chance of pursuing higher education and finding an adult job where deficits are seen as eccentricities rather than handicaps.

Imagination and creativity. Gifted children with AS use imagination in several ways. They may have imaginary lands, languages, and games. Kenneth Hall (2001), an exceptionally gifted boy with AS, reported that he had an imaginary land in his room. He was King, but he was not superior to others. Also, though there were strict safety rules, there were no territories. Kenneth also involved his friend, Neil, in his play. Neil was able to make up rules for the land, and was Prime Minister. Kenneth also had a portal to a parallel solar system in which everything was reversed. There children started out with the most difficult math and ended up learning what two plus two is.

Some gifted children with AS tell complex and imaginative stories. Some stories are quite original while others are based on putting together many other stories they have heard or read. Other children without AS, especially in preschool and early elementary years, may want to play with the gifted child with AS who acts out these stories in a director's mode, as if putting on a play.

Gifted children with AS may be visual thinkers who develop creative solutions to problems. Edward, age nine, an exceptionally gifted boy with AS, liked to think about the Big Bang and to hypothesize what there was before the Big Bang. His idea was that there were a series of universes, each starting from the endings of the one before. He could visualize how this might have occurred. More examples of creativity in gifted children with AS are presented in Chapter 5.

Early development. In their early years, gifted children with AS learn to speak and to use more complex vocabulary at an earlier age than more average children with AS. They also use more specialized words from an area of interest from an earlier age. However, not all gifted children with AS show advanced language skills. Several at the Gifted Resource Center of New England, despite very high IQ scores, were average or somewhat delayed in speech.

Many gifted children with AS learn to read in early preschool years, and comprehension may not lag behind decoding. In later school years, reading may continue to be advanced, and ability to comprehend will continue to increase. Some gifted children with AS maintain high ability to read nonfiction but have lower comprehension of fiction. This is due more to difficulty with metaphorical language than to actual comprehension.

Gifted children with AS who are interested in numbers may be mathematical prodigies who can continue to accelerate in math through college-level courses. Harry, the little boy described at the start of this chapter, was a child whose math abilities were outstanding. He continued to progress in mathematics and took part in the Johns Hopkins CTY program, scoring one of the highest mathematics scores in the state at age 13.

Test profiles. The profile of strengths and weaknesses of gifted children with AS can be wider than for more typical children with AS. For example, verbal skills can be in the IQ 200 range, with writing skills in the average range. On the Vineland Adaptive Behavior Scales, a scale of adaptive and social functioning, social interaction may be SS 36, a score in the very far below average range, but similar to that found for many average children with AS; however, the discrepancy between this score and verbal IQ will be greater. Thus, gifted children with AS may have greater ability in verbal tasks, and in figuring out the correct answers to social interaction scenarios presented as a story or test, but will have as much trouble as other children with AS in actually performing socially.

Comparisons of gifted children with AS to typical gifted children

Special interests. Gifted children with AS, like other gifted children, have absorbing interests and acquire large amounts of factual information about the interest. Like other gifted children, those with AS will give lengthy and elaborate responses to questions in areas of knowledge and interest. They have a desire to learn new things, especially factual and conceptual knowledge. Unlike other gifted children, those with AS may collect information and categorize it but may not connect it to anything else they are learning. Many do not make the subtle comparisons other gifted children make to other fields of knowledge. Because they do not easily see a big picture, it is more difficult to see how a trend in one area may be like a trend in another. There are exceptions to this with some of the most gifted children, as in the example above with Edward.

Gifted children, both with and without AS, are able to immerse themselves in material of interest. Hyperfocus can lead to creativity. The amount of imagination and creativity as well as commitment to a topic can lead to being productive, as Aaron was with his piano playing and composition. Many gifted children with AS are perfectionists who want to perform perfectly and are willing to practice until they do. Thus, they are able to work hard for their goal.

Though gifted children with AS can hyperfocus on a creative endeavor, they have more trouble being creative than gifted children without AS. This is both because their ideas are very different and because it is hard for them to go from the idea to the reality. Jacob, an extroverted gifted boy with AS, loved to tell stories he created. However, though his stories had many interesting ideas, he had trouble putting together a coherent sequence of events. He focused on details too much, and when one idea reminded him of another, he switched to the new idea without any transition. His stories were hard to follow and didn't seem to have a focus, so it was hard to tell what his story was really about. Thus, though Jacob was original and creative, he had trouble with communicating his story to others.

Like gifted children without AS, those with AS can be high achievers in a variety of fields including math, writing, literature, science, social studies, foreign languages, debating, drama, chess, music and art, and competitions of various types. Gifted children with AS can be especially talented in mathematics and science. They may be interested in new theories even in childhood, as Edward was. They can have savant-like skills or even be a prodigy in music, math, chess, and other areas.

Early development. Gifted children, with and without AS, show similar precocious development of language and verbal expression. Their early descriptive and factual memory is advanced over age mates'. Many gifted children with AS, like other gifted children, are early readers, spellers, writers, and mathematicians.

Cognitive development. Gifted children with AS show more variability on IQ test profiles than other gifted children. They show wider discrepancies of Verbal and Performance scores, and they show wider subtest scatter. Thus, gifted children with AS will show some scores below average, while most gifted children show lowest scores above average. Lowest subtest scores for most gifted children tend to be in visual-motor functioning. Their scores are not low, just not as well developed as verbal and nonverbal reasoning scores. The scores that are lowest for gifted children with AS tend to be visual-perceptual subtest scores. Also, scores on tests of social knowledge, such as Comprehension on the WISC-III, are often lower. Visual-motor functioning is often below average.

This means that in terms of academics, gifted children with AS show more difficulty with output of work, especially written work. They also show subtle language problems that other gifted children do not show; those with AS are much more literal. For example, Gillberg (1991) described one boy at age 15 with an IQ of 132. He thought his mother's statement about a friend, "She was on the way to getting better," referred to a street address. In his mind, the friend was going there (p.142).

Though advanced in reading skills, gifted children with AS have more trouble than gifted peers in analysis of literature for metaphor, irony, and in following a theme.

Social/emotional. Like other gifted children, those with AS can show a high level of moral development. Their concepts of fairness and justice can be advanced, and they can adhere to high ideals of following rules, being honest and fair. On the other hand, they can have difficulty applying the rules in a flexible manner.

Like other gifted children, those with AS are more asynchronous than average children. Unlike other gifted children, those with AS are much less mature and act like much younger children in social situations. While other gifted children may lack friends because they cannot find others who share their interests, or play at the level of sophistication they need, they know how to socialize at an appropriate level. Those with AS, however, do not know how to make friends or play in sophisticated ways. Given another gifted child with similar interests, they will not be able to interact at an appropriate level.

Gifted children with AS are much less mature and, unlike the gifted child with AD/HD, they do not show variability in maturity. Gifted children with AD/HD act maturely at times and immaturely at others. Those with AS act below age level most of the time.

Positive aspects of AS

While the focus is often on the negative traits and symptoms seen in AS, there are positive aspects to AS that also should be noted. Not only are these positive aspects strengths of people with AS, but also they are part of what can give AS some positive social value. Thus, individuals' strengths can be used to ameliorate and accommodate for some of the weaknesses of AS. Positive aspects can benefit society as a whole.

Attwood and Gray (1999) described positive traits that could be viewed as part of AS. Adapted from their list, and from descriptions of Gillberg (2002) and Ozonoff *et al.* (2002), these include the following:

Social interaction

- Interpersonal relationships are characterized by complete loyalty and dependability. The person with AS will never stab someone in the back or underhandedly compete for a loved one's affection. If a person with AS thinks of someone as a friend, that person is a friend forever.

- Relationships are free of sexism and other biases. The person with AS has an ability to take others at "face value." Thus, they are much more interested in what the person will do with them, and very much less interested in whether that person is viewed favorably or not by others. This, of course, has both positive and negative aspects.

- People with AS have an ability to speak their minds regardless of social context. This means they do not put on airs or suck up to the boss or try to sugar coat something to manipulate you into doing something they want. Instead, they are upfront about what they think. You might not like it, but you know where they stand.

- People with AS have the ability to pursue personal ideas or perspectives despite conflicting evidence. Thus, once they are convinced of something, they will pursue it to its end. This can be positive because they are not easily swayed by others' opinions, nor do they give up because someone tries to implant doubts.

- People with AS have a great desire for seeking an audience or friends who are enthusiastic about unique interests and topics. If they can find friends who share a particular interest and are willing to invest as much as they do in it, then they have a great deal to offer.

- People with AS have a recognition of order and a desire to follow rules; they recognize patterns of how things work. Because of this, they are apt to want to follow the rules and pursue things in an orderly manner. They are good to have as guides for meetings because they will remember and apply all of Robert's Rules for conducting meetings. They are also good classifiers and pattern finders, and can understand trends.

- People with AS are interested in conversations that are significant; they prefer to avoid small talk and superficial conversation. Because of this they focus more on topics of interest to them. If you are interested, you can learn a lot from listening.

- People with AS seek sincere, positive, genuine friends with a sense of humor. In fact, once they relax, people with AS can show a wonderfully offbeat and clever sense of humor. Some know a great many jokes, especially truly good puns. People with AS also like to share pictorial puns and cartoons. Some even draw them. This sharing of humor makes people with AS fun to be around.

- People with AS are truth tellers and like others who also tell the truth. They tend to believe the best of everyone until proven otherwise.

Cognitive

- People with AS show an advanced vocabulary and an interest in words. Those with strong verbal skills and vocabulary are good Scrabble partners, and good at doing crosswords and puzzles of various types. They are fun to play with because they know so many obscure words. Some even write crossword puzzle books and dictionaries.

- People with AS who are visual thinkers have an interesting way of looking at things. They use visual thinking and tend to talk in pictures too. These people are fun to play with in doing puzzles, tangrams, and chess because they are so good at thinking of unusual ways to try the same thing.

- People with AS are especially good at noting and recalling details. They are helpful in work that requires knowledge of facts, details, and memory. They are often exceptional at the recall of details often forgotten or disregarded by others: names, dates, schedules, routines.

- Some people with AS can have a photographic memory and can even recall specific road routes and directions from an early age. They can give precise and clear directions.

- People with AS have a passion for gathering and cataloguing information on a topic of interest; they show a voluminous memory for facts related to a special interest, and can have an encyclopedic knowledge of one or more topics.

Personal/emotional

- People with AS have acute sensitivity to specific sensory experiences and stimuli: for example, hearing, touch, vision, and/or smell. They may have unusual sensory experiences such as synaesthesia. This makes them interesting to know. Having such unusual sensory experiences gives a different perspective on the world and it can be interesting to know how their world looks to them.

- People with AS are trusting of others, even charmingly naive. Many, while having been hurt by others, still maintain a belief in the possibility of positive relationships, and continue to try to make and have friends.

- People with AS can be caretakers of others and can be compassionate. Some are engaged in important causes to end world poverty, hunger, and war.

Conclusion

Gifted children and adolescents with AS have a dual challenge. They are often exceptional at abstract thinking and at acquiring knowledge; they have advanced skills in many areas and are eager to learn. When passionately interested, they have a real potential for doing things that are worthwhile in adult life. On the other hand, they suffer from severe deficits in social awareness, social interactions, and social cognition, and these deficits interfere with social and emotional functioning. In helping gifted children with AS, it is important to work on their areas of deficits to encourage as much growth as possible. At the same time, it is vital that these gifted children be afforded the chance to develop areas of strength and interests. Their interests are the key to adult success. Gifted children with AS need to learn enough social ability to negotiate the adult world and function in a job. However, it is important to find a job that will suit their interests and talents:

one that will not rely heavily on social cognition. Planning and working towards this goal is an important task of adolescence.

Temple Grandin has suggested that if we eliminated the genes that caused autism (and AS), we'd also eliminate many of the gifted and talented people like Einstein. She goes on to suggest that the really social people are not the ones who make new discoveries; they are too busy socializing (Attwood and Grandin 2000). It is hoped that we can nurture the talents of our future great discoverers with AS while helping them learn the skills they need to navigate the essential social and emotional aspects of adulthood.

> The fools! They do not know that half may be worth more by far than whole.

> Hesiod
> *Works and Days*, 1.42

Chapter 4

Cognitive Issues: How Those with a Different Mind Think

Tom

By age 12, Tom had started to fail in school. Though he had been in gifted classes through 6th grade, in 7th grade he was having difficulty keeping up. His winter-term report card was shocking to his parents. He had gotten "D"s in two subjects! Teachers complained that Tom was not doing adequate written work. He often did not complete assignments, and failed to hand in reports and homework. He also had difficulty writing in class. On class essays, he wrote little, and what was written was off the topic. Tom's points did not quite fit the answer required, and his writing was disorganized. Tom's class participation, however, was quite good. His comments showed that he understood the concepts well. In fact, many of his comments were very insightful, and well above the level expected for students of his age. Nevertheless, teachers who had Tom for English, social studies, and French all thought he was not working to his potential, showed little persistence, and did not care about his work.

Tom did quite well in some subjects. Math, science, shop, band, physical education, and art were outstanding. These teachers praised Tom's efforts, persistence, and talent. In math, he was the top student, and his teacher thought he should be accelerated into the faster-paced honors algebra course. His science teacher praised his curiosity, excellent questions, and thoughtful answers to science questions. His teachers in art and music praised his exceptional talent and hard work. Tom's parents were puzzled. It almost seemed like they had two children named Tom who went to Ryder Middle School.

Prior to 7th grade, Tom's work had been adequate because homework didn't count. Since he did so well on tests, he always received good grades. It was evident to his lower-grade teachers that Tom knew the work. His difficulties with writing were less evident because he had a good imagination and could dictate creative stories. In fact, the class acted out several of Tom's stories as part of a cooperative story-writing venture. Tom invented the story; someone else wrote the script. Since his school encouraged the arts, Tom was able to sing and draw his way through book reports and other writing projects with ease. It was only in the higher grades when he had to actually write down material that his problems were more evident.

Tom, a gifted boy with AD/HD, showed areas of strength in concept formation, getting the big picture, using creativity and imagination, and in formulating math and science hypotheses. He showed deficits in working memory, prioritizing, organization and planning, goal setting, and sustaining attention. He showed slow work speed and difficulty with tolerating frustration. He also had specific difficulty with written expression. These deficits have all come to be recognized as inefficiencies in executive functions.

Stuart

Stuart's troubles started in 3rd grade with notes from his teacher about his behavior. According to the teacher, Stuart would not do any assignments in which he was not interested. She saw him as oppositional and disruptive, especially when he would insist on doing something his own way. Stuart was an excellent student in reading, math, science, social studies, and spelling. What he would not do was write stories or do worksheets. He also did not like art and never finished any of the projects. When he had to do a class project, he would not work with any of the other children. He felt they never wanted to do his ideas and he was not interested in any of theirs. On the other hand, when Stuart liked a topic, he could be enticed to do projects and reports about it, and these reports were usually outstanding.

By 8th grade, Stuart had more difficulty. He had trouble writing reports on assigned topics. Even if he did a report, it was returned with a lower grade than he expected, and with comments about not being organized and missing the point. Stuart stated that he hated writing things down and didn't see why he had to take notes or do outlines of chapters. He preferred to listen in class, and he could recite the lesson back verbatim.

Stuart also had more difficulty with reading comprehension. While he breezed through books on facts, he struggled with novels assigned by his teacher. Taking tests was less satisfying than previously. If he had a fill-in-the-blank or multiple-choice fact test, Stuart did well, but he had trouble with the beginning essays now required. He also still had to do most assignments his own way whether or not this was successful.

Stuart did do well in some subjects. He was the star Spanish student in the class and could remember, almost verbatim, all the conversations from the book. He was also excellent at drama for the same reason. In addition, he could mimic voices and accents quite well. Stuart won the district geography bee in 8th grade. He knew a tremendous amount of factual material about maps, countries, terrain, and history.

Stuart loved words. He enjoyed word searches, anagrams, crossword puzzles, acrostics, and jumbles. In his spare time at home Stuart wrote crossword puzzles, acrostics, and word searches on various topics. He also made up puns. Stuart recalled dialogue from books, movies, television, and plays that he had seen. His speech and his writing (when he did any) were peppered with pieces of this dialogue. A favorite was Monty Python. In fact, Stuart would recite large parts of *The Life of Brian* and other Monty Python favorites whenever he even thought someone might listen.

Stuart, a gifted child with AS, showed strengths in verbal reasoning, memorization, foreign languages, spelling, and creativity. He was very detail-oriented and loved to collect facts and pieces of dialogue. He showed deficits in prioritizing, planning and organization, goal setting, mental flexibility, part-to-whole relationships (getting the big picture), dealing with complexity, shifting attention, using strategies for correcting mistakes and problem solving, generalizing from one instance to a whole, changing work speed and sustaining effort, using prediction, and with performance on demand. These suggest deficits in central coherence and executive functions.

Cognitive processes common to gifted children

Both Tom and Stuart are gifted children, though both struggle with deficits that prevent their showing how gifted they are. Nevertheless, what they do share in common with other gifted children are advanced cognitive abilities in abstract reasoning, concept formation, insight, and love for learning. Like other gifted children they are immensely curious and eager to learn, especially in areas of interest. There they show great passion and persistence, just as do other gifted children. Like many other gifted children, Tom and Stuart have distinct learning styles. Tom is a visual learner while Stuart learns better through auditory means. However, their learning styles are less flexible than those of other gifted children, and they cannot easily compensate if material is taught in a different style. Unlike other gifted children, Tom and Stuart process information more slowly, and work less efficiently. In addition, they have more trouble with the output part of learning. For example, they have difficulty putting together a coherent demonstration of their learning, and often cannot show what they know due to their inefficient executive functions. Nevertheless, abstract reasoning, concept formation, and insightful learning are strengths.

The focus of this chapter

Insight and abstract reasoning abilities aren't all that are needed to be successful in most endeavors. While abstract reasoning ability and concept formation are the main strengths of gifted children, those with attention deficits have difficulty showing what they know. This can be due to their distinct learning styles and to deficiencies in executive functions.

We can think of abstract reasoning ability, learning styles, and executive functions as a sort of computer system. Abstract reasoning ability tells us how many things the computer can do. Does it only monitor the functions of your car? Can it let you access all the resources available on the Internet like a home PC? Is it one of the computers that serves as a systems monitor like an Internet server? Abstract reasoning ability is sort of like this: it tells us how "smart" the computer is, how many different types of things it might be able to do.

We can think of learning styles as the type of operating system the computer runs on. Is it Windows, Mac OS, or Linux based? Each operating system looks at material in different ways, and they are not very compatible with each other. Learning styles are similar.

Executive functions tell us how efficient the computer is. How big is its memory; how fast does it work; does it have shortcuts that save time and space? How well does it do when using multiple software programs at the same time? Executive functions are like this. They tell us how efficiently the brain uses information.

In this chapter, the following are described:

- How reasoning ability and concept formation are expressed in gifted children.

- The advantages and limitations of several learning styles.

- Descriptions of the cognitive executive functions and how they affect performance.

- Suggestions for accommodation and remediation of deficits.

Abstract reasoning ability and concept formation

Gifted children, including those with AD/HD and AS, excel at reasoning ability. This means that all gifted children are more advanced at using abstraction than are other children. However, abstraction isn't necessarily only verbal. Abstraction occurs in many different cognitive realms: for example, the visual. The important thing is that abstraction leads to formation of concepts in an area of endeavor. In using abstract reasoning abilities, gifted children may categorize, make associations among material, see the next logical step, and find the underlying concept. Many also form hypotheses about how things work and then test out their ideas. They develop sets of rules, and figure out patterns. They also ask themselves questions, and then set about finding out a way to think about the answer, a sort of paradigm or thought experiment. Not all gifted children ask original questions, but those who do show precocity in the type of questions asked, and the age at which these questions are first asked (Rogers and Silverman 1988; Silverman 1993d). Asking questions is a way that many young gifted children show advanced abstract reasoning ability.

Questions asked by gifted children

Young gifted children ask many interesting questions. Those children with AD/HD ask the same sorts of questions as other gifted children. Those with AS tend less to ask questions than to make observations that reveal their precocious thoughts.

Many of the questions asked by young gifted children are about the big issues of life and death. Emmanuel, at age three and a half, asked how far outer space went on, and where did it come from. When his mother explained about the Big Bang Theory, he asked where the Big Bang came from, and then where God came from. At age seven, he was more interested in how the brain is connected to the soul, and how we think. Who people are, and how they become individuals, also interested him.

Many young gifted children are fascinated by the concept of time. The young gifted child might start to ask what time is, and when time started, as if time were a separate entity. Ian, a boy with AD/HD, at age six asked if there was anti-time before the Big Bang. Benjamin, another gifted boy with AD/HD, at age three asked if time would run backwards if the earth revolved in the opposite direction. The level of knowledge, conceptual complexity, and reasoning ability required to ask these questions differs qualitatively from the type of question asked by a more average six-year-old, Jeff: "Where did clocks come from?"

Gifted children may develop their observations into questions which show the underlying complexity of their thinking. This complexity is important because most small children ask questions and show curiosity. It is not that gifted children only ask questions that are complex and precocious; they also ask many of the typical questions of average children. Nevertheless, just the fact that they ask complex questions at all suggests that their intellectual development is different from the average because such questions are not expected from children of their age.

Hollingworth (1942) discussed the need for logically coherent answers to questions when children reach a mental age of 12 to 13 years. For some gifted children, especially exceptionally and profoundly gifted children, this need may occur as early as age five.

Gifted children not only ask more complex questions, but also demand more complex responses. A simpler explanation is not satisfying because it doesn't allow the child to add to the developing concept already in place when the question was asked.

Complex answers are required both to questions of complexity, and questions that are more typical of age peers. Thus, the more average child might ask where heaven is located, and would be satisfied with an answer that provides a physical location: for example, above the clouds. The young gifted child, asking the same question, might start to argue that above the clouds is the rest of the atmosphere, and then outer space, and that heaven could not really be located there. Because the young gifted child knows so much more information about the universe, and because the level of complexity needed to answer the question satisfactorily is so much greater, young gifted children are not satisfied with easy answers.

Hypotheses about the nature of things

Many gifted children, from an early age, develop hypotheses about where things come from, why certain things happen as they do, and how things work. They seek explanations for the observations they have made or for ideas they may have heard. These explanations are not always correct. For example, many young gifted children appear to hypothesize that after one grows up, there comes a time when one then grows down again, and becomes a baby.

The literature describes hypotheses developed by young gifted children. Hollingworth (1942) discussed Child A who, after being read the Eugene Field poem about the gingham dog and calico cat who fought and ate each other up, protested that this was a logical impossibility. A child who makes this sort of observation, at age three, has developed a hypothesis about what logical means.

Gifted children with AD/HD do form hypotheses about the nature of life and death, as well as about science and math. As do other gifted children, some gifted children with AD/HD try to think of ways of finding the answers. Most gifted children with AS do not seem to develop hypotheses. The few who do are exceptionally high IQ children. For example, Edward, age nine, an exceptionally gifted boy with AS, liked to think about the Big Bang and hypothesize what there was before the Big Bang. His idea was there were a series of universes, each starting from the endings of the one before.

Highly gifted children often develop interesting hypotheses to explain how things happen. Five-year-old Peter, a profoundly gifted boy, around Christmas time discovered and read Stephen Hawking's book, *A Brief History of Time*. At about the same time he saw a special on television in which Big Bird worried about how Santa Claus would get down all those chimneys. Peter applied what he had learned from Hawking's book and came up with a solution. Peter's solution was based on the idea of being able to control the forces generated within a black hole. By using those forces, Santa would become long and thin, and time would slow down, thereby allowing him to both fit in, and visit, all those chimneys on Christmas Eve (Morelock 1997). Contrast this with the reasoning of four-year-old Molly, a gifted girl with AD/HD. She was fascinated with maps and spent hours studying them. Near Christmas time, as she was studying a map of the world, she said to her mother: "One man, one night? I don't think so, Mom." Peter used his reasoning ability as a way of answering his questions so he could continue to believe in Santa, while Molly's reasoning led her to start to disbelieve.

As gifted children get older, their hypotheses become more sophisticated. John Matthews, age eight (Matthews 1980), described to his father an idea that had been puzzling to him: "Daddy, why don't I see you double because I have two eyes, and I can see you with each one by itself?" (p.8). Over time, John developed a theory of binocular vision which, while not accurate, did enable him to follow the path of light through the eye into the brain.

As gifted children develop reasoning ability and skills in producing reports and projects, their hypotheses become more research-oriented. Kate, a gifted girl with AD/HD (described in Chapter 1), decided for her junior high-school science fair to study whether there were basic differences in how boys and girls of different grades viewed girls' math and science ability. In effect, she replicated the work of several adult researchers. The following year, she developed an attitude questionnaire to research the topic of liking for these subjects among students of different grades, comparing how girls in co-educational environments versus girls in single-sex environments viewed themselves. Kate obtained highly significant results suggesting that both boys and girls viewed girls as less talented in math and science. Kate is typical of many gifted young adolescents, able to do quite impressive work to answer questions based on their own interests.

The derivation of rules and algorithms

Many gifted children are fascinated with numbers and patterns. Some derive relationships between numerical entities starting from an early age. They literally invent math for themselves. Gross (1993) described Richard who, at age four, could do mental arithmetic in binary, octal, hexadecimal, and decimal systems.

Tom was this sort of math student, able to solve unknown problems by applying rules he did know. Harry, the gifted boy with AS in Chapter 3, noticed patterns in numbers, and was adept at multiplication using these. In fact, gifted children with AS are particularly good at seeing patterns and developing rules about them. Ozonoff *et al.* (2002) described an adolescent girl with AS who noted that one researcher preferred clothing with horizontal stripes, and another, clothing with vertical stripes. The researchers had to go home and examine their own closets to note the accuracy of this girl's pattern recognition.

Some gifted children derive original algorithms. Eric, age nine, a gifted boy with AD/HD, developed an original mathematical formula. His teacher told him that he had developed a new theorem, but Eric corrected him, saying that it was only a hypothesis as he hadn't yet tested it with all possible sets of numbers (Lovecky 1994a).

Another such gifted student was Aaron, who was interested in mathematics and astrophysics. At age 12, Aaron thought about how time might be visualized in the universe as a multidimensional system. He imagined the three dimensions of length, width, and height as lines in three directions, with time as a line intersecting these. At the second level, time became a plane, intersecting planes of length, width, and height. At the third level, all were cubes. He also could imagine a fourth set of dimensions, hypercubes or tesseracts, thus 16 dimensions in all. From this model, he was able to visualize how the universe might currently work, and how it might have been formed from a singularity.

By developing themes, rules, and algorithms, gifted children, much earlier than age peers, determine how relationships among concepts interact. This can then lead to further development of knowledge in the field of exploration, and to new work as the child develops variations on the rules, or looks for exceptions and tries to explain them.

Cognitive reasoning and asynchrony

Observations of many of the children seen at the Gifted Resource Center of New England suggested that they exhibited a range of thinking styles and levels of abstraction depending on interests, task, and temperament. This range of levels of abstraction within the same child is called *asynchrony*. It means that the child may simultaneously be capable of dealing with a high degree of abstraction, and yet not question whether Santa Claus exists or not, as in the vignette above about Peter. The realness of the concepts may not be as important to the child as solving the theoretical problem. Thus, Peter could use Stephen Hawking's book to solve a puzzle about Santa's visit.

This type of asynchrony may mislead parents, teachers, and other adults into thinking the gifted child is more cognitively advanced in all areas than he or she is. Parents and teachers need to be careful about this because gifted children may not really understand all of the concept they are discussing, and they may not be emotionally ready for a topic they can discuss intellectually. Nevertheless, it is the ability to ask high-level questions, to wonder about the world, and to formulate interesting and original ideas about things that differentiate gifted children from average. Despite the many questions average children ask, they do not advance to the level where they spontaneously ask questions like those described above. The gifted child indeed has a qualitatively different mind.

Learning styles

In general, gifted children learn material faster, in more depth, and with greater complexity than other children. They also make connections among different aspects of the material that can lead to new insights. Most people have a distinct style of learning. While there are many different types of learning styles, two major ones are visual-spatial and auditory-sequential.

Cognitive styles not only impact how one learns, but also how one experiences the world. Someone who experiences the world visually has a different take on things than someone who is more auditory. Someone who is a big-picture thinker sees things differently than someone who is detail-oriented. West (1997) described the two hemispheres of the brain as two different modes of consciousness. The left hemisphere is verbal, using words and language to convey meaning. The right hemisphere is pictorial. The left hemisphere is sequential and analytic; the right holistic and synthetic. Thus, the left hemisphere can be thought of as auditory (verbal), sequential, and analytic, while the right hemisphere is visual, holistic, and intuitive.

Many gifted children are combined learners. They are easily able to integrate both auditory and visual aspects of experience. They can learn rote material, yet also envision the bigger picture. Some gifted children, though, are more oriented to one particular style. While many are more flexible and can learn in another style if needed, some gifted children are "wired" for one style only, and can only learn in this style. Stuart, described at the start of this chapter, was an auditory learner. Though he learned step by step, he needed the big picture pointed out to him and a step-by-step delineation about how to get there. If this was not done, Stuart missed the point. If he learned a problem one way, he could only solve it that way. He often insisted on doing things his own way because that was what he felt comfortable doing, even if it didn't work particularly well. Stuart's extreme style meant he was inflexible and unable to generate a suitable solution by slightly changing what he had learned to fit a new situation.

Gifted children like Stuart who seem "wired" only one way need to be evaluated for underlying learning problems. They are not oppositional, as Stuart was accused of being, because they insist on one way of doing things. Indeed, without special training, this is the only way they can function.

Right brain / left brain?

Intuition versus logic, visual-spatial reasoning versus verbal reasoning, the arts versus sciences are all dichotomies that reflect differences in how we view styles of reasoning and learning. The idea of right-brain versus left-brain thinking, in broad terms at least, is somewhat based on actual brain functioning. That is, the left side of the brain, on the whole for most people, is more concerned with verbal and sequential functioning, and the right brain, on the whole for most people, with nonverbal and holistic functioning. This is by no means the sharp dichotomy it may at first appear to be because different aspects of tasks are handled by different parts of the brain, and the brain works as an integrated unit.

Gifted children who show nonverbal, or right-brain preference in style are holistic. They are good synthesizers of information: that is, they are good at looking at separate pieces of material and then jumping instantly to the whole underlying concept. They envision the solution first, then set out to prove it. They are more intuitive, holistic, and nonlinear in thinking.

Gifted children who are more verbal and left brain in preference love facts and learning how facts relate to each other. They are sequential, logical, and analytical. They go step by step in building up an argument to a conclusion. These are children who make classifying systems for themselves after they have accumulated information. They also love seeing where each new piece of information fits and how it verifies or defeats their particular hypothesis, using both methods of logical deduction and statistics.

Most gifted children are more balanced thinkers, able to use both visual-holistic or auditory-sequential methods, though they may have a preference for one or the other. Nevertheless, they can adapt to the other style without too much effort. Thus, they build a big picture, but think about whether the facts make sense. They are good at logic and intuition, seeing the whole picture but also having strong sequential skills.

Studies of verbally and mathematically talented youth, those who did exceptionally well when taking the SATs (Scholastic Aptitude Tests) before age 13 (Benbow and Minor 1990), suggested differences in cognitive styles. Mathematically precocious students scored higher than verbally precocious students on spatial ability, nonverbal reasoning, speed, memory, and mechanical ability, while verbally precocious students scored higher on verbal reasoning, general information, and written expression.

Benbow and Minor also found that the presence of exceptionally high verbal ability increased the likelihood of high mathematical ability: that is, most of the verbally precocious students also scored high on mathematics (over 500) on the SATs. The reverse was not true. Mathematically precocious students did not, in general, score high verbally. (They scored over 700 M but less than 430 V on the SATs.) This suggests that verbally gifted students tend to be more even in cognitive development, and to have learning preferences that more fully utilize cognitive styles of both right- and left-brain thinking, while mathematically gifted students tend to be more one-sided, and more spatially, rather than verbally, talented.

Visual-spatial or right-brain learning styles

Linda Silverman (2002), in her book, *Upside-Down Brilliance: The Visual-Spatial Learner*, described extensively characteristics of visual-spatial learners. She suggested that up to one-third of all school children have this learning style. Silverman (p.70) described 26 traits of visual-spatial learners. Children identified as visual-spatial learners do not exhibit all of these; however, the majority of traits are identified in visual-spatial learners. An individual with these traits

- thinks primarily in images
- has visual strengths
- relates well to space
- is a whole-part learner
- learns concepts all at once
- learns complex concepts easily; struggles with basic skills
- is a good synthesizer
- sees the big picture; may miss details
- is better at math reasoning than computation

- learns whole words easily

- must visualize words to spell them

- is much better at keyboarding than handwriting

- creates unique methods of organization

- arrives at correct solutions intuitively

- learns best by seeing relationships

- has good long-term visual memory

- learns concepts permanently; does not need drill and repetition

- develops own methods of problem solving

- is very sensitive to teacher's attitudes

- generates unusual solutions to problems

- develops asynchronously

- may have very uneven grades

- enjoys geometry and physics

- masters other languages through immersion

- is creatively, technologically, mechanically, emotionally, spiritually gifted

- is a late bloomer.

Visual-spatial learning encompasses preferences for visual explanations, better visual memory, holistic information processing, intuitive thinking, emotional learning, metaphoric learning, dealing with tasks in parallel (that is, working on several at once) liking open-ended discussion and experience, preferring first to gain an overview of material (that is, the big picture), and being a whole-to-part learner who often learns all at once by synthesizing patterns.

Visual-spatial learners like to picture things. Asked to think about a problem, they will use a picture or spatial schema or find a mental pattern. These gifted children can be very creative, quick to grasp concepts and find patterns. They excel at tasks that require inductive reasoning, holistic thinking, and seeing complex relationships among parts. Silverman suggested that visual-spatial learning was like art. When an artist has developed an image for a painting it is there, complete and permanent. It does not need to be rehearsed or practiced; it does not improve with drill or review.

People who are visual-spatial thinkers and learners are good at a variety of tasks. West (1997) described scientists (Michael Faraday, James Clerk Maxwell, Albert Einstein), inventors (Nikola Tesla, Thomas Edison, Leonardo da Vinci), mathematicians (Henri Poincaré), poets (William Butler Yeats), and national leaders (Winston Churchill, George S. Patton) who were especially gifted with visual-spatial thinking. Visual-spatial thinking also occurs in music and art. Mozart was supposed to have seen the entire movement of a symphony in his mind before he wrote a note (Silverman 2002). Artists certainly use visual-spatial thinking in their work. Other areas that might also use visual-spatial thinking include sewing, especially design; cooking, especially pastry making; and business, especially entrepreneurship, planning sales campaigns, developing marketing concepts, fundraising, and other big-picture endeavors.

Visual-spatial thinking can be exhibited by quite young children. Silverman (2002) listed a number of areas in which visual-spatial thinking can be seen from an early age: puzzles, art work, building things, interest in numbers, visual memory, spatial perception, maps and geography, vivid imagination, mechanical interest and ability, taking things apart, music, mazes, and computers.

Raymond, a gifted boy with AD/HD, was interested in anything that had to do with building things. He liked to invent using electronics parts, and also to build toys of his own design from Lego and Capsela pieces. His Christmas wish, at age five, was to get a particular motor so that he could build several items he had designed. When he got the motor, he spent months happily building these things. Raymond continued to design and build complex and original designs from Lego, Capsela parts, and eventually from electronic components. He enjoyed building his own robot and then programming it. He also enjoyed inventing devices to do simple tasks using electronic parts. One of his devices was designed to water the family plants. It was clear that his long-term passions were for the spatial and mathematical. Contrast this with Tolan's (1985) report of her son RJ's experience with Capsela. He played with it intensively over a short time period in which he did nothing else, a marathon of Capsela building. Yet once he had accomplished all the objectives of that kit, and learned the basic principles, he never touched the set again. His Capsela episode had more to do with learning the concepts offered by the toy as rapidly as he could, rather than seeing the toy as a means to further develop other visual-spatial concepts of his own creation. Raymond, in contrast, continued over the course of several years to build increasingly complex and integrated products. While quite adept spatially and mathematically, RJ appeared to be more of a balanced learner, whose creative interests lay in other areas.

Visual-spatial learners, because they are holistic, have weaknesses in sequential thinking and sometimes in language functioning. Nevertheless, most visual-spatial thinkers are also quite creative in language. They are adept at metaphoric language, as well as at language that describes concepts. Silverman (2002) thought that visual-spatial thinkers lack verbal fluency, not verbal ability.

In addition, visual-spatial learners have trouble with step-by-step or logical organization, planning, thinking of details, and learning. They are poorer at basic skills and this can impact on reading, spelling, and math computation. This may mean they do less well in school and may not be labeled gifted when programs depend on sequential learning.

THE WEAKNESSES OF VISUAL-SPATIAL THINKING

In addition to weaker sequential skills, there are a number of disabilities that can affect people with visual-spatial thinking styles. These include dyslexia, Central Auditory Processing Disorder (CAPD) and AD/HD.

There is a group of visual-spatial thinkers who have more difficulty with auditory processing and language. West (1997) described their difficulties in learning to read, that is, their dyslexia. In fact, West (1997) described how visual thinking, pattern recognition, creativity, thinking in visual images, holistic thinking, and spatial intelligence can result in dyslexia. His conclusion was that dyslexia is a mixed disorder with positive as well as negative attributes. In fact, the very visual strengths that allow such wonderful nonverbal reasoning are associated with corresponding deficits in language functioning.

Silverman saw increased learning problems and auditory processing disorders including CAPD. This means that, in addition to poorer ability to process sequential material, children with CAPD have poorer auditory memory, difficulty with auditory attention to directions, trouble focusing on exact meaning of complex sentence structure, difficulty getting the main point of material, trouble prioritizing among details for relevant or irrelevant, and difficulty ascertaining how qualifiers such as "if, maybe, since, because, however" change sentence meaning.

GIFTED CHILDREN WITH AD/HD

Many visual-spatial thinkers do not have AD/HD. On the other hand, many children with AD/HD are nonsequential and may be visual-spatial thinkers. Silverman (2002) discussed this overlap in her book and suggested that many of the traits of fluidity of thinking, intuition, and big-picture synthesis that are found with visual-spatial learners are also found in AD/HD.

Hallowell and Ratey (1994a) suggested that people with AD/HD are more right than left brain in learning and thinking preferences. Those with AD/HD dislike logic and linear reasoning, but instead prefer holistic thinking. They form the whole from little information, use the visual and emotional to construct ideas, and think in patterns and rhythms rather than words. This means also that they are exceptionally good at intuition. Yet Hallowell and Ratey also explain that many with AD/HD cannot articulate the ideas and insights that come to them. These authors see those with AD/HD as actually "trapped" in their right hemispheres so they can't articulate the holistic ideas they have. To do so would involve a transfer to more left-brain thinking in which logic, detail, and analysis is involved. In effect, they are blocked from producing the ideas they have and cannot easily share them fully with others. This is Tom's problem in writing. He cannot figure out how to get from the picture he has in his mind of the story to what to write on paper. Tom sees the story as a movie moving in his mind, complete with color and sound. He feels completely unable to translate this to written form. He hasn't a clue how to start. Even if he writes a few sentences, he feels it isn't at all what he has in mind and soon gives up from frustration.

Gifted children with AD/HD who are visual-spatial learners differ from other visual-spatial learners in being less able to articulate or demonstrate their ideas to an audience. As Hallowell and Ratey described, they have the holistic picture, the new concept, the interesting insight, but translating it to an expressive form is much more difficult than for other visual-spatial learners because of executive function deficits. Also, gifted children with AD/HD differ from other visual-spatial learners in being more asynchronous in development of skills, in emotional expression, and in intensity of expression.

Some gifted children with AD/HD who are visual-spatial learners are so impulsive and stimulus-driven that they never form an accurate big picture. These AD/HD children need to work quickly. They skim the surface of material and cannot stop to consider contradictions or incongruities. That is, they get the gist of something by grabbing onto one part that is the most stimulating, or novel, and base their conclusion on that part rather than on the whole. So, though they are visual-spatial thinkers and form wholes readily, they are mistaken in what they perceive. Once they have done a piece of work, correctly or incorrectly, they feel they have mastered it and refuse to redo it. They just want to move on. However, they may not know the concept adequately, quite unlike other visual-spatial learners.

Gifted children with AD/HD who are visual-spatial learners may be more intuitive than other visual-spatial learners. This means that they can be even more creative, as well as more idiosyncratic, in their thinking. Gifted children with

AD/HD may overuse intuition. This occurs particularly in situations where all the parameters are not obvious, and when logic and reason need to be applied. At this point, their more divergent responses miss the mark. On the other hand, using their intuitive powers allows gifted children with AD/HD to perform exceptionally well in situations where the parameters are not yet set. When improvisation or guessing is required, then these children are at their strongest. They are also the most likely to think of new responses to situations, to see the aspect that has eluded others, and to see things from a different perspective so that old time-worn solutions may not be the first they develop. This allows flexibility and creativity.

Gifted children with AD/HD who are visual-spatial learners can be successful using strategies that build upon their strong abilities to visualize, integrate, and make patterns of material. Creative learning tasks that utilize the student's special interests will help focus attention and increase motivation through some of the struggles with weaker areas.

SUGGESTIONS FOR VISUAL-SPATIAL/HOLISTIC LEARNERS

- Use methods that emphasize visualization in performing tasks, especially those related to basic skills of reading, math, and spelling. For example, emphasize word families by color coding them. Color math signs to direct attention to them.

- In problem solving, use methods that show the big picture, and allow students to develop concepts by intuiting an answer and then checking data to see if they are right. Use pattern finding and induction to solve problems.

- Use visual models and diagrams to accent weaker organizational skills based on sequencing. Use time lines to help with sequencing. Make a book of math facts and help the child to see all the patterns. For example, for all but the seven times table, there are tricks to enhance memorization of multiplication facts. The four table is the two table doubled. The eight table is the four doubled. Let the child play with the combinations. Give the child unknown problems and let him or her solve them, then try another problem to check the hypothesis. De-emphasize timed tests.

- Go from the big picture to smaller steps. Thus, give the big picture, the major concepts, and finally the details that need to be attached to the concepts. Teach outlining by showing the outline already completed and then go backwards to the next biggest parts, and the next, until the last part is the skeleton. Show how it matches an outline in a chapter of a text.

- Improve organization, especially of written work, by teaching brainstorming and then organization of ideas using graphic organizers such as idea nets, webs, outline skeleton to be filled in, and so on. Show how to figure out what belongs with what; for example, use categories.

- Improve listening skills and verbal short-term memory by having the child look at the adult's mouth while instructions are being given. Then have the child repeat the instructions until they are correct (Silverman 2002).

Visual learners who are not holistic

Gifted children with AD/HD frequently show a preference for visual-spatial learning; however, some gifted children with AD/HD are such slow processors of information that they do not think holistically. Instead, they form partial wholes, or wholes based on erroneous information. Then, they have more trouble with interpreting meaning. These slower processors may actually have quite good visual-spatial skills, and will perform to a high level on tests of nonverbal reasoning ability. What gives them more difficulty are those tasks that require holding material in mind while operating on it or dealing with complex material in several sensory modalities. For example, Colin had difficulty thinking of a topic for his high-school senior project. Though many topics were of interest, Colin could not figure out what he would actually do. He might want to do something with travel in it, or maybe he'd put on an exhibit of some kind. He only had the vaguest idea, and could not see himself actually doing anything. Consequently, he had no clear idea of what his project might look like, or even what he'd really be doing. Colin lacked the ability to see the big picture. He also did not how to take an idea and add more parts or pieces until he had elaborated details enough to build a big picture. This elaboration of an initial idea might have been a substitute strategy. Since he also lacked sequential skills, he had trouble breaking any task down into small parts. The combination of not being able to visualize the whole project and the difficulty thinking of the parts left Colin feeling defeated. On the other hand, Colin was highly intuitive, a wonderful musician and poet who used visual images to good effect in his creative work. Colin learned best by looking at pictures and making diagrams. He liked maps and geography. He also loved to learn languages which he did by immersing himself in the language. While Colin had 18 of the visual-spatial traits listed by Silverman (2002), he was not a holistic learner.

It can be helpful to some non-holistic visual-spatial learners with AD/HD to slow down the presentation of material and to decrease the necessity for rapid response, so they can focus more on the big picture; nevertheless, some still may need to work so slowly that the big picture never is completely formed. These students need the big picture presented to them first.

Gifted children with AS and other autism spectrum disorders can be visual thinkers. They think in pictures, and words become a series of pictures as they hear them. This means that thoughts are also pictures. Material that cannot translate to pictures is more difficult to understand. Thus, people with AS and other autism spectrum disorders are often good at visual tasks like maps, puzzles, and visualizing systems like subways and highways. Temple Grandin, for example, a brilliant woman with AS, described her thinking processes as almost entirely visual. She is quite creative and sees her designs at a distance, or displayed before her so she can rotate them in her mind and see different aspects. She also experiences her own memory as a videotape that she can replay exactly as she first saw an object (Grandin 1995).

People with autism spectrum disorders tend to come from families with a higher than average number of physicists, mathematicians, and engineers (Baron-Cohen *et al.* 1998). The visual style of thinking that is necessary for these professions suggests that these strengths may run in families, and so be present in those with AS. The visual strengths found include visualization or mental picturing of objects, mental rotation of objects in space, finding hidden figures, finding visual similarities and differences, memory for shapes, patterns and pictures, and seeing patterns and sequences in visual material.

On the other hand, while an important aspect of visual-spatial thinkers is holistic thinking, people with AS and other autism spectrum disorders appear to lack holistic thinking. Though they may be excellent at visualization, they are not very good at constructing the whole from its parts. Unlike the holistic learner who instantly sees the whole, people with AS see the parts without seeing them as a whole. This is due to weak central coherence. For example, in doing a jigsaw puzzle, they work by putting shapes together, not by constructing a picture. Many can construct the puzzle just as well upside down or with the picture removed because that isn't what is important to them in the construction.

Difficulties with facial recognition are an example of difficulty with visualization of wholes. In facial recognition, most people experience the face all at once. They immediately recognize another person. They also know how another person feels by looking at their face. People with AS have trouble seeing faces as a whole. They are slower in recognizing faces because they have to put the parts together. For example, in doing a puzzle of a face, most people know where to put the individual parts based on knowing how faces look. The gifted child with AS will treat the pieces as objects to be fitted together by shape without regard to knowing how the face goes, even if they articulate they know the puzzle is a face. Furthermore, instead of seeing emotions all at once, they have to analyze how faces look in each part to recognize emotion. Wide-open eyes mean surprise or shock.

A problem with the visualization of wholes has important correlates in the social realm. Forming visual wholes has a lot to do with forming whole social pictures. A lack of understanding of how social and emotional aspects of experience interrelate is a handicap. Just as the pictures on the puzzle pieces are irrelevant to the person with AS in making the puzzle, the expressions on faces, the nonverbal body language, and tone of voice are irrelevant in making social decisions. Instead, social decisions are made based on what the person with AS thinks is most striking.

Among the gifted children with AS seen at the Gifted Resource Center of New England, some showed visual-spatial skills in such activities as designing maps, doing puzzles, drawing highways and train systems, designing computer websites, computer programming, making animated drawings, designing robots on computer, building with Lego, both with bricks and through Lego Mindstorms, and origami folding. This reflected excellent visual-perceptual skills in mental rotation of objects, seeing the parts of a whole quickly, recall of visual objects and images, sequencing visual objects, and finding embedded (hidden) figures. On the other hand, these same children also showed visual-spatial weaknesses in some areas, especially in finding visual figures against different backgrounds, making wholes from component parts, planning visual tasks, and eye–hand coordination, especially in handwriting. None of the children seen could be classified as holistic, big-picture thinkers, even when they scored much higher on visual-spatial tests than average. Thus, gifted children with AS who are visual-spatial thinkers are not holistic.

SUGGESTIONS FOR VISUAL BUT NOT HOLISTIC LEARNERS

- Many of the suggestions for visual-spatial learners still apply to those who are not holistic. They need visual images to learn well: that is, pictures, diagrams, time lines, and charts. They need a decreased emphasis on time and more emphasis on space. They need use of compensatory devices such as word-processing programs, spell checkers, and calculators.

- Visual-spatial learners who are not holistic need the big picture given to them first. Then, they need the big picture broken down into component parts. At the end of a lesson, the big picture is put together again from the parts. For example, to teach a child how to get dressed, the parent would say, "We are going to have you learn how to dress yourself." This might be followed by a reason why this would be useful. Then the parent would place a picture of a fully dressed child at the top of a chart. The parts of getting dressed would be discussed and each step placed on the chart step by step, using drawings or pictures. Finally, the chart would end with a picture of a fully dressed child, and a "Good Job" chip the child could put into a jar to use for a future reward.

- Children with difficulty building to a big picture need to build a repertoire of parts that can be added together to make a whole. Thus, they need to know the parts of academic tasks, or of social and emotional expectations. For example, a parent could make a book of facial expressions. First the whole expression is pictured, then the parts that make that expression. Reading the expression can be done part by part and added up. Over time, as the child learns that slitted eyes means anger, he or she can react more quickly.

- Gifted children with AD/HD, like Colin, need models of the completed task. Thus, Colin needed to see how an idea was developed into a project. He needed to see how that idea was first visualized, then to see how it might be elaborated. Once Colin elaborated an idea, he then would need help sharpening the idea into a feasible project. Thus, at every step, Colin needed help in learning the next step. In the last part, Colin would develop a series of tasks he would do to complete the project and describe them in detail. This would all have to occur before Colin could even start a project.

Auditory-sequential or left-brain learning styles

Auditory-sequential learners are usually good students. School is geared towards their learning style, with step-by-step instruction, practice and drilling of facts, and building to a bigger concept. Gifted children who are auditory-sequential learners are good at most school subjects. They learn to read on schedule, are excellent spellers, have legible handwriting, and do well in math. In fact, they are good at math problems that require showing the steps they used to solve a problem. To these children, math can be a language, and they are proficient at languages. These gifted children also show exceptional ability in written expression, English, science, social studies, and foreign languages.

Gifted children who are auditory-sequential learners do especially well with fact-based learning that requires memorization and categorization, or depends on rule-based applications. In fact, children who win spelling and geography bees and do well in national foreign language competitions are usually auditory-sequential learners. Auditory-sequential learners learn the structures taught by school on how to learn. They understand outlining, can define parts of speech, and can memorize math facts. This does not mean they necessarily like learning all of these things, but they can do so.

Silverman (2002) listed some of the strengths of auditory-sequential learners. In general, these are the opposite of the strengths of visual-spatial learners. Thus, instead of learning better with pictures, auditory-sequential learners learn better with words. Based on observations of the gifted children at the Gifted Resource Center of New England, auditory-sequential learners excel at:

- using words
- using logic
- logical inference; what goes in this blank space...
- deduction
- time sequences; if...then
- a...b...c ordering
- following oral directions
- memorizing facts
- knowing what ought to come next; knowing the rules and forms so they can deduce it
- building parts to a whole
- recalling conversations
- convergent thinking; how are these two alike
- categorical ordering: find the commonality
- details of language, parts of speech, grammar, and usage
- foreign language learning, because they pick up rules, structures, and vocabulary quickly.

People with auditory, left-brain learning styles enjoy working quickly on parts without needing to know the whole. This means they can solve problems by deduction, using step-by-step reasoning to determine logically how something ought to be. These students build on previous learning by adding details to what they already know and then come up with a more elaborated argument. They are good at developing a hypothesis, supporting a thesis, and seeing if the facts match the question. They are often good outliners because they can follow directions to identify the main topics. This means these students are good at picking out the main points, the most important topics, and seeing how subtopics fit within the larger scheme. Auditory-sequential learners are rewarded in schools with high grades because they are so good at following what the teacher wants.

Many famous people have been creative using an auditory-sequential style. For example, Sigmund Freud, Margaret Mead, Eleanor Roosevelt, Martin Luther King, Jr., Clarence Darrow, and William Jennings Bryan all were known for their facility with words. This does not mean that these famous people did not also have strong visual-spatial skills, but that their auditory skills were predominant enough to persuade people to listen to their ideas. Auditory-sequential learners can excel in teaching, psychology, jurisprudence, philosophy, linguistics, accounting, editing, science, social studies, law enforcement, and in many other areas.

Auditory-sequential skills can be detected from an early age in gifted children. These gifted children develop language earlier than age peers, and often speak in full sentences prior to 18 months of age. They are often early readers and writers. Many are good at spelling from the time of preschool years. Ryan could spell words such as "scythe" at age five, and he had learned to read at age two. Many of these gifted children enjoy imaginative play and have imaginary playmates. They enjoy acting out what they have read, and also they will compose new scenarios based on variations of what they have done before. From an early age, many gifted children with strong auditory-sequential skills engage in argument and debate, especially with their parents. They want logical reasons why they can and cannot do things.

WEAKNESSES OF AUDITORY-SEQUENTIAL LEARNERS

Most auditory-sequential learners who have visual-spatial weaknesses are never noticed because their deficits are subtle. Thus, mild difficulty synthesizing parts to a whole may not be very important in the general classroom. Mild deficits in organization and planning, reading maps and finding unknown locations by map, having a sense of how far away something is, or how big or small compared to another object, remembering what is seen, using inductive means to problem solve, or flexibility in problem solving all can affect children who are primarily auditory-sequential learners. However, there are ways to compensate that utilize auditory-sequential skills. For example, a poor map reader learns to get verbal directions, and one who has trouble with visual memory makes lists, and always puts things back in the same place.

Because girls tend to be less exposed to spatial materials in general, they often have had less practice at some types of skills. It is important, therefore, to assess how much opportunity for practice a person has had when determining their weaknesses. Gallagher and Johnson (1992) showed that when given timed tasks of mental rotation, gifted male adolescents tended to outscore gifted females. Yet if allowed to work at the task on an untimed version, scores were more nearly equal. Thus, both boys and girls may be adept at spatial tasks, but boys, who generally have had more practice, can perform much faster than girls.

SUGGESTIONS FOR AUDITORY-SEQUENTIAL LEARNERS

- Auditory-sequential learners love words. Encourage speaking and listening skills by reading aloud and having gifted children read aloud. Use books on tape including books of poetry and plays. Go to plays and poetry readings. Memorize and recite poetry.

- Encourage oratory and debate on particular topics. Have these gifted children take opposing sides in turns, so that they argue each side of an issue. Since these gifted children love to argue, teach them the rules for fair arguments.

- Use verbal compensations for visual-spatial weaknesses: oral directions, taping and listening to lectures, using subvocal self-directions and plans, making up stories to recall material that is not sequential.

- Teach these gifted students to use compensatory sequential skills for spatial weaknesses. List the steps to solve a problem, make a book of math and science formulas and their solutions, as well as applications to particular problems. Put things into categories and rank order them.

- Teach these gifted students study skills based on auditory-sequential strengths: outline, recite, put into categories and hierarchies, memorize lists of things that go together or sound alike. Make up lists of rules and instances that conform to and differ from the rule.

- Encourage children without much experience with visual-spatial material to play games and do tasks that require learning some of these skills: mazes, hidden pictures, connecting the dots, simple origami, building models from kits following the directions (bird houses, car models, Lego and other building toys, electronic kits), playing games that require visual-spatial strategy such as Set, Mancala, Go, and chess.

Auditory learners who are not sequential

Gifted children with AD/HD and some visual-spatial deficits can be auditory learners, but they may not be sequential. In fact, they have a mixed learning pattern in which they fail to get the big picture, and have trouble with using parts to build to the whole. These gifted children often have difficulty with completing work because the sequential skills involved are too difficult for them. They don't understand how steps follow one on the other. They also don't see how to get to the solution. They are intuitive but perceive the wrong thing because their big-picture skills are not well developed.

Some gifted children with AS also fall into this pattern. Though they fit many of the characteristics of auditory-sequential learners, they are poor at picking out the main points, and deciding what is the most important and what is subordinate. To them, all the points are similarly important. This deficit arises from their extreme difficulty with part-to-whole relationships. It is difficult to assess relevancy when one does not know how parts relate to each other, or what the big picture is. Because of these deficits, gifted children with AS are often good students in subjects that emphasize memorization, use of basic skills, and their applications, but they are poorer at those that require organization of content, such as mathematics and written expression.

There are a proportion of people who are auditory-sequential learners who have more severe problems with visual-spatial learning. These people have NVLDs. As described in Chapters 2, 3, and 9, people with NVLD have right-brain deficits that affect many areas including the following (Denckla 1991; Rourke and Tsatsanis 2000; Thompson 1997).

- *Visual-spatial-organizational skills* such as organization and planning, problems with spatial perception, synthesis of visual-perceptual material, left/right orientation, visual memory, problems visualizing what was seen previously, visual-motor organization and integration, tactile perception, mental flexibility in novel problem solving.

- *Motor coordination deficits* such as poor handwriting, difficulty with balance, athletic skills, especially coordinated skills like jumping jacks, fine motor skills involved in dressing and eating.

- *Language deficits* in metaphoric language, problems recognizing incongruities in verbal and visual situations, problems with verbosity and inappropriate talking, needing to talk to do tasks, or know where other people are in space.

- *Academic skills deficits* such as math, reading comprehension, and written expression.

- *Deficits in social awareness and social judgment* including misinterpretation of social situations, poor reading of nonverbal body language, poor reading of facial expression, problems reading the intentions of others, deficits in social prediction of behavior.

Many children with NVLD have trouble with the organizational part of school tasks. They have trouble planning what to do. They even have trouble organizing their own thoughts. Thus, written work is difficult. Not only do they have to coordinate thoughts and handwriting, but also they have to think of what to say, and how to say it, all at the same time. Because many children with NVLD have particular trouble with multistep tasks, they are defeated by written work. For example, Alex, age 12, could not think of anything to say. Given a picture prompt, he was unable to think of anything to write. He became stuck. Given some help generating ideas, he then could not figure out which he should do first. Given help with that, he still did not quite know how to start. Alex needed specific scripts about what to do to write a short piece: how to generate ideas, how to group them, how to select the first one, how to decide what to say.

Gifted children with AD/HD can have NVLD. In fact, it is important to discriminate whether weaknesses in visual-perceptual-motor tasks are the result of attention problems and work speed, or if they truly constitute an NVLD. Evaluation needs to based on more than the Performance section of the Wechsler Intelligence Scale; usually a battery of tests that evaluate visual-perceptual functioning (both timed and untimed), in both written and nonwritten formats, needs to be performed to fully assess weaknesses. These children need specific evaluation because they will need more than American with Disabilities Act (ADA) AD/HD 504 accommodations in order to function well in school even when very gifted.

Gifted children with AD/HD who have NVLD are very disorganized. They forget and lose things. They have trouble organizing projects. They have goals but have trouble seeing how to get to the goal. Details sidetrack them from the main task. They insist on doing certain things, such as solving math problems, only their own way, and are impervious to considering alternate ways. Often, these children insist they are right no matter what. They have trouble thinking clearly in social solutions as well, and may have social deficits because they can't see social cues clearly and do not really get the big picture. In addition, slower processing means that their response time is slower. Finally, what is most pertinent in a situation is what is most prominent to them rather than what is most related to the goal of the situation. This means their behavior and responses seem inappropriate.

While gifted children with NVLD and AD/HD perform some tasks by using part-to-whole relationships, they have deficits in guessing the whole. With milder forms of NVLD, they take a much longer than average time to figure out what the bigger picture is. Thus, processing speed is affected more than actual ability to put parts together to see the whole. These are children whose first attempt on a visual-perceptual task is poor, but who do significantly better with time and mild practice. This helps them to consolidate the material into their longer-term memory, so the next time they encounter it, they do recall the whole.

Gifted children with NVLD and AD/HD can hyperfocus on small details or problems and obsess about them. It is hard for them to let go of these worries or feelings. In fact, small incidents that occurred will come to mind over and over. Thus, some have obsessive-compulsive tendencies as well as AD/HD.

Gifted children with AS may also have NVLD (Klin *et al.* 1995; Rourke and Tsatsanis 2000; Volkmar and Klin 2000). Like other children with NVLD, children with AS have trouble with organization, planning, getting the big picture, dealing with part-to-whole relationships, and mental flexibility. Gifted children with AS show particular deficits in organizing their own talking and writing. They have trouble with using strategies, and so cannot effectively plan work. They are inflexible and are prone to rigid thinking.

These children also have a tendency to overgeneralize from one instance. Thus, if something happened once in particular way, they think it will always happen in that same way. For example, if on the first day of school, the teacher gave out papers in a certain way, the next day the child with AS would expect the same thing to occur. Another aspect of this occurs when something negative happens. The gifted child with AS then wants to avoid repeating the unpleasant aspect again by avoiding the whole situation. Once they are stuck, it is hard to change. Part of the problem for these children is their limited perspective. Because they can see no other solutions to their dilemmas, they feel there are none. Then, even given another option, they cannot conceptualize how it applies to them and their situation.

Rules also can appear to be rigid to them, since there seem no other options but obeying them. Thus, Robert was upset that his friends sat together at lunch, and he was left out. It turned out that in Robert's mind, the school rule of no overcrowded tables meant that he could not sit there as he would have had to bring over another seat. To him, this would have been overcrowding. The fact other students regularly brought over other seats did not matter to Robert. He was stuck in his definition of overcrowding.

Gifted children with AS and NVLD are so easily overwhelmed by too much complexity that they focus on a part. In the face of a situation in which they feel overwhelmed, they retreat to previously learned solutions or rules and try to apply these. Because they only have a few options in their repertoire and cannot generalize to similar situations very well, they act inappropriately. Also, they miss essential clues, especially those that are subtle and nonverbal.

Severe NVLD does produce deficits similar to those found in AS. Whether this is sufficient to produce the entire set of problems is not known at this time. Certainly, there are other aspects of AS related to underlying problems with social attribution that may not be associated with NVLD. However, it is not an either/or question.

SUGGESTIONS FOR AUDITORY LEARNERS WITH NVLD

- Encourage use of reading and listening to learn new material. Saying the material aloud to oneself can improve retention. Describing visual material aloud can help the child to figure out what to do. For example, giving verbal instructions can aid in organization of material in a visual format. Also making up a verbal story can help the child recall visual material.

- Use tasks that involve logic and deduction to solve problems or arrive at a conclusion.

- Teach brainstorming and encourage the child to think of pros and cons in comparing alternatives. This is effective for children who tend to see only one solution. For those who have trouble brainstorming, have them tell all they know, free associate, think of categories, think of another situation in which the problem might occur and solve that. Think of all the possibilities and then eliminate all those that do not fit the criteria.

- Encourage memorization of facts, but show how the facts relate to a bigger concept. Discuss the bigger picture. Thus the causes of the Civil War might be listed as slavery, states' rights, and economics, but the bigger picture was why each side felt it absolutely necessary to fight. What did each side really hope to gain?

- In teaching a new concept, start with the big picture, the concept, or the goal, then teach the steps, parts, facts in sequence, then go to the big picture again and show how the parts add up to the whole.

- Teach why things are done a certain way so students don't just memorize steps.

- Avoid visual overload: place fewer problems on a page, allow use of blockers or folding so less is seen at once, use large-hole graph paper, or regular lined paper turned sideways to keep problems lined up, avoid work pages that require finding material in a visual field – for example, pages where the child colors all the answers that are "3"s.

- Build on strong verbal skills in rote memory, phonetic analysis, vocabulary, and general knowledge.

- Allow use of compensatory mechanisms such as calculators and word processors.

Executive functions

In general, gifted children who do not have AD/HD, AS or other learning or emotional problems do well in academics. They are able to accelerate in many subjects because they perform well above age peers. Nevertheless, there is some evidence that gifted children vary in their ability to use executive functions efficiently. They may not do better than age peers on some types of self-monitoring. In contrast, gifted children with AD/HD and AS, as well other learning problems, tend to be below average in efficient use of executive functions.

Research on gifted children in general suggests a mixed picture. Alexander *et al.* (1998) suggested that eight-year-old gifted children did not reliably distinguish among different types of memory or understand how to selectively focus attention. They did not understand how to learn something new or that certain things might be distracters. Even if they knew some strategies, these gifted children did not know how to use them appropriately.

Carr, Alexander, and Schwanenflugel (1996) demonstrated that gifted children have more cognitive knowledge about how the mind works and can apply strategies someone else taught them to very different types of problems. However, they had more trouble using strategies learned on their own, especially in applying them to use on similar types of problems to the training problem or maintaining the strategy use over time. That is, they learned the strategy for that one problem and did not necessarily see other problems as similar.

Markham (1979) found that gifted children were no more adept at breaking out of a set and using another strategy than were average children. On the other hand, Dover and Shore (1992) found gifted children did better on using strategies within a specific area (such as math problem solving). For example, once they got the idea of how to pour water between buckets, they could solve problems of any type that had to do with measuring water using different volumes of buckets without measuring marks. Zimmerman and Martinez-Pons (1986) and Dover (1983, cited in Shore and Dover 1987) demonstrated that gifted children used self-regulatory learning strategies more frequently and skillfully than did average children.

Older gifted children, age 13 and 14, were found to show differential performance in working memory. Verbally precocious youths showed increased memory for words while the mathematically precocious showed increased recall of digits and locations. When speed was examined, the verbally precocious youths showed enhanced speed of encoding material into memory. Thus, adolescents with different types of giftedness showed different patterns of efficiency of working memory (Dark and Benbow 1991).

There is evidence that underachieving gifted children are less well developed in their use of self-monitoring skills. Risemberg and Zimmerman (1992) point out that these students fail to set appropriate goals, choose ineffective strategies, fail to monitor progress, and fail to evaluate their end result.

Underlying the difficulties of children with AD/HD, including gifted children, are deficits in executive functions that have a specific impact on learning. Gifted children with AS also have specific deficits in some aspects of executive functions that impact learning on a variety of tasks.

Executive functions and gifted children with attention deficits

Deficits in particular executive functions affect the efficiency of learning in those gifted children with AD/HD or AS. There are a number of executive functions that are important in learning new material, in integrating material with what is already known, and in demonstrating mastery of material through written expression. These executive functions include: paying attention; working memory; internalization of speech; arousal, activation, and effort; and holistic and sequential performance. Each of these will be discussed below.

Paying attention

Gifted children with AD/HD have difficulty with focusing and sustaining attention. They may also have trouble shifting attention from less relevant to more relevant things, or have trouble shifting to a less preferred task. They are easily distracted by material that is tangential and they are apt to go off onto tangents that are interesting. They have trouble with attending to more than one aspect of material at once: for example, content and spelling, or spelling and handwriting. Grace, age ten, had difficulty completing work because she could not pay attention. She had trouble sticking to the task, and found herself daydreaming partway through. She also found she forgot important parts of tasks such as checking her computation, or remembering to check that she had done all the parts required.

Gifted children with AS have trouble with focusing on tasks of less interest to them. They need the stimulation of the interest to do the task at all. They are easily distracted by irrelevant material especially if it involves their own thoughts or associations. Both children with AD/HD and AS may have trouble with hyperfocusing in inappropriate situations. Stuart found himself distracted by his inner dialogue. When he disliked a task, or felt bored, he stated to daydream, recalling parts of his favorite Monty Python movies. He was often surprised by how much time had gone by, and how little work was done.

The consequences of poor attention are poorer ability to think about the task at hand, to finish work, to have work fit the expected parameters, and to perform tasks that are important but of less interest. Difficulty paying attention means that directions are missed and materials lost or forgotten. Also, trouble with hyperfocusing means the child can do significant amounts of work of good quality when interested, especially on self-selected topics, but may have trouble performing on other tasks.

Suggestions for improving attention

- To help children focus and sustain attention, use high-interest materials with defined goals. Also children need to be taught to recognize when they have lost focus and to learn to refocus. This could be done by stopping the child periodically to see if he or she is focusing.

- Teach strategies to focus such as talking to oneself about the task, dividing the task into smaller parts and doing each part in a short time, and saying the directions subvocally as the task is done. Ned, a very successful young adult with AD/HD, in high school taught himself to focus on academic tasks by using this method.

- Have the child note particular types of distracters. Make a list of these and focus on one each week. A distraction "zapper" can be used as the distraction is noted. Tom found it was helpful to chew gum or squeeze a ball when he had to listen to a verbally presented lesson. This kept him more focused and less apt to fidget. Another child who is easily distracted by unexpected noise might use ear plugs or white noise as a blocker. For interrupting thoughts, some children can focus if they write down the distracting thoughts.

- Dealing with hyperfocus is not easy. When children become stuck, it can be difficult to get them to move on. Setting and enforcing a time or page limit can help them to stop. However, this may mean the adult has to put a hand over the page, turn off the computer, or steer the child to another activity. Positive practice sometimes helps. The child cooperates in learning to stop and change activity. First a mildly interesting task is selected, such as a cartoon the child has already read many times. The child reads the cartoon, and the parent stops the reading and gets the child to move onto another interesting task on command. It may take a lot of practice until the child is able to do this. Then, more interesting tasks are chosen so that it requires more attention to stop, disengage and reengage in another interesting task. After a series of steps of engaging in more absorbing tasks, disengaging and switching, the second task chosen is less interesting: for example, taking a shower or eating dinner. Over time, given small enough steps and enough practice, children who hyperfocus can learn to attend when asked to do so. Successful approximations are rewarded.

- In order to focus adequately, some children will need stimulant medication; otherwise they will be unable to do enough work to learn important skills.

Working memory

Gifted children with AD/HD have difficulty with working memory. Working memory includes short-term memory, prioritizing, sense of time, and appropriate use of rules to guide behavior.

SHORT-TERM MEMORY CAPACITY

Gifted children with AD/HD have difficulty with hearing and remembering directions, recalling facts on demand, memorizing math facts and spelling words, and forgetting to do parts of math problems or parts of questions.

The consequences of short-term memory deficits are that children have more difficulty recalling what to do, remembering all the parts to be done, recalling specific material, and memorizing material; they forget what they are saying and lose things. They also fail to do chores and other tasks at home and do not recall instructions or messages given by others. These deficits affect all areas where memory plays a part. Tom often forgot things. He would leave the house without his books, lunch, gym equipment, projects, band instrument, and coat. Coming home from school, he forgot books he needed for homework, his lunch container, dirty gym clothes, notes to be handed to his parents, and other belongings. Once he even lost his Game Boy. Tom's parents usually rescued him by bringing the forgotten objects to school, and were so used to doing this that they did not even see it as a problem.

Gifted children with AS have less trouble with short-term memory. Unless they also have AD/HD, they usually have quite good short-term memory for facts, directions, and rules. They are not very good at following directions though. This is not so much because they forget them but because they don't understand the meaning of the directions, or see the relevancy to themselves. Stuart had trouble with directions that would state: "Go 200 yards and turn right." He didn't know how far right he should turn. He would get so focused on how far "right" was, that he didn't think of the obvious – what object or path he was supposed to see next.

Suggestions for improving short-term memory

- Use checklists so the child can check off each part of the directions; checklists also can remind children to check for errors. Mental lists are also helpful. For example, to teach children what to do for a morning routine, first there would be an actual written checklist. As the child learns to manage this, the parents would teach the child to mentally rehearse the list until it became easily recalled. Then, the child needs to be cued when to use the list. Before the child left the house he or she would go over the mental list and make sure it was all completed.

- Provide written criteria about task requirements so the child can refer back to them and know exactly what is expected. This is useful at home for chores, as well as at school.

- Provide for both oral and written directions and some practice trials before starting a new task.

- Use compensatory tools like hand-held spellers, calculators and word processors to enhance ability to focus on content.

- Use placeholders so children can work on one part at a time. Write down part of the material for them so they fill in the rest. Have them write down part of the process as they go along, or work on parts one at a time.

- To enable the child to remember things for a short time use a "mantra" approach. That is, the child says the thing to be recalled over and over until it is completed. For example, sent upstairs to put on his shoes and shirt, Tom would go to his bedroom saying "shoes and shirt" over and over until he had put them on.

- Some children with AS need help in seeing the obvious. Stuart needs to be taught to look at the next direction and stop to think what clues he has about what to do next.

PRIORITIZING

Gifted children with AD/HD cannot efficiently follow through on tasks that require summarizing or paraphrasing because they can't decide what is relevant and what is not. They cannot pick out the main point. Also, because they are good at seeing the whole big picture, many gifted children with AD/HD do not know how to make that picture smaller, to give just the outlines or main idea. They see it as a movie in their minds, and all the details are important. Difficulties with prioritizing mean that the child has difficulty with choosing among options, deciding which is most important and which is subordinate. This affects decision making as well as school tasks. One of the reasons writing was so hard for Tom was that he could not prioritize ideas into any order. All of his ideas seemed good, and he didn't know where to start. He had no idea how to take the ideas and make an outline. Picking out the most important idea made no sense to him. He could not tell what made any idea the most important.

Gifted children with AS have difficulty with prioritizing because all the parts of the task seem of equal importance to them. They can omit part without any idea that the part is needed to make sense of the material. These children don't always know why they are doing a task so they don't know what the goal is. They can't summarize or prioritize because they can't see what the big picture is. Stuart usually used the idea he liked the best, often the idea that was most related to his own interests, or something he wanted to know more about. As he discussed this idea, he put in material as he thought of it. He had no idea when material did or didn't fit with the topic. It was important to him to go off on tangents because that explained a point he wanted to explore. He didn't recognize that a reader would not be able to follow his thought processes.

Suggestions for improving prioritizing and summarizing

- To teach summarizing skills, have AD/HD students brainstorm all the possible ideas, and then rank order them from most to least important. Discuss what makes an idea more important in a certain context. Have them then pick out the five most important ideas, and the five least important. For students who cannot tell if ideas are important, give a topic with a preset number of ideas about that topic that you, the teacher, have selected. Have the students rank order these in order of importance according to different categories. Then have some challenges where the list of ideas is not initially given, but let the students brainstorm and pick out the most important ideas, and then compare them to the teacher list to see if they are correct.

- Practice developing main ideas by using texts that have bold-faced print for main ideas. Show students how to use the typeface to predict the importance of ideas.

- Use special worksheets that focus only on the ideas of picking out the most commonplace and the most unusual points in a passage. Have challenges that look for irrelevant material in math problems and in stories. Write some silly stories that have irrelevant material and discuss what the material does to the clarity of the storyline.

- Give students with attention deficits the goal to start with. Show why something is relevant. They won't see it otherwise. Often these students need lessons in commonplace thinking.

- Have these students write summaries of small events in their lives and show how to make these succinct. Discuss when to elaborate and when not to do so. Make models of summaries and compare to the whole story.

SENSE OF TIME

Because students with AD/HD have trouble holding events in mind, they have difficulty judging how much time has passed or how much time will be required to do something, so they wait too long. They have more trouble planning for the future. Because they can't hold time in mind, it is hard to think about when class material is due, or the necessity of handing in homework or studying for a test.

Both gifted students with AD/HD and with AS have difficulty with long-term planning. They have trouble with knowing how long it will take to reach a particular goal, and tend to underestimate the time needed. Thinking ahead to what is required, to deadlines and to consequences, is just as difficult for gifted children with AD/HD as for other AD/HD children. Procrastinating is a big problem for these children.

Gifted children with AD/HD have trouble with getting work in on time. They always plan to do better but do not take the actual steps needed to make a change. Because they have trouble with recalling past consequences, they get into trouble for the same problems again and again. Tom's problems in 7th grade were based partly on his poor sense of time. He had no idea when projects were due, how long they would take, or what the long-term consequences were for not doing them. He lived in the moment and planned to improve later.

Gifted children with AS have a different sense of time than most people. While able to tell time accurately, they have trouble sensing duration. Thus these students don't know when time is passing, or how much has passed. When intrigued with a special interest, time has no meaning. Also, when hyperfocusing on a task – for example, reading a comic book or playing a computer game – it is particularly difficult to disengage these students. They have no sense that other people are waiting or that it is time to leave, or change activities. Stuart had trouble disengaging from favorite activities. As described above, he had no sense he had spent so long daydreaming about Monty Python while not doing any work.

Suggestions for improving time management

- Give warnings about how much time is available and when there is just time to finish up. Use time lines to help students figure out how long something will take, first within a class period, later within a week or month. Tie longer time lines to specific dates on a calendar. Help with the time aspects of organization and planning by setting mini-deadlines and have students meet these. This means having a specific goal that has to be completed by that time. Make mini-deadlines daily to weekly.

- Have children practice how to judge how long something will take. Have them predict ahead of time how long it will take to do something, and then see how close they come to judging the total actually used to do a good job.

- Even in upper grades, have children with AD/HD and AS hand the homework directly to the teacher each day. Over time, one day a week can be assigned for the child to remember him- or herself. First, the child would be reminded that this is the day to remember handing in homework. For example, before leaving home, parents could remind the child, and at school the guidance counselor or resource teacher could provide an additional reminder. Subsequently, the reminder would be faded out, and additional days added for independent recall.

- Send notes home to parents about deadlines and missing schoolwork. Parents do want to know and can help the child better manage work completion, handing in work, and working efficiently on longer-term projects if they do know what is due or missing.

USING RULES TO GOVERN BEHAVIOR

Gifted children with AD/HD may know the rules, but because of poorer capacity to think about several aspects at once, it is more difficult to apply rules in the moment. These gifted children approximate rules. They think almost is good enough. They don't see what the fuss is when adults want more compliance. Impulsivity is another aspect of difficulty in adhering to rules. Thus, gifted children with AD/HD need to learn to think before they act. One of the reasons Tom had trouble with work completion was his noncompliance with the exact requirements for projects. He had so much trouble doing the work that he never got all the parts done. He also felt that some of the parts really didn't matter, so he didn't do them. One book report required several questions to be answered about each chapter, a list of idioms used in the book, and a book cover. Tom never did all the questions nor did he do the list of idioms. Then he was surprised when his grade was barely passing.

Gifted children with AS tend to be very rule-conscious, but have trouble seeing nuances and exceptions to rules. They have more difficulty understanding what some rules mean: that is, they miss the basic assumptions. Also, when needing to pursue their own goals, rules imposed by others have less importance.

Suggestions for improving rule adherence

- Consequences need to follow soon after a problem occurs. The best consequences are those that teach children with AD/HD to think the next time before acting. Thus, practicing how to do the tasks or conform to the rule can be effective. This sort of positive practice has the child do the action the correct way five times in succession.

Then, the child and adult make conforming to the rule a particular goal that will be targeted that week. When the rule is violated again, additional practice is required.

- Gifted children with AD/HD may need help in understanding why they have to do some things in a set order or certain way. While some things can have alternate ways to reach the same goal or answer, others do not. Differentiating which tasks need conformity and which allow multiple approaches is important in teaching rule adherence, as gifted children with AD/HD have disdain for rules they think are arbitrary. It can be helpful to these students if they have to derive satisfactory rules for some tasks. Discussing the idea of custom and tradition can help with understanding and acceptance. Also, knowing the derivation of certain rules helps students recall them; for example, why we use the "i" before "e" rule in English spelling, and where the exceptions originate.

- Gifted children with AS need consequences to be specific to the act so that they learn why there is a consequence for what they did. Because these children have trouble with "if…then" reasoning, it can be helpful to portray consequences as sequential: "First this happens, then this."

- Gifted children with AD/HD need to learn when they can approximate the rules, and when they need to comply exactly. Thus, on a first draft, any kind of effort to produce ideas is acceptable, but a final draft needs all the rules for format, mechanics, and so on followed. Playing at home for fun allows improvisation on a musical instrument but playing in the orchestra does not. Children with AS, on the other hand, need to learn that there are times when rules can be broken. In essence, they need rules about when they can break rules.

Internalization of speech

Internalization of speech includes planning and goal setting, self-direction and instruction, course correction and problem solving, and generalizing from one specific to a whole class of items.

Gifted children learn to internalize speech gradually from preschool years to about age eight (Daugherty, White, and Manning 1994). First children spoke aloud, gradually shifting to whispers, and then to internal speech. Even at age eight, however, many gifted children were still less well developed in use of internalized speech, and were more like age peers. On the other hand, young children with AD/HD tended to lag behind age peers in learning to use self-talk, and in learning to internalize this speech to give themselves directions and instructions (Barkley 1995, 1998).

Gifted children with AD/HD are much less able to talk to themselves to plan an approach to a difficult task, or to try a different strategy if the first fails. In essence, the person using internalized speech mentally rehearses plans, strategies, and formulation of rules. Gifted children with AD/HD are less able to use internalized speech and so have more difficulty with this type of planning.

Gifted children with AS have trouble with internalized speech because they don't know *what* to say to themselves. They don't know the words to use that would let them do the task. They also can't change plans or try another strategy because they don't have any alternatives. However, children with AS do use internalized speech for well-learned tasks, and can be taught to use it as part of using scripts.

PLANNING AND GOAL SETTING

Gifted children with AD/HD have trouble planning ahead and setting appropriate goals because they are more focused on the short term. When they do set longer-term goals it is difficult for them to think about the steps they need to take to reach the goal.

Gifted children with AD/HD often assume things that others would not: for example, that the book they need will be at the library waiting for them when they choose to go get it. This does not mean they have called and asked that the book be reserved for them; rather, they never think someone else might take it out. Thus, they wait until the last moment to get the book and are surprised that it is checked out. Of course the book report then isn't done, and the child feels it is not his or her fault; after all, the book wasn't there. This is very typical of the poor planning ability and difficulties with making rules for themselves that are common with gifted children with AD/HD.

Difficulties with goal setting and planning have academic consequences. These difficulties mean that the gifted child with AD/HD often does not complete or hand in homework, or finish long-term projects on time. Parts of assignments are forgotten. Also, students may only understand part of the material because they have missed the rest so learning may suffer. Over the long term, gifted students with AD/HD can suffer underachievement and failure.

Gifted children with AS have particular difficulty with planning and problem solving because they have no idea what the goal should be. Therefore they don't know what to do. They also do not know how to break the goal down into steps they can take. If someone else breaks down the plan into smaller steps, the steps may still be too big. For example, a book report would include as a first step going to the library to get a book. Everyone assumes children know how to do this: ask a parent to take you to the library. Once there, select an appropriate book. The child with AS doesn't think to ask a parent to go to the library. If they are taken there they don't know how to select an appropriate book. The first step for the AS child needs to be a lot smaller: make a plan for asking a parent to help you get a book. Because children with AS need such tiny steps they don't know how to use language to help themselves solve problems. They can't say to themselves, "Well, I don't know how to get a book. What can I do about that?" On the other hand, once they have mastered the process of what to do, they will form an internal rule about it. The next time they will immediately ask a parent to take them to the library.

Gifted children with AS have trouble with planning and goal setting for every new task. They also have difficulty with tasks that are slightly different from ones they know well. They find it hard to apply the idea of planning or setting a goal when the situation is in any way open-ended. This is because they can't originate plans and goals. What they do well is to memorize plans. Thus, scripts of what to do are helpful. Given a script, a child with AS can then use self-talk to remind him or herself what to do and how to do it.

Suggestions to improve planning and goal setting

- When teaching goal setting to gifted children with AD/HD, use short tasks with specific goals to be described by the student. Have students set goals for themselves about what amount of work they can do and in what time span. Have them use time lines and other visual structures to help them see how a linear plan can be laid out.

- Practice brainstorming what obstacles can occur and how to overcome the most likely ones. Use sequential plans for more logical, linear learners. "First this, then this, then last." For spatial learners use more visual plans – all the parts drawn out, or made into pictures, and then arranged in an order they could be done. While some of these practices will also work with gifted children with AS, they may need the goal spelled out for them, and the steps broken down into smaller pieces. Then, contracting how much can be done will be more successful.

- Use activities that require students to think ahead. For example, they might try to use their own eye movements to mentally trace out what a dot-to-dot picture might be like. Then they could use their finger, and finally draw it. Use of mazes, tangrams, Lego sets, and other building toys can teach visual planning. Use of Scrabble grids, acrostics, and tongue twisters can teach auditory planning.

- For students who have trouble with goal setting and making a plan, make the steps smaller. Use scripts that describe every step. As the child learns sequences of small steps, combine them into bigger steps. Have a plan for what to do when they don't know what to do. Plan an activity around the child's main interest. Set a goal with children about what they will do, and have them try to set small steps to the accomplishment of the goal.

SELF-DIRECTION AND INSTRUCTION

As most children do tasks, they give themselves verbal directions. These directions are audible in very young children but become more internalized as the child matures.

Gifted children with AD/HD have trouble internalizing this private speech. Either they don't use it at all, or they vocalize aloud long after peers have turned to internalized speech. Ned still studied by repeating material aloud to himself even when he was in college. He had found this an effective way to learn. He also talked aloud to himself as he did tasks, giving himself directions and instructions. When he could not do this, he had more trouble focusing. Bill, at age 12, was asked how he read directions and guided his performance as he went along on a particular task of crossing out "3"s on a grid of paper. Bill said he just looked at the paper. When specifically asked, he said he never talked to himself, nor was he aware of a "mental voice." Just looking at the paper was inefficient: he missed many of the "3"s, and crossed out other numbers.

Gifted children with AS are likely to verbalize aloud as a means of reminding themselves what to do. Like the AD/HD children, they act like much younger children in vocalizing aloud what they are doing. Fred talked out loud as he did tasks at school. He was oblivious to his effect on the other children who were distracted by his loud voice.

The consequences of poor self-direction and instruction are not doing what is expected, not following directions, forgetting part, or becoming mired in a distraction or detail. Children who have difficulty with self-monitoring and self-direction don't see how fast or slow they ought to go, what strategies they ought to use, or what to do if they encounter obstacles. Children who talk aloud to themselves are also seen as a problem in class. While they may be talking aloud as a way of organizing their own performance, they are distracting others.

Suggestions for improving self-direction and instruction

- Some gifted children with AD/HD or AS have trouble knowing what the directions mean, so they don't know what to do. That is, while they can read the words and know their meaning, the idea behind the directions is elusive. Thus, they need models of how to do an example with the directions. They also need to be checked partway through the task that they are still following the directions.

- After students learn to self-direct their actions using talk-aloud techniques, these can be faded to whispers, and finally internal speech.

COURSE CORRECTION AND PROBLEM SOLVING

Gifted children with AD/HD have trouble with correcting mistakes. They often don't notice the errors, and make no plans to go back and check work. These children also have difficulty with problem solving because they don't talk to themselves about alternative plans. They choose the first option they think of. The consequences of difficulties with course correction and problem solving are uneven results. Gifted children with AD/HD do exceptionally well one day, and much less well on another day, even in the same subject. By forgetting to check their work, they miss careless errors and that decreases test grades. They may make wrong assumptions because they don't ask if the answer makes sense given the questions; they just do what they first assume and don't think about it again. In adolescence, some of these students write creative and thoughtful papers that are not on the topic assigned. They may be rebelling by writing what they want to write, but many of these students with AD/HD genuinely don't understand what they did wrong.

When Grace reached high school she had difficulty with written assign-ments. She liked to write, but her insights into the material were unusual and she had difficulty backing them up with appropriate quotes. Many of her ideas were not well elaborated so her English teacher had trouble knowing what point Grace was trying to make. It was clear to Grace, and she thought she had made it clear to the teacher. To Grace, her teacher was just being picky.

Gifted children with AS have trouble with course correction because they can't think of alternatives. They are not good at problem solving and are inflexible in using the solutions they know even if these fail over and over. They can't think of anything new to do. Thus, it is difficult to solve problems that are somewhat different from the ones they were taught. Also, while these children are often good at finding errors in mechanics (grammar, punctuation, spelling), they are poor in finding errors in reasoning. They can't ask themselves if something makes sense or not because it is hard for them to know what makes sense to others. Their reasoning makes sense to them. Stuart answered some test questions with his own associations to the material. This led him off on tangents that really did not fit the answer required. Stuart had trouble thinking of another answer. Each time he looked at the questions, he associated to the same tangent, and the same train of thought. Therefore, it must be correct.

Suggestions for improving course correction and problem solving

- Have students assess how they know if an answer makes sense. Work on the underlying assumptions they have made. See how they thought about the plan and execution of the task and where they went off on tangents. Work on the idea of what makes something make sense. This is easy to do in math, but can be done in other areas with silly stories or wrong facts. Teach children how to make up little rules for themselves about knowing if an answer is right or makes sense. Gifted children with AD/HD need to ask themselves if something makes sense in context. Asking if something makes sense is also a good strategy for AD/HD children who miss steps or work carelessly.

- It can be helpful to gifted children with AS to work on commonplace ideas. When their reasoning doesn't make sense, discuss what they thought was being asked and see how they reasoned out their response. Then, work with them on what the question meant. A list of key words for school questions and their meanings is helpful. Games that require the student to guess the most popular response or the most common meaning can also help children with AS make sense of school questions.

- Make mistakes on purpose. Ask children with AD/HD to find them and correct them. Challenge them with mistakes in spelling, math facts, grammar, and wrong answers in knowledge areas.

- In proofreading work on tests and before handing in papers and projects, have students proofread by using their fingers as guides on each word and symbol. Don't depend on eyes alone to see errors. Read the text aloud and see if grammar makes sense.

- When a gifted child shows a rigid and inflexible thinking style, give him or her an alternate strategy to try. If it works, have him or her tell why it works. If the child is afraid to try a new strategy, doesn't know how to do so, and so refuses, have an adult try it with the child and see why it worked. See if the child can brainstorm another idea to try. Have the child learn several different types of strategies to use on different types of work.

GENERALIZING FROM ONE SPECIFIC TO A WHOLE CLASS OF ITEMS

Gifted children with AD/HD have difficulty generalizing from one specific instance to the whole class of items. They tend to focus on the moment and don't think of the implications. They don't plan or organize work, but go with what seems most obvious. This means they have trouble learning to generalize. They also then have trouble with thinking of the bigger rule or class, but attend more to the specific instance. Though many gifted children with AD/HD are adept at finding the underlying rule and then using it to solve other types of problems, some gifted children with AD/HD are more stimulus-bound and need to learn each separate problem as if it were entirely new. Dave could never apply what he had previously learned in math problems. Each time, he had to relearn the material and apply the new step. Thus, when he learned to multiply and divide fractions, he did not see how that applied to anything. He could do these operations on paper and pencil problems but could not apply them to word problems. Later, in pre-algebra, he acted as if he had never seen fractions before and had trouble applying the rules he'd previously learned.

Gifted children with AS have particular trouble generalizing from one specific to a whole class because they don't see how things are related to each other very well. On the other hand, they can also overgeneralize because they don't see how some things are different. George ate some eggs and then was sick. He was convinced he got sick because of the eggs, and thereafter refused to eat eggs. In fact, he would avoid eggs in packaged ingredients as well. George had overgeneralized since there was no evidence at all that his illness had anything to do with the eggs.

Gifted children with AS will overuse the same solution for many different types of problems because they don't know what else to do, and because they don't notice that there are differences among the problems. They hone in on the one feature that is the same. Stuart had trouble learning to generalize when to use certain greetings. Thus, he had been instructed to say, "Thank you," "Excuse me," or "I'm sorry". At first, he only said these with cueing. Later, he learned to use these expressions spontaneously but it was not always appropriate when he said them. Once he even apologized to the door after banging into it!

The consequences of deficits in generalizing from a specific instance are difficulty with cause and effect thinking, trouble devising strategies that will work for a whole class of problems, and trouble thinking of alternatives if the first does not work.

Suggestions for improving generalization

- Have gifted children with AD/HD and AS work on noticing similarities and differences in work. What makes something the same or different? How many points of similarity are needed to say two things are similar, and how many differences to say they are different?

- Use sorting chips to help children learn to think in new categories: all the red sharp tools, curvy handles, use for cooking, etc. Pick out several items and see if the child can guess the category and vice versa. Sort faces cut from magazines and newspapers into feelings and expressions that are similar. Discuss what makes them similar. What makes them all look sad?

- Work on generalizing given several pieces of information. For example, make up stories that have several facts that can be made into a general statement. Model how to determine what the generality is.

- Work on logic problems and the rules for deducing a generality. Work on generalizing language through making general statements about the meaning of old sayings and proverbs. What does it mean when we say, "A watched pot never boils?" Is it true?

- See if, given a number of statements that are related, these gifted children can find the relationship. See if they can determine a common rule they can use to cover several similar examples of work. For example, can they devise the rule for silent "e," or to recall the nine times table. Are there rules that can be devised for behavior? When should people use quiet voices, for example?

- Children with AS who overgeneralize need to work on when not to use the rule. Thus, once a rule is learned and is part of the child's repertoire – such as saying, "Thank you" – a list of times when one would not do so is also needed.

Deficits in arousal, activation and effort

Deficits in arousal, activation, and effort include difficulty being aroused and activated, sustaining effort on tasks, working quickly, and performing consistently
good-quality work.

DIFFICULTY BEING AROUSED AND ACTIVATED

Gifted children with AD/HD have a difficult time starting tasks, maintaining attention, and completing tasks. Procrastination, slow work speed, and loss of energy
partway through a task are typical. Distractibility is another aspect. Children who
are easily distractible have trouble with sustaining activation and effort. To them
each part of the task seems separate – what they do in between distractions. Tom
often put off his homework and projects. He had trouble getting started on them,
and when he could not feel any enthusiasm for doing them, he would tell himself
he would do them later. What would finally activate Tom to work was an impending deadline, but often he left work so late that he could not meet that deadline,
and so he did not finish. Rather than hand in partly completed work, he pretended he had forgotten to do it.

   Gifted children with AS also have deficits in arousal. Their deficits arise from the
slower processing speed and difficulty making sense of the whole. Thus, they
have trouble getting started. They also have trouble doing tasks that are not
intrinsically interesting. The stimulation of being very interested is needed to
arouse their attention. Without it, it is hard for them to focus. Finally, they are
easily distracted by internal thoughts and associations related to their own
interests, as often happened for Stuart as he thought of his own preoccupations
and interests instead of doing tasks.

   The consequences of low arousal and difficulty with procrastination are that
things don't get done. School work is inconsistently performed, and work often
takes up all of the child's time. This is because the long period of procrastination
takes away from doing other things. Also, these children are seen as lazy. Because
work isn't completed, they miss out on treats and rewards. They also may miss
learning essential skills because they didn't do the necessary work.

Suggestions for improving low arousal

- Before starting tasks that involve focused attention, many children
  with AD/HD or AS need physical activity. Engaging in a rhythmic
  physical activity such as running, aerobics or warm-up stretches can
  improve concentration by increasing arousal.

- Try to make the work as stimulating as possible. Children who are slow to arouse need the stimulation of interest and enthusiasm to energize them.

- Plan for the time needed to become aroused. For example, if the child is difficult to rouse in the morning, plan enough time that arousal can be slow. It also helps to have a set routine to follow to get started in the morning.

- Following a routine to get involved in tasks also can be helpful. For example, doing tasks in a certain place and using the same materials can set the mood to work. To get started it can be helpful for some children to do a few easy problems. For others it is better to start with the most novel task. For people who have trouble starting, it can be useful to break the work down into tiny parts and to do each part in a short time period.

- If doing a task seems overwhelming, have the child set out to do a small part. When this is completed either go on to another small part, or change to do another type of task. Thus, in learning French vocabulary, practice half the list, then do something else, then try that half again and add another quarter of the list, and so on until the list is learned. If doing a chore seems overwhelming, have the child do half of two chores. Someone else can complete the other halves. The goal is to teach how to break through procrastination.

- Teach children to praise themselves for completing tasks. Over time, self-praise, as well as moderate praise from others, does provide motivation.

SUSTAINING EFFORT ON TASKS

Gifted children with AD/HD have trouble sustaining effort. They daydream and forget what they are doing. Because they have trouble getting going, they miss or forget directions, and may miss part of the task. It is hard to get them motivated to do nonpreferred tasks. Gifted children with AD/HD work less consistently than other children. Some, especially those with Inattentive Type AD/HD, can be exceptionally slow.

Juggling all the parts of tasks at once is difficult. Thus, gifted children with AD/HD can think of content but not handwriting or spelling. This makes sustaining effort more difficult since they have to work much harder to do all the aspects of a task that others can do automatically. By middle school they have immense difficulty completing work within the allotted time. If they are in advanced classes, the workload can seem overwhelming, yet they need the stimulation of the advanced work to perform at all. Conversely, it is much harder for them to arouse their attention and effort to perform tasks they already know. Unlike other children with AD/HD, gifted children with AD/HD have more difficulty doing familiar, well-learned tasks. Tom had trouble focusing on tasks that he thought were boring or repetitious, especially if he already knew how to do them. In the lower grades he rarely did any of the assigned homework because it consisted of practice math examples and writing spelling words five times each. Tom already knew this work and felt it was a waste of time to do it, so he didn't. Later in middle school, he still did not do homework he considered a waste of time, like book reports and grammar exercises, but he didn't know all the work anymore. Consequently his test grades dropped, and he was on the verge of failing.

Gifted children with AS have difficulty sustaining effort on tasks because they need the stimulation of preferred tasks to keep their focus. Without such interest, they cannot sustain attention over time. Gifted children with AS also show difficulty completing tasks that require much organization, especially tasks that require organization of written work. Unlike gifted children with AD/HD, gifted children with AS often have mastered rote tasks exceptionally well, and do well on basic skills like decoding new words in reading and spelling. They can enjoy showing their mastery by getting perfect papers. When effort is poorly sustained, the consequences are often poor work completion and poor grades, especially in middle and high school. Stuart did not have trouble completing most of his school work, unless it required writing something he had to create, such as a story. He had trouble answering open-ended questions and giving an explanation for something that was not obvious. On these types of tasks, Stuart made little effort because he didn't know how to do the task.

Suggestions for improving work effort

- Give less work in a time period for those gifted children with AD/HD who have trouble sustaining effort. Give just enough work that it can be finished within the time frame with some effort.

- Gifted children who have trouble sustaining effort need shortcuts. They also need to have part of the information learned so they can focus on the rest. For example, difficulty sustaining effort affects tasks such as reading longer books. The way around this is to allow the child to read a synopsis of the plot first or to listen to the book on tape, then to read it. Knowing the plot and characters decreases the need to attend to so much.

- Have some tests and projects count for double and decrease the number required. Allow taking long tests in two parts in high school and college.

- Decrease homework to a manageable amount. If the child has a lot of trouble completing even minimal homework, it may be that the child's ability to work in the evening is poor. For example, children on medication often have to do homework when medication has worn off, and they can't focus. These students benefit greatly from daytime study periods. Children with AS often expend all their energy all day conforming to school expectations and then cannot do any more work at home. They need less practice work than other students because they master basic skills quickly. Thus, reducing this kind of work is helpful so they can work slowly on longer-term projects and more complex work.

- Some types of tasks are especially difficult for children with AS, and they need guidelines about how to do the task, and help in starting. Tasks such as writing original stories on an assigned theme, answering open-ended questions, or using inference to figure out a conclusion will be especially difficult.

- Children who procrastinate need a time limit for how long they are allowed to work; then they have to stop. Help them decide what to do within the time period and set a plan for how to get going. Work that wasn't completed will need to be done in the morning prior to school or on the weekend. Some parents of gifted children with AD/HD who procrastinate and don't complete homework have had success with having a Saturday study hall at home during which incomplete tasks are finished even if the teacher will no longer accept them for credit.

SLOW WORK SPEED/POOR QUALITY OF WORK

Both gifted children with AD/HD and those with AS can work quite slowly and need more time on tasks than others. Often they produce much less work than age peers within the same time period.

Some gifted children with AD/HD or AS do not work quickly on tasks but take their time because they want the paper to be perfect. To them, the goal is not to complete the work, but to do so without any mistakes at all.

Ethan was such a perfectionist that he was very slow to finish any tasks. He would not erase, so he started over whenever he made a mistake. Since he made some mistakes on each attempt, he never finished anything. He had the same problem when he practiced the piano. Once he made an error, he started over again. Only when he could play a piece all the way through without an error was he satisfied. He had trouble with the concept that errors while learning were acceptable as opposed to errors while performing. To him, even a first attempt ought to be perfect.

The consequences of a slow work speed are less work completed, and fatigue on tasks that others find easy. These students feel easily overloaded and make many errors as they fatigue. Tasks such as writing require immense effort because they cannot translate thoughts to paper quickly and also their handwriting speed is slower than average. As they progress in school, these students have trouble finishing class assignments, tests, and homework.

Gifted children with AD/HD are variable in the quality and quantity of work they are able to produce. Children can appear not to know something, yet a day later score 100% on a more difficult test. Variability also can be seen in discrepancies among subjects, between homework and test grades, and between grades and standardized tests. This may occur because of the variable effort the student is able to make. It also may reflect interest in one aspect of the curriculum and not another.

Gifted children with AS show variability of effort and quality. These children produce more depending on interest and ability to do the particular task. Thus, on a new type of problem they are less able to work because they cannot intuit what to do in the same way others do.

If the quality and quantity of work are inconsistent, the consequences are that the child and teachers often have no idea how capable the child is. The child does not learn study skills, but relies on trying to be a quick study because it does not seem that studying is effective. It becomes more difficult for these children to learn to monitor progress because they have no sense of how they are doing. What seemed like good effort does not necessarily bring a good result. Some students give up trying at all. Variability in work quality has consequences for high school and college when placement depends on grades and effort. Many schools are reluctant to place gifted students with variable grades in honors classes, yet these students will not do better in more average classes. In fact, they may do worse. Thus, if Tom was removed from honors English and placed in the average class, he would not produce higher grades. His grades would likely be the same, and he'd be more bored.

Suggestions for improving slow work speed or poor quality of work

- Decrease the amount of work to be done and allow more time for its completion.

- Decrease the amount of writing the student has to do by giving papers that require more circling, underlining, and single words than writing out material. For those tasks that require longer explanations, try using a scribe or an oral report. Allow use of a computer in class.

- Prioritize work so that the most important is done first. Because some of these children spend all night doing school work even in elementary years, limit the amount of homework required and allow parents to act as scribes. Parents will need to set time limits so they have the child complete homework at a reasonable time in order to have some recreation time.

- For young children who do not complete work in class, sending it home for completion is often counterproductive. For the slow worker it is better to decrease the amount of work. If this is not enough, the child may need further intervention: for example, resource help.

- It is important to assess if part of the problem is a need for perfection. If perfection is the child's goal, then limiting the amount of practice work, setting time limits, and focusing on quality of ideas, not handwriting, is important. For those who need to write perfectly, use a computer so mistakes are easily fixed.

- Allow some of the lowest grades for each student in the class to be dropped. Allow extra credit work to improve grades. Allow test retakes for all students.

- For younger children who do poorly on a paper, have them tell you the answers orally and see if they know them. They may have lost attention. Allow these students to redo some tasks, or do alternate tasks to show what they know.

- Teach study skills specifically to students with AD/HD and AS. Help students practice skills enough so they become automatic, as they do in music or sports.

- Keep students who are bright, but doing less well, in honors courses. Supplement their work with extra help, tutoring, and alternate projects. They need the mental stimulation while they learn executive function skills.

Holistic / sequential performance

Difficulties with holistic and/or sequential performance were covered in the section on learning styles. Gifted children with weaknesses in both areas have difficulty with written language, prediction of events, and with demand performance.

Barkley (1997) postulated that an important executive function is the ability to break information apart and then to recombine it into new wholes (reconstitution). This analysis and synthesis allows for problem solving, imagination, and creativity. When the child with AD/HD cannot wait, but responds impulsively, there is less chance that this analysis and synthesis will happen.

DIFFICULTY WITH ORGANIZING WRITTEN WORK

Gifted children with AD/HD have difficulty breaking bigger tasks down into smaller ones and also going step by step to build to a conclusion. This means they have particular difficulty with written expression. Many cannot write more than a sentence or two. Difficulties with elaboration, organization, and development of a theme are issues. Tom had trouble with written expression because he could not get his ideas down on paper. He had trouble translating from the picture in his mind to the words on a page. He also had trouble organizing content so it would have any sequence. What was clear in his mind was disorganized on a page. Tom was much better at dictating his work because he could verbalize the sequence more easily.

Children with AS have trouble with writing because of both organizational deficits and difficulties understanding how to develop ideas into a whole. Thus, these students can have trouble writing even a sentence if they have to decide what to write. They can write sentences if they have exact directions. Also, they can write long pieces that are creative and elaborated, but they don't follow a plot or theme so the reader never quite gets the point. Stuart would write if he had to do so, but much of what he wrote was taken from other things he had read or heard. He would not see that his work was not original because he had put the dialogue and characters into a new setting.

The consequences of poor writing ability occur when much of school work in higher grades depends on adequate written expression of ideas and concepts. The student is less able to produce quality work, and show what is known. Thus it can be difficult for teachers to evaluate what a student knows.

Suggestions to improve writing skills

- Have younger students, and those with writing problems, dictate pieces into a tape recorder or to a scribe. Then have an adult transcribe some of these pieces into book form and have the student illustrate them or select pictures to illustrate them. Try to write as many pieces as possible so the child has practice in generating content. For students who cannot think of what to write, brainstorming techniques or use of picture cues will be helpful. Use of graphic organizers can help to organize material as described in the section on learning styles.

- Taking a central idea, start to have students dictate a sentence about it. Add another sentence. Add more elaboration to the sentences by adding adjectives and other modifiers. Use models for students who do not know how to generate material.

- As students gain facility in writing, separating handwriting from generation of content will continue to be important. Thus, use of a computer word processor, scribe, or voice-recognition programs will be necessary. Have the students work on writing daily using a variety of modalities such as journals, stories, essays, reports, poetry, opinion pieces, arguments they have to defend, and criticism of an idea. Final drafts will be made of some pieces by completing them and attending to format and mechanics. Reading sentences aloud to see where commas and periods should be placed is often helpful.

- Some students will need scripts that teach them exactly what should go into a piece of writing, and they need to follow the script to produce a written piece.

- Use of a writer's workshop where students read work aloud to others, produce their own books, and put on readings of works completed also improves writing.

PREDICTION

Gifted children with AD/HD have difficulty making the connection between now and the future. Because of this they have trouble understanding how consequences result from actions. Thus, they have trouble saying to themselves, "If I do this, then…will happen." Because they live more in the moment, consequences are not foreseen. Thus, these gifted students are often surprised by the outcome. It can seem incredible to parents and teachers that a gifted student can't predict that he or she will fail if work isn't completed, but often he or she can't. Failure is always a surprise. Somehow the student never thought that there wouldn't be enough time to make up work or get better grades. They also seem unaware of how many missed assignments or poor grades there were.

Problems with prediction occur when the gifted child with AD/HD tries to deal with certain types of work that depend on making inferences and predicting what an author meant, or how a trend will develop. It can be hard to figure out how to pick out the right answer from all the material. Some gifted students with AD/HD also have trouble with prediction in social as well as in academic contexts. Though they are better than age peers at predicting in hypothetical situations, in real life they cannot juggle all the details, nor easily interpret a complex situation, as it is happening, in order to say and do the best thing.

Gifted children with AS have difficulty with prediction because they don't see how things relate to each other. Not only do they have deficits in executive functions, but problems with central coherence also make it difficult to think of what a possible future might be. Consequently, they can't imagine what might be an outcome of a situation they have not experienced. Young children who do not have AS can predict consequences because they have some ability to think ahead and see they will displease adults; children with AS do not have this concept.

Older children with AS, especially with high verbal skills, learn how to make predictions of hypothetical situations but have difficulty doing so in real life. Because they don't see the relevancy of things to themselves, or because they don't see all the parts, they make false assumptions and base predictions on only part of the information. The complexity involved in integrating all the aspects of a situation, and the fast reaction time required in real life, defeats them.

Difficulty with prediction can precipitate emotional crises. Children with AS are locked into the moment, cannot foresee any other possibility or outcome, and can only deal with how they feel right now. Olivia, age ten, described in Chapter 3, loved to hold and pet my dog. However, she tended to hold the dog too tightly and disregarded warnings not to do so. Consequently, the dog was removed from the room and Olivia was told she wouldn't be allowed to pet the dog the following week. She raged and screamed for several hours. Olivia couldn't see what she had done wrong. A list of rules for being with the dog, and consequences for disregarding the rules, was drawn up, and after her week's deprivation of the dog's presence, Olivia was allowed once again to pet her. Olivia now behaved more appropriately. Olivia's difficulty was that she could not predict the consequences of her behavior. She also did not see how she was hurting the dog. Thus, she was surprised and angered by the outcome. While deprivation of the dog taught her to behave with the dog at the Gifted Resource Center of New England, she was not able to generalize to other similar situations.

The consequence of difficulty with prediction is that these gifted students don't know how to judge their own behavior. In academics, they don't know when they have done enough, or whether they have satisfied criteria. They tend to use the first answer they think of rather than being able to predict the best answer. In terms of behavior, they tend to think their intention is what counts because they cannot predict what others will think or feel about what they are doing. Then, they are surprised by the outcome.

Suggestions for improving prediction

- Play games of strategy and luck with students and have them try to predict what will happen. Discuss the laws of probability, and how people make judgments based on knowing the odds or having an idea about the likelihood something will occur.

- Work on making predictions of answers through estimating. In math, the best way to estimate is to round off the number to the nearest big number and then perform the operations. Teach math tricks for estimating.

- To figure out the best-fit answer give several choices ranging from wildly wrong to possibly right and have students give reasons why they choose an answer. Work on what the reason behind the question was since most students with AD/HD and AS have no idea that there is a reason questions are asked. Help students figure out what is the best thing to focus on in order to answer in the most succinct and appropriate way.

- Help the student to understand how to use contextual clues to make predictions. In a story, list the clues that lead to certain acts and then ask for a prediction based on these explicit clues. As students become more adept at making these predictions, have them find their own clues.

- Understand that some of the emotional crises that occur with gifted children with AS are due to their lack of ability to predict consequences, see the big picture, and know what they are supposed to do. To them their intent is what counts the most. To help them to understand better, parents and teachers need to use a social story (see Chapter 7) to describe what happened. They need to set up a list of rules about appropriate behavior, and they need to make explicit exactly what the consequence will be and why. This will help gifted children with AS to get the connection between their actions and the consequences. As they learn the rules, and the explicit consequences, work on predicting other consequences that are less obvious, as well as on predicting consequences for similar but slightly different situations.

DIFFICULTY WITH DEMAND PERFORMANCE

Gifted children with AD/HD have difficulty with retrieval of material on the spot. They cannot easily organize material that they are learning so they can find it again. They also are slow to think of answers, and retrieve them just as the material moves along to the next idea. Children with AD/HD do not know how to get going, find the material they have learned, and produce it efficiently. Another aspect of this is demand performance. Rapidly extracting material from the mind is difficult for children with AD/HD when a specific response is required. On the other hand, when they are in charge, words often flow and they can present material amusingly and with good detail. Thus, despite some trouble with demand performance, many gifted children with AD/HD actually do better giving verbal answers and making speeches. While Grace had difficulty getting her work in on time, she was a champion talker. Yet, if asked to explain an answer on the spot, she had trouble thinking of anything to say. Engaged in a conversation about the same topic, information would flow out of her. Too bad her teachers never heard her just talking.

Gifted children with AS have difficulty with demand performance because they have trouble figuring out what is wanted. If questions and their answers are clear, then these children answer readily. They do well in demand performance for tasks they know by rote, but poorly when they have to devise the content, especially for open-ended questions. Children with AS can be clever at covering up their problems by using memorized dialogue, stories, and answers as responses. Their extensive recall of verbal material allows for excellent demand performance at times. However, the material produced can be inappropriate when it does not really fit the intent of the question.

Suggestions for improving demand performance

- Help gifted children with AD/HD deal with retrieval problems by coaching them in the use of categories, associating, guessing, and thinking of all they know about the topic. On tests use material that embeds the answer in the question like multiple choice or word banks.

- Allow time to organize thoughts. Let the student start with an example, and explain the example. Teach students to think of the answer and mentally rehearse it before they start to answer.

- For those students who have trouble with demand performance because they don't know what to say, teach how to form an opinion; for example, thinking of one answer, and then an opposite point of view.

- Teach how to make choices by exploring pros and cons, or using a chance-related technique like a roll of dice or "eeney meeney miney moe." Whatever is picked is then weighed for pros and cons.

Conclusion

Gifted children with AD/HD and AS have both strengths and weaknesses. This chapter has described some of the weaknesses in each learning style and in executive function skills. It is equally important to attend to the cognitive strengths of these children. Because of their strong abstract reasoning ability, they need a differentiated educational program that will allow them to progress in areas of strength while providing support for weaknesses through accommodations and remediations. Gifted students with AD/HD or AS should participate in gifted programs, along with other gifted students. They will need some accommodations, but can do the work in many areas. Accelerated learning, enrichment programs, on-line learning through Johns Hopkins or Stanford's CTY programs, mentors, and special projects also are options.

I think, therefore I am.

René Descartes
Discourse on the Method, Part IV

Chapter 5

Finding Flow: The Wellspring of Creative Endeavor

Stephen

Stephen, age nine, was very interested in science and math. He especially liked making things from blueprints and schematics he developed himself. Things with patterns were easy for him to learn. What is more, he was quite adept at finding the patterns within the material himself, then instantly recalling all of it once he had recalled the patterns. Stephen also loved the sea, and had acquired a vast store of knowledge about sea animals, ocean currents, sailing vessels, whale migration routes, and life in the extreme depths of the deepest ocean trenches.

In 5th grade, Stephen entered the school science fair with a project that grew from his love of the sea combined with his love of numbers. Stephen had learned about the pattern used by the chambered nautilus in building successive parts of its shell. Stephen's project, called "Mathematics of the Chambered Nautilus," studied how this sea animal used the Fibonacci number pattern. Each turn of the spiral made by the animal is a factor of 1.618 from the center. This logarithmic spiral is also found in other aspects of nature. Stephen included information on cows, bees, and rabbits illustrating famous Fibonacci problems. He also described how many plants use Fibonacci sequences in leaf distribution, seed-head growth, and flower petal arrangement to allow for maximum packing of many elements into a smaller space. Stephen's project won first place at his school science fair.

Sarah

Sarah, age nine, loved music. She composed songs in the car as she was driven to school, and she liked to sing them to her parents. Sarah also loved to play the piano. When she was three and four she used to sit for over an hour, and music would pour forth from her. As she became older, and started more formal lessons, music flowed in a different way, much less spontaneously. She still clearly heard the music in her mind, and knew how the music should sound as she played it, but she could not always translate from her mind to the keys. She mourned the loss of her earlier effortless playing. Nevertheless she was determined to play well and continued to compose. Over time, her music assumed a depth and richness that was more satisfying.

Both Stephen and Sarah are especially creative gifted children. Stephen enjoys the process of finding unusual patterns, but he also enjoys showing his ideas to others via his projects. Sarah is more interested in the flow of her music from her mind through her hands. Her joy is in playing. The end product matters but less than the flow of music. Sarah's compositions are never finished. She constantly changes them and adds new aspects. Sarah's creativity is her improvisation.

Creativity: Both process and product

Gifted children can't help being creative. They play creatively. They add interesting insights to their schoolwork. They also are able to add details to, and further extend, a basic idea. In fact, they seem to live in a creative zone. Much of their lives seems to be taken up with periods of flow (Csikszentmihalyi 1996): that is, a state of focused concentration and energy in which ideas pour out and the person is caught on the novelty and pull to bring the idea to fulfillment. This flow accompanies all creative acts and is felt as highly rewarding by the person; it is that focused joyful state one feels when totally involved in a satisfying activity.

Gifted children are often creative in an area of interest. The excitement of finding out something new, of developing a new idea, or answering a question they have posed encourages them to continue to pursue more involvement, as Stephen did. Learning, and doing, for its own sake is characteristic of gifted children. The lively curiosity of the toddler and the inquiring and penetrating insight of the adolescent or adult are related phenomena.

Both Stephen and Sarah engaged in a creative process, and both ended up with a product. Yet, if asked what was most important, each would emphasize something different. Stephen would emphasize finding and making things, seeing if his ideas work, and wanting to share them with others. Sarah would emphasize the joy from she gets from playing well, from having the music flow well through her, letting her be an instrument upon which it plays as much as the piano. Which aspect of creativity is emphasized depends on the needs of the child and the special skills and talents each has, as well as particular personality traits. It also depends somewhat on the age of the child and on the child's particular interests.

The focus of this chapter

In order to understand the interaction of giftedness and attention deficits in creativity it is useful to explore different aspects of attention deficits and creativity. In this chapter the following topics are explored:

- What is creativity?
- The development of creativity from childhood through adolescence.
- Creativity and attention deficits.
- Cognitive and affective aspects of creativity and how these are affected by attention deficits.
- Suggestions for enhancing creativity.

What is creativity?

People usually think of creativity as originality – coming up with a new idea. Much of creativity research has been about how people come up with original ideas. Are they the result of inspiration or insight? Do they just happen or can original thinking be nurtured? Researchers who think about creativity as originality look at insight and problem finding. Getzels and Csikszentmihalyi (1976) suggested that creativity came from an internal tension the person tried to reduce by finding the problem, defining the problem in a new way, and then solving the problem. The emphasis on problem finding was a significant contribution in how creative people delineate their life's work.

Creativity can be the result of exceptional mental flexibility. Because the creative person is so flexible, he or she is able to consider multiple solutions and alternative perspectives. People who are especially good at this type of thinking tend to be divergent thinkers: they have both many ideas and unusual ideas. So, if one solution does not work, they always have something else in mind. Think of Thomas Edison as he tried out all the possible filaments for his new invention, the electric lightbulb. People who study mental flexibility focus on divergent thinking ability, visualization, and primary process thinking.

Creativity can be the result of other factors though. A creative person might put two different aspects of something together and come up with something different, or see how two things that look very different are actually related in some way. For example, understanding the relationship of bacteria to mitochondria, the energy makers in our cells, is an exciting new concept in genetics.

People who discover new relationships often do so by observation and comparison. Thus, they have a good ability to take apart two things, and see how they might be similar or different. This then allows a reasoning by analogy – seeing a likeness between one thing and another. If a cockle burr attaches by tiny hooks, maybe clothing also could be fastened this way. Voilà! Velcro was developed.

Creativity can arise because of an elaboration on and development of an original idea. This is what artists and musicians do when they improvise. Monet, with his studies of water lilies, experimented with light by improvising on the one theme of the water-lily pond. Elaboration also can result in a whole new work, as for example Aaron Copeland's "Appalachian Spring" which builds on the old Shaker hymn, "Simple Gifts." The focus of people who study reasoning by analogy and elaboration of old ideas is on problem solution, as well as insight.

Torrance (1966) has extensively studied creative production in children through use of the *Torrance Tests of Creative Thinking*. These measure divergent thinking ability by looking at fluency of ideas (how many are generated), flexibility (how many different categories are used), originality of response, and elaboration of details. It is known that fluency (how many different ideas are generated) influences creativity scores. The more ideas that are generated, the more likely it is that some will be original. Divergent thinking ability is measured by the fluency of ideas in children (Runco 1993). However, some researchers (Cropley 2000; Fishkin and Johnson 1998; Runco 1991) also caution that divergent thinking ability is really a measure of creative potential rather than of creativity *per se*. Nevertheless, if only one measure of creativity can be given, the literature suggests that it should be divergent thinking ability, especially the *Torrance Tests of Creative Thinking* (Cropley 2000).

The development of creativity

In this section, the development of creativity from early childhood through adolescence will be explored. In each section, examples will include gifted children without attention deficits, gifted children with AD/HD, and gifted children with AS. A discussion of asynchrony and how it affects creativity will be included.

Younger gifted children

Younger gifted children may develop a finished product, but most do not. What then constitutes creativity in these gifted children?

Piirto (1992), based on material she collected from questionnaires and in interviews, reported that young gifted children were exceptionally imaginative, had imaginary playmates, tended to be fantasy prone, and made up imaginative scenarios with toys. Shmukler (1985) described a relationship between imaginative play and divergent thinking in young children, and thought that imaginative play in young gifted children was creative expression. Young children who were more imaginative in play were observed to be more creative in story writing than less imaginative children (Gottlieb 1973).

Young gifted children also play with ideas. As was described in Chapter 4, even very young gifted children show evidence of creative questioning, hypothesis making, and noticing patterns and rules. Some of these ideas can be developed into thought experiments by quite young children. For example, when Danny was age four years and one month, he lived in an older house with pine board floors that had slanted with the settling of the house. One day he said to his mother, "This is called the inspiration about a golf ball sliding down the hill. It's the curve that's making the golf ball slide down the hill. In the hallway, one side is bent down to here, and one side is bent down to here." (He gestured accordingly with his right and left hand.) "The middle is up. That means the house is curving with the Earth. That is why my golf ball rolls down the side."

The use of imagination, curiosity, and exploration of ideas and materials are play for gifted children. This kind of play is intensely involving. In young gifted children, under the age of nine or so, creativity is primarily play. Children engage in creative endeavors because they are fun to do. Like Sarah, described at the start of this chapter, Brandon Mausler – a seven-year-old boy with an autism spectrum disorder, and one of the Temple Grandin Award Nominees for 2001 – has loved playing music all his life. He composed 30 original pieces within one year (Future Horizons 2002). Sam, age five, a very gifted boy with AD/HD, loved playing with atoms. Actually, he had a set of colored balls representing atoms that he used to form different types of molecules. His idea was to see if he could reproduce particular molecules in model form and if he then could invent molecules and predict what they would do. Sam spent hours playing with these models. When he finished one model, he would go onto another. What was important to Sam was the fun he had in making his discoveries. Indeed, the fun aspect of creativity is sometimes lost in all the studies of what makes for creative thinking in older children and adults.

Young gifted children also show their creativity in a variety of imaginative activities. These gifted children play with imaginary companions, do role playing, imagine scenarios, and play out dramatic scenes from books, television, and their own stories. On the whole, the higher the IQ, the more likely a gifted child is to use fantasy and dramatic play themes, and to prefer interacting with other gifted children rather than doing something solitary (Wright 1990). Even young gifted children with AD/HD or AS can be quite imaginative in staging dramatic scenes for classmates to act out, with the classmates being very willing participants. Like young gifted children without attention deficits, those with AD/HD or AS may lead fantasy adventures that are attractive to other children who are willing to participate in whatever roles they are assigned. This ability to lead play by having ideas and directing others only lasts so long though. By the end of 3rd grade most children start to learn games and sports. Instead of being willing participants in recess games of dramatic play, they prefer other activities governed by rules, and start to consider fantasy play rather babyish. At home, however, many will still enact fantasy adventures, especially Harry Potter and Star Wars.

Fantasy play lasts longer for many gifted children. In fact, it is not uncommon for even young adolescents to still engage in fantasy play with siblings and friends. Some even continue fantasy play into adulthood by joining medieval societies and organizations that stage historical re-enactments. Some join ongoing role-playing games. Some of these gifted young people have AD/HD or AS, but many do not.

Many of the gifted children at the Gifted Resource Center of New England had imaginary companions or impersonated imaginary characters. Some had one ongoing imaginary entity; others changed often. One little boy had an imaginary baseball team and played imaginary games with plays and scores he could describe in great detail. Some children created whole countries, civilizations, or planets, complete with maps of the terrain, knowledge of ecology, the customs, dress, war strategies, and conquests. Some children went on to develop whole languages for the places and to have conversations with imaginary beings from these places.

Other gifted children had elaborate fantasies in which they required participation from their whole family. As was described in Chapter 3, one little girl with AS, Abby, age five, required her family to pretend to be Pilgrims, making them eat out of pretend trenchers, and wanting only foods Pilgrims would have eaten. Justin, a six-year-old boy with AD/HD, and his seven-year-old sister, Allie, dressed in medieval clothes, and had the family pretend they lived in a castle. This involved cooking foods over the fireplace, using candles for light, playing medieval games, and doing medieval crafts. Periodically there were battles to protect the castle from invaders.

It is important to emphasize that it is the play aspect, the fun, the process of making something that is important to the child, not usually the product. Children create for the love of it, not to make something for the reward or for societal approval. Their fun is sustained by their experience of "flow" (Csikszentmihalyi 1996). For young children, play is all about being in flow. Watching young children pretending something is a good example of a flow experience. The concentration, energy, and motivation of the child engaged in the doing of the action produces the feeling of flow.

The fact is most young children simply do not yet value products. Laura, at age six, enjoyed making many paintings at home. Yet, once they were finished, she lost interest in them. Her mother kept them in a portfolio, but Laura would have been content to let them be discarded. It was doing them that was important to her, not the end result. This is the case with many young children when they create something. The project is discarded as soon as the fun goes out of it. Thus, creativity for young gifted children should emphasize how they play, and whether they use complex ideas and are willing to risk trying out things that might not work. The real question is whether the play of the child produces the flow experience, the joy of doing for the fun of it, because this is the key to learning how to work on more complex projects.

Older gifted children

Like Stephen, described at the start of this chapter, many older gifted children start to value the products they make as much as the process of making them. Stephen felt it was fun to discover the Fibonacci sequence, and then see for himself how it worked in nature, in addition to the descriptions he had read.

Older gifted children may focus on an area and spend considerable time mastering it. These gifted children feel a "rage to learn" (Winner 1996). They may study an area of interest in great depth and detail for a prolonged period of time. These particular interests may develop into recognizable products as an extension of the child's development of expertise. While these children are not prodigies, they still may, at an early age, produce an original contribution. For example, Hollingworth's (1942) Child "E" produced an original contribution in his study of the Pentateuch, the first five books of the Bible, at age ten.

Gifted children with a "rage to learn" may actually have many interests that they pursue, studying some in depth, others more superficially. Some ideas are thoroughly researched, others merely perused briefly. Ideas come from many sources: school projects, an area of interest the child has researched, a pattern noted, or an original observation. Stephen's school science fair sparked his interest in marine creatures, and his reading introduced him to the concept of Fibonacci spirals. Some of the Nicholas Greene Scholars, selected by the National Association for Gifted Children (NAGC) each year, show creativity in what they present as part of the selection process. For example, David Appel, a 1998–99 Distinguished Student, wrote about his journey into science. He became interested in aerogel, an ultra low density glasslike substance used to collect interstellar dust. It has at least 800 other uses as well. David learned how to make aerogel, and entered a number of science competitions based on his knowledge, applications, and ingenuity. He won a number of prestigious awards, felt he had learned an immense amount of science, and solidified his desire to become a scientist. David Nolan, another 1998–99 winner, wrote, "My Paper Voice," the story of how he became interested in writing poetry. He described himself: "It was as if I had been blind all my life. Then someone suddenly turned on a light and I could see the colors in all their glory" (NAGC 2001).

Some children are creative in the arts, and start in elementary school to take lessons and engage more seriously in their study. Sarah, for example, at age eight, was already learning advanced piano pieces. At age ten, Kenneth Hall, an exceptionally gifted boy with AS, published his own book. *Asperger Syndrome, the Universe and Everything* (Hall 2001) is a very funny, charming and insightful book into what it is like for Kenneth to have AS.

Kate Kingston, a ten-year-old girl with AS, and a Temple Grandin Award Nominee, has always had a special interest and love for animals. She trains dogs to be therapy dogs. Recently, she invented a "Kwik Release" collar for dogs (Future Horizons 2002).

Among the older gifted children at the Gifted Resource Center of New England, Aaron, a boy with AS, at age 12 was composing original music compositions on the piano and keyboard. Eric, at age nine with AD/HD, developed an original mathematical formula. Jessica, age 11 with AD/HD, developed a study for her science fair to assess the differences between how boys and girls in the 6th grade recalled verbal material. She had also wanted to compare her results to their learning of visual material but her teacher would not allow her to do this complicated a study. Nevertheless, Jessica found that the 6th-graders recalled less than half of the material presented to them. Several children wrote both poetry and novels prolifically. Several drew cartoons. Lonnie's were particularly adept at pointing out the foibles of other people and institutions.

Gifted children play with ideas and materials as if they were toys. These are children who have many different types of interests, and are creative in a number of different areas. Amanda, age ten, a Davidson Young Scholar who liked to think of new house designs and perhaps wanted to be an architect when she grew up, made many blueprints of houses, and from these built models. After building them, she would then modify them as she added new ideas and learned more about what famous architects had done. Her houses were usually works in progress, never really completed. Amanda was also immensely talented in music, playing the violin in the State Youth Orchestra. She loved to sew and had made soft sculpture as well as clothing for herself and her little sister. The year she was eight, she made her Easter dress. Amanda's finished products were just for herself. Aside from some quilts she made for charity, and music recitals, she had little interest in showing others, outside of her family, what she had done. Like many of the other gifted children in this study, the focus was on the fun of the project, not on what could be done with it.

Gifted adolescents

Older gifted children and young adolescents have the ability to amass large amounts of information on a topic, to make associations between what is known and what is not, and to extend knowledge by analogy. These children become experts on a topic and collect information as others collect Pokémon cards. As they get older, knowledge and interests can coalesce into experiments and testable hypotheses. When these children reach middle- and high-school years, they are more apt to want to do something with their knowledge rather than just absorbing a mass of facts. These children have come far enough in intellectual and creative development that they can now use their abilities more broadly.

Children who previously were more content to study an instrument want to be part of an orchestra or form their own band. Many of them have experienced the different pleasure that comes from creating something as a group that is more than could be created individually, such as playing a symphony. Others are more ready to delve deeply into individual research ideas.

By high-school years, many of these students have taken the coursework that will enable them to work more closely with an adult mentor in the field. Caitlin, at age ten, became interested in the development of language in young children. With the help of a mentor from a nearby college, she was able to develop her interest by making and analyzing tapes of small children learning to talk. Later, her interest developed further into how language develops in children with autism, an area she has begun to research in her late teens.

Marguerite Richardson, a high-school student with AS, and a Temple Grandin Award Nominee, used her art to design educational programs used throughout her school. She won her state award for web page design. She developed a holiday card line as a business venture, and her t-shirt design was used as a fundraiser (Future Horizons 2002).

Luke Jackson, a gifted 13-year-old boy with AS, published a book that not only describes AS in adolescence, but also gives helpful hints to teens with AS on topics ranging from sleep, to school to bullying to dating. Luke's book *Freaks, Geeks and Asperger Syndrome* (Jackson 2002) ends with a delightful explanation of common idioms.

Some of the adolescents with AD/HD or AS who have come to the Gifted Resource Center of New England engaged in many creative pursuits. Gareth, with AD/HD, in 7th grade started to turn his knowledge and interest about the Middle Ages into activities. He attended a group that re-enacted scenes from medieval times. He built a forge, and made medieval weapons and even his own chain mail. He also became interested in medieval foods and started to cook meals, using these foods, for his family. Gareth's interest continued through his young adult years; he spent many weekends actively engaged in what was now his hobby. As for his creative development, Gareth became a chef who specialized in desserts, eventually attending a school for pastry chefs. Gareth is a good example of a gifted boy whose creativity was apparent in his original pastry designs, and dessert creations, as well as his costumes for medieval events. Like many other gifted children, Gareth's playing with his interests brought him joy and satisfaction.

Kate, described in Chapter 1, is a gifted girl with AD/HD. In junior high school, she developed a science-fair project that examined attitudes of students in several local high schools towards math and science ability in boys and girls. Despite many obstacles, she was interested enough in this work to continue it through the next year, comparing how girls in co-educational environments versus girls in single-sex environments viewed themselves. Kate obtained significant results suggesting that boys and girls viewed girls as less talented in math and science. Kate later presented her project to the School Board to express her concern about the attitudes she had found expressed by both pupils and teachers about girls' abilities.

Tyler, a very gifted boy with AD/HD, through high school and college wrote clever satirical poems and op-ed pieces for the city newspaper on a variety of topics of current interest, including government politics. His wit and riposte were exquisite.

Seth, a very gifted adolescent with AS, was an excellent programmer, so much so that starting in high school he was employed in the computer department of a major university, developing programs for various departments. He was the only computer consultant to the university who needed working papers.

The problem of asynchrony

Gifted children experience asynchrony when their ability to conceive of a creative idea does not match their ability to express that idea. They also experience asynchrony because they do not yet have the life experience to allow them to fully express what they know. Thus, they may not have developed the critical skills, wide knowledge, or ability to draw conclusions from confusing data when working on a project.

Asynchrony occurs when gifted children do not have the technical skills to translate their feelings into a medium. This may mean they do not have the technical expertise yet, or they lack the way to produce the creative idea within a medium. Thus, Amanda does not yet have the expertise to do the technical building that will allow her to make exact models of the houses of her dreams. She has the raw ideas, can make some constructions from blueprints she has designed, but cannot yet capture what is in her mind. Thus, she tries out some of her ideas in three dimensions, but feels frustrated with what she has built.

Children who compose music – like Sarah, the girl described at the start of this chapter, or Aaron with AS – sometimes report the frustration of not being able to get their ideas into the notes they play. They have a mental version of their music, but somehow cannot yet translate it to the instrument. Some can translate it to the instrument, but haven't the expertise to translate it to written notes.

Children who have the largest gaps between ideas and ability to produce them may also be the most original. The more original the idea, and the less it is an extension of what else the child has already produced, the less well the child may be able to translate it to a project or product, like Amanda who could not yet build a model of her exact dream house. Asynchrony may be one of the reasons that in childhood the most original thinkers produce few of their ideas in any sort of product form, and we don't hear about them until they reach adulthood and can produce what they can conceive.

Freeman (1994) discussed another type of phenomenon which she saw occurring in schools. Gifted children who were high achievers were not usually the most creative thinkers. She thought this was due to a choice the children had to make between achieving or creating. High achievement in school subjects seemed to suppress creative endeavors. In fact, many children, by age nine or ten, are loaded with school work and activities. They have little free time and so have no solitary, unscheduled time in which to follow individual creative pursuits.

Another aspect has to do with media influence. Many gifted children are not original in their ideas because they are so programmed to think in certain ways by what they hear and see on television, from video games, movies, and peers. When a young gifted child first learns to play creatively, and to produce creative dramas or stories to enact, the influence of media can curtail original ideas. Compared to what the media produces, one's own ideas may seem dull and lacking in intensity. This is much more the case than in previous generations. Even when children used to act out the plots of books they had read, they were able to imagine their own version. Today, all the action is already programmed, and this programming destroys original ideas. Having seen the movie, how many children now have an original idea about what Harry Potter looks like? What is not programmed – the intentions, feelings, thoughts, and consequences – is often not part of children's play, especially for young boys who focus on action. Asynchrony arises between what the child deems important to create and what the media suggests is the way to do it. Children who conform to the media message are less creative.

Gifted children who are unusually creative are often doubly different from age peers. They differ not only in how they think, but often also in how they act. That is, these gifted children tend to think in uncommon ways, and so often do not reflect the opinion of the status quo. They are often more fantasy-prone, more divergent in their thinking, less likely to see the common underlying assumptions, and less likely to go along with popular opinion. They also are less likely to do what everyone else is doing and do not see the value of following popular fads. They are less conventional in what they express as beliefs, and follow their own interests more than doing what someone else wants.

For some gifted children, doing one's own creative work is seen as less socially acceptable and can lead to social rejection. If the gifted young person follows peer opinion, does activities with peers, and values what peers' value, there is little time for creative work. The gifted young person may feel creative work is not valued and may give up doing it. If the gifted young person persists in creative work it is because the intrinsic value of doing so outweighs any outside opinion about its worth. Often, if the young person persists and becomes known for creative work, his or her individualism and originality becomes more socially acceptable. Thus, sometimes, creative gifted young people can garner respect for marching to their own drummers.

Creativity and attention deficits

In this section of this chapter, creativity in gifted children with AD/HD and AS will be described. This will include a portrayal of the characteristics of creativity for each group.

Gifted children with AD/HD

Hallowell and Ratey (1994b) observed that many people with AD/HD are "creative, intuitive and highly intelligent" (p.74). In fact, creativity is seen as a special strength. Gifted people with AD/HD may have specific elements that favor creative thinking. Hallowell and Ratey included traits such as greater tolerance for chaos than usual, greater responsiveness to impulses, the ability to hyperfocus at times, and hyperreactivity of the mind. These elements mean the person with AD/HD is less prone than usual to put data into specific categories, more likely to go with unusual ideas and see where they lead, able to focus to a greater than average degree on things of interest, and more likely to be thinking constantly about things. All of these elements enable the person with AD/HD to use imagination and impulse creatively.

Hallowell and Ratey's ideas about the relationship between AD/HD and creativity are based on anecdotal material. Research on the creativity of children with AD/HD is meager. Alessandri (1992) found that creativity expressed in the free play of average children with AD/HD was below average. Funk *et al.* (1993) found performance on tests of figural creativity (nonverbal tests that assess originality, fluency, and flexibility of ideas through drawings) to be below normal. Barkley (1997, 1998) hypothesized that both verbal and figural creativity assessed via fluency tests would be decreased in children with AD/HD because of deficits in recombination ability, an executive function. That is, people with AD/HD have particular difficulty taking apart verbal and visual wholes into component parts and then recombining them with new elements added or substituted.

Nevertheless, in other studies evaluating the association of creativity with AD/HD, Shaw (1992) studied bright children with AD/HD and found their high levels of stimulation seeking, as well as their ability to use incidentally acquired information, visual imagery, and problem solving in creativity tasks, discriminated them from other children. Shaw and Brown (1990) assessed close to 100 children with AD/HD and IQs above the 84th percentile on a range of tasks that included visual cognitive tasks, problem solving, and creativity. The children with AD/HD showed higher creativity using visual material than did the children without AD/HD. Shaw and Brown hypothesized that these children may show increased flexibility and originality because they attend to different aspects of the environment than others, and so discover more diverse material. Thus, Hallowell and Ratey may well be right about their own observations of creativity and AD/HD, at least in people of above-average intellectual ability.

In his book *In the Mind's Eye*, West (1997) explored the relationship between the ability to visualize and creativity. An important aspect of visualization is the ability to form new wholes by transforming what was there before to something new, or by elaborating on an older idea. People who are creative see instantly how two things might go together in a new whole. People with AD/HD are often very good at this kind of visual thinking. They are holistic thinkers and problem solvers. Thus, they have unusual insight into problems, based on a new conceptualization of the material.

Another form of holistic thinking occurs when the person with AD/HD has a vision of how something will look when it is completed: for example, how a ballet might look as a whole rather than as an assembly of parts together. In fact, people with AD/HD tend to be very good at forming the big picture. The problem for them is breaking it down into smaller parts, or attending to important aspects of the big picture aside from the whole. These wholes are more than the sum of their parts: that is, by being a whole, they impart a type of information that each piece added together did not do. Thus, attending to the details means the creative person with AD/HD has to change focus and may lose the vision that fueled their work. This is because it is especially difficult for people with AD/HD not only to hold the big picture in mind, but also to think of important details about the production aspect of the project. "The Devil is in the details" is a saying that was probably invented by someone with AD/HD.

Holistic thinking underlies many new concepts. Not all people with AD/HD who are creative use holistic thinking. However, those who do use it produce many interesting ideas and products.

Gifted children with AD/HD who are highly verbal may also be unusually creative. These children depend on recalling what they have heard. They often have very good memories for dialogue, discourse, and what they have read. They love word play and may invent their own words to describe feelings or actions that they know no words to describe. These children are good at creating new ideas by finding similarities among different verbal entities. For example, Brian, age eight, with an IQ in the 180s, loved history. He spent hours deciding on alternate outcomes for particular events, depending on the shifting of particular parameters that had occurred at the time. Suppose General Patton hadn't gotten these reinforcements just then: what would have been the likely outcome? Brian had AD/HD and difficulty with writing. His ideas and associations were often transcribed by his mother as he dictated them to her. He liked to study civilizations, and once he had grasped the essentials of the civilization, he mentally roamed through history finding similarities to other cultures. He liked to collect ideas, not only about history, but also about governments, economics, science, art, and philosophy.

CHARACTERISTICS OF CREATIVITY AND AD/HD IN GIFTED CHILDREN

Cramond (1994) noted that many of the characteristics associated with AD/HD are also associated with creativity, and wondered if creatively gifted children were being misdiagnosed with AD/HD.

The problem of overlap of the traits of creativity with those of AD/HD occurs not at the extremes of behavior, but with people who show milder traits or symptoms. Children who have severe AD/HD are difficult to manage. They may be full of creative ideas, but they are also full of behaviors that are provocative, disruptive, and often dangerous. No one looking at these children will claim that they are being misdiagnosed.

At the other end of the spectrum are highly creative people with mild AD/HD symptoms. They may actually have AD/HD but, if they do, it really does not interfere much with their lives. They may experience mild problems with organization, or impulsivity, but they are mostly productive. In childhood, they may not get all of their school work done, but they are not disruptive to others, and they generally get by with good grades. Where they really shine is in their creative endeavors. In adolescence, some of these children become more problematic for authority figures as they try to carve out their own identities and come in conflict with the status quo. This does not occur because they have AD/HD, however, but because they are unconventional and challenging.

The most difficult group to assess, the ones Cramond (1994) felt are misdiagnosed, are those with moderate degrees of AD/HD symptoms and high levels of creativity. These are the students whose creativity and eccentricity are disruptive, troublesome, and frustrating. When focused on something they love, these students produce prodigiously, but they may not work in any other area. They have difficulty with the executive functions that allow for planning and executing a project, even one of their own choosing. Many of these students can only do things their own way. Because of their AD/HD symptoms, they are limited in the options they see to solve problems, yet can produce many creative ideas about intellectual interests. They are less flexible in doing tasks assigned by others, even while they are immensely flexible in how they view their place in society. They march gladly to their own beat, unaware of the difficulties they produce for others and even for themselves.

Gifted children with AD/HD symptoms who are creative are quite likely actually to have AD/HD along with their high creativity. Indeed, their AD/HD may be part and parcel of their giftedness. That is, what makes them AD/HD also makes them creative and vice versa. As with dyslexia, the negative symptoms need to be acknowledged and addressed so as to enhance their lives. No one says to leave the dyslexia alone and never mind if a child can't read. No one says that dyslexia is misdiagnosed and it's really creativity. Instead, what happens is diagnosis of the disorder and remediation using techniques that will help. Remediating dyslexia does not change creativity. The same should hold true for gifted children with AD/HD who are creative. The symptoms of AD/HD need to be assessed and, if the child has AD/HD, appropriate remediation and accommodation is needed. Otherwise, the risk is that the child will not learn needed skills and will have greater difficulty later trying to learn how to produce and complete work. At the same time, creative abilities need to be fostered, or the child is at risk for losing interest and motivation in learning. Thus, the question is not whether a child is being misdiagnosed. What should be asked instead are questions about what the symptoms are, and what they mean, how troublesome they are, and what remediations would help the child to develop most fully.

Gifted children with AS

The literature about the relationship of AS and creativity is largely anecdotal. In fact, the only research is circumstantial as it involves the relationship of imagination and autism spectrum disorders. While imagination and creativity are related, they are not the same.

Scott and Baron-Cohen (1996) assessed imagination in children with autism by asking them to draw both possible and impossible objects such as a house or a man (that is, they had to draw a picture of a man that was impossible, like a two-headed person, using their imagination alone). The children with autism were unable to do this at all. Leevers and Harris (1998) followed up with studies that eliminated the aspects of executive functioning that required the children to shift attention and have a plan. Instead, the children were required to complete only one aspect of a picture in either a possible or impossible way ("What kind of head could you draw that would be impossible for a real person to have?"). The differences between the children with autism and those who did not have autism disappeared. Indeed, some of the children with autism chose unusual ways to make impossible pictures, ways that were highly imaginative and clever. Furthermore, children with autism were able to imagine novel combinations of elements so long as they were visual. Kavanaugh and Harris (1994) suggested that children with autism visualize novel combinations. They may even create this way. Temple Grandin (1995) described her own visualization of parts stored in her mental "video library" that she recombined in order to make a new design.

Hans Asperger (1991) thought that the children he saw were immensely creative. He stated that these children were able to produce original ideas; indeed, they could only be original. Language was a special area of creativity, with quite original words used and unusual descriptions. For example, one boy described the difference between stairs and ladders as: "The ladder goes up pointedly and the stairs go up snakedly" (p.71).

Asperger thought that these children showed an originality, not just of language, but also of experience. One boy, at age seven and a half, described how mirrors worked; he had figured it out for himself. Asperger mentioned a child he knew who observed the natural world, ordering facts into systems and making up his own theories. The child had formed the ideas based on his own experiences since he had read or heard little about the topics.

Some of the children studied by Asperger had developed unusual systems for solving complex math word problems, well above what they had been taught in class. All of these children seem quite creative.

Special interests can be another source of creativity in people with AS. A special interest may be unusual, but its main function is to provide the individual with pleasure and enjoyment. Interests are not always creative, though they are passionately developed.

Creativity is nevertheless found in children, adolescents, and adults with AS. Anecdotes about the creative use of language abound. Kenneth Hall (2001) described his fascination with language and invention of humor in his book.

Some young people with AS are also creative in the more traditional sense of producing new products. A perusal of the 2001 Temple Grandin Award Nominees shows children who wrote books and told stories, played music and composed, used art to design a curriculum for their school, designed web pages, dealt with bullying, wrote newspaper articles about the treatment of animals, and invented a "Kwik Release" dog collar (Future Horizons 2002). Kenneth Hall (2001) described how he created imaginary inventions for Wallace & Gromit & Co., an imaginary company he formed. He printed out invoices and statements for the various inventions using his stepfather's computer programs.

While imagination is deficient in many people with autism spectrum disorders, it is not deficient in all. Attwood (1998) described creative imaginary play by young children with AS. Some children created imaginary lands, drew comic book superheroes, or created fantastic stories.

The type of imagination needed to make predictions about social events is deficient in people with AS. That is, they cannot foresee consequences or alternatives with people, or imagine another person's point of view or feelings. On the other hand, creative imagination, the ability to see another aspect or an unusual connection among things (words, visual parts, ideas), is not at all lacking, and may be highly developed in some people with AS.

Both Asperger and Attwood have attributed great advances in science and art to people with AS. Attwood (1998) described the thinking associated with AS as "different, potentially highly original, often misunderstood, but not defective" (p.126). More recently, Temple Grandin has suggested that if we got rid of the genes that caused autism, we'd also be getting rid of many of the gifted and talented people like Einstein. She goes on to suggest that the really social people are not the ones who make new discoveries; they are too busy socializing (Attwood and Grandin 2000).

THE PROCESS OF CREATIVITY IN AS

People with AD/HD tend to be holistic, and big-picture thinkers and creators. They get the idea first and then gradually fill in the details. For example, gifted children with AD/HD who built spacecraft or alien vehicles from construction toys often visualized what the end would be before starting the construction. Children who created musical compositions heard them playing as a whole piece in their minds. Children who wrote stories saw the entire story played out before them. People with AS, however, with weak central coherence, appear to create in a different manner.

Because people with AS readily see the component parts within a whole, hyperfocus on one part, and take a long time to shift attention from part to part, they are less apt to form a notion of the whole. While this is inhibiting in many areas of functioning, it may be an asset in some aspects of creativity. For example, in studying each part for a longer time, the person may notice much more about the part, and may notice unusual relationships among parts. This is called segmented information processing, and use of this type of thinking appears to underlie some savant skills (Hermelin 2001).

People with AS also use visual thinking and pictures. Visualizing an object and studying it in all its dimensions can lead to ideas about how to change something and see how it might look from a distance, rotated, or inverted. Some people with AS who create may be like Temple Grandin, who has a vast catalogue of parts in her mental video library that she tries out until it seems like her mental image might be right for her project. She can extract each part from the previous whole, rotate or invert it, exchange it for another part, or change its shape, and then see how the new part changes the whole. By adding together known parts, and altering parts in wholes, she then creates a new image (Grandin 1995). This type of elaboration on a known quantity is an important type of creativity. Visualization may also lead to original ideas that are then tested out as, for example, Einstein's visualization of riding on a beam of light helped him to understand the idea of relativity.

Much of the research on creativity in gifted children and adults seems geared towards processes that require big-picture thinking. For example, in schools, many projects require thinking up a new idea. Imagining something novel is more difficult for children with AS. They are much more able to imagine novelty if they do not have to invent it totally themselves. Thus, drawing an imaginary creature totally from scratch is something most kindergartners enjoy doing, but is a task that is bewildering to children with AS. They need a different way to tap into the process involved. For example, telling them to think of several animals they know and take some parts from each to make an imaginary animal will enable them to do the task. Consequently, in evaluating creativity in children with AS, it is especially important to use procedures that actually allow the child to show ability.

Cognitive and affective aspects of creativity

In this section of this chapter, the cognitive and affective aspects of creativity and how they are affected by the attention deficits of AD/HD and AS will be described.

There have been many hypotheses about what constitutes creativity. Sternberg and Lubart (1993) suggested that creative individuals initiate ideas that are out of synch with what others think. Over time they are able to bring these ideas to fruition, and to convince others of their worth. They then move on to another novel idea. Sternberg (1991) hypothesized many subparts to each of the theories to explain how people think and innovate. Creative people need a combination of six resources, such as: intellectual processes like divergent thinking, problem definition, and insight; knowledge within a domain; styles of thinking that focus on making one's own rules and working independently; personality traits such as tolerance of ambiguity, moderate risk taking, and willingness to persevere; intrinsic and extrinsic motivation; and a supportive environment (Sternberg and Lubart 1993). How well do these aspects of creativity apply to AD/HD and AS?

Cognitive aspects of creative ability

Cognitive aspects include divergent thinking ability, problem-solving ability, problem-finding ability, and visualization and primary process thinking.

DIVERGENT THINKING ABILITY

Divergent thinking is the ability to look at material in new, unusual, or novel ways (Lovecky 1991, 1993). In fact, divergent thinking is associated with the potential for certain types of creative performance (Runco 1991). High scores on certain creativity tests do appear to correlate with later creativity in adulthood, especially tests of divergent thinking (Torrance and Safter 1989). Divergent thinking ability has often been defined as having aspects of fluency, novelty, synthesizing and analyzing abilities, complexity, redefinition, and evaluation (Guilford 1967). Torrance (1966) defined divergent thinking as fluency, elaboration, and originality.

It has been noted that popular responses appear first when children are tested, and only as more ideas are generated are more original responses elicited. Thus, the number of ideas generated was an important variable. The number of ideas generated can be related to intelligence (Borland 1986; Hocevar 1980), and if only the number of ideas generated is measured, divergent thinking ability is closely related to intelligence (Moran *et al.* 1983a, 1983b, 1984). This effect changes if only original and imaginative responses are counted.

Newer research by Runco and associates (Runco 1993) suggested that tests of divergent thinking are more effective as predictors of creativity if they define both problems and solutions; that is, the solution has actually to be able to solve the problem presented.

In general, the research on divergent thinking, its relationship to creativity, especially as determined by paper and pencil tests, and its value for use in gifted programs is debatable. Whether divergent thinking is related to intelligence is only one confounding variable. Piirto (1992) and Fishkin and Johnson (1998) reviewed much of the research and its limitations.

Gifted children with AD/HD often show flexibility of ideas, unusual ideas, and unique combinations of ideas. Divergent thinking ability appears to be present in many (but not all) gifted children with AD/HD. In fact, this is their creative gift: the ability to generate unusual and original responses to verbal and visual material. This is evident in formal assessments when these children give highly unusual responses to tasks such as Similarities on the Wechsler Intelligence tests. The task for the examiner is to then evaluate whether the response is merely idiosyncratic, and not scoreable, or whether it fulfills the criteria for a higher-level response. Gifted children with AD/HD tend to give higher-level unusual responses. Thus, the children not only give unusual responses, but also get to the essence of the question.

Many of the gifted children with AD/HD who came to the Gifted Resource Center of New England showed divergent thinking ability. Humor is one area in which they showed divergent thought and creativity. They repeated jokes, made up jokes, and drew jokes as parts of cartoons. Some were quite good at producing jokes, from an early age. Many also enjoyed word play and were fascinated with the multiple meaning of some words. Others were divergent thinkers in music improvisation and composition. Writing poetry is another area in which divergent thinking allows images to be used in unusual ways to convey feeling; several of the children were quite gifted poets. Several of these children were described earlier in this chapter.

There is a group of gifted children with AD/HD, however, who are exceptionally divergent. Many of their test responses were not scoreable because they associated to part of the material presented and then went off on a tangent. They were caught on the novelty of part of the response, or they only comprehended part of the question and responded on that basis, but in an unusual way. Scoring their responses meant that the examiner had to question more to figure out what they really did know.

Divergent thinking can be a great asset for gifted children, but for the most divergent children such thinking has negative aspects. For example, Talley, age eight, was such a divergent thinker he found it difficult to do anything except in his own way. He could turn any task into a challenge for himself, but his challenges often did not fit task requirements. Talley felt frustrated and singled out for criticism. He could not see that his responses were off the point because he could not discriminate relevant from irrelevant responses. Talley was difficult to assess because his need to do things his own way interfered with performance on even simple tasks. For example, on a task on which he had to name as many animals as he could in a set period of time, he decided to name mythological beasts. Even when the directions were clarified (name any animals), he stuck to his own agenda and obtained a low score.

Many children with AD/HD have trouble with these tasks because they cannot generate enough words to fulfill the criteria. This sort of task, called a demand-naming task, requires quick recall from memory. Talley had trouble with the task, not because he was deficient in quick recall from memory, but because he was so divergent. Talley's type of responding was likely to decrease his scores on many types of tests, so it was difficult to get a true idea of his potential. For example, since the class of mythological beasts is much smaller than the one of all animals, even if Talley had been an expert in naming mythological beasts, his score still would likely be lower than what he could potentially do with a bigger class to choose from. On the other hand, Talley was exceptional at generating unusual solutions to "what if…" types of questions. On the *Torrance Tests of Creative Thinking*, he scored exceptionally high on all the figural creativity tests, as well as on verbal tasks.

Gifted children like Talley who are exceptionally divergent thinkers are idiosyncratic in their approach to life as well. They tend to see their own way as best and have great difficulty listening to anyone else's ideas. Some of these children are quite creative. Their unusual ideas can lead to a totally different approach or concept. However, many are not creative because their tangents are not productive.

Gifted children with AS exhibit high levels of divergent thinking. This idiosyncratic thought is unusual and may be creative, but often is not. The reason children with AS are so unusual in their thinking is that they have no idea what the more common responses ought to be. They respond from their own experience, which is not only limited, but often reflective of their difficulties in seeing the bigger picture or shifting focus to another aspect of a problem.

Often, when children with AS were unusual in their responses to test items, these responses were lower level because they reflected a focus on a part of the problem rather than the whole. However, some of the most highly gifted children with AS who were evaluated at the Gifted Resource Center of New England were well able to develop high-level responses.

Gifted children with AS viewed the world differently from others. Some of these views were incorporated into interesting creative productions. One boy, Oliver, designed his own planet, with two languages and several countries who regularly had battles and shifted alliances according to political issues. Alicia, in childhood, told long stories about pop stars and her imaginary relationship with them. In young adulthood, she wrote a novel and several books of poetry.

Is there such a thing as being too creative? If by that one means too divergent in thinking, the answer is "yes" because some ability to place the divergent production within a context of other work is necessary. Without awareness of structure or the relationship to other parts of a larger domain, divergent thinkers only produce interesting images. That is a problem for some gifted children with AD/HD and many with AS.

PROBLEM-SOLVING ABILITY

Osborn (1963) and Parnes (1962) described different aspects of "Creative Problem Solving," defined as the ability to solve problems in unusual and innovative ways. Osborn focused more on the idea of "applied imagination" while Parnes developed specific programs designed to enhance problem solving skills for bright children. Nevertheless, these slightly different focuses utilize the same underlying divergent thinking strategies to solve problems. The process consists of a series of five steps: fact finding, problem finding, idea finding, solution finding, and acceptance finding. Much of the creativity training in schools, especially in gifted programs, is a version of creative problem solving. Piirto (1992) made the point that such creativity is fun, but may be of limited usefulness for gifted children. Creative problem solving doesn't help gifted children learn to solve real-life problems, partly because it can be difficult to recognize what the problem is.

Another approach to problem solving comes from the work of cognitive psychologists studying thinking processes. Experimental problems, such as abstract puzzles for students to solve, are typically used. While there is a big difference between the ability to solve such problems and the creation of something new, the gap is not so big as it might appear. For example, Simon (cited in Simonton 1994) conducted informal "field experiments" using problems of historic significance. In one such experiment, subjects were given a problem to solve that would require deriving Plank's formula for black body radiation. Many did so. Simonton (1994) also described a similar experiment with college students given data to examine that required a derivation of Kepler's third law of planetary motion. Several of the students successfully found the relationship required. Thus, it would appear that those types of problem solving that require more abstract reasoning ability may be related to creative production.

Research on insight by Sternberg and his colleagues is another branch of problem-solving research. Insight research ranges from descriptions of the inspired solution, to moments of illumination, to the "aha!" experience. Research with gifted children on tasks of insight suggested that they scored significantly higher than average children, and they tended to use particular strategies such as selectively recombining elements of the problems in order to solve them. Average children did well if specifically taught these strategies, but the gifted children used them spontaneously (Davidson 1986).

Gifted children with AD/HD appear to be good at solving different types of problems. They are especially good at generating new solutions to open-ended problems: "Just suppose...then what?" Insight and use of intuitive skills can be seen with these children. Some of the children who are exceptionally gifted in math can solve problems they have never seen before. Talley, described above, was such a boy, as was Stephen, who noted the relationships between Fibonacci numbers and patterns in nature. Both of them could look at an unknown word problem, and use what math skills they did have to figure out the answer. On one problem, Talley was able to say, "You add all these up, and you get 4,006,952 as an answer, then you divide by the seven cats, but I don't know how to do that. We haven't learned how to divide big numbers yet." One boy solved a myriad of addition, subtraction, and multiplication problems using only addition, as that was all he had learned how to do.

Some gifted children with AD/HD were good problem solvers in mathematics but tended to do only part of the problem, then jump to the answer. If they were the type of math student who did need to sequence each step, their answers were wrong. If they were the type of math student who reinvented math as they did each problem, they were usually correct. This latter type of student often did not use paper and pencil, but did most of the work mentally. Some of these exceptional math students were so adept at seeing to the core of a problem that they did not know the sequential steps taken by most other people. They just saw the answer instantaneously. This type of insight is a special strength for the creative mathematically gifted child. One special aspect of this mathematical insight was that they could guess answers with exceptional accuracy. However, on well-known problems, some made computation errors though they knew the procedure. This tended to be the result of attention problems or problems with working memory.

Gifted children with AD/HD can be quite good at problem solving, but their solutions are not always good ones. The best solutions solve problems of real-life importance to the young person. For example, Roger used his writing ability to cement some friendships in the new high school he was attending. In middle school, Roger really hadn't fit in well. His school was so small there were only a few other boys in each grade, and they rejected Roger. In the much larger public high school, he started to make friends in some of his classes, especially robotics, one of his favorites. However, Roger also loved to write and started a novel. As he slowly made friends, he incorporated all of them into the ongoing saga he was writing each day. Like a soap opera, his new friends came back to find out what would happen next. Their adventures and dilemmas were written over a two-year period, and all of the real-life friends enjoyed seeing how Roger would incorporate high-school issues into his novel.

Gifted children with AD/HD are especially good problem solvers in areas of special interest to them. Kevin, age ten, loved drama, and was especially adept at his roles, but found that he was less spontaneous when taking medication. On the other hand, if he did not take it, he was disruptive and had trouble learning his lines. Kevin's solution to his problem was to use the medication most of the time, but not for the actual performances when he already knew the part very well, and could manage his behavior in the context of the larger performance.

Other gifted children with AD/HD have attempted to solve problems of hunger and poverty by actively doing something to work for a good cause. Tiffany worked to help children at a homeless shelter by putting on a talent show. The price of admission was the donation of some art supplies for the shelter's art therapy program.

Problem solving is used to a high degree in playing computer and video games, and in making original constructions with building types of toys. These are often favorite activities of gifted children with AD/HD, especially boys.

Problem solving doesn't always work with gifted children with AD/HD. Sometimes the solutions they find are not realistic enough, or the child has no way of implementing them. These gifted children can get stuck into one mode of thinking. They do not have the strategy of flexibly switching categories to think of another type of response, so they keep generating the same sort of response, but get less and less effective. Jeremy, though immensely creative in art, music, and story telling, could not get his projects finished. A lot of the problem was with decision making: Jeremy had trouble finding a topic he liked and sticking with it. He would pick something, then have second thoughts, or find another idea he thought he would like better; this impeded him from actually doing enough work to finish anything, though he started a good many things. He insisted he had to solve the problem by himself, and resisted any suggestions about how he might make a choice. Unfortunately, he also couldn't stick to the plans he made that would allow him to make choices more effectively.

Some gifted children with AD/HD, like Talley, are so idiosyncratic that the solutions they do generate only work for one problem and are not generalizable to other similar problems. Finally, many gifted children with AD/HD, like other children with AD/HD, have trouble seeing cause and effect, and so find it difficult to think of effective solutions to everyday problems. Thus, gifted children with AD/HD can be quite effective problem solvers, and quite creative in many endeavors, but may be unable to use their creativity to solve their everyday difficulties.

Gifted children with AS can be excellent at solving problems within their areas of interest. They can be quite creative in how they formulate problems and then solve them. Brendan, age six, read about and developed classification systems for all the dinosaurs that ever lived. These were based on his own ideas about how dinosaurs were related to each other and to other mythological and fantastic beasts he read about. He also could classify any dinosaur by its latest scientific classification.

Gifted children with AS can, at times, be quite creative at solving real-life problems, including how to manage some of their own issues. Seth, age ten, had to wear a face mask in his dusty school due to severe asthma. Since he was teased about it, he decided to do something to change the situation. So he asked permission from the principal to tell the school about his problem at the next assembly. He had prepared a short speech that explained what his problem was and why he had to wear the mask. The principal tried to talk him out of appearing before the whole school, but Seth was insistent. He was sure that if he just explained to the others why he had to wear the mask for medical reasons, they would stop teasing him. His speech went very well. He was asked many questions and, at the end, several other students volunteered that they had asthma too. After that, fewer episodes of teasing occurred.

While gifted children with AS can be quite good problem solvers about situations of interest to them, they are notoriously poor problem solvers about most other types of problems. Often they get set in or stuck on one way of thinking about or doing something, and have great difficulty being persuaded that any other solution is even possible. Brendan often had trouble with even simple choices. He simply couldn't choose; it required more flexibility than he had to be able to think of one thing as more desirable or more important than another, especially when he was not especially interested in either one. Even flipping a coin was difficult for him. He thought the coin might not get the choice right.

PROBLEM-FINDING ABILITY

Problem finding is the mode of the moment. What this means for gifted children in school programs is a focus on finding real-life problems to solve in a particular domain of endeavor. Problem finding is the ability to find interesting questions and observations around which to focus new work.

In an interesting study Getzels and Csikszentmihalyi (1976) studied the ability of art students to find problems in their artwork. This was accomplished by having them use a variety of objects presented to them to use in forming their own pictures. The use of the objects in the finished product was then judged by professional artists for originality and craftsmanship. The scores obtained were used to formulate an index of problem-finding ability. Five years later students were judged on success as artists and those who were most successful as problem finders were also most successful as artists. When the artists were closer in age to mid-life, the correlation between earlier problem-finding ability and success was much lower (Getzels 1987). Why the decrease in relationship occurred is not known but it could be related to the fickleness of public taste, the difficulties of attaining eminence rather than early popularity, or perhaps the gaining of further skill by those artists who initially scored lower on problem finding.

There are alternative points of view. Runco (1994, cited in Runco and Nemiro 1994) suggested that because many creative problems are found accidentally, special skills in problem finding may not be essential for creativity. Creativity, in his view, involved more than problem finding and problem solving. Further, Runco and Nemiro (1994) suggested that problem finding was defined as problem identification and problem definition. Thus, both finding an interesting problem on which to focus and recognizing a problem found accidentally are part of creativity.

Some researchers have suggested that those problems with no known set solution require more creative thinking (Getzels 1964; Getzels and Csikszentmihalyi 1976). Their focus on discovered problems has set the stage for increasingly complex work on problem generation and problem finding. This has led to a vision of creativity as related to finding interesting real-life problems on which to work.

Gifted children with AD/HD do well with problem finding. Because they are so imaginative, they can think up unusual questions and set interesting challenges for themselves. Many of the children who asked the most interesting questions in this study had AD/HD. Ian, age six, thought about a potential battle between Godzilla and a black hole and asked himself who might win. He concluded that Godzilla would. Stephen, the boy featured at the start of this chapter with the interest in Fibonacci numbers, asked questions he tried to solve with his science project. Eric derived an original mathematical formula (Lovecky 1994a). Eric, who was nine at the time, is now in college, taking accelerated courses. With an IQ in the 190s he is adept at both finding and solving problems. Still, his AD/HD is problematic because Eric has often had trouble with work completion and impulsive behavior.

In general, gifted children with AD/HD who have trouble with problem finding appear to be those who are not very independent or self-directed. They also appear to need a lot of outside stimulation to focus and organize themselves, and they tend to get this by working quickly, skimming the surface of tasks, and using material that is visually complex but may not require much analysis from them. Also, children who are rigid or who have trouble with recognizing intrinsic rewards may also have difficulty with problem finding because the only activities that feel rewarding enough for them need to be highly stimulating and immediately rewarding.

Gifted children with AS sometimes can show problem-finding skills in special areas of interest. In effect, the special area is a problem the child has set to investigate and learn about. Sometimes, in this process, insight and original thought develop, and the investigation is creative. Interesting ideas may arise because of unusual details noted by the child, or because of seeing something in a new way. Tony, age 12, loved humor, especially cartoon books. He noted that the funniest cartoons relied on visual puns, so he set out to see what made these jokes funny. He studied cartoon joke books and read several books written on the subject of humor itself. He made a chart of what things make jokes funny, and then combined different aspects. Tony started to make up some of his own jokes, usually puns, that he had others rate for "funniness." Eventually, he was able to discuss what it was about some jokes that made them funny, and how he could use these jokes in certain situations to get others to laugh.

Some gifted children with AS have difficulty with the unusual associations they make to material. For one thing, no one else understands what they mean. Often, they give only a part of the meaning and expect that others know what they are thinking, so they explain too little. This means their way of looking at material may be new, but may not be particularly effective or useful. Thus, while they may make many novel associations to material, they may be unable to take further steps to develop ideas into problems to research.

VISUALIZATION AND PRIMARY PROCESS THINKING

Primary process thinking is the first thought that is associated to a newly introduced idea. So is the stream of ideas that flow when they are not being censored. We use primary process thinking especially when we daydream or free associate. Intuition is another form of primary process thinking. We go with what we feel rather than analyzing it. Primary process thinking is unconscious: that is, it is not directed. An example of primary process thinking occurs when someone has a problem and goes to sleep. Upon waking in the morning, the solution pops into mind.

Visualization and primary process thinking have been recently recognized as important precursors of creativity. This recognition has come from both the cognitive processes area of creativity, and from those who focus more on unconscious processes. Also, new emphasis in the field of learning disabilities, especially dyslexia, has suggested that the very cognitive deficits that cause dyslexia may also be responsible for creative thinking (West 1997). See Chapter 4 for further discussion.

The uses of visual images, spatial concepts, and pattern recognition are all important aspects of visualization. Visualization includes not only what one sees directly, but also what can be imagined as shape or image. Thus, visualization techniques actually include many fields or domains of thought. Gardner (1983) suggested that an original thinker is one who makes unconventional but apt associations across domains using visualization. The comparisons gave rise to the recognition of unusual patterns or similarities among different items that brought new insight. These patterns and images were recognized as analogies or metaphors.

Visualization techniques are used in many types of creative work. The product that is developed can range from an almost entirely visual-spatial concept to an integrated auditory-visual one. West (1997) described a young computer expert who could visualize the design of an entire graphics system in his mind, and could see "the rhythm and pulsing of the data" moving through the design circuits (p.269).

Some creative individuals also move among several modes of thinking. They can think of visual images and move them to more verbal descriptions or vice versa (West 1997). This type of thinking also has been seen in some studies of gifted children (O'Boyle and Benbow 1990).

The ability to think in visual and spatial images has been noted for many well-known creative people. Root-Bernstein (1987) discussed a type of mental visualization used by creative scientists. George Gaylord Simpson could visualize an image of a whole forest including the underlying geology, and then watch as this changed from one geological age to the next. Barbara McClintock, the Nobel Prize winning geneticist, was able to visualize the results of her experiments before actually looking in the microscope at the chromosomes of her corn plants (Keller 1983). Einstein, in his early years, was exposed to a type of visual thinking called "Anschauung," which was one of the predisposing factors in his using mental imagery in forming the special theory of relativity (Miller 1984).

Other sense modalities also can serve as a means of projection; for example, Mozart heard all the parts he had written at once, as a whole (Root-Bernstein 1987). Gifted children also may be able to utilize this type of projection.

Primary process thinking also can involve visualization. In this aspect of visualization, intuition about what might happen next, how something ought to be, and what something might look like from the inside is prominent. Fantasy proneness, the ability to fantasize easily, can be related to visualization as the person imagines. Fantasies are often running series of pictures within one's mind's eye. The child who is highly intuitive sees things as wholes, experiences constantly changing perceptions about the world, and is often fantasy prone and a visual thinker as well.

It is important to recognize that creativity can also be verbal. While visualization is a special aspect of creativity, people who are predominantly verbal also may be exceptionally creative. For example, Edgar Allen Poe's poem, "The Bells," is an example of an auditory creative piece. It depends on sound rather than visual images to portray the feelings of the author. Much of creation in the fields of music, literature, history, philosophy, and cultural anthropology, among others, depends on verbal encoding of ideas rather than initially visual ones. As in the visual realm, translation to a more balanced mode using both verbal and visual modes to expand the initial concepts is important.

Gifted children with AD/HD often have well-developed visualization skills. For example, many of the math students who reinvent math with each problem are exceptional at visualization. Many of the gifted children with AD/HD in this study had excellent visual-spatial and visualization skills. Building with construction toys, and making complex three-dimensional original creations with household objects and art supplies, all suggested strong ability to visualize. Some children made their own costumes for plays and Halloween. Others created entire dramas with props, scenery, and characters all developed through visualizing them first. Children who built spacecraft or alien vehicles from construction toys often visualized what the end would be before starting the construction. Amanda liked to visualize building her own houses, thinking what the blueprints she drew would look like in real life. Also, some of the children, like Stephen, used visualization skills in scientific projects.

Other gifted children used their imaginative skills as fantasy. Fantasy can involve visualization, but also may involve other sensory modes in a richly integrated tapestry of experience. Gifted children often have rich fantasy lives, with imaginary playmates, and extensive role playing. These children have fun with their imaginations and, as described earlier in this chapter, may continue fantasy play well into adolescence.

Some gifted children with AD/HD involve themselves in making their entire lives into dramatic and unusual stories. Some of these become rather fantastic, especially with younger children. They simply get carried away on the excitement of the story and do not stop to think about whether it is true, or even if it is believable. Because it is so vivid, it appears as if it must have happened.

Jeremy, age 14, was quite dramatic. His whole life seemed to be one intense incident after another. These were related by Jeremy with a certain amount of pride, as if he were the starring character in a movie about his life. Jeremy also lived in a world filled with characters that he invented for his various stories in progress. These imaginary people were wonderfully creative, with finely detailed personalities. When Jeremy described a character, that person lived in the space of the moment, that creative space made when communicating a grand idea. Jeremy wasn't very interested in developing written stories. He was content to let this imaginary world exist in his own mind. The challenge for Jeremy in his later high-school years was to find ways to use his marvelous divergent thinking and primary process fantasizing in real creative projects that would allow him a way to function successfully in adulthood.

Gifted children with AS may have highly developed visualization skills. Grandin (1995) discusses these skills in her own life and how they enable creative production. Some of the gifted children who came to the Gifted Resource Center of New England used visualization skills to describe creatively how they felt. Seth, age 14, used a visual image to describe his loneliness: "Imagine a point on a line. Now, imagine that the line isn't there anymore."

Children with AS may live in fantasy worlds. Richard (Bosch 1970, cited in Attwood 1998) described an elaborate dream world, a world full of peace and happiness where nothing evil happened. Other gifted children with AS who have created imaginary worlds are mentioned in the literature (Asperger 1991; Attwood 1998; Grandin 1995). Kenneth Hall (2001) vividly described his excursion into the portal, his parallel solar system. Williams (1992) described how, as a child, she would withdraw into a type of self-induced hypnotic state where her mind would fill with colors, sensations, and rhythms, an extreme state of primary process thinking.

Several of the gifted children with AS at the Gifted Resource Center of New England created imaginary worlds. Oliver created his own world with several continents and countries, languages, and battles. Abby, at age six, described a rainbow world where rainbows lived before they came to earth.

For some of these children, the distinction between fantasy and reality can be blurred at times. Some even appeared to have imaginary companions; however, unlike those of other children, the imaginary companions of these children with AS appeared to be almost alter egos. That is, the child became the person or animal created, and insisted parents follow scripted roles as well. Luke Jackson (2002) described the wild imagination of one of his friends that led him to be a monkey or crocodile. Kenneth Hall (2001) described his involvement with the portal, in which he became an alter ego, Ken, who acted exactly the opposite to the real Kenneth.

Several children at the Gifted Resource Center of New England insisted that fantastic things really happened, and seemed to have difficulty with the line between pretending and reality. Stuart, age nine, told a long story about how he was almost hit by a train. Since he lived near the MTA rail line in Boston, this was of some concern, especially since several people had recently died on the Amtrak line not too far away. However, as his story progressed, and he talked about being able to outrun the train, and to jump over the 12-foot fence, the story was revealed for the fantasy it was. Less clear was the story about how his peers attacked him at school with sticks during recess. Sadly, that story turned out to be true.

Affective aspects of creative ability

Affective aspects of creativity include a tolerance for ambiguity and having motivation and persistence.

TOLERANCE FOR AMBIGUITY

A tolerance for ambiguity is important in creative production (MacKinnon 1962). More recently, Mumford and colleagues (Mumford *et al.* 1994) measured the "adaptability" – that is, the combination of openness, mastery, and tolerance for ambiguity – of college undergraduates on familiar, unfamiliar, and novel tasks. Those who were most adaptable could sustain performance, tolerate frustration, deal with the unknown, and engage in tasks that required a degree of self-discipline. They were also more productive on creative problem-solving tasks.

Gifted children with AD/HD may show a greater tolerance for ambiguity. Hallowell and Ratey (1994a, 1994b) suggested that many people with AD/HD have a greater tolerance than usual for chaos. Because he or she is bombarded by distractions, the person with AD/HD learns to live with ambiguity. Things don't always make sense, so the person learns to make a unique sense of things. This can result in big mistakes, but may also produce creative insight into something from a different perspective.

In addition, ideas just jump into mind. When random ideas jump into mind, they can be a self-distraction, but they can also be productive. Children like Jeremy, who could not get his work done, also have fluency of ideas. Jeremy had so many ideas that picking among them was too difficult. He lived with the ambiguity of contradictory ideas by never committing himself to any one idea. Thus he got little done. Stephen, on the other hand, was able to use his flow of ideas more productively to explore how to apply his original idea about Fibonacci sequences to other aspects of nature. Sarah had a flow of music, especially when she was very young. She was totally nonselective – all ideas flowed right out of her into what she played. Only later on, when she developed more skills at composition, did she start to choose among musical ideas, and have to tolerate the necessity of choosing one over another.

At times, contradictory ideas can form a new whole by connecting in an unusual way. This is how humor is often developed – the juxtaposition of absurdity makes something funny. That's why many gifted children with AD/HD are so good at witty comments and sarcasm.

At other times, though, tolerance for ambiguity becomes uncritical acceptance. Thus, gifted children with AD/HD may not able to determine whether their answers meet criteria, are a good fit for a question, or whether they even make sense. Since the child lives with so much ambiguity, all options seem equally likely and possible. How then can they pick out one main idea or select a best-fit response? Because they see so many possibilities, all seem equally valid in one way or other, even ideas that are contradictory. Gifted children who are good at tolerating ambiguity may also be good at understanding multiple points of view, each from a separate perspective. This can lead to creativity as the child thinks of new points of view and different perspectives.

Some gifted children with AD/HD have more trouble with ambiguity. For example, what should the child do when the teacher clearly thinks only one answer is right and the child can think of several? Dealing with the foolishness of others is another type of tolerance of ambiguity. Those gifted children, including those with AD/HD, who have a burning need for truth and an intolerance of imperfection have great difficulty tolerating ambiguity. Nevertheless, they may be quite creative in their chosen area.

Finally, some children with AD/HD tolerate ambiguity because they don't notice that two ideas actually are contradictory. The child is able to examine these ideas because each is compartmentalized, and only one is considered at any point: its pros and cons weighed as if it were the primary idea then. Thus, these gifted children never think that one answer must be ridiculous because it could not fit the data. The answer is considered only on its merits as an answer. The parts that fit are noted and those that do not are ignored.

Gifted children with AS live in worlds filled with contradictions and ambiguity. Because they have so much trouble with part-to-whole relationships, they cannot assess very easily the validity of particular ideas as opposed to others. Nothing makes much sense. Opinions are especially difficult to understand because they don't seem based on anything concrete. The gifted child with AS can only see his or her own opinion, which is regarded as a "right" answer. Thus, these children try to stick to the one right answer, the one way they have developed to deal with a problem or the one rule they know, whether of not it exactly applies. They become stuck into inflexibility and rigid responding.

Gifted children with AS are creative because of their ability to look at something in a new way despite the fact that many things don't make sense. They can improvise upon a theme once they are clear about the theme. They elaborate well on an idea they have considered, and they show an insight into problems that is unusual and novel. Hermelin (2001) described several people who were savants in music. One of them was exceptionally able to improvise on a presented work. Other savants, as well as gifted children with AS, like Aaron, were able to improvise and create new musical pieces.

Some gifted children with AS are quite good at using ambiguity and contradictions in making up puns. Because they are alert to the double meanings of words, it is easy for them to immediately see several meanings of each word, and from that to produce witty puns. Kenneth Hall (2001), when he heard his mother say, "That's a turn up for the books," replied: "And a potato too if they really want it." (If you don't get it, think of the pun for "turn up.")

On the whole, however, people with AS do not tolerate ambiguity well at all. Tolerating means knowing that things are contradictory and being able to live with a lack of clarity. It means one doesn't need to know what will happen next, but can go with the flow. People with AS need to know exactly what will happen next. It is only when they have complete control over something of interest that they can improvise on the known, and develop it into something new.

MOTIVATION AND PERSISTENCE

Motivation and persistence are important aspects of creative production. Csikszentmihalyi, Rathunde, and Whalen (1993) conducted a longitudinal study of talented adolescents to discover what affected development of their talent. Integral to the study was the concept of motivation. These researchers thought that adolescents would do an activity if they enjoyed it, and if they did it well.

The enjoyment from achieving excellence within the field of talent is what Csikszentmihalyi (1996) called "flow." When skills and challenges are balanced, the person is most likely to feel harmony, and thus flow occurs. Over time, this leads to more complexity of experience because to maintain the flow new skills are developed and then new challenges formulated (Csikszentmihalyi *et al.* 1993).

In a state of flow, actions and awareness are merged, distractions are excluded from consciousness, there is no fear of failure, self-consciousness disappears, the sense of time becomes distorted, and the activity becomes autotelic: that is, worth doing for its own sake (Csikszentmihalyi 1996). Flow is part of the intrinsic motivation that leads to high productivity. Without flow, much of the creative work of individuals would not be accomplished.

In their study of creative adolescents, Csikszentmihalyi *et al.* (1993) found that flow predicted the commitment of these teens across several different types of creative endeavors. However, those gifted in science and math felt less engaged in, and less excited by, their work than those in art, music, or sports. This may have had to do with the direct sensory involvement with their material for those in art, music, and sports. However, those in math and science were more aware of the longer-term benefits of their work, and felt they would gain career rewards in the future in ways that those in the arts, music, and sports could not.

Sternberg and Lubart (1993) suggested that motivation is an integral part of creativity. They distinguished between motivators that were more internal, and those that were external. Motivators were divided into two main classes: task focusing and goal focusing.

Task-focusing motivators are intrinsic. They are the energy, drive, or desire that leads to concentrated attention and work on a task. Task motivators include desire to achieve excellence, self-actualize potential, experience intellectual novelty, or feel pleasure with a certain subject. Other studies have shown a clear relationship between intrinsic motivation and creative performance (Amabile 1983; MacKinnon 1962).

Goal-focusing motivators are extrinsic. They use a task as a means to an end, and separate tasks from the goal. These motivators include wanting fame, money, recognition, approval, or other externally produced rewards. Sternberg and Lubart (1993) pointed out that extrinsic motivators are often useful to creativity: for example, when the reward does not remove attention from the task, when task-focusing motivation is already strongly present, and during the latter stages of creative work when details can be more tedious.

Motivation can change over time. Different types of motivators are more effective at the start of work, and others at the end; some matter more for tasks that are less directly future-oriented. Certain motivators may also depend on personality: that is, some people need more immediate and tangible rewards to work at all.

Gifted children with AD/HD can show great persistence in areas of their own choosing. Some are immersion learners who love to delve into material and learn all there is to know about a topic before moving on to another. Some persist in learning about one area all their lives. Thus, on self-selected material, gifted children with AD/HD can be quite motivated. Carly, with AD/HD, was passionately interested in marine life from kindergarten through 4th grade. Every school project had to be related in some way to marine life. Finally, towards the end of 4th grade her teacher would no longer allow her to do any more projects on marine life. Carly then had to do other projects but became much less involved in school work, and much less passionate about learning.

Gifted children with AD/HD are highly motivated to work on self-chosen material and material that is stimulating. When these children can hyperfocus and get into a state of flow, they can produce exceptional work. This can include work in any area of endeavor from the arts to the sciences. Thus, Gareth, described above, entered into hyperfocused flow states while working on his forge and making chain mail. He also hyperfocused when he was captivated by the prospect of making a new cake design for one of the Medieval Society's tournaments. Ted, mentioned in Chapter 1, discussed how he felt time disappear when he got into designing websites. Several hours later he would come to with a shock that so much time had passed unmarked by him. Both Gareth and Ted found their work highly pleasurable and, therefore, intrinsically motivating.

Persistence and motivation are required for a person to achieve any creative work. Some gifted people with AD/HD, however, have much more trouble entering into a hyperfocused state that leads to any productive work. They can hyperfocus on television or computer games but not on other tasks.

Thus, when the gifted person with AD/HD has trouble with creative production, it may be that the level of skills is not enough to meet the challenges required to do the project. It may be that the person cannot stick with the project long enough to reach a flow state. Also, since flow is intrinsically rewarding, being unable to sustain attention can interfere with attaining the level of positive hyperfocus necessary to enter into the flow state. Thus, the person with AD/HD never feels rewarded by the work.

Motivation needs to be sustained by intrinsic rewards through much of the process. Extrinsic rewards can be helpful to children with AD/HD, but may not be readily available in creative work. For example, the reward may be so far distant that effort fades. The extrinsic reward visualized may be unrealistic (fame and fortune) or may become a distraction itself, as when the person starts to daydream about the future reward and not the creative work. On the other hand, small extrinsic rewards, given in the short term for small portions of creative work, can be enhancing. Some gifted children with AD/HD plan so they can play computer games after they have done a portion of creative work.

Persistence can become a problem when the person with AD/HD has too many associations and ideas to direct energy to work on one idea. Thus, work on an idea gets disrupted by another idea, and working on that one by another. Some people produce so many creative thoughts that creative thoughts themselves become a distracter. Like Jeremy, this sort of person has wonderful ideas and starts many projects, but rarely completes any because the next novel idea is so intriguing the person starts to follow it, and so on through a long trail of incomplete projects.

People who change projects frequently may always be in a state of creative process and stimulation, because of the constant novelty they engender, but this is not truly flow. In the end, they do not feel rewarded because they have not accomplished their goals. People who are always in the process of changing things, of developing and then dropping ideas, are hyperreactive to the environment. The trick is to harness the creative energy and use it productively (Hallowell and Ratey 1994a, 1994b).

Gifted children with AD/HD are especially likely to have difficulties with the skill side of creative production. Coaching the child who has lower skill levels and providing compensatory techniques can help the child develop both creative ideas and skills. Thus, allowing a gifted child with AD/HD who has visual-motor dysfunction to dictate stories can result in more creative stories than if actual handwriting of the story is required. Working with a tutor in junior high might have been helpful to Jeremy; in this process, Jeremy would have been assigned small pieces to write using one of his characters doing one action. Because he would not have started with a whole story, he would have had more chance to develop skills slowly until he was able to put several parts together into a series of sketches that intertwined.

Since creative work is the work they love, most gifted children with AD/HD strive to overcome whatever problems they have with the production side of creativity. Sarah, mentioned at the start of this chapter, was able to compose music. Her music changed over time from primarily primary process flow of music to more thought-out and developed compositions. She had no trouble entering into a state of flow or working on her music. She also enjoyed perfecting various pieces to play for enjoyment. Sarah is typical of many creative gifted children with AD/HD.

Gifted children with AS can be remarkably motivated and persistent when engaging in an activity of choice, especially a special interest. Some of these become creative. For example, Aaron was an excellent composer. He loved piano and not only played quite well, but also composed sophisticated pieces with complex themes.

Motivation for these gifted children on creative tasks is always intrinsic. In fact, it is difficult to find extrinsic rewards that are motivating. Sometimes the best extrinsic reward for another task is time to work on their own interest. However, extrinsic rewards can be helpful during the production part of a creative project. Because output can be difficult for many of these children, they may not want to complete a project. In this case, time to work on their own work, or the chance to do a pleasurable activity like reading or playing computer games, can serve as an extrinsic motivator. Sometimes, though, the child needs adult structure in order to finish: for example, by getting help in breaking the production part into tiny steps.

Because children with AS hyperfocus, it can be difficult for them to leave ideas and material they find interesting to work on other things. When gifted children with AS engage in their favorite pastimes, they enter into a state of flow. Whether these are creative or not, leaving them appears to be painful.

Gifted children with AS have difficulty with persistence when required to do tasks in which they have little interest, or that they already know well. While some like to work on well-known tasks and dread doing anything new, many gifted children with AS do not see the point of doing things they already know or that seem boring to them. In fact, they will not do these tasks. Gifted children with AS need material tied to what they have already learned or to a special interest in order to enhance motivation and persistence.

Gifted children with attention deficits who are not creative

Not every gifted child with AD/HD is creative, no more than every gifted child is. Some of the gifted children with AD/HD who are not very creative are very highly gifted children who like to gather information and become experts in a field, but who have little new to contribute. Others seem to have limited ability to solve unfamiliar problems. Some gifted children with AD/HD appear to have creative ideas, but are unable to incorporate them into any project. If the circumstances are right, ideas might flow, but then the child is unable to use the idea in any activity.

A number of gifted children with AD/HD need immediate rewards. They seek activities that are high in extrinsic rewards and need a great deal of extrinsic stimulation. Their own ideas are not stimulating enough to keep them focused. These children are often thrill seekers.

Gifted children with AS who are not creative appear to be very inflexible in thinking, have fewer broad-ranging interests, and not much curiosity. Thus, they are satisfied with what they are told about a subject and never ask questions about it (though they do question why they have to do it). Their interests are very limited in scope: for example, playing computer games, or collecting things with limited possibilities, such as bottle caps or matchbook covers. Thus, they are not presented with problems that require a creative solution. Gifted children with AS who have wide-ranging interests and find learning things satisfying can be more creative because they come across more unstructured material.

The gifted children with attention deficits who came to the Gifted Resource Center of New England ranged from very creative to having little creativity at all. Some were creative on some occasions, but rather conventional on others. It seemed that sometimes they became locked into certain ways of thinking and were unable to get unstuck. Brainstorming did not work at these times; they just tended to repeat ideas. They had little knowledge about using strategies such as grouping like things, or switching categories to a different type of response. They had difficulty with making predictions. Because they went along doing a task without thinking of a possible goal or any possible outcomes, these gifted children had no means of knowing if they were on the right track. Thus, even if they had creative solutions, they did not try them out for long, or they gave up easily if the first attempt wasn't correct.

Suggestions for enhancing creativity

- Have quiet places where children can retreat to daydream. Make sure there is unstructured time each week that can be used for imaginative play and daydreaming well into the teen years. If a child is interested in specific lessons, allow them, but leave enough time that free play with the materials of the lesson can happen. That is, the child plays with the piano, as well as plays set pieces.

- Not all creativity depends on divergent thinking processes; much is involved with convergent thinking as well. Thus, gifted children need to develop both types of skills. Divergent thinking involves what is different, unusual and, novel. It means taking something apart, and seeing how meaning could alter given a different point of view. Convergent thinking requires putting things into context, synthesis of material with other material, finding how new material fits in the context of what is already known, and comparing and contrasting things to see what new aspects can be discovered. How are a dog and a tree the same?

- It is important to recognize the different processes that underlie creativity for children with autism spectrum disorders. Much of the research on creativity is geared to children who are big-picture thinkers. For children with AS, having to produce something novel, or to be creative in verbal formats, may be impossible. When giving assignments or projects that require creativity, teachers and parents should assume that gifted children with AS will have trouble thinking of a topic and executing it. They will do best if they can do a variation on something already known to them, and have a visual model of previous work.

- Creative work has often been inspired by witnessing the pain and hardship of others. Picasso's *Guernica* is a depiction of the pain felt from the Spanish Civil War in 1936. When gifted children with AD/HD or AS feel touched by an event around them, that can be the trigger for creative inspiration, especially in the arts, and sometimes in the sciences as well.

- Creative work can be used to overcome obstacles to learning. Thus, a gifted child who has difficulty with an area of learning (for example, writing) can be led to express creative content that overcomes the obstacle. The child can dictate a creative story that is written down for him or her. Later, as writing skills improve, the child does the actual physical act of writing, perhaps on a word processor. Parents and teachers can also use creative teaching techniques to maintain interest in subjects with which some children have difficulty.

- Special interests can lead to or impede creativity depending on how intense they are, how much time they take from the day, and how geared they are to develop independent and different solutions. Playing computer games, Pokémon, or Game Boy is not a creative activity because there are only a certain number of set solutions allowed to solve the problem of the game. Limiting the time allowed on these types of activities while slowly building skills in more open-ended activities can build creativity.

- Special interests that have an open-ended component can lead to creativity as the creative person begins to ask questions and wonder about aspects of the material. Gifted children with these sorts of special interests need more time allowed in which they can develop creative aspects of their interests.

- Since much of the research on the early lives of creative people suggests that reading was an important activity, parents need to read to children from books above their reading level. As the child develops reading facility, the family can take turns reading. Reading plays and poetry aloud is also exciting. Children can also be encouraged to memorize poems and plays for recitation. Having the feel for language, and having complex language within one's memory, allows a child to use words with more facility.

- Model one's own creative work. This means engage in one's own work and share some of the joys and hardships of it with gifted children. Discuss with them problems of obstacles, time constraints, use of deadlines, how one got started, what is important about the work, what part was inspiration and what was hard work, and where the joy of creating lies. Discuss the satisfaction in working hard and doing one's best work, not just when projects are completed, but at the small points along the way, so children get the idea that there is satisfaction in finishing steps. Talk about the concept of flow, when time stands still and one is one's work, and why that is the greatest joy.

- Work with children sometimes. Help them get started on projects. Let them see that the process of flow in doing something feels good by experiencing it with them in some endeavors. Sample some of the masters together and discuss the parts where one is carried off by the work. Work with the child on a creative enterprise where he or she directs the action. This keeps the parent or other adult as guide and companion and helps prevent adults from taking over the child's work and "doing it right."

- Help creative children who never finish anything by selecting one of their ideas on which to work. Structure the experience: when the work will be done, what kind of help will be given, and so on. Break the task down into tiny parts and help the child to accomplish the parts. Reward the completion of each part by using small pleasures such as time on computer or reading. Then, celebrate the finishing by putting the work into a special portfolio. Sometimes working for a competition can enhance finishing; the goal of writing poetry could be to send it to a contest, or perform it at a poetry reading.

Conclusion

Creativity for gifted children is play, even when they are engaged in making some type of product. The product endpoint is not so important, though, as is the fun of doing the work. Creative work is only worth doing so long as it has some aspects of fun. When it becomes only hard work or is done to meet another's expectation, then it is no longer creative. Thus, the process is as important as the product. Gifted people who are creative do not stop being creative, even if they achieve little in the way of recognition. It is not the recognition that makes them creative but their own inner connection to their material. The process of becoming one's whole self, of using all of one's potential to benefit oneself and others, should be the goal of gifted people.

> If a man does not keep pace with his companions, perhaps it is because he hears a different drummer. Let him step to the music which he hears, however measured or far away.

Henry David Thoreau
Walden, Conclusion

Chapter 6

Emotional Intelligence
and Emotional Giftedness

Ross

Ross, age eight, had been a difficult baby to comfort. He screamed through the night, as well as the day. In fact, for a baby he seemed to need little sleep. He was very active and liked to explore objects from quite an early age. He was always touching things, pulling things, and banging things. He had a very strong will. It was obvious what he wanted even before he could talk. As Ross grew into toddlerhood, he had frequent tantrums ranging in intensity from giving single piercing shrieks to full-scale hitting, kicking, biting, and throwing things with accompanying continuous screaming. Tantrums could be set off by telling Ross "No," saying "Later," or needing Ross to do something he didn't want to do.

Even in early elementary years, Ross still had tantrums in public places when tired, hungry, or bored. He became upset and acted out if his expectations were not met. For example, some of the children on his baseball team had play dates after practice. Ross wanted a play date every week and would have a tantrum as soon as practice was over when he found out he had no play date, even if the family had discussed this in advance and planned another fun activity, such as eating out at his favorite restaurant. Ross's preconceived ideas about what should happen, and his inflexibility in tolerating change, sparked his upset. This sort of emotional outburst was also common at school. On the other hand, Ross could be very sweet and endearing. He liked to do nice things for people, and to surprise them with a drawing, treat, or toy that he wanted to give them. Occasionally he did chores spontaneously, saying that he thought it would be a nice thing to sweep the floor for his mom who was busy with the baby.

Madison

Madison, at age eight, was very quiet, daydreamy, and shy. She was noted for her fears at school and home. In fact, Madison had many intense feelings and they were difficult for her to manage. As a baby, at 11 months of age, she had been cuddly and even clingy, with an exaggerated fear of strange faces. She was not very exploratory but was content to sit and look at one thing for several minutes.

In elementary school, it took Madison a long time to warm up and feel comfortable in new situations, or places where she felt overwhelmed, like the lunchroom at school. She preferred sitting with one or two friends. If forced to engage in group activities, she often cried. Madison also disliked physical activity and avoided it as much as possible. Since she had asthma, she did miss physical education on very cold or hot days. On the other hand, she used creative excuses to avoid going to gym at all. Once she told a new gym teacher that she had only one lung and so couldn't run. Madison was a perfect student academically, but needed a great deal of reassurance that she was doing the correct assignment or doing things as her teacher wished.

In her own small circle, Madison was a very good friend. However, her close friends weren't in her classes, so Madison felt lonely and was without a partner for school projects. Madison had wonderful ideas for these projects. Often her ideas were the most creative in the class, but she felt stuck in groups with students who did not want to try her ideas or allow her to do what she liked.

Derrick

Derrick, age eight, had very intense feelings. He had been difficult to calm as a baby. Also, he did not seem to enjoy the games other infants do, like peek-a-boo. His mother could not get him to look at her, or to look at what she was showing him. In fact, she commented on what an independent baby Derrick was. It was almost as if he didn't need her at all except for food and body care. Derrick's emotional reactions were intense in toddlerhood. He had tantrums when interrupted or when he was frustrated. He disliked changes and transitions of any kind and fought them.

Derrick also showed inappropriate responses to other people's expressions of pain or upset. For example, his father dropped a large book on his foot and four-year-old Derrick laughed uproariously. He asked his mother why daddy was behaving like a funny clown jumping all over like that. When he was age eight, his mother reported that feelings lasted a long time, and Derrick could not stop feeling upset for several hours. On a trip to the ice-cream store, Derrick didn't like any of the flavors listed. Since they didn't have his favorite, cookie dough, he threw a fit. Even hours later, Derrick could not get over the fact that the store hadn't had the ice cream he liked, and he obsessed about it until bedtime. Needless to say, no one else in the family got any ice cream either.

Derrick enjoyed music, loving to listen to pieces by various artists from different musical genres and time periods. He loved hard rock as much as classical. He also enjoyed playing music on his keyboard. Derrick had a large repertoire of pieces he could play by ear, and he enjoyed practicing them until they were perfect.

Ross, Madison, and Derrick are all gifted children who had difficulty with emotional regulation. Other aspects of emotional knowledge and control were also troublesome. Ross and Madison, with AD/HD, had difficulty with controlling behavior when upset or thwarted. Derrick, with AS, also had difficulty reading emotional cues and understanding the emotions of others. He had trouble with empathy and perspective taking. The emotional and behavioral difficulties described for these three children are all aspects of emotional intelligence.

The focus of this chapter

The concept of emotional intelligence reflects recent thinking about emotional regulation and interpersonal relationships. In this chapter, topics discussed include:

- The concept of emotional intelligence.

- Emotional intelligence and IQ.

- The development of emotional intelligence.

- Emotional intelligence and attention deficits.

- Attention deficits and the core emotions of giftedness.

The concept of emotional intelligence

Mayer and Salovey (1997) defined emotional intelligence as several different abilities. These include the ability to accurately perceive, evaluate and express emotion, to access and/or generate feelings so as to facilitate thought in emotional situations, to understand feelings, and use them in social interactions, and to regulate emotions to encourage emotional and intellectual growth.

Emotional intelligence is further divided into four branches: the perception, appraisal, and expression of emotion; emotional facilitation of thinking;

understanding and analyzing emotion and employing emotional knowledge; and reflective regulation of emotions to promote emotional and intellectual growth. Emotional intelligence helps people to monitor emotions in themselves and others, to discriminate among various feelings from different points of view, and to know how to use emotional knowledge to guide thought and action. Emotional intelligence has both an internal emotional and intellectual part, and an external emotional and social part. In this chapter, there will be more focus on internal emotion and intellect; and in the next chapter on social competency, more focus on emotional and social factors.

Characteristics of emotional intelligence

Based on Mayer and Salovey's (1997) description of emotional intelligence, the following characteristics were adapted.

The ability to perceive accurately, appraise, and express emotion is comprised of: identifying feelings; knowing one's own feelings, including the idea that one may feel more than one feeling at a time; identifying feelings in others, especially when different from one's own; feeling empathy and sympathy; expressing feelings accurately; and discriminating between accurate and inaccurate expressions of feelings and words – that is, knowing when affect does not match content.

The ability to use emotions to facilitate thinking is comprised of: aspects of using past experience and self-knowledge to judge situations based on emotions generated; separating feelings from content so one can analyze meaning appropriately; being able to shift emotions based on thinking about situations; and using emotions to facilitate problem solving and creativity.

The ability to understand and analyze emotion includes knowing how to recognize feelings and use appropriate verbal labels to define nuances of feelings; understanding relationships between emotions and relationships; understanding complex emotions in self and others; being able to use another's perspective to develop accurate empathy; and recognizing and formulating how to make the transition from one feeling state to another.

The ability to use thinking to regulate emotions includes staying open to feelings, even negative ones; engaging or detaching from emotions depending on their usefulness and appropriateness for a situation; monitoring the expression of emotions in self and others for clarity, reasonableness etc.; modulating one's own feelings and expressions of them while still recognizing the underlying content they suggest; and assessing the appropriateness of any expression, its intensity, and its possible effect.

As can be seen from the above descriptions, emotional intelligence involves some of the traits also described as executive functions: recognition of feelings and how they relate to actions, separating emotion from content of messages, regulation of sensitivity and intensity of emotional expression, timing of emotional expression, toleration of frustration, and modulating behavior by thinking before acting. These are all problematic for gifted children with AD/HD and/or AS, and will be explored in more detail later in this chapter.

Emotional intelligence and IQ

Studies by several researchers have suggested that the construct of emotional intelligence is a useful one. Mayer, DiPaolo, and Salovey (1990) found that people who were better at detecting emotion on faces, and recognizing emotion in abstract designs and in colors, were better also on measures of empathy. Mayer and Geher (1996) found that scores for identifying emotional perception of characters in situations were related to SAT scores, empathy, and emotional openness.

What the concept of emotional intelligence suggests is a range of abilities in emotional functioning. We might think of emotional intelligence as a minimal level of competency required to deal successfully with many different types of people and social situations. People who have less emotional competency have trouble with regulating emotions and dealing with relationships. Those who are more emotionally competent may be emotionally gifted.

Emotional intelligence does not depend on IQ. However, people who are below average in intelligence will still have difficulty with the thinking part of emotional competency. Analyzing emotions will be difficult for them, and they will have trouble with accurate empathy because empathy in adulthood requires reasoning ability. On the other hand, some with exceptionally high IQs will be low in emotional intelligence.

Mayer *et al.* (2001) showed that adolescents who were more verbally adept tended to have higher scores on emotional intelligence measures as well. In addition, Gardner (1983) cited examples of high interpersonal intelligence (usually people who can influence others, such as leaders) and intrapersonal intelligence (often people who can detect and symbolize feelings, such as writers or psychologists). Almost all of those described were quite high in IQ. Thus, those who are especially emotionally competent may have higher verbal reasoning ability, and verbal intelligence may be a necessary, but not sufficient, requirement for higher emotional intelligence.

Emotional giftedness

Gifted children, while usually emotionally competent, may not be emotionally gifted. To be emotionally gifted requires an unusual ability to understand the self and/or others. Those children who show emotional giftedness are, from an early age, especially aware of their own feelings, and how these influence interactions with others. For example, when Madison was in 3rd grade, she became so fearful that she could not sleep at night. She called her parents into her room during the night, explaining in great detail exactly what she felt. Her father faithfully came and comforted her. One day, she told him that she knew coming to her room meant he was losing sleep, and maybe they needed to find some other ways to allay her fears instead. As Madison worked with her father, she was able to see her fear at more of a distance. She learned that she could put the fear away from her and fall asleep by "putting it at the side of her mind." Thus, it was there but no longer bothered her so much. It is noteworthy that Madison's fears first arose from her empathy with the suffering in the world. However, her solution also arose from her empathy – in this case, her concern for her father's needs.

Children who are emotionally gifted are aware of the feelings of others and know how to use accurate empathy. They try to be mutual in their dealings with others at a much earlier age than expected. Empathy includes recognition of feelings in others, the ability to project oneself into another's situation, and the ability to imagine situations that are different from one's own experience. Samantha Smith, at age ten, wrote to the then Soviet Premier, Andropov, because she wanted to tell him about her fears of nuclear war. She thought that people in the Soviet Union were not so different from Americans in wishing to stop such a war from happening. Her letter was answered, and she spent some time in the Soviet Union, seeing for herself that Soviet citizens were, indeed, not so different from people she knew. Samantha's visit was one of the first openings of the Soviet Union to outside visitors (Smith 1985).

Many children who are emotionally gifted are highly empathic and compassionate. Empathy allows these gifted children to see the plight and pain of others, feel sympathy, and try to end such suffering. For example, Helena, age 12, started a charity club using the Internet. She and her friends ran an auction to raise money for charity. After they reached their goal, they decided how to distribute the money: so much for the local soup kitchen, some for the zoo, and some for children overseas. Once they spent the money, they elicited more contributions of articles to auction, and continued the process.

Emotional giftedness includes emotional intelligence and can be noted starting from an early age. The three-year-old who can deal with peer conflicts by negotiating fair turns is likely emotionally gifted, as well as advanced in concepts of fairness for his or her age. Thus, emotional giftedness also suggests advanced concepts of fairness, justice, truth, honesty, and other moral attributes.

Emotional giftedness implies emotional creativity. An ability to understand the perspectives of others, at an age when one has not yet had much life experience, suggests an ability to use imagination and emotional openness to perceive the similarities and differences among people. Emotional imagination allows both a unique perspective and an ability to develop alternate points of view. This is the child who is labeled "an old soul" because his or her comprehension of others is so much deeper and more complex than would be expected not only for a child, but for almost anyone.

Development of emotional intelligence

The development of emotional intelligence depends on acquiring both a firm sense of self (identity) and an understanding of how selves interact in relationships. These two processes occur together from the earliest days of life, and are related to interactions between the infant and the primary care-giver. As Ainsworth (1964) and Stern (1985) have shown, it is the process of early attachment between primary care-giver and child that leads to the formation of identity, since identity means both who one is, and who one is in relationship with others. Formation of identity occurs through the phenomenon of *maternal attunement* to the child's earliest emotional expressions, and *mutual delight* in the interactions between parent and child (Ainsworth 1964). In the attunement process, the parent helps the child develop as an individual by following the baby's lead. Then, the parent mimics and plays with the movements and sounds suggested by the baby.

Not only does the baby need the care-taking parent's engagement in play, but also in expanding emotional and social repertoires. Initially, it is the parent who responds, matching the baby's level of intensity and tempo. Over time, the baby also contributes to the interaction by responding to the parent. Babies start to imitate parents at only a few months of age. They imitate facial expressions and emotion, as well as actions. Babies also observe the facial expression of the parent when it is directed to a particular object. This is called *social referencing*. This means the baby looks at the parent to see how the parent feels about the object, and then assumes that same facial expression. That is, the baby copies the presumed mental state of the parent as shown by facial expression (Gopnik, Capps, and Meltzoff 2000; Stern 1985).

As mutuality develops, the child and care-taking parent both experiment with variation and elaboration of an introduced behavior. Being responded to in a closely imitative manner, and developing the capacity to follow the parent's lead, allows the child to experience empathy in relationship.

Over time, as the relationship between parent and child develops, both parties introduce new material. They do this by showing objects to each other. For example, the mother points to a cat sleeping on the bed, and says, "See the kitty." The baby looks where she points. Babies also point out things to parents, who follow and look too. This is called *shared joint attention* – two people attending to the same thing at the same time (Stern 1985). This sharing of attention occurs by age 15 months for average children, and may occur sooner for some gifted children.

This complex set of interactions between baby and parent is more than just mirroring or imitation. It involves embellishment of the original behaviors so that increasingly complex interactions are built. Because the baby can influence the parent, he or she experiences feeling understood, accepted, and loved in his or her expression of feelings. Feeling understood, and having an influence on the parent, then gives rise to the beginnings of an independent self (Ainsworth 1964; Stern 1985). The parent, moreover, increases or decreases the baby's level of emotion. This aids soothing and self-regulation. The process of mutual attunement is vital in the child's learning to regulate emotion. Also, over time, the secure attachment that arises allows the child to develop independence and trust in others.

For emotional competency to develop, children need to experience the processes of maternal attunement and reciprocal influence, including social referencing and shared joint attention. When these processes go awry, children display problems with attachment, emotional regulation, and ability to form relationships. The process of attunement can go awry for a number of reasons. It can occur because the parent is emotionally unavailable to the child, or because the child has deficits that prevent him or her from participating. For example, a child with a difficult temperament, who cannot be easily calmed, is at risk for relationship problems if the parent cannot find ways to attune to and help him or her learn to regulate emotion (Ainsworth 1964; Thomas, Chess, and Birch 1968).

Children with AD/HD who are fussy, have erratic schedules, or who do not attend well to parents' efforts to engage them are especially at risk. Some children with AD/HD only notice high-intensity stimulation. The lower-intensity stimulation offered by parents' voices or looks may go unnoticed. These children may create their own high-intensity stimulation by head banging, kicking, and crying. One baby, Chuck, a gifted child with severe AD/HD, cried unless he was constantly swung in the rocking swing or taken out in the car. He needed to be bounced and jumped to calm down. At age two, he attempted to engage in high-risk behaviors such as climbing on the stair banisters at the top of the landing and trying to walk like a circus performer.

Fortunately, most children with AD/HD are less intense in their needs for stimulation. However, their poor ability to focus and sustain attention may mean they miss parental cues and are less able to follow these cues. Early hyperactivity may mean these children are more interested in moving than in looking. Attuning to a more active baby can be challenging, but parents can follow the child's lead. Some parents have shaped their baby's behavior by first attuning to the baby, as any parent would, but then enticing the baby's following of their cues. If they are ignored, they change the cues until the child can follow them, and slowly decrease the level of intensity required.

Lewis and Michalson (1985) reported a study by Brown of a child named Felicia, studied from birth to age eight. As an infant, Felicia was difficult, being especially demanding, intense, and driven to explore. Nevertheless, there was evidence of mutual attunement and mutual regulation between mother and child. The mother stated that she served more as a passive partner, allowing the child to lead the way, in order to avoid premature confrontations with her.

Gifted children with AD/HD who came to the Gifted Resource Center of New England had parents who kept their children from dangerous activities, but allowed free exploration in which they also participated, following the child's lead. Anecdotal parent reports of gifted children with AD/HD suggested that for those children who appeared securely attached, early attunement was intensified around activities chosen by the child. One parent described the process as "learning to listen" to what her child was really asking when she made what seemed like overwhelming demands for attention.

Children with AS are more likely to have difficulty with efforts at maternal attunement because they may not attend to parental cues. Thus, they do not imitate gestures, movements, or mental states of the parent. They don't follow the parent's lead, look at the parent for cues, or respond reciprocally. The parent may follow the baby's lead, but without the baby noticing and following back – that is, engaging in a mutual activity with the parent – the baby with AS has difficulty learning about relationships. This deficit of social referencing (Gopnik *et al.* 2000) and shared joint attention (Baron-Cohen 1995) appears to be present in young children with autism and AS and signals that they are not establishing developmentally necessary relationship patterns.

Why is this? One hypothesis is that the child with AS sees the world in parts. It takes so long to shift attention from one thing to the next that the child cannot process wholes. Thus, the baby sees the eye of the parent and focuses on that.

Several seconds later the baby shifts to the mouth. Shifting so slowly means that the child never gets a clear picture of the whole as other children do. Thus, the world is made up of parts and the child misses vital information. Instead of being able to look at the parent to see what he or she is feeling about an object, the child with AS continues to look at the object. If a parent points out an object, the baby cannot shift attention quickly enough to see it too. Consequently, the child with AS does not experience social relationships, but only gets part. The rigid routines that develop, and the focus on narrow interests, may be ways of coping with this problem (Ratey and Johnson 1997).

As children with AS become older, they are more content to play on their own, to study objects that they select, and to look at sights of interest to them, never sharing these with a parent. In fact, parents report they carry the whole burden of the relationship with their children with AS. One parent of a gifted child with AS reported how she cried the first time her very gifted son brought something to show her. He was five years old.

The young gifted children with AS who came to the Gifted Resource Center of New England varied in their early ability to share with parents. If they were sharing objects or material about their favorite interests, they had no difficulty engaging with parents around these. On the other hand, it was universally difficult to get them to pay attention to something the parent initiated unless it involved an interest of theirs.

The development of empathy

Like identity, development of accurate empathy is a process that begins with mutual attunement and continues throughout childhood. The development of accurate empathy is essential for emotional competency because dealing with interpersonal relationships depends so greatly on it. Without empathy, mutual relationships do not develop.

During the process of early attachment, mutual attunement grows to become mutual empathy (Gilligan and Wiggins 1987). First, the infant receives empathy from the parent. In the reciprocal interaction that develops between them, the child becomes attuned to the parent's feelings even though he or she is not yet able to label what the feelings are. By 12 months of age, the average child is able to detect the feelings of parents and respond to them. By 18 months of age, children are able to respond to feelings of siblings, friends, and others.

Hoffman (1994) described the development of empathy in young children. In earliest life, empathy is immediate as children experience the feelings of the other as their own. At this stage, they react to distress in others by seeking comfort for themselves. As young children progress through the first year of life into the second, they start to experience others' feelings as separate from their own and as belonging to the other person. This parallels development of identity. At this stage, children will try to directly comfort another by doing for the other what would comfort themselves: for example, bringing their own mother when the other child's mother is also present.

As children grow older, direct empathy becomes more inferred, and is experienced less directly as internal feelings, and more as understanding the cues put out by the other that suggest particular feelings. Then the young child makes an association about how such a situation might make them feel, and they act accordingly. As children learn to infer empathy, they recognize that what will relieve another's distress may be different from what might relieve their own. For example, they may need their teddy bear, but the other child needs a special blanket. At this point, both empathy (feeling the other's pain within) and sympathy (distress for another without feeling their feelings directly) are in play.

As development continues, and children expand their capacity for abstract reasoning, they are able to imagine feelings that are different from their own. As they become able to view another's perspective, empathy begins to encompass how the situation might feel and look to another. This is the beginning of mutuality as both people struggle to accurately understand the feelings and perspectives of the other.

Children with AD/HD may have difficulty with empathy. While not a universal trait, decreases in empathic awareness occur in some children, especially those with associated ODD. These children have trouble reading emotional cues unless they are intense. They also are self-centered and feel that only their own feelings count. They may appear to be empathic at times, because they choose to be kind or caring, but only because it is a means of asserting control.

Other children with AD/HD have difficulty with empathy because they are overloaded by too much incoming information, or because they are flooded by their own feelings. T.E. Brown (2001) described emotion taking over thinking, like "a computer virus of the mind," so that the person can't attend to how another feels. The lack of attention to others because of their own intense emotions means that these children cannot offer empathy unless they feel calm and focused.

Braaten and Rosen (2000) found that boys with AD/HD were less empathic than other boys. They also had more difficulty matching emotions of story characters with their own. These boys also showed more sadness, anger, and guilt than other boys. Difficulties with empathic responding do not necessarily occur due to a lack of empathy, but more to a lack of attention to those factors that require empathy: the other person's perspective and feelings.

Gifted children with AD/HD, like other children with AD/HD, can appear to show a lack of empathy. Some appear actually to have less empathy; they are more self-centered and seem to care most about their own feelings and needs.

Some gifted children with AD/HD feel great personal distress at feelings they pick up from others. They are so sensitive that they may try to avoid negative emotional situations in order to avoid feeling overloaded by the pain of another's suffering.

While some gifted children with AD/HD are quite adept at understanding and responding empathically, they miss the subtle ongoing emotional cues offered by others. Thus, while capable of empathy, and empathic in many situations, they also miss cues to show empathy, have difficulty sustaining empathy over time, or show empathy variably.

There are gifted children with AD/HD who are quite empathic, and have little difficulty in showing their empathy for others, despite other problems with AD/HD. These are children who, despite having AD/HD, are emotionally gifted.

Children with AS have great difficulty with empathy. They typically do not know what empathy feels like. In a situation where others would show some concern, young children with AS miss the emotional significance entirely. Either they don't notice the emotional significance of the event or they focus on the wrong aspect, as did the boy who laughed when his father jumped up and down in pain after dropping a heavy object on his foot.

As they grow older, some children with AS learn that certain situations require an expression of sympathy. In these situations, they can respond sympathetically and with concern, but on a limited basis. That is, concern is short lived, expressed once, and then the event is over so far as they can see. Also concern is not continuous. Thus, Derrick might remember to ask about his therapist's broken finger, but a minute later will forget about it and want to play a game that requires use of that finger.

Another aspect of difficulty with empathy occurs when the child with AS does not see how the emotional aspect of the situation affects him or her. "Why should I care?" they ask. "It didn't happen to me."

Some children with AS appear able to feel the negative feelings of others, but do not know how to respond appropriately. Like very young children, they feel flooded by negative feelings of their own, and so try to avoid them. Jack, an 8th-grader with AS, withdrew from situations in which he felt negative emotions directed at him or others, even if not directly stated. An introverted boy, he did not like being the center of attention at any time, but especially if he felt the situation was negative. Jack often asked people if they were mad at him, because he couldn't tell if they were or not. He could only feel their negative affect, and didn't know why they felt this way.

Emotional intelligence and attention deficits

In this section of this chapter, how attention deficits affect emotional intelligence will be described. Executive functions related to emotional intelligence will be discussed and suggestions made to improve functioning.

Gifted children with AD/HD

In each subsection below, the difficulties of children with AD/HD will be described and how gifted children with AD/HD differ will be delineated.

Children with AD/HD have difficulty with many aspects of emotional intelligence (Brown 2002), and gifted children are no exception.

Children with AD/HD have been found to be less accurate in interpreting emotions in themselves and others. Cadesky *et al.* (2000) asked children with AD/HD, children with Conduct Disorder, and children with neither diagnosis to assess the emotional meaning of facial expressions. Those with AD/HD and those with Conduct Disorder were less accurate than average. Those with AD/HD made more random errors, suggesting they missed specific cues, while those with conduct disorders tended to interpret expressions as angry, indicating they misinterpreted facial cues. Norvilitis *et al.* (2000) found that children with AD/HD and their parents were less adept at appraising, expressing, and modulating emotions in themselves and others.

Many gifted children with AD/HD have difficulty with assessing facial cues and understanding how another is feeling. If the situation is broken down for them, or replayed slowly, they are much more able to assess what was going on, and what facial expressions indicate. Ross just reacted with anger at what appeared to him to be an arbitrary decision by his parents to go home. They never gave him any warning, he thought. However, when they discussed the situation, Ross was able to recall the cues that he had been given: several warnings that it was time to pack his belongings, his parents putting on coats and calling to him, and their saying goodbye to others. The tone of their voices, their frowns, and their increasingly intense body language were further cues. Ross needed to learn to attend to these cues.

Barkley (1997) suggested that people with AD/HD have difficulty with managing emotional and arousal states. They have trouble recognizing how feelings contribute to events and behavior. Consequently, they have difficulties with emotional self-control. Children with AD/HD tend to be more emotional than age peers, and to react with more emotional intensity to small events that others would brush off. They also show decreased objectivity in responses to events. This means that children with AD/HD cannot so easily set aside their immediate feelings to deal with what has happened. They also have trouble stepping back to see another's perspective, or to consider another's feelings. Children with AD/HD have great difficulty separating feelings from the content of the message, so they also have trouble dealing with frustration. They have trouble modulating behavior so they don't think before they act, and they have difficulty with timing behavior so that it is appropriate.

T.E. Brown (2000b) described emotional control as necessary for focus of attention. Emotional memory of an event arouses further emotion that can derail or enhance attention. Memory of previous failure, as well as intense feelings of frustration, being overwhelmed, or disliking the task, all affect attention negatively. Conversely, great interest or liking for a topic can produce hyperfocusing and good performance. Children with AD/HD show deficits in emotional intelligence due to deficits in executive functions (see Chapter 2).

Gifted children with AD/HD show many of the problems of other children with AD/HD, but they are also different. Moon *et al.* (2001) studied three groups of boys: gifted boys with AD/HD, average boys with AD/HD, and gifted boys without AD/HD. Though the number in each group was small (only three), results were interesting.

The gifted boys with AD/HD in the study were found to be less mature than either other gifted boys, or other boys of their age with AD/HD. The gifted boys with AD/HD showed poor regulation of emotion, easily became emotional, and were easily frustrated. They tended to overrespond to situations. Socially, they were impulsive and made inappropriate physical contact with other children. They described themselves in extremes: with exceedingly positive or exceedingly negative characteristics. They engaged in irresponsible, irritating, and annoying social behaviors.

In contrast, the boys with AD/HD and more average intelligence were less poorly adjusted; however, they had more difficulty with school-related emotional adjustment than the other boys and were more prone to frustration because the school work could be quite difficult for them. They also over-responded to situations and became overly emotional.

The three boys who were gifted without AD/HD did not appear to show great emotional intensity, reactivity, or immaturity. They were judged to have excellent emotional adjustment at home and at school.

The gifted children with AD/HD who came to the Gifted Resource Center of New England showed similar behaviors: impulsivity, tantrums, sulking and other forms of anger, refusals to comply, and indignation at what they considered unfairness by teachers or parents. They showed a lack of ability to modulate behavioral and emotional responses by arguing, complaining, and crying, as well as acting without forethought.

Executive functions, emotion, and AD/HD

Emotional intelligence is related to executive functions, especially as regards the regulation of emotion and its use in complex situations. Because executive function deficits are part of AD/HD, it follows that these deficits are likely to affect emotional intelligence in people with AD/HD.

Specific emotional aspects of executive functions that are problematic for gifted children with AD/HD include separating emotion from content, recognition of feelings and how they contribute to behavior, difficulty tolerating frustration, difficulty thinking before acting, and assessing appropriateness and timing of behavior.

SEPARATING EMOTION FROM CONTENT

Gifted children with AD/HD, particularly those who are hyperactive, react first, think second. They hear the emotional aspect or the emotional tone, and miss the message. This leads to a focus on how they are feeling rather than what they are doing. Things happen so quickly they cannot stop and think about the intent of an action, either their own or another's. They misjudge and misinterpret. They can't easily step back from their feelings and assess the situation in a less emotional manner. This impedes problem solving. Thus, they are more apt to react than thoughtfully to plan an action. Ross had this difficulty; many of his tantrums were related to his misinterpreting what was meant. This could occur because he interpreted messages such as "maybe" as promises. Then, when they did not occur, he was furious. He lost all sense of being able to think of an alternate plan or enjoy an alternate activity.

When emotion is intense and overwhelming, children with AD/HD have trouble thinking about what the message says, and so they miss vital pieces of information. This is especially the case with conditional statements like "if...then." All they hear is the end part of the sentence. Consequently, they overreact or take something to be a promise that was conditional on their action. Ross often missed statements such as, "If you finish your homework, you can watch cartoons." Instead, he became focused on the cartoons and demanded to watch them now.

When gifted children with AD/HD make mistakes or misbehave, their own emotional response may delete the message of what they did wrong. All they can focus on is how they feel. Once they feel better, the problem, in their eyes, is over. In fact, they can barely recall what it was about. What they do recall is how they felt. This can be frustrating for parents who still feel upset over the child's transgression. Paul felt so badly about the mistakes he made that he could not forgive himself. In fact, he felt that whatever anyone said to him about the event made him feel even more guilty. Since he couldn't stand how bad he felt he would have a tantrum full of self-hatred and rage. In effect, Paul felt that he was so negative about himself that others shouldn't scold him on top of it. After all, he had already punished himself. When adults would chastise or punish him for the misbehavior, he felt overwhelmed by the negativity. Paul lost all sense of what he did wrong and how he might remedy the situation.

Suggestions for improving separation of emotion from content

- Gifted children with AD/HD who react first and miss the message need to slow down so they have a chance to stop and hear what was really said. This can be done by breaking the message into two parts and asking after each part what was meant. Then, put the whole message together. Have them repeat the content and tell you what they think it means. Correct misconceptions. For example, "When homework is done, you can watch cartoons," can be broken down into: "First, do homework. Then, watch cartoons." Ask which happens first: homework or cartoons?

- Teach what conditional phrases mean by using physical examples. If we build this tower too high, it will fall. What will happen when the tower is too high? Move to less concrete examples, and show how conditionals work in real life. For more abstract concepts, discuss the idea of possibility and how it is different from probability. Thus, there are many possible flavors of ice cream but it is probable that the store will have only a few of them.

- When gifted children with AD/HD have trouble because they are stuck on wanting something to happen a certain way, practice with them, as if in a movie, other possible scenarios and outcomes. Then, in the real situation remind them of the fictitious outcomes and their solutions. See if any apply now.

- When the child makes a mistake about content (has a tantrum or perhaps thinks something will never happen), spell out exactly what will be required to have something happen.

- For those children who have trouble with sustaining memory for what happened in the past, dictate material into a journal that is kept over time. As the problem repeats, look at what solved the problem last time.

- For those gifted children who have tantrums when they feel guilty and upset over their own actions, wait until they are calm and have them state what the problem was. Then, teach brainstorming and other problem-solving methods. Discuss how much blame should go into a mistake. Make a rating scale with ten being a mistake that led to a great disaster, and one a tiny error without much consequence. Have them rate their mistakes on this scale and discuss how much guilt is reasonable to feel for particular offenses at different points on the scale. Discuss how what they feel isn't equivalent to what they did. Thus, hurting someone's feelings is more of a problem than making a mistake on a test but isn't so big as driving and drinking. The goal is to get them to be less overresponsive to small errors and more able to find solutions to problems without so much upset.

RECOGNITION OF FEELINGS AND HOW THEY CONTRIBUTE TO EVENTS

Gifted children with AD/HD, like other children with AD/HD, often have trouble knowing what they are feeling, and how that feeling contributes to what happens next. For example, a child who was teased is angry and bent on revenge. He will not be able to see what he did that led to the teasing: for example, that he was teasing first. Because they don't detect feelings quickly or accurately, gifted children with AD/HD have difficulty with interpretation of the meaning of events. Because they are more sensitive than other children with AD/HD, gifted children with AD/HD have more trouble with their complexity of feelings about events and people. It is more difficult to separate out what led to all their different feelings. Because they are so much more intense and reactive than other children with AD/HD, gifted children with AD/HD have more difficulty sorting through all their feelings and deciding which is the one to act on.

Children with AD/HD have difficulty with recognizing feelings in themselves and in others. Because they are apt to miss cues or randomly see some cues and not others, they are more apt to get only part of the picture. They also have trouble with seeing the other person's perspective because their own feelings are so intense, and they have less ability to focus on all the aspects of the situation at once: what they feel, what happened, what the other person might feel, why they might feel that, how to deal with the situation, and so on.

Gifted children with AD/HD can focus too much on what they feel and forget to think about the rest of the picture. For example, they can be so involved in arguing for their own way that they forget that their feelings are not all that count. Gifted children with AD/HD can argue much more convincingly for their own way than other children with AD/HD. They use facts and logic in an attempt to overwhelm their adult opposition. Their arguing is based on their own feelings, but their tools of arguing are based on their skills as gifted reasoners. Thus, they can be formidable opponents; however, the use of logic and argument can keep some gifted children from learning to think of others' feelings. Instead, they become more invested in seeing the situation as a game or competition they need to win.

Suggestions to improve recognition of feelings and applications to situations

- Practice labeling feelings. Discuss what the gifted child with AD/HD was feeling in different types of situations. Make up a feeling book that describes situations that have occurred in the child's life and describe what was felt and what happened as a result.

- When the child has been carried away with feelings, dissect situations to see what complex feelings were present. Which ones were recognized at the time, and which later? Which were acted on, and which not? Think about what feelings the child had and how intensifying them or decreasing them contributed to the event. Practice what he or she might have said or done instead. Discuss how feelings are related to actions and to consequences.

- Identify trigger points that lead to negative feelings and behaviors. Target one of these at a time and work specifically on replacing the inappropriate action with a more thoughtful one.

- When gifted children with AD/HD try to use argument to get their way or to excuse their actions, practice perspective taking. This means they have to argue alternate points of view and think about the issues and feelings of others involved. Then, work on a fair solution.

- Teach children how to excuse small mistakes, minor irritants, and human failings, both in themselves and in others.

- Practice having gifted children say, "I'm sorry." Work on forgiveness rather than revenge as a way of enhancing planning ability and tolerance.

TOLERATING FRUSTRATION

Children with AD/HD are well known for their difficulty tolerating frustration. This occurs because they need to have immediate rewards or high stimulation and cannot perform well when a situation requires longer periods without immediate reward, overcoming obstacles, or feeling unable to do the task immediately. However, children with AD/HD also give themselves negative emotional messages that increase frustration. At the first sign of difficulty they tell themselves the task is impossible, and then they feel angry they have to do it. Struggling to do something difficult is a skill many never learn.

Another aspect of poor frustration tolerance is little experience with being patient. Children with AD/HD need to have everything happen immediately. Waiting for something to occur is frustrating because these children don't know what to do unless they are doing something all the time. Also, some are so used to receiving constant high stimulation that they are unable to deal with situations that require a slower approach, more planning, or waiting for the parts to come together.

To children with AD/HD, feeling frustrated is a very negative feeling that they would rather avoid. Learning to work through frustration towards a goal is more difficult than for other children because their feelings are so negative.

Gifted children with AD/HD may have more trouble tolerating frustration than average peers with AD/HD because the gap between what they want to do and what they can do is so much greater. The gifted child can see the whole picture in his or her head, wants to hurry and get there, and is impatient with details, mistakes, and obstacles. Since the projects conceived may be more complex and require more work than an average project, these gifted children with AD/HD may feel more frustration when trying to accomplish something so hard.

Gifted children with AD/HD may show poorer frustration tolerance due to their much higher need for complex mental stimulation. When not involved in tasks that produce hyperfocus, they do not feel sufficiently rewarded. This then leads to poorer frustration tolerance for less stimulating tasks. On the other hand, for tasks that are more stimulating, gifted children with AD/HD can show greater frustration tolerance than usual because they become so deeply involved in the task.

Suggestions for dealing with poor frustration tolerance

- First, children need to recognize when they are frustrated. The body signs of frustration (fast breathing, tension, intense feelings of "I can't") need to be explored with the child and rank ordered from least to most intense. Then, when they recognize the impending symptoms of frustration, they can avoid a tantrum by attending to the feelings and body signs.

- Have the child identify what is frustrating about a task: is it too hard or too easy, undesirable, boring, has too many parts to do, or feels overwhelming? By identifying the frustration, the child may be able to find a solution: do part now and part later, change tasks, ask for help, ask for harder work, do it quickly, or use imagination to make it challenging. When the task is done, have a reward: a fun activity.

- Frustration zappers can be effective. These consist of relaxation techniques to relieve tension. The child can stop the task and breathe, tighten up and release muscles, or use positive talk. ("I can do this. I know how.")

- Teach planning skills and organizational skills so the child can overcome obstacles, know where to start, know how to divide the task up etc. Also, teach skills about how to overcome simple obstacles: try again, skip that one and do the rest, find the easiest or most interesting.

- Teach the child how to become actively involved in tasks by asking questions about the material, getting the big picture and having an end goal, and setting a self-chosen reward that occurs when the task is complete. Parents and teachers can also use timers to set apart spaces of time to do a part of a task. "Do this part before the timer goes off."

- Work on cultivating patience in all areas of life. Plan activities that require waiting until they can happen, and describe each step of the process of waiting. Brainstorm with the child things they can do while waiting. As each part of a task is completed, mark it off and think about how it feels to be patient. When feeling impatient, purposely slow down, try to explore the good parts of the task, and focus on the positive feelings that can occur.

ACTING WITHOUT THINKING, AND ACTING BASED ON FEELING

Children with AD/HD have trouble with impulsivity. Part of the problem is the emotional tag that comes with stopping oneself. To be able to stop, a child has to know what to do next. Children with AD/HD do not know what to do next and feel overwhelmed if they have to try to think of alternatives. Though they often regret impulsive actions, stopping themselves also has an emotional price. Furthermore, impulsivity can be driven by emotion. Once the emotion overtakes the child, thinking of alternatives does not seem possible or even desirable to the child. For example, a child with AD/HD who is teased may feel so angry all he can do is think of revenge. At that moment, he cannot stop himself, and even if he is stopped, he may not see an alternative as desirable.

The intense needs of gifted children with AD/HD can lead to more difficulty with impulsivity, especially when gratification comes from engaging in complex and intense stimulation. When these activities produce feelings of reward and accomplishment, it can be difficult to get the child to attend to more mundane everyday activities such as relationships with others and feelings. The impulsive gifted child who loves video games, for example, is least likely to be able to stop and think about other people's feelings when wanting to play.

Acting before thinking can come from intense feelings. Gifted children who feel strongly about something will act on their feelings before considering whether that is the best plan. Also, because they tend to be big-picture people who get the gist of a situation, gifted children with AD/HD can come to erroneous conclusions about the meaning of comments and situations. That is, they have only grasped part of the information, and jumped to conclusions based on the part they perceived. This can result in poor judgment.

Suggestions to improve impulsive responding

- Work on a program of "Stop, Feel, Think, Act." This type of program tries to put some time between the impulse to act and the action.

  Stop is accomplished by trying to have the child think of ways to slow down. Imagining a stop sign, taking a calming breath, centering oneself as sports stars do before a game, counting to ten before starting, looking at the directions, following the rules: all are ways of stopping.

  Feel means to think about the feelings experienced because of the idea, event, or task. Try to induce pleasant feelings by telling oneself, "I can do it."

  Think means to plan, to decide on how to do something, follow directions, and ask oneself about what will happen next. Thinking requires looking at alternative perspectives, and underlying assumptions such as intent of actions. Make a prediction about outcome.

  Act means to do the task or action and then see what happened. Did the result match the expected outcome? Why or why not?

Doing this type of program requires focusing on one part at a time and building skills while helping children feel positive about accomplishing the parts.

- For difficult situations where an angry response is most likely and results in the most negative behavior, think about the trigger, and plan ahead of time what to do when it happens. Then plan what to do next. For example, Ross's parents decided that the way to avoid tantrums at baseball games was to tell Ross that he would never have a play date right afterwards. Play dates would be planned for another day, and Ross would earn or lose the chance to have them based on his baseball behavior. If Ross started to act up at the game, he was reminded of the plan, and given one chance to pull himself together.

- For children whose main positive feeling comes from intense stimulation (for example, from computer games) limit time on the computer and work on gaining skills in other areas of social and emotional functioning. Playing complex board games with others can be a part of this. There are rules to be followed, a slower pace, sportsmanship to be considered, and interactions with others. Another alternative is to have the child participate in a different type of activity entirely such as charity work. The goal will be to develop compassion and empathy while changing the types of stimulation that will produce satisfaction. Building a house, working in a food pantry, or taking part in a community effort to clean up a waterway can use a lot of energy and produce positive feelings.

- When gifted children with AD/HD have a tendency to jump to conclusions, they need to slow down and get the bigger picture. Have them verbalize the big picture or the main theme of the emotional situation. What are the underlying assumptions? What do the other people think and feel? How do people know when they are right? What are good ways to handle different types of situations? All of these topics can be sources for discussion with children and adolescents.

ASSESSING APPROPRIATENESS AND TIMING OF BEHAVIOR

Children with AD/HD have trouble with emotional timing, so they miss the subtle sequence of low-level emotion that is ongoing in an interpersonal interaction. Then, they do not respond appropriately. For example, a friend is quiet and sad, but the child with AD/HD does not notice and continues to talk about a movie seen recently.

Assessing appropriateness is also a problem because of the tendency to act based on feeling. Thus, behavior is not congruent with what should happen next, but with what the child is feeling. The more intense the feeling, the more likely it is the child will have difficulty stopping to notice nuances and cues about what is going on, and what to do next. Sometimes the inappropriateness arises from the lack of a frame of reference. This occurs with gifted children with AD/HD who are ahead of age peers intellectually, but may be at age level or below emotionally. An appropriate frame of reference arises when there are peers appropriate to one's reasoning and emotional level. If gifted children with AD/HD have no such peers, they may only have their own experience to fall back on, and thus can make errors in judgment.

Timing of the expression of feelings is difficult for gifted children with AD/HD. Because they can feel so passionate and intense about situations, they have trouble letting go of intense feelings, waiting until the right moment to express their feelings, accepting refusals from others, or accepting limits that they don't agree with. When this occurs, gifted children with AD/HD are likely to argue intensely and for a prolonged period with the authority, or they ignore the authority and act upon their feelings.

Some gifted children with AD/HD have an exquisite sense of timing for humor. They can play the role of the class clown, and know the exact moment to act up, say something funny, or do an imitation. This intuition is coupled with positive feelings for the esteem received by making everyone laugh. However, they have trouble assessing the moment when such behavior will be viewed with indulgence by their teacher and when it will be problematic.

Suggestions to improve assessment and timing of behaviors

- For children who have trouble assessing situations because they have a limited frame of reference, try to widen the frame by using hypothetical scenarios about the feelings of different people. Use books and movies as a jumping-off point. Try to supply a different reference point in a mildly emotional situation: what else could be happening; what else could someone be thinking or feeling? What is the opposite point of view to the one the child has, and could he or she think of how it might be to think and feel in that mode on a particular issue?

- When children feel thwarted, they have particular difficulty assessing what is the best thing to do. Think of problem times at home and with friends and think ahead to what might be an appropriate response. When would be the best time to act upon the urge? What can the child do instead if acting on the urge is inappropriate?

- Gifted children with AD/HD and intense emotions have a tendency to argue for what they think is right. It is important to assess with them specific times when arguing is appropriate and when it is foolish. Within a family, list the things that can be negotiable under certain conditions and which things are not negotiable. In school, discuss which rules are flexible and which are not. Have the child work on articulating the interpersonal consequences of continuous arguing.

- Class clowns need some lessons in judging the effect of their humor. How could they predict whether it will be accepted or not? It depends on the teacher's mood, the seriousness of the topic, and the appropriateness of the comment or act. All of these can be discussed. Building relationships based on humor can be an effective way to break the ice or defuse problems, but the person using humor needs to assess the potential effect. Predicting what the other person is feeling is often a helpful means of assessing what effect humor will have.

Gifted children with AS

In each subsection below, the difficulties of children with AS will be described and how gifted children with AS differ will be delineated.

Children with AS have difficulty with most of the aspects of emotional intelligence (Brown 2002). They have trouble with understanding feelings in self and others, understanding facial expressions, seeing the link between affect and behavior, using feelings to direct behavior, using emotion to enhance relationships, and modulating their own feelings and behavior. As with children with AD/HD, some of the problems are related to deficits in executive functioning. However, others are more related to deficits in recognizing social meaning and in understanding others' perspectives. Children with AS show emotional difficulties that arise from their underlying deficits in Theory of Mind and central coherence as well as executive functions.

Difficulty in understanding feelings in self and others affects emotional functioning in gifted children with AS. Some of these gifted children do learn to understand how they feel, and how their behavior affects others, but they don't understand why it should. Consequently, gifted children with AS can make some statements about the effects of behavior on others, and they may even have a good understanding of what they feel. The relevance of their feelings and behavior to what happens with others, though, is more difficult. Derrick understood that snapping his fingers made other people feel annoyed, but he would not stop. It didn't bother him if they were annoyed, so he kept on snapping his fingers. Doing so made him feel calmer, and that was most important to him.

Children with AS have difficulty reading facial expression. Inferring complex mental states from images of the eyes is particularly difficult, and is related to deficits in particular brain systems. Instead of using the areas most people use for facial recognition, those with autism spectrum disorders use areas of the brain more related to recognizing objects. Thus, faces appear to have much less social and emotional cogency for those with AS (Baron-Cohen *et al.* 1999; Schultz *et al.* 2000). Because they have difficulty seeing emotions in faces, people with AS have difficulty attending to expressed emotions in others.

Gifted children with AS have the same difficulties noting facial expression and understanding how it conveys emotion as more average children with AS. Gifted children, however, can learn to assess some aspects of facial expression, relate it to strong emotions, and use that information in dealing with others. Stuart, described in Chapter 4, learned how people in his family expressed feelings on their faces and, provided he was paying attention, could respond appropriately. Olivia, described in Chapter 3, on the other hand, never noted what others were feeling because her own feelings were always so intense. She could not pay attention to facial expression or even expressed feelings because her own feelings were so much more significant than what others were feeling, and her feelings lasted so much longer.

Emotional deficits in AS

Children with AS have deficits in recognizing, labeling, and identifying feelings; in dealing with obsessive, repetitive, and restricted feelings; dealing with frustration; dealing with transitions; assessing other people's feelings; and monitoring and assessing the appropriateness of their own behavior. They have difficulty managing feelings and in using feelings in interpersonal relationships. In each part of this section of the chapter, the problems of children with AS will be described, and then how gifted children with AS may be similar or different.

RECOGNIZING, LABELING, AND IDENTIFYING FEELINGS

Children with AS have difficulty identifying feelings. They do not know what they feel nor how what they feel is reflected in their behavior. Thus, even in late adolescence and adulthood, people with AS have difficulty identifying feelings when asked what they feel. While many have learned to identify pure and strong feeling states – sad, angry, happy, scared, worried – they have much more difficulty with mixed feeling states and complex feelings. Derrick could not identify easily what he felt when he moved to a new higher-level school. It wasn't quite happy or sad or worried; he just couldn't say.

One of the reasons for poor identification of feeling states is not only a lack of associating feelings with particular labels, but also difficulty in actually feeling anything much of the time. George, a gifted adolescent with AS, often said he wasn't feeling anything. If asked, he would reply, "Sort of blank." Because he had so much trouble feeling anything, he assumed others also felt nothing. Thus, George had particular difficulty getting the idea of predicting feelings in others using their facial expression. In fact, George's own face did not match what he said he felt. He would frown but say he was happy, or look peaceful and say he was angry. George had trouble with the idea that others were making assumptions about what he was feeling based on his facial expression. He would insist that wasn't how it was, and that other people ought to know how he felt.

George had very little idea of how different facial expressions looked. He didn't know how eyes or mouths looked if someone was angry as opposed to happy. It was little wonder he had little idea of how he looked either.

Gifted children with AS have trouble with self-disclosure because they don't have the words to describe their inner feelings. Though they can describe an object or one of their interests in exquisite detail, they have no idea how to talk about feelings. Even when they can identify their basic feelings, it is difficult for them to say why they feel this way, or how what they are feeling is connected to what happened. It is especially difficult for them to describe complex feelings. Thus, while they may learn how to identify a feeling, talking about the feeling and sharing feelings with others remains difficult throughout life. For example, George could say he felt sad about something that had happened, but he could go no further in talking about his sadness. To him, saying he was sad summed it up. This meant he also had less means of receiving comfort, because he did not know what would be comforting to him either.

Some gifted adolescents with AS have a degree of self-knowledge about their feelings. In conversations, although they are not good at small talk or discussing how others feel, they are good at discussing their own emotional experiences (Ratey and Johnson 1997). Unfortunately, they also don't monitor the appropriateness of what they say. Derrick, as an adolescent, was able to dissect his feelings and trace how they had led to his behavior. He knew when he was teased he was likely to get angry and try to get back at the teaser. He also knew that he was likely to get into trouble if he did so. Nevertheless, Derrick had great trouble in the moment stopping himself from responding to teasing. Part of the issue was that he felt justified in getting revenge. Derrick went so far as to provoke incidents since, in his mind, he was still angry at what had happened and needed to extract more retribution. Thus, he addressed his tormenter as "Bully Boy."

Suggestions to help children with AS learn about feelings

- Use pictures that illustrate how different expressions of feeling look on different people's faces. Cutting these from magazines and newspapers can be interesting so long as posed pictures – advertisements for example – aren't used. Advertisements don't really show full facial expression of the displayed feeling. Use the pictures to illustrate what makes different expressions different: eyes, mouth, shape, direction of gaze, and so on.

- Make a picture journal of all the ways faces can look angry, sad, etc. Start to discuss faces with more complex emotions and how these look. Have the child look carefully at parents' faces and guess what expression is being displayed. Tell the child which cues you, the adult, use to know what he or she is feeling: tightly scrunched eyes, open yelling mouth – angry or frustrated.

- When children with AS say they feel nothing, or blank, they are probably correct, but need coaching in how to feel. Use models of how someone might feel in a similar situation. Discuss what the feeling would feel like inside the body. Help the child translate "blank" to more subtle expression of feeling – okay, peaceful.

- When children with AS don't know what they feel, try to have them guess. Use a multiple-choice format. Use a mirror so they can look at themselves and decide if the feeling matches inside and out. Have them assume, on purpose, expressions of happy, sad, and angry and see which feels most like their current feelings. Also, see if they can remember a time when they felt a particular feeling and what caused the feeling. Getting a present they wanted made them feel happy. Can they think about it now and remember what happiness felt like? Some children with AS will be able to do this, but some will not.

- Work with gifted children with AS on how and when to self-disclose feelings. Help them to elaborate on an initial feeling statement by giving close-ended choices. (Is it more like happy or more like sad?) Then, state the elaborated feeling description in several sentences. Make a feeling script. When…happens, I feel…because… I also feel a little…and a little… I will (calm down, remember good things, enjoy this feeling).

OBSESSIVE, REPETITIVE, AND RESTRICTED FEELINGS

Children with AS can become stuck on certain feelings. Because their thinking is rigid and no other alternatives seem possible, these children feel stuck in impossibility or helplessness. Nothing has ever worked before, and nothing ever will. However, these children are stuck on one viewpoint. They cannot conceive that there might be another even if it is pointed out to them. It isn't their point of view, so it isn't imaginable. Getting stuck on one point of view is a particular problem for gifted children with AS. They can think of so many possibilities in other areas that it seems surprising that they get so stuck in emotional functioning. Adults are less willing to believe the gifted child with AS is truly stuck and sees them instead as stubborn or manipulative.

Another variation of this "stuckness" occurs when a strong negative feeling is associated with an event. Because it happened once that way, the gifted child with AS is convinced it always will. Thus, the child will attempt to avoid situations in which the negative feeling occurred. Joseph, age 13, was convinced that because he had been teased on one occasion in the school lunchroom, he could not ever eat at that table again. When George got sick after he had eaten scrambled eggs, he was convinced the eggs were to blame and refused to eat them again. It is almost as if these children become behaviorally conditioned, and they go on to develop what seems to be a phobia about the food, place, or activity. However, it is not a true phobia, but rather the result of rigid feeling and thinking that allows no alternative.

Once a feeling has become associated with a place or event, it can be difficult to change. Joseph did not think he could feel positively about eating lunch at that cafeteria location even if there were entirely different people at the table. His negative feeling was stuck on that particular table. Oddly enough, he could eat lunch with people who teased him if they all sat at another table.

Some gifted children with AS have intrusive thoughts and feelings. They are highly imaginative, but lose control of their imagination, and start to obsess about negative thoughts and feelings. Bradley blurted out exceptionally negative comments in class: "I'm going to kill you all. You'll see the bloody mess." Olivia with great openness, and no hesitation, told her teachers how she'd create blood and gore. Some children report experiencing extremely frightening and horrible feelings, images of blood and mutilation. These thoughts and feelings can be stated without any sign of disturbance, with great glee, or with a massive flooding of anxiety. Hans Asperger (1991) described several children in his original study with these sorts of feelings and behaviors.

Such feelings and verbalizations may be the result of the emotional immaturity of the child who cannot appreciate the effect of cheerfully talking about an interest that other people find repugnant. One boy appeared to be more interested in how the circulatory system worked in his discussions of blood and gore (Dewey 1991). Dewey discussed the possibility that such thoughts are verbalized by children with AS because they are so socially immature. A threat that might be made by an angry four-year-old child without AS – "I'll make you drive 100 miles without your seat belt fastened!" (p.193) – sounds more ominous when uttered by a ten-year-old child with AS. Careful assessment is required when feelings or behaviors like these occur or are reported by gifted children with AS, to determine if they have become attached to this negative way of stating anger, or if they are experiencing obsessive-compulsive thoughts, are depressed, have Tourette Syndrome, or even are psychotic.

Suggestions for improving obsessive and rigid thinking

- When the child with AS becomes stuck on a feeling and tries to avoid something based on the feeling, it can be helpful to explore what the child is trying to avoid. Joseph associated the table with the anger he felt. One thing that helped Joseph was seeing all the tables removed for a school dance. When they were replaced, none of them was in the exact spot where Joseph had felt anger. Meanwhile, he started to work on how to deal with being teased, and how to release anger more safely. Once he was more able to handle his feelings, he was less likely to associate them with a place.

- Gifted children with AS, who rigidly respond to a problem based on intense feeling, need help in identifying the triggers of their feelings, in setting up scripts of what appropriate responses would be, and in using a plan to try to use a new approach. Also, these children need some methods of decreasing how long they continue to feel the feeling. Derrick, who had to get revenge for being teased, might identify the specific words that made him feel so angry. The words he said to himself to prolong the anger would be determined. If Derrick had no internal words but reacted because he saw the situation occurring again, he would need to identify what were the scene triggers. Then, he would need a plan of action, and a script of what to say and do instead of calling his opponent, "Bully Boy."

Finally, he would meet daily with an adult who could help him evaluate how his plan was working.

• Obsessive rumination about a feeling can also occur. Jillian would talk continuously about a situation she found upsetting, saying the same words over and over, asking for reassurance, and never being reassured for more than a moment. This obsessive questioning in and of itself helped Jillian handle her anxiety, but it drove everyone else crazy. Attempts to limit how many times Jillian could say the same words or ask the same question were somewhat successful in decreasing her obsessing. Giving Jillian words to say to herself to counter her worries did not work. She was unable to use these even with cueing. Medication to decrease obsessive rumination helped significantly.

• Those gifted children with AS who blurt out, or seem to feel, horrifying thoughts and feelings may not be helped by techniques that foster suppression or changing to less powerful images. It is hard to cue children with AS to follow these directives. A behavioral treatment plan may be helpful for some of these children using tiny steps and tiny goals. Medication may also be helpful in decreasing the intrusive thoughts.

DEALING WITH FRUSTRATION

Children with AS are easily frustrated. They have so many things they want and need to have just so, and real life isn't like this. It is so frustrating to count on the bus arriving at the same exact time each day, and then have it arrive late or early. It is frustrating to need to eat your breakfast in a certain way, and that day mom decides she needs to have you eat it in the car because the alarm didn't go off and you are late for school. Unlike the frustration of children with AD/HD, children with AS feel upset when things are different from their very rigid expectations. This is because these rigid expectations are what helps them make sense of a chaotic world. When the routine changes, they can't see the central likeness of the situation to what they expect (we will still get to school). Instead, these children feel as if since that piece was destroyed, the whole will be different (you can't go to school a different way, or late, and so on). Ratey and Johnson (1997) describe this rigidity as if the AS person could not connect how events that lead to the same result come together. Thus, one man they described always came into the house through the front door. It was as if to him coming into the house through the back door was a totally different experience, whereas most people know that either door takes them to the same goal.

Children with AD/HD are more apt to feel frustrated if they cannot do something they want to do, are told "No," or feel thwarted. Children with AS feel frustrated by these things too, but experience more intense frustration if things change. Most children with AD/HD can weather having a green rather than blue mug for breakfast. The child with AS cannot. To him or her it is as if the world suddenly changed.

Gifted children with AS can become very frustrated when things change unexpectedly. Because they are so bright, it can be difficult for teachers and other adults to understand what all the fuss is about. Why can't Joseph, who is in middle school already, do math without his favorite pencil? That just seems so silly. Yet, to the gifted child with AS, doing the math is part and parcel of doing it with that pencil.

Gifted children with AS also become frustrated when told, "No," when they are made to stop doing their favorite activity to do something else, or if they want something right now and they are not allowed to have it. These gifted children show their frustration with tantrums, refusals to do the appointed task, or ignoring what is being said to them. With gifted children with AD/HD, a secondary reward can be substituted for the desired item, or the child can understand the idea of working to get what he or she wants. Gifted children with AS, for all their intelligence, do not see why they should do things they don't want to do. If it has no point they can see, they refuse to do it. Nevertheless, gifted children with AS do learn to do tasks so they can get more of what they want. When they have a behavior contract, and know ahead of time what to expect, they can cooperate in doing tasks that are not their choice.

Suggestions for dealing with frustration

- Pick your battles. It is especially important with gifted children with AS that parents and teachers allow harmless idiosyncrasies. Thus, if George won't eat eggs, don't fuss about it but provide other foods. At the same time, let your child know that there are harmless and not so harmless idiosyncrasies. For the latter, some changes may have to be made.

- Work with gifted children with AS to see more solutions to problems. If the first does not work, what alternatives do they have? Thus, if Joseph is dedicated to using a certain favorite pencil for math, he might need a supply of similar pencils, or he might need some ideas of what to do if his pencil is lost or forgotten.

- Gifted children with AS can work for rewards, if the reward is something they want. Extra time for

- doing their favorite activity, a new piece of equipment for their activity and so on can be earned through use of a behavioral contract and point system for completing small steps.

- Some gifted children with AS become very frustrated if they are unable to perform perfectly. They need to start over and over and never finish because they inevitably make a mistake. When gifted children with AS are extremely perfectionistic, it is advisable to break work down into tiny steps that can be completed in a short time and give rewards for doing so. The goal is to complete the work, so de-emphasize exactness; in other lessons, accuracy can be the focus. The child will need to learn strategies to enable him or her to be more accurate: for example, using a spell checker or calculator.

- When gifted children with AS become frustrated because they cannot have what they want, they can learn how to accept a negative reply. One way to do this is to make a plan of how to handle being told, "No," and having a list of alternatives of what to do. For example, the child could ask for something else, or ask when the desired activity or object will be allowed. He or she could develop a plan for use of the desired activity: for example, every day from three to four, playing computer games is allowed.

DEALING WITH TRANSITIONS

For both children with AD/HD and those with AS, transitions can be difficult because they involve stopping one activity, requiring children to organize themselves and move to do something else. Children with AD/HD have trouble with all aspects of transitions as do children with AS. One important difference between children with AS and AD/HD, though, is their approach afterwards. If children with AD/HD had difficulty with a transition, they are able to recognize that they have made the other person feel angry because they did not get going. Those with AS do not make this connection. They are not trying to annoy or manipulate adults, but instead, are simply trying to cope with the disorganization they continuously experience.

Because gifted children with AS become hyperfocused on activities, it can be very difficult to have them change to a less desired activity. Some do not pay attention to warnings or time limits. These children seem to enter an alternate universe where time has no meaning. In fact, they would not care if they never ate dinner or slept.

Trying something new can be a source of great stress for gifted children with AS. While they gladly rush ahead into the unexplored depths of computer games and new books, these children are unable to attempt trying new foods or new experiences. Not all gifted children with AS are this rigid; some do enjoy new experiences. It depends on what it is. Joseph enjoyed traveling to Europe with his family. He had little trouble with different foods and was eager to try them. Derrick, despite his difficulty with foods, enjoyed going to San Francisco. His parents had planned a low-key trip that included doing activities Derrick enjoyed, and finding restaurants that served foods he would eat.

Suggestions for improving transitions and need to change

- Give children with AS warnings about impending changes. Make sure they know what to expect next. Use visual charts and schedules so they can see the sequence of activities. Knowing what will happen next then allows them to learn how to shift attention. It can be helpful to use a script to practice stopping an activity without finishing it while moving onto the next (see Chapter 4 for suggestions for dealing with hyperfocusing). This method, with a lot of structuring, can also work with computer games. However, even with a lot of practice, it is hard for children with AS to stop playing computer games on command, and the best thing parents can do is to limit playing to times when they will not need to make a sudden change.

- While most children can eventually learn how to deal with planned transitions, emergencies are very difficult for children with AS. Because they do not recognize an emergency as something that will need all their time and attention, they don't see why they should have to stop what they are doing, or do something differently. Playing "emergency" can be helpful. This involves developing a set of scripts about what to do when an emergency is declared. For example, if there is a cue word, such as "emergency," the child has to stop, listen, get certain supplies, go to an assigned place, and wait. Separate scenarios for fires, tornadoes, and such will also be needed. Practice these scenarios and have the child actually perform the actions. If a real emergency occurs, the child will be prepared.

- The feelings of panic that arise when children with AS have to hurry need to be addressed by parents and schools. As with emergencies, practicing how to hurry and under what conditions hurrying may occur will allow the child to feel less anxious and more in control. Allowing the child to pick out some aspects of what could be done to hurry can be helpful in getting him or her to do these things. For example, on days when the bus is missed and the family has to hurry, what foods can be eaten in the car? How about an emergency take-along kit for hurry-up days? Practice filling up the kit and then plan the scenario like a movie script. Then have the child act it out. For example, get in the car and go with the kit. If the child is very rigid – "apples need a knife and can only be eaten at the table" – what else can be substituted? Practice pays off later on in real life.

ASSESSING OTHER PEOPLE'S FEELINGS

Not only is it difficult for those with AS to assess and feel their own feelings, it is difficult to read what others are feeling and to use that knowledge of feelings in interpersonal relationships. Part of the problem is the difficulty of children with AS in understanding the emotional significance of events for others. They focus on the event itself and miss the emotional content. This is the opposite of what AD/HD children do: they focus on the feeling and miss the message. Those with AS focus on the message and take it literally. The emotional content that would modify the message, let them know if it is serious or a joke, or let them know the other person's feelings is not processed.

Thus, children with AS miss context, misinterpret the meaning of content, and miss nonverbal messages. They tend to be literal and concrete. Sarcasm and other subtle emotional displays based on voice tone or body posture (for example, rolling the eyes) are missed as cues. It is as if people with AS live in an almost gray world while everyone else experiences color. Gifted children with AS are easy to tease because they miss the innuendoes and body language of peers. They also don't understand sarcasm in adults. For example, when a teacher is sarcastic, the gifted child with AS is apt to take him or her literally. Often these children do not know how to respond, and thus do the wrong thing.

Not being able to read emotional messages means that behaviors are misread and intent is misinterpreted. People with AS are more apt to think others do things on purpose, that accidents were intended to happen, and that being overlooked is being purposely ignored. Derrick thought the store didn't have his favorite ice cream on purpose. However, it should be pointed out that it is not only children with AS who misinterpret others' behavior. Often, other people misinterpret the behavior of the child with AS.

People with AS also have trouble with assessing the appropriateness of their own and others' behaviors. In a famous series of stories about social situations

(Dewey 1991), people with HFA (many of whom would be classified as having AS now) were asked to determine if particular behaviors in the stories were normal, rather strange, very eccentric, or shocking. Their responses were compared to college students without AS. The people with HFA tended to misinterpret the behaviors as more normal, or they recognized the strangeness of the behavior but gave idiosyncratic reasons why it was strange. Thus, the way people with AS interpret what others are doing is different from most people.

Because people with AS have trouble with holding two points of view in mind at once, they tend to stick to one, their own. They then assume that everyone else feels the same way about something. They have limited ability to see things from another point of view without changing their own minds to that point of view too. Yet it is possible to change their minds. When they change, it is as if all the feelings generated by the first point of view never happened. Lara's parents divorced when she was 11. Because things were now different, Lara could not adjust. She had trouble with the idea that she was supposed to go to her father's new apartment to see him. In her point of view, things should not be different. Dad should still live with them. So she refused to go with him to the new place. When he tried to force the issue, Lara cried and screamed for the whole afternoon. They never actually got out of the car, because Lara would not get out. By meeting Lara in the car, taking her to favorite neighborhood places, and slowly getting her used to Dad's new life, her father got her used to his new status. Finally, he took Lara to his apartment and, despite some trepidation, it went fine. Suddenly all of Lara's anxiety about Dad and the divorce disappeared as if it never had been, and she could hardly recall what she had felt just a few hours before. Changing Lara's point of view changed her feelings.

Gifted children with AS have as much trouble assessing people and situations as other children with AS; however, they are so intelligent that adults cannot believe they have not acted negatively on purpose. Joseph, in middle school, was told by the school bus aide to get off the bus, but he was busy reading his book. When she asked again, he told her, "In a minute..." Since this was behavior he used all the time at home, and it was acceptable, he didn't understand why the bus aide became angry at him. He would have gotten off the bus; he just needed to get to end of the chapter.

Gifted children with AS get into trouble because of their rigid adherence to rules and routines. They point out rule violations by both other children and adults. Will saw boys smoking in the hallway at his high school, and immediately went to the office where he announced, in front of several other students, about the smoking violation. When the principal brushed off Will's complaints, he became indignant. "Aren't you going to do something?" he yelled. Will was punished for yelling at the principal. The injustice of this made Will have a tantrum, and things escalated until his parents were called to school. It was difficult for Will to see that he might have been more successful if he had talked to the principal in private, or understood that it might take some time for the principal to do something about the smoking.

Suggestions for improving assessing people and situations

- Over a long period of time, adults need to work with children and adolescents with AS to explain the strange customs and thoughts of other people. These children need scenarios, feelings, and points of view explained over and over until they can start to make some judgments themselves that are accurate. Making up hypothetical situations about how people might feel, and what they might expect as a response, is another technique to be used. When something has happened, replaying it and discussing the other points of view can be useful.

- Working on point of view and intent is especially important for children with AS who think things are purposely done against them. Working on defining an "accident," and how to tell what behaviors have a high probability of being accidental, is important in learning about intent.

- Practicing points of view with children with AS can be challenging. One game that can help is to suggest several possible ideas and views that a person might have, and then to use clues to figure out which ones might fit which person, sort of like the mystery game *Clue*. Thus, by using clues, one might determine that the person with the Save the Whales t-shirt probably also has a particular point of view about logging in rain forests. Later, using clues about how the person looks and acts can give information. Some people with AS, especially adolescents and young adults, respond to the idea of forming a hypothesis and then looking for evidence about the hypothesis. Thus, would my mother like the same thing I do? Would she feel the same way I do about a movie? What evidence could I use to find out? What questions could I ask? How would I know when it is a good time to make a complaint, or ask for something?

- It is important to work with gifted children with AS on when and how to report rule violations. As gifted children with AS become adolescents, they need to learn that teens in general tend to disregard rules, and some of these need to be reported and some don't. Frank discussions about rights and needs of self and others are important. The gifted adolescent with AS needs to know when they might also violate rules and customs, such as touching others. Luke Jackson (2002), in his book on AS for adolescents, addresses this issue quite nicely.

MONITORING AND ASSESSING THE APPROPRIATENESS OF EXPRESSION OF FEELINGS

Children with AS may have extreme and inappropriate emotional responses to what seem minor issues. They can have trouble modulating emotional expression and trouble realizing why they reacted as they did. People with AS resemble younger children in their expression of emotions, so they look immature. Many still have tantrums well past the age when others have outgrown such extreme expressions of emotion. Also, because of their preoccupations with their own interests, these children and adolescents appear more self-centered. For very bright children with AS, such extreme expressions of emotion and lack of self-control are incongruous. Not only do gifted children with AS react negatively, they react out of all proportion to the problem. The asynchrony between their ability to reason about other topics and their ability to control emotional responses is much greater than for gifted children without AS. Will's story, above, is an example of a gifted boy with AS who had trouble modulating his emotional response when the principal didn't act as upset as he was over the smoking.

Some people with AS have difficulty with controlling emotional responses to frustration, anger, and upset. The tantrums of young children with AS that include physical aggression may not disappear as the child enters adolescence or even young adulthood. If upset, they revert to total loss of control, only they are bigger now and more destructive. The problem isn't that these older children and teens are more aggressive than earlier, but that they haven't learned more acceptable ways of showing extreme feelings. They still react emotionally as they did when they were age two. Some gifted children with AS who have difficulty controlling emotional responses and aggression feel justified in being angry and using whatever physical means they have to express their intense feelings. "I had to do it," they say. "It was the only way to get rid of my anger."

Many children with AS feel deeply hurt when criticized (Attwood 1998) and do not have the means to deal with criticism. If criticized, they react with tantrums. Some incorporate self-images that are negative, such as "bad boy." Many also have difficulty letting go of extreme feelings of anger, guilt, and hurt. They brood upon these and even turn them into obsessions. This is due to their seeing part of the picture and then getting stuck on it. Gifted children with AS have even more things to feel badly about. Because they can see more deeply into an issue, but also lack perspective, they are more apt to come to a negative conclusion and then to overfocus on it. Because gifted children with AS can only see their own point of view, it feels as if as if they are all alone in the world in suffering the particular negative emotion. Therefore, they take each negative instance as proof that they, or the world, are bad.

Suggestions for dealing with inappropriate and extreme emotion

- Older children and teens who engage in inappropriate and extreme responses to emotion will need specialized intervention in which their behavior is part of an overall plan for helping them attain control. While they may not see any reason for self-control, programs that use rewards specific to their interests, and break behaviors into small enough steps, can improve functioning. Christopher, age 16, a gifted boy with AS, attended a small private high school for boys with autism spectrum disorders. Here he learned to build positive behaviors. As he did so, his frustration decreased and his aggression was less easily aroused. He also was given some reality lessons in what could happen if he were aggressive at his age. They went to visit the jail, and it was pointed out to him that if he went there because of his aggression, he'd have to give up all the things he liked because jails didn't allow them. This helped him control himself.

- For younger children, aggressive behavior occurs because of a lack of positive coping skills. Building these skills by breaking behaviors to smaller units and offering rewards can be helpful. However, changing the child's environment is also helpful until he or she learns better coping skills. Thus, parents with a gifted child with AS need to know that they can't spring surprises on their child and expect appropriate behavior. Their child can't *ever* "go with the flow." Using a book like Ross Greene's (1998) *The Explosive Child* can alleviate many battles between parents and children.

- Gifted children with AS who develop negative self-concepts are very sensitive to criticism. It is helpful to use a matter-of-fact tone of voice, lay out the rule violation, discuss how to remedy the problem, and then offer praise for the positive aspects of self-restraint seen, for doing something to remedy the problem, and for having good intentions. Often gifted children with AS hear too much criticism; they do not receive many positive comments, then, so they tend to disregard those they do hear. Use reward systems that allow the child to measure individual progress and give access to favored activities coupled with positive comments about progress.

Attention deficits and the core emotions of giftedness

Emotional characteristics of giftedness

From the time of Terman (1925) and Hollingworth (1942), many have listed emotional characteristics related to giftedness. These include capacity for emotional depth, deep attachment to people and animals, emotional intensity, sensitivity, empathy, self-awareness, passion, and the rage to learn (Roeper 1982; Silverman 1993a, 1993d; Winner 1996). Roeper thought the capacity to understand and transform perceptions into intellectual and emotional knowledge was important. Lovecky (1993) described excitability, sensitivity, perceptiveness, and entelechy (an internal vital force directing one towards a goal) as emotional characteristics of giftedness.

Well-adjusted gifted children appear to have many of the characteristics of emotional intelligence. They are positive in outlook, and sensitive to their own feelings and those of others. They have a strong sense of integrity and are emotionally well balanced. They try to be fair in their own dealings with others. They are self-directed, independent, and well motivated when working on appropriate tasks. Gross (1993) described Gabrielle, age six with an IQ of 168, as happy in school and popular with the other children. She was known to be quite definite about those she liked, and those she did not, and why. She was exceptionally able to articulate insights into her own feelings and other people's behavior.

The superior emotional adjustment of gifted children starts early in life. For example, the Harvard Project (White 1985), which studied six-year-old gifted children, found them exceptionally able to get and hold adult attention in socially acceptable ways. The children showed a variety of mechanisms and chose the one that would work best for the situation. They were good at using adults as resources after they first tried something, but could not do it themselves. They were able to express affection and mild disappointment appropriately to adults and to peers. They were proud of their achievements, and spontaneously, yet without bragging, were able to talk freely about them. They showed a desire and capacity for appropriate competition. Finally, many also engaged in fantasy play. The roles chosen were future oriented rather than driven by the past (adult roles were chosen as opposed to being a baby, for example).

The issue of asynchrony

Gifted children vary in degree of emotional maturity both from age peers and within themselves. Thus, while much more mature, on the whole, than age peers, gifted children's emotional development is not commensurate with intellectual growth. In some areas, gifted children may be as mature as adults, and in others, more like age peers.

Levels of maturity can also vary over time, especially as developmental issues come into play. Thus, the young adolescent, who is trying to become independent of parents, may act less maturely about restrictions than even a short time before. Life experience also plays a big part in development of maturity, and this cannot be rushed; consequently, emotional development still takes time and lags behind intellectual development. This means gifted children may often be able to discuss emotional issues intelligently, but may be much less able to act on them.

Emotional asynchrony occurs when there is a mismatch of inner and outer states. Gifted children may be cognitively ready to ask questions, but may not be emotionally ready yet for the answers. For example, a highly gifted 2nd-grader may have a reading level that would allow her to comprehend *The Diary of Anne Frank*, but would not be emotionally ready at age six or seven to deal with either Anne's own emotional growing-up issues or the horror of the Holocaust.

Emotional asynchrony may occur when gifted children are accelerated by being placed in an advanced grade without thought to their emotional vulnerability. Thus, topics may be discussed in health class, art class, or in the lunchroom that are age appropriate for the classmates, but not appropriate for gifted children. While able to understand these cognitively, gifted children still lack the life experience needed to have an emotional stake in these issues. They simply aren't at the developmental stage of classmates yet. This type of asynchrony does not occur for all gifted children. Some are able to imagine the experiences by having read very widely, and being quite empathic themselves. Thus, while they may not have fallen in love themselves yet, they may know why it brings anguish to a classmate or a character in a novel read in class. In addition, some gifted children may have a wider range and depth of emotional experience and expression than even older classmates. They seem born older and are wise beyond their years.

The emotional core of giftedness

Giftedness is composed of more than intellectual advancement and reasoning. Giftedness also has an emotional component. People who are gifted are both intellectually advanced and emotionally more complex. Both intellectual and emotional reasoning is advanced over age peers.

Emotional intensity, reactivity, and sensitivity are considered to be the core emotional traits associated with giftedness (Piechowski 1986, 1991; Roeper 1982; Silverman 1993a; Winner 1996). In addition to the characteristics of emotional intelligence, these three traits are found in varying degrees in gifted children, and provide additional aspects to emotional intelligence. Children who have exceptional ability in perspective taking, empathy and compassion, concerns about moral issues from an early age, and show emotional imagination may also be emotionally gifted.

Gifted children with AD/HD and *gifted children with AS* show more variability in the core emotional aspects of giftedness than other gifted children. Like other gifted children, they show more intensity, reactivity, and sensitivity in emotional perception and responses. However, since they are also having attention deficits, the emotional aspects of giftedness add another aspect to the emotional issues presented by AD/HD and AS.

EMOTIONAL INTENSITY

The concept of emotional intensity refers to the energy, strength, and vehemence of a response, thought, or feeling. Intensity can mean a high degree of emotional excitement, a depth of emotional feeling. As it is applied to giftedness, it can mean both the depth of experience and the passion with which one pursues an endeavor. Winner's (1996) "rage to master" encompasses intensity, as does the concept of entelechy (Lovecky 1992b). Csikszentmihalyi (1996) described the state in which creativity occurs when the world falls away, and one becomes one's creative endeavor. His concept of "flow," which arises during this state, is another example of the passion felt by gifted people when trying to master something. Flow is both a state of intellectual readiness, and also an emotional state of commitment and passion.

Emotional intensity, the passion that compels an endeavor, is also related to conation, or will. That is, the motivation to do things comes from a well of intense passion that energizes and drives achievement. Motivation, in this sense, has to do with psychological drive. Motivation relies on other underlying skills such as ability to set goals, to sustain working even with obstacles, and to feel rewarded. A feeling of reward occurs when a person feels positive during the process of working and positive about the result. This is called intrinsic motivation: that is, the rewards come from within. Gifted children who feel an intense drive to accomplish, learn, discover, and invent all have high intrinsic motivation.

Emotional intensity also can be more negative, both to the gifted individual and to those around. When intensity is too great, life becomes difficult to bear because too much is felt and there is no way of safeguarding the self from the power of the feelings perceived. These gifted children are unable to take a mental step back and gain some perspective, or allow things to happen in their own time. They feel a sense of urgency to act and change things. If channeled, this great passion can be directed positively, but often intense individuals are also exceptionally sensitive and then feel overwhelmed by the depth of their feelings.

Gifted children with AD/HD feel things intensely, and react on the basis of these feelings. Like other gifted children, they can feel passion in learning new things and in pursuing their own interests. When motivated to learn, they can become immersion learners, people who need to hyperfocus on material until it is mastered, learned in depth, or construed in some new way. Like other gifted children, those with AD/HD feel more intense feelings, have a greater depth of feeling, and feel more subtle feelings. It is as if their emotional color wheel has many more hues than what most people experience. Thus, more feelings are available to gifted children with AD/HD. Some gifted children with AD/HD are able to use their feeling color palette effectively in relationships. Their own awareness of their feelings and their behavior can be exceptional. Like other gifted children, those with AD/HD also can be nonconformists and question authority due to the intensity of their beliefs and feelings about issues.

Gifted children with AD/HD are different from other gifted children in their difficulty managing their intense feelings. Though some are exceptionally self-aware, they still may not be able to control how they act. These children and adolescents are aware of their errors as they make them, but they cannot correct their actions before the fact. Others are less self-aware and have more of the problems with awareness of feelings, labeling of feelings, and dealing with intense feelings that more average children with AD/HD experience.

Gifted children with Inattentive Type AD/HD process emotional material more slowly than others, just as they process cognitive material. Thus, it takes time for them to process the emotional, cognitive, and social context. Consequently, they react less quickly. Some of these children have difficulty labeling their feelings because they have trouble describing exact nuances of feeling. If Simon were asked how he felt, there would be a long pause while he thought about it, then he would answer, "A little sad, a little lonely, a little bored, a little frustrated." He would go on to explain what had caused all of these feelings.

The experience of intense feelings is unsettling. In addition, gifted children with AD/HD may still have the same difficulties as other children with AD/HD in recognizing what they are feeling at any one time, and in how their feelings affect their own behavior and its consequences.

Some gifted children with AD/HD become cognitively and affectively locked onto an idea or feeling and then cannot easily let go of it. Simon would see a scary movie and then feel scared for days as the images replayed themselves in his mind. If he started worrying about something, he could not stop. This locking onto an idea or activity is why transitions can be so difficult for so many gifted children with AD/HD; it is hard to shift attention once it is set on something highly stimulating.

Another aspect of intensity for a certain percentage of AD/HD gifted children is the need to do things their own way. These gifted children ask compelling questions, argue, question authority, and do not conform to expectations they consider foolish. Their intensity about the issue can be extreme. It can feel like life and death when, to others, it is a minor point. These gifted children find it hard to give up their own point of view to consider another perspective, and they have difficulty listening to other people's opinions.

Gifted children with AS, like other gifted children, have strengths in emotional intensity. The passion of doing an endeavor of their choosing is much greater for gifted children with AS than for other gifted children. Not only do they put all their intellectual energy into their passion, but also their emotional energy. Gifted children with AS also have a passion for learning. Of the gifted children with AS at the Gifted Resource Center of New England, 17 of 30 had a great desire to learn all they could about everything. In this way, they were like many other gifted children. They also desired to do a good job. Doing their work well was a source of pride and positive feelings. They had high standards for their achievement, but even on ordinary tasks often tried to do their best. A few, especially those with the highest IQ scores, also wanted to be the best, and strove to become so. Another aspect of their intensity was their willingness to try to learn skills they knew they were poor at, such as social skills. These children did their best in trying to learn these skills too, though it was also much more frustrating when they failed at them.

Unlike other gifted children, problems with intensity of gifted children with AS were much more noticeable in everyday endeavors. They were passionate about their interests, but their passion was more limited. Other gifted children would be passionate about their interests too, but they weren't usually the focus of their whole lives.

While other gifted children are nonconformists and question authority because of their ideals, those with AS tend to be nonconformists because they live in their own worlds. They aren't rebelling against society but are less aware of society. Those who do question authority, especially in teen years, tend to focus more on specific issues rather than the problems of all of society, as many other gifted children do.

Gifted children with AS have difficulty with overfocusing. They obsess, sometimes for years, about emotional events that occurred in the past that they found disturbing. Also, they find disturbing many more types of events than do other gifted children, or more average children with AS. Toby, therefore, worried about sharks in the ocean near the family's summer cottage on Cape Cod. He also feared there might be sharks in the backyard pool at home. Though he knew this was a ridiculous idea, he still would not go in the pool. He tried to argue about it based on his prodigious knowledge of shark attacks in the USA. When it was pointed out to Toby that no sharks had been sighted near his family's summer home in decades, he countered with all the attacks by sharks on the Eastern Seaboard in the past century. Not only could Toby enumerate the sum total of shark attacks, he could describe which had been fatal. In fact, he drew attention to the fact that most shark attacks happen in the United States in Florida, but that even in areas in which no sharks had attacked in decades, such as Virginia Beach, a shark had killed a boy in 2001. It was hard to defeat the logic of such a response, and difficult to help Toby to see that sharks in the ocean were a different matter than fear of sharks in his outdoor New England pool.

Decision making is difficult for many gifted children with AS. If they need to make a decision about something, these children become exceedingly anxious. Because they have so much emotional intensity, they worry they will make the wrong decision. Because of their limited abilities in perspective taking, they act as if a "right" decision were a particular attribute of a situation or choice, and they have to guess what it is. The idea that there might be individual preferences that could change across situations is difficult for them to grasp. Some of the rigid insistence on doing things a certain way certainly alleviates the need to make decisions. Toby had difficulty deciding if he would go on a class trip because they were going to eat in a restaurant, and he didn't know if they would have any of the foods he would eat. He also didn't want to take his lunch because no one else was doing so. This made it impossible for Toby to find a solution. What did finally work for Toby was an extension of choices. Once he was able to allow input into the problem by a supportive adult, he was able to see that there might be alternatives he had not considered. For example, since he liked most breakfast foods, he might be able to order those for lunch, or he could eat a big breakfast and eat fruit for lunch. This made going on the trip more possible for Toby. In fact, once on the trip he found that the restaurant chosen had some food he did like.

Other children need specific work on learning how to generate more ideas, alternatives and options.

Suggestions for dealing with emotional intensity

- Recognize the ways in which the child is intense. Is it about mistakes, worries, too many feelings that are overwhelming, or due to a tendency to hyperfocus on an event?

- Help gifted children with AD/HD and AS to rate feelings on degree of intensity. Use a color chart ranging from light to deep hues. Discuss which types of feelings are most intense and which types of events trigger them. Discuss how there are gradations of feelings and intensity. Discuss when feelings seem excessive for the event.

- When gifted children with AD/HD and AS become stuck on worries and frightening images, try to help them to replace the image with a more positive one. Add distance by pretending the feeling is behind a shield or use thought stopping in which the child purposely changes to thinking about another activity. Try to put the worry or fear "to the side of the mind." Imagine the image with a different outcome, or think about it and slowly change it, so it is more positive. These suggestions work better for gifted children with AD/HD. For those with AS, setting limits on how much they are allowed to think about the image or worry works better. Thus, they can think about it five times; after that they have to tell it to go away by blanking it out or thinking of or doing something else.

- Channel intensity into positive activities of interest to the child; support his or her causes and passions. When gifted children feel intensely negative, try to get them to think about their fun activity or passion.

- Teach gifted children with AS how to make decisions. First the child needs to learn to generate alternatives by thinking of what they already know about the topic, free associating, thinking of another item in the same category, changing categories, or looking for ideas that impact different sense modalities. Then the child is taught to think of pros and cons for each alternative. Pros and cons include feelings, consequences, and effects on self and others. Thirdly, the child picks one alternative to try out. Then the child evaluates if the idea or option worked. If it didn't, why not? What else might work?

Finally, the child tries to look at the longer-term positive and negative consequences.

EMOTIONAL REACTIVITY

The concept of emotional reactivity refers to proneness to quick emotional responding, as well as proneness to particular modes of responding. Is the gifted child patient or quick to act, able to wait and allow others to express themselves, or quick to try to fix things? Gifted children who are well adjusted are able to delay gratification and act positively for their own and others' benefits. They show self-control when appropriate, yet are able to be spontaneous in their expression of emotions.

A second aspect of reactivity is quickness of response to change a situation. Thinking quickly under stress, using humor to deflect negative words, and having the quickness of wit to see immediately what needs to be done to change the tone of a group, or to refocus energy in positive ways, are aspects of reactivity.

Another aspect of emotional reactivity is resiliency: that is, the ability to cope with stressful situations by using inner resources. In general, children who are resilient are able to use emotional reactivity positively; they seek out new situations, act with self-reliance, and show independence. They are able to develop a source of refuge from stressful environments through interests, hobbies, and intellectual pursuits. They elicit positive responses from adults and ask for them for assistance. They develop a social network that does provide support. Finally, they have a sense of incorporating something that is larger than themselves (Anthony 1987; Werner 1984).

The underlying mechanism that allows these gifted children to cope so well is their use of *cognitive appraisal* (Lazarus 1993): that is, their ability to evaluate if a stress is harmful or not. Gifted children as young as age nine have used cognitive appraisal to cope with various stresses. This early use of cognitive coping measures to help with emotional stress appears related to gifted children's precocious development of abstract thinking, reasoning, and problem-solving skills (Bland, Sowa, and Callahan 1994). The cognitive appraisal process included both problem-solving skills (changing behavior to influence environment) and emotion-focused coping skills (changing one's own interpretation of the situation).

Resilient gifted children tended to use withdrawal and self-imposed time-out to deal with stressful and negative feelings. They created challenges for themselves and sought ways of getting their needs met. They were assertive and stood up for their rights to create challenge and stimulation for themselves (Sowa *et al.* 1994).

Emotional reactivity can be more negative. Those gifted children who react excessively to small stimuli and minor irritations are easily upset. They may have trouble making transitions, calming down, and using self-soothing techniques. Indeed, if they are upset, they often have little means of calming down, until the emotional storm is over.

Gifted children who have trouble with emotional reactivity are less independent. Some are so dependent they cannot function without an adult present to help them to organize their behavior. Also, while very needful of challenge and stimulation, they have more trouble with frustration or finding ways to challenge themselves. They often need adult intervention in problems other children handle on their own.

Gifted children with AD/HD, like other gifted children, can respond quickly and decisively. They often have the energy to do many things, particularly activities that focus their energy. Those gifted children with moderate AD/HD often find that sports that focus energy, including martial arts, can help them focus on academics.

The emotional reactivity and intensity of many gifted children with AD/HD is a problem at home, school, and in community activities. The behaviors seen in babyhood and early childhood may not change much as the child grows into adolescence. DeGangi (1991) who studied "regulatory disordered" children found them to be fussy, irritable, intolerant of change, to have hyperarousal to environmental stimulation, trouble with sleeping, mood regulation, feeding, and transitions. These same children in adolescence still throw tantrums, are inflexible, and have trouble with regulating mood and affect.

While other gifted children are more emotionally resilient, those with AD/HD show immature coping strategies. Moods may change fast, and some gifted children with AD/HD rapidly shift from cheerful to miserable if a slight problem occurs. This degree of emotional reactivity also produces tantrums, often at ages when others have outgrown such responses to minor stress. Thus, Luke, at age 16, threw a tantrum at home, kicking, screaming, and throwing things, because his favorite shirt was in the laundry and he couldn't wear it to school. Ten minutes later, after he had calmed down, he was talking about getting his driver's license.

Dealing with angry overreaction is a particular problem for many gifted children with AD/HD. Because they are gifted, they are more able to use logic to argue the merits of what they want. Because they are intense, they argue all the more vehemently. They also bargain and negotiate well because they can problem solve in the abstract. In reality, though, it is hard to get them to keep their end of the bargain. This is especially the case if they have had the reward first. Then, anger and overreaction are likely to result when it is time to do the promised work. In fact, what has happened is that the immediacy of the reward, what makes it feel rewarding, has faded and all that is left is negative affect towards the chore or task they don't wish to do.

Anger also results when gifted children with AD/HD feel thwarted and unrewarded in everyday life. To them, life feels like a series of unpleasant tasks they need to continually redo, all for little or no reward. The stress of this builds up until the child has a tantrum. While gifted children with AD/HD have difficulty with the aspect of resiliency that requires forethought (cognitive appraisal – see Lazarus 1993), they have little difficulty bouncing back after an explosion. Thus, while they have poor planning skills and cannot easily think ahead to change their own feelings or the situation, they are resilient in not holding onto the negative feelings.

Another form of poor resiliency occurs for gifted children with the Inattentive Type of AD/HD. Falling apart means crying, worrying, obsessing, or complete withdrawal from the problem. These gifted children can fade out, retreat, and do nothing. They feel unable to begin. Some develop psychosomatic symptoms, reporting that certain types of work gives them a stomach ache: for example, answering questions at the end of a chapter. Others just avoid the task by daydreaming, doing something else, or even actively retreating into their own fantasy world.

Brooding about the meaning of things can contribute to overreaction. When combined with rapidly changing emotions, the brooding over small mistakes, overconcern about worries, or fears of being overwhelmed can lead a proportion of these gifted children to react with panic attacks when they feel totally helpless. At times, these panic attacks take the form of suicidal feelings and the acting out of suicidal gestures. Children who react in this way need immediate support so they will not follow through on their threats. They need additional help in learning to recognize the feelings that lead to the panic, and ways to self-soothe and decrease the negative affect.

Gifted children in general require mental stimulation. Those with AD/HD are no different, but they also require other types of stimulation. Zentall *et al.* (2001b) discussed optimal stimulation theory with respect to gifted AD/HD boys. In their study, children with AD/HD were chronically understimulated and attempted to provide stimulation for themselves with their hyperactivity, impulsivity, and daydreaming. Gifted boys with AD/HD were more likely to prefer stimulation in the form of imagination, visual-spatial activities, and cognitive and language-based activities such as dramatics, humor, role playing, creating games, making and building things, etc. Depriving students of these activities did not improve behavior. That is, if these activities were removed because a child did not complete an uninteresting task, such as cleaning bedrooms or finishing classroom work papers, performance did not improve. Zentall *et al.* (2001b) hypothesized that withholding activity only decreased stimulation in an already understimulated child, making it harder to do the unchallenging task. Thus, the stimulation needs of the gifted AD/HD children are intense, much more so than for gifted children without AD/HD.

Kutner (1999) described another phenomenon that contributes to the problem of intensity for gifted people with AD/HD. These adolescents and adults seemed to attribute the boredom they experience to the task, as if boredom were an intrinsic property rather than a measure of their emotions or motivation. Thus, if they rated the task as boring, they were unable to accomplish it. That is, they equated intensity of interest with "doableness." Consequently, they could only do tasks they found very stimulating. Also, Kutner noticed that while hyperfocusing on a task, people with AD/HD continually assessed how likable the task was. The more likable, the more focus.

Gifted children with AS, like other gifted children, often have a lot of mental and emotional energy to use for activities. They especially like to explore the physical world, and to see patterns in nature, numbers, science, and other areas. This readiness to see patterns enables them to be creative, to have some insight into how the physical world works, and to form hypotheses about the nature of things. Like other gifted children, reactivity takes the form of delight in mastering these bodies of knowledge. Some children with AS also see human patterns, and are gifted at seeing dynamics. They can describe the patterns of dynamics, but miss the emotional impact and the social significance. Thus it can seem that they are more adept at social functioning than they really are.

Gifted children with AS also show emotional reactivity in their endeavors with others. While they are not resilient in the sense of coping well with stress by using cognitive appraisal, they do show remarkable bravery in trying again when they have failed. While some can get stuck into negative obsessions and avoidance when negative events have occurred, others will try again, especially if they feel adults have tried to make things different. Some of these children and adolescents also do try problem solving. For example, Michael Niebauer, a 2001 Temple Grandin Award Nominee, worked on changing the bullying he was undergoing at school. He confronted his principal, his tormenters, and other peers and told them about the history and causes of bullying. He also offered a plan to deal effectively with it. This made the bullying decrease significantly (Future Horizons 2002). Other gifted children with AS willingly use the solutions of adults if they feel safe enough to try them; they are much more amenable to using adult support than are gifted children with AD/HD.

Unlike other gifted children, those with AS have difficulty because they over respond to small problems. They react quickly and out of proportion to the stimulus. Harry, first described in Chapter 3, would give a sudden loud shriek when frustrated. While one might expect this kind of scream from a preschooler, it was disconcerting in a ten-year-old boy. Harry would give this sort of scream whenever he lost a game or had to stop doing something he was overfocused on. Harry also found it quite difficult to calm down once he was upset. This was especially so if the trigger was internal. When Harry was in one of his worried states, it was almost impossible to get him to focus on anything else.

Harry also had trouble with too much stimulation and would act very immaturely and inappropriately when overstimulated. For example, at a church party, he became wild, running around, hitting others, screaming, and jumping over chairs. He had no awareness that what he was doing was inappropriate. In fact, he focused on the fact that several two-year-old children were doing similar things and then felt picked on because more was expected from him.

Gifted children with AS are much less resilient than other gifted children. That is, they are much more prone to stress, have poorer coping strategies, and are much more likely to become anxious and depressed than other gifted children. Because their coping skills are so poor, they are much more likely than other children of their age to show emotional outbursts. These outbursts are more intense, triggered by less, and exhibited in situations where others of their age would never show anger or upset.

Suggestions for dealing with emotional reactivity

- Many of the suggestions previously described in this chapter are applicable in helping gifted children with AD/HD and AS to become less overreactive to small events. Some of these included identifying triggers (stop...feel...think...act), learning problem-solving strategies, assessing the result of their reaction, and discussing how it might have happened differently.

- Gifted children with AD/HD and AS can learn to be more emotionally resilient if they can learn coping strategies such as self-calming techniques. Use of relaxation techniques, engaging in meditation practices, removing oneself from the problem to calm down, and actively working to decrease anger all will produce a calmer state. Then, the gifted child can learn to use problem-solving strategies to deal with the issue.

- Gifted children with AD/HD and AS who are quick to react and quick to change mood will need help in learning how to connect their feelings with events. If they can identify the feelings that lead to upsets, they can learn to calm down before they have a tantrum. They might use some of the skills of gifted children who are resilient: recognizing impending upset, giving themselves a self-imposed time-out, or learning when it is appropriate to ask for adult help. After a tantrum, these gifted children will need to work on understanding how others may still feel; that is, while the problem may seem over for them, it is not over for others. Others' feelings may continue for longer and the consequences suffered by the child are due to the long lasting effect on others. For example, Luke cannot throw a tantrum about his shirt and then expect that his parents are going to think he has sufficient self-control to drive a car.

- Help gifted children with AD/HD and AS learn to recognize that things happen in their own time. However frenzied a person is, the speed with which something will occur does not change. Therefore, these gifted children need to learn to do something else rather than try to hurry things along: do something else while waiting; plan when the event will most likely happen; plan what to do if obstacles present themselves; and have an alternative plan if necessary.

- Gifted children with AD/HD and AS are less apt to be overly stressed if they feel adequately stimulated. They need mental and physical stimulation that engages them in positive ways and that builds skills over time. Engaging in hobbies and individual sports is useful. Learning a martial art is so popular with children with AD/HD and AS because it teaches body control, emotional control, centering, focusing, and calming techniques in a socially acceptable manner.

EMOTIONAL SENSITIVITY

The concept of emotional sensitivity refers to the capacity for sensation or feeling, or to acuteness of feeling. It also means having a capacity and appreciation for the aesthetic, for imagination, and for physical sensations. In the sense used in this chapter, sensitivity means sensibility: that is, having the capacity for understanding emotions. Thus, sensitivity means awareness of one's own feelings, ability to perceive complex feelings, ability to perceive and understand another's feelings, ability to perceive another's perspective, and the ability to feel empathy, compassion, and caring for others.

Mendaglio (1995) attempted to find a consensus definition of sensitivity that also fit with his clinical experience in working with gifted children and adults. He divided sensitivity into intrapersonal and interpersonal aspects. Both of these have cognitive and affective aspects.

Intrapersonal sensitivity was divided into self-awareness and emotional experience. Self-awareness referred to self-knowledge: that is, being able to reflect on how one is the same and different from others (cognition). Emotional experience referred to awareness of one's own emotional states. This requires a focus of attention on feelings in order to discover what they are and how intense they feel (affect).

Interpersonal sensitivity was divided into perspective taking and empathy. Perspective taking referred to the ability to imagine what others are thinking and feeling. This ability to look at something from another's point of view is what is commonly referred to as "walking a mile in another's shoes" (cognition). Empathy meant either the vicarious experience of perceived emotions of another (experiencing them as inside the self) or perception of another's frame of references as if from the other's point of view (affect). When empathy is vicariously experienced, it does not require overt expression, only feeling. When empathy incorporates the perception of another's frame of reference, it requires doing something about another's pain (Mendaglio 1995). Thus, gifted children who feel another's sadness and can articulate it, even to themselves, have empathy whether or not they do anything for the other person. Note, though, that feeling another's feelings within oneself is a developmentally earlier level of empathy as defined by Hoffman (1994), while the ability to act based on trying to alleviate another's inferred feelings is developmentally more mature.

Empathy, as defined by Mendaglio from his search of the literature, may reflect different definitions based on different groups of different ages. Observations and anecdotes don't usually describe the level of empathy exhibited by the gifted child. Thus, what may appear to be different types of empathy may be different levels of development. Some children may still feel others' feelings within themselves directly, because they have not yet learned the cognitive and emotional skills that would provide perspective.

Gifted children with AD/HD, like other gifted children, show exceptional sensitivity. This sensitivity is manifested by awareness of their own needs and feelings. Also, many of these gifted children are unusually able to think about how others might view a situation and what their feelings would be. For example, Madison, described at the start of this chapter, was able to think about social dynamics displayed among her circle of friends. She also could describe the dynamics operating in her classroom. She was sensitive to what the rules for participation were, though she didn't feel that she could follow them herself. To do so would have been dishonest, because she would only have been pretending to like certain people in order to be popular.

Madison was also deeply loyal to her friends. She did not let squabbles get in the way of friendship, but tried to understand what had happened, and what to do to help everyone feel better. Madison was also empathic with the less popular students, and tried to include some of them in activities. Madison could have difficulty with empathy at times. She ignored cues that a friend needed her to listen, but she was genuinely contrite if her friend told her to stop talking and listen. Madison was quite self-aware of her attention lapses and their consequences.

Like other gifted children, those with AD/HD can be devoted to the ideal and miss the reality. For example, Kayla, age 12, a gifted girl with AD/HD and an NVLD, wanted a perfect friendship. She knew all about how to be a friend, but she missed the point that friends aren't perfect. Kayla often ended up with hurt feelings because she thought friendship meant her friends should not even talk to someone else on her street when they were visiting her. Kayla had the ideal but lacked the ability to put it all together with real people. When engaged in one of these episodes, her empathy towards her friends disappeared – though, at other times, she was quite empathic and caring about their needs.

When gifted children are sensitive, there is the danger that they will be overly sensitive about their own feelings. Being overly sensitive means having feelings that are easily hurt. The immaturity of many gifted children with AD/HD, their overfocus on certain aspects of their own needs, and strong feelings of unfairness that arise can result in situations where feelings are hurt. Many gifted children with AD/HD do not focus on others' perspectives to the same degree as most children of the same age. Instead, they focus more on their own needs and feelings. More mature children are less apt to overly personalize criticism or situations that require negotiation. Less mature gifted children with AD/HD are more apt to see those same situations as unfair or personally negative, and therefore will experience more feelings of personal hurt.

Another aspect of sensitivity for gifted children with AD/HD is the over-internalization of blame for small transgressions. These children blame themselves and feel responsible in situations where others would not see fault. Thus, Paul felt negativity from adults around him, but felt it must be related to him and what he did or didn't do. It was hard for Paul to realize that the adults might just be having a bad day. On the other hand, Paul also could ignore strong cues that he was displeasing others. His classmates wrote in an assessment of his cooperative group work that "Paul has good ideas, but he doesn't pay attention to anyone else." "Paul doesn't listen to us when we brainstorm ideas; then he doesn't know why we did things and he gets mad." "He doesn't know when we are getting mad at him, because he isn't listening."

Gifted children with AD/HD, like Paul, may be so sensitive they have difficulty with criticism. Because they cannot read subtle cues well, they miss parts of experience, then they insist on their own way. That leads to a poor outcome, and they are criticized for it. They feel the criticism is unjust and too harsh. What they don't see is why the criticism happened. For them, criticism is not a helpful learning experience. They simply don't notice that everyone is criticized, that criticism is not necessarily negative, and that they can learn something from mistakes made.

Gifted children with AS, like other gifted children, can show self-awareness. Some gifted children with AS are able to spontaneously discuss their problems and personality traits. While this is unusual for children with AS, some gifted adolescents with AS have been able to bring up their "selfishness" or "bad tempers." These traits are brought up because they want to try to do better. Jillian, for example, brought up her selfishness and wanted to learn how to be unselfish. She thought learning to be unselfish would allow her to make more friends. As we worked in therapy, this focus allowed her to learn other social skills she was lacking, such as giving the other person a turn in talking and thinking about what the other person might want to do at the mall. Thus, Jillian's self-awareness, limited as it was to start with, gave her a bridge to make some real changes.

Like other gifted children, those with AS can be deeply moved by the aesthetics of an experience. The mood created by music or art, dance or even nature can be a source of deeper connection and emotional satisfaction. In the same way, a sensitive connection to animals and nature is shown by many young gifted children and adolescents with AS. In fact, while they have trouble feeling empathy for people, many of the gifted children and adolescents with AS were especially tuned into how animals feel. Some of these gifted adolescents were also able to appreciate the pain of other people at a distance. Patrick, age 12, could discuss the suffering of people in Africa living in a drought area. He wanted to find ways to send them money.

Unlike other gifted children, those with AS are extremely sensitive to the environment and quickly become overstimulated and wild in behavior. Their feelings are easily hurt when criticized. They feel some things are criticisms that are not, yet miss essential criticism because they cannot bear to hear it. Kolby, age 12, could not stand any criticism about his personal habits. Even though his hygiene was inadequate, he would not listen to suggestions from his parents that he needed to shower or brush his teeth. When he went to the dentist, he got angry at the dentist's critique of his oral hygiene. The dentist learned not to use words but to let the plaque-coloring solution speak for itself. Seeing a mouth full of red did tell Kolby that he had to do a better job of taking care of his teeth. His parents only wished there was a body hygiene coloring solution to tell Kolby he needed to shower and use deodorant. Kolby's high intelligence (IQ 150+) was not at all helpful in reasoning with him.

Other gifted children with AS may be more willing to listen to criticism but are sensitive to how it is put. If criticism is put into neutral tones, they are much more able to listen without feeling hurt and angry. Thus, if they are given ways to focus on content and what to do, they are more able to handle suggestions about changing things.

Gifted children with AS are less sensitive to understanding how their behavior and choices affect a situation. Kolby didn't understand how his poor hygiene affected his chances of making friends. He did want friends but could not see the relationship between how looking and smelling good to others might lead them to want him as a friend. It was more important to Kolby that he feel comfortable to himself, and that meant keeping the same clothes, same smell, and same feel of his body. To Kolby, how he looked and felt was normal, and people should accept him for it; otherwise, they were unjust and prejudiced. Kolby's giftedness allowed him to think of arguments that made logical sense but were not socially relevant. What did finally help Kolby to change was a contract with his advisor at school, who was also his Spanish teacher. If he showered three times a week, he would not have Spanish homework on those days.

Suggestions for dealing with emotional sensitivity

- Gifted children with AD/HD and AS who are sensitive and easily hurt need to learn what types of things are most likely to hurt their feelings. Then, they can learn how to defend against the pain they feel. For example, they can avoid situations when they might be hurt. They might learn to question what is being said to them, and have a script of answers that stop the other person from continuing. They can learn how to talk to themselves about what hurt them, and offer themselves soothing words. Gifted children with AD/HD can learn to measure their hurt against bigger hurts and keep a score chart of all the hurts in the world. This can change their perspective and minimize their own pain.

- When gifted children with AD/HD and AS overreact due to sensitivity and hurt feelings, it can be helpful to explore with them what they expected, what were their underlying assumptions, and how realistic were their worries.

- Criticism is difficult for many gifted children with AD/HD and AS. For one thing, it is unexpected. Therefore, it helps to warn the child that what will be said next is not going to be pleasant. Give the criticism a rating prior to giving it, and follow up with something positive. Then, ask them how they would rate both the negative and positive comments. Work with them on increasing the positive rating. Plan for how to deal with the criticism (fix a mistake, apologize).

- Gifted children with AD/HD and AS, especially when younger, are quite sensitive to the environment. Therefore, it is important that parents and teachers take into account reactions to stress that occur due to sensitivity to noise, light, crowds, fatigue, or boredom.

- Gifted children with AD/HD and AS benefit from immersion in the arts, especially music, painting, dance, drama and so on. These children also benefit from exposure to beauty of all kinds, including nature. This immersion can later be used to build scenarios of remembered good times and pleasant places. Thus, when feelings are hurt it can be healing to listen to uplifting music or recall a beautiful place far from here.

Conclusion

Gifted children with AD/HD and with AS show emotional strengths and weaknesses. The weaknesses of these children place them at risk for further emotional and social problems.

Some aspects of emotional intelligence are problematic for gifted children with AD/HD. In particular, they are less adept than other gifted children at using emotions to facilitate thinking because they have trouble separating feelings from content and remembering the past enough to incorporate into current planning. They have trouble with using complex emotions in complex situations because of difficulties with assessing appropriateness and timing of behavior. They also have trouble with regulating emotions and using emotions to regulate behavior. This is due to problems with making the connection between cause and effect, being able to focus on all of the situation at once, dealing with low frustration tolerance, and impulsivity. Like other aspects of functioning, gifted children with AD/HD, on the whole, seem to know what to do in the abstract. They can do the appropriate thing if not too overwhelmed or upset. They do know how to think about and use feelings in positive ways. Their problem is one of use of executive functions and output. That is, the same difficulties that arise for showing what they know intellectually (written language, succinct and to the point verbal responses) also affect them emotionally.

Nevertheless, gifted children with AD/HD do show strengths in identifying and assessing emotions and in using emotions to deal with others. In the gifted children with AD/HD who came to the Gifted Resource Center of New England, use of empathy was particularly striking, as was the quality of caring about others. Thus, even while some aspects of emotional intelligence gave gifted children with AD/HD difficulty, on the whole, they were not deficient in abilities, only in their execution. In fact, some gifted children with AD/HD, even while having difficulties, also appear emotionally gifted in their ability to understand themselves and others, in their ability to feel for others, and in their compassionate responses and seeking after justice. In this, they are more like other emotionally gifted children than like others of their age.

Those gifted children with AS had much more difficulty with all aspects of emotional intelligence. Unlike those with AD/HD, gifted children with AS actually lacked skills and concepts; it wasn't just a matter of timing or using self-restraint properly. Gifted children with AS had much more trouble with all four aspects of emotional intelligence: the ability to perceive accurately, appraise, and express emotion; the ability to use emotions to facilitate thinking; the ability to understand and analyze emotion; and the ability to use thinking to regulate emotions. Despite their many problems, though, these gifted children have an innocence and trust in the ideal that makes being with them immensely worthwhile. That is why despite their deficits in emotional and social skills, gifted children with AS often attract other people who will care for and nurture them. And that, in itself, is a gift.

> Self-reverence, self-knowledge, self-control,
> These three alone lead life to sovereign power.
>
> Alfred Lord Tennyson
> *Oenone,* l.141

Chapter 7

Social Cognition
and Interpersonal Relationships

Phillip

Phillip, a gifted boy with AD/HD Combined Type, was first described in Chapter 2. Phillip loved school. He enjoyed knowing things, and especially sharing it all with his classmates and teacher. Though immensely creative and imaginative, Phillip was not much liked by peers because he needed to be the center of every group. He dominated classroom discussions and required much of the teacher's attention. Even in 1st and 2nd grade, the other children complained that Phillip took over everything. On the playground, things were no different. Phillip wanted others to play with him, but he had little idea of how to play co-operatively. He did not know how to join in play. Instead of waiting for a turn or asking if he could play, he jumped right in. Then, he insisted the others were doing the activity wrong, and should change certain rules. Phillip didn't have the idea of working towards a group goal; instead, he felt things ought to be the way he wanted them.

Even when Phillip did manage to start playing cooperatively, he often lost interest and wandered away, or he lost focus. Soon, the other children were angry because he wasn't paying attention to the game. Phillip was a poor loser; he tried to cheat or made negative comments about others if he were losing.

At home, Phillip had two friends whom he did invite over to play. They were somewhat younger boys who enjoyed the same sorts of imaginative role-playing games as Phillip. He had such a good imagination that he and his friends could play for an entire afternoon with a few props. With no set rules, there was less chance for conflict to arise. Also, none of these games required focused attention. There was always the chance to stop and smell the roses, even while hunting enemy spies. Phillip also loved card games with strategy like Pokémon and Magic

Cards. At age eight, he was able to play with the complex Magic Cards with older peers, and he often won.

Kayla

Kayla, a gifted girl with AD/HD Inattentive Type and an NVLD, liked to have one or two best friends. In elementary school, she had enjoyed the company of a few girls who lived near her and were in her classes. Most of Kayla's activities with these girls were action-oriented. She liked to skate, bike, swim, and play board games. Kayla began to have trouble with friends in 5th grade. One of the girls in her group moved away and, with this, the others seemed to find new friends. Kayla had trouble sharing her old friends with newer people; she wanted their exclusive attention. Kayla's feelings were often hurt when she discovered that one of the girls she had thought of as her friend had gone to the mall with someone else, and not invited her too. Kayla had trouble understanding how a person could call her a friend and yet not always include her. Kayla's mother also started to notice that Kayla was having more trouble attending to friends even when they were at her house. Kayla expected the friend to do what she wanted, and for as long as she wanted. The friend wasn't supposed to talk to anyone else on the street, nor to have any interaction with Kayla's cute baby sister. If the friend didn't follow these "rules," Kayla would go off in a huff and sulk. Kayla didn't like many of the new activities her friends were discovering. While she did like going to the mall and buying clothes, she didn't like her friends giggling at boys. To Kayla, going to the mall was more functional and not so much a social experience. Of course to her friends, it was the opposite. Soon her friends thought Kayla immature and babyish. By the time she was in 7th grade, she had no friends.

Derrick

Derrick, a gifted boy with AS, was first described in Chapter 6. At age 11, Derrick very much wanted friends but had little idea of how to act appropriately: he monopolized conversations, made irrelevant comments, and interrupted. Derrick also had trouble with being friendly. He might run up to someone and start talking to them, but he didn't greet them, or look at them. He never waved and smiled at people he knew when he met them. He didn't know how to act like a friend either: for example, doing nice things for another person, or inviting someone to join him. Furthermore, he often ignored attempts by others to include him. He acted as if they were intruding on his privacy. Other than computer games, Derrick had no interests in common with other boys his age. However, he didn't want to play games with others, even over the Internet. What he wanted to do was to talk about the games in great detail and discuss how he had beaten certain obstacles.

When other boys teased him, Derrick didn't know how to react. He wanted them to stop and got angrier and angrier if they continued. If pushed too far, Derrick exploded and lashed out. By the end of middle school, Derrick was bullied on a regular basis by boys who had discovered how to get him to lash out while looking innocent themselves. Derrick had no clue how he was being manipulated and he was always in trouble. The only classmates he trusted were two girls who came to his defense and tried to protect him.

Commonalities

Phillip, Kayla and Derrick are three gifted children with deficits in social functioning. Phillip has trouble modulating and monitoring his behavior. His AD/HD brings deficits in executive functions that affect social functioning as much as they affect functioning in intellectual and emotional areas. Thus, Phillip has trouble with aspects of self-regulation, self-monitoring, controlling frustration, using appropriate social rules, predicting outcomes and consequences of acts, and timing of behavior, all of which have an impact on friendships. It is not that Phillip lacks social knowledge; in fact, he knows quite well in the abstract what to do. What he has trouble with is dealing with the complexity of situations and controlling his expression of feelings and behaviors to match the situation.

Kayla has trouble reading social cues, as well as moderating her behavior. She has trouble with realistic expectations for friendship. She doesn't know how to maneuver the more complex relationship demands of late childhood and early adolescence. Kayla's AD/HD means she is inattentive to important aspects of relationships: she misinterprets events and jumps to false conclusions. She also has trouble processing all the aspects of the situation rapidly. In fact, she is still processing part while the situation moves on in another direction. Because of her NVLD, she is more apt to misread cues, and to fail to see the big picture. Then, she gets stuck on her own interpretation and is unable to modulate her ideas and see things differently. In the more complex interactions required as girls enter adolescence, when friendships depend on mutual sharing and mutual empathy, she has less ability to process all that is required for friendships.

Derrick has difficulty understanding the basic ideas of interpersonal relationships. While he wants friends, he doesn't really know what friendship entails. He misses the social relevancy of his actions. He has trouble with the idea of reciprocity, and he has trouble noting others' perspectives, intentions, or feelings. He cannot accommodate to others' needs. Thus, as he moves towards adolescence, Derrick misses out on the give and take of mutual kidding and teasing, sharing of mutual activities, of feeling like he belongs to a group, or of helping a friend deal with adversity or sadness. Derrick's AS means he has trouble reading others' intentions, and making predictions about how others will feel, think, and behave. He has trouble getting the big picture and is apt to go off on a tangent of interest to him. He misses social cues and does not know what the expected responses are. He also has trouble with social attribution: that is, seeing certain social rules as relevant to him and his situation.

The focus of this chapter

These three children exhibited difficulties with social functioning. They had trouble with both knowing and using the skills needed for successful interrelationships with others; that is, they had difficulty with social competency.

In this chapter, the following are examined:

- The overall social adjustment of gifted children.

- The concept of social competency – social knowledge, social perspective taking, engaging in social behaviors, developing good interpersonal relationships and friendships, and feeling accepted by a social group – as a basis for understanding the social strengths and weaknesses of gifted children with attention deficits.

- The development of social competency for gifted children with AD/HD, particularly as relates to deficits in executive functions.

- The development of social competency especially as viewed though some of the underlying social deficits of gifted children with AS.

Social competency and giftedness

In this section of this chapter, the social adjustment of gifted children and their social competency will be described. Each section will also discuss how gifted children with AD/HD and AS are similar to and different from gifted children who do not have attention deficits.

The social adjustment of gifted children

Gifted children who are the best socially adjusted, have friends with similar interests, and do well both socially and emotionally are those with intellectual potential in the mildly to moderately gifted range (IQ 125 to 155). Hollingworth (1926) called this the "optimal range of intelligence." Gifted children in this range of intelligence are not so gifted that they are very different from their peers; thus, they are more accepted by these peers. They are busy with many school and peer-related activities and are often popular. They are at the top of the class, may be the valedictorian, are class leaders, and are often elected to student offices.

Hollingworth suggested that to be a leader, it was most desirable for people to be about 30 to 40 points above the general norm of the IQ range of the group being led. Then, the leader's ideas would be looked upon positively and followed by the group members. Children who are much higher in IQ, even if they have outstanding leadership ability, might never get to exercise their talents in this area, Hollingworth thought, because they are too different from the peer group being led and their ideas would not be understood. Thus, such a person could only be a leader in a group with other higher IQ people (for example, a think tank).

Research on social adjustment often gives a varied picture. In the period prior to Terman's (1925) famous study of over a thousand gifted students, it was generally accepted that gifted children were poorly adjusted social misfits. Terman, and later Hollingworth (1926), helped dispel the myth of the gifted child as an isolated and socially maladjusted individual. In fact, gifted children were found to be above average in emotional and social adjustment. More recent research has continued to find positive social adjustment in most gifted students. An overview of the research by Robinson and Noble (1991) suggested that most gifted students had positive relations with peers. They were seen as more mature in play interests, social understanding, choice of friends, and world view.

Yet others, who have examined the adjustment of different groups of gifted students, have found more evidence of poorer adjustment. McCallister, Nash, and Meckstroth (1996) made the point that when social psychologists evaluated social adjustment, gifted children usually had high scores and few concerns evident, but clinical reports showed a different picture. Indeed, some groups of gifted children showed poorer adjustment, more isolation, and lower popularity.

Highly gifted children as a group (IQs over 150) tended to exhibit more difficulties with social adjustment, had more difficulty finding peers, and were more likely to feel lonely and isolated. Of the children studied by Terman and Hollingworth in the early 20th century, the ones with the most social adjustment difficulties were among the most highly gifted (IQs of 170+). Among groups of gifted children, 20 to 25% of the most highly gifted had difficulties with social and emotional adjustment (Gallagher and Crowder 1957).

More recently, a study of the most highly gifted children participating in the Johns Hopkins Talent Search found that those most at risk for developing problems with peer relations were the most verbally advanced adolescents

(Dauber and Benbow 1990). Exceptionally verbally precocious adolescents saw themselves as less popular, less socially adept, more introverted, and inhibited. Mathematically precocious students, on the other hand, felt less social stigma and had much higher self-concepts. In fact, they were much more like moderately gifted verbally and mathematically talented children.

The authors hypothesized that it was easier for the mathematically gifted to fit in because their mathematical gifts might be less obvious in everyday activities at school, while verbal gifts might be more prominent all the time.

Another aspect might have been the gender ratio since most of the extremely mathematically gifted were male, while the verbally gifted were more predominately female. In fact, from a young age, gifted girls may be seen by nongifted peers as lower in popularity and as having negative personality traits. It depends on how they display their giftedness. If they appear to be too different, gifted girls may be rejected as not fitting into the social milieu (Luftig and Nichols 1991). Finally, it is also possible that some of the most verbally gifted were weaker in visual-perceptual skills, and had the social difficulties that accompany NVLD, or mild AS.

Exceptionally gifted children (IQs over 160) are more at risk for feeling different, isolated, and socially unacceptable. Janos and Robinson (1985), however, emphasized that the social isolation of these children might have been less social rejection and more the absence of a suitable peer group: that is, peers at their level with similar interests. Others have made the same point. In fact, Terman (1925) recognized that many exceptionally gifted children were loners by choice. They were not disliked or rejected, but felt they had little in common with age peers. Winner (1996) thought that many such gifted children wait for the right relationship and use their solitary times to further develop their talents. Many of these children are introverts and so both need, and value, time alone.

Gifted children with AD/HD, like other children with AD/HD, have difficulties with social adjustment. Moon *et al.* (2001) reported that the three gifted boys with AD/HD in their study were less emotionally and socially mature than either gifted boys without AD/HD, or the more average boys with AD/HD of their age. Socially, they were impulsive and made inappropriate physical contact with other children. They tended to overrespond to situations. They engaged in irresponsible, irritating, and annoying social behaviors. They were tolerated by gifted peers but not usually picked as work or play partners. In school, they were not selected as friends by other gifted students, and were described as "friendless loners." Nevertheless, outside of school, they did have friends who fit more with their aggressive or imaginative styles.

In contrast, boys who were gifted without AD/HD did not appear to show great emotional intensity, reactivity, or immaturity. They were judged to have excellent emotional adjustment at home and at school. However, social relationships were more difficult for two of the three boys.

The gifted children with AD/HD who came to the Gifted Resource Center of New England showed a range of social adjustment. There were some who were exceptionally social, had many friends, and fit in well with the social groups at school; some were even school leaders. Others struggled through middle school looking for friends, but suddenly blossomed in high school. Louis, age 13, found himself involved in the social life of his new high school. He was on the basketball team, became a delegate to the Model UN Program run by his school, and ran for student council. With all of these new activities, he also found it easy to make friends. He loved his classes and found his teachers challenging but fair. He felt he was really thriving in this new environment; not only was his social life greatly improved over middle school, but also his grades increased dramatically.

Most of the gifted children with AD/HD did experience some difficulties with social interactions and friendships. They tended to be less mature than other gifted children, less able to form lasting relationships, and less able to deal with negative interactions with others. Gifted boys with AD/HD tended to be attention seeking, controlling, aggressive, and/or disruptive to peers. They showed poor frustration tolerance, became angry and quit activities, or had difficulty with winning and losing. They were negative to peers, could not support a group goal, and had little idea of how to plan play activities that their playmates would also enjoy. They did best with one-on-one relationships and in structured activities. Phillip enjoyed imaginative role-playing games with his two good friends. He also did well in structured individual sports activities such as karate and swimming.

Gifted girls with AD/HD tended to have more conflict with friends, to be left out of social interactions, and to play alone more. They had more trouble negotiating the complexities of relationships, especially the subtle things that girls rely on. Thus, they were less there in the moment for friends, less empathic, and less able to listen to peers. They wanted to do all the talking or planning of activities. In fact, they did best if they planned activities ahead of time but had some alternatives if the first didn't work out. Kayla did best playing board games at her house. She also did well when she and one other girl went to see a movie together at the mall, then had something to eat and came home. This provided enough structure to the event that Kayla could relax and have fun without losing control.

Some boys and girls with AD/HD were less disruptive but more socially isolated. They had more trouble tracking conversations, following along with what peers wanted to do, and joining in. These children also tended to be bullied by others because they didn't know how to deal with even friendly teasing and fooling around.

Gifted children with AS have rarely been specifically described in the literature. However, those reports that do exist of children who were gifted (Cash 1999; Donnelly and Altman 1994; Neihart 2000) suggested that they suffered from the same deficits in social adjustment as did other children with AS. Earlier studies by Asperger (1991) and Gillberg (1991) also suggested severe deficiencies in social understanding and social relating. Gifted children with AS differed from more average children with AS, though, on knowledge of social perspectives, since that appeared related to verbal intelligence. The gifted children with AS who came to the Gifted Resource Center of New England showed many difficulties with social adjustment: they were immature for their ages, and exhibited social and play skills many years younger than expected. They either did not interact with others spontaneously or did so inappropriately. They did not understand social rules and showed little ability to share in social relationships except as one-sided vehicles for their own needs. Thus, they did not understand the idea of reciprocity in relationships. They did best with adults, or with peers who were intensely interested in the same specialized area of interest and didn't mind listening to trivia about the interest. Boys who liked the same computer games and collected the same types of cards were able to have some limited friendships with others. George was able to relate to some of his middle-school peers around Yu-Gi-Oh cards and trivia. The relationships worked because no one was actually listening very much; all of the boys were talking at once.

Aspects of social competency

Social competency refers to the ability to deal effectively with others. It involves knowledge of social cues, social norms, and expectations; the ability to take another's perspective and to use empathy; the competence to use prosocial behaviors appropriately; the skill of developing friendships and positive interpersonal relationships; and the capacity to feel a part of some social group. On the whole, research suggests that gifted children exhibit social competency.

SOCIAL KNOWLEDGE

From an early age, gifted children show greater social maturity in play interests, choices of friends, and degree of socialization (Janos and Robinson 1985; Robinson and Noble 1991). That is, they want to do the things older children do, to play with older children at games older children enjoy, and they act more like older children in ability to understand some social rules. Roedell (1989) studied preschool gifted children and found higher levels of ability to solve theoretical social conflicts. These children also knew more ways than average children to interact cooperatively; however, they did not necessarily do so. What they required was social experience, as well as social understanding, to develop more mature social interaction skills. Consequently, these gifted children were no different from age peers in their ability to control behavior.

Social knowledge refers to understanding how the social world functions. Knowledge of how social interactions work is essential for positive relationships. A more mature child knows how to solve common social problems, how to deal with conflict in a fair way, and how to join in with others. From an early age, the socially mature gifted child understands the social rules of play. For example, Rod, age five, wants to play with the older boys, but he knows they will consider him too little. One way to get them to let him play might be to have a skill they need. Thus, Rod chases balls for the boys and throws them back until the older boys see how well he throws. Tina, age eight, wants to play with her ten-year-old classmates, but she knows that they think she is too young since she skipped two grades. Tina watches them playing jump rope at recess. Later she catches the eye of Maria who is both good at jump rope and who talks to her in class. Tina asks Maria if she will teach her the jump-rope routine so she can play too, which Maria does. Following Maria's lead, the other girls allow Tina to play.

Children with AD/HD often have deficiencies in social knowledge. Guevremont (1990) described high rates of aggressive and negative behavior, self-centered behavior, and poor prosocial skills as responsible for the social rejection of children with AD/HD. More recently, Stormont (2001) found reasons for social rejection to include inappropriate social behaviors, social knowledge deficits, and negative interactions with peers and teachers.

The gifted children with AD/HD who came to the Gifted Resource Center of New England were often deficient in conversation skills, especially in the idea of turn-taking and letting the other person talk while they listened. They also had some trouble, especially under age eight, with game playing. While able to play sophisticated games according to rules, they had trouble letting others take their own turns. Instead, they tried to throw the dice "to help" others or to move their playing pawns. They acted as if only they should perform any of the game activities even if they recognized it was someone else's turn. The knowledge of how to let others take a turn was difficult for them. Phillip needed constant cueing at first to allow others to take a turn free of his "help." He was allowed an extra reward chip every time he was able to restrain himself without cueing.

During the wait for his turn he learned to focus on thinking about how he would answer the questions asked of the other players. After their turn was over, he could give his answer. Gradually, Phillip's turn-taking ability improved.

In both real-life situations and games that required answering questions about social skills, gifted children with AD/HD usually knew the correct answers. The exceptions seemed to be those situations in which an impulsive response was elicited or the character had to deal with anger. Knowledge seemed more lacking there. If games specifically targeted anger control, the gifted children with AD/HD soon learned the techniques illustrated by the games. After that they knew and could generalize to other games similar ideas about appropriate strategies. Applying them in real life was a different matter. Because Phillip had so much trouble with self-control, especially of anger, he agreed to participate in a program at home that would target how many alternative strategies he used instead of having a tantrum. A list of possible alternatives was compiled, and Phillip's parents laminated it and put it on his bedroom door. He also had a chart on which he would mark each day the number of each of the strategies used (for example, number one was punch a pillow). At the end of the day, he received reward chips for using alternative strategies for incidents that would ordinarily have elicited a tantrum. At the end of the week, chips were counted, and Phillip received new privileges or treats based on how many were earned. In the initial weeks, Phillip was given chips for use of strategies even if he used the same one all the time. In later stages, he had to use several strategies each week. This method helped Phillip gain control over his angry outbursts.

Children with AS lack social knowledge by definition. They do not know what to do in situations that most children find easy to understand. Children with AS also behave inappropriately because they lack knowledge of other people's thoughts, feelings, and intentions.

In particular, social reasoning is deficient: that is, knowing what is the appropriate thing to do in a situation and which behaviors are regarded by others as inappropriate. Dewey (1991) described how adolescents with AS and HFA made mistakes in determining what was appropriate in a series of social stories, such as when a young man in an elevator going to a job interview asks a stranger if he could borrow a comb. Compared to college controls, the people with autism spectrum disorders thought some behaviors were inappropriate that the college students did not, yet missed the inappropriateness of some of the behaviors described.

In general, children with AS have difficulty knowing social rules, knowing how to attract and join in with others, understanding the subtle language of nonverbal communication, starting and maintaining a conversation, and knowing how to work for a group goal. The child with AS stands out as different and odd.

Gifted children with AS who came to the Gifted Resource Center of New England shared the same difficulty with social reasoning and social knowledge as more average children with AS, and it caused the same types of inappropriate behavior. However, the reactions of people to gifted children with AS who display inappropriate behavior can be more pronounced than those given other children with AS. Because the gifted AS child stands out academically as so bright, it is hard for others to accept that the inappropriate behavior arises from a lack of social knowledge. Inappropriate behavior is thus often seen by both peers and adults as intentional. This is particularly the case with inappropriate comments. Derrick had great difficulty in school because he kept addressing one of the boys who teased him as "Bully Boy." He couldn't see that doing so antagonized the boy and led to more problems for Derrick. To Derrick, the other boy was a bully, so he was only telling the truth.

It is especially difficult for gifted children with AS to understand that even if a comment is true, it should not be said. The truth is the important feature to gifted children with AS because the social relevancy of hurting others' feelings is something they have to learn. Thus, the gap between social knowledge and intellectual reasoning is much wider than for other gifted children, even those with AD/HD.

SOCIAL PERSPECTIVE TAKING

Social perspective taking allows people to predict what others are thinking, feeling and intending. Social perspective taking – that is, what children know about other people's behaviors – starts to develop quite early, in preschool years. Dunn (1987) described toddlers who understood the social interaction of teasing. Some of the children in her study started teasing as early as 14 months of age by provoking and annoying a sibling: for example, by removing a child's comfort object or favorite possession, by destroying a valued possession or game, or by frightening another. One child of 18 months scared a sibling by getting a toy spider the sibling feared and shoving it at her. By 24 months of age, verbal teasing was also evident.

Gifted children showed advanced skills in social perspective taking. Given sets of items to place by following directions that required noting their own and another person's perspective (visual perspective taking), preschool-age gifted children scored higher than average children. On tasks of conceptual perspective taking the children were asked to predict which of a group of objects a friend would like as a birthday gift. Many of the young gifted children made appropriate choices at a younger age than average. These young gifted children also understood kinship roles and gender concepts significantly earlier. Affective perspective taking – that is, identifying feelings from facial expressions – also was present in many young gifted children from early preschool years. In general, gifted children appeared to go through the stages of social cognition earlier than other children (Abroms 1985).

Young gifted children often develop imaginary companions. The presence of an imaginary companion allows gifted children to try out new roles, as well as to have a friend who is agreeable to doing anything the child wants. Thus, children who develop imaginary companions are higher in intelligence on some tests of verbal intelligence, in creative story telling, and on tasks of Theory of Mind (ToM). Thus, from early preschool years, they were much more able to imagine another person's perspective and take it into account in forming conclusions (Taylor and Carlson 1997).

The implications of this are that young gifted children are less rooted in their own perspective and are more able to start to see things from a broader perspective from an early age. This gives rise to children who can think about the needs of others, care about others' feelings, and who will share with others because they can see how it feels to be in others' shoes.

Perspective taking is related to the development of empathy. Sympathy for another's distress, trying to find something to soothe another, caring about another's feelings, and acts of generosity and compassion all can occur early in the development of some gifted children. Perspective taking thus has emotional, intellectual, and social components, and young gifted children who develop the ability to take another's perspective in early preschool years also develop an earlier awareness of the similarities and differences of others.

Children with AD/HD were found to have deficits in social perspective taking when compared to children without AD/HD (Mckinna 1999). However, these results were more marked for older children with AD/HD and less for younger, most likely because deficits are more noticeable in older children from whom more is expected.

The gifted children with AD/HD who came to the Gifted Resource Center of New England generally were able to describe the perspective of the other person. This was found to be the case in board-game playing and in discussing real-life situations. However, there was a gap in knowing in the abstract, and thinking about the other's perspective, when in the throes of emotion. When angry, many gifted children with AD/HD cannot think of the other person's perspective at all, even in retrospect. That is partly because recalling the incident recalls their anger all over again. It was especially hard to think of the other's perspective if they felt an injustice had occurred. Luke, at age ten, fought constantly with his younger brother, age three. When the little boy broke one of his Lego constructions, Luke hit him rather hard, and called him many terrible names. Luke felt justified at the time because he had worked so hard on the Lego. When he was punished for hurting his brother, he acknowledged that he was wrong to hit him, but failed to see the harm in calling him names because he had harmed Luke's toy. He couldn't see how badly his words hurt, nor how bad his brother felt at breaking his Lego. Later, the little boy asked his mother why Luke hated him so much.

Another aspect of deficient perspective taking occurred when gifted children with AD/HD acted impulsively. Afterwards, they were usually remorseful because they could think of the other's feelings and point of view.

Children with AS have deficits in social perspective taking. This deficit is what is studied in ToM tests. Even when children with AS can pass many of the easier ToM tasks, they still have difficulty understanding several orders of perspectives (what did Mary think that John thought that Mary thought?), and thus they have difficulty understanding other people's perspectives. Happé (1994) studied people with autism spectrum disorders who passed ToM tasks and found they used less appropriate descriptions of actions when presented with story situations. They had trouble understanding how the characters thought and what they should do.

Gifted children with AS who came to the Gifted Resource Center of New England had difficulty with understanding other people's perspectives and feelings. If they practiced, some of these gifted children learned what the expected answer should be when presented with a hypothetical situation, but in real-life interactions, other people's points of view were still difficult for them to ascertain. Like other children with AS, they assumed there was only one point of view: their own. Derrick, at age 11, played a therapeutic board game about anger control. He had trouble seeing why the boy in the presented vignettes would perform certain actions to calm down. These wouldn't be things he would do, so they made no sense to him. In fact, Derrick had difficulty seeing why his temper tantrums were disturbing to other people. He couldn't assume the perspective of two characters discussing a problem. Derrick wondered how he was supposed to know what they were thinking; after all, he wasn't there.

PROSOCIAL BEHAVIORS

Learning social behaviors is more an issue for young gifted children than older ones. By early elementary school, most gifted children know basic social skills such as sharing, turn-taking, helping, and considering the feelings of others.

They know how to be fair and how to play according to rules. In fact, basic social skill development starts very young. Young gifted children were shown to be especially adept at getting and holding an adult's attention in socially acceptable ways as early as ten months of age (White 1985). These gifted children had a variety of mechanisms to use for engaging adults (such as asking questions), which they varied according to the situation.

Abroms (1985) suggested that prosocial behaviors did not necessarily develop earlier, or at a faster pace, in preschool gifted children than in more average children. Gifted children took turns, shared, helped, and communicated feelings of distress and anger about the same way as did more average children. What gifted children were advanced in was knowledge. They knew more about social skills than age peers. For example, in playing games, young gifted children knew about taking turns, and that each person takes a turn. Unlike age peers, these preschoolers did not think they should have all the turns, but were able to wait patiently while others took a turn too. What young gifted children had more difficulty with were other aspects, such as the concept of fair turns (for example, who should go first, or how long a turn should last). This develops at a later age. Abroms suggested that "the bottom line...was: 'Let's share. I'll go first'" (Abroms and Gollin 1980, cited in Abroms 1985, p.207).

This asynchrony between social knowledge and social action may occur because young gifted children do not develop all aspects of social skills at the same rate. Also, life experience may play a part (Lovecky 1995). Since they play advanced games, young gifted children may have the idea that they should go first as many game rules suggest the youngest goes first. Finally, if they mostly play with adults, young gifted children are usually indulgently given the first turn. When playing with gifted age peers, fair turn-taking may be sorted out quickly. Silverman (1993a) described several anecdotes of young gifted children who were well advanced in prosocial behaviors such as sharing, turn-taking, and caring about others. A parent questionnaire for a four-year-old gifted boy read:

> A is an exceptionally gentle and kind boy. I have never seen him hit or push and, in fact, have had to teach him that it is not good to let his little brother hit him... He has an intense love of games and frequently seeks out adults to play with him. When he plays with his friends, he will help them find the best move in a game and deliberately lose – all the while telling his friend how good they [*sic*] are at the game. (p.63)

Children with AD/HD are often socially rejected because of their poor behavior and their lack of prosocial skills. Children with AD/HD often lack knowledge of such prosocial skills as sharing, taking turns, initiating activities in a positive way, asking appropriate questions, making social conversation, using cooperative behavior, giving compliments, joining activities smoothly, saying "yes" to requests, and controlling affect when angry. Even in adolescence, poor social behavior such as disruption of activities, annoying others with irritating behaviors, excluding others, engaging in rule violations, unfriendliness, teasing, cruelty, lying and stealing, and immature interests all resulted in social rejection for teens with AD/HD (Guevremont 1990). Pelham and Millich (1984) described problems joining conversations and group activities, poor turn-taking, and irritating behavior as resulting in peer dislike. These children were not so rejected as those who were also aggressive, but they were still unpopular.

Gifted children with AD/HD who came to the Gifted Resource Center of New England exhibited many of these difficulties. Not only did they seem to lack knowledge of some of the social skills but, even more, they lacked the ability to put them into practice. Thus, as mentioned above, they might try to take all the turns in playing a board game, or blurt out answers on someone else's turn. They might get up and wander away if it wasn't their turn, or act silly and disruptive. Many had trouble with winning and especially losing. When Phillip lost a game, he would get angry and bend the game pieces, or throw the game on the floor. If he even thought he would lose, he would start to cheat, or decide he wanted to stop playing. He didn't behave much better when he won. He would gloat, make negative comments about the other players, and brag about what a great player he was. The gap between Phillip's ability to play difficult and advanced games using sophisticated rules and his ability to act appropriately was often marked, especially when he played with older children.

Not all gifted children with AD/HD had these problems. Some were quite good at conversational skills and game playing, but had more trouble with choosing an activity, sticking with it, or engaging in reciprocal interactions. They knew the prosocial skills but still did not really get the idea of how to connect with and join in with peers.

Children with AS lack prosocial behaviors. They do not know how to perform them nor do they see why they should. When other young children first learn prosocial behaviors in preschool years, children with AS are totally preoccupied with their own agendas. In elementary school, while other children know many of the social skills needed to navigate social life, children with AS have few skills. Thus, at a much older age than others, children with AS still need to learn basic social skills such as taking turns, waiting, listening, offering positive comments, joining in, basic conversation skills, helping, and cooperation. Even through adolescence and into adulthood, young people with AS may still be deficient in these basic skills. Also, while they may learn the rules for taking turns and waiting, children with AS have more trouble cooperating and making positive comments because the rules about when and how to do this are less clear. Children with AS are rule bound. Once they learn the rule, they will follow it, but cannot generalize or add a new rule on their own.

Gifted children with AS who came to the Gifted Resource Center of New England had to learn prosocial skills in the same way as more average children with AS. Being gifted means they have more ability to learn the basics of rules quickly, but they still have as much difficulty applying rules to complex interactions and in novel situations. Indeed these gifted children, while so knowledgeable in academic areas, are so immature about social skills. Will, age 16, was eager to take part in conversations in his high school. He especially wanted to talk with girls, so he followed several girls around trying to engage them in conversation. After he followed them into the girls' locker room, he was told in no uncertain terms to leave them alone. Will was devastated. He hadn't intended to follow them into the locker room. In fact, he was so intent on getting their attention he wasn't looking where they were going.

DEVELOPING FRIENDSHIPS AND POSITIVE INTERPERSONAL RELATIONSHIPS

Wright (1990) studied the play of gifted children in special preschools for the gifted. Overall, these children were found to be immensely social, turning activities that were usually more solitary into social interactions. For example, instead of solitary painting at an easel, they took turns painting portraits of each other. Wright noted that these children could be cooperative, but because of their leadership abilities, several might compete. Thus, their level of play was often more associative: that is, the play lacked organization or a common goal. Children in the study showed extremely high levels of complex dramatic and imaginative play. They developed their own imaginative play storylines alongside others, by adapting ideas, rather than all playing on one common theme. The higher the IQ of the children as a group, the more likely they were to use fantasy, to use dramatic play themes, and to prefer these over construction toys.

Imaginative play is highly prevalent in young gifted children and is the basis for forming some friendships. For young gifted children, fantasy play promotes group interactions with many types of peers. Thus, gifted children can have an idea and others will want to play it out. Usually, though, gifted children remain in control of the play. Thus, while they may build on the ideas of others, they are not acting cooperatively to produce a group effort. What they are doing is leading others by the strength of their imaginations. Gross (1993), Hollingworth (1926), Silverman (1993d), and Terman (1925) described the fascination of gifted children for fantasy and pretend play.

Young gifted children appear to engage in pretend and fantasy play for a number of reasons. Gross (1993) suggested that gifted children invented solitary games based on fantasy themes because they had difficulty dealing with the compromises they might need to make in their own interests, and knowledge of rules to play with more average children. The invention of an imaginary play friend satisfied the need for social interaction at their own level of maturity and with their own interests. Also, such fantasy games were quite complex and allowed the gifted children to use much more abstract reasoning and organization than most play with average children would allow.

The formation of friendships is difficult for many gifted children because of their advanced interests and desire for more mature relationships. Terman (1931) suggested that precocity is a complicating factor in developing social relationships. Hollingworth (1931) suggested that the child whose interests and intellectual development are far advanced from average will have difficulty relating to age peers. For example, Antoine, age three, wanted to share his favorite video with his preschool class. It was *The Nutcracker* ballet. At age four, he tried to explain what a black hole was to the class. When they didn't understand the difference between implosion and explosion, he tried to explain further with the example of import and export (Silverman 1998). How could Antoine find a friend in preschool? Preschoolers pick friends because they will play together, but all through childhood, friendship depends on shared common interests. How frustrated and lonely Antoine must have felt.

Finding friends is a challenge for gifted children, especially those at the higher end of intellectual potential. These children differ significantly from age peers in understanding of social perspective taking and also in expectations for friendships. Children who are more advanced in social perspective taking act more like older children in their friendship needs. For example, they may be at a higher level of understanding about reciprocity in relationships at an age when others are still more apt to see a friend as someone who lives nearby, or who likes the same things.

This advanced understanding of friendship presents a dilemma for gifted children. No longer satisfied to be the sort of friend age peers expect, they look to older children to meet friendship needs. When gifted children choose friends who are much older, they are trying to deal with their loneliness by finding a peer who is like them in mental age: that is, at about the same level of cognitive development (their *mental-age* peers). Nevertheless, this brings problems of its own. For one thing, older peers may have interests that are still discrepant from those of the gifted child. Thus, Chad might be able to play complex board games with older children but may not have the emotional sophistication to participate in games for adolescents. If he likes unusual games, he may be too different from older children, even if they might be able to play the games. Thus, if he likes an odd type of role-playing game when everyone else is playing *Dungeons and Dragons*, he may still not have anyone with whom to play.

Young gifted children who have much older playmates may find that the interests of the older children are not developmentally appropriate. The six-year-old who plays with ten-year-olds will be with children who likely have a lot more freedom of movement and ability to control their own time. They may be playing video games, seeing movies, and reading books that are not developmentally appropriate for a six-year-old, even an unusually mature one. In general, older children are just more used to having greater independence than is usual, or safe, for younger children.

As gifted children become older, their interests may become more like some mental-age peers, but aspects of some topics of discussion, or places peers are allowed to go, are still too mature for the gifted child. The ten-year-old gifted child who is friends with a typical 15-year-old may be exposed to adolescent topics such as sex, drugs, violence, romance, off-color jokes, and strivings for autonomy and independence that are not yet appropriate for a younger child. Thus, though mental age may be the same, emotional needs may be quite different.

Mental-age peers also know only part of the gifted child. Unless they are also true peers, mental-age peers cannot know the complexity of what giftedness really means to the gifted person, and how that difference really feels from the inside.

For gifted children, then, the goal is to find not a mental-age peer, but a *true peer*, another gifted child who can share interests and friendship expectations at about the same level (Roedell 1989). A true peer really fits: that is, he or she has a similar need for depth and breadth of perspective, has similar expectations of the friendship, and shares some interests. True peers are difficult to find, yet finding such a peer is absolutely essential to further social and emotional development, and to allow gifted children to learn how to have in-depth relationships. Having a true peer as a friend allows gifted children to grow in identity and connection to others through interactions with a person who really can know the whole gifted child.

Finding true peers is difficult. While gifted children yearn for these special friendships, they often make do with age peers and somewhat older children. This can meet some needs, especially for the sports-minded child who spends spare time in team sports. Also, boys who tend to be more activity-oriented may find peers who enjoy the same activities, even if they cannot share all the nuances (construction toys, robotics, rocketry, electronics, computer). It may be more difficult for gifted girls when they reach the level of friendship in which mutual sharing of thoughts and feelings constitutes much of the process of the friendship. Girls who are unable to find true peers feel something is missing, that underneath they are different and not really understood.

Some gifted children are so hungry for friendship with a true peer that when they finally meet someone who has the same yearning for depth as themselves, they become friends even if major interests are different. What they emphasize is the similarities they share, their depth of passion, their unique ways of looking at something, jokes and humor, and the little everyday things that matter in a close friendship. Such friendships are often maintained over time and distance for many years.

Children with AD/HD are often rejected by peers due to their annoying and aggressive behaviors, poor social skills, and negative comments to others. Many of them have few friends. In fact, Guevremont noted that many children with AD/HD, starting from preschool years on, preferred playing with younger children because they were socially successful with less mature children who allowed them to dominate the activities. Unfortunately, once rejected by peers, children with AD/HD tended to remain rejected. As many as 30% were still rejected four years later, and maintained their rejected status even if they moved into new social groupings (Guevremont 1990).

Gifted children with AD/HD also have difficulty making and keeping friends. Moon *et al.* (2001) described the rejected status at school of the three gifted boys with AD/HD whom they studied. Nevertheless, at home these boys did have some friends. Two had friends who were as aggressive and active as they were. The third had a friend who enjoyed the same type of imaginative play.

The gifted children who came to the Gifted Resource Center of New England had a variety of friendship situations. Some gifted children with AD/HD had no friends. These tended to be either the most aggressive or the most shy and socially inhibited. The aggressive children were more actively rejected, the withdrawn children mostly ignored. Those gifted children who played on sports teams tended to have more friends. Only a few were really popular though. Indeed, most of the gifted children with AD/HD had some difficulty with friendships. Difficulties ranged from rejection, to fights, to feeling hurt, to being teased. Like Phillip, many of the boys had a difficult time managing anger, dealing with teasing, and knowing how to be part of the group. They had trouble with prosocial behaviors and often aggression. Like Kayla, many of the girls had trouble feeling part of the group. They tried to be too domineering with their friends or had trouble being interested in the topics of conversation. Almost all of the children yearned for friends who would appreciate them for their gifts.

Finding true peers is as difficult for gifted children with AD/HD as for other gifted children. Having limited interests, a high need for stimulation, and a lack of patience with the reciprocal nature and slow process of building a friendship all can make finding true peers difficult. In addition, gifted children with AD/HD can appear self-centered because their needs are so great they forget about others' needs. All Ted, age 13, was interested in was computers. He was so interested in his work in building websites that he ignored how this felt to his friends. Ted was appalled when he was confronted with his self-centeredness, but he didn't know what to do. He did apologize, but knew he would have a hard time not monopolizing the conversation again. He just could not tolerate other topics; they bored him so much he felt like he was going to fall asleep. Ted needed help in finding ways to keep focused by asking questions about the other person's topics, by developing more interests, and by starting to realize that conversations were not fact-imparting ventures, but aspects of mutual sharing.

Some gifted children with AD/HD have trouble with sustaining interests. Thus, even when they find others with similar interests, they may not have the patience to continue with the interest to the same depth or level as the gifted child without AD/HD. Also, some gifted children with AD/HD have more limited interests. These more limited interests are often narrow stimulus-seeking endeavors that may not be as satisfying to other gifted children on a longer-term basis. Thus, while most gifted boys do like video games, as they develop a friendship they also want to do other things.

The activity level of the child, high need for stimulation, and the need for novelty and change may militate against the development of a close bond with a child with a similar interest. Friendships rely on the participants having about the same level of commitment to an interest, the same level of ability to pursue it, and the same level of continuing interest in the activities that constitute it. If one participant needs to change activities constantly, or pursue new ideas, the other may be frustrated and dissatisfied. This is not to say that gifted children with AD/HD do not find true peers. It depends on the level of expectation of the parties concerned. Thus, a relationship that might not seem like a true peer to another gifted child without AD/HD may be exactly what the gifted child with AD/HD needs. Often gifted children with AD/HD find friends, even true peers, through their use of fantasy play. Several children at the Gifted Resource Center of New England were fascinated by fantasy, including medieval weaponry, and costumes. Some of them were also Davidson Young Scholars who met at some of the regional gatherings. When they discovered their mutual interests, they knew they had found true peers.

Those with less ability to form close relationships have particular difficulty developing longer-term and in-depth friendships. As friendships develop from side-by-side companionship to reciprocal interactions, to mutual expressions of interest and concern, the gifted child with AD/HD who is out of synch will find it harder to develop true peer relationships with other gifted children.

Children with AS are often socially rejected because of their poor social knowledge, social skills, and social judgment, which results in inappropriate behavior. It is very hard for children with AS to make and keep friends.

Gifted children with AS have great difficulty finding peers among either average children or gifted children without attention deficits. They are unlike either, and therefore have less chance of finding friends with whom they will fit. Thus, finding true peers is extremely difficult for gifted children with AS. Who would a true peer be? For some children with AS, a true peer is someone with whom they share a special interest on a deep level, and to whom they are able to relate in their own way. However, if the interests of the friend change, the child with AS may lose the friendship because it may be based on nothing more than the sharing of an interest, and not on other similarities of personality, likes, and beliefs.

Gifted children with AS who came to the Gifted Resource Center of New England showed the same difficulties in finding friends as more average children with AS. They had more trouble finding true peers than did other gifted children. Those who had the most success in finding friendships were those placed in structured environments where they were coached by other gifted students while working together with them. Olivia, first mentioned in Chapter 3, was placed in a small learning setting at school, and peers were brought in to share her school day. It was a special privilege to eat lunch with Olivia or join her for a board game during a break. Gradually, Olivia was integrated for part of the day into a class for gifted children. Her classmates were trained to coach her on what was expected in terms of work and behavior. Olivia was quite willing to listen to her peers and to start to take steps to moderate her behavior.

Some gifted children with AS can find friends in small groups: around a special interest, in a community activity group, or in a small church school group. Some gifted children with AS do well if they live in a small town and attend school with the same peers, or go to a small private school with the same classmates over the years. Liane Holliday Willey (1999), an adult with AS, described just such an environment in her book, *Pretending to Be Normal*. Tony, first mentioned in Chapter 5, lived in a small town and attended a small elementary and middle school. This enabled him to make some friends because he was with the same classmates through most of his school years. Tony also attended the small congregational church in his town, and made his confirmation with his friends the same year he graduated from middle school. Because of all their shared experiences, Tony and his classmates regarded him as part of the group.

Serendipity may also play a part in building a bridge to acceptance from peers. Ryan, age ten, applied to a small parochial school in his area after difficulty fitting in to the public school. On the day he went for his initial visit, one of the 3rd-grade girls yelled to everyone on the playground, "Harry Potter is visiting our school!" Immediately, all the younger children crowded around Ryan and wanted to play with him on the playground, accompany him to lunch, and stand next to him in line. The 5th-graders thought it was funny. Though Ryan resembled Daniel Radcliffe, the actor who played Harry Potter in the movie, to an uncanny degree, they knew he wasn't Harry Potter. Still, they enjoyed the joke and issued their own invitations to Ryan.

Some gifted children with AS who are home-schooled find true peers as part of attending group activities geared to home-schoolers. Not only do they find a variety of children of different ages who might share interests, but they also find adults who may be willing to serve as mentors in areas of special knowledge. Aaron, described in Chapter 3, who composed music and constructed mental images of math theorems, was home-schooled for several years. During this period, he was able to invest time in music composition and mathematics. Aaron's university math tutor also had several other students at about the same level as Aaron, and he decided to teach them as a group. After the lessons, the boys usually arranged to spend more time together at one or another's house. Thus, Aaron found true peers who met both academic and social needs.

Siblings who do not have AS can be a source of true peers. This is particularly the case for younger gifted children with AS who love fantasy play and will enact scenes from books and movies. Siblings who are willing to enact the assigned roles and who are able to take the scenes in a different direction can be, for the gifted child with AS, a valuable source of learning how to negotiate a relationship while engaging in a loved activity. At the Gifted Resource Center of New England, it has been noted that those gifted children with AS who have siblings seem to engage in more play activities and appear somewhat less demanding of attention than those who are only children.

Finally, special interests can be a starting point in finding a true peer. Given interests in common, other aspects of friendship can be constructed, especially if the peer is willing to instruct and help the gifted child with AS to negotiate social situations.

FEELING DIFFERENT AND FEELING ACCEPTED

Fitting in with age-peer expectations is difficult for many gifted children. If they try to blend in and be like others, they have to give up to some degree their exceptional achievement and intellectual pastimes because these are not what more average age peers value. If they continue to appear gifted, usually by showing that they like school and achieve high grades, they risk being left out of peer groups because they are seen as not fitting the group norm.

Young gifted children compare themselves to age peers and see themselves unfavorably. This reference to the perceived norm from which they differ is called "norm-referenced" behavior. As most children become aware of the standards of peers, they try to conform. However, most children only begin to see these differences at about age seven or eight, while gifted children may see them at age four or five (Gross 1999). As gifted children begin to recognize the ways in which they differ from others, discomfort arises because conforming is not as easy as it is for the more average child. These gifted children then experience a lack of acceptance from others for differences they do not understand. Thus, age peers may not want to play with gifted children because their advanced ideas of play are incomprehensible. The gifted child then is likely to see this as a fault within the self ("They don't like me…I am not likable." Tolan 1987, p.185), rather than as a result of not being matched with the right peers.

Since age peers are the only peer group the young gifted child knows, the standards of this group then are the norm. What the gifted child loves the most, learning things, is not valued by peers or by society at large. Gross (1998) refers to this love of learning as "the love that dare not speak its name" because of societal disapproval. Thus, gifted children are presented with two options: to wear a mask and act like others by underachieving, or to achieve and risk not being accepted.

Some gifted children do conform, yet others choose to achieve quietly in school and develop outside interests that take up much of their time. In these outside interests, there is an opportunity to meet other people who support achievement. Thus, gifted children who elect this option belong to community groups in which a variety of ages are part of the activity. It is only when children are forced into the exclusive company of age peers that lack of acceptance is so painful.

Even in adolescence, the dilemma of not fitting in brings pain. However, adolescents have a number of coping mechanisms they use. Cross, Coleman, and Stewart (1993) studied gifted adolescents taking part in summer programs for bright adolescents in Tennessee. This study examined how gifted high-school students felt about themselves and their peers. Gifted students reported feeling that peers regarded them as different, and that the summer program was the first time they felt they could really be themselves. Most of them also reported that they dealt with difference at school by downplaying it in one way or other: for example, making disclaiming statements about achievements ("I was lucky"). About half felt they could not be their real selves at school. For many gifted children, the first time intellectual achievement is accepted is in college.

Gifted girls experience the forced choice dilemma to a greater degree than do gifted boys at all levels of potential. In this forced choice dilemma (Silverman 1986), gifted girls have to choose between an identity of being different, and even unfeminine, because of choosing to continue to achieve, or an identity of being a "regular person" – that is, someone who goes along with group norms. Gifted girls, in fact, may have to face two forced choices: hiding a love of learning to fit in with average peer norms (the dilemma of gifted students) and the choice forced on all intelligent women who try to achieve in a masculine-dominated world (AAUW 1992; Sadker and Sadker 1994). All gifted young women face this latter choice starting from early elementary years. Bell (1989) suggested that already by 4th-grade, many gifted girls had started to lose confidence and lower their expectations and effort.

Gifted children with AD/HD have as much, or more, trouble fitting in and feeling accepted as other gifted children. Because gifted children with AD/HD must struggle so much with managing behavior, some may be less socially accepted no matter what else they do. If achieving or being popular is a choice (the forced choice dilemma), these children do not get to choose. In fact, the only choice is whether they can find some peers, and achieve to an acceptable level. Thus, the forced choice dilemma may be different for these children. Some may be able to achieve to a high level despite AD/HD, and choose to do so. What these students are able to choose is whether to achieve or not, not how socially acceptable they can be.

Those gifted children with AD/HD who are socially acceptable on the surface may have other aspects of choice with which to struggle. For example, Jay, age 14, had to work exceptionally hard to make good grades because of his learning problems and AD/HD. Despite his gifted IQ (130 range), he made "B"s if he really tried. Jay gave up trying in 9th grade. He refused all help that was offered so he failed English and barely passed his other subjects. He decided at that point that he would not go to college, and he changed his friendship circle from college-bound peers to more average peers. With these he played computer games. Jay chose to underachieve because he felt he just could not keep up with his gifted peers. What came so easily for them cost him so much struggle, and Jay felt he had little in common with these students. He felt more at home with those who were not struggling. Jay's social choice cost him dearly, because he had trouble after he graduated finding a satisfactory job. In fact, Jay really felt quite lonely and longed for the days when he was young, and achievement was not such an issue.

The forced choice dilemma for gifted children with AD/HD may mean that those who choose to underachieve do themselves lasting damage since they actually may miss essential skills not easily learned at a later date. Those who achieve at the cost of social acceptance may find themselves lacking essential social skills in later years because they did not continually learn refinements of their childhood skills. This knowledge, once lost, is not easily learned in later years. Gifted children with AD/HD when faced with the forced choice dilemma have potentially more to lose no matter what they choose to do. Guidance, special gifted classes, and monitoring are all the more essential for this group of students in order for them to develop as full persons.

Gifted children with AS have difficulty fitting in and being accepted by either age peers or other gifted children. If they are lucky, they may be part of a group that includes many diverse people. This group then serves as a support and also gives advice on social skills.

Some gifted children with AS are well aware that they do not fit in, and that other students reject them. These students are at risk for depression because they want friends and want to be like other students. Will, Derrick, and Stuart all wanted very much to fit in and be accepted. Despite having some friends, all of them felt that they were not accepted by most of the other students and were in fact openly rejected, as well as teased and bullied.

Other gifted children with AS, especially in elementary school, are unaware that they are different and not accepted. These children think that everyone is their friend. Harry, described in Chapter 3, took little notice of others unless he needed them for his purposes. If asked about friends, though, he thought that everyone in his classroom was a friend. For his seventh birthday, he invited everyone in his class of 16 to a party at the Science Museum. About half the students accepted and came. Sadly, Harry was never invited to any of their birthday parties.

While other gifted children struggle with the forced choice dilemma – whether to be socially accepted or achieve at their potential – those with AS have no choice, because there is nothing they can do to be socially popular. Also, gifted children with AS have no idea that someone would actually choose underachievement to fit in. The idea of underachievement is alien. Once these children have acclimated to the idea of what school is about – that is, doing things the teacher wants – they become good students. They have to do their work and get good grades. When underachievement does occur, it is because the child is not interested in the subject at all, or in later school years feels negatively towards the teacher, perhaps thinking that the teacher is unfair. If provided with the chance to use their interests in class projects, gifted children with AS become star pupils. Achievement is what they know how to do.

Social competency and gifted children with AD/HD

In this section of this chapter, the social rejection that can result from AD/HD will be described and the underlying executive function deficits that contribute to social difficulties will be explored. In each subsection below, the difficulties of more average children with AD/HD will be examined and the differences shown by gifted children with AD/HD described.

Social rejection and AD/HD

It has been estimated that as many as 50 to 60% of all children with AD/HD experience some form of social rejection from their peer group. More than 30% retain their rejected status over four years and maintain it despite joining new social groups (Guevremont 1990). At every age level, children with AD/HD engage in behaviors that peers find bothersome.

The social difficulties of children with AD/HD arise because of the problems they have with executive functions, especially separating feelings from content, having a poor sense of both past and future, using self-directed inner speech appropriately, and breaking apart and recombining information. The results of these deficits are: overly intense affective responses in social situations, getting locked onto negative responding, poor perspective taking, poor delay of gratification, difficulty with cause and effect, impulsivity, difficulty using foresight and planning, difficulty with rule-governed behaviors, poor timing of responses, lack of seeing social cues, poor flexibility in responding, and difficulty assessing at once all the social parameters that are present. The end result is negative, irritating, and impulsive behavior that drives peers away.

Gifted children with AD/HD-Combined Type show many of these difficulties with social functioning. Generally, these gifted children do best in one-on-one contact or with only a few peers. They do least well when they have to function as a group working towards a group goal.

Children with AD/HD Inattentive Type have problems with social interactions. They are slow processors who feel that things go too fast, and they can't keep up. In social situations they miss the nuances, or process so slowly that by the time they reach a conclusion or think of something to say, the topic has long passed. In fact, they have been mentally absent and don't even know what was said next.

Children with AD/HD-Inattentive Type have problems with social timing because of their processing deficits. They appear to miss important aspects of conversations, and so say inappropriate things, or they say something at the wrong time. Both they, and others, can then misunderstand what is going on.

Gifted children with AD/HD Inattentive Type are often not socially rejected, but instead may be ignored. These children tend to do best when they feel familiar with the situation and the people. They also do well if they have a role to perform that requires more focus on a goal. They do least well in a large group with an ill-defined goal.

Social rejection of girls with AD/HD starts in preschool and gets more pronounced with age (Berry, Shaywitz and Shaywitz 1985; Brown, Madau-Swain, and Baldwin 1991; Gaub and Carlson 1997;). In fact, the social rejection of girls with AD/HD is more severe than that of boys with AD/HD. For one thing, girls with the Inattentive Type of AD/HD are as likely as girls with the Combined Type to be rejected (Berry, Shaywitz and Shaywitz 1985). Girls with AD/HD tend to have fewer friends, and more trouble maintaining friendships over time. In general, they also have higher levels of negative features to their relationships, such as conflict and verbal aggression (Blachman and Hinshaw 2002). Nadeau *et al.* (1999) suggested that the social climate in which girls operate is very different from that of boys because girls are more verbal and socially interactive. Their relationships require sensitivity to others and cooperation. In this sort of atmosphere, girls with even mild difficulties with verbal expressiveness and self-control, who tend to demand attention, and seem insensitive to subtle social messages – that is, those with AD/HD – will stand out.

Gifted girls with AD/HD who have difficulty with the subtle interactions of girls' social networks do stand out as different and are often rejected. Sometimes the problem occurs because the gifted girl does not value the group norms as Alissa, introduced in Chapter 2, did not. She felt that the norms were unfair because other girls arbitrarily selected some girls to be left out and ostracized. She did not want to go along with group games like this.

Some gifted girls with AD/HD like Kayla, described at the start of this chapter, had more difficulty understanding the unwritten rules of girls' social networks. Kayla, age 12, spent much of her spare time on the Internet instant messaging her friends. Kayla usually ended up crying after a session on the Internet because invariably someone would make a comment that would hurt Kayla's feelings. Her mother read some of the communications and thought that Kayla had two problems. She was exceptionally sensitive and took offense very easily to comments that were somewhat ambiguous. Perhaps they weren't meant as Kayla took them. On the other hand, much of the problem seemed to center around two girls who were the popular girls at school and whose friendship Kayla wanted. They seemed to know just what to say to get Kayla angry. Kayla's mother wondered if Kayla was dealing with some of the subtle bullying that girls can do, and that Kayla seemed not to understand. In truth, Kayla could be rather annoying as her mother well knew. She talked too much and was immature for her age. She had no finesse or sophistication. She made social mistakes like interrupting and not saying nice things about the right people; she demanded peers' attention. Conversely, she was a true and loyal friend once someone got to know her. Fortunately, Kayla related well to adults, and her relationships with these interested women served as a protective factor, and helped her social skills to develop. Like other girls with AD/HD who have good relationships with adults, and an ability to play alone in meaningful ways, Kayla showed less anxious or depressed behaviour then she otherwise might have (Mikami and Hinshaw 2003).

By middle-school years, when most girls encounter subtle encouragement not to compete with boys, not be too competent, and not be too assertive, a girl who has difficulty with self-control will be seen as disregarding societal norms. Also, she may find it difficult to continue working hard to achieve as she starts to get mixed messages about the value of female achievement.

Executive functions and how they relate to social competency

Gifted children with AD/HD, like other children with AD/HD, can have difficulty with executive functions related to paying attention, working memory, internalization of speech, part-to-whole relationships, emotional control, and delay of gratification. These lead to social problems such as difficulties recalling rules on the spot; noting social cues; using social problem solving; generalizing from one social situation to the next; predicting intentions, behaviors, feelings and consequences; inhibiting inappropriate behaviors and level of activity; acting without thinking; tolerating frustration; and developing a rhythm and timing of behaviors. Gifted children with AD/HD can also be aggressive, disruptive, and lacking in social skills and prosocial behaviors.

WORKING MEMORY

Children with AD/HD have difficulty when they have to hold the complexities of a social situation in mind while quickly deciding what is the appropriate thing to do. Because they have trouble with attention, these children may not perceive all the critical aspects of the situation. They also may not be able to attend to necessary aspects such as the other person's feelings, triggers that upset them, the need to think of the goal, and how to modulate behavior to fit the circumstance.

Children with AD/HD also have difficulty with remembering appropriate rules and expectations at the time of the social interaction. Thus, if asked later, they can state the rule, but in the heat of the moment, they do not think of it, or they misapply it.

Gifted children with AD/HD are likely to exhibit social difficulties based on poor working memory in group situations. When playing with one friend, the complexity of the situation is less likely to be as overwhelming as in a group. Also, in a group, gifted children with AD/HD are competing to have their ideas heard. When they try to induce the group to go along with an idea they want, gifted children with AD/HD are less apt to be able to consider all the aspects of a situation. This is especially the case if their ideas of what to do are more sophisticated than those of the group in general. Then, the gifted child with AD/HD has to deal not only with managing behavior in a group, difficult for most children with AD/HD, but also dealing with the asynchrony of more advanced or complex ideas that are misunderstood by peers. One of Phillip's difficulties with peers was his insistence on wanting to do things his own way. In playing a game on the playground, he wanted to change the rules so they would be more challenging. The other children wanted to play by the rules they already knew.

Suggestions to improve social working memory problems

- With the gifted child, try to identify particular situations and triggers that result in social conflict. Once identified, think of one or two ways the child can focus on the group goal, and on presenting an idea. For example, the child could restate the group goal before giving an idea: "Our goal is to decide on a game to play together." In giving an idea, the child needs to think of how to relate it to the group goal. "Maybe we could each suggest a game, or we could look at all the games we have and vote on them?" Practice several situations with the child.

- With the gifted child, look at situations that went wrong and see if a common problem arises. "Each time you interrupt, the other children get mad. How else could you get their attention?" One way might be to devise a rule: let two others talk, then the gifted child can talk again.

INTERNALIZATION OF SPEECH

Children with AD/HD have difficulty with internalization of speech in social situations because they have difficulty planning what they will do next in playing with others. They forget to ask others what they want to do, and forget to try alternatives if their first suggestions don't work. Monitoring their own behavior is a problem because children with AD/HD are not aware of how loud they are or how much they are interrupting others. They are unaware of how much they move around and of how much they touch others. Also, children with AD/HD forget social rules such as not taking other people's turns and waiting patiently for their next turn. Instead, they are apt to wander off or be disruptive. This means they also do not support other children's play with positive comments like "That was a good move." They are more apt to use negative comments with peers, and to engage in conflict when they are not receiving immediate attention.

Gifted children with AD/HD are likely to act in all of these ways. Whether they play with age peers or older children, their ability to monitor and plan their activity is a problem. If added to this is the gifted child's need for higher intellectual stimulation and novel experience, the result is poor social relationships with both age peers and other gifted children. When Phillip invited a friend over to play, he would forget rules about treating his friend as a guest, and instead would want to play computer games while his friend watched. He just could not stop himself. Even if he gave his friend a turn playing the computer game, Phillip could not watch his friend play; either Phillip told him what to do, or he wandered off to do something else.

Suggestions for improving social internalization of speech

- Pick one behavior at a time to target: for example, not taking all the turns in a board game. Make this the goal of playing the game and see if the child can restrain him or herself from touching the dice or other player's pawns during the game. Select an alternative action with the child: for example, sitting on his or her hands or squeezing a rubber eraser. Have the child say aloud on the first few turns: "I am going to squeeze this eraser after I finish my turn to remember to keep my hands off the dice." Each round, cue the child to stop and think; then, if the child has been successful, give a check mark on sheet of paper. Keep track of how many checks are earned, and praise improvement. Sometimes eating something crunchy or sour will allow the child to focus more on self-restraint. Once one skill is mastered, move onto another: for example, saying nice things to the other players.

- Discuss with the gifted AD/HD child how to play fairly. Planning what is fair requires thinking of other players' points of view and feelings. Deciding on fair rules, especially rules that allow a variety of ages and abilities to play a game, allows gifted children to plan and use strategy for a group goal.

- Teach the gifted AD/HD child how to talk to him or herself about a situation. For example, what are the signs that others are getting annoyed? A mental conversation that might be modeled for the child might be: "Oops, Marty is telling me to stop talking. I must be talking too much. I need to close my mouth and let two other people have a turn before I talk again."

PART-TO-WHOLE RELATIONSHIPS

In social situations, part-to-whole relationships include the ability to predict what will happen next, as well as what are people's feelings, intentions, and beliefs.

Some children with AD/HD have trouble in social situations because they are unable to figure out the whole. They tend to overfocus on part or to jump to conclusions based on one aspect. Often the aspect they judge a situation on is the most outstanding to them: that is, the one that has the highest intensity rather than the one that is really the most important. This makes accurate prediction difficult. Consequently, children with AD/HD often misunderstand the intentions of others and think they did things on purpose that were unintentional. Thus, if plans had to be changed, they are unable to see the big picture that sometimes things don't work out as planned, and they feel instead that the thing was changed on purpose to be mean to them.

Zentall, Cassady, and Javorsky (2001a), using stories about social events, found that children with AD/HD, compared to children without AD/HD, had trouble focusing on the main story events, providing relevant predictions for future outcomes, maintaining a positive outlook on future events, and providing more than one socially acceptable solution to a social problem. If the researchers, however, had the children with AD/HD reconstruct the story, they had much less problem, scoring more like peers without AD/HD. Thus, children with AD/HD make poor predictions because they do not have readily available in memory the cues about the situation, and they focus on the wrong part because they have less sense of the whole.

Alternatively, many children with AD/HD are big-picture thinkers. They have trouble attending to the details. In social situations they get the gist of what is going on but ignore specific cues. Thus, they focus on the big-picture goal of playing the game but miss the nuances of the social interactions, the social cues being given about their behavior, and the cues about other people's feelings.

Timing and rhythm of behavior is another area of difficulty. Children with AD/HD have trouble with knowing when to do things. Thus, some social behavior is inappropriate because it is done at the wrong time or in the wrong rhythm. Children with AD/HD have trouble joining in games with others because they don't note the rhythm of the group, but press ahead with their own agendas. They miss the waiting time others employ to get used to someone new; instead, they barge right in and miss the cues about whose turn it is. They also have trouble with the rhythm of conversations: whose turn it is to talk, how to get the floor, how to interrupt correctly, how to introduce new ideas, etc.

Children with AD/HD have trouble with predicting how people will behave towards them. Because they cannot see their own actions, they are surprised when someone reacts negatively to what they are doing. In their eyes, they aren't doing much at all, and why that should bother anyone, they don't know. Children with AD/HD also have trouble with emotional prediction: how what they feel results in their acting a particular way, and that their actions will bring certain social consequences. They miss the connection between cause and effect.

Gifted children with AD/HD have these same difficulties. However, there is a bigger gap than for other children with AD/HD between what they may be able to understand cognitively and what they are able to actually do in a situation. Thus, if they are given a hypothetical situation about something a boy did and how angry his parents would be, gifted children with AD/HD would answer correctly, and might even embellish the answer with comments about how the boy should stop and think, or what trouble he might get into. Given this very same situation at home, though, they will not see a connection between how they acted and the resulting parental anger. They will not feel parents are justified in their anger, nor will they see what the big deal is. After all, they didn't intend for the consequences to happen.

Gifted children with AD/HD, more than average children with AD/HD, argue with parents and teachers about problem behaviors. They have a very difficult time accepting the authority of adults unless they see it as reasonable or just. More than other children with AD/HD, gifted children with AD/HD feel equal to adults and think logical arguments ought to decide outcomes. Gifted children with AD/HD have trouble with the idea that logic doesn't solve all problems and that other factors matter more. They also are not always logical about arguments they call logical. If they can defeat a parent or other adult because they can manipulate them, use knowledge the adult does not have, or simply wear the adult down, they can feel justified in doing whatever they want.

If parents make the mistake, especially with very young children, of giving in to logical arguments or allowing the child to manipulate them, their gifted child with AD/HD will soon be unmanageable. Tyler, age 14, described in Chapter 5 for his creativity and sharp wit in writing newspaper commentary, was also a wonderful debater at school. As part of the school debate team, he helped win several regional and national matches. At home Tyler also was known for his debate skills. However, the rules that applied in formal debates at school somehow didn't apply to Tyler's debates at home. He also failed to acknowledge that some things were not open to negotiation. In fact, Tyler felt that he should have equal rights with his parents, and therefore they didn't have the right to tell him, "No," if he could give a good reason for doing something. In his mind, his idea of logic was all that mattered.

Suggestions for improving problems with part-to-whole relationships in social interactions

- Take real-life situations and discuss what the child predicts the people in that situation were feeling and thinking. Then, what did happen next and why? Did the result relate to how the people thought or felt about the problem?

- After a negative incident has occurred with a child, plan a review time when the child has calmed down in which people will say what they were expecting to happen and why. Discuss the possible outcomes given the feelings, thoughts, and expectations of the participants. Discuss what else might have happened given a different set of expectations.

- When gifted children are upset with friends, it is useful to analyze the situation as a big picture: what was the goal of the interaction; how did the events of the situation lead to the goal or not; what changed the goal; and when were obstacles encountered? Then, the details need to be explored: how did each party feel? How did their feelings relate to the failure of the plan? Where did things go wrong? What one thing would have positively changed the picture?

- Adults need to learn how to deal with the arguments of gifted children with AD/HD. This means limiting what they are allowed to argue about. Thus, some things in the family are not negotiable, and there is no arguing about these. Some things are negotiable, and good reasons for doing or not doing are allowed, but not as the result of an argument. That is, the child has to calm down and present a proposal to the parents for the change he or she wants. For example, a child might be allowed to decide when and how he or she will do tasks, but not whether he or she will do them. If tasks are too easy or too boring, adults may listen to the complaints and then decide if the task is important to do. The idea is not to let the child argue the adult out of performing a necessary task, but listening to the reasons the child has for feeling negatively and trying to help with those. On the other hand, some boring chores, like taking out the trash, need to be done anyway, and no one is exempt from experiencing and dealing with this type of boredom.

- Older gifted children with AD/HD who have gotten into the habit of arguing with parents need a planned approach that changes the parameters of the situation so that arguing no longer works. Changing the parameters means parents and other adults need to reset how tasks are accomplished, how positive attention is obtained, and how negative behavior is discouraged. In some families this will only be accomplished if there is a major refocus on responsibilities and privileges. Some parents can use books on managing AD/HD problems but also may need professional intervention.

EMOTIONAL CONTROL

In social relationships, emotional control includes the ability to recognize feelings in self and others, to separate emotion from the content of the message, to monitor and control behavior, to tolerate frustration, to deal with intensity, and to use appropriate rhythm and timing of behavior, all of which affect interpersonal relationships.

Children with AD/HD have difficulty with emotional control in social situations because they have trouble dealing with all the aspects of the situation at once. They also may have trouble reading their own feelings and those of others. Because of this, they are apt to misinterpret situations and act inappropriately. Children with AD/HD have trouble recognizing their own feelings because they may not feel them unless they are very intense. Because they are not used to recognizing or labeling the nuances of less intense feelings, they have trouble noting triggers for feelings. Thus, until they feel intensely, they may not realize they are scared or angry.

Children with AD/HD also have trouble recognizing feelings in others because they cannot focus on the complexity of emotional expression in social situations. Thus, they miss the low-intensity expression of feelings because they are focused on other things, including their own feelings. They miss such cues as tone of voice and mildly negative expressions of feelings. That is why many parents remark that their children with AD/HD do not listen until they are screaming at them. This neglect of more subtle feeling also has consequences for friendships. Especially in older childhood and adolescence, as children grow to rely more on mutuality and reciprocity, the emotional part of reciprocity is missing for those with AD/HD.

Separating feelings from the message being given is hard for many children with AD/HD. If they feel negative about doing something, nothing that is said will help. If they feel picked on, nothing said about what they did will be heard. If things are said with great intensity, they will hear only that part of the message and miss the part said with lower intensity. Thus, children act based on hearing only part of an emotional message. This has a great impact in relationships because what they think they hear may not be at all what was said. Later, the person with AD/HD will insist they were told what they thought they heard. Even if it were tape recorded during the telling, they will often still insist they are right.

Interpersonal relationships that require subtlety, timing, waiting, and patience are difficult for older children, adolescents, and adults with AD/HD. Noting the feelings of another, listening with empathy, focusing on what the other is saying, offering supportive comments, suppressing negative comments, thinking about the effect of words before saying them, and suppressing inappropriate humor are problems for people with AD/HD.

Gifted children with AD/HD have particular trouble with emotional control in relationships. Being gifted brings both intensity and sensitivity. Thus, the gifted child with AD/HD is more intense and sensitive than the average child with AD/HD, and also the gifted child who does not have AD/HD. The added intensity and sensitivity brings more complexity to feelings the gifted child with AD/HD needs to manage. Unfortunately, one of the problems these children face is less ability to deal with emotional and social complexity; thus, they have an added disadvantage in social situations. Paul, age 13, mentioned in Chapter 6, was such a perfectionist that he immediately assumed any comment made by anyone that suggested disappointment or frustration was his fault. Thus, he apologized constantly. He was exceptionally sensitive to any negative feelings of others and thought that it was his job to make them feel better. His friends got to the point that they never wanted to tell Paul anything bad because it would upset him so much. Thus, Paul started to miss out on developing intimacy in his relationships because he could not bear negative feelings.

Having increased intensity means that gifted children with AD/HD feel and react even more extremely than other children with AD/HD to frustration and negative messages from others. They feel more passionately about ideas, emotional events, ideals, and moral dilemmas than others, and they have a harder time accepting the limited amount anyone can do to solve world problems. This intensity makes it hard to be with them, hard to comfort and support them, and hard to help them live in this world. As a consequence, gifted children with AD/HD can take too personally events most others see at more of a distance.

The sensitivity of gifted children is also increased for those with AD/HD. Sensitivity runs the gamut from feeling more hurt feelings, to feeling deprived of what they think is due them, to feeling too much empathy towards and pain from others. Sensitivity to one's own feelings and to those of others promotes positive social interactions. For example, children who exhibit a high degree of prosocial behaviors such as altruism, sharing, taking turns, helping, and making positive comments generally make and keep friends. Thus, sensitivity, used the right way, can promote friendships. However, gifted children with AD/HD can have difficulty feeling too much sensitivity. When they feel too internally sensitive, they have difficulty attending to the feelings of others and to what else is going on in the situation. This leads to trouble predicting outcome or using effective problem solving.

Those who are too sensitive to others' feelings have trouble setting appropriate boundaries so they are not carried away on the feelings of others. If too sensitive to others' feelings, they miss the part of the message about what needs to be done, what other parameters are important, and how to solve a problem effectively while considering all aspects of the situation. They may be so caught on the feelings that this is all they attend to.

Gifted children with AD/HD may experience themselves as unpopular both because of their poor emotional monitoring in interpersonal situations and because of their giftedness. Thus, not only do they behave in an inappropriate and annoying manner towards others, but also they have few interests in common with which to build bonds. They have higher expectations for friendship than do age peers, but may act too intensely for other gifted children to tolerate. Not only may they have more depth and perceptiveness into human behavior than other children, but also they may act less maturely and have less insight into their own failings. Thus, finding friendships is much more difficult for gifted children with AD/HD than for gifted children without AD/HD. Sydney, first described in Chapter 2, was disliked by the other girls because of her intensity and ex-uberance. Sydney understood why the other girls didn't like her, but she couldn't help herself. Changing Sydney was like trying to change the wind. It was only when she was older and more able to manage team sports, debate, and drama that Sydney was able to develop female friends – girls who also loved activity and intense movement. Until then, she played more with boys.

Suggestions for improving emotional control in social situations

- Work on labeling lower-intensity feelings. With some children this means showing them the cues they miss when they do not look at faces or think about the tone of voice. Practice using different voice tones and emphases to describe different feelings. "I want some of that" changes meaning if different words are emphasized. "I want some of *that*" is quite different from "I want *some* of that." By starting to direct attention to what words are being emphasized, children with AD/HD are able to learn to listen to more subtle modes of expression, and to react more to the content of the message.

- After an incident has occurred, it is helpful to discuss what the interpersonal consequences of the eruption might be. It is important to teach children with AD/HD that the problem doesn't just go away when they stop being angry. Instead, they need to do something to actively repair the relationship, such as making the other person feel better by apologizing, and taking steps to change the behavior.

- Dealing with intensity can be difficult. It can be helpful to identify how the child shows intensity. Toning down intensity requires awareness of feelings and of effect on others. Thus, gifted children with AD/HD who are too intense need to learn how to stop and check the responses of others. Are their eyes getting glazed? Are they backing away? Are they arguing or getting angry and the child doesn't know why? Has the child been doing any of the identified intense behaviors: talking too much, being too close, touching, arguing, controlling, whining?

    Once the gifted child has identified a behavior as too intense, having a plan to stop is also important. For example, Phillip can learn a rule. When he is given a signal that he is talking too loudly, he can lower his voice, and finish his sentence, then ask a question to allow the other person to talk.

- When the gifted child with AD/HD has adopted an ineffective strategy for dealing with intensity and complexity in social situations, such as Paul's apologizing, it is helpful to teach more positive coping strategies. Paul needed to learn that he wasn't responsible for all the negative feelings he perceived, and that trying to change them only kept people from trusting that they could share them. Paul could learn to tolerate negative feelings by using emotional distancing techniques such as putting a pretend glass wall between himself and the feeling, pretending the feelings are washable and can be rinsed off him after an encounter, using relaxation techniques so he can focus on his breathing and not the negativity, and learning to focus on the other person's needs.

• Children who overfocus on their own intensely sensitive feelings need to improve sensitivity to others' feelings. When ordinary events result in hurt feelings, it can be helpful if adults are able to talk about other aspects of the situation. For example, Kayla's feelings were hurt because of what her friends wrote when she was sending them instant messages. Helping Kayla get over the hurt means analyzing the situation with her to see what the trigger was for the hurt. How did the hurtful comment come about? How does she know it was intentional? If it was intentional, what would she like to do about it? If this girl always hurts Kayla's feelings, maybe Kayla should consider ignoring whatever she says, or just not being her friend. In other words, Kayla needs an interpersonal plan to deal with situations in which she feels hurt. The solution depends on what happened and why. Maybe Kayla is so annoying she unintentionally provokes anger in others. On the other hand, maybe Kayla needs new friends.

• Help gifted children with AD/HD who are rejected by classmates to find their own special strengths and joys. If friends are not available at school, try other places, and look for a variety of friends of different ages and sexes. Retry activities again a year or so later if the child cannot handle them at first. Sydney was too active for drama at age six, but able to participate in a children's theater at age nine. She also became involved in street hockey with the boys in her neighborhood, and went on to play field hockey in middle school where she was a star player.

DELAYING GRATIFICATION

Children with AD/HD have difficulty with delaying gratification: that is, putting off immediate gain for a later reward. They are invested in the moment and in the most intense stimulation the moment can bring. Children who cannot delay gratification have difficulty with social relationships because much of social responding requires delaying gratification for a future attainment. Thus, to have a friend means being patient and letting the friendship unfold. It means not demanding things right now, but waiting to see what happens as people get to know one another. The "can't wait" aspect of AD/HD means that sustaining relationships over time is difficult, as is dealing with nuances of expression and feeling, building positive common goals, and negotiating conflicts.

Gifted children with AD/HD have trouble delaying gratification for the reasons described above. In relationships, because they are sensitive to how different from others they are, they are more likely to have trouble finding others with whom they fit.

Gifted children with AD/HD who are high stimulus seekers have the most trouble with long-term, close relationships. Unless these gifted people with AD/HD can find others who enjoy the same pace, friendships won't last long. This type of gifted person with AD/HD does best with several friendships built around active and exciting engagements, or a central enterprise: for example, a theater group that puts on a series of plays. The friendships are built around the play productions. Another example is a ski club where interactions are around skiing different trails in different places. The high stimulus seeker, as an adult, often tries to find a spouse who can manage longer-term relationships for both partners. Kyle, age 12, loves go-cart racing, riding his dirt bike, and doing tricks on his skateboard on the ramp he built in the front yard. Kyle is always on the go, and his friend, Mitch, is just like him. Together, the boys attempted to persuade Kyle's father to allow them to go camping by themselves for a week during the summer. They intended to do it survival style, taking nothing but a knife and some matches. Kyle's father consented, but only if he went too. Since he was an excellent woodsman, the boys agreed.

Gifted children with AD/HD who are less needful of high stimulation can have trouble sustaining relationships because of difficulty delaying gratification. They want things to happen now, and according to their own expectations and standards. In relationships, they need immediate feedback and immediate support. When others are not available to provide this, they may become exceptionally disappointed in their friends and feel rejected.

Another aspect of poor ability to delay gratification in relationships is boredom. After an initial period in which the relationship seemed perfect, the gifted child with AD/HD becomes rapidly disillusioned and bored. Once the newness has worn off, so has the excitement of the relationship. The aspect of friendship building that relies on slower, less intense repetition of events and experiences is experienced as boredom. While gifted children with AD/HD vary in their ability to delay gratification, those with the most difficulty also have the most difficulty sustaining long-term relationships.

Suggestions for improving the delay of gratification in social situations

- Gifted children with AD/HD need to work on the rhythm of relationships. Using stories as well as real-life situations, adults who work with gifted children with AD/HD need to explain relationships as a sort of dance, in which the music goes faster and slower, but one needs to be aware of what the pace is at any one time. Listening to the rhythm of the interaction gives cues to what to expect next. Sometimes the pace can be speeded up by taking particular actions, such as calling a friend and issuing an invitation. Other times, the pace has to be tolerated.

- Those gifted children with AD/HD who become bored with friends and constantly seek new relationships have a difficult time learning another pattern because it is the novelty of the relationship that keeps them involved. If these children learn how to inject their own novelty into relationships, they can learn to sustain them better. This means picking tolerant friends who are interested in a variety of things and are always open to new ideas and activities. Then, the easily bored gifted person with AD/HD can introduce new ideas and activities and find someone eager to share the adventure.

Positive social aspects of gifted children with AD/HD

Gifted children with AD/HD, because they are somewhat less mature than other gifted children, tend to be more naive and trusting. This means they also believe in ideals to a greater degree than age peers and are much more like other gifted children in their approach to truth and loyalty in friendships.

Gifted children with AD/HD as a whole tend to be quite generous and kindhearted to others if they perceive them to be in need. Partly because they are impulsive and give no thought to the consequences, some are generous with their possessions. Material things mean little to them in the moment. They may want the latest video game, but they also will give away items that others found valuable just because they are asked. How generous they are depends on how much value they place on any object at any time, and this can vary even with the same object over time. Nevertheless, there are many gifted children with AD/HD who are unselfish, compassionate, and caring about others.

Gifted children with AD/HD are often very enthusiastic about new things and new ideas and are willing to try out new activities. They can be risk takers or adventurers depending how they channel their enthusiasm. The passion of these children is also important because if they find someone or something to love, they are immensely loyal, passionate about the pursuit, and eager to commit themselves to the cause. If their energy is channeled they are enthusiastic partners in change. Socially, their passion and enthusiasm get them involved. They also can get others involved and passionate about a cause as well.

Gifted children with AD/HD are often very funny. Many are class clowns and are quite entertaining. The problem is that they can become disruptive and irritating because they don't know when to stop. Nevertheless, many of the people who become our greatest comedians were class clowns in childhood (Fern 1991). These gifted humorists, according to research, were able to tell jokes that, because of their sophistication, peers did not get. Many developed an appreciation for and created jokes that were well beyond the level of age peers. Eric, for example, at age nine (Lovecky 1994a), when told by his mother that they had to eat and run, quipped, "You mean like carnivorous panty hose?" The use of humor defuses many social conflicts, and the gifted child who can use it in this way has a social advantage no matter what his or her other problems may be.

Social competency and gifted children with AS

In this section of this chapter, the social rejection that can result from AS will be described and the underlying deficits that contribute to social difficulties will be explored. In each subsection below, the difficulties of more average children with AS will be examined and the differences shown by gifted children with AS described.

Social deficits and AS

Children with AS have primary social deficits in understanding and interacting with other people. These deficits in functioning can lead to problems with social communications; social interactions; making and keeping friends; understanding social rules; understanding appropriateness of actions; lack of reciprocity and empathy; recognizing, monitoring, and modifying inappropriate social behavior; and using emotions appropriately in social interactions.

The current hypotheses about the underlying deficits in AS include problems with executive function, central coherence, and Theory of Mind (ToM). It seems useful to think of social problems as having a relationship to one or more of these three aspects. However, which of the three aspects results in particular deficits is not really known yet, nor is it known which is the major cause of AS. However, for the purposes of this book, all three aspects will be discussed as if certain deficits arose from each specific one.

Like children with AD/HD, children with AS have deficits that may be the result of deficiencies in executive function: attention (especially shifting attention), working memory, internalization of speech, part-to-whole relationships, emotional control, and delay of gratification. These lead to social problems such as difficulties shifting from one situation to the next, shifting attention to deal with the changing focus of a conversation, noting social cues, using social problem solving, generalizing from one social situation to the next, inhibiting inappropriate behaviors and level of activity, and developing a rhythm and timing of behaviors.

Social deficits that may occur due to problems with central coherence (making wholes from component parts and imbuing these with social relevancy) include difficulties with part-to-whole relationships, formation and use of social imagination, having a sense of the future, social problem solving, overliteralness of interpretation of social meaning, integrating complex social meaning, understanding facial expression, and understanding verbal and nonverbal communication.

Social deficits that may be related to ToM mechanisms include difficulties with understanding social relevancy; problems with understanding the feelings, thoughts, and intentions of others; making predictions of behavior; problems with understanding basic social rules; and problems understanding social reciprocity, feeling empathy, and starting and maintaining friendships.

The social deficits of children with AS have some fundamental differences from those of most children with AD/HD alone, even when children with AD/HD have deficits in social functioning. Children with AS have much more difficulty understanding the social basis of behavior, and how that social basis controls the actions of people. Children with AD/HD have a different set of basic assumptions about people than those with AS. For example, Phillip may become very angry and aggressive, but he does recognize that other people don't like his behavior, and that it is desirable for him to change it.

Children with AS, however, do not recognize the social basis for controlling actions. Derrick is more likely to feel no reason to change his behavior based on his effect on other people. His own feelings count most because that is all he can really process. Thus, it is much more difficult to convince Derrick that he needs to control himself so as to not hurt others' feelings, because he doesn't see this as a goal. This basic lack of comprehending social significance and relevancy could be thought of as deficits in ToM and lack of central coherence. Derrick does not see how behaviors have a social impact because he doesn't understand social relevancy. It makes no sense to him that how he behaves affects how someone else feels. He also has less ability than others of his age to appreciate the differing points of view and feelings of others. Thus, he has no perspective about why conflicts occur or what he could do to change them; all he is aware of is how he feels.

Children with AS have less social imagination (despite often having a wonderful imagination in other aspects). They cannot see themselves as any different than they are right now. When caught in an unpleasant interaction, they also see no way to change things. Selecting an alternative strategy requires the ability to imagine something different. A lack of social imagination also means that children with AS have no sense of the future. Like children with AD/HD who have a poor sense of the future, children with AS have trouble predicting what will happen next. The poor sense of the future, however, seems somewhat different in children with AS than in children with AD/HD. Because children with AS have so much trouble seeing the whole (weak central coherence), they have no sense of what the bigger picture could be, or what could possibly happen. One of the reasons that people with AS have rituals and routines, a strong need for sameness, and a dislike for change is their inability to make predictions. Consequently, everything that happens is a surprise – it's unpredictable and this causes anxiety.

A lack of social imagination, a poor sense of the future, and difficulty making predictions based on having only part of the picture mean that people with AS have immense trouble in dealing with all the nuances of relationships. They just don't get what social relationships are about. Breaking the code of relationships means that people have to be able to have a sense that something has social significance. It's like dyslexia and breaking the code of reading: if there is no correspondence between the sound and symbol, the person learning to read does not understand how letters make up words and sentences and convey meaning. In the same way, because there is difficulty attaching social significance to events and relationships, the person with AS has trouble understanding the meaning of the units of social behavior that make up social relationships. Thus, at a very basic level, AS appears to be a disorder of making social attributions.

The symptoms of AS that result from this basic lack of social attribution vary in severity among individuals. Thus, while all children with AS have social deficit problems, some are more impaired overall. In addition, differences in personality traits such as motivation, persistence, patience, and outgoingness can all affect how the child with AS fares in attempting social interactions. Finally, intelligence does matter. Gifted children with AS have more ability to learn social rules. They have more complex interests, and more ability to share those interests at a complex level of development. Thus, while some gifted children with AS have few or no interests, many have interests in areas that allow a great deal of scope for learning and interacting with others. On the other hand, gifted children with AS have a bigger gap between their strengths and weaknesses than most other children, and this gap can be misinterpreted by others as "won't do" rather than "can't do."

Areas that are commonly affected by AS include: appreciation of social cues; understanding social rules; recognizing, monitoring, and mediating inappropriate behaviors; developing social communication skills; and developing friendship skills.

APPRECIATION OF SOCIAL CUES

The reading of social cues involves the ability to notice, understand, and act on subtle verbal and nonverbal social messages from others.

Children with AS have difficulty noting social cues. They have trouble seeing facial expressions and knowing the significance of what particular facial expressions mean. They also have trouble with understanding the subtle social cues that signal how people in social situations act. For example, when two people interact, a certain rhythm develops in who talks and when. People also know how to signal that they have something to contribute or wish to change the subject. Social cues also give indications about what people mean with their words. The same words may mean different things in a different context.

Social cues let people know the context within which to act. Is it appropriate to show levity, or need one be serious? Social cues also give social feedback: for example, about feelings and intentions, or about comfort with current behavior. For example, talking louder and softer can be a social cue to emphasize certain feelings or to tell someone else to be more or less loud in their speech. All of these social cues are difficult for people with AS.

Gifted children with AS have difficulty with social cues in the same way as other children with AS. Because they are so bright, with instruction gifted children with AS can learn to read basic facial expressions. They can learn what tones of voice mean and how to assess what to do from a tone of voice. They can learn to listen for cue words that indicate a change of subject. What is more difficult is putting it all together at once: learning the rhythm of social interactions and reading social context to determine the expectations of others. Will, age 16, had the most trouble with subtle social cues. He had difficulty knowing when it was acceptable for him to approach a girl and talk with her. He missed the subtle cues that indicated a lack of interest or a desire for him to leave. Part of the problem was that Will so much wanted a girlfriend that he was apt to ignore cues that he might have otherwise seen. On the other hand, he really did have difficulty with comprehending body language and subtle signs that the other person was turned off to him.

Suggestions to improve reading social cues

- Practice tones of voice by exaggerating the tone and teaching the child what characteristics to listen to: for example, a loud harsh voice often means displeasure, a light soft voice a more positive message. Make tape recordings of various voices: surprise, anger, embarrassment, happiness, scolding, praise and so on. Have the child identify by tone what was meant by the message. Discuss with the child what words mean negative or positive messages. Make lists of the "yes" and "no" words.

- Teach the child with AS the cues that indicate how people give each other feedback in social situations. For example, nodding means a positive response but doesn't always mean agreement. It means the person is listening. List the other ways that suggest someone is listening. Practice with the child noting these cues and using them him or herself.

- Teach the child with AS how to interrupt politely. Work on how and when to interrupt, and when not to do so. Make a list of social virtues for everyone to follow: being polite, showing you are listening, waiting quietly, smiling, etc.

- One way to work on determining social context is to teach children with AS to watch others and see what they are doing. Then, the child has to assess if the activity is a good or bad thing to do. How would the child know? Make a list of the times it is necessary to be serious (not laugh, be quiet, listen carefully) and when it is allowable to be less serious (laugh, be silly, choose what you want to do, talk out loud and so on). Imitating the children who are the best role models is a way for children with AS to learn social context. Adults will need to help the child choose appropriate role models and behaviors to imitate.

UNDERSTANDING SOCIAL RULES

The rules of social engagement are especially difficult for children with AS. These social rules determine how to engage with people, how to treat people, how to deal with negative feelings, and how to interact cooperatively. Social rules are often unwritten, a part of the intuitive knowledge most other children learn through social contact. For example, there are social rules about not interrupting others, and rules about how to interrupt. There are rules about joining in, and about recognizing signs when one is not invited – a private conversation, for example. When rules can be made explicit, it is easier for children with AS to follow them.

Rules that apply to engaging others include such skills as making eye contact, recognizing interest from others, knowing how to join a group, how to issue an invitation, how to kindly discourage someone, how to disengage from a group, and how to enter into a group rhythm. Children with AS need to have skills broken down into smaller parts and to practice each part separately. Thus, Derrick would learn how to look at another person to see if he or she were looking at him. Derrick also would learn to use eye contact as a means of checking if someone were listening. At the end of each sentence, or each time he took a breath, he would look up and check the other's eyes. Derrick also would learn to look where others are looking to see what else is going on.

Gifted children with AS have difficulty following social rules of engagement as much as do other children with AS. However, another problem for gifted children with AS is the need for additional rules about being ahead of others academically or being smart. Gifted children with AS need rules about not sharing information about grades, class ranks, IQ, or sometimes age. While it is generally not advisable to tell gifted children their IQ scores, some find out on their own. They read psychologists' reports or see school records. Then, gifted children with AS may start trying to relate to other people around the topic of how high an IQ each has. Also, if they are advanced and are taking courses at a younger than usual age, it is helpful for them to learn not to comment on age or degree of advancement. Harry, described in Chapter 3, read the psychologist's report after he was tested. He knew what an IQ was and loved the idea of standard deviations which he had looked up on the Internet. From there he was able to calculate how far his score was above average. Harry saw no reason not to share this news with his classmates. In a matter of fact way he described how they were all at the norm (that is, average) and he was not. His classmates laughed at this; they already knew he wasn't normal. This just gave them more reason to tease him.

Suggestions for improving knowledge and use of social rules

There are a variety of techniques that have been developed to teach children with AS the rules of engagement.

- *Social Stories* (Gray 1998) provide social structure. The child hears a synopsis of the situation, a statement of social cues, and what other people's expectations might be. The stories also provide a reason for following a social rule, and run through a short scenario of what to do. Providing the reason for following the social rule is especially important because having a reason for doing the behavior helps the child with AS to make sense of the rule. Since children with AS lack social imagination, they don't know why people do social things; often it doesn't make sense to them. Helping social actions make sense ensures the child will learn the rule and then follow it. A variation on social stories is Carol Gray's *Comic Strip Conversations*, a graphic that illustrates what others might be thinking, as well as saying, in a particular situation. Color is used to illustrate emotional content (Gray 1994, 1998).

- *Social scripts* are useful. These give more of a step-by-step sequence of yes/no prompts, and what to do. For example, if Derrick wants to ask a schoolmate to go to a video arcade with him, he might call and use a script.

"Hello, this Derrick Smith. Is Brian there?"

("*No.*") "May I please leave him a message?"

("*Yes.*") If Brian is there: "Hi Brian, this is Derrick. My dad is taking me to the Arcade this Saturday, and he said I could ask a friend to come, and I'd like to ask you. Would you be able to come?" (Wait while Brian asks his parents.)

1. ("*Yes.*") "Great! We could pick you up at your house at 11 a.m. Is that time okay for you?" (Wait while Brian asks his parents.)

("*Yes.*") "I'll look forward to seeing you Saturday. Goodbye."

2. ("*No.*") "Too bad. Well, maybe we can go some other time then. Have a good weekend. Goodbye."

Social scripts try to include as many variations of response as possible so the child is prepared for several responses. Otherwise, the script will not be useful.

- *The rules of the (social) road* (Bolick 2001) include many tips on politeness and positive behavior for adolescents such as: don't stare; don't make negative comments about race, religion, clothing, or hairstyle; don't walk between people who are having a conversation; when talking to people in authority over you, be respectful; don't swear or use slang; don't make judgments about other people. Bolick

also has rules about keeping secrets, not giving out personal
information to strangers, not forwarding an e-mail without the other
person's permission, and not agreeing to meet people found on-line.
These are all very useful and can be made into scripts and lists of
rules to remember.

Gifted children with AS are very adept at learning social stories and scripts, and
following rules, once they know what the rule is and why it should be followed.
Because they are gifted children, these children with AS are often more loyal to
following rules, and there are more reasons that can be given as a rationale for following a particular rule. On the other hand, these gifted children encounter more
complex situations where social scripts may fall short, or where social stories are
more difficult to write. For example, Seth, at age 12, won a national Spanish
award and had to give a speech in Spanish. Learning the speech was easy.
Learning the social script about what to do when accepting the award was difficult. Because the award presenter said something different than expected, Seth's
script didn't have a response. However, his father had included a "What to do if
the unexpected happens," and Seth had been instructed to say, "Thank you." That
worked well enough.

SOCIAL SKILLS AND PROSOCIAL BEHAVIORS

Social skills (as opposed to knowledge) are needed to enter into social engagement and conversations with friends, as well as interactions with strangers. Social
skills include the ability to monitor and modulate intensity of behavior and to
assess if behavior is appropriate or inappropriate for time and place.

Children with AS have difficulty with social skills and prosocial behaviors
such as taking turns, waiting, paying attention to others, listening, sharing,
cooperating, helping, saying positive comments, and refraining from inappropriate behaviors. Both knowing social rules and being able to perform social
behaviors are important for successful social engagements. Thus, even when
children with AS know what to do (knowledge of a social rule), putting it into
action can be difficult. The child with AS may misjudge when to use the rule. The
child may use the rule appropriately, but be too intense in its application. There
may be conflicting rules, and the child with AS doesn't know how to judge the
situation and infer what to do. For example, one social rule is that it is polite to
share. However, there are also times when one ought not to share. If Derrick only
knows the rule about sharing, he may have difficulty when he doesn't want to or
cannot share. Suppose Tom wants to borrow Derrick's homework answers or his
comb? Suppose Derrick wants something, and someone else doesn't want to
share?

Rules also evolve over time. What was appropriate when a child is five or six is no longer so at 13. Thus, both knowledge and performance of social skills need to evolve over time so the child learns how to deal with more complex situations and higher social expectations. Sometimes it is useful to explain rule changes to children with AS in developmental terms. Knowing that children have tantrums when they are preschoolers, but try to control themselves as young teens, is helpful to the child with AS struggling to understand why people now have a more negative reaction to what he or she has always done.

Gifted children with AS also have trouble with social skills and prosocial behaviors. They have difficulty inhibiting inappropriate behaviors such as making inappropriate comments, intruding into peer activities, interrupting, talking too much and giving no one else a turn, ignoring peers and teachers, saying negative things about peers and teachers, and controlling group activities. Stuart, described in Chapter 4, talked too much, and at inappropriate times, about Monty Python. He turned every conversation into a monologue. His peers were tired of hearing about *The Life of Brian* and other plots. Even those who once had liked Monty Python themselves just wanted him to shut up.

Inappropriate behaviors can occur because of problems with processing and timing. That is, the behavior itself is not inappropriate, but its expression at that time is wrong for the situation.

Since children with AS often have much slower processing, more difficulty taking in complex situations, more trouble seeing the whole instead of only part, and problems with smoothly reacting in synch with the event, they not surprisingly react long after the causative event has passed. Inappropriate behavior can also occur because the child with AS responds to the feature of the situation that is most pertinent to him or her rather than what might be needed, given the whole. For example, Will wants to say hello to a certain girl in his high school. He waits in the hall outside her class until the bell rings, then he stands in the way of the other students trying to leave the room as he tries to talk to her. Even when the other students tell him to move, he just ignores them, because all his attention is focused on the girl and his goal of talking to her.

Inappropriate behavior also includes rituals, tics, stereotyped behaviors, and rigid insistence on sameness. Eccentric behaviors can be inappropriate such as eating unusual food combinations, eating with a spoon or fingers instead of a fork, or refusing to touch certain materials.

Suggestions for dealing with inappropriate behaviors

- Make a list of inappropriate behaviors exhibited by the child. Try to ascertain if they are the result of timing, slow processing, or inexperience – or are they rituals, preoccupations, or eccentric behaviors? How important are they? Pick out the ones that cause the most social problems.

- Poor timing and inappropriate expression due to inexperience can change with practice. Using scripts and social stories, discuss when it is appropriate to do certain things, and when is it not. Will needs some practice about how to approach a girl, when to do so, and what to say. He needs to be told that right outside the classroom is not the best place. Alternatives can be suggested – talking to her at lunch, before a class they both take, or at her locker.

- Children with AS need to learn to listen for key words that tell them to stop behaviors or do something else. "Not right now," " Please stop," "I don't want to," "I'm not interested," "No!" are all words they need to learn to pay attention to.

- If the inappropriate behaviors are the result of rituals and eccentricities, limiting the time and place of their expression can help somewhat. In other words, Derrick could indulge his passion for wearing political buttons at home, but not school. Derrick could have finger foods that are appropriate for school, packed as a lunch, if he refuses to eat with tableware. He can be taught that it is necessary to eat with tableware in some situations such as a fancy restaurant, a wedding, at someone else's house for a holiday meal; that is, in some situations the only choice is using silverware. He may need lessons in using tableware efficiently.

- To get the child with AS to change an inappropriate behavior, it is necessary to have a plan in which the child also participates. The behavior is broken down into smaller steps, and each step is learned separately. For example, to teach Will to think about timing in greeting others, he might first make a list of places where it is dangerous to stop and talk to others, as well as places where it is inconvenient to do so. Next, he can help identify when it is appropriate to greet others (before class versus in the middle of a lesson). Will can try to keep track of avoiding the wrong places and picking the right places and see how many people he greets. He can then gradually extend this process to other aspects of timing in greeting others: for example, how to tell when they will be receptive to a comment from him, or how to catch their attention.

- Sometimes it is better to change the environment than to try to change the child. For example, if the child will only eat some foods or wear some items of clothing, these can be made as attractive as possible. Good table manners can do much to alleviate problems of eating unusual foods in unusual ways. Thus, it is more important to eat with one's mouth closed, and not slurp one's food, than it is to eat what other students eat for lunch. Work on table manners at home and school using positive reinforcement. Dewey (1991) suggested that one way to do this is to praise the child for the attempt at using a table skill, no matter how imperfectly it is done, or even if the skill happened by accident. For example, Derrick used his napkin once and his mother then said, "Derrick, I've noticed you've been using your napkin much more recently instead of your sleeve. I'm really proud of you." Anytime Derrick then even reached in the vicinity of his napkin, his mother repeated her praise. Soon, Derrick actually was using the napkin spontaneously.

- Have the child keep a chart of progress. In the lives of children with AS, so many behaviors are worked on for so long, it can seem disheartening. Nothing they ever do is enough. Keeping track of progress then can help in building esteem for what they already have accomplished.

- Try to find alternatives for some of the more annoying inappropriate behaviors. For example, if Joseph, mentioned in Chapter 6, likes to tap his pencil in class and this makes an annoying noise, he could tap on a surface that does not make noise. However, the sound may be what is most important to Joseph, and then other alternatives need to be found. For example, Joseph might do well if he could listen to headphones with sound in them. Then he might not need to tap.

COMMUNICATION SKILLS

Problems with communication skills include difficulties understanding the context and nuances of social use of language, difficulty with conversation skills, and problems with inappropriate remarks.

Children with AS have difficulty with social language: that is, language that depends on context to convey social meaning. This is the case with both nonverbal and verbal communication. For example, whole conversations can be accomplished with looks and facial and bodily gestures that convey meaning to others without a word ever being said. Many aspects of relationships are nonverbal. Conveying interest in someone, making contact across a room, showing approval and disapproval, flirting, even making a plan can all be accomplished with a look and a glance. For example, Martha looks at Rob. He nods at her, and she smiles. He makes a slight movement with his head towards the door, and she nods. Soon they both leave the room. Children with AS miss these nuances.

Meaning that is conveyed by words in a particular context may be missed. Irony, sarcasm, and use of metaphor and symbolic language can be taken literally by the child with AS. Sayings such as "Let sleeping dogs lie" and "Don't judge a book by its cover" make sense to them, but on a literal basis. The social meaning is not understood. Indirect requests by others may also be taken literally. Stuart's grandfather said to him, "Don't you think it would be a good idea to turn off that video and go to bed now?" Stuart said, "No," and didn't understand why his grandfather became annoyed with him.

Conversation skills can be especially problematic for children with AS as they grow older. They need to be specifically taught such conversation skills as the idea of talking and listening turns; the idea of a beginning, middle, and end in a conversation; how to start, and maintain, a conversation; and how to introduce a topic, show that one is listening, ask appropriate questions, stick to the topic, and change the topic.

Children with AS need to learn how to avoid making inappropriate remarks about others or themselves. If they inadvertently interrupt or make an inappropriate remark, they need to learn how to apologize.

Gifted children with AS have a great deal of trouble with conversational skills because they often have so much to say on a topic that there seems to be no good stopping place. Also, many gifted children with and without AS, especially boys, think the goal of a conversation is to convey information, not to have a social experience. Thus, those with AS are at an extreme end of the gifted boy tendency to want to tell everything they know, and to assume the listener doesn't know anything, but is willing to learn by hearing them discourse on the subject. Most gifted boys, though, can give up the conversational floor if prompted. They allow questions and will explain things. There is room in their discourse for the other person. Also, other gifted boys look to see if the listener is still attending and will try to clarify what they mean. All of these aspects are very difficult or even impossible for gifted boys and girls with AS.

Gerald, age 14, a gifted boy without attention deficits, was discussing a new science-fiction book he'd read. As he went on and on, telling me the plot, I said, "Gerald, stop! I want to read it myself. Don't spoil it for me." Gerald immediately stopped, and changed the topic to some of the concepts he had found interesting in the book which were also present in other books he knew we had both read.

Contrast this with Stuart who had nothing to say when I asked him not to tell me the plot of the newest Harry Potter book. He could not separate the content of the plot from what he liked about the book, nor could he pick out a theme to talk about that might encompass other books we had previously discussed. Even when I picked out the theme, he had trouble thinking of a way to discuss it that didn't include telling me the plot of the newest book. (Do you think if would be a good idea if we really had a Magic World like Harry does? If I was a friendly Muggle, how would you explain the point of Quidditch matches to me?) Stuart also had trouble thinking of a different topic since he couldn't discuss this one. In fact, Stuart was "stuck" on the newest Harry Potter book and, when prevented from talking about it, had no other topics available.

Gifted children with AS have trouble with the social context of communication. They miss the nuances of language, especially the nonverbal aspects. Because they are advanced in language skills in other areas, though, they get more practice in analyzing sarcasm, metaphor, and proverbs than other children with AS. Some of the gifted children with AS who came to the Gifted Resource Center of New England were quite good at detecting sarcasm after some training, and became expert at using it themselves. They also memorized the metaphorical meaning of proverbs and so could use them appropriately in class work and in conversation.

Suggestions for improving social communication skills

- Work on conversational skills by taking one skill at a time and targeting it. Break it down into smaller parts if necessary. Provide scenarios when the child would use this skill and practice at home and in school everyday. For example, Derrick learned to start a conversation by making a list of possible conversation starters. After he had said hello and been acknowledged, he asked a question or two: "What are you up to?" "How are you doing?" "How was your weekend?" "What's that book you're reading?" He also had some statements he could make: "I can't believe all this homework!" "I am so glad it's the weekend!" As he learned to talk for a minute or two, Derrick was also taught how to extend the conversation by asking a nonpersonal question: "Did you see that new movie [fill in name of a movie] yet?" "Do anything interesting this weekend?" As Derrick progressed, he introduced more topics.

- To teach Derrick the reciprocal nature of conversation, he was told to envision a conversation as a ball game. The goal was to hold the conversation ball for a sentence or two and then pass it back to the other person. If he forgot and started to talk too long, he was signaled to pass the ball. Eventually Derrick did get the idea, and while not very smooth at changing back and forth, he did develop a sense of how much time he ought to talk before asking the other person a question.

- Some movies and television videotapes can be helpful in teaching children with AS to notice nonverbal language. Thus, on a video, when a sequence is found that illustrates giving a message with a look, it can be replayed showing the child the essential features. On machines that allow slow motion, slowing down the speed may help the child to process more readily what happened.

FRIENDSHIP SKILLS

Children with AS have difficulty making and keeping friends. They have difficulty knowing who is a friend, and they have trouble with the give and take of friendship. They are susceptible to teasing and to manipulation by others because they are so naive about the intentions of others.

Making and keeping friends

Making and keeping friends is difficult because children with AS can't negotiate the many complex aspects of relationships. The need to attend to so many things at once is difficult even when these children have learned some basic play and friendship skills (take turns, cooperate, be a good loser). Consequently, children with AS do better with one person at a time rather than a group, so they can go more at their own pace. This allows them to be more aware and more able to use skills they have practiced.

It is difficult for children with AS to know who is a friend. If asked about friendships, many of these children described all the children in the class as friends. They often wanted to invite the entire class to a birthday party as Harry did for his seventh birthday. Despite the fact other children actually were rather mean to them, many of these children still thought of anyone they knew as their friends.

Most important though, these children lack an idea of what friendship is. When asked what makes a good friend, children with AS respond with a list of actions a friend should not do, as opposed to describing attributes of a friend (Attwood and Gray 1999).

Gifted children with AS who came to the Gifted Resource Center of New England behaved similarly. They could not think of any positive attributes other than: "A friend is someone who is nice to you." They were unable to describe what nice meant except in negative terms: that is, a friend would not tease, or name call, or get up and walk away from the table when they sat down to lunch, or trip them. Partly this was the result of how they had been treated. Given a list of friendly and unfriendly behaviors, several gifted children with AS described in detail how they were the subjects of specific unfriendly behaviors. On the other hand, they recalled fewer of the more positive behaviors. The positive behaviors included people greeting them, smiling at them, saving them a place in line, waving at them in a store, asking them over to play at the pool or on a playground, and so on. It is not that these positive behaviors never happened. In fact, parents reported they did, though the frequency may have been lower than for more average children. The problem was that gifted children with AS did not recognize the friendly behaviors, did not respond in kind, and initiated few of these behaviors themselves. Even at age 16, Will had difficulty greeting other students when he saw them in town. Though he desperately wanted friends, he had a difficult time knowing what to say when the meeting was unexpected. It was not that he didn't notice or recognize the student he met, as is the case for some children with AS; instead, he had trouble organizing an appropriate and rapid enough response.

Children with AS have difficulty with the reciprocal nature of friendship. As with conversational skills, children with AS fail to see that friendship requires an interplay of two people. Thus, it is hard for these children to respond appropriately to friends' requests, to offer friendship, to show they care about the friend, to offer positive support, to share feelings – all the things that friendships require as children move into middle school and adolescence. Children with AS are socially immature and act much more like children in preschool (playing alongside a friend) or early elementary school (sharing an activity).

If they are lucky enough to have family friends, children with AS may have the support of friendship without having to expend most of their energy finding the friend. Also, some children with AS have compassionate peers who include them and instruct them in appropriate social skills. The idea of modeling other children, especially in adolescence, has been described by other people with AS such as Liane Holliday Willey (1999) and Temple Grandin (1995). Both used modeling as a means of learning how to navigate the social world that was so confusing in its complexity. The modeling allowed each to break the complexity down into tangible units that could then be worked on. Meanwhile, adolescents like Tony, mentioned in this chapter, feel they are part of the group, accepted and valued by the group, and supported by the group.

Gifted children with AS have difficulty making and maintaining friendships because they are so odd, and because they really have more difficulty finding people with whom to share their interests. As described earlier in this chapter, finding peers at their level of interest, passion, and comprehension is very difficult. Some gifted children, though, do form relationships based on teaching their special interests, especially if these are in fields peers find interesting, such as computers and math.

Introversion/extroversion

Children with AS vary in their desire for friendship. Some children with AS are very isolated loners who appear to feel more comfortable with their own company, and so ignore peers. These children tend to be more introverted. They feel less desire for friends and have more trouble approaching other children at all. They tend to be more withdrawn. If asked, they will say that they have no friends. Some yearn, though, for one true friend, even though they might not be sure exactly what a friend would be like. Jack, described in Chapter 3, was introverted and preferred reading to socializing. He liked doing his own activities, and preferred that he didn't have to share any of them with anyone else. He wasn't particularly interested in making any new friends. He felt the two friends he had known from infancy were enough.

Children with AS who are more extroverted are more ready to approach other children. They like the excitement and energy of being with others and want to go to school to be with other children. More extroverted children with AS make attempts at friendship, and think that others are their friends if they even have their acquaintance. Extroverted children with AS are just as inappropriate in behavior, as annoying, and as lacking in social skills as the more introverted children with AS. However, being with other children does result in more chance for instruction by peers in social skills, more chance for friendship, and more chance for acceptance. Derrick, an extroverted boy with AS, tried to make friends by jumping into the middle of games and conversations. He interrupted others' conversations and was annoying with his inappropriate comments. He also intruded in games by telling others what they were doing wrong, or standing in the way and talking when others were trying to play.

Teasing and bullying

Children with AS are especially vulnerable to negative behavior from peers. Teasing and bullying are a problem for many children with AS. In earlier childhood, many do not recognize that teasing is negative. They look on it as information. If that information is incorrect, they try to correct it using a logical response. If the information is silly or fantastic ("pickle-nose" or "butt-head"), these children go to great lengths to explain the logical fault.

In early childhood, some children with AS are quite aggressive towards peers who intrude on their space. When a curious peer is kicked or hit by the child with AS, they may try to hit back. Sometimes, because children with AS do not appreciate personal space, they intrude too much and so are shoved or tripped in retaliation for what appeared to other children as aggression. To the child with AS, the retaliation will seem to appear without cause because events are disconnected in time, and the child cannot form the big picture. In this case, though, the other children may complain that the child with AS is the bully.

In later childhood, as they become more aware of the negative intent of teasing, children with AS may feel more hurt. This is especially likely if there is a physical aspect to teasing as well. Children with AS feel bewildered when someone comes up and pokes them or trips them. By middle childhood years, other children may make those with AS into targets because they are so different and vulnerable.

In middle school, teasing may reach a crescendo. Children of this age can be very mean to each other. Anyone who is different and does not have a powerful group of friends is likely to be a target. Often feelings are acted upon without much thought for consequences by even average children with no problems. Thus, it is easy to be part of a gang that teases those who are defenseless, and it is in middle school that many children with AS report brutal teasing and bullying.

Children with AS rarely tease. In fact, they usually do not understand what teasing means. It requires an ability to understand what will annoy another person and what to do to ensure that they will be unable to retaliate. If they can retaliate in kind, they win the teasing bout. Teasing requires an idea that the other person will be "gotten," something those with AS do not comprehend. Children with AS will retaliate for teasing by using aggression, telling the teacher, or using logic, but other children don't consider this to be "in kind" retaliation.

Some children with AS appear to tease pets or younger siblings too much. This is not the same as garden variety teasing. This behavior results from the child with AS not comprehending that the pet or sibling is being hurt; often the child thinks affection is being offered, or they see their action as fun and the reaction as silly.

Arguing

Gifted children with AS argue with adults and peers. They are intelligent enough that they can outargue most adults. Roselyn, age 12, argued constantly about why she should have the rights and privileges of an adult, including driving a car. Once a person was old enough to reach the pedals of the car and see over the steering wheel, she thought they ought to be able to take the driver's test and, if they passed it, be able to drive. She also thought that once a person reached the age of reason, which she set at about 12, they ought to be able to vote, drink, smoke, and decide if they wanted to go to school or not. Roselyn thought that if someone only gave her a chance she could do an adult job and would be able to pay for the things she wanted; therefore, she ought to have this option. She did recognize that not all children were ready for it, and that some children might be exploited if parents had the option of deciding if they were going to school. Nevertheless, she thought that society ought to make exceptions based on ability rather than basing everything on age. She thought rules based solely on age were silly.

Some gifted children and adolescents with AS have trouble dealing with the fact that most people are less intelligent. They may regard others with some disdain for being less knowledgeable on subjects they consider simple. Like the philosopher Wittgenstein, they find it difficult to tolerate the presence of some people, "feeling 'wounded' by the crudeness of their company" (Gillberg 2002, p.129).

Suggestions to improve friendship skills

- In addition to some of the social skill training methods described above, children with AS benefit from structured activity groups in which their needs are the main focus. Social skills groups in which skills are broken done into smaller parts and practiced within the group and at home and school can be helpful. In addition, children with AS need specific instruction in how to make friends and how to maintain friendships.

- Andron (cited in Ozonoff *et al.* 2002) described a technique called "narrating life" in which the adult talks aloud about what he or she is doing and gives reasons for what is done, how problems are solved, what social cues are being given, and so on. Ozonoff *et al.* (2002) provided an example of using the technique on a shopping expedition. The mother talked about why she bought certain brands, what to do when she couldn't find something in the store, how to know whom to ask, why she chose a particular checkout line, how to wait and what to do while waiting, how to pay and what to do if one way doesn't work, and finally, as she left the store, a comment on the friendliness of the cashier, how she had liked chatting with the cashier, and how, if she couldn't think of what to say, she mentioned the weather. The same kinds of running commentaries can be made for other social enterprises such as phone calls, invitations, greeting someone seen at a store, meeting people at church, or talking to others at lunch at school.

- Tony Attwood (cited in Ozonoff *et al.* 2002) described friendship files. These are index cards on which the child with AS writes relevant information about peers such as attributes, interests, likes and dislikes, and favorite games and activities. This information provides a structure then for the child with AS to develop appropriate topics for conversation, compliment others based on their attributes, and find activities they and their friend might enjoy together. Having a structure for constructing activities allows the child with AS to plan, think about the other's desires and likes, and have some knowledge about what would feel positive and negative for the peer.

- Attwood (1998) described a Circle of Friends as a method of helping children with AS identify what behaviors are appropriate with different people, and how to think about relationships. Thus, at the center of the circle is the child, family, and close family friends, then school friends, then acquaintances. Behavior that is appropriate in the inner circle, such as touching and kissing, is not appropriate in the third circle or beyond. Another form of the Circle of Friends (Ozonoff *et al.* 2002) puts the child at the center, then family, then adult supports like teachers, then friends. In the classroom the teacher asks for volunteers to be part of the Circle of Friends. These child volunteers are trained to help by greeting the child with AS, offering helpful instruction, and being with him or her for an activity. The volunteer friends receive weekly support and help in working with the child with AS. Ozonoff *et al.* (2002) described how a neighborhood Circle of Friends was formed and maintained.

- For the gifted child with AS, there is no reason that a Circle of Friends could not include interested gifted children as peer partners and supporters. It is especially nice if they share the interest of the gifted child with AS, but even if not, sharing activities can build a relationship.

- Gifted children with AS have social interactions built around complex interests that others also share. Because they are so able to abstract, know so much about a topic, and are usually eager to share their knowledge, they can be valuable members of groups that work around an interest such as ornithology or herpetology. Children who know enormous amounts of information about astrophysics, dinosaurs, computers, and other topics have many others who work in the field and participate in endeavors in which a bright student may be welcome. These mentor relationships can be the source of friendship and academic advancement.

• Coaching in friendship skills, especially by peer volunteers, needs to continue through high school, especially as the gifted child with AS starts to become romantically interested in others. While some children with AS lag years behind age peers in wanting sexual and romantic relationships, others want to be just like age peers and have a boy- or girlfriend, even if they are still quite emotionally immature for their age. It is then helpful if peer coaches are supported in helping the adolescent with AS in recognizing exploitation and superficial playing with feelings. Discussing "friendship first" with teens with AS can help them avoid some of the hazards of being dumped too quickly in a romantic relationship. Bolick (2001) has many suggestions for adolescents with AS, and their supporting adults, about sexuality and intimacy in relationships.

• When children with AS are teased, the environment (school, camp, recreation center, home, church) has a special onus to be responsible and work to promote an atmosphere in which individuals are appreciated for their unique qualities. Teasing is not permitted in these places. If it occurs, remedial action is taken.

   It is important to assess why certain children are teasing. Are they excited by the power they feel? Are they angry at the child they tease for bothering them? Are they trying to fit in with others? Is teasing a game to them, a test of manhood? Children who tease for reasons other than enjoying being mean, and feeling power over others, can be gotten to cooperate in a teasing ban. To do this requires educating them about AS and other learning problems that result in unusual behaviors. Then, these children are engaged in brainstorming ways to help the child with AS to get along, make friends, and feel safe. They can become peer coaches and effective volunteer friends, and earn interpersonal esteem and rewards for promoting a positive atmosphere and being a true friend.

   Children who bully, on the other hand, because they enjoy being mean, need help in directing their impulses to power in other directions. They also need monitoring and supervision, with consequences for bullying.

   If a Circle of Friends and peer mediators can be effectively set up, this is often enough to mitigate much of the teasing that occurs. Not only are these children involved in activities in which their self-interest is to keep peace, but they also serve as a brake on the other students. For example, just by being with other children most of the time, the opportunity to isolate the child with AS decreases. If the child with AS is accompanied by an adult aid or peer friend, there is less chance the bully will attack.

Having worked with gifted children with AS who were bullied and teased quite severely, it can be said with confidence that in schools in which there is a cooperative atmosphere, a desire for each student to be an accepted individual, and where teasing and bullying are not permitted, students feel safe and teasing and bullying do not occur very much. In schools in which the administration has turned a blind eye and said, "Boys will be boys," teasing and bullying are inevitably present and brutal. Girls tease and bully too. They spread rumors and suddenly start leaving out a previously accepted girl. They make fun of the girl who does not fit in, especially teasing her about clothes and relationships. Several children with AS have been traumatized enough to develop Post Traumatic Stress Disorder.

- Adults who work with gifted children and especially adolescents with AS need to be aware of the possibility of teasing and bullying, especially in its more subtle forms. Teachers, principals, counselors, and other school personnel should be vigilant and proactive. Steps to educate other students about AS, and how students with AS act, as well as efforts to directly intervene when students with AS are teased are necessary. Many of the ideas about Circles of Friends and Peer Buddies can be helpful in warding off teasing because the student with AS is in the company of others. At times, an aide assigned to the child with AS can be helpful in both spot-teaching social skills and defusing bullying.

Positive social aspects of gifted children with AS

While AS is generally viewed as a deficit in social awareness, there are certain traits that people with AS share that can be socially positive. Gray and Attwood (1999) proposed a new term called "aspie" that would allow certain traits to be seen in a new light.

Some of the the traits suggested by Gray and Attwood include: peer relationships that are characterized by absolute loyalty and perfect dependability; people who are free of sexist, ageist, and cultural bias and who accept others at face value; people who feel able to speak their mind; people who enjoy friends capable of enthusiasm for unique interests and topics, and who love details and trivia; people who do not make continual judgments or assumptions about others; people who are interested in making significant contributions to conversation, preferring to avoid ritualistic small talk and superficiality; people with a determination to seek the truth; and people who have an exceptional memory and a love of word-based humor and pictorial metaphor.

Many people with AS do find ways to manage social interactions by adulthood. Some find spouses who direct their activities. Some are remarkably patient and loyal people motivated to learn about friendships. They may attract others who are willing to carry more of the burden of initiating and maintaining friendships because the person with AS is so endearing. Some maintain relationships through their interests and activities, such as research and teaching.

Indeed, by adolescence, a few of the gifted children with AS in this study were willing to share information and to instruct in a topic or skill area in which they had expertise, such as chess playing, computers, or math, without any thought of getting payment for it. They also were willing to listen to advice, particularly information-based advice. If they were in error, and it was pointed out, they were usually willing to change their data to match the new facts in evidence. They loved humor, especially cartoon humor that involved puns, visual jokes, and visual incongruities. *The Far Side, Close to Home,* and other such cartoon books were special favorites and they were eager to share these with friends and adults.

Conclusion

Some gifted children with AD/HD have many friends and do well in social interactions; others have no friends and show many social deficits. It depends on the severity of the AD/HD, as well as on personality traits such as having a positive outlook and being cheerful or easygoing.

Gifted children with AD/HD share in common with other gifted children a desire to fit in and be accepted, and a wish for true peers, those people with whom they will be most deeply known and accepted. They are also more intense, passionate, and sensitive than average. They are unlike other gifted children, though, in the difficulty they have managing friendships because of deficits in executive functions. Gifted children with AD/HD need social learning interventions that allow them the chance to interact with other gifted children in creative projects that enable them to show their best selves, while learning specific social skills.

Gifted children with AS are like other gifted children in their intensity and exquisite sensitivity, though those with AS are more extreme in these traits than

Different Minds

other gifted children. They also share with other gifted children a desire for knowledge and a means to share that knowledge with others that will bring some recognition. Gifted children with AS differ from other gifted children in their difficulties navigating social interactions based on their primary social learning disability. This keeps them from having friends and participating with other gifted children in mutual shared endeavors. Children with AS do not share the intimacy that occurs when other gifted children work together on a mutual deeply held cause. They miss the camaraderie that results from being with true peers: for example, at some of the summer projects and Talent Searches. Gifted children with AS need specific instruction in all aspects of social learning, and they especially need the intervention that allows them to be part of a group of gifted children who will serve as peer coaches and mediators.

Finally, both gifted children with AD/HD and AS need the chance to work with a mentor in their field of interest, not only to allow them to advance academically, but also to serve as a model of how to relate to another person around an interest.

The real friend...is, as it were, another self.

Cicero
De Amicitia, XXI

Chapter 8

Moral Development: Moral Reasoning and Compassion

Emily

At age six, Emily knew that Santa Claus was unfair. She had noted that there were good children in her class who never seemed to have anything. These children received little from Santa. Others, who seemed to Emily to already have many toys, bragged about all that they had gotten. This made no sense to Emily. To her, if Santa were really fair, he would have brought more toys to those who had little.

As she grew older, Emily was known as "The Fairness Person" in her family. If there was any issue about fairness, Emily was sure to be there giving her opinion about the best thing to do. "It's not fair" was her rallying cry about so many things, ranging from who got the biggest cookie to whose turn it was to get first choice of a video to rent to how they ought to decide whose turn it was to do the hated chore no one wanted to do: cleaning the bathroom. Emily was a strong arguer, too, and her parents had to be careful that they didn't just give in because she presented a logical argument. In fact, her more forceful arguments often lacked logic or they missed the point.

Emily's ideas about fairness varied. At times, she was most concerned about what was fair for her. She presented arguments why she should have certain privileges, or not receive a punishment, or not have to do a chore. Other times, she was concerned about fairness for other people. As in her observations about Santa, Emily was exquisitely sensitive to injustice, as shown in fairness to others. She also was aware that fairness wasn't always about getting an equal amount of something, but that it depended on what was needed. From an early age, she had an idea of the big picture when it came to what everyone ought to be able to have. She believed in equal opportunity, but had little patience with people she felt were purposely stupid about something. This trait got her into trouble in middle and high school when she made her feelings known about various teachers. Emily did not suffer fools gladly.

Emily often refused to do work she considered beneath her intelligence, no matter what the cost. She also failed to hand in work, and argued in class about work. Emily's parents worried about her increasingly lower grades, especially in subjects where she had to write. She claimed she could do the work but chose not to do it; however, she usually said this after the fact, and it seemed less an act of rebellion than one of defense. Emily, of course, claimed that the teachers were unfair and that even if she handed in work, they did not appreciate her efforts. Thus, if she wrote a paper, the teachers wouldn't understand it and would give her a "B" instead of the "A" she deserved just because they were unfair and unable to recognize the value of her unique ideas. Emily's parents worried about her failure to treat others with respect and with generosity rather than harsh judgments. With Emily, it seemed that the quality of mercy was indeed strained.

John

When John was age seven he became a vegetarian. He carefully thought out what this might entail. He found sources of alternate protein needed by children to ensure proper growth, and explained to his parents that he based his beliefs on caring for the entire ecosystem. His belief was that all living things deserved to live. Thus, he would not even kill an insect, but insisted that his parents release it back into the outdoors. As he became older, John was drawn to Tibetan Buddhism and started to study these beliefs. At first, he was very taken with them, and determined to become a Buddhist, but later he incorporated beliefs from many systems of thought into his personal coda. This enabled him to look at several sides of a problem: for example, how to feed hungry people without destroying the ecosystem in which they live.

John was exceptionally sensitive to the pain of others, and he wanted to relieve the pain he witnessed. If he knew about people suffering from a disaster, he worked to raise money, send supplies, and increase awareness of those around him about the problem. During the 9/11 crisis, John was driven to call friends and see if they were all right, to collect money and supplies, and to send letters of support to the emergency personnel and firefighters.

John was almost too sensitive to pain. He was also exceptionally empathic and could almost feel the pain of others himself. John felt upset by his sense of helplessness to really change things. He tried as hard as he could, but still many bad things occurred, and he felt overwhelmed by the pain of others' suffering. To help him, his parents tried to limit his exposure to the news, and discussed how we know more about what happens because of 24-hour news, but that bad things have always happened and people have had to cope and grow strong anyway. John's parents worry that his sensitivity and empathy may lead him to be depressed, because the truth is he cannot change even a small fraction of the suffering around him. It would be good if John could develop more of a shell, something he could retreat to, or place between himself and the worst of the ravages of the world.

Adam

Adam, age 12, liked rules and regulations. When going to a new place, one of his first questions was whether they had any special rules he should know about. Adam was probably the only person who actually read the student manual when he arrived in middle school. Certainly, he was the only one who actually knew all the regulations and obeyed them. What was more, he tried to point them out to the other students too, something they did not appreciate. This made no sense to Adam. After all, why weren't they obeying the rules? The rules were very clear. They were even written down for all to read. That someone might not care about minor rules was more than Adam could comprehend.

Adam was very good at certain kinds of rules. He knew, could obey, and even made up rules with definite "yes...no" polarities. He was not so good about rules that had more leeway. Actually, Adam did not understand the idea of leeway. Why have a rule if someone wasn't going to have to obey it? On the other hand, Adam was very good at extending rules to other situations. Thus, once Adam learned the meaning of the "Golden Rule" about treating others as we would like to be treated, he really tried to be nice to others, and to treat them courteously and with respect. After all, this was how he wanted to be treated.

Adam was a naturally kind person. He loved animals and had many pets at home. He spoke out when he saw other boys mistreating a dog, going so far as to take the dog home with him and trying to find its owner. He liked working at the animal shelter – one of the few places where he didn't obey the rules, but tried to find homes for all the animals.

Adam's parents worried about his literalness with rules and his lack of flexibility. They found themselves having to obey rules they had set up when Adam was younger because he refused to change them even when no longer needed. Adam also was inappropriate in how he expressed his ideas about rules. For example, he didn't know when to stop obeying them. Thus, he raised his hand at home to ask a question, although even he could see it was silly to do so when only he and his mother were home. His parents worried about how he'd fare in later life if he could not be more flexible about rules.

Commonalities

Emily, John, and Adam are all gifted children with issues arising from their strong moral views. All three of them showed a high degree of moral development, but also variability in that development. Thus, Emily was advanced in her ability to reason and argue for moral justice, but she found it difficult to temper her ideas with empathy and concern for others on a personal level. She often had to win. Emily's friends and relatives told her she'd make a good lawyer because of her abilities, but Emily differed. She felt lawyers had to make too many compromises. She'd prefer being a judge or maybe a philosopher. Emily had mild AD/HD Combined Type. Her symptoms were rather subtle and she had coasted along until middle school without actually doing much work. In middle school she rebelled, because the work was actually difficult to do, and she had trouble sustaining attention and working for what she considered to be little reward. While Emily was right that she knew a great deal, she was wrong about how brilliant her work was. Her ideas were wonderful, but she did not know how to develop them well. She was used to winning by arguing people into the ground, and that didn't work on a paper where one had to support statements and give examples.

John was exceptionally compassionate and empathic in dealing with people both in his personal life and on a global scale. The problem for him was that he had less ability to limit the amount he suffered as a result of others' pain. That impacted his effectiveness in looking at the big picture and trying to find equitable solutions for several parties with conflicting interests. It also overwhelmed him with so much pain that he was depressed when he could not fix a problem. John's relatives and friends thought he might become a minister or psychologist, but John wasn't sure. Maybe there were other jobs he could do that would allow him to really change the world. He thought that former president Jimmy Carter had the right idea. John was a boy with AD/HD Inattentive Type whose anxiety masked many of his AD/HD symptoms. In fact, his sensitivity, empathy, and caring were where he focused his energy. Otherwise, he was a rather absent-minded professor who was off in his own dream world.

Adam was especially sensitive to the issue of right and wrong. He was excellent at understanding a moral conflict and playing it out according to specified rules. In adolescence he was good at debating, and knew all of Robert's Rules for conducting meetings. Anytime there was a dispute, Adam was called to keep things civil by following proper procedures. Adam's difficulties came with trying to interpret vague rules and situations. Adam's relatives thought he would make a good professor, and that is what Adam wanted to do. Adam was a boy with mild AS. Because he attended school in a small town, and was so bright, he was not seen as strikingly different, and so was never referred for evaluation. Other students saw him as rather too good, somewhat obsessive and compulsive about rules, and someone they didn't include when they wanted to party, or discuss mischief they were planning.

The focus of this chapter

Emily, John, and Adam showed different aspects of moral development. Emily and Adam focused strongly on concepts about rules and how they govern behavior. Emily saw morality as fairness, Adam as adherence to a canon or law. On the other hand, John adhered more to a concept of morality as empathy and compassion for the suffering of one's fellow beings. To John, justice required that suffering be alleviated in relationships and in the wider world.

Moral development follows two main paths: empathy and compassion, and moral reasoning. In this chapter, the following are explored:

- The two main theories of moral development (empathy and compassion, and moral reasoning).

- The development of moral awareness in children through the development of empathy and rules-based reasoning.

- The relationship of giftedness and moral development.

- How the strengths and weaknesses found in AD/HD and AS are brought to bear on the development of empathy and compassion, and moral reasoning.

Theories of moral development

In this section of this chapter, the two main theories of moral development will be discussed. Because Kohlberg's theory (1984) was developed first, it will be discussed first, even though, in later sections of this chapter, empathy will be discussed first.

Moral development has two major threads. For some, moral development is seen principally as the ability to reason about universal principles of justice and fairness (moral reasoning and judgment). For others, it is a matter of ability to empathize with, and act to alleviate, others' suffering (compassion). Both reasoning and compassion are necessary in formulating moral actions; however, it is the relative importance of each that distinguishes different theories.

Two of the main modern theories of moral development, Kohlberg's (1984) and Gilligan's (1982), are based on long-standing, underlying philosophical arguments about the basis of moral development. Each is a stage theory in which people develop from one stage to the next as they grow in ability to make complex judgments. Where these theories differ is on how people make judgments.

Kohlberg's theory

Kohlberg's theory (1984) focused more on the use of abstract reason to draw conclusions about what ought to be done to achieve justice and fairness in a particular situation. Altruism, compassion, and empathy are less important than are principles of justice, and are not the main part of the reasoned process of coming to moral decisions. The moral reasoner is one who knows that a moral decision is required, understands that principles need to be applied universally, and then makes a decision based on abstract principles of justice and fairness. Kohlberg's theory follows Piaget and Inhelder's (1969) thinking about the stages of mental development in children. Because Kohlberg's (1984) theory is based on the ability to reason abstractly, young children are not seen as being able to reason about moral issues yet; they are pre-moral. Only when people are able to reason abstractly, use principles of justice applied universally, and separate their own feelings about the particular person from the issue are they seen as moral reasoners. This does not usually happen before adulthood, though the seeds can be seen in mid-adolescence.

In Kohlberg's theory, there are three stages of development, each separated into two substages. People progress through the stages as they grow in ability to reason. At the earliest *preconventional* stages, children define what is good or bad based on the consequences: that is, is the action rewarded or punished? A good boy or girl won't steal a cookie or disobey because they will be punished.

At the next substage, children are more reciprocal, but see doing moral actions in terms of how they affect the self. Other points of view can be considered. In this substage the child has the idea of doing good so that others will do good to them in return. Justice is seen as "an eye for an eye," the idea of negative reciprocity thus also defining justice. He hit me, so I am justified in hitting him back. We will help our neighbors because they help us.

In the *conventional* middle stages, conformity is what guides behavior. At the third substage, conformity is to do what one thinks others would approve. What is expected for one's role is also important. By this stage, people are able to start to reason abstractly, and to see identity in relation to others and to larger groups. We should obey the rules because that is what our parents would want us to do. We help others because it is the right thing to do; besides, what goes around comes around.

In the fourth substage, the reference group becomes larger and more abstract than one's own family or familiar authority figures. At this level a person who is moral supports, maintains, and justifies the concept of institutional order. Loyalty to institutions as well as duty is operational. We obey sets of rules because they are conventions we honor such as the Ten Commandments, or the laws of the state or nation.

At the final, *postconventional* stages, people look to universal principles to define actions. In the fifth substage, social perspective taking is the rule. People are able to critique rules and want to change them if they are unjust. Some values and principles are seen as universal, beyond the rule of even the majority. In general, a person at this level evaluates the greatest good for the most people, but not at the cost of minority rights. Since I think homelessness is wrong, I need to work to end homelessness; if I think it is wrong to go to war, I need to object and work for peace. The Golden Rule is really lived.

In the final, sixth stage, which few people are seen to reach, universal ethical principles are most cogent. Social perspective taking is more relative, and moral imagination is required. A just action is one in which a person is detached from particular individual interests to take on the perspective of every person or group to be considered. The principle is just if the outcome is fair and just to all concerned. In this substage a person needs to have a world perspective: for example, thinking of the rights of all nations and peoples in dealing with an issue such as hunger or poverty.

Kohlberg does not see most people achieving the final stage. Indeed, many are at the third or fourth substage all their adult lives, though some remain at the second stage. Progress is forward only: that is, once someone has passed through a stage, they do not go backwards.

While Kohlberg did not see children as moral reasoners because they cannot yet reason abstractly, some studies have shown high-IQ elementary school age children to reason at the postconventional level, a level few adults obtain (Arbuthnot 1973; Gross 1993; Janos and Robinson 1985; Kohlberg 1964).

Gilligan's theory

Gilligan's theory (1982) described the interrelationships among people as most important in moral development. These relationships, which are based on empathy, grow and develop from a child's earliest moments of life into complex relationships based on mutual care and altruism. The earliest experiences of empathy are one-sided. As the person develops through childhood to adolescence, relationships grow more complex. They become reciprocal and, later, mutual. At a final stage, relationships weave among self, family, and community to encompass all of humanity. As relationships become more complex, and empathy more mutual, moral decisions are made that affect all parties in the relationship. Gilligan's theory is a stage theory; however, stages are not rigid and movement between stages does seem to occur.

Gilligan (Gilligan and Wiggins 1987) described "co-feeling," a stage of empathy development in which a person can experience feelings different from his or her own. A co-feeling person participates in another's feelings, engaging with him or her rather than standing aside and judging and observing. Whereas Kohlberg (1984) requires an uninvolved participant for higher-level moral actions, Gilligan (Gilligan and Wiggins 1987) requires an engaged other. Care – that is, compassion for the other – is based on standards of authentic relationship. It is principled and can also involve conflicts or dilemmas based on deciding how to deal with differing needs and differing viewpoints.

A moral action requires an individual to think about inequality. Since attachment and connection to others are essential in this view, inequality implies a disconnection. How to deal with inclusion and exclusion as connection and disconnection is the root of a moral life. As we connect to others very different from ourselves, we, *de facto*, are making things more equal in the sense of giving to each what is needed. As we connect to humanity in the largest sense, we are obliged to see that all beings receive our co-feeling and care. This type of thinking reflects sensitivity towards others as opposed to a focus on reasoning about what is a principled or unprincipled act.

While Kohlberg's (1984) theory has been directly tested with gifted children, especially through the use of the Defining Issues Test (Rest 1979), there has been little direct application of Gilligan's (1982) theory to the gifted. Like many other researchers, Gilligan appears to use some data from gifted children, but does not distinguish between data obtained from gifted children and more average subjects. For example, an extensive study at the Emma Willard School illustrated the moral decisions made in the context of relationships with other girls (Gilligan, Lyons, and Hanmer 1989). Many of the girls described appear to be quite gifted.

Dabrowski's theory

Dabrowski, a Polish psychologist, whose work has been described and interpreted by Piechowski (1986, 1991), suggested a stage approach theory that specifically studied gifted youth and adults. Dabrowski developed a theory of emotional development that was based on observations of his gifted subjects. Piechowski (1991), in interpreting the theory, noted that gifted youths, like gifted adults, feel a deep longing for ideals in life, such as justice, fairness, honesty, and responsibility. They are also extremely compassionate. These youths also expect that adults ought to be able to do something to right the wrongs of the world and may be profoundly disappointed by their lack of doing so.

Dabrowski's theory (Piechowski 1986) does not specifically discuss young gifted children. Dabrowski focused on adolescents and adults; thus, his theory required both life experience and ability to evaluate concepts in order for people to develop further in emotional and moral complexity. Like the theories of Kohlberg (1984) and Gilligan (1982), Dabrowski's theory suggests stages of development (five), with growth towards an ideal of self-actualization in the final stage, realized by few. The end point of Dabrowski's theory is described by a stage of universal caring, similar to the highest stages of Kohlberg and Gilligan's theories.

For young gifted children, the applicability of Dabrowski's theory lies in his description of exceptional emotional sensitivity and intensity that can accompany giftedness. As the child grows into adolescence and identity is formed through evaluation of personal values, the person may develop through Dabrowski's stages.

Piechowski (1991) described a number of adolescents who appeared to show potential for the kind of inner growth in both emotional self-awareness and moral sensitivity described by Dabrowski's theory. For these adolescents, the development of self is accompanied throughout life by growth in moral sensitivity, integration of universal concepts of justice and fairness, and universal compassion. Thus, Dabrowski's theory combined aspects of both Kohlberg and Gilligan; unfortunately, Dabrowski's theory is not very well known in the USA.

For the purposes of this book, both Kohlberg and Gilligan offer aspects of unique understanding of moral development. Thus, both theories are considered to be useful. How any particular person balances the two aspects of principle and compassion delineates how they reason about any particular moral issue. On the whole, some people seem more predisposed to acting on principle, and others to acting with empathy and compassion. However, it is not as simple as either Kohlberg or Gilligan would make it appear. Thus, in some circumstances, it is better to to use an abstract principle, in others to use empathy and compassion; which predominates depends on the individual and the circumstances.

The development of moral awareness

Moral awareness arises from the earliest interactions between parents and infants. As young children learn empathy, they learn about caring for others, the basis for compassion. As young children learn about rules and how they are used in guiding behavior, they learn about fairness and justice.

The development of empathy

Hoffman (1994) argued that the experience of empathic feelings is important in the development of moral understanding. Parental explanations to children about the cause of others' distress, especially if accompanied with a strong affective component, are especially effective in promoting altruistic behavior in the children.

Hoffman described the development of empathy and its direct application in young children to relieve others' distress. He showed how this was the basis for moral decisions. As described in Chapter 6, in earliest life, empathy is immediate as children experience the feelings of the other as their own. At this stage, they react to distress in others by seeking comfort for themselves. As young children progress through the first year of life, they start to experience feelings as separate from their own and belonging to another. At this stage, children will try to directly comfort another by doing for the other what would comfort themselves: for example, bringing their own mother when the other child's mother is also present. The action of the young child in alleviating pain in another is at least in part motivated by a desire to alleviate the suffering they feel from the received feelings.

As children grow older, direct empathy becomes more inferred, and is experienced more as understanding the cues put out by others that suggest distress. Then young children make an association about how such a situation might make them feel, and they act accordingly to decrease the other's pain, with the recognition that what will relieve another's pain may be different from what might relieve their own. Also, children start to realize that there may be times when it is better not to interfere and try to help: for example, to avoid loss of face for another.

At this point, both empathy (feeling the other's pain within) and sympathy (distress for another without feeling their feelings directly) are in play. Hereafter, people experience both empathy and sympathy in caring for another. As children evolve the ability to feel empathy and sympathy for another's life condition, the real start of compassion – direct elicitation of internal feelings – does occur. In fact, the more strongly one feels internally what it might be like to be homeless, hungry, unjustly imprisoned, a child laborer, the more intense the resolve to do something may be.

Hoffman also discussed factors that add to or detract from a person's willingness to help once empathic and sympathetic feelings are aroused. Thus, cognitive components become important. For example, being seen as an innocent victim, seeing oneself as responsible in some way for the other's plight (guilt), feeling angry at the perpetrator for the injustice done, or seeing the injustice as worse due to the character of the victim all can change the response of the person involved.

Hoffman does not see his description as a stage theory *per se*. However, few children will have the experience to know how society, as a whole, operates to create victims of injustice, and fewer still will know what is required to right an injustice. Thus, most children can deal with moral dilemmas which involve empathy and sympathy, but not those which primarily involve abstract principles of justice or injustice.

The development of rules-based reasoning

To develop sensitivity to moral issues, children must also understand rules and standards: both the format of the rule and the reasons why we have rules. Dunn (1987) described young children's increasing understanding of social rules and explanations for consequences. During the second year of life, children regularly explored, experimented with, and violated rules. It was the emotional responsiveness of the parent, and the mutual interaction between parent and child, that enabled children eventually to modify behavior and incorporate the standards within themselves. Parental disappointment, disapproval, and anger at rule violations, for example, helped children to learn about unacceptable behavior (Kagan 1981).

Dunn (1987) made the case that in early years children learn both positive and negative behaviors from their relationships. Not only do young children respond empathically to others, they also respond in negative ways such as teasing. Some of the children in her study started teasing as early as 14 months of age by provoking and annoying a sibling: for example, by removing a child's comfort object or favorite possession, by destroying a valued possession or game, or by frightening another.

By 24 months of age, verbal teasing was also evident. However, this is not all that transpires. Parental responsiveness, and the mutual interaction between parent and child, enabled children eventually to modify behavior and incorporate rules and standards within themselves (Kagan 1981). Parents and children engaged in discussion of rules and their limitations. Children explored the qualities of people and objects (were they good or bad, perfect or broken, clean or dirty?). These contrasts helped young children learn about standards and how to judge them (Dunn 1987; Kagan 1981).

The work of Dunn, Hoffman, and others suggests that even very small children can be responsive to the distress of others and will attempt to remedy the situation. Young children develop internal ideas about how things ought to be by questioning rules and contrasting standards. This is seen as the basis for moral behavior. The early empathic response of children to parental distress develops into responsiveness to parental disapproval and anger. Thus, the early maternal attunement described by Ainsworth (1964) and Stern (1985) is the basis for development of a personal identity, empathy for others, and for development of a rules-based internal standard that becomes moral reasoning of right and wrong.

Giftedness and moral development

The literature suggests that, starting from an early age, many gifted children show evidence of awareness of the importance of moral concerns in their empathy for others, compassionate responses to the plight of others, idealism, and concern about world issues, as well as in their advanced understanding and judgment of moral issues (Galbraith 1985; Lovecky 1997; Roeper 1989; Silverman 1993c, 1994). Both threads – of empathy and compassion, and moral judgment of fairness and justice – were noted.

Empathy and compassion

In this section of this chapter, the literature on empathy and compassion in gifted children will be explored, problems with empathy and compassion will be examined, and particular strengths and deficits of gifted children with AD/HD and AS will be described.

Roeper (1995a) described her experiences with gifted children of preschool age at the Roeper School. These children were noted to comfort others upset over their separation from parents. The consoling children described to adults an awareness of knowing how the upset children felt, based on remembering how they had felt previously.

A gifted child who experiences empathy and compassion for the suffering of others can feel the need to do something. This need can be intense and consuming. For some of these children, watching suffering causes them to suffer too, because they are so sensitive and aware. For the most sensitive children, the suffering of others can seem almost too painful to bear. Hollingworth (1942) described a boy of nine who "wept bitterly at how the North taxed the South after the Civil War" (p.281).

Silverman (1994) suggested that advanced moral sensitivity is an essential feature of being gifted; she described a number of unusually compassionate children who were intensely aware of world issues or the feelings of others.

Silverman suggested that the greater the moral sensitivity and asynchrony of gifted children, the more vulnerability they experience. Thus, very young, highly compassionate children are especially vulnerable when they express moral concerns about problems of the world. They risk being overwhelmed by the pain they feel since they have not yet developed effective ways to deal with strong emotional content. That is, they may still be at the stage in which empathy is experienced directly, so they feel the pain of others intensely within themselves.

Gifted children have the ability to understand suffering in a wider context than most age peers. Consequently, they are out of synch in the development of internal boundaries that would help them deal with the societal issues they notice. For example, it may be difficult to explain to a very young gifted child why we can't alleviate homelessness. To the child, the solution is simple: build houses and give them to poor people. That building houses on a large scale cannot easily be accomplished with limited resources is difficult to explain to the child. It is even more difficult to explain the problems that mental illness and alcoholism cause that result in homelessness, and how hard they are to alleviate. Because there is a gap of experience as well as knowledge, the young gifted child may be exceptionally compassionate, but not be able to appreciate the value of efforts that are made for the homeless (Habitat for Humanity, local shelters and soup kitchens, Traveler's Aid, local efforts to rehabilitate housing and sell it for low prices, etc.). The young gifted child who feels empathic distress for others may not have the capacity to turn the internal feeling he or she has into action. It may be exceptionally distressing to the child who feels suffering intensely not to have a ready and satisfying solution.

Another aspect of exceptional empathy can be a less clear delineation of the boundaries of responsibility, fairness, and even compassion. Some gifted children have trouble with the idea that they cannot control everything and make problems go away. They feel responsible even if no one could solve the problem at hand. They also may feel responsible for everything that happens, thinking that they only needed to care more or try harder. Some try to deny themselves pleasures in order to give enough to others. There are many anecdotes of young gifted children who wanted to give away all their Christmas toys and other possessions to the poor.

On a shopping expedition, three-year-old Crissy told her mother that she did not need any new clothes. She also would not allow her mother to buy her toys even though her mother had planned several purchases with money Crissy had recently received from relatives. The only purchase Crissy would allow that day was a pair of shoes since she had outgrown her old ones. Instead, she wanted the money to be given to the poor (Lovecky 1997).

Silverman (1994) described Sara Jane who, at two-and-a-half years old, observed a television news report about an earthquake that hit Russia. She asked her parents to send the money in her piggy bank. The following Christmas, she requested that her presents be given to needy children. Her family obliged. At age six, Sara Jane contacted a local soup kitchen and organized a Christmas drive for food, clothing, and gifts for needy children.

Some gifted children are moved, not only by suffering, but also by universal principles of justice and responsibility for others. These are children who have the capacity to look beyond the immediate situation and to take on a more universal perspective. For example, Winner (1996) described 12-year-old Hilary who became a vegetarian due to a strong belief that it is morally wrong to kill animals.

Problems with empathy and compassion

Not everyone grows up to act in moral ways. Even gifted children who appear to have early concerns about others, the environment, pollution, war and peace, and issues of fairness and justice do not all grow up to be exceptionally sensitive to moral issues.

Roeper discussed how gifted children's sense of justice and ethics can be lost through an overemphasis on conformity. When conformity rules the world in which gifted children live, they often respond by creating a subculture of beating the system, getting around the rules, and manipulating. They start to do things for personal gain and learn that "might makes right." Anyone who thinks differently is seen as an idealist, someone not to be taken seriously (Roeper 1995b). Since most gifted children are pressured to conform, they become sensitized to the expectations of society to be less idealistic, less altruistic, and less ethical, and over time show less moral awareness. Those children who conform less to societal expectations, the ones who do not suffer fools gladly, retain more moral awareness through adolescence.

The need to conform starts at birth, but is kept at bay for many gifted children until they reach formal schooling. Then, the process of lowering expectations, doing things as peers do, and using popular pastimes to ensure social success can also decrease moral sensitivity. This can be the case even among those gifted children who were exceptionally compassionate or sensitive to injustice in early childhood. Silverman (1994) described one boy who was extremely sensitive to injustice but became "desensitized" after he entered school.

My own earlier observations with gifted children (Lovecky 1994c) suggested that many young gifted boys, even as they worry about the environment and show concern for homelessness, poverty, and war become, nevertheless, fascinated with violence. As they compete with age peers and become immersed in peer culture, especially media-driven pastimes, these boys begin to see violence as an acceptable solution to interpersonal conflict. This can have a number of different ramifications, including loss of previously held ideals about justice and caring.

Gifted children with AD/HD

Gifted children with AD/HD can be exceptionally empathic and compassionate. Some take on causes and give their energy to helping others. Some have more trouble with organizing both their feelings and behavior, and despite good intentions may not accomplish anything helpful.

The rapid responding of some gifted children with AD/HD can result in meeting challenges spontaneously and with great passion. This may be the best thing to do, and many such actions have benefited others, but it may also be a disaster if the action does not really suit the problem and is more the result of impulsivity. For example, Martha was saving her allowance to go on a school trip. She also heard about a campaign to raise money for the local food bank, so she donated all of her money to the food bank. When it came time for the trip, Martha had too little money to go. What she had not considered in her generosity was how she'd feel being the only one not going on the trip. Martha hadn't intended to miss the trip, and she didn't really make a choice to give the money rather than go. She just had not considered the consequences. Martha did have a very kind heart, and there were many examples of her generosity to family and friends. What Martha had to learn was how to make better decisions about her generosity so she wasn't ruled by her feelings and need to do something right that moment.

Many gifted children with AD/HD are like Martha. They are compassionate and generous to a fault. Some of the most spontaneous and generous people also have AD/HD. This occurs partly because they may place little importance on ownership of possessions. Some have trouble with interpersonal boundaries, so who owns a thing means little to them. It can also mean they are just as generous in early years with others' possessions as they are with their own.

Exceptional empathy and sensitivity can be a source of both joy and pain for gifted children with AD/HD. Since they don't stop to weigh consequences, but go with their empathic feelings, they notice the suffering of other people. Like John, described at the beginning of this chapter, these gifted children can almost feel the pain of others themselves. They may feel a sense of helplessness in trying to change all the bad things they experience in the world, but they can't ignore them either. Like John, they feel driven to help in any way they can. Nevertheless, they may neglect other important aspects: for example, whether a different action, such as a community effort, might not be more effective in helping.

Another aspect of exceptional empathy may be delayed development of learning how to externalize empathy. Thus, at a much older than expected age, some gifted children with AD/HD continue to feel others' feelings directly within themselves, and they desire to stop the feelings of pain by trying to fix the problem. Also, these gifted children with AD/HD may be exceptionally sensitive to moral principles that suggest to them that not helping is wrong. To know someone is suffering and not help is something they cannot tolerate. These passionate, empathic children, like John, feel obliged to do something to alleviate whatever the negative situation is that they see – feed the hungry person, give toys to poor children, build houses, etc. The very drivenness that can lead these gifted children with AD/HD into trouble in other situations can also bring great satisfaction in these contexts.

PROBLEMS WITH EMPATHY AND COMPASSION

Gifted children with AD/HD can exhibit deficits in empathy and compassion due to intense need for stimulation, as well as desensitization to the suffering of others.

Some gifted children with AD/HD suffer from a real deficit in being able to understand and apply the language of feelings either to themselves or others, and only intense affect is felt or noticed. These children have more trouble with generating empathic responses. They may still act generously, but only when they see a clear need. They can be aroused to sympathy and compassion for others as part of a group effort or school project. Sometimes they will notice a specific need and then do something themselves. For example, Albert, age 13, liked to work with little children. They made him feel important and useful. So he asked the librarian at the local library if he could help at the Saturday story hour each week. He loved doing this work, and the library staff thought him to be a mature and responsible young man. His family, who rarely saw this side of Albert, wondered why he did not show some of this empathy at home instead of his generally self-centered behavior.

Empathy and compassion are most difficult for those gifted children with AD/HD who need intense stimulation. Because they are so driven to seek pleasurable stimulation, they don't notice the needs of others. If those needs are pointed out to them, they might wish to help, but will find it difficult to do so because organizing an effort to help someone else is beyond their abilities. These children can respond to clear-cut, short, very structured projects with high stimulation. In these projects, they do not do any of the planning; their role is to perform in a high-stimulation activity that raises money or otherwise does good. For example, Kyle, age 12, was willing to collect cans of food for his school. He visited all the people who lived within a six-block radius and told them what he needed and when he would be collecting. On the appointed day, he collected the food while riding his skateboard. He took each load to his father who had the family car parked halfway down each street. Later, with his father, Kyle brought the food to the drop-off point at school.

Desensitization to the suffering of others can be a problem for gifted children with AD/HD, especially boys. These gifted boys can become addicted to the stimulating effects of fast action and violent conflict in media. They are often quite adept at solving complex computer and video games, but like those best that move fast and kill the participants. They see their high scores as proof of their prowess and masculinity. These gifted boys with AD/HD spend most of their spare time engaged in playing games, talking about them, or thinking about strategies to use to beat the game. Thus, they also lose the opportunity to engage in pastimes that might teach them alternate social and interpersonal skills. If all these children have as a guide in problem solving are fast-moving, violent solutions practiced over and over, with little practice in negotiating, giving the other the benefit of the doubt, helping others, or weighing what is most fair and just for all, it is little wonder they grow up to lack essential interpersonal skills, even if they are not overtly violent in their own behavior. Unfortunately, there are several thousand studies that show a relationship between watching aggressive content and later overt aggressive acts in young boys who have difficulty with self-regulation and impulsivity.

The culture of violence teaches young gifted boys that excitement is preferable to intellectual challenge, that high arousal and intensity of response is what counts most, and that living on the edge is preferable to a reflective, contemplative state. This means that gifted boys with AD/HD who already have difficulty with impulse control are pushed to be more impulsive and thrill seeking. Boys who might have found some satisfaction in quieter intellectual pursuits now find these unstimulating and boring. The biggest problem, though, is the disconnection that results between the witnessing of others' suffering and the need for intense stimulation. Thus, the stimulation aspects are first noted and are more intensely recalled than the aspects of human suffering.

Suggestions to improve problems with empathy and compassion

- Gifted children with AD/HD who feel suffering too intensely, and feel overwhelmed by others' suffering, need to build some boundaries and safety. This means learning how to put some distance between the self and the witnessed suffering. One way to do this is to help these children talk about what they would want to do in an ideal world to help, as well as what might really be possible. Have the child perform helpful acts in the context of the family doing them together. For example, work for an organization that builds homes for the poor like Habitat for Humanity. Actually building a house can help a child feel that something concrete is being done, one family at a time.

- Discuss with children how charities work to help many people. Visit some local charities and discuss how many people are helped and in what ways. Discuss what other efforts might be needed that are not now available. Are there ways for the gifted child with AD/HD to join in efforts to develop projects of interest to him or her? Check out local foundations that distribute charitable funds. Some of these are open to new projects.

- Discuss the limitations of helping, and what we can do when things are beyond our control to solve. Is a partial solution better than none at all? What about situations where no one is able to help? In terrible situations some people serve as witnesses to show the world that the terrible thing happened. Others serve as historians to record the numbers of problems in an area over time. Finally, just writing about something can make changes. A letter to the editor of the local paper, participating in a citizens' grassroot Internet campaign of letter writing, or writing to a government official or representative can start a process of change. This can also happen if the letter is sent to a foreign country: for example, as part of Amnesty International's letter-writing campaigns. Amnesty's letter-writing campaigns have resulted in the freeing of many political prisoners.

- As parents and teachers, be aware of the asynchrony in young gifted children with AD/HD between thinking and actions, having a desire to help and the lack of ability to manage emotionally the feelings involved, and wanting to participate and having difficulty planning and carrying out a project. Promote the desire and help the child by structuring the process. For example, set a goal of collecting money for a particular charity and then meet the goal.

- Be especially aware of how problems with impulsivity in gifted children with AD/HD affect moral behavior. Help these children understand that consequences count. Teach them to be responsible for what happens even if they did not intend it. Teach them to figure out what to do instead.

- With those children who think of themselves first, and think that their own needs are paramount, discuss the problem of always needing to be at the center of attention and how other people feel. Those who show difficulty with reciprocity because they are self-centered need lessons about giving when they will not receive anything. For example, plan with them how to think about, make, or buy a gift and not have a gift in return. Discuss selfishness and when thinking of oneself first is best, and when it is not.

- For children who have difficulty with using empathy and compassion because they are impulse ridden, plan activities that will allow them to do a small task that leads to a larger whole. For example, like Kyle, gifted children with AD/HD might first concentrate on collecting cans of food for a food drive. When a predetermined number have been collected, these are then brought to the food bank. A second part of the project might be signing up to help sort cans at the food bank for a Saturday. A third aspect might be to help deliver cans and other goods to distribution points, and see how the food is used. In this way, the impulsive child still accomplishes a project, feels positive, and can relate more readily the next time he or she hears about hunger. Other such projects might be used to build compassion for people suffering in other ways.

- Help children discuss the culture of violence and how it affects them in school, in the community, and within themselves. Discuss the relationship of feeling aggressive and dominant, and playing violent video games. Most likely children will deny there is a relationship. Limit violent media in your home and let your children know you disapprove of their playing such games and viewing such movies when away from home.

- Teach ten ways to defuse anger and repair relationships. These might include: take deep breaths to calm down; give oneself a time-out; write out why one is angry and what precipitated it; think of what the underlying problem was or the bigger picture; listen to why the other person is angry and empathize before answering; think of how the future might be different with this person (for example, does the relationship need some changes); own up to mistakes; apologize for one's actions; accept an apology from another; don't carry a grudge.

Gifted children with AS

Gifted children with AS have difficulty with empathy, especially in the immediate moment. Attwood (1998) suggested that the diagnostic criteria that people with

AS lack empathy should not be taken to mean that they lack completely the ability to care for others; rather, they are confused by the emotions of others and have trouble expressing their own emotions. Tantam (1991) suggested that unconcern for others is not a universal characteristic of those with AS; on the other hand, there is also a small minority of people with AS who show very little empathy and can even react violently when frustrated, including attacks on animals, small children, and their parents. Those with particular difficulty with reading nonverbal cues have the most trouble with empathic expression.

Gillberg (2002) described empathy as a form of "mentalising" or ToM skill, and concluded that people with AS are severely delayed in development of this skill. Even by adolescence, children with AS do not develop empathy skills commensurate with peers because they lack the requisite ability to assume another's perspective.

While the literature does offer many examples of lack of empathy in children and adolescents with AS, it is important to recognize that some gifted children with AS are compassionate and want to help others, relieve suffering, and work for causes to aid animals and the environment just like other gifted children. Thus, there can be a difference between the ability to understand another person's feelings and perspective in the moment, and an ability to comprehend and want to help relieve another's suffering.

For example, Kyle Middleton, a young man with AS, was recently nominated for the Temple Grandin Award in part for his outstanding work protecting animals and the environment. Using his writing skills, Kyle has written to newspapers, but he also has visited rodeos and circuses, handing out flyers about the treatment of caged animals. He began a letter-writing campaign to companies which tested products on animals. He received an Honorary Guardian of Nature Award from the World Wildlife Fund. Kyle, nevertheless, still suffers from social challenges (Future Horizons 2002).

Gifted children with AS at the Gifted Resource Center of New England, at times, expressed ideas of compassion for others. Patrick, age 11, expressed concern for world hunger, especially in Africa, a continent that fascinated him. Not only could he recite all sorts of facts about different African countries, but he genuinely cared about the threat people were suffering from drought and famine. He was eager to collect money to send to relief organizations.

Ryan cared about the rainforest and its destruction which he had learned about in Sunday school. He was eager to earn money to send to organizations devoted to saving the rainforest by harvesting rainforest products. Ryan had a yard sale with his family, and also sold cookies and lemonade throughout one summer.

PROBLEMS WITH EMPATHY AND COMPASSION

Like gifted children with AD/HD, gifted children with AS can feel overwhelmed by the suffering of others and try to shut it off by not acknowledging it or by purposely avoiding it.

Seth, age 14, described how overwhelmed he felt by the suffering of others. He wanted to help when he heard about a disaster, but felt so paralyzed by the immense feelings generated that he could do nothing. Then he felt sad. Seth never read newspapers or watched television news in order to avoid feeling overwhelmed. What he preferred was someone asking for his help in a small way that allowed him to gather his resources. Thus, he was willing to help with the annual church food drive for the community food bank, and he liked to save part of his allowance so he could have some money to contribute to charities.

Adam, on the other hand, found it difficult to respond to charitable appeals or situations that others approached with compassion. He thought that people ought to take care of themselves, and it wasn't his job to do that for them. He had little conception of the needs of others. His feeling was that it wasn't him, so he didn't need to think about the problem.

Some gifted children with AS are more apt to personalize some aspects of an incident and relate to the victim's suffering based on their identification; however, some may also relate to the perpetrator for the same reason.

Bruce, age 15, was very upset after the Columbine shootings. Because he had been teased quite mercilessly at school, he identified with the students who did the shooting. What he focused on was their humiliation over the years by their peers. He could understand just why they shot others, though he was clear to state that he thought he would never choose such a method of getting even. In his mind, getting even was justified, though he might choose some other method that didn't involve blood. Fortunately, Bruce was actually not a violent boy at all. Nevertheless, he had trouble looking at the larger picture and seeing that shooting was an immoral solution. While most people with AS do not have this much trouble understanding the moral issue at stake, there are some who do.

Violence in video games and media raises some important questions with regard to gifted children with AS. Like gifted children with AD/HD, those gifted boys with AS whose only guide in interpersonal problem solving is fast-moving, violent solutions, practiced over and over, may not learn appropriate ways to deal with conflict. The problem of desensitization to violence, especially through the media viewing, is different though for gifted children with AS. The danger is not only that they will become desensitized to violence, but also that they have not learned to be sensitive to people's needs to start with. So, if they play violent computer games and watch violent media, they will use these as learning tools for how to behave if frustrated or upset, especially if they see no wrong in hurting others. While most people with AS abide by laws and would never hurt another, there is a small group who are aggressive and stimulated by violence. These children and adolescents need restrictions on what types of games they are allowed to play, as well as limitations on the amount of time spent on video games, so they can develop other pastimes and skills.

Suggestions for improving empathy and compassion

- Separate the teaching of empathy skills from the teaching of compassion. This will enable the gifted child with AS to focus more readily on the goal of caring about suffering. Empathy in everyday relationships is much more difficult to learn, and requires many small lessons in recognizing feelings in the self, and others, correlating these with body and facial cues, and learning how to assume the point of view first of a similar other, then a less similar other. It involves learning about the reciprocity expected in relationships, first as taking turns, then as offering support, then as giving and receiving in a mutual way. This requires years of work and many small lessons each day by a variety of people in the child's life: parents, teachers, other adults, friends, peers at school, and finally acquaintances.

- Since gifted children with AS often love books and reading, the use of books about how different people live and their everyday problems can serve to help bridge the gap between the child's immediate cultural background and that of others. Though gifted people with AS are often less aware of people's differences, and so are more tolerant of idiosyncrasies, they do need to learn about how people in different places can have problems particular to their lives: for example, famine in Africa caused by prolonged drought. The use of books of interest to the child can be helpful if the lesson is made explicit for the child, and a script based on the lesson developed. Remember some of the child's best friends are books.

- Compassion can be taught through targeting some of the child's interests. If the gifted child with AS likes animals, teaching compassion for the suffering of animals can be a model for both future work with animals and in human relationships as well. Thus, a small project around taking care of animals can be a start. The child with AS could collect bags of food for the local animal shelter. He or she could write letters and make posters about animal rights. Informing people about the needs of animals who work – such as police dogs, circus animals, and so on – can increase the child's awareness and compassion. Then the child might work to help provide animals for people who live in foreign countries. The Heifer Project donates animals that people use to improve their standard of living. A flock of chicks grows to be chickens which produce eggs, manure for fertilizer, feathers, and meat for the poor families. Each family that receives animals has to produce more and give at least one to another family. The gifted child with AS can learn about how a small investment in caring provides a large benefit for the community.

- As described above for gifted children with AD/HD who have trouble organizing themselves to work on projects, small charitable projects that lead to large outcomes can also be useful for gifted children with AS. However, children with AS need more instruction about why the project is being done, what the bigger picture is, and why it is desirable to do the project. While obvious to children with AD/HD, such concepts are not obvious to those with AS.

- Video games need to be carefully selected for children with AS. While on-line and playing games, children with AS need frequent monitoring. Since computers are a favorite activity for many people with AS, in later years it is important to discuss the meaning of violent videos and games and why some people watch and play them. Discuss also the effects on people who are easily upset and what expectations society does have for appropriate behavior; that is, the person with AS needs more emphasis on the unreality of violent fantasy games.

Moral reasoning

In this section of this chapter, the literature on moral reasoning in gifted children will be explored, problems with moral reasoning will be examined, and the particular strengths and deficits of gifted children with AD/HD and AS will be described.

Gifted children have been shown in the research to be advanced in their reasoning about moral concerns. Sensitivity to moral issues was noted in gifted children as far back as Terman's (1925) studies of gifted children. These early studies described gifted children as trustworthy and morally advanced.

Hollingworth (1942) described how good and evil in the abstract can come to be troublesome for exceptionally gifted children. Hollingworth mentioned specific traits of character related to moral development. Child D was noted to show a "refusal to lie, loyalty to standards once adopted, readiness to admit to just criticisms, unselfishness and amiability" (p.121).

Many current-day gifted children have also been described in these terms. These gifted children hold to high moral standards for themselves, and often for others. They believe in truth, honesty, loyalty, and fairness. Gross's (1993) studies of children with IQs over 160 found them well above age peers in conceptuization of moral concepts such as fairness, justice, responsibility for self, and responsibility towards others. Other examples are to be found in Silverman (1993c, 1994).

A number of writers have shown gifted children to be advanced in making moral judgments: that is, deciding what is right under various conditions. On the Defining Issues Test (DIT) (Rest 1979), a series of tasks based on Kohlberg's (1984) premises, Janos and Robinson (1985) compared both radically accelerated college students and two groups of highly gifted high-school students with a group of typical undergraduate college students. They found that the three groups of highly gifted students scored higher on the DIT, thus exhibiting higher levels of moral reasoning and judgment than did the more average students. Howard-Hamilton (1994) found that gifted high-school students scored well above the norms for age peers on the DIT.

Gross (1993) found that two of her exceptionally gifted students, by age 12, scored on the DIT above the level for college students. Thus, many gifted students may also be advanced in moral reasoning.

Problems with moral reasoning

Gifted children may find that their attempts at moral reasoning are misunderstood. Often asynchrony occurs because they are so much in advance of what peers and adults expect. Also, gifted children can have such high moral standards that their expectations for others are disappointed. Not able to suffer fools gladly, they point out the lapses of adults and peers alike.

THE PROBLEM OF ASYNCHRONY

While advanced moral reasoning allows gifted children to make more mature decisions about moral issues, nevertheless such advancement may have its costs. Gross (1993) discussed the ramifications of being advanced in moral reasoning. The children in her study showed more intense awareness in thinking and feeling, which set them apart from age peers. For example, Ian's views of ethical and moral issues such as justice, fairness, and personal responsibility were above high-school level when he was age ten. Fred, who at age 12 scored as high as college students on the DIT (Rest 1979), was teased and mocked for his advanced interests in psychology and philosophy. The result for these children was feelings of alienation and isolation from peers at a time when most children have a satisfying peer group with whom they can share values.

Another area of difficulty for many gifted children arises from their advanced understanding of rules, and what makes certain rules fair or unfair. Tim, age four, worked out a means of sharing the one train set with his preschool playmates: all would take turns. To Tim, fairness meant taking turns, not necessarily of equal length. Nicholas, age eight, developed a concept about fairness that stated that no one should be left out of playground games. Tiffany, age nine, worried about the cliques in her class. She tried to make sense of why other girls thought these were acceptable. In Tiffany's conceptualization, fairness meant exclusivity was wrong. Caroline, age 11, felt it wasn't fair that she should have so much while others had so little; each month she gave part of her allowance to charity. Notice the different ideas about fairness, and how each is developed in a context of relationship to others.

Some gifted children, from an early age, show a tendency to question rules they feel are unfair or unjust, not only with adults but also with peers. For example, Nicholas was upset over how the boys at school treated each other. He complained about the unfairness they showed in choosing sides in games, in changing rules partway through, and in not letting certain children play. Nicholas was usually welcome to play because he was a good player, but he chose not to play after several of the smaller boys were excluded. He and these boys decided to form their own games and allow anyone to play. This sort of challenge to the norms of his peer group worked for Nicholas because he was popular, but it may not for other gifted children.

Those gifted children who have the most difficult time with conflicts about the fairness of rules are those who hold rules as absolutes, while peers still feel rules are approximations. Adam was an extreme example of such a child, due to his AS.

It is not only rules about games that are problematic, but also rules about behavior. Many gifted young adolescents question authority in ways that are difficult to answer, as Emily did. These young people are advanced in reasoning ability and in ideals about justice, but do not see the adult's point of view. At times, the resulting collision of values is difficult to negotiate and the young person becomes disillusioned. Many disagreements in schools over attire, what can be printed in the school paper, and opinions that may be expressed in class or in assigned written work fall into this category. Since many of these young people are operating on adult levels of reasoning, but younger levels of emotional maturity or life experience (asynchrony), they may feel that theirs is the only way. In some cases these young persons will have a true vision and need to find a way to change things; in other cases, they will need to find ways to work for compromises.

THE PROBLEM OF SUFFERING FOOLS GLADLY

As was the case for Emily, many gifted children and adolescents find it difficult to "suffer fools gladly." Hollingworth (1942) was one of the first to note the problems gifted children often had in dealing with the lower standards, lesser expectations, and decreased moral sensitivity of others – both peers and, especially, adults. Because they are likely to be very different from others in thought, action, interests, and intentions, gifted children may find it difficult to comprehend why others behave as they do and to tolerate these differences. This is particularly the case with what the gifted child experiences as stupidity. Many young gifted children find themselves in trouble with adults for correcting errors, trying to talk about their interests, and questioning adult standards. It is especially galling to these children when adults espouse a standard but then do not obey it. Thus, many a gifted child has been puzzled and upset by adults' failure to follow the Golden Rule. Hollingworth suggested that these children needed to learn to live with human foibles, to understand that others around them would fall short of standards and, in fact, often not be the best they could be. This is termed "suffering fools gladly" with the gifted child learning to suffer the foolishness and tolerate the differences.

These gifted children often see issues as larger than life. They feel deeply about causes and want others to make the same deep commitments they do. They are passionate, intense, and sensitive, as well as perceptive and intuitive. When adults and peers around them are disappointing because of shallowness or imperfection, these gifted children try to correct, admonish, and intervene so that things will be set right.

Suffering fools gladly means learning to deal with the ordinariness of life, rather than finding life to be the glorious adventure promised in fantasy or the ideal. It means dealing with the less than ideal and finding ways to be happy anyway. The problem is most acute for those with a high degree of perceptiveness and intuitiveness (Lovecky 1992b), who are exceptionally fair and truthful themselves. Thus, they cannot conceive why adults cannot be as kind, just, fair, virtuous, and truthful as they are. That adults might not want to know the truth, be corrected, or learn a better way to do something is shocking. For those gifted children who still are at more of an either/or stage, truth can be very rigidly defined; even differences of opinion can be difficult to tolerate. Because there is only one objective truth to them, the idea of a range of cases, a judgment of exceptions, and a differing definition is difficult to accept. Thus, these children's moral judgments tend to be more rigid, especially in concepts about right and wrong.

Gifted children who have trouble suffering fools gladly often have strong views on the issues of fairness and justice. These views are the basis for strong opinions that lead to arguments in parenting and teaching them. These gifted children have such strong ideals that they cannot be easily satisfied with a weaker response than what they expect. Often the gifted child is right about the principle, but wrong about the context or the solution. Inexperience about life, and about how people act, leads to frustration that others cannot be what the gifted child expected. Sometimes it will be important to work with such youngsters about how to accomplish a realistic goal; other times, they may need help in understanding why things won't work out as they foresee.

Mika and Meckstroth (2001) suggested that learning the "Platinum Rule" would be beneficial. Instead of the Golden Rule in which treating others as we would like to be treated is the focus, gifted children need to learn to respect the fact that not everyone else wants what they want. Therefore, they need to learn to understand and be compassionate towards others' differences.

Gifted children with AD/HD

Gifted children with AD/HD may be indistinguishable from their gifted peers in terms of moral reasoning. Yet the literature also notes that more average children with AD/HD may be immature in their ability to make moral judgments. There have been no studies of moral reasoning of gifted children with AD/HD; thus, it is not easy to ascertain how gifted children with AD/HD really compare with others.

In the literature about AD/HD, more average children are seen as having deficits in moral judgment because of inability to internalize rules and standards, as well as in inattentive, overaroused, and impulsive behavior. Douglas (1972; cited in Barkley 1997) noted the relationship between attentional/impulsive control and deficiencies in moral development. Moral reasoning was found to be less well developed in hyperactive/impulsive and behaviorally disordered children (Nucci and Herman 1982). Furthermore, delays in the development of moral reasoning were found to be predictive of disruptive and aggressive behavior in school, in decreased social competency, and decreased social status (Bear and Rys 1994).

There is also a group of children with AD/HD and ODD who are deficient in knowing what is the right thing to do. These children look to the most stimulating aspect of the situation to guide behavior. They consider defying rules to be fun and stimulating (Melnick and Hinshaw 1996). These children also lack, even on social problem solving tasks, the ability to predict what a character might do next, what might be the outcome in a story, or what could have happened given the initial premise. Argumentativeness, defiance, anger, aggression, teasing, stealing, and lying are particular problems with this group of children. Thus, this group of children appear more deficient in moral reasoning, as well as in behavior; they are the ones who appear to have feeble consciences and less empathy.

Weiss and Hechtman's (1993) longitudinal study of children with AD/HD through their adolescent and adult years indicated that it is only those with antisocial tendencies and conduct disorders who showed lower moral reasoning or deficits in moral behavior in early adulthood.

Barkley (1997, 1998) suggested that deficits in moral reasoning are related to deficits in specific executive functions such as verbal working memory or self-directed inner speech. These particular executive functions help construct a recall of the past and a sense of the future so a person can delineate cause and effect through recall of experience. Also, along with this, an internalization of rules and standards is important, as is building specific rules into more general or meta rules. Being able to recall standards, and to compare one's actions to these standards, allows for the development of conscience. While not specifically tested with children with AD/HD, evidence does exist that rule-governed behavior along with working memory gives rise to moral reasoning and moral regulation of behavior (Hayes, Gifford, and Ruckstuhl 1996; Kopp 1982).

Perhaps the best way to think about moral reasoning and AD/HD is to analyze the problems these gifted children have with executive functions and how these impact moral judgment.

USING RULES TO GOVERN BEHAVIOR

Gifted children with AD/HD who came to the Gifted Resource Center of New England showed some difficulties with using rules. Though they knew what to do, doing it in the heat of the moment was difficult. This was due to their variable attention, poor self-modulation, and difficulties with delaying gratification. They also had some difficulty with using time and seeing the future. Thus, long-term consequences mean less to them than to gifted children without AD/HD.

Variability is often a problem for gifted children with AD/HD, since the environment never feels the same from moment to moment to them, and they never act the same. Thus one minute the young gifted child with AD/HD may comfort a peer, yet the next minute impulsively act aggressively. As mood shifts, and as the child's perceptions undergo a rapid change, behavior can erupt without clear connections to an antecedent event. Using rules to guide behavior means having both a sense of the rules needed, being able to draw them from memory quickly, and being able to stop impulsive responding in order to apply the right rule at the right time. Thus, while gifted children with AD/HD may do very well on a Kohlbergian-type moral reasoning test, where they have to supply theoretical answers, they may still have trouble making good judgments from moment to moment.

Some gifted children with AD/HD show strengths in rule-governed behavior. They not only know the rules, but also the intent of the rules. They have a good sense of right and wrong, and many have very high personal standards for some aspects of behavior. Madison, age ten, a gifted girl with AD/HD described in Chapter 6, broke her teacher's timer when she accidentally knocked it off the desk. No one was in the classroom at the time, and Madison debated whether she should tell on herself or not. She didn't think the teacher would be able to figure out who had broken the timer, but in the end, she decided to confess because it was the right thing to do.

Having high moral standards means that gifted children with AD/HD have thought about the rules in terms of right and wrong, just and unjust, fair and unfair. Like gifted children without AD/HD, those with AD/HD have developed clear ideas about what different aspects of moral reasoning mean to them. Thus, they have developed ideas about what is truth, justice, honesty, fairness, and loyalty. For example, Alissa, age 11, a gifted girl with AD/HD, wondered if it was honest to say her science project was finished when she hadn't put that much effort into it. When she received an "A", she wondered if she had really cheated. Kevin, age ten, a gifted boy with AD/HD, decided it was a lie to pretend to go to sleep but then read with a flashlight under the covers for several hours. It wasn't a lie, though, if he had really tried to go to sleep, but could not.

Some gifted children with AD/HD have high personal standards but show gaps in awareness of the full meaning of those standards. Charles, age 14, had been a vegetarian for the past two years. He had strong convictions that it was wrong to kill any living thing. He prepared his own meals so that he would not trouble his mother with having to make two dinners. He considered that he had high moral standards and would not cheat, lie, or steal. Though exceptionally honest about everything else, Charles lied frequently about his school work. He did not do homework and his grades suffered; however, he lied about his grades until his report card arrived. Charles did not consider lying about his homework to be lying because he did not consider doing homework important. Because he did not wish to do it, lying about it was acceptable.

Some gifted children with AD/HD have very high standards for themselves and cannot possibly live up to them. When they fail, they are so disappointed in themselves, and feel such guilt, they become depressed. Paul, a gifted boy with AD/HD described in Chapter 6, took every project to an extreme. He set goals for himself far above the requirements of any teacher. Then he had difficulty following through, and he rarely completed anything. When the deadline had passed, and the day of reckoning was upon him, Paul felt so guilty he could not live with himself. He felt he had failed not only himself, but everyone else too. In fact, he saw his failure as a moral problem – he had failed the trust of others that he would do as he had said. Paul's feelings about his failure took over his whole sense of being so that it was impossible for him to think about what he might have done to meet more realistic standards. The problem for Paul was twofold. His expectations for himself were unrealistically high; he thought ordinary standards were too easy, so he should set himself harder goals. He also saw ordinary failings as breaking trust. When he failed, he could not see that his original idea had been unwieldy.

INTERNALIZATION OF SPEECH

Internalization of speech allows monitoring of behavior, as well as time to think of a plan and to execute it. It also allows thoughtful analysis of what is going on and reflection on the bigger picture. In terms of moral development, this means that gifted children with AD/HD may have more trouble than other children with stopping to think of what is the best thing to do and changing plan if the judgment was faulty. They have difficulty understanding how rules fit together into bigger rules to become guiding principles by which one might act. Gifted children with AD/HD who are impulsive, need high levels of stimulation, and are reactive may have greater difficulty even seeing the bigger picture, the "why" of what they should do. Since they act in the moment, experiencing each moment as new, disconnected almost from the one before, they are not able to develop principles by which they might live. This then leads to acting at a less mature level. Luke, age 16, a gifted adolescent with AD/HD described in Chapter 6, saw nothing wrong with having a tantrum because his favorite shirt was in the laundry. He thought he had a right to express his anger. Since he didn't physically hurt anyone, why shouldn't he scream and yell if he was upset? He saw no connection between his immature behavior over his shirt and his parents' decision that he was not mature enough to get his driver's permit. He thought they were arbitrary and unfair.

Some gifted children with AD/HD show strengths in internalization of speech because they are able to see the big picture and to make appropriate plans.

Some are adept at using strategy to overcome obstacles. Thus, when confronted with the need to decide on what is the right thing to do for themselves and others, they are able to stop and think. Colin, age 17, a gifted boy with AD/HD described in Chapter 4, attended some courses at a local university even though he was still in high school. He made friends with several of the college students and spent his spare time with them. One night, his college student friends started drinking and became rowdy and noisy. Colin took the public bus home so that he would not get into trouble. One of the college students was arrested later on that night for disturbing the peace. Colin's other friends, though, complimented Colin on showing good judgment in going home.

Like gifted children without AD/HD, those with AD/HD may be able to understand how rules fit together into bigger rules to become guiding principles by which they might act. These gifted children with AD/HD evolve a personal philosophy of right and wrong from an early age, and use it to guide behavior. Andrew, age eight, a gifted boy with AD/HD, was often in trouble for his antics and mischievous behavior. Yet, when confronted with wrongdoing, Andrew never lied. He always admitted his culpability and took the consequences. Andrew didn't mean to misbehave; he was very high-spirited, but he did know lying was wrong and refused to try to excuse his misbehavior with a lie. To Andrew, if he was wrong, it was his responsibility to own up.

UNDERSTANDING CAUSE AND EFFECT

Difficulty understanding cause and effect can have an impact on moral reasoning. For example, if a child with AD/HD does not know what will happen next, given certain actions, it is difficult to make decisions that reflect good judgment. If decisions are not based on good judgment, they are not based on moral principles but on immediate feeling. Thus, impulsivity, poor working memory, and difficulty with delaying gratification all have a role in poor decision making. When children with AD/HD have difficulty understanding cause and effect, they also have difficulty conceptualizing consequences and understanding how to change behavior. Thus, these children have trouble learning from past mistakes and have trouble making a good plan for the future.

Some gifted children with AD/HD may have advanced ideas about moral reasoning, but may still be unable to control their own behavior. They may think teasing is wrong but be unable to resist doing it, or they may only define one type of teasing and not see a similar act as just as reprehensible. They may want fairness, but have difficulty allowing another child to share the attention or have a fair turn. They may hate cheating, but not be able to stand losing, so they change the rules. They may be able to spend a lot of time discussing what is fair and just, but no time considering whether they are being fair. Fairness sometimes means getting what they want first, then others may have a chance. They may care very deeply about a friend's feelings, but are unable to sustain the attention to listen to a friend's dilemma before jumping in to fix it, and they may insist on fixing it their own way without allowing their friend to choose if that solution is satisfactory. They would never think of stealing, but they are so forgetful they walk off with a friend's ball, then forget to return it despite pleas from the friend.

The gifted child with AD/HD likely does not intend for the negative consequence to happen. If intentions counted most, they would always be innocent. Unfortunately, consequences count more for most people, and they ascribe intent based on the consequences. It is difficult for most people to think of someone who does something that a moment's thought would suggest was stupid as innocent of a bad intent. Thus, gifted children with AD/HD are continually at risk for being misunderstood and misbelieved about what their actions may mean, but they are also at risk for excusing the consequences based on their intent. It is important to work with gifted children with AD/HD to accept responsibility for the consequences of their actions while learning how to stop their impulsive behavior.

Gifted children with AD/HD show asynchrony in the understanding of cause and effect, as well as of consequences. For short-term consequences that are the direct result of their own behavior, gifted children with AD/HD are apt to act more like average children with AD/HD. They forget what they are supposed to do and act on the spur of the moment. Ross, age eight, a gifted boy with AD/HD described in Chapter 6, had trouble playing games with others because he needed so much to be in control. If he even felt he was losing, he would accuse the other players of cheating or refuse to play anymore. Ross had no idea of the consequences of his accusations. He could not see that he was being unfair, only that he thought others were. Soon, other children would not play games with Ross, and they started to tease him about being a "loser."

Gifted children with difficulty controlling impulsivity and a poor idea of the big picture tend to have a view of justice that is an "eye for an eye." They are quick to enact revenge for wrongs done to them and slow to reciprocate the good.

Some gifted children with AD/HD are able to understand the longer-term aspect of cause and effect for moral actions. They see the big picture and want to work to make things better, more fair, more just, or more peaceful for themselves and others. Though they may be less able to control impulsivity about their own lives, they show great ability in moral reasoning. They seem able to take a mental step back and reason out the thing to do that would be just for everyone. Bob, age eight, a gifted boy with AD/HD, decided that teasing was a form of injustice because it was based on prejudice. He felt the suffering of the children who could not help the traits about which they were taunted. This caused Bob to wonder why it was acceptable to tease about physical traits like weight when it was not acceptable to tease about race or religion.

Vanessa, age 14, a gifted adolescent with AD/HD, worked with others at her high school to set up a group that would help students negotiate conflicts and use peaceful solutions for interpersonal problems. Vanessa believed that it was possible to have peace in the world, and it should start with those closest to us: our friends, acquaintances, and classmates. Vanessa also took part in statewide demonstrations for peace, and was one of the students to march on Washington to persuade President Bush to let UN inspections have a chance to work instead of going to war with Iraq.

THE PROBLEM OF SUFFERING FOOLS GLADLY

Gifted children with AD/HD have difficulty suffering fools gladly. For some, the definition of foolishness is whatever those in authority want them to do that they do not want to do, or find difficult to do. Like Emily, described at the start of this chapter, rather than saying that they could not focus on an assignment, or forgot to do it, they say that they considered it beneath their intelligence, too easy, childish, or stupid. Sometimes the assignment is unchallenging, but that really isn't the problem; the problem is that these students do not know how to tolerate mediocrity. Some of these students really do need more stimulation and a faster pace, and rebel against those who hold them back. At the same time, they have trouble doing more in-depth work, and want to speed across the curriculum, skimming the surface as fast as possible. The tension of this can produce anger and disrespect for authority.

Because of their problems with intensity, behavioral and emotional reactivity, impulsivity, and sensitivity, gifted children with AD/HD have more difficulty than gifted children without AD/HD in learning to be tactful. To be tactful requires being able to put a feeling on hold, wait for an opportunity to act, think ahead about how to say something and think about the ramifications. With an impulsive style, this is almost impossible for the child. Also, since the child with AD/HD can't so easily take another's point of view, can't wait until a better time, and can't easily measure cost, these gifted children often cannot tolerate even everyday imperfection in themselves or others. The impulse, the drive to do it now, and the inability to think ahead means the child will blurt out corrections, make what seem to be rude and thoughtless comments, hurt others' feelings by focusing on the fact instead of the effort or intent, and have trouble changing to a less critical mode. Emily had little patience with people she felt were purposely stupid about something. When her history teacher wanted her to stop correcting him in class, Emily thought he was being stupid. Why teach something erroneous when she could easily correct it? She also had trouble with the slow pace of the class and did not see why the teacher spent so much time on material that was obvious if one had read the chapter. Often, Emily was the only one with her hand raised to answer questions, and she would become angry when the teacher would purposely call on someone else who didn't know the answers. That, she thought, was a waste of time. Emily had two problems with her history teacher: she was very bright but had no appropriate outlet for her knowledge and ideas; also, she was impatient with people who made mistakes or needed time to grasp concepts that were easy for her. She was loud in her criticism and unyielding in her opinions, showing no tact or caring for the feelings of the other students.

For the gifted child with AD/HD, suffering foolishness ungracefully has moral ramifications because others, both adults and peers, see the child as overly critical, inflexible, rather inconsiderate, and lacking in empathy. Teaching gifted children with AD/HD how to deal with the minor changes, differences, and imperfections of life is vital in helping them learn appropriate social skills, especially as they reach the ages when the social expectation is for empathy and mature moral judgment.

Suggestions for improving moral reasoning

- Gifted children with AD/HD have a gap between knowledge of right and wrong and ability to carry out appropriate actions. Often, this is due to impulsivity and poor judgment. Thus, it is helpful to replay situations and discuss the right thing to do, and how to judge what that is. What are the clues? What did the child predict would happen? Practice after the fact, and replay problem situations so the child gets practice in doing the right thing versus just being scolded for doing the wrong thing.

- Problems like lying, dishonesty, and cheating need to be addressed whether the child intended the negative outcome or not. Some gifted children with AD/HD learn to lie automatically about things such as school, homework, chores, and other responsibilities. Since they don't cheat on tests, or steal or lie about things they consider important, they rationalize that lying about school work doesn't count. Discussions and consequences around personal integrity are important. It does matter if a person lies about work, and the gifted child's attempt to excuse this type of dishonesty by saying that it wasn't a worse type of lie doesn't make it right.

- Intentions matter, but so does outcome. Gifted children with AD/HD can have good intentions but if they don't make plans, or think about consequences, they are still responsible for the consequences. That is often a difficult concept to get across. These gifted children feel it shouldn't count because they didn't intend it to end as it did. Thus, if Tom throws a baseball in the house, and it breaks a mirror, whether he intended to break the mirror or not, he has to find a way of replacing it; that would be the appropriate consequence. If he broke the mirror in a fit of rage though, he would not only have to replace the mirror but suffer additional consequences for his loss of control.

- Gifted children with AD/HD can benefit from discussions and lessons on values. What do they think are important principles by which to live? What is a lie? What does honesty mean? How should a friend be loyal? Suppose their friend is taking drugs or threatening suicide? What are the gray areas in their moral reasoning? When is it acceptable to them to tell a lie? What do they think are moral principles that everyone in the world should follow? How do we deal with differences of opinion about what is the best thing to do? Work on family and community morality. Model moral dilemmas for children and think out the ramifications of various solutions. Discuss ideals in the adult world and universal principles that you, the adults, find helpful. Discuss what led you to accept particular standards. Tell children about some of the moral dilemmas you faced as a child and how you solved them, and also whether that was a good solution or not.

- Offer books, movies, and other media that explore values such as honesty, truth, caring, truthfulness, and fairness. Develop a children's book discussion group to explore issues based on a moral precept such as: was Matilda right to have gotten revenge? What about Harry Potter? In *Tuck Everlasting*, would you choose immortality or not?

- Discuss the issue of suffering fools gladly and how it relates to ideals. For gifted children with rigid ideas and not much leeway for the ordinary parts of life, work on seeing more than one viewpoint or having more than one definition of what a standard might be. Frankly discuss human failings and how people strive for an ideal but usually don't meet it. The ideal is worth having, but one needs to be tolerant of genuine efforts that are less than perfect. Discuss when to make a stand about an issue and when not to accept someone's standard as adequate. When gifted adolescents with AD/HD have difficulty with the slowness of pace in class or the ignorance of classmates, help them by both discussing the need for tolerance of others who need more help to learn and by trying to find ways to improve their curriculum.

- Discuss teasing as a moral issue. What is the relationship between teasing and prejudice? Is it okay to tease about some things and not others? What about friendly teasing? How does one tolerate difference? What should one do about peers who tease and encourage a culture of teasing to fit in?

Gifted children with AS

The literature suggests that children with AS have the ability to respond to moral precepts. Gillberg (2002) suggested that people with AS can appear quite undisturbed by the suffering of those near to them, but can be deeply involved in ethical, moral, and philosophical issues. Some also fight for particular causes. However, while these children have high moral standards, they can be rather rigid about their beliefs, and then make decisions based on these beliefs which may not fit the situation.

Ozonoff *et al.* (2002) suggested that because adolescence is a time of ambiguity, especially in social situations, children with AS tend to develop rigid moral and religious beliefs as a way of coping. They may try to apply these inappropriately: for example, a teen who reads about the meat packing industry, decides to become a vegetarian, and then points out to classmates and cafeteria workers at school all the health dangers inherent in eating meat (Ozonoff *et al.* 2002). The problem wasn't trying to educate and influence classmates and school personnel; many gifted children have similar agendas. The problem was how the girl in the vignette went about her mission. She might select the wrong time and place: for example, telling her classmates at lunch that their food was disgusting, or describing slaughterhouse practices as they were eating, without any sense that they would not want this information.

Perhaps the best way to think about moral reasoning and AS is to analyze the problems these gifted children have with executive functions and how these impact moral judgment.

USING RULES TO DIRECT BEHAVIOR

On the whole, people with AS are very much guided by rules. Once they know a rule, they will follow it. Thus, internalizing rules is not as much of a problem as it is for some children with AD/HD. However, gifted children with AS may disregard rules they think are silly or that they cannot follow. Derrick refused to follow rules he thought were stupid; thus, he refused to stand in line for the bus. He would stand in line for lunch because that made more sense to him. At lunch, standing in line allowed an orderly approach to the food table, so everyone could eat during their brief lunch period. For the bus, though, it didn't matter in what order people got onto the bus, so why stand in line? Like other children with AS, Derrick had trouble with understanding the intent of rules.

Another problem for children with AS is the rigidity of their moral codes. Thus, while they believe in truth, fairness, loyalty, and honesty, they may not have many ideas about how to express these. Gifted children with AS can have mature ideas about moral concepts, yet be strikingly immature about how they put these into operation. Thus, they are able to state moral principles and have high codes of conduct. Many would never tell a lie or steal anything. It would not occur to them to cheat in a game or set out on purpose to say mean things about others. If they tell an authority about a classmate breaking a rule, it is because the classmate broke the rules, and the child with AS has to rectify this. It is not seen by the child with AS as a means of getting the other child into trouble. Adam, described at the beginning of this chapter, knew all the rules and obeyed them. What was more, he tried to point them out to other students too, something they did not appreciate. This made no sense to Adam. After all, why didn't they obey the rules? The rules were very clear. They were even written down in the middle-school student handbook. That someone might not care about minor rules was more than Adam could comprehend.

Gifted children with AS do not make many exceptions for their rules. Gifted children without AS will make some discernment about when lies are acceptable (to save someone's life, for example, or keep a friend out of trouble), when a person might be forgiven for stealing, and so on. Those with AS see no exceptions. Furthermore, they don't understand why anyone would tell lies or steal or cheat. Thus, while having a high moral code, they have no ideas about human foibles, because that is what is learned through empathy. Will, age 16, described in Chapter 6, was clear in his knowledge that smoking was not allowed at school. Though he was right about the need for the principal to enforce the rule, Will was too adamant and impatient, so he ended up having a tantrum and being the one in trouble.

There is a group of children and adolescents with AS who are less truthful, honest, and loyal. They are more apt to tell lies, steal, cheat at games, and tell on others to get revenge. These gifted children with AS seemed to regard rules as applying only when it was important to them. Thus, they expected other people to obey the rules, but if they didn't like the rule, or see a reason for it, they disregarded it as Derrick did about lining up for the bus. These gifted children with AS tended to be those with the highest IQs. They also tended to have more AD/HD symptoms. Thus, they also were more impulsive, and had less fully internalized rule-governed behavior.

It is important to note that some actions that seem like a disregard for certain rules are not purposeful. Thus, Joseph, described in Chapter 6, had trouble getting off the school bus because he was reading and didn't really attend to the fact that it was time to leave. He told the bus aide he'd be ready in a minute and kept on reading to the end of the chapter. Joseph didn't intend to break the rules; he was hyperfocused on his book and hadn't learned how to stop and change focus quickly.

UNDERSTANDING CAUSE AND EFFECT

Gifted children with AS can have difficulty with consequences, prediction, and cause and effect in social situations based on their difficulties in comprehending how others think and feel. Thus, they do not predict the effects of what they might say or do, nor can they, in the aftermath, understand why something didn't work out. In the area of moral issues, these gifted children do not see how their absolute definitions of what is right and wrong inhibit social functioning.

Since these gifted children don't understand areas of gray, they don't easily forgive transgressions. Also, they mistake what is done and said to them and then hold it against the other person. Will was a bagger at a local supermarket for the summer. While on the job, he was asked by another worker to carry groceries out to a customer's car. Will didn't know what to do; he felt manipulated by the other worker. It hadn't occurred to Will that all the baggers were supposed to help customers carry groceries. Even when this was explained to him, he had difficulty grasping that he hadn't been asked to do the other worker's job. So he complained about the incident for days. Finally, he was fired for having a poor attitude. Will did not understand why he was fired.

Some gifted children with AS may have advanced ideas about moral reasoning, but may still be unable to control their own behavior. The gifted child with AS does not intend for the negative consequence to happen. Negative consequences happen as a result of the poor understanding of the child with AS, and the difficulty with negotiating social interactions, as with Will above.

DIFFICULTY WITH PART-TO-WHOLE RELATIONSHIPS

One part of the deficits experienced by people with AS appears to be their inability to easily make wholes from component parts. Instead they focus on a part and come to an idiosyncratic interpretation of the whole. In moral development, this means that people with AS can have trouble developing a systematic code of behavior based on thought-out principles of universal fairness and justice. Thus, in general, most people with AS will have difficulty, in the larger sense, developing a system of justice that looks at universal needs, the weighing of justice and compassion, and mitigating factors, as well as individual circumstances. Indeed, being able to understand universal ideas of freedom, justice, and compassion is at an advanced level in Kohlberg's theory (1984). Therefore, it is unlikely that people with AS would develop ideals of moral concepts that are much in advance of conventional ideas, and be able to enact them. In fact, what most young adults and adolescents with AS seem to do is either adopt conventional ideas, and struggle to understand these, or develop idiosyncratic ideas that may come into conflict with the law or the rights of others. Sometimes, even while thinking that a principle is right – for example, that stealing is forbidden – the person with AS may not see what he or she is doing as stealing.

For example, Matt hacked his way into the high-school computer system. He then called the principal to report how easy it was to break in, and erase, steal, or change data so that the high school would enact the safeguards that he would give them. In this way, no one else could do as he had done. He was outraged when he was arrested. In his view, he had done a very moral thing by helping the school improve its computer safety system. He could not see why he was being charged with a crime. If someone else had done it, well, then they would have done a crime, because they might have harmed the school, but he hadn't.

Helping a boy like Matt requires focusing on the moral principles involved and setting priorities about which matters most. That is, permission is required to enter or change something that isn't one's own, and that rule has a higher priority than preventing possible future damage. Both acts – that is, breaking into the computer system and preventing damage – affect property rights and feelings of being intruded on. The most important aspect is that Matt actually broke in; others only might have done so. Alternative actions also should be explored with Matt: for example, talking with the principal about a demonstration of how easy it would be to breach security.

Some gifted children with AS do develop personal moral codes about right and wrong, good and evil, fairness, justice, truth, honesty, and loyalty. Like other gifted children without AS, explorations of moral issues can start in early childhood and continue into adolescence.

Byron, a gifted boy with AS, at age four started to ask about good and evil. He was interested in traditional puppet shows in the Southeast Asian country he was visiting. Byron became fascinated by the puppet shows and learned all the ritualized stories. In the stories, good characters entered from stage left and evil ones from stage right. However, evil characters who had once been good entered from the opposite side. This led Byron to ask about what had turned the character from good to bad. What had made him start to live a bad life and decide on a course of evil? Byron went on to write his own stories about good and evil, developing plots and characters that explored the question of what makes something evil, as well as how good can control evil. In later childhood, he was interested in the abstract concept of good and evil, how it develops, and how it can be controlled in people's lives.

Because of their emphasis on abstract principles of moral reasoning, gifted people with AS may make moral decisions that are based on the greatest good for the most people. Because gifted people with AS don't see difference among people as important, they can be much more tolerant of idiosyncrasies than most other people. On the other hand, the differences that might lead to sympathy for a person's difficulties or condition may also be unnoticed. Thus, justice may not be tempered with mercy.

THE PROBLEM OF SUFFERING FOOLS GLADLY

One of the problems for gifted children with AS is that they have no means of telling what others intend. In fact, the whole idea of intentionality is difficult for them. If they do not understand the idea of intention, then it is very hard to make predictions about others' moral behavior, especially if it is different from what they would do. Because so much of life is about gray areas, intentionality, and pre-diction, these gifted people choose religious or moral codes that are designed to tell them how to behave and what to expect. Of course, since others don't actually follow these codes exactly, the person with AS may feel compelled to tell them what they are doing wrong.

In this way, gifted children and adolescents with AS have difficulty suffering fools gladly. However, this type of difficulty in suffering the foolishness of others comes from underlying deficits in understanding others' perspectives, not from trouble dealing with the ordinariness or general lack of thoughtfulness or precision in others as is the case for gifted children without AS. Nevertheless, some with AS also find it difficult to tolerate foolishness in the sense of stupidity or ignorance. The philosopher Wittgenstein, who likely had AS, was noted for having feelings similar to this. He was said to find it almost "intolerable to get along with people from the working classes, because he felt 'wounded' by the crudeness of their company" (Gillberg 2002, p.129).

Suggestions improving deficits in moral reasoning

- Gifted children with AS have difficulty with the appropriate application of rules. They are not usually trying to do wrong, but are misinterpreting a situation. They may only have one way of thinking about a rule and use that way in all situations. As the gifted child with AS becomes an adolescent it is useful to discuss old rules, when they are applicable, and when they are not. See if the child can generalize about the rule. Make up a list about when to use each variation.

- Discuss what the intent of some rules is meant to be. With the gifted child with AS, discuss the concept of gray areas and how much leeway rules may have. For example, most people break the speed limit: why do they do this; how far over the limit is permissible; when is it a bad idea to break the speed limit; how bad are the consequences for breaking the speed limit? What rules in the child's life have leeway, and how can they weigh the cost of breaking rules at the wrong time?

- Some gifted children with AS have long memories for negative events that occur. They can obsess over the incident, bringing it up over and over and asking the same question each time. It can be helpful to introduce the idea of "letting go of the past." What this means is that some incidents and feelings are labeled obsolete, and after they have been reworked a number of times and it is not productive to discuss them anymore, they are written down and put into an "obsolete box." Physically put them into a box. Then, if the child tries to bring them up again, he or she is reminded they are obsolete ideas or feelings and that new ones are needed. In fact, it is time to go on and not be stuck. Using a script about getting unstuck can get past the barrier of not being able to see beyond the current negative feeling.

- As the child gets practice in letting go of negative incidents, parents and teachers can start to practice "forgiving others." This means that the gifted child with AS is taught via scripts and stories that other people are allowed by each of us to make some mistakes. After the mistake is over, and whether or not it can be fully rectified, we try to go on, and we don't bring it up again. We try to have better feelings about the people instead of mistrusting them. Explain the kinds of everyday things people commonly forgive. Discuss what might be unforgivable: situations where a person is not trusted or has to earn trust again. Make a list and, over time, add to it the things the gifted child with AS has learned to forgive.

- Gifted children with AS can develop idiosyncratic codes of behavior because they don't see what they do as wrong. Thus, like the children with AD/HD and NVLD, children with AS need help in thinking about what kinds of moral values they should have, and what to do if they see someone else not behaving as their code would suggest. Continuing work on understanding other's ideas, opinions, perceptions, and beliefs are all in order.

Conclusion

Like other gifted children, those with attention deficits may show advanced moral development. Gifted children are likely to be advanced in empathy and compassion and/or moral reasoning, the two strands of moral development. Because of this they are likely to be more advanced than age peers in understanding moral issues. They are also likely to have concerns about the suffering of others and feel a need to find some way to alleviate that suffering.

Like other gifted children, those with AD/HD can develop moral reasoning to a higher than average degree. However, because of deficits in executive functions, gifted children with AD/HD have more difficulty in the moment acting on their knowledge. Thus, they may know more about what is right and wrong, and have adopted advanced concepts about fairness, honesty, truth, and responsibility, but have trouble putting these concepts into practice in everyday situations. Gifted children with AD/HD also, like other gifted children, show advanced concerns about others and feel great empathy and compassion. For some, there is a strong need, as for other gifted children, to try to change things. Others have more scattered organization and energy and need specific projects to tap their compassion. Like other gifted children, those with AD/HD find suffering fools gladly can be a great burden.

Gifted children with AS, like other gifted children, can have high moral codes based on reasoning moral principles as absolutes. A small number of these children do appear to understand moral concepts as universals, such as the idea of freedom and what it entails, but, more usually, gifted children with AS appear to have adopted more conventional ideas, or have developed idiosyncratic ones based on their own interpretations. Most gifted children with AS do develop good moral values, and often are extremely honest, truthful, and responsible. Like other gifted children, those with AS can be compassionate, especially in caring for the environment and animals. They can care about people in a charitable enterprise: for example, caring about hunger or homelessness. Unlike other gifted children, though, they have difficulty with empathy in everyday life, and there is a separation of empathy and compassion for gifted children with AS that does not occur for other gifted children.

All gifted children need opportunities to discuss ideas about the concepts they develop around moral as well as intellectual issues. Caring adults can help them to discover their own internal resources while providing the intellectual, emotional, and moral support needed to integrate reasoning and compassion into wise moral choice.

> The sense for abstract justice which some persons have is as eccentric a variation, from the natural-history point of view, as is the passion for music...

> William James
> *The Moral Philosopher and The Moral Life*, I

Chapter 9

Issues in the Assessment of Gifted Children with Attention Deficits

Brett

Brett, age 11, was referred for an evaluation due to underachievement at school. He was slow to start assignments, and slow to complete them. He disliked writing and tried to avoid it as much as possible. However, if his mother allowed him to dictate work, he was able to accomplish some; left to do it on his own, nothing was usually completed. Brett's parents were worried about his apathy for school work. His mother thought that he needed to learn self-discipline, but he didn't seem to be doing so.

His father thought maybe something else was wrong. Brett reminded him of himself as a child. In fact, Brett's father still had many of the same issues with getting himself to do routine work. He described himself as creative, thinking up new ideas, and getting very excited about new projects. Then there would come a point where the newness would have worn off, he would start feeling bored, and it would be hard to continue. The family's resources varied considerably as he went through these cycles. After a period of concern, he always bounced back and found something else that would make money.

Brett was like that too. He enjoyed creative activities, but rarely finished anything. He wanted to do it all: music, poetry, science experiments. He loved to read and was a fountain of information about the most obscure and arcane subjects. Brett knew everything from the theories behind the formation of black holes to the tenets of major philosophies. Brett also loved playing Nintendo. He thought the perfect vacation would be to spend all his time playing video games.

Brett's teachers were puzzled by his behavior. He didn't act out in school, though he could be somewhat disruptive with questions and comments. He tended to dominate class discussions, but then he knew a lot, and usually made good contributions. On the other hand, Brett's written work was nothing special. He never seemed particularly bright when he answered questions on school papers; his work was average at best.

It was true that he fidgeted considerably. In fact, by the end of each school day his desk had mysteriously ended up several feet from where it was in the morning. Still, he wasn't really a behavior problem. He just never seemed to get any work done.

Brett's parents were worried. They saw a boy who was still fascinated by science and math, but only if he originated the project, and only until he lost interest. They were glad he still shared his knowledge with peers in class, but how long would that last? Soon he'd be an adolescent who might not think it was very good to be smart. Also, his preoccupation with video games worried them. Already they were having fights with Brett over what games he was allowed to play, as well as for how long he could play them. Left to his own devices, Brett would play all day.

What they wanted was a boy who had some interest in learning in school, did reasonably well, and had a few outside interests. They also might prefer one who did his chores, but they would settle right now for one who did his homework.

Brett's parents went for the second report card conference. As they spoke of their concerns, a picture of a smart boy who was having some sort of difficulty coalesced. Both teachers and parents expressed concerns about Brett's school work, his apathy, his difficulties with writing, his time playing video games. His good points were also considered: his contributions to class discussion, his good solutions to problems, his wonderful poetry, his zany sense of humor, and his kindness to other children.

Still, Brett's behavior raised questions: was he lazy, and needed prodding? This didn't really seem to work, actually. Was he AD/HD? He did seem spacey at times, but, on the other hand, he didn't act up like many of the hyperactive children the teachers had known. It was agreed that Brett needed a professional assessment. Though the school would do such an evaluation under the special education law, Brett's parents decided to get a more comprehensive evaluation privately.

Michael

Michael was age eight when he was referred for an evaluation. His 3rd-grade teacher reported that he was stubborn in class and refused to do assignments. He also was defiant, not verbally so much, but more in just doing as he pleased. For example, his teacher, Ms Gardner, had told him she didn't want to hear him sharpening his pencil so loudly again. Michael stood at the pencil sharpener for

20 minutes turning the handle very slowly. When she asked him what he thought he was doing, Michael said he was sharpening his pencil quietly.

Michael's performance was very erratic. He seemed to do exceptionally well in some subjects and very badly in others. He won the school spelling bee and the school geography bee. He seemed able to solve complex math problems, yet he seemed to misunderstand the simplest instructions. When the teacher asked the children to look at a picture of a garden in their math books to get clues as to how to solve the problems, Michael couldn't figure out what to do. He didn't seem to see the clues even when they were pointed out to him. Nevertheless, given the problem without the need for picture clues, Michael quickly solved it. Michael knew many facts about science and social studies topics but refused to write about them; he usually avoided written work.

Michael's behavior in class was quite disruptive at times. He called out answers constantly, interrupted the teacher, and corrected her if he thought she was wrong. He often reminded her when it was time to do things, and he got upset if the schedule was changed. For example, if the class was to see a movie instead of having math class, Michael protested and almost had a tantrum.

Finally, Michael had increasing problems dealing with the other children. Until 3rd grade, they had been quite tolerant of his erratic behavior but now were less forgiving of his disruptions, which took away from their time with the teacher or their fun activities. He also did not know how to join games, take fair turns, or wait without interrupting. Everything had to be his way and his peers were getting tired of it.

At home, Michael had a number of preoccupations and routines that occupied most of his time. He liked to read and to play video games, but he especially liked maps, and spent long hours making maps, tracing maps from the atlas, and planning trips using different auto routes. Each day he would tell his parents and sister about all the different ways they could get from his house in Massachusetts to some distant place. Michael also loved zip codes and had memorized the zip-code book. Give him a town or city and he could tell you the zip codes. What was more problematic, though, was getting Michael to engage with the family in any activities they planned. Unless it was a place he liked, it was difficult to get him to go.

Homework was a special nightmare. Michael would do spelling and math homework, but refused to write anything. If his parents allowed him to dictate to them, he was somewhat more able to perform writing tasks. Homework often took hours.

At the first report card conference of the year, Michael's parents and teachers expressed concerns about his school work, his stubbornness, his strange difficulty with obvious directions, his apathy except for subjects he liked, his difficulties with writing, his problem with peers, and his unusual interests. His good points were also considered: his great store of general knowledge especially about geography, his spelling and math ability, his persistence when he was motivated, his good contributions to class discussion, his unusual outlook on the world, and his sense of humor.

Still, Michael's behavior raised questions: was he just lazy and in need of discipline? As with Brett, that didn't really seem to work. Was he oppositional for some unknown reason: for example, some sort of strange learning disability? Did he have a vision problem of some sort? Maybe he had AS. The teacher had seen a television special about this disorder, and Michael seemed to have some of those characteristics. It was agreed that Michael needed a professional assessment. Though the school would do such an evaluation under the special education law, Michael's parents decided to get a more comprehensive evaluation privately.

The focus of this chapter

In this chapter, the following issues are discussed:

- The steps in assessment of gifted children.

- Evaluation of gifted children with attention deficits.

- Intellectual, achievement, neuropsychological, and behavioral and personality assessment.

- Special issues for clinicians, teachers, and parents.

Steps in the assessment of gifted children

This section of this chapter will explore what assessment is; presenting problems and how they vary; typical presenting problems for children with AD/HD, NVLD and AS; questions about the initial visit; and how to decide how much testing to do to answer specific questions about gifted children's issues.

What is assessment?

Assessment is an evaluation of a person using multiple means of gathering information upon which a clinical opinion will be based. Assessment may include testing. Testing means the standardized administration of a psychological instrument, such as an IQ test, in exactly the same way each time. Testing produces results usually reported as numbers. Assessment is more than testing though. It also includes observations, answers given to questions pertaining to life experiences, material obtained from other sources such as report cards, an extensive history of early development, and knowledge of family, medical, school, and social history. In addition, the clinician performing the assessment makes clinical judgments about ability to interact appropriately with others, as well as temperament and ability to deal with stress and frustration.

In the context of this book, assessment includes evaluation of symptoms and strengths and weaknesses; it utilizes both standardized tests and clinical judgment to determine the needs of the gifted child. Testing thus can include measures of intellectual ability; neuropsychological functioning including executive functions; learning and memory; language functioning; visual-perceptual-motor functioning; social and emotional development; and academic achievement. Assessment also includes free-play interviews, structured interviews, history taking, behavior checklists, use of portfolios, and interaction with the examiner throughout the entire time the child is evaluated. For the purposes of this book, evaluation and assessment are used synonymously; testing can be part of both of them.

Presenting problems

Parents typically bring children for assessment because they have a question or concern that they are hoping to answer. Presenting problems, those symptoms or concerns that are the reason for wanting the evaluation, include questions about behavioral, learning, and social and emotional issues. Parents are not always aware they are posing questions, and may not be aware of the limitations of testing in answering their concerns. Thus, parents sometimes ask questions of particular tests that cannot be answered by that test. It is therefore important to be aware of what questions are being asked, and what the limitations of testing are.

Typical questions developed from presenting problems include the following:

- *Cognitive levels.* How bright is the child? Is he or she so advanced that a special curriculum is needed? Is cognitive functioning in language and visual-spatial areas similar or are there specific cognitive strengths and weaknesses?

- *Achievement.* Why isn't the child working up to potential? Is the work too easy or too hard? Is the child unmotivated? Does the child have an attention or learning problem? Is the child a perfectionist or anxious?

- *Motivation.* Is the child bored because the curriculum is too easy? Is the curriculum not stimulating enough? Does the child need particular types of work to hold attention, or deal with a learning disability? Does the child require frequent reward and/or structure to do tasks? What sorts of work does the child have the most fun with and enjoy doing?

- *Behavior.* When is the child most likely to behave well? Are there particular triggers noted as a prelude to misbehavior? Is the child unable to suffer fools gladly? Is it an authority issue? Is the child impulsive or hyperactive? Is the child frustrated? Is asynchrony the problem: that is, the child is advanced and can't see why he or she shouldn't give the correct answer, or point out another way to do the problem? Does the child seem to miss essential pieces of the directions or make assumptions others do not?

- *Emotional states.* Is the child rigid or easily upset? Are transitions difficult? Is the child fearful or, conversely, fearless and disregarding of life and limb? Does the child talk about killing him- or herself? Is this an exceptionally sensitive or intense child? Does the child recognize feelings in the self and others?

- *Friends and social skills.* Does the child have few or no friends? Is the child the victim of teasing? Does the child seem oblivious to social cues? Is the child inappropriate? Given that the child is so bright, why doesn't he or she know the language of simple social interaction? Is the child lonely; what can be done to find friends at the same level? Why are there so few children with the same interests? How can gifted children meet others like themselves?

In formulating what the evaluation can answer, parents, teachers, and psychologists all need to have some input into the process of determining how advanced the child is, what sorts of issues are important or problematic, and how intense or frequent they are. Testing helps to answer what may underlie particular issues. For example, a child who is unmotivated may need a variety of tests to rule out a learning, attention, or emotional problem, especially if being given challenging work does not improve matters considerably. Conversely, information about the child's life outside of school can help to answer the question of motivation in other activities. A child with many interests, who follows through at home on chores, and can do complex work in more challenging courses is likely understimulated. However, such a child still may have an undetected attention problem that is more noticeable when work is not self-chosen.

PRESENTING SYMPTOMS VARY

Brett's presenting problems – apathy, poor concentration, poor motivation, failure to do work, failure to hand it in, not listening, and little interest in activities other than computers – might have a number of causes. Brett might be very bored by too easy a curriculum. He might have a learning disability or processing problem. Maybe he has an attention deficit. He might be depressed. Or maybe he is just the kind of boy who has nothing in particular wrong with him, but has no real motivation.

Brett's parents and teachers filled out behavior checklists such as the Child Behavior Checklist (Achenbach 1991a, 1991b), the ACTeRS scales (Ullmann, Sleator, and Sprague 1997), the Conners Rating Scales (Conners 2001), and the Brown ADD Scales (Brown 2001). It was noted that no clear picture emerged. Brett was scored moderately above average on problems that reflected poor motivation, low arousal, difficulties with memory, difficulties with sustaining interest, and somewhat poor social skills. However, he was not really hyperactive, was average for oppositional behavior, and showed varying results on attention focus. On some scales he scored above average, and on others he was average. Some symptoms of anxiety and depression were also noted. These checklists, though they indicated some problems, also did not give a clear picture of what was the main, underlying problem. Thus, Brett's parents decided to have a full assessment battery that would include intellectual and academic skills, memory, learning style, executive function skills, language skills, visual-motor functioning, and social and emotional functioning.

Michael's presenting symptoms included some difficulties with achievement, behavior, and social skills. He was described as motivated in things he liked but not willing to work on things he disliked. He also misinterpreted some directions and instructions and had trouble with outbursts in class.

Behavior checklists such as the Child Behavior Checklist, ACTeRS scales, Brown ADD Scales, and the Conners showed erratic patterns with anxiety high, as well as oppositional behavior. Teachers ranked attention with two different answers for each item: high if he liked the task and low if he did not. Effort, arousal, and motivation also were variable. On the Asperger Syndrome Diagnostic Scale (Myles, Bock, and Simpson 2001), Michael was scored high by his parents on items related to deficits in communication, social skills, maladaptive behaviors, and friendship skills. His overall score fell into the range strongly suggestive of AS.

Nevertheless, though these scores gave some indications of the underlying problems, Michael's parents decided to have a full evaluation to formulate recommendations that would fit their child's particular strengths and weaknesses.

A TYPICAL PRESENTATION OF GIFTED BOYS WITH AD/HD

Generally, it is gifted boys from ages 8 through 14 who are referred. In earlier years, they were seen as good students who may not have finished assignments, but did well anyway. At the time of referral, the gifted boy seems unmotivated. Grades are erratic and are related to how well the boy likes the subject, the teacher, the time of year, and other external factors since performance waxes and wanes. As the boy struggles to bring up grades in one subject, grades in others fall. The boy gives many excuses for this but does not recognize that he is unable to provide the consistent effort across the board to achieve success in all subjects. Procrastination is a big piece of the problem as well. Given a deadline for a project, the boy waits until the night before to start, even if the project clearly requires several days' efforts. Amazingly, much of the time the boy pulls it off, gets the project done, gets a passing but not especially good grade, and vows next time he'll do more ahead of time. But, like all his promises, it's soon forgotten.

A TYPICAL PRESENTATION OF GIFTED GIRLS WITH AD/HD

On the whole, gifted girls with AD/HD often present differently than gifted boys. Gifted girls are less likely to be hyperactive in elementary years, and more likely to compensate because they are so bright. They are less likely to be noticed as having any difficulties. In worst-case scenarios, very gifted girls who are not hyperactive, but have AD/HD Inattentive Type, may appear average in achievement. Sometimes, symptoms appear minimal in gifted girls until they reach puberty. At that time, symptoms of AD/HD may increase (Nadeau *et al.* 1999). Certainly, as school work becomes more complex in upper grades, deficits in executive functions may be more of a problem for girls who have previously relied on their memory and rapid learning without having to study.

Gifted girls with AD/HD may initially present with symptoms of vague unhappiness and lack of stimulation in school, but they also can present symptoms that mask the AD/HD, such as anxiety and depression. Practitioners who are less familiar with how AD/HD may manifest in girls may miss the underlying AD/HD and treat only the depression or anxiety. This is especially the case for girls first developing symptoms of underachievement and depression in middle-school or high-school years. In cases of presenting depression and anxiety, an evaluation of those symptoms needs to be done first. Only when depression and anxiety have decreased can a more formal assessment be undertaken if questions about attention deficits, learning problems, executive functions, memory, or processing still persist.

Gifted girls who have AD/HD Combined Type do show hyperactivity but may show less disruptiveness than boys. These gifted girls can be highly energetic, creative, restless, and fidgety. They often talk a lot to peers and may engage more in social interactions than in completing school work, especially when the school work is repetitive or too easy. This type of gifted girl with AD/HD has many of the same problems as gifted boys with AD/HD in managing and self-monitoring behavior, but she is less likely to get into trouble.

GIFTED CHILDREN WITH ATTENTION DEFICITS AND NVLD

These gifted children often initially present symptoms of disorganization and inattention. Difficulties with slow work speed, poor planning of tasks, and not following directions are often given as presenting symptoms. These children drift off in the middle of a conversation, forget what they are doing in the middle of a game, and do everything very slowly. School work takes them a long time, and they don't complete it because the amount of energy they have to devote to work seems much less than other children. It takes them a long time to start, to continue, and to end each task. Along with this, they are forgetful, lose things, and seem overloaded by too much of anything. Gifted children with NVLD may also present symptoms of perfectionism and obsessiveness, along with rigidity and absentmindedness. They have difficulty with changing course when presented with obstacles, often only see one solution to a problem, and insist they are right even when they can be proven wrong. Underlying problems of missing the big picture and being too concrete and literal also are evident. Most children with NVLD have some social skill deficits, and these can vary from mild problems with timing to the severe problems associated with AS.

Like other children with AD/HD or AS, those with additional NVLD may be very verbose. They talk on and on without saying very much, and ignore the saliency of the topic to the question or occasion. A high percentage of children with AD/HD and NVLD also appear anxious and/or depressed.

A TYPICAL PRESENTATION OF GIFTED CHILDREN WITH AS

Gifted children with AS typically present symptoms of difficulties with social skills and social awareness. They are socially inept, have few or no friends, and act inappropriately in social situations. However, especially when the child is younger – for example, prior to 3rd-grade – presenting symptoms may reflect more concerns about uncooperative behavior than about social deficits. This is because preschool gifted children with AS may not yet stand out as so different from age peers in play skills, especially on a busy playground. In fact, if the child has a good imagination and can involve age peers in acting out fantasy, he or she may even appear to be a leader. It is only later that the lack of reciprocity and difficulty understanding social cues become more apparent.

Presenting symptoms often include uncooperative behavior at home and at school, rigid thinking, need for sameness and routine, rigid adherence to routines, peculiar or narrow interests, and difficulty going with the flow of things at home or school. Presenting symptoms of children with AS focus on poor interpersonal relationships, lack of reciprocity, lack of social engagement, poor communication skills, preoccupation with particular interests, motor clumsiness, and sensory integration deficits, in addition to deficits in executive functions.

The initial visit

The initial visit is vitally important in determining the extent of evaluation needed. That is, the initial concerns reported by the parents and the observations made during the first visit become a means of determining what else needs to be answered about this child. Thus, it is important to find out if behavior observed is typical of the child. How the parents perceive behavior is also important. Do they see it as typical of a child of that age or as an indication of a problem? What about the child's teachers? What do they report about achievement and behavior?

A child who acts very differently in the test situation than either at home or school may be anxious, and it is important to know this. Sometimes, though, a child will choose an initial visit to reveal problems that were not suspected previously, such as abuse; thus, behavior needs to be looked at not only in context, but also as a possible message about the child's problems and feelings.

THE INITIAL INTERVIEW

One of the most helpful sources of information about gifted children is the initial interview with the parents and a play interview with the child. Previous researchers have valued the amount and types of information gained by both informal and formal interviews with parents (Feldman and Goldsmith 1986; Gross 1993; Hollingworth 1942; Silverman 1993b). These authors have collected a wealth of information on preschool gifted children that suggests that parents are well able to document early advanced developmental progress in their children. Certainly, young gifted children's advanced skills in language, reading, and general development usually continue to be as advanced in later years.

In the case of young children from disadvantaged backgrounds, parent information often provided insight into children's skills that could not have been obtained from other sources (Borland, Schnur, and Wright 2000; Borland and Wright 1994; Wright and Borland 1993).

INFORMATION GATHERING

Direct history taking provides information about the developmental history of the child. This may consist of an oral question and answer period, or a set of written questions to which the parents and teachers can respond. Information on birth history, early infant behavior, attainment of developmental milestones, temperament, language development, presence of early academic skills, and indications of curiosity, imagination, and empathy should be assessed. A medical/physical history (including number of ear infections, strep infections, allergies and medications taken, previous accidents and illnesses, history of any abuse, current physical status, and level of motor coordination), history of social functioning, and previous school history also will be needed.

Observations of the child and parents would include aspects of interpersonal relationships such as eye contact, communication skills, spontaneous interest in others, offering to show others an interest, ability to listen to and tolerate another's point of view, ability to hold a simple conversation, ability to use prosocial skills such as turn waiting, not interrupting, sharing, etc. In addition, emotional reactivity, dependence/independence, introversion/extroversion, play skills, imagination, and curiosity should all be assessed by observation of the child interacting with parents, examiner, and play materials. A practitioner can learn much about how a child deals with such aspects as winning and losing, understanding of strategy versus luck, memory skills, and social skills by use of play or art materials. During this time, a mental status evaluation also will occur. This is an evaluation of expressive language ability, concentration, level of vocabulary use, affect, self-control, and emotional and social functioning.

Outside information in the form of copies of school report cards, samples of children's school work (including their best and most problematic pieces), and copies of previous standardized testing from schools or from previous evaluations is needed. These all give information about how the child has functioned over the years and are, therefore, part of the history taking.

A portfolio constructed by the parents and child of the child's best work, interests, and talents is a useful adjunct. These materials would consist of representative samples of the child's art work, writing, and other enjoyed activities. Children can bring pictures of their Lego constructions, small pieces of sculpture, models they have built, and designs they have developed. Also, audio and short video tapes of the child performing music pieces, dance, or acting can be viewed. All of this material gives a picture of the child at his or her best, doing what is most interesting and enjoyable. A contrast of the levels of these pieces with what is obtained in testing can point out problems, as well as special areas of strength.

Structured inventories can provide information from parents and teachers about the development and interests of gifted children. Osborn (1998) developed an adaptation of the Deslisle Questionnaire that covers questions about how children feel about themselves, their friends, and their abilities. Silverman (1993b) developed a checklist to help parents determine if their children may be gifted. At the Gifted Resource Center of New England, a multipage questionnaire is given to parents to fill out, with the suggestion of using anecdotes whenever possible. From this questionnaire comes a wealth of information about the child not easily obtained anywhere else. Information ranges from favorite activities and skills to moral and spiritual issues.

How much testing to do?

A full assessment, including testing of cognitive, achievement, learning and memory, executive functions, auditory and visual processing skills, and emotional and social functioning, is quite expensive and can take several days. The question then arises if all of this needs to be done. The answer is complicated. How much testing needs to be done is determined by the questions to be answered. An assessment of AD/HD or AS, for an average child, can often be made using a structured interview, checklists, and observations. However, such an assessment will not answer questions about the level of cognitive functioning, or if there are learning disabilities. In particular, with gifted children, assessments do need to focus on level of cognitive ability and whether the child has, in addition to AD/HD or AS, learning disabilities since these are not easily diagnosed by observation or through a simple IQ or achievement test. Also, it is not always clear from a simple assessment using an interview, observations, and checklists whether a gifted child has AD/HD (or sometimes AS). The brighter the child, the more likely it is that it will be difficult to diagnose the underlying causes of problems at school and home. Thus, gifted children often do require more assessment than more average children.

A PLAN OF ACTION

A plan should be developed by the end of the initial visit. It should include decisions about what questions the parents want answered by the assessment and what instruments and observations will best decide the answer. How much testing, how long it will likely take, and the estimated cost should be discussed and made clear. Parents will need to contact insurance companies to see if the assessment will be covered and if they need to arrange for preauthorization. They should also ask their insurance company how many hours of assessment and what types of assessment are covered, since most insurance companies only cover tests that lead to mental health diagnoses; usually they will not cover the academic part of testing. Many companies will not cover practitioners outside of their own network. Parents need to be aware that they are responsible for the cost of testing unless a specific contract is otherwise made. For example, some school systems will pay part of the cost as an independent evaluation of children who have or possibly need Individual Educational Plans.

It should also be noted that some problems only become evident in the course of actual assessment. For example, some children come for intellectual assessment to help determine what type of academic environment would be best for them since they are bored and unhappy with the current arrangement. In the course of the assessment, difficulty with concentration, poor organization and planning, difficulty with self-monitoring of behavior, and difficulties with memory can be noted that warrant further evaluation. A child may appear to show a problem with visual-perception or visual-motor skills. It may become evident that a child has trouble listening to long, complex sentences or with word retrieval. All of this would require further testing to assess.

The evaluation of gifted children with attention deficits

The evaluation of gifted children differs in some respects from the evaluation of more average children. Gifted children's higher-level abstract reasoning ability, ability to see things globally, and breadth of knowledge all mean that more time and somewhat different materials need to be used in testing. In this section of this chapter, various issues about testing gifted children will be described.

- *Ceilings.* Because gifted children know so much, their evaluations will include more material: that is, they will reach material usually administered to older children. By age 10 or 11, they may not reach stopping criteria but instead run out of items. This limits the amount of information that may be obtained from some tests because the child reaches the ceiling too quickly. This may limit an accurate assessment of strengths and relative weaknesses.

- *Testing time.* Another aspect of testing gifted children is the length of time assessment takes. Intelligence tests that typically take an hour for an average child can take much longer for a gifted child because the gifted child answers so many more questions. For gifted children who are slower, more reflective thinkers, testing time may be more than double, and fatigue may become a factor. Also, gifted children with attention deficits may not show typical patterns on IQ tests. It depends on how the total testing time is broken up. For example, the novelty of the tasks and the one-on-one attention can keep some children with AD/HD focused, especially if the examiner breaks the testing time into several short sessions as occurs in many school settings. Thus, examiners have to evaluate long enough so that the child actually has to focus under less than ideal conditions. Then, deficits may appear.

- *Extent of knowledge.* It is important to be sure that gifted children have actually reached the limit of their knowledge. If the test chosen is too easy, or has too low a ceiling, the extent of the child's ability may not be determined. Gifted children with attention deficits may miss many easier items but get more difficult ones correct. If a strict stopping criteria is used, the child will not show the extent of ability. What is really being measured, then, is not knowledge or ability, but the attention span of the child. Thus, it is important to test to the point that it is certain that the child really cannot do any more items. For example, on one test, Perry correctly completed 15 (out of 23) more items after the stopping point. Had the testing stopped at the stopping point, Perry would have obtained a score in the severely below average range rather than a score in the superior range. Which score is more representative of Perry's ability? Well, if he really was incapable, he would not have been able to complete more difficult items. Thus, the second score is the more accurate assessment of his *ability*. The first score, though, gives the examiner important information about Perry's *executive functions*, especially how he may perform at times on standardized tests, when he is not paying attention, and when he has to work within a time limit.

- *Elaboration of material.* Because gifted children can be knowledgeable about so many areas, they tend to assume that adults are as knowledgeable. Thus, they may give telescoped answers because they assume the examiner will know what they mean. It can be difficult to get this type of child to elaborate on responses. To them, they have already told you the answer, and they don't see why you want more. In these cases it is important to explain testing parameters to the child, such as how much material is needed to get a score. It also can be helpful to get the child to give an example and then explain the example, or to pretend the examiner is a Martian and does not understand. Some gifted children also become stuck on one way of responding and will simply repeat their answer if asked for another reason, more information, or clarification. It can be difficult to assess what this type of child really does know. However, others show a pattern of vague responses that slowly become more focused and, if pressed, the child will suddenly blurt out the correct answer all at once with good elaboration. Often this occurs as the next question is read. Thus, it is important not to accept the first vague answer as the final answer if the child shows evidence of higher-level ability on other items. Diagnostically, a rigid child and one who answers as the next question is read have very different underlying deficits, even though both have trouble elaborating.

- *Level of difficulty.* Many young, exceptionally bright children feel insulted by being asked very easy material. Some don't understand that the material is so easy and look for the trick. They answer that they don't know because it really does not occur to them that the examiner is asking such an easy question. Thus, Bobby, age seven, a profoundly gifted boy described in Chapter 1, could not respond to an easy question about how to make water boil. All he had to answer was "Put it on a stove," or "Heat it." Bobby, however, was unsure what was being asked, so he didn't answer. Later, when asked about the phenomenon of boiling, he was able to describe the process and give an accurate account of what made water actually boil.

  If, prior to testing, it is explained to the child that some of the material will be "easy, baby questions," then when the child is stuck, a reminder that this is one of those easy questions may help the child to realize that an obvious answer is what is wanted.

- *Use of incentives.* In evaluating gifted children many will be delighted to be tested, and will have fun showing what they know. On the other hand, very young children and those with AD/HD, AS, or other problems may be less than delighted to perform. Using incentives, such as points for trying hard that will translate to a small reward at the end of testing, is very helpful in motivating the more reluctant child. So is having a break partway through with the chance to eat a special snack brought from home.

Intellectual assessment

In this section of this chapter, intelligence testing in general and the various IQ tests used with gifted children will be discussed.

Most intelligence tests in use today give several scores that help to pinpoint cognitive areas of strength and weakness. Variations among scores within a test, and among scores for different tests, give a picture of abilities in different areas. Intelligence tests can be a good measure, all other things being equal, of a person's ability to reason abstractly. However, there are a number of reasons why intelligence tests might not show a person's true ability. For example, the test may not measure the person's areas of strength adequately. Other reasons include fatigue, lack of interest in the task, slow cognitive processing on timed tasks, lack of experience with the type of test items used, lack of education and lack of opportunity to achieve skills, poor attention, anxiety, lack of rapport, and extreme immaturity or youth so that the child does not realize the importance of the set of tasks and cannot respond adequately. Even shyness with strangers can decrease scores, as can depression and peer pressure not to look too smart. Consequently, a score may be low for many reasons other than that the child is incapable. For that reason, on intelligence tests that break tasks down into domains, Borland and Wright (1994) suggested that the highest score is most likely the best estimate of ability. On tests that include factor scores, the highest factor score is the best estimate. This is especially important to bear in mind with gifted children with AD/HD, AS, and other learning and behavioral problems. Using this score as a basis, scores in weaker areas can be compared to give a better picture of the cognitive strengths and weaknesses of that particular child. Then, a plan that encompasses both strengths and weaknesses can be drawn up.

Ranges of intelligence have been developed for most tests clustering around a mean of 100. Depending on the Standard Deviation (how much variability the population shows), subdivisions of average (90 to 110), above average (110 to 120), superior (120 to 130) and very superior (130+) are made for scores at or above the mean. A similar division occurs for scores below the mean. Recently, as more children have been discovered in the very superior category, this has also been further delineated into mildly gifted (120 to 139), moderately or highly gifted (140 to 159), exceptionally gifted (160 to 179) and profoundly gifted (180+). Osborn (1999) listed slightly different ranges, as does Gross (1993).

A child in the IQ 180 range is as different from one in the 130 range, as a child in the low average range (IQ 80) is from a gifted child in the 130 range. To assess the potential of children above IQ 160, the Stanford-Binet LM has been the only assessment instrument that has been able to differentiate among levels of giftedness; however, the Stanford-Binet 5 will also do so in the Interpretive Manual.

Out-of-level testing for children, using tests usually administered at older ages, can be advantageous in expanding the ceiling for extremely bright students. Some of the older IQ tests allowed young children to progress as high as they could, even through adult levels. This is not the case with most modern IQ tests. Thus, use of tests such as the SCAT (School and College Ability Tests) or PLUS tests for elementary-age children, and the Scholastic Aptitude Tests (SATs) for middle-school students through the Johns Hopkins University, Duke University, University of Washington, and other Talent Searches, can provide information about the extent of verbal and quantitative abilities. Each of these tests has particular strengths and weaknesses that are important to know when testing gifted children. A review of the use of out-of-level testing can be found in Stanley, Keating and Fox (1974).

The Wechsler Intelligence Scales

The Wechsler Intelligence Scales have a long history of use in the United States, as well as other countries. There are editions in several languages other than English including Spanish and Chinese. The test is divided into two main subareas: verbal and performance. Verbal items are those that are administered verbally and require verbal responses. The performance items are administered using a verbal explanation and demonstration, and the response required is performance based: putting together puzzles, assembling block design patterns. The Wechsler tests include: the Wechsler Preschool and Primary Scale of Intelligence (WPPSI), the Wechsler Intelligence Scale for Children (WISC), and the Wechsler Adult Intelligence Scale (WAIS). The Wechsler Abbreviated Scale of Intelligence (WASI), a four scale brief test, covers ages six to 89.

The different Wechsler tests for different age groups tend to be similar in their advantages and disadvantages because of similar construction. Each age group also brings particular sets of advantages and disadvantages to each test.

The *Wechsler Preschool and Primary Scale of Intelligence – Third Edition* (WPPSI-III), the most recent revision, has two levels: for children ages two years through three years, 11 months, and ages four through age seven years three months. The new revision has three verbal and three performance subtests at each age level. For the older group, the core Verbal subtests are Information, Vocabulary, and Word Reasoning. Also, there are several supplementary tests that can be included in the assessment. For the older age group these include: Comprehension, Similarities, Receptive Vocabulary and Picture Naming. The core Performance subtests include Block Design, Matrix Reasoning, and Picture Concepts. Supplementary subtests include Symbol Search, Picture Completion, and Object Assembly. One of the verbal and one of the performance supplementary subtests can be substituted for a core subtest to determine the Full Scale IQ (FSIQ) Score.

Advantages are that the test has a long history of use and has been normed with minority and disadvantaged children. Its items are attractive to young children and the practice of varying verbal with performance subtests allows for decreasing boredom and maintaining interest. The testing time for the most recent revision has been considerably shortened, so it is easier to test small children quickly, and the previous reliance on bonus points for speed to achieve higher performance scores has been eliminated.

Disadvantages include the use of fewer subtests to determine the scores. Since the examiner may substitute one supplementary verbal and one supplementary performance subtest to form the FSIQ, depending on which subtests are chosen, FSIQ can vary. The new core subtests may be useful, but until they have been used diagnostically in clinical settings and compared to previous material used to assess functioning, they are an unknown quantity. Also, the verbal subtests that have been relegated to supplementary status were useful in assessing young gifted children's language and verbal reasoning skills. In testing gifted children, the loss of subtests which measured abstract verbal reasoning ability at high levels (Similarities and Comprehension) is important. Also, the Sentence Memory subtest from the previous edition has been eliminated and thus there is less ability to assess verbal memory. Another disadvantage is that young gifted children near the age limit of the test (after age five and a half or six) can reach test ceiling: that is, run out of items before reaching stopping points (usually so many incorrect). This means the child's potential will not be adequately tapped by the test.

Julia Osborn, who has extensive experience in assessing young gifted children, has suggested that examiners who test young gifted children should not administer the WPPSI-III to children over age six because the items in many of the subtests are too easy. For example, there are not enough difficult designs on the Block Design test. She further suggested that examiners of all children, gifted or more average, administer Comprehension as a measure of ability to use expressive language. For gifted children between ages four and six, she suggested that the supplementary tests (Similarities, Comprehension, and Object Assembly) all be administered, as well as a test of sentence memory, in order to more fully assess children's skills (Julia Osborn, personal communication, January 21, 2003).

The *Wechsler Intelligence Scale for Children –Third Edition* (WISC-III) is the test used most often with gifted children, ages six through 17. In addition to the FSIQ score and the scores for the verbal area (VIQ) and performance area (PIQ) there are four further factor scores: Verbal Comprehension, Freedom from Distractibility, Perceptual Organization, and Processing Speed. In addition, each of the main subareas is further subdivided into a number of subtests.

On the WISC-III, the verbal subtests include Information, Similarities, Arithmetic, Vocabulary, Comprehension, and Digit Span. The performance subtests include Picture Completion, Coding, Picture Arrangement, Block Design, Object Assembly, Symbol Search, and Mazes. Digit Span, Symbol

Search, and Mazes are not included in the overall IQ scores as they are considered supplemental tests.

The main advantages of the WISC-III are its good standardization sample using minority and diverse socioeconomic groupings, and its appeal to a wide variety of children. It also is constructed in such a way that scores can be easily compared to standardized tests of achievement. Furthermore, its alternating verbal and performance format helps children to maintain interest through the entire administration. Administration time is not onerous for most elementary or middle-school age children.

The disadvantages of the WISC-III in testing gifted children are several. The extreme use of awarded bonus points for speed of response on five performance subtests, and one verbal subtest, penalizes children who are reflective thinkers, have difficulties sustaining attention and concentration, have motor-construction difficulties, or tend to be less willing to take risks, and so are slower to respond to unknown tasks.

It is also more difficult to ascertain the meaning of test scatter for gifted children: that is, the amount that scores vary from each other. Current research suggests that both larger than usual verbal versus performance discrepancies, and differences between highest and lowest subtest scores, are more common for gifted than average children (Fishkin, Kampsnider, and Pack 1996; Webb and Dyer 1993) on both the older WISC-R and the WISC-III. When assessing more average children, discrepancies between verbal and performance scores, discrepancies from the mean score for subtest scores, and subtest scatter from highest to lowest scores are often used as the basis of suggesting attention and/or learning problems. Thus, with gifted children, the discrepancy alone is not sufficient to suggest there is a problem; on the other hand, with very large discrepancies, the chances that lowest scores are significant areas of weakness rises, and this suggests the need for further evaluation in an individual.

Because there are so many issues around the efficacy of bonus points and the problems of unusually large test scatter for gifted children, it is recommended that the highest score obtained be used as a determinant of giftedness. Thus, VIQ (Verbal IQ), VC (Verbal Comprehension Factor), PIQ (Performance IQ), or PO (Perceptual Organization Factor) may be a better estimate of ability than the FSIQ. This is particularly the case with large VIQ and PIQ differences. Thus a child who scores VIQ 144, PIQ 100, and FSIQ 126, with VC 148 and PO 116, is likely best described by using the VC score to describe potential. The discrepancies from this score, especially on the performance side, bear further examination. They may be indications of perceptual or attention difficulties, but could also be indications of nothing more than a slower, more reflective thinker who does not respond well to timed items.

The *Wechsler Intelligence Scale for Children – Fourth Edition* (WISC-IV) was released in 2003. Test descriptions (and a phone discussion with Psychological Corporation's representative) suggest that it is a somewhat different test than the WISC-III. Several subtests have been eliminated (Mazes and Picture Arrangement) and some previous subtests are available as supplements only (Arithmetic and Information). New subtests such as Word Reasoning, Matrix Reasoning, Picture Concepts, Letter–Number Sequencing, and Cancellation have been added. Some of the new subtests assess working memory and processing speed in more complex ways than on the WISC-III. In the next two to three years, while the new test is being evaluated by clinicians and compared in research studies to the older version, the WISC-III will likely continue to be used by many clinicians.

The Kaufman Tests

The *Kaufman Assessment Battery for Children* (K-ABC) has a large standardization sample that follows the US census in both socioeconomic levels and ethnicity of subjects. The test is designed to assess children within a small testing range of items so that most children stop being tested when the stopping point for their age is reached. If all items are passed, however, testing continues until the first error is made. This testing method allows for a relatively less frustrating sample of tasks for most children, but may penalize those gifted children who are inattentive and miss easier items. Also, while much of the test is untimed, it is heavily dependent on nonverbal skills. Only in the achievement area are verbal skills heavily weighted. Thus, this test is much better for children who have language problems, or are non-English speaking, but it does little to identify the particular strengths of gifted children with high verbal abstract reasoning ability. Morelock and Feldman (1992) suggested that the K-ABC is an inadequate instrument for assessing the abilities of most gifted children.

The *Kaufman Brief Intelligence Scale* utilizes two measures of vocabulary and visual matrices to assess ability. Kaufman offers it as a brief screening for eligibility to gifted programs. While each subtest is highly correlated with general intelligence, many other areas are not evaluated, such as verbal reasoning ability or quantitative reasoning. Thus, use of the Kaufman needs to be supplemented by other measures.

The *Kaufman Adolescent and Adult Intelligence Test* does not measure the more traditional skills and abilities measured by children's tests or other tests available for adults. Verbal analogies, vocabulary, similarities, verbal comprehension, matrices, quantitative reasoning, number series, and short-term memory items are often seen as best measures of intelligence. Kaufman's test looks interesting in its reliance on inferential reasoning, convergent thinking, immediate learning, applications to problem solving, and deductive reasoning. Supplementary tests measure short-term memory. However, it may be difficult to compare results, in terms of similar abilities, to other tests of intelligence or to tests taken during childhood years.

The Stanford-Binet Intelligence Scales

The Stanford-Binet Intelligence Scales have a long and venerable history in the testing of gifted children beginning with Terman's (1925) famous study and including Hollingworth's (1942) studies of exceptionally gifted children. The Stanford-Binet Fourth Edition is a revision of the 1960 version of the older Stanford-Binet Form LM; however, it is really a very different type of test, following more the modern tendency to divide tests into a number of factors rather than a single IQ score. The Stanford-Binet 5 continues the modern idea of several types of intelligence, and the use of several factor scores.

The *Stanford-Binet Intelligence Scale – Fourth Edition* (SB-IV) has four main factors: Verbal Reasoning, Visual/Abstract Reasoning, Quantitative, and Short-Term Memory. Depending on the questions being asked by the evaluation, subtests can be selected to show different types of abilities. These can be combined in a variety of ways to obtain a composite score. The test measures intelligence from age two to young adulthood, though not equally well at all ages. Indeed, for the youngest and oldest children, test scores are not very reliable due to problems with the test itself. For example, with the youngest children, under age four, the materials are less attractive and even confusing. The test directions are not very clear and the test is too long. Nevertheless, a shortened test (three verbal tests, Bead Memory, and Memory for Sentences) was effective in identifying preschool children for gifted programs (Kitano and De Leon 1988).

At the older ages, children may finish all the items without reaching the stopping point. This means the test ceiling, the highest obtainable score, differs at different ages. By late adolescence, the ceiling is much lower, and the highest possible overall score obtainable is 151, compared with 164 in preadolescence.

Other disadvantages of the SB-IV include ceiling effects for some very gifted children, by age seven, on some of the most valuable subtests, such as Pattern Analysis, a block design test. Some tasks, like Copying, may also depress scores of primary-age children with visual-motor deficits who are otherwise exceptionally capable. While at younger ages, there is validity in the reproduction of geometric figures as a measure of intelligence, visual-motor copying at older ages and with handicapped children is less valid. Certainly, experience in testing hundreds of gifted children at the Gifted Resource Center of New England suggests that the majority tend to have more average visual-motor skills no matter what their other skill levels are.

The biggest problem with the SB-IV is the loss of valuable information that had been tapped by the older Stanford-Binet LM in the area of verbal abstract reasoning. The Similarities and Differences, Verbal Absurdities, and Proverbs all provided insight into how children think and what level of abstraction they can use. The newer Binets (and all the Wechsler tests) lacks this useful delineation.

Despite its disadvantages though, the SB-IV has many advantages when used appropriately. It is largely untimed, and so reflective thinkers are not placed at a disadvantage as they are on the Wechsler tests. The SB-IV has some unusual subtests in the Quantitative and Abstract/Visual Reasoning realms. For the gifted child who is a visual-spatial thinker, the SB-IV allows exploration of visual-spatial strengths with tasks such as Pattern Analysis, Matrices, Paper Folding and Cutting, Absurdities, Bead Memory, and Memory for Objects. It also allows more exploration of mathematical ability with Quantitative Reasoning, Number Series, and Equation Building tests. The biggest advantage though is the fact that the examiner can choose which subtests to use, can go above the child's age to explore advanced ability, and can go beyond the stopping point if the child seems knowledgeable since every correct answer counts. This allows examiners to know when a child really has reached a ceiling rather than being limited by poor attention or impulsivity.

There are many difficult items that can tap abilities. If a young child achieves beyond the highest norms listed, an approximate age-equivalent score can still be obtained for some raw scores by using page 136 of the supplementary manual. This allows an approximate measure of exceptional ability for young children.

The *Stanford-Binet Intelligence Scale – Fifth Edition* (SB-5) was released in 2003. Some of the subtests from SB-IV, as well as from the older Stanford-Binet Form LM, have been incorporated into this version; others have not been. This revision is divided into verbal and nonverbal realms. There are five factor scores: Fluid Reasoning, Knowledge, Quantitative Reasoning, Visual-Spatial Processing, and Working Memory. Each of these is composed of both verbal and nonverbal tests. Which tests are administered depends on age, as the test progresses from age two through age 85+. The use of routing and starting points, stopping criteria, and ceiling criteria keeps the testing time within reasonable bounds for most people. How well the new SB-5 will compare to the older versions in identifying gifted children, and in serving as a clinical instrument, remains to be seen. It is supposed to supplant previous versions. The Interpretive Manual includes a method of assessing IQs below 40 and above 160 with the highest obtainable score IQ 225+. If this is a good enough test, it will replace the need to test further on the outdated Stanford-Binet LM when a child reaches test ceiling. Whether this will be the case or not, though, will only be determined after the test has been in use for a while.

On the positive side, gifted children from several areas of the country served as part of the standardization sample. In fact, 33 children from the Gifted Resource Center of New England were part of the standardization sample. These included gifted children with AD/HD, gifted children with AS, and profoundly gifted children.

Some of the subtests from previous versions of the Stanford-Binet not repeated in SB-5 may be useful to examiners of gifted children, particularly for those children who are exceptionally gifted, or who have possible disabilities. Subtests that might be used as an adjunct include (from the Stanford-Binet LM) Proverbs, Similarities and Differences, and Vocabulary. For some children who are visual-spatial learners, subtests from the SB-IV can be a useful adjunct: Pattern Analysis, Paper Folding and Cutting, Equation Building, Bead Memory, and Memory for Objects. Continued use of tests of auditory sequential memory such as Memory for Digits and Memory for Sentences also may prove useful as adjuncts to the very difficult working memory subtests on the SB-5.

The *Stanford-Binet Form LM* has been useful as a supplementary test for those children who reach ceiling on other intelligence scales. This is because it has a much higher ceiling. It was designed initially to test the abilities of average adults as well as children. Thus, there are many more difficult items for very bright children. The way the test is designed also allows out-of-level testing: that is, beyond the norms listed in the test manual. Other advantages include a gradual increase in skills needed as the child continues through the test, a mix of items so that the child does not get bored with a long list of similar items to perform, and the use of attractive toys and materials for very young children, with very clear directions for even the youngest. The test covers a wide range of ability levels. Over the course of my career using the Stanford-Binet LM, the lowest IQ obtained by an individual was 10, the highest 230.

The biggest disadvantage in using the Stanford-Binet LM is the outdated norms, the newest of which are from 1972. Also, the test is very different from what modern-day examiners are used to; it doesn't have the same theoretical framework. Ethical considerations are also an issue. In general, psychologists are required to use the most recent edition of tests to obtain a valid assessment. However, it is not intrinsically unethical to use an older test if there is a good reason to do so. The American Psychological Association has given the opinion

(Rimm 1991, cited in Silverman and Kearney 1992) that determination of such use is up to the clinical judgment of the psychologist and should be based on why the test is needed. In the case of the Stanford-Binet LM, there will likely continue to be a need for its unique assessment of exceptional verbal ability until such time as another assessment instrument effectively measures verbal abstract reasoning as well as the Stanford Binet LM has through the years.

The Stanford-Binet LM is not a very good test for children who are less highly verbal, whether because they have auditory processing problems, hearing loss, speak another primary language, or just tend to be more visual-spatial in their abilities. Also, minority representation in the original standardization was minimal, though the 1972 norms do try to remedy this. On the other hand, African-American children with good verbal skills can do well on this test. Some of the original highest scoring children at the earlier part of the 20th century were African-American boys and girls (Kearney and LeBlanc 1993). Despite these disadvantages, the Stanford-Binet LM will continue to hold some advantages for assessing exceptional verbal reasoning ability when used as a supplement to other more recently normed tests.

Which test to use?

Decisions about which is the best test to use to evaluate intelligence depend on both the developmental history taken from the parents and the purpose for which the evaluation is being done. Children with a history of verbal precocity, early reading ability, and a large fund of general knowledge will likely do well on both the Wechsler tests and the Stanford-Binets in elementary and middle-school years. On the other hand, due to the timed nature of the WISC-III, it is not the first choice for elementary-school age children who are reflective thinkers, slow to respond, or have motor coordination problems or attention deficits. In these cases, use of the Stanford-Binet tests has been more effective in delineating children's strengths. The newest versions of both the Wechsler and Stanford-Binet will need to be assessed over time to determine best use for different populations.

It should also be noted that professionals who test children often base use of a particular test instrument on their own experience and comfort. Many who have not previously assessed gifted children do not know the differences among tests. These psychologists may not select a test based on obtaining a best view of the child's strengths and weaknesses, but rather on familiarity with a particular test. Thus, some will use the K-ABC because that is what they most often use with young children in their clinic, and these instruments offer invaluable information about average children. However, they are not adequate assessment instruments for the gifted.

For example, Max, age eight, was administered the K-ABC and scored a Sequential Scale Score of 93, a Simultaneous Scale Score of 114, and a Mental Processing Composite of 106, all within the average range. Testing on the WISC-III a few months later showed a VIQ of 143 (very superior), PIQ of 100 (average), and FSIQ of 125 (superior). Since Max had three WISC-III scaled scores over 17 (vocabulary, similarities and comprehension), at age nine years four months he was administered the Stanford-Binet LM and scored IQ 172, in the exceptionally gifted range. Had Max's parents listened to the first psychologist, who told them they had an average child with no special needs, he would have experienced even more frustration in school than he did. As it was, programming for Max was difficult, but he was able to be advanced in several areas and also to receive some help in areas of weakness. Max was an exceptionally gifted boy with AD/HD whose slower processing decreased scores on the K-ABC as well as on the Performance part of the WISC. Despite his difficulties, Max will likely start college with several Advanced Placement (AP) course credits as he is already taking advanced courses in high school. Thus, it is really important in assessing gifted children to be knowledgeable about the testing instruments, as well as about how gifted children differ from more average peers.

BRETT'S INTELLECTUAL ASSESSMENT

Brett's assessment started with the WISC-III. He obtained the scores shown in Figure 9.1.

WECHSLER INTELLIGENCE SCALE
FOR CHILDREN – REVISION III

FULL SCALE IQ	SS	130	Very Superior
VERBAL IQ		133	Very Superior
VERBAL COMPREHENSION		137	Very Superior
FREEDOM FROM DISTRACTIBILITY		101	Average
PERFORMANCE IQ		120	Superior
PERCEPTUAL ORGANIZATION		122	Superior
PROCESSING SPEED		106	Average

VERBAL		PERFORMANCE	
SUBTEST	SCALED SCORE	SUBTEST	SCALED SCORE
Information	15	Picture Completion	15
Similarities	16	Coding	11
Arithmetic	12	Picture Arrangement	9
Vocabulary	17	Block Design	15
Comprehension	18	Object Assembly	15
(Digit Span)	(8)	(Symbol Search)	(11)

Scaled Scores of 9 to 11, average; scores of 6 or less, below average; 15+, very superior

STANFORD-BINET INTELLIGENCE SCALE FORM LM

IQ 149

Figure 9.1 Intelligence test scores for Brett

Brett scored, overall, an FSIQ in the very superior or gifted range. He scored in the very superior range on Information, Similarities, Vocabulary, Comprehension, Picture Completion, Block Design, and Object Assembly. Brett was good at recalling information, at comparing two concepts and telling how they are alike (water and orange juice, for example), defining words, understanding social norms (what would someone do if they see a fire, or why should a person not tell a lie), finding missing details in pictures, making designs with blocks, and assembling puzzles. Brett was more average on mental arithmetic, copying symbols quickly, rapidly scanning to find similar symbols, and arranging pictures in order to tell a story. He was low average on recalling sequences of digits.

The examiner would also observe Brett's behavior during testing to assess if he paid attention, whether he used strategies to approach problems, how concise his answers were, and whether he went off on tangents; this would help the examiner determine if further testing was warranted. In this case, Brett was noted to forget what he was saying and lose his train of thought. He needed questions and directions repeated several times. He tended to trail off on his verbal answers and needed to be refocused to complete them. While he was quite quick and accurate on some of the performance tasks, he had trouble with organizing his approach on others.

What Brett's testing protocol suggested was some difficulties with doing timed items quickly and accurately, holding information in mind, sequencing, and attention. His Freedom from Distractibility score – an indication of difficulty with attention, auditory short-term memory, and auditory sequencing – was only average. Also, there was a difference between his total score for the verbal side and the score for the performance side of 13 points. The difference between the scores for verbal comprehension and perceptual organization was 15 points, which is significant. However, Brett appeared to be slow in starting and performing timed tasks, and he did not earn many bonus points for speed. His score for perceptual speed was only average.

Brett's testing suggested that he might have an attention problem, but also could have difficulties with motor organization, motor planning, and speed. Brett could have AD/HD but, in addition, he could have a learning disability or processing problem. Thus, while suggestive of problems, the WISC-III alone did not give enough information to decide what really caused Brett's difficulties.

What the test did show quite well was that Brett was a gifted child with some difficulties. He also had two scores in the highly gifted range (Vocabulary and Comprehension) and might score in this range or higher on the Stanford-Binet LM. Brett also was good at reasoning on both verbal and nonverbal tasks.

MICHAEL'S INTELLECTUAL ASSESSMENT

Michael, like Brett, was administered a battery of tests to help pinpoint strengths and weaknesses, and to make a determination of the underlying problem. Like Brett, Michael was administered the WISC-III. Michael's results are in shown in Figure 9.2.

WECHSLER INTELLIGENCE SCALE
FOR CHILDREN – REVISION III

FULL SCALE IQ	SS	133	Very Superior
VERBAL IQ		139	Very Superior
VERBAL COMPREHENSION		136	Very Superior
FREEDOM FROM DISTRACTIBILITY		137	Very Superior
PERFORMANCE IQ		120	Superior
PERCEPTUAL ORGANIZATION		122	Superior
PROCESSING SPEED		109	Average

VERBAL		PERFORMANCE	
SUBTEST	SCALED SCORE	SUBTEST	SCALED SCORE
Information	17	Picture Completion	12
Similarities	17	Coding	11
Arithmetic	18	Picture Arrangement	18
Vocabulary	19	Block Design	15
Comprehension	12	Object Assembly	9
(Digit Span)	(15)	(Symbol Search)	(12)

Scaled Scores of 9 to 11, average; scores of 6 or less, below average; 15+, very superior

STANFORD-BINET INTELLIGENCE SCALE REVISION IV

	SAS SCORE
Absurdities	53
Pattern Analysis	67
Matrices	58
Number Series	74
Memory of Objects	53

Standard Age Score (SAS) of 44 to 55, average; 68+, very superior; 74+, highly gifted range

STANFORD-BINET INTELLIGENCE SCALE FORM LM

IQ 165

Figure 9.2 Intelligence test scores for Michael

Michael's WISC-III showed him to be a gifted child, scoring in the very superior range. However, his profile showed a significant difference between the verbal and performance scores of 19 points. Michael's areas of strength were in general information, knowledge of similarities, mental arithmetic, knowledge of words, memory for digits forward and in reverse, sequencing pictures to tell a story, and putting blocks together to make a design. His scores were all in the very superior range. Michael's areas of weakness were in knowledge of social norms, finding missing details in pictures, copying symbols quickly, putting together puzzles, and rapidly scanning material to find identical symbols. These scores were all in the average range, with Object Assembly (the puzzles) somewhat lower, in the low average range.

Michael's verbal scores were fairly high except for Comprehension, a test of social knowledge. Michael had inadequate answers for simple social questions such as what to do if you lose a friend's toy, or if someone teases you. Michael also became stuck on an answer and could not give another reason when a question asked for two. Thus, he became interested in discussing lightbulbs on one question and could not then get to the essence of the question. This type of tangential response to an aspect of the whole was typical of other areas of performance too.

On the performance side, Michael showed weaknesses on Coding and Symbol Search due to his slower motor speed in copying and his distractibility in searching for symbols. He had some trouble noting details in pictures, but his biggest problem was on Object Assembly. Michael had difficulty putting the puzzles together, and only was able to finish one of them. He appeared to have difficulty understanding how the parts might fit together to make the whole. What he did was to turn pieces over and around without much regard for the details printed on each piece.

Michael was also administered part of the SB-IV to evaluate some aspects of nonverbal performance that are not assessed by the WISC-III. Michael was administered the Pattern Analysis test. This Block Design task does not depend on speed to obtain a high score; however, Michael's performance was just about as good as on the WISC-III Block Design test. Michael scored about as well on Number Series as he had done on the WISC-III Arithmetic. Michael scored only average on a test of noting Absurdities in Pictures (what was silly about a picture of a girl skating on her hands, for example) and on a test of recalling a series of pictured objects. He was high average on a test of nonverbal reasoning, Matrices.

Michael's test profile suggested that he might have an attention problem, and deficits in visual-perceptual-motor functioning. Michael could have AD/HD but, in addition, he could have an NVLD, or processing problem. Thus, while suggestive of problems, the WISC-III alone did not give enough information to decide what really caused Michael's difficulties. Also, Michael's other problems in the area of social behavior were not addressed by the WISC-III evaluation.

What the test did show quite well was that Michael was a gifted child with some difficulties. Michael scored in the highly gifted range (SS 17+) on a number of subtests on the WISC-III including Information, Similarities, Arithmetic, Vocabulary, and Picture Arrangement. He was, thus, further assessed on the Stanford-Binet LM.

PATTERNS FOUND IN ASSESSMENT WITH THE WISC-III

Factor scores (Verbal Comprehension, Freedom from Distractibility, Perceptual Organization, and Processing Speed) have traditionally been used as a means of indicating AD/HD and/or learning disabilities. Each of the factors is composed of several subtests. The scores for Freedom from Distractibility (composed of Arithmetic and Digit Span) and Processing Speed (composed of Coding and Symbol Search) are most important in determining AD/HD. However, factor scores are not necessarily a valid indicator of problems for gifted children with AD/HD. For most children with AD/HD, Freedom from Distractibility plus Processing Speed is lower than the other two factor scores. In fact, research (Mayes *et al.* 1998) suggested that for average children with AD/HD, these two factor scores and the subtests that comprise them are the lowest scores. Furthermore, for about a quarter of children with AD/HD, Digit Span and Arithmetic are two of the three lowest subtests, something not found with average children who do not have AD/HD. Thus, for average children the Freedom from Distractibility score may be a good indicator of possible AD/HD, but is this the case for gifted children? Chae *et al.* (2003) found when comparing a sample of gifted Korean children with AD/HD with a sample of gifted children without AD/HD, the only significantly different score was Coding. Digit Span and Arithmetic did not differentiate the gifted samples.

Research at the Gifted Resource Center of New England (Lovecky 1999) analyzed the WISC-III and Stanford-Binet LM patterns of 250 gifted children with AD/HD tested at the Center. Results suggested that at least some of the time, gifted children can have AD/HD and still have Arithmetic, Digit Span, Coding, and Symbol Search scores in the highly gifted range; in fact, at times these scores are among the highest obtained by the child. The percentage of gifted children with at least one of those four scores in the highly gifted range (SS 17 or higher) was 50%. The percentage of gifted children with AD/HD with at least one of these four scores in the gifted range (SS 15 or higher) was 67%. On the other hand, the percentage of gifted children with one of these four scores just average is 50%, but only 25% of gifted children with AD/HD show two of their three lowest scores as some of these four. Brett followed a more usual pattern with Digit Span, Coding, and Symbol Search among his lowest scores. Picture Arrangement was also low, and was his second lowest score, not part of the usual pattern.

A pattern on WISC-III subtest scores found for some children with AS shows highest scores on Information, Similarities, Vocabulary, and Comprehension, with lowest scores on Arithmetic, Object Assembly, and Coding (Ehlers *et al.* 1997). Michael's profile was somewhat different from this with weaker Comprehension, and higher Arithmetic. He showed weaknesses on Coding and

Symbol Search. Object Assembly was his lowest score. Michael did exceptionally well on Arithmetic and Digit Span. These latter two were among his highest scores.

Areas of greatest strength on the WISC-III for the gifted children at the Gifted Resource Center of New England, were shown on Information, Similarities, Vocabulary, Comprehension, and Block Design. Also, a significant number were also very high on Arithmetic and Digit Span, like Michael. These latter children appeared to do so well on Freedom from Distractibility because they are especially drawn to numbers. These are the children who are exceptionally gifted in mathematical reasoning, computation, and problem solving. They often invent math for themselves and can solve unknown problems. Anything with numbers in it is recalled accurately and quickly. Thus, this group has no trouble with holding math in working memory or recalling long strings of digits. Some of these children are also able to recall long strings of letters as well. They appear to have strong memories for symbols in general.

Because research suggested that gifted children may have greater amounts of scatter throughout their WISC profiles (Fishkin *et al.* 1996; Silver and Clampit 1990; Webb and Dyer 1993), WISC profiles need to be evaluated in the context of other assessment material including behavioral observations and specific tasks that call for use of executive functions, memory and learning, organization, and planning, as well as reasoning and knowledge. Whenever a large discrepancy is found, the reason should be investigated. It should not be assumed that this is "just normal for gifted children."

What patterns will be found with the newer Wechsler and Stanford-Binet tests will only be determined over the next few years. Current patterns may no longer be valid.

STANFORD-BINET FORM LM ASSESSMENT

Brett scored an IQ of 149 on the Stanford-Binet LM. His score placed him within the highly gifted range. Brett shows significant potential on abstract verbal reasoning tasks. Brett scored high on knowledge of words, knowledge of similarities and differences, verbal problem solving, finding what was incongruent in sentences, mathematical reasoning, and logical reasoning. Brett scored slightly weaker, though still well above age level, on spatial reasoning, memory for designs, visual and auditory sequencing, and visual organization and planning.

Michael's Stanford-Binet LM score placed him in the exceptionally gifted range with an IQ of 165. Michael showed areas of strength in verbal reasoning ability, knowledge of words, knowledge of similarities and differences, mathematical reasoning, knowledge of compass directions (verbal spatial orientation), verbal absurdities (how a verbally administered sentence is silly), memory for digits forward and in reverse, and memory for sentences and passages, as well as visual memory and verbal fluency (number of words said in a short time period). He was weaker on verbal problem solving, ability to interpret proverbs, spatial orientation and visualization, and organization and planning. The Stanford-Binet LM gave a much broader interpretation of his verbal strengths which was useful in planning appropriate recommendations for him.

At the Gifted Resource Center of New England, there were a number of children with either AD/HD or AS who scored over IQ 180 on the Stanford-Binet. Of the total number of children with AD/HD or AS scoring over IQ 180, 44 had AD/HD and 11 had AS. However, some of the highest scorers – that is, five children with scores over 200 – had AS. This suggests that very bright children need further assessment in order to plan adequately for them.

The mean Binet LM score of this group was IQ 194 and the mean WISC-III FSIQ was 142. This 52-point difference becomes important not only in planning for the child's education, but also in other aspects of assessing the child. Scores nearer average on some tasks then suggest much more difficulty than for children who have smaller discrepancies. On the other hand, strengths are much higher than expectancy for a child of that age, and these strengths can be an important aspect of compensating for weaknesses.

Tests of academic achievement

In this section of this chapter, achievement testing in general and the various tests used with gifted children will be discussed.

Assessment of gifted children also should involve academic testing to evaluate academic strengths and weaknesses. Not only is it important to know how much a child is advanced, but also to know how the advancement manifests. Also, discrepancies in achievement among academic subjects may point to particular strengths and weaknesses. Discrepancies between intellectual potential and achievement may point to learning disabilities.

Children with similar IQ scores will show very different areas of strength and weakness. One will be advanced in math and science, another in reading and social studies. A third will be an excellent writer but poorer in science. Some will shine in everything; others will show learning disabilities despite their excellent potential. Thus, in making recommendations to schools on programming for children, knowledge of academics is important.

A number of different achievement tasks can be used to assess different aspects of achievement. For example, in reading, word recognition and decoding, knowledge of phonics, fluency and rapidly of reading, ability to sustain reading over longer passages, and reading comprehension all can be tested.

To assess academic achievement specific batteries can be utilized or different tests can be used to assess different skills. Some of the different achievement batteries include the Woodcock-Johnson Achievement Tests; the Kaufman Test of Educational Achievement; the Peabody Individual Achievement Tests; Wechsler Individual Achievement Test; and the Wide Range Achievement Tests, among others. There are also many individual tests one can use to build an appropriate battery to assess a particular child's functioning.

The *Woodcock-Johnson Achievement Tests* (WJ-III) are currently in the third revision, and contain 22 subtests that are administered over about one-and-a-half hours. The evaluator can vary which tasks are administered to tailor the battery to specific needs for information, and may also combine the material with that elicited from other assessment measures. The test ceiling is high in the elementary years so that highly achieving children have enough ceiling to show their ability.

The advantage of using the Woodcock-Johnson Achievement Tests is that many schools also use them and so recognize the validity of high scores. In fact, the range of scores on many of the subtests over many ages range up to the highly gifted level. Grade comparisons as well as age comparisons are also possible from kindergarten through post high school. This is especially useful for children out of synch for the usual age for a grade. For example, children who are quite gifted but repeated or delayed kindergarten can be compared to both age mates (who are in a higher grade) and grade mates. Children who are about to skip a grade can be assessed to see both how they compare to age mates, and how they will compare to students in their new class. Home-schooled children can be compared to both age mates and to grade expectations for material they are covering in their individualized learning.

Disadvantages include the need for a computer to have the test scored. Previous versions used tedious and numerous calculations by the examiner to obtain and compare scores. Also, the reading comprehension test depends on the Cloze method of filling in a blank with an appropriate word. This method may miss reading comprehension problems for those who have more trouble sustaining attention or making inferences. Writing samples also is problematic in only requiring the writing of sentences, versus a whole paragraph. These difficulties can be overcome by use of supplementary tests but this does add to the testing time. Another disadvantage is that despite high ceiling scores for elementary ages, by middle school, students' scores are apt to be much lower, even if they get almost all items correct. In fact, the overall highest scores are lower than on the previous edition of the test (WJ-R). Tom, described in Chapter 4, had been assessed on the WJ-R in 4th grade, and had scored in the highly gifted range at SS 165. In 7th grade, despite being at the top of the math class, Tom scored only in the superior range on broad mathematics, SS 128. Tom knew how to solve most of the difficult word problems on the WJ-III but did not yet know all the computational math; thus, he did much less well than expected given his advanced math achievement in school.

The Gifted Resource Center of New England uses the Woodcock-Johnson because of its high ceilings. Its construction also allows easy comparison to other tests of achievement and to intelligence tests. Partial batteries are also possible using tasks that have high ceilings for gifted children combined with measures that better test reading comprehension, written expression, and spelling.

The *Kaufman Test of Educational Achievement* consists of five measures: mathematics applications, mathematics computation, reading decoding, reading comprehension, and spelling. The test takes about an hour to administer and is easy to score. There is a wide age range from 6 to 18, 1st grade through 12th grade. There are also spring and fall norms which increase test sensitivity to the variations in achievement that occur after long vacations. Finally, the separate spelling score is useful, and the reading comprehension is based on actual reading of passages and answering questions. Disadvantages include no preschool norms, no written language score, and no test of general knowledge in science, social studies, and other subjects. Also the mechanics of written language other than spelling are not tested.

Supplementary tests can be used for these disadvantages, but at the cost of increased testing time. Osborn (1999) prefers use of this test with young gifted children due to its ease of administration and shorter administration time.

The *Peabody Individual Achievement Tests – Revised* (PIAT-R) consist of six subtests: general information, reading recognition, reading comprehension, written expression, mathematics, and spelling. The test has two levels of written expression, one designed for young children who are not yet writing fluently. The upper level requires the actual writing of a story in response to a picture. The age ranges are 5 through 18, kindergarten through 12th grade. Advantages of the PIAT-R are its decreased need for a verbal response on reading, math, and spelling – the child points to a response. The test takes about an hour and is fairly easily scored. There are both age and grade norms. Disadvantages include not knowing if a child's written spelling is similar to the score obtained by pointing to a correct response. The test does not involve complex reading comprehension but only requires responding via a picture to a sentence. Math is multiple choice, not allowing the examiner to see if a child is actually able to solve problems but is making computational errors. Also the examiner cannot see how the child goes about solving unknown problems.

The *Wechsler Individual Achievement Test – Second Edition* (WIAT) is a companion test to the Wechsler Intelligence Scales which allows direct comparisons with intellectual potential to determine learning problems. The test is both age and grade normed, with fall, winter, and spring-based norms. It takes about one to one-and-a-half hours and consists of eight subtests: basic reading (decoding), reading comprehension, mathematics reasoning, numerical operations, spelling, oral expression, listening comprehension, and written expression. Advantages are that the WIAT is often used in school systems and can be part of a comprehensive battery of tests that assess memory and learning, as well as intellect and achievement. The disadvantages include a lack of preschool norms, and norms that don't go high or low enough. Thus, they may not adequately assess the abilities of gifted children. Also, if the WIAT is compared to the Wechsler tests, and used as a basis for determining learning disabilities, the amount of discrepancy between potential and achievement may be underestimated because attention deficits can also reduce IQ scores, especially on the Wechsler tests.

The *Wide Range Achievement Tests – 3* (WRAT) include reading recognition, spelling, and math computation. Age ranges go from 5 to 75 and administration time is 15 to 30 minutes. Scoring is exceptionally quick and easy. As a screening device the WRAT offers quick assessment of basic skills but is unable to provide sufficient information about the ability to apply these skills. For example, one child with AS scored SS 149 in reading, 155 in spelling, and 85 in arithmetic due to her nonverbal learning problems. Her reading comprehension and written expression (assessed by other tests) were well below the reading and spelling scores found on the WRAT by several years. In fact, her scores illustrate the dangers of depending on such a screening instrument alone. The publishers of the WRAT have recently developed an extended version that covers some of these concerns.

Achievement tests that supplement batteries

Tests of reading ability include the Test of Reading Comprehension (TORC-3), Gray Oral Reading Test, and many others. The Test of Reading Comprehension is composed of a number of subtests that assess different aspects of reading comprehension including vocabulary, sentence sequencing, and paragraph reading.

Tests of written language include the Test of Written Language – 3; Test of Early Written Language – 2, and others. There are also tests of spelling, handwriting, and knowledge of written language mechanics.

The Test of Written Language is used at the Gifted Resource Center of New England to assess ability to write at more length. Children from ages 7½ through 17 may be evaluated by this test which requires writing a story in response to a picture. The ability to write a coherent story, contextual vocabulary, spelling, grammar, and punctuation are all assessed. They also can be compared to tasks which measure each of these abilities in isolation to determine the abilities of children to use known skills in writing. This is an excellent supplement for many other achievement batteries that do not focus on these aspects of writing.

For younger children, ages three through ten, the Test of Early Written Language is available. It measures abilities in basic written language skills such as grammar and spelling, as well as ability to write a story when provided with a picture cue. The skills in basic writing are not separately delineated so a separate measure of spelling may still need to be administered. Since both the Test of Written Language and the Test of Early Written Language allow the writing of only one draft, are timed, and require writing to a particular picture that may not interest the child, results can vary considerably from the child's actual ability. One of the advantages of having portfolio material is that it allows comparison with a sample of the child's best work. Both ability to generate ideas and ability to produce a more polished product can be evaluated.

Tests of mathematics are available but mathematics is one area that is adequately covered by most achievement batteries. For younger children (ages 5 to 14, grades K through 9), Key Math can be useful with its separate emphasis on number knowledge, computation, and applications in several unique areas such as estimation, geometry, and problem solving. Spring and fall norms are also available for both age and grade.

Brett's achievement testing

Brett was administered the Woodcock-Johnson Achievement Test – III, the Test of Written Language – 3, and the Test of Reading Comprehension – 3.

Brett's scores indicated that he was exceptionally strong in reading comprehension, reading vocabulary, reading decoding (reading words), reading fluency (the number of easy sentences read quickly), mathematics computation and reasoning, spelling, editing, and general knowledge. Brett was weaker on word attack skills, mathematics fluency (the number of easy math problems done in a limited time period), writing samples (writing sentences to a set of directions), writing basic skills, handwriting, and writing fluency (the number of quick short sentences that can be written in a limited time). On subtests that were areas of strength, scores were in the superior to very superior range. On subtests that were areas of weakness, scores tended to be low average to average.

On the Test of Written Language, Brett wrote an interesting story and scored in the superior range overall. His use of complex sentence structure and vocabulary were high. Mechanics and spelling, within the context of the story, were high average. The actual construction of the story was high average. This was partly due to Brett's slow handwriting. It took him a long time to start, and to do the task. By the end of the 15-minute time period, he had not completed the story, but was really only introducing the main characters and plot. This meant he didn't fulfill some of the task requirements and so his score was lowered.

On the Test of Reading Comprehension, Brett was able to answer most of the questions correctly, and so scored in the very superior range on paragraph reading. He was more average on following directions but was close to the ceiling of this test, and had really only missed two items that he had overlooked.

When Brett's achievement was compared to his school standardized tests and work papers, he was found to be misplaced in reading: that is, he was placed at a level much lower than his test results. No wonder he was complaining of boredom! Analysis of his most recently read books did suggest, however, that Brett had some trouble sustaining interest and attention on books at his true reading level, which was three years beyond grade level. What he did enjoy were books that were somewhat above grade level. These he read with ease and concentration. Recently he had just finished the newest Harry Potter book, had enjoyed all the Redwall books, had loved all the Lemony Snickett books, and was trying Philip Pullman's *The Golden Compass*, though it was somewhat of a struggle for him.

In math, Brett was performing several years above grade level and was certainly bored with the standard curriculum. He was ready for a more challenging math program.

In writing, Brett's finished products from home were much more developed than his Test of Written Language piece. Brett hated to write, and often tried to do the least amount he could. If he was at home and his mother was monitoring, he did much more and better work. At school, he left work unfinished. Handwriting was another problem for him. Though his writing was legible, he was slow and tired easily, complaining that his hand hurt if he had to write very much. Dictating helped and Brett was learning to keyboard, hoping that he would do better on a word processor or computer.

In spelling, Brett usually got 100% on grade-level tests but explained that he often forgot some of the words once the test was over and then had to restudy them later. When he wrote, he was apt to spell a word several different ways in the course of his composition.

Like many other gifted children with AD/HD, when tested, Brett scored high in some academic areas. Even his areas of weakness were about grade level. His school would never pick him out as a student with special needs, except for his behavior and unfinished work. Nevertheless, like many children with AD/HD, Brett struggled with organizing his thoughts, and with written expression, basic reading skills, working quickly on timed items, and handwriting. These scores did not, however, reveal why he had so much trouble handing in work and doing long-term projects. It wasn't that they were so far beneath his ability level that projects were boring; in fact, Brett would be very excited about his ideas. It was bringing them to fruition that seemed more the issue. Brett's parents worried that if he was struggling like this at the end of 6th grade, by the time he reached high school he might give up. Also, he was getting too discouraged that math was so unchallenging. It was decided to look further at underlying cognitive processes to further assess executive functions and memory.

Michael's achievement testing

Michael was assessed on the same achievement tests as Brett. Michael showed areas of strength in reading decoding, word attack skills, reading fluency, reading vocabulary and reading comprehension. In math he showed areas of strength in math computation and reasoning, as well as number series. He was very high on the mechanics of writing: spelling, editing, and knowledge of punctuation and capitalization. In fact, his only areas of weakness were in math fluency, writing fluency, and writing samples (writing sentences according to directions). Areas of strength were all in the superior and very superior range. Areas of weakness were in the low average to average range.

The Test of Written Language was also administered, but Michael would or could not do it. By the end of the 15-minute period, he had completed only the title. This gave him a score in the deficient range (SS 68). When allowed to dictate a second story to his mother, he scored in the low average range. Mechanics and use of language were high average, but his story construction was quite low, and well below grade level.

On the Test of Reading Comprehension, Michael scored at the 95% level, and his errors were all on questions requiring inference.

An analysis of Michael's achievement testing suggested a learning disability in written language, both in producing material and in handwriting. He also showed subtle weaknesses in reading when asked to make inferences. His difficulties explaining proverbs on the Stanford-Binet LM, given his other very high scores, suggested he had some subtle language deficits in understanding metaphoric language.

Neuropsychological assessment

In this section of this chapter, neuropsychological assessment in general and the various tests used with gifted children will be discussed.

Many gifted children will need neuropsychological assessment to answer the question if they have AD/HD or not. Children may look inattentive in class and not complete work for a variety of reasons. Just being bored can produce many AD/HD-like symptoms that disappear if the child is given appropriate, challenging work. On the other hand, some of these children will be able to work well on topics of interest, especially if self-selected, but cannot work on less stimulating ones. Still others have little they find interesting for long. Thus, an assessment that describes the child's abilities on a variety of tasks, makes comparisons among different tasks of executive function, and assesses memory and learning style will contribute to understanding both strengths and weaknesses, and will help in the determination of AD/HD, learning styles, and learning disabilities.

Neuropsychological assessment is also useful for children with AS in determining areas of cognitive strength and weakness, especially subtle underlying deficits, and in formulating recommendations about academic, social, and emotional goals.

None of the neuropsychological tests, in and of themselves, can provide a definitive diagnosis of either AD/HD or AS. What the tests do show is the pattern of abilities that, along with behavioral observations, lead to a better understanding of the underlying neuropsychological functioning of this particular child. In that context, the diagnosis is formulated.

Neuropsychological assessment of gifted children with attention deficits

GIFTED CHILDREN WITH AD/HD

There are no definitive tests to measure if a child does or does not have AD/HD. Even the various types of brain scans are done retrospectively. That is, given a large group of children with AD/HD compared to a non-AD/HD sample, brain scans can show statistical differences in children with AD/HD. These differences are particularly noted in the frontal brain areas (site of executive functions), the basal ganglia (the organizer of brain functions), and the cerebellum (modulates emotion and higher levels of cognition) (Giedd 2000). However, this does not mean one can use a brain scan to detect AD/HD. The differences found are statistical differences within and between groups, not for individuals. Even having the same profile on an MRI (magnetic resonance image) as the group mean for children with AD/HD does not mean necessarily that any individual has AD/HD.

Continuous performance tests are often used to assess AD/HD by measuring attention: ability to focus, divide, and sustain attention, as well as ability to perform rapidly and accurately, and to inhibit responding when appropriate. There are several types of continuous performance tests which measure attention to a test stimulus or to avoiding a target stimulus. Some tests of continuous performance are visual (Conners 1995) and some auditory or combined (Baker, Taylor, and Leyva 1995; Greenberg and Kindschi 1996, cited in Gordon and Barkley 1998). Most of these tests measure the ability to correctly signal the appearance of a target item, to inhibit responding to a target item, or to do both. Correct identification of AD/HD requires training in the use of these tests. Both false positives (identification of AD/HD when not present) and false negatives (missing a valid diagnosis) can occur. Test results are susceptible to factors such as anxiety (Epstein *et al.* 1997). Continuous performance tests that measure number of target items correct are also related to intelligence, achievement, memory, and learning scores (Aylward, Gordon, and Verhulst 1997; Chae *et al.* 2003). There is also evidence that gifted children with AD/HD score higher on many of the norms of continuous performance tests such as the T.O.V.A. (Chae *et al.* 2003). The discrepancy from expectation based on their intelligence needs to be taken into account.

Tests of executive functions may be used to describe dysfunction in planning, organizing, monitoring, flexible thinking, use of strategies, and rapid and accurate working.

Generally, there is agreement that AD/HD is a disorder of executive functions. There is great inconsistency across studies about the degree to which particular tests discriminate dysfunction in frontal lobe processes that determine executive functions, and thus would identify AD/HD (Barkley, Grodzinsky, and DuPaul 1992). On a battery of tests measuring executive function, no two persons will score identically, nor will any particular test be definitely impacted by AD/HD. That is why a variety of tests is used. The particular areas of executive function strength and weakness are important to determine in order to formulate specific goals to help the child compensate.

Research of specific deficits in executive functions of children with AD/HD has found deficits in unmedicated children with AD/HD on spatial short-term memory, spatial working memory, set-shifting ability, and planning ability. Spatial recognition memory was also impaired compared to a group of control subjects (Kempton *et al.* 1999). Deficits have also been found for children with AD/HD in performance on the Tower of London, a planning and reasoning task

(Culbertson and Zillmer 1998); in encoding memory, especially verbal working memory and inhibition (Denckla 1996); in tasks of controlled reasoning and processing such as performance in solving mazes, and in gross motor output (Carte, Nigg, and Hinshaw 1996). Pearson *et al.* (1995) found waxing and waning in attention over progressively longer time intervals within a task. Other deficit areas found included attention and progression through the initial stages of verbal memory formation (Mealer, Morgan, and Luscomb 1996). Even in preschool boys with AD/HD, neuropsychological differences were found in motor speed and coordination, visual-spatial construction ability, and verbal, spatial, and short-term memories (Mariani and Barkley 1997). In adults who were not diagnosed with AD/HD until adulthood, neuropsychological tests, such as the Paced Auditory Serial Addition task, Delayed Free Recall on the California Verbal Learning Test, verbal fluency, and Wisconsin Card Sorting Tests, classified subjects into correct diagnostic groups 75% of the time (Jenkins *et al.* 1998).

The picture is much less clear with girls. It has been noted that difficulties with executive functioning are less prominent with girls who have AD/HD. They tend to have impairments in attention and achievement, but less impairment on executive functions than boys with AD/HD (Seidman *et al.* 1997). On the other hand, Biederman *et al.* (1999) reported no differences between boys and girls with AD/HD in patterns of deficit in executive function. Part of the issue may be sample size or IQ, or perhaps that both boys and girls with AD/HD are such a heterogeneous group that there may be several subtypes with different patterns of strengths and weaknesses (Conners 1997). Certainly the gifted girls seen for neuropsychological evaluation by the Gifted Resource Center of New England appear to show deficits in executive functions similar to those of boys.

GIFTED CHILDREN WITH AS

A number of researchers equate AS with the presence of an NVLD (Ehlers *et al.* 1997; Klin *et al.* 1995). That is, AS is seen as the most severe type of NVLD. Others, such as Attwood (1998), suggested that an NVLD may occur but is not a defining feature of AS. In fact, some people with AS show exceptional visual-spatial skills. Thus, while many children with AS will have an NVLD, some will not. It is important to note that with exceptionally high IQ children, NVLD may be present, but can be subtle given the child's high level of skills. Because most of these children are tested on tests that have lower ceilings or evaluate the child according to age-level norms, the presence of an NVLD may go unnoticed. For example, Stuart, with an IQ over 200, scored equally well on the WISC-III on verbal and performance IQs. A few subtests were slightly lower (Comprehension,

Object Assembly) but these were still in the superior range, so it did not appear that Stuart had an NVLD. However, given Stuart's high verbal intelligence, non-verbal skills in the superior range were areas of weakness. Other tasks with a higher ceiling confirmed Stuart's NVLD and problems with central coherence.

Current studies of how children with AS perform on neuropsychological tests, especially tests of executive function, are sparse. On tests of executive function, Berthier (1995) found that, compared to controls, children with AS performed less well on the Wisconsin Card Sorting Test, the Tower of Hanoi, and the Road Map Test. Ozonoff, Rogers, and Pennington (1991) found that individuals with AS, and those with autism, did less well on the Wisconsin Card Sorting Test and Tower of Hanoi. Also found were difficulties in shifting cognitive set, making plans about how to order an activity, in use of pragmatic language, and difficulties with word finding (Landa 2000).

THE NEUROPSYCHOLOGICAL EVALUATION

To administer and interpret neuropsychological instruments requires special training. Not only does it matter what each particular test may show, but also the patterns underlying the whole battery need to be formulated.

There are a wide variety of neuropsychological instruments available. These are used to determine adequacy of brain functioning in a number of different areas. For example, some tests evaluate differences based on brain damage, developmental expectations, or learning differences.

The amount of testing that is done, the instruments used, and the way the evaluation is reported depend on the philosophy and training of the evaluator, as well as the purpose of the evaluation. Some evaluators (neuropsychologists) only perform neuropsychological evaluations. Others also may do other sorts of evaluations and/or therapy as well. These evaluators may be neuropsychologists or clinical psychologists. Some psychologists use a set battery; others base their selections on the initial history and add instruments as they progress, depending on initial findings. Some base interpretations strictly on age scores and deviations from average; that is, children are assessed to see if they are normal or not. Other psychologists assess not only the scores, but also the process elements of the assessment: the behavior during testing, deviations from the child's mean score, or deviations from expectations based on the child's intellectual potential.

Neuropsychological instruments have a theoretical basis about brain functioning upon which interpretation depends. Neuropsychological tests can be part of set batteries based on particular philosophies of neuropsychological functioning. Currently, the Luria-Nebraska and its variations, the Halstead-Reitan and its variations, and the NEPSY are all widely used. These batteries, while based on somewhat different philosophies of brain functioning, assess motor functions, tactile functions, speech and language, memory, attention, executive functions, and visual-perceptual functions. If done carefully by a qualified examiner, neuropsychological tests are as effective in assessing brain dysfunction as an MRI.

In addition to using all tests in a particular battery, many psychologists compose their own batteries consisting of tasks designed to assess memory, intelligence, sensory functions, language functions, attention and executive functions, tactile and proprioceptive feedback, and visual-perceptual and motor functions. Most psychologists who use neuropsychological instruments select among the wide variety available. They choose instruments that assess auditory versus visual perception, visual and auditory processing, short- and long-term recall, working memory, rapid learning and amount of forgetting over time, ability to be mentally flexible, monitor performance, vigilance and attention, motor and visual-motor functioning, spatial and proprioceptive functioning, and the ability of the brain to integrate functions in a complex manner (what is called simultaneous processing of material). They also assess intellectual functioning, and some assess academic functioning.

A good source of information about various psychological and neuro-psychological assessment instruments is Spreen and Strauss's *A Compendium of Neuropsychological Tests* (1998). In addition to descriptions of various tests, the authors provide information about where to order tests in the USA, Canada, and sometimes the United Kingdom. Also, for some tests that do not require much material, and are in the public domain, norms are provided for different ages.

Neuropsychological instruments used to assess learning functioning, AD/HD, and AS include the following:

- *Tests of language and auditory processing*: Boston Naming Test; Test of Pragmatic Language; Expressive One-Word Picture Vocabulary Test; Receptive One-Word Picture Vocabulary Test; Token Test for Children; Test of Auditory Reasoning and Processing Skills; SCAN-C: Test for Auditory Processing Disorders in Children – Revised; Test of Language Development.

- *Tests of memory and learning*: California Verbal Learning Test – Children's; Children's Auditory-Verbal Learning Test; Wide Range Assessment of Memory and Learning; Test of Memory and Learning; Children's Memory Scale; Benton Visual Retention Test; Rey-Osterrieth Complex Figure – Delayed Memory.

- *Tests of visual-perception and visual-motor integration*: Bender-Gestalt Test; Beery-Buktenica Developmental Test of Visual-Motor Integration (VMI) – 2; Developmental Test of Visual-Perception – 2 (through age 10 years 11 months); Developmental Test of Visual-Perception-A (Adolescent and Adult); Benton Facial Recognition Test; Benton Judgment of Line Orientation; Test of Visual-Perceptual Skills – Lower Level; Upper Level.

- *Tests of executive functions*: Wisconsin Card Sorting Test; Children's Category Test; Stroop Color-Word Test; Verbal Fluency Test, FAS Test, Cancellation Tests; d2 Test of Attention; Trail Making Test; Rey-Osterrieth Complex Figure Test; Benton Finger Localization Test; NEPSY (includes the Tower of London Test); Continuous Performance Tests including Conners' Continuous Performance Test; Auditory Continuous Performance Test; Tests of Variables of Attention.

- *Other tests*: Portions of some of the various tests of intelligence such as Bead Memory, Memory for Objects (SB-IV), Digit Span, and Coding (WISC-III) are also useful as tests of executive function or memory. Some of the new subtests on the WISC-IV and SB-5 may be useful in assessing processing speed and working memory. In addition, there are other tests that measure motor speed, tactile performance and memory, visual-kinesthetic memory, shape discrimination, and sensory integration that are available and useful in certain types of assessments.

While some of these assessment procedures and instruments are better than others, remember no instrument alone is sufficient in determining whether gifted children have attention or learning problems. The clinician is the most important variable. The best assessment instrument in the world is only as good as the person administering the test, observing the child, and doing the interpretation of findings.

Psychologists, clinics, and school systems that follow rigid criteria in determining deviations from age expectations, or in eligibility for services, may miss gifted children who indeed have AD/HD or are learning disabled but who can compensate some of the time, especially in one-on-one situations, when tasks are novel, and when they are motivated and interested. Being seen by multiple evaluators can provide a variety of viewpoints, but also can obscure findings when children are rushed from one to another, or have only a short time with each examiner. Since gifted children's attention may not flag with shorter tasks and novel situations, shorter assessments may miss difficulties with sustaining and dividing attention. Missing these difficulties will matter when the child is confronted with longer tasks and higher-level work using more mature levels of executive functions.

Because of very high intelligence, some gifted children are misidentified. Children who are bored because the curriculum is too easy may look bored, restless, and inattentive. Some may act out and look like children with AD/HD. On the other hand, children who are highly gifted and have AD/HD may be able to score above average on many tests. If scoring below average is the criteria for diagnosing a disability, many gifted children with real disabilities will be misdiagnosed as having no problems.

Gifted children with AS are more likely to be diagnosed with AS if their symptoms are even moderate, but the emphasis is on their deficits and less on their strengths as gifted learners. Thus children with AS with IQs as high as 200 can have significant special needs, yet also need advanced programming. On the other hand, gifted children with mild AS may not be diagnosed at all and may miss needed services for both social deficits and cognitive weaknesses.

Because many neuropsychologists use batteries which have the average child as a standard, gifted children with disabilities may be missed if tested on tasks that only use age norms as a cutoff. Thus, the use of process testing in which the child is compared to his or her own highest scores better shows both strengths and deficits. A child with IQ 165, who scores average on a test of mental flexibility or planning and organization, has a huge deficit in these skills, and will likely have trouble in taking courses geared for older students who can perform at higher levels on these skills. All assessments at the Gifted Resource Center of New England are process assessments.

BRETT'S NEUROPSYCHOLOGICAL ASSESSMENT

Brett was assessed using tests of executive functions such as the Rey-Osterrieth Complex Figure, Trail Making, Cancellation Tests, d2 Test of Attention, Wisconsin Card Sorting Test, Stroop Color-Word Test, and Finger Localization Test. Measures of memory and learning were also used that included the California Verbal Learning Test – Children's Version, parts of the Wide Range Assessment of Memory and Learning, and Test of Memory and Learning. Brett was administered tests of language functioning that included Receptive and Expressive Vocabulary Tests, the Token Test for Children, the FAS Test and the Verbal Fluency Test. Finally, Brett was administered tests of visual-perceptual-motor functioning such as the Beery Developmental Test of Visual-Motor Integration, and the Developmental Test of Visual-Perception – A.

Brett's test results suggested that he had mild auditory processing deficits. He had some trouble remembering complex directions presented in an auditory format. It took him some time to start tasks, and he was easily overloaded, especially with competing similar material such as more digits, another story, more words. Brett showed an interference effect when given competing material so that his performance dropped considerably. Performance on memory items then improved after a delay, suggesting that it took him some time to consolidate material into memory. Brett showed a combined verbal and visual learning style, especially if material was repeated several times. Brett did best with verbal and visual material with some context, but which did not include an overload of too many details.

Brett showed some deficits in planning, and organization for complex material. When presented with a complex geometric figure to draw (the Rey Complex Figure), he was very careful when copying it, but even so was not able to accurately make lines meet. Thus, his score for organization was slightly below average. When asked to recall the drawing immediately after finishing it, he recalled the outline well, and some of the details. However, he forgot most of how the inside of the design was arranged, but his score was about average for his age. Later on, when tested again after a delay, he recalled a few more details but still focused mostly on the outline. Brett appeared to be more of a big-picture learner who got the gist of things but was more vague on details. Over time, he improved on memory of these details, but still focused more on the big picture.

On a test of mental flexibility (Wisconsin Card Sort), Brett scored well above average. He was good at problem solving and was able to flexibly change parameters to meet changing needs of the task.

Brett also did well on rapidly performing on well-learned material, and on a task of quickly recalling familiar material from memory, in the very superior range. However, he was less adept at recalling material that was unfamiliar, and he seemed to have some trouble thinking of words and names.

Brett had some trouble on a task on which he had to rapidly cross off all the target items. He missed many of the items and also crossed off some that were not target items. His score for concentration was low average. His error score was also low average: that is, he performed at a low average level. On the other hand, he did cross off many items. Thus, Brett worked quickly but not very accurately.

Visual-motor functioning was average. On visual-perceptual-motor functioning, scores varied somewhat. His scores for items that required a motor response, such as writing, were low average, while scores for tasks that measured visual-perception alone (visual closure, visual figure-ground, form constancy) were in the superior range. Thus, Brett was quite good at quickly seeing the whole when given part, at locating figures against various backgrounds, and at finding hidden figures.

His more age-level skills in planning, organizing, recalling material from memory, working quickly and accurately, and dealing with competing material all suggested deficits in executive functions. However, his above average visual-perceptual skills suggested that Brett did not have an NVLD so his lower WISC-III performance skills were more related to processing speed and AD/HD than to perceptual deficits. Other children with AD/HD may show entirely different patterns of scores on these tests.

MICHAEL'S NEUROPSYCHOLOGICAL ASSESSMENT

Michael was assessed using tests of executive functions such as the Rey-Osterrieth Complex Figure, FAS Test, Verbal Fluency Test, Trail Making, d2 Test of Attention, Wisconsin Card Sorting Test, Stroop Color-Word Test, and Finger Localization Test. Michael was administered tests of language functioning such as the Token Test for Children, Test of Pragmatic Language, and Expressive and Receptive Vocabulary.

Measures of memory and learning were also used that included the California Verbal Learning Test – Children's Version, parts of the Wide Range Assessment of Memory and Learning, and Test of Memory and Learning. Michael was administered the Benton Facial Recognition Test, as well as tests of facial memory. Finally, he was administered tests of visual-perceptual-motor functioning such as the Developmental Test of Visual-Motor Integration (VMI), and the Developmental Test of Visual Perception – 2.

Results of Michael's evaluation of executive functions showed deficits in flexible thinking. On the Wisconsin Card Sorting Test, a test of figuring out the sorting principle being used, Michael had trouble with thinking of alternate responses. If he was wrong, he tended to keep repeating his mistake and sorting by the same principle. He also lost the sorting principle five times and then had to start over. On the FAS test, a test of naming as many words as he could within one minute starting with a particular letter of the alphabet, he was in the very superior range. He had trouble, though, naming all the animals he could think of within one minute because he decided to name only dinosaurs. Thus, his tremendous knowledge of animals was not called into play. Michael showed slower than average speed and average accuracy on tasks of attention and vigilance. He had no trouble with tests of localizing touch on his finger tips. All of these results suggest difficulty with flexible thinking, problem solving, following rules, and working quickly.

On tests of language functioning, Michael was able to score in the very superior range on both receptive and expressive vocabulary. In fact, he was above the norms for his age on the test. He did well on a test of following complex directions. He was able to recall a long list of words read to him five times at a superior level, and he did not forget them over time. On the other hand, he scored low average on a test of pragmatic language. He had trouble with describing things to another person and understanding sarcasm, irony, and metaphor.

On tests of verbal memory, Michael scored mostly in the very superior range. He was especially adept at digit and sentence memory, but scored in the superior range on memory for stories. Visual memory was slightly lower, but he did score high average on recalling details of pictures and locations of designs. He also did well if he had to recall which design he had seen from an array of five.

On tests of memory for faces, Michael was well below average. After a delay, he recalled even fewer faces. His score on the Benton Facial Recognition Test was also well below the mean for his age. It was evident in watching him that he tried to recall the faces by picking out features to use. Since many of the faces had these same features, this did not work. He seemed unable to recall faces as a whole.

On tests of visual-perceptual-motor functioning, Michael had much difficulty with drawing the Rey-Osterrieth Complex Figure, a complex geometric figure drawn from a model. He tended to draw it in small pieces as an assortment of triangles loosely connected to other parts. His drawing was below the 10% level for organization. After drawing the design he had to recall it from memory. Drawing it immediately from memory, he drew many triangles and some details, but he did not have most of the salient underlying features that would make it a whole. Thus, he forgot parts and put some in the wrong place. When he had to draw simpler geometric designs, he did somewhat better, and his production was low average. On tests of visual-motor skills, Michael scored low average. On tests of visual-perceptual skills (what he perceived without having to write or draw), he scored higher, more in the high average range.

Michael's results suggest he had trouble with noting visual details, recalling faces accurately, organizing visual material on a page, planning an approach to a problem, paying attention consistently, developing a picture of a whole, visualizing social scenes, interpreting complex material, and holding several aspects of things in mind at once (for example, size, sequence, number, and color). He had trouble shifting set and tended to stick with strategies that were not working. His visual-motor functioning was especially poor: he had trouble with motor organization and planning, and scores were certainly exceptionally discrepant from his verbal intellectual potential. He had difficulty with inhibiting responding on a task that required such inhibition. On a test of pragmatic language he missed all the questions that had to do with more subtle interpretation of meaning, as well as those that had to do with interpreting metaphor. He was outstanding in verbal fluency, in rapidly responding to stimuli, and in use of reasoning skills, and in visual and auditory memory. Michael's neuropsychological profile showed the deficits in executive functions, subtle language skills, organization and planning associated with AS.

Behavior and personality assessment

In this section of this chapter, behavior checklists and personality assessment in general and the various tests used with gifted children will be discussed.

It is important to evaluate the child's emotional and social strengths and weaknesses as part of the whole picture. Understanding how the child views the self and others, whether the child can understand another's perspective or feelings, how well the child understands cause and effect, the ways in which he or she understands responsibility for what happens, how authority figures are seen, how the child handles stress, what value he or she places on emotion and how well emotion is integrated into behavior, and what understanding and value the child has for feelings about family, school, and peers, as well as specific problems of self-esteem, anxiety, fears, depression, and isolation from others, are all necessary to form a picture of the child.

There are a number of different types of assessments of emotional and social functioning. These include checklists filled out by parents, teachers, and child; paper and pencil tests of emotional functioning; and projective tests which assess underlying psychological constructs such as defenses, reality testing, view of the world, interpersonal interactions, and use of emotion.

Behavior checklists

Parents and teachers may be asked to fill out forms that ask about presence of specific behaviors in the child. Typical behavior checklists include the Child Behavior Checklist, Conners Rating Scales, ACTeRS, Brown ADD Scales, and the Behavior Assessment System for Children, among others. Adaptive functioning can be assessed with the Vineland Adaptive Behavior Scales. In addition several checklists that assess AS symptoms are also available including the Asperger Syndrome Diagnostic Scale (ASDS), Autism Spectrum Screening Questionnaire, Attwood Scale, and the Gilliam Asperger Disorder Scale.

None of these has been standardized specifically on gifted children, though the Brown ADD Scales have included gifted subjects.

The Child Behavior Checklist has been used in several studies on gifted children, and has generally not found them to have any particular emotional problems as a group (Cornell *et al.* 1994; Gallucci 1988; Gallucci, Middleton, and Kline 1999). Using the Behavior Assessment System for Children, Nail and Evans (1997) found gifted adolescents to show fewer indices of behavioral-emotional maladjustment than average students. Thus, gifted students in general are found to be emotionally well-adjusted. But what about gifted children with AD/HD? These children have not been studied using checklists commonly used with parents and teachers. In fact, even with average children, these checklists may not give the whole picture. They are susceptible to halo effects (under- or overestimating problems), differences in raters' perceptions about what terms mean, and differences in the child's behavior that may actually be present in different environments, and with different people (Mandal, Olmi, and Wilczynski 1999).

Recent research with several of these checklists found that no checklist, or subscale from any checklist, could discriminate between Inattentive and Combined Types of AD/HD. However, the most useful way to use the checklists was to use cutoff scores for subtests of attention and hyperactivity. Thus, on the Conners Rating Scales, a cutoff of 1 SD above the mean on either attention or hyperactivity scales was likely to find most of the AD/HD children and not falsely identify others with AD/HD-like symptoms. The biggest problem with all the checklists, singly or in combination, was the misclassification of children who did not have the disorder. Therefore, use of behavior rating scales in clinical practice needs to be done with caution (Forbes 2001).

At the Gifted Resource Center of New England, however, other problems have arisen. It is not at all uncommon for rating scales to miss AD/HD in gifted children. Unless the child is very hyperactive, behaviors such as inattention, forgetfulness, impulsivity, and disorganization may not be viewed as serious. Parents of gifted children may, in fact, view these behaviors as part of their child's giftedness, and resulting from boredom with inappropriate work. Thus, even if present, parents may discount the behaviors, and not mark them on the checklists. These parents may or may not be correct about the cause of their child's problems, but professionals assessing gifted children need to be aware of this type of halo effect.

When marking checklists, parents and teachers may see a slightly different child because the child may behave differently in different environments. Thus, in school the child may have many difficulties but not at home, because at home the parents are able to stimulate the child adequately, and expectations for close attention are less prominent. The criteria for diagnosis of AD/HD by DSM-IV requires problems in two areas, but with many gifted children the problems may be more subtle and seem limited to one situation. For example, Phillip, age seven, was very disruptive at school, but his parents kept him very busy at home with things he liked to do and didn't demand much of him, so the problems they saw were much milder.

Another problem can occur when parents are so familiar with their children's behavior, it has ceased to bother them. It doesn't seem like such a big problem anymore so the parents mark checklists as if the problems were mild. Finally, some parents see their child's behavior in a different light then others do. Perry, age nine, was very disruptive at school, and though his parents denied that he had any problems at home, it was evident from watching them in the initial meeting that they hadn't a clue about what was expected behavior and what was not. They saw Perry's disruptiveness as evidence of his independence and disregard for things that were not important. In fact, Perry's parents were very much like him. They talked over each other, interrupted, squabbled, disrupted each other's train of thought, and seemed to live with continual chaos. They saw this as normal and, therefore, did not see Perry as having any unusual problems.

It is important to assess how the child does in social and community situations such as eating in restaurants, behaving at movies, concerts, and museums, and modulating behavior at birthday parties, the pool, church school, and sporting events, both when the child watches and when the child participates. Thus, questions about activity level, ability to join in an ongoing activity, and need for special treatment are all useful.

Teachers may have difficulty with checklists because checklists don't describe exactly what the gifted child with AD/HD does to disrupt things: for example, adding additional information to every discussion, or correcting the teacher's errors. Furthermore, the gifted child may be very inattentive, but the work is so easy that it can be completed with almost no effort, so inattention is not noted by teachers. It is only when the work becomes more challenging that the child's difficulties may come more into focus. However, some gifted children with AD/HD are able to function until high school, college, or even graduate school years.

The problems that occur with behavior checklists for AD/HD are less apt to occur with AS, though when AS is very mild, the symptoms can be mistakenly attributed to giftedness and the difficulty finding a suitable peer. In these cases, parents may not see behaviors on checklists as applicable to their child. Nevertheless, the social problems of most gifted children with AS are so outstanding that parents see them as problematic.

Paper and pencil assessments

Assessments of self-esteem, anxiety, depression, and personality may be measured by self-report instruments such as the Self-Esteem Inventory, Reynolds Child Depression Scale, Reynolds Adolescent Depression Scale, Beck Youth Inventories for Emotional and Social Impairment, Adolescent Psychopathology Scale, and many others.

Self-report measures with gifted children with AD/HD or AS administered at the Gifted Resource Center of New England may not show problems that do exist. For one thing, adolescents often refuse these measures, especially adolescents with AS. Those who do take them underreport problems. This occurs because these adolescents are less apt to want to share how they really feel given specific questions, or because they don't feel that way right at that moment. Also, if a symptom occurred more than a few days ago, some adolescents with AD/HD may not even recall that it occurred. Consequently, gifted children with AD/HD may have as much trouble with longer-term memory for emotional events as other children with AD/HD. Thus, if a symptom is not evident right at that moment, they may discount it. Younger children are more straightforward and tend to report items more honestly; however, they too may not recall anything that occurred more than a short time previously.

Gordon, age 15, despite making threats to harm himself two days before, scored only average on depression inventories. When asked about his responses, he was surprised. To him the feelings of despair and unhappiness that had led to his threats were so long in the past they were no longer applicable. Gordon no longer felt that way, would never feel that way again, and the problem was resolved as far as he was concerned. Gordon's projective testing, on the other hand, showed more underlying depression and difficulty making sense of things. Boredom and frustration also appeared to increase his anxiety and feeling of unease. Thus, Gordon, despite his current more positive feelings, was still very much at risk. Indeed, two days later he threatened to stab himself when he became frustrated, getting out a knife and holding it to his throat.

Self-report inventories are very useful if children accurately report symptoms; reported symptoms can serve as a jumping-off place to decide on intervention. However, when a child or adolescent with a known emotional problem does not reveal it on an inventory, care needs to be taken that the inventory is not accepted at face value, and that the child or adolescent receives needed support and care.

Projective assessments

As part of a clinical evaluation by a psychologist, projective assessment instruments can be employed to assess emotional and interpersonal functioning. These might include the Thematic Apperception Test, Tasks of Emotional Development, Rorschach, Projective Drawings, Draw A Person, and others for children. While none of these has been specifically constructed for gifted children, all will (given a competent person making the interpretation) give a full picture of the underlying psychodynamic structures.

Special knowledge of the problems of gifted children and adolescents is needed, however, to give the evaluator a perspective on how the child's perception of his or her difference from average may contribute to the view of self and others, and be part of underlying depression or anxiety. Thus, in reporting the results of projective testing, the degree of isolation and feelings of difference shown in the projective material may reflect an inability to make interpersonal contact, but may also reflect the lack of true peers with whom to interact.

BRETT'S PROJECTIVE TESTING

Brett's assessment showed a boy who was a big-picture thinker. Because he assessed things so globally, he sometimes had trouble understanding the smaller contributions of particular incidents as antecedents to problems. For example, in stories he constructed, Brett saw characters as having trouble making decisions and choices that led to good outcomes. Even when they made good decisions, fate intervened and a bad outcome occurred. Brett felt helpless and unable to alter things in his own life. To him, fate determined how things turned out despite his best efforts. In the end, he felt maybe it was better not to try. On the other hand, Brett's interpersonal abilities and his warmth were seen as strengths. He showed high creativity and intelligence, as well as a sense of humor. Thus, while Brett's projectives showed evidence of underlying anxiety and worry – depression – he also had the intelligence and creativity to make some changes if he could be supported and helped to make them come about.

MICHAEL'S PROJECTIVE TESTING

Michael's assessment showed a boy who had great difficulty making sense of the world. He tended to overfocus on part of a situation and then to see the whole in terms of this initial impression. Often his impression was not accurate or salient. Thus, he had a tendency to misinterpret what was going on. Also, Michael showed difficulty with interpersonal relationships. He had little idea of how others thought or felt. He rejected several of the projective story cards saying that he had no idea what was going on. In others, he named objects in the pictures but expressed no relationship among the objects or people. Michael also had trouble with cause and effect, and understanding consequences. He showed signs of anxiety and depression as well, but had little idea of how to deal with strong feelings or upset. Michael's projectives supported the diagnosis of AS, and suggested how fragmented his world was and how hard he had to work to make sense of the relationships among things and people.

Special issues in assessment

In this section of this chapter, specific issues pertinent to psychologists, teachers, and parents will be described.

Issues for psychologists and psychological examiners

In evaluating gifted children, the following are important.

1. Experience with gifted children. If the psychologist does not have any experience with gifted children, he or she should not be evaluating them. To say giftedness does not matter is to ignore the reality of what impact giftedness has on children and their families. If a psychologist with little experience wishes to gain more, there are currently many sources on the Internet (see Resource List, Chapter 10) and through books and conferences that will increase knowledge. Then, when assessing gifted children, it will be possible to tell what is the result of giftedness and what is the result of psychopathology.

    If the examiner is an expert on giftedness but does not know much about AD/HD or AS, then it is also necessary to learn more to avoid seeing all symptoms as manifestations of giftedness and to be able to recommend means of compensating for weaker cognitive areas. Read about AD/HD and AS, get permission to watch assessments of average children with these disorders, and go to conferences. In the USA, CHADD (Children and Adults with AD/HD) is an excellent resource for AD/HD. There are several conferences for AS. Tony Attwood also travels offering local conferences in the USA each year.

2. When assessing gifted children, it is important to use tests with high enough ceilings. Otherwise, it is difficult to tell what strengths and weaknesses are truly present. Also, with too low a ceiling, the difference between strengths and weaknesses is compressed so it appears as if the child is not as different as he or she may really be. Recommendations based on a faulty assessment of symptoms can be harmful to the child and family.

3.   In assessing the child, use a process method so that the child's own strengths are the measure of weakness rather than age-norm cutoffs. Also look for variability in performance. Does the child miss easy questions and get harder ones? Also, if the child goes beyond the stopping point of the particular test, even if he or she reached stopping criteria, does performance improve considerably? This is an indication of an attention problem.

4.   Make recommendations in terms of the child's strengths as well as weaknesses. For weaknesses suggest compensatory mechanisms that will allow for higher-level work instead of only lower-level rote work, even if the child needs remediations. Gifted children who are understimulated by the work never will learn it.

5.   Use portfolios to see what the child is capable of doing at home on topics of interest. This also is a measure of ability.

Issues for teachers

1.   When asked to assess a gifted child on a behavior checklist, try to determine how much the child varies in behavior and attention within the day as a means of understanding the child's functioning. Unless the child is very hyperactive, symptoms may be more subtle and will require careful observation from teachers about when they occur and how they compare to the child's best and worst times (rather than to the average child's norm).

2.   Add anecdotes and written evaluations to supplement the checklists. With gifted children with AD/HD, the comments teachers make are more diagnostic in many areas than the score on the checklist. For children with AS, it is helpful to know what types of work give the child the most trouble. Include sample papers when possible.

3.   What turns the child onto learning? When is the child eager and excited about a topic? For how long? How much structure does the child need to accomplish the task? Are there complaints about boredom, as well as about work being too easy or too hard? The same child may make both complaints on different days. For abilities that appear especially high try to see if out-of-level standardized testing can be done. A child who scores very high in reading needs an adjusted curriculum and is not helped by testing that cuts off a year above grade level.

4. Look for the child with splinter abilities – that is, outstanding abilities in one or two areas and more average performance in other areas – especially if performance varies across days. Such a child may be learning disabled, AD/HD, or AS, as well as gifted. If particular children are known for their insightful answers but usually get mediocre grades, they may need further evaluation. Children who are brilliant but do not do their work, complain about how much they have to write, and daydream need an evaluation especially if grades are dropping.

5. If a gifted child acts bored and complains about the level of the work, give the child more challenging work to determine if this helps to decrease negative behaviors, inattention, and lack of work completion. If challenge does help, the child may still have AD/HD, but may improve the level of inattentiveness.

6. With inattentive children with writing deficits, try to use compensatory methods and see if these help. Measures such as allowing dictation, more time on tests, and use of a computer may decrease the child's problem.

7. Don't assume in middle school that children whose grades drop are suffering from poor motivation or too much social interest. That may be so, but poorer performance may also be the result of a learning or attention problem that has gone undetected because up to now the child could compensate.

8. Children who are socially marginal also need evaluation. Some are loners because they have nothing in common with most other age peers, but are socially skilled when they meet true peers. Others need help in learning how to make friends and to establish social skills that are lacking.

9. Read about both giftedness and AD/HD, and giftedness and AS. Learn about useful websites. Go to some conferences and see what the issues are. You will learn information that will be invaluable in dealing with this special population. If you are gifted or have AD/HD or AS yourself, you can be a special resource for many children.

Issues for parents

1. Make sure that whoever assesses your child has knowledge about giftedness. It is also important if you suspect a problem like AD/HD or AS to select an evaluator who has experience with these disorders and other childhood problems. It may not be possible to find one

psychologist who is knowledgeable about both giftedness and childhood problems, so you may need two. However, make sure that both people are willing to work together, and that neither has a bias about giftedness or the prevalence of childhood problems in gifted children.

2.   Know what you want to ask of the evaluation. Make a list of specific questions and ask about the limitations of tests in answering these.

3.   When accumulating information to bring with you, bring samples of best and worst school work and standardized tests performed. Bring samples of work your child does for fun – take photos, bring tapes. One family brought pictures of a child's extensive rock collection and a computer printout showing how he classified all the samples he had. Others have brought short audiotapes of music composed by the child, writing, drawings, etc. Also bring a list of books read by your child in the past few months.

4.   When filling out checklists and surveys, be honest. Think of how your child behaves on both best and worst days. Don't underrate behaviors. If the form says, "Compared to the average child…" what it means is how often does the behavior really occur. A parent would expect a number of tantrums from a two-year-old, but not from a seven-year-old. Thus, compared to the average seven-year-old who does not display a lot of tantrums, how does your child look?

5.   Ask for written recommendations and make sure the psychologist will write suggestions for both strengths and weaknesses. Expect to have a feedback session and make sure this is part of the process. Some psychologists just send the report.

6.   Prepare the child for the assessment in a positive way. Many parents tell children the purpose is to learn about how they learn, and that they will be doing lots of things, some more like games and some more like school work, to see what is the best way for them to learn. This also will help to develop more interesting lessons at school and fun things to do at home.

       Try to make sure the child sees this as a fun experience. Most testing is fun, and children enjoy the experience. If your child does not, call the evaluator and discuss why. Some children need extra encouragement or a different approach to helping them feel reassured when faced with difficult material. Some shy children may need more rapport building before the testing, and some may need more careful limits set.

7.   Make sure you know what the process of assessment will be and try to plan accordingly. A parent who comes for an assessment with a child who has stayed up late is doing the child a disservice. If you decide to go to one of the centers known to work with gifted children to have your child tested, make sure you take jet lag and fatigue into account. You really can't expect your child to do his or her best work if it's the equivalent of 4 a.m. your time, and you have just arrived.

On the day before the evaluation make sure the child has enough sleep and is prepared to go the next day. That is not the day he or she should have a sleepover or go to one. Make sure the child is not sick. Testing children with mild colds makes little difference, but children with ear infections, getting over the flu, or with high fevers can't work very well. Some children lose as many as 25 or 30 IQ points when tested sick.

If the child is taking medication, tell the evaluator. Some medications affect testing such as asthma drugs and antihistamines. Children on stimulant medication need to take it. If this is a drug holiday, this is not the best time to test the child. It does matter.

Inform the evaluator of any allergies the child has. There is nothing like getting to a place and finding out they have a resident cat and the child is allergic. This can severely affect testing. If snacks are provided by the evaluator and your child is allergic or fussy, bring your own. Not only will your child feel better, but he or she will get what he or she likes.

8.   Don't expect to be with your child during the evaluation. Evaluations usually go much better for the child if he or she doesn't feel the parent is watching. There are some exceptions to this, but it does violate test guidelines, so only in very special circumstances should the parent be present. If the child is too young to separate comfortably, he or she is too young to be tested adequately. Most people will not assess young children (under age four) for intellectual potential unless they suspect mental retardation. Other learning problems and AD/HD are not usually even considered until the child has been to school. Thus, it is rare that a child younger than six is evaluated for these.

9.   Keep your copies of the evaluation safe. Don't rely on the evaluator to always have extra copies. They do keep files, but finding your child's file and making another copy will cost you extra, and evaluators do move away, and you may not be able to find them again.

10.   Reassessment will be needed for children with learning problems or attention deficits at about three-year intervals, and sometime before the

child takes the SATs if he or she has had a recommendation to take extended time or untimed tests as part of the evaluation. Parents need to plan accordingly for this, especially as more insurance companies are requiring prior approval and only approve for medical necessity, not for reevaluation purposes.

At the end of an evaluation, recommendations need to focus not only on accommodation and remediation of deficits, but also on enhancement of strengths. It is only by building on strengths that gifted children are motivated to achieve.

Brett's evaluation showed a moderately gifted and creative boy with AD/HD and anxiety. His biggest academic problems were slow work speed and poor handwriting. He needs accommodations such as use of a word processor, decreased workload for written work and help with organization and planning, including help in breaking projects down into manageable chunks. Brett needs to learn study skills tailored to his mixed learning style. He requires stimulation to keep him focused and motivated. Stimulation could be accomplished by acceleration in mathematics, and use of a mentor to develop projects in areas of interest. Brett should participate in the school's gifted program. Brett might also benefit from a trial of stimulant medication to help with his concentration and impulsivity. Psychotherapy around managing the asynchrony associated with both AD/HD symptoms and giftedness would likely decrease his anxiety.

Michael's evaluation showed an exceptionally gifted boy with AS, a NVLD and anxiety. Michael's biggest school problems were symptoms associated with his AS, both those related to understanding what was required in assignments, as well as in social functioning. Michael needs an Individual Educational Plan that would address written work deficits, handwriting deficits, difficulty with getting the big picture, problem solving deficits, poor organization and planning, and subtle language deficits. Michael also needs a program to address his social deficits including a social skills group, and a Buddy System. Michael needs higher-level work commensurate with his level of ability in his areas of strength to stimulate motivation and to decrease negative behavior. He could benefit from doing projects in areas of interest, accelerating in mathematics, participating in an advanced reading program, and learning a foreign language or Latin. Michael would benefit from working with gifted peers. He also would need interventions to decrease stress and anxiety.

For to be possessed of good mental powers is not sufficient; the principal matter is to apply them well.

René Descartes
Discourse on the Method, Part I

Chapter 10

Resource List for Parents, Teachers, and Professsionals

Books

Gifted children

Bireley, M. (1995) *Crossover Children: A Sourcebook for Helping Children Who are Gifted and Learning Disabled*. Reston, VA: The Council for Exceptional Children.

Csikszentmihalyi, M. (1996) *Creativity: Flow and the Psychology of Discovery and Invention*. New York: HarperCollins.

Gardner, H. (1983) *Frames of Mind: The Theory of Multiple Intelligences*. New York: Basic Books.

Gross, M.U.M. (1993) *Exceptionally Gifted Children*. New York: Routledge.

Kerr, B.A. (1985) *Smart Girls, Gifted Women*. Columbus, OH: Ohio Psychology Publishing.

Lynch, M.D. and Harris, C.R. (2001) *Fostering Creativity in Children, K-8: Theory and Practice*. Needham Heights, MA: Allyn and Bacon.

Piirto, J. (1992) *Understanding Those Who Create*. Dayton, OH: Ohio Psychology Publishing.

Roeper, A. (1995) *Annemarie Roeper: Selected Writings and Speeches*. Minneapolis, MN: Free Spirit Publishing.

Rogers, K.B. (2002) *Re-Forming Gifted Education: Matching the Program to the Child*. Scottsdale, AZ: Great Potential Press.

Silverman, L.K. (ed) (1993) *Counseling the Gifted and Talented*. Denver, CO: Love.

Silverman, L.K. (2002) *Upside-Down Brilliance: The Visual-Spatial Learner*. Denver, CO: DeLeon Publishing.

Webb, J.T., Meckstroth, E.A., and Tolan, S.S. (1982) *Guiding the Gifted Child: A Practical Source for Parents and Teachers*. Columbus, OH: Ohio Psychology Publishing.

West, T.G. (1997) *In the Mind's Eye. Updated Edition*. Amherst, NY: Prometheus Books.

Winner, E. (1996) *Gifted Children: Myths and Realities*. New York: Basic Books.

Attention Deficit/Hyperactivity Disorder

Barkley, R.A. (1995) *Taking Charge of ADHD: The Complete, Authoritative Guide for Parents.* New York: Guilford.

CHADD (2000) *The CHADD Information and Resource Guide to AD/HD.* (*www.chadd.org*).

Hallowell, E.M. and Ratey, J.J. (1994a) *Answers to Distraction.* New York: Pantheon.

Hallowell, E.M. and Ratey, J.J. (1994b) *Driven to Distraction.* New York: Pantheon.

Hartmann, T. (1993, 1997) *Attention Deficit Disorder: A Different Perception.* Grass Valley, CA: Underwood Books.

Hartmann, T. (1996) *Beyond ADD: Hunting for Reasons in the Past and Present.* Grass Valley, CA: Underwood Books.

McConnell, K., Ryser, G., and Higgins, J. (2000) *Practical Ideas That Really Work for Students with ADHD.* Austin, TX: Pro-Ed.

Nadeau, K.G. (ed) (1995) *A Comprehensive Guide to Attention Deficit Disorder in Adults.* New York: Bruner/Mazel.

Nadeau K.G., Littman, E.B., and Quinn, P.O. (1999) *Understanding Girls with AD/HD.* Silver Spring, MD: Advantage Books.

Quinn P.O. (1997) *Attention Deficit Disorder: Diagnosis and Treatment from Infancy to Adulthood.* New York: Bruner/Mazel.

Ratey, J.J. and Johnson, C. (1997) *Shadow Syndromes.* New York: Random House.

Rief, S. (1998) *The ADD/ADHD Checklist: A Easy Reference for Parents and Teachers.* Paramus, NJ: Prentice Hall.

Robin, A.L. (1999) *ADHD in Adolescents.* New York: Guilford.

Silverman, L.K. (2002) *Upside-Down Brilliance: The Visual-Spatial Learner.* Denver, CO: DeLeon Publishing.

Asperger Syndrome

Andron, L. (2001) *Our Journey Through High-Functioning Autism and Asperger Syndrome: A Roadmap.* London: Jessica Kingsley Publishers.

Attwood, T. (1998) *Asperger's Syndrome: A Guide for Parents and Professionals.* London: Jessica Kingsley Publishers.

Attwood, T. and Gray, C. (1999) *Understanding and Teaching Friendship Skills.* Available from Tony Attwood's website (*www.tonyattwood.com*).

Bolick, T. (2001) *Asperger Syndrome and Adolescence.* Gloucester, MA: Fair Winds Press.

Frith, U. (ed) (1991) *Autism and Asperger Syndrome.* Cambridge: Cambridge University Press.

Grandin, T. (1995) *Thinking in Pictures.* New York: Doubleday.

Hall, K. (2001) *Asperger Syndrome, the Universe and Everything.* London: Jessica Kingsley Publishers.

Jackson, L. (2002) *Freaks, Geeks and Asperger Syndrome.* London: Jessica Kingsley Publishers.

Myles, B.S. and Southwick, J. (1999) *Asperger Syndrome and Difficult Moments: Practical Solutions for Tantrums, Rages and Meltdowns.* Shawnee Mission, KS: Autism Asperger Publishing Co.

Ozonoff, S., Dawson, G., and McPartland, J. (2002) *A Parent's Guide to Asperger Syndrome and High-Functioning Autism.* New York: Guilford.

Stewart, K. (2002) *Helping a Child with Nonverbal Learning Disorder or Asperger's Syndrome.* Oakland, CA: New Harbinger Publications.

Willey, L.H. (1999) *Pretending to Be Normal: Living with Asperger's Syndrome.* London: Jessica Kingsley Publishers.

Williams, D. (1992) *Nobody Nowhere.* London: Transworld Publishers.

Related and coexisting problems

Barkley, R.A. and Benton, C.M. (1998) *Your Defiant Child: Eight Steps to Better Behavior.* New York: Guilford.

Greene, R. (1998) *The Explosive Child.* New York: HarperCollins.

Haerle, T. (ed) (1992) *Children with Tourette Syndrome: A Parent's Guide.* Rockville, MD: Woodbine House.

Kranowitz, C.S. (1998) *The Out-of-Synch Child: Recognizing and Coping With Sensory Integration Dysfunction.* New York; Skylight Press.

Papolos, D. and Papolos, J. (1999) *The Bipolar Child.* New York: Broadway Books.

Thompson, S. (1997) *The Source for Nonverbal Learning Disorders.* East Moline, IL: LinguiSystems.

Social skills

Frankel, F. (1996) *Good Friends are Hard to Find.* Los Angeles: Perspective Press.

Gabor, D. (2001) *How to Start a Conversation and Make Friends.* New York: Fireside Press.

Gray, C. (1994) *Comic Strip Conversations.* Arlington, TX: Future Horizons.

Gray, C. (2000) *The New Social Story Book, Illustrated Edition.* Arlington, TX: Future Horizons.

Mayo, P. and Waldo, P. (1994) *Scripting: Social Communication for Adolescents.* Eau Claire, WI: Thinking Publications.

Nowicki, S. Jr. and Duke, M.P. (1992) *Helping the Child Who Doesn't Fit In.* Atlanta, GA: Peachtree Publishers.

School skills

Cumine, V., Leach, J., and Stevenson, G. (1998) *Asperger Syndrome: A Practical Guide for Teachers.* London: Fulton.

Dendy, C.A.Z. (2003) *Teaching Teens with ADD and ADHD: A Quick Reference Guide for Teachers and Parents.* Bethsda, MD: Woodbine House.

Faherty, C. (2000) *Asperger's... What Does It Mean to Me? Structured Teaching Ideas for Home and School.* Arlington, TX: Future Horizons.

McConnell, K. and Ryser, G. (2000) *Practical Ideas That Really Work for Students With Autism Spectrum Disorders.* Austin, TX: Pro-Ed.

Moyes, R.A. (2001) *Incorporating Social Goals Into the Classroom: A Guide for Teachers and Parents of Children with High-Functioning Autism and Asperger Syndrome.* London: Jessica Kingsley Publishers.

Rief, S.F. (1993) *How to Reach and Teach ADD/ADHD Children.* San Francisco: Jossey Bass.

Zentall, S., Goldstein, S., and Dimatteo, R. (1999) *Seven Steps to Homework Success: A Family Guide for Solving Common Homework Problems.* Plantation, FL: Specialty Press.

Publishers

The ADD Warehouse (*www.addwarehouse.com*) 800-233-9273.

Free Spirit Publishing (*www.freespirit.com*) 800-735-7323.

Future Horizons (*www.futurehorizons-autism.com*).

Jessica Kingsley Publishers (*www.jkp.com*).

Mindware (*www.MINDWAREonline.com*) 800-999-0398.

Prufrock Press (Gifted and Talented) (*www.prufrock.com*) 800-998-2208.

Roeper Review (*www.roeperreview.org*).

Organizations and websites

Gifted children

Gifted Canada
(*www3.bc.sympatico.ca/giftedcanada/*).

National Association of Gifted Children (US)
1707 L Street NW
Suite 550
Washington, DC 20036.
Parenting for High Potential
Gifted Child Quarterly
(*www.nagc.org*).

National Association for Gifted Children (UK)
540 Elder House
Milton Keynes
MK9 1LR
(*www.nagcbritain.org.uk*).

New South Wales Association Gifted and Talented Children
(*www.nswagtc.org.au*).

New Zealand Association for Gifted Children
(*www.homestead.com/nzagc/files/intro.htm*).

Attention Deficit/Hyperactivity Disorder

CHADD (Children and Adults with AD/HD)
   8181 Professional Place
   Suite 201
   Landover, MD 20785
   800-233-4050
   Attention: for families and adults with AD/HD
   (*www.chadd.org*).

CHADD of Canada
   National Office
   1376 Bank Street
   Ottawa, ON K1H 743
   613-731-1209
   (*www.chaddcanada.org/*).

The Learning Disabilities Association
   4156 Library Road
   Pittsburgh, PA 15234
   412-341-1515.

National Attention Deficit Disorder Association
   1788 Second Street Suite 200
   Highland Park, IL 60035
   (*www.add.org*).

Asperger Syndrome

Asperger's Asssociation of New England (AANE)
   1301 Centre Street
   Newton, MA 02459
   (617) 527-2894
   (*www.aane.org*).

Autism Society of America
   7910 Woodmont Avenue, Suite 300
   Bethsda, MD, 20814-3067
   301-657-0081
   (*www.autism-society.org*).

Autism Society of Canada
  129 Yorkville Avenue Ste 020 Road
  Toronto, Ontario MSR-IC4.

The National Autistic Society (UK)
  393 City Road
  London EC1V 1NG
  020 7833 2299
  (*www.nas.org.uk/l*).

Other useful websites

Gifted children

  Awesome Library – Special Education
  (*www.awesomelibrary.org/library/special_education/gifted/Gifted.html*).

  CTY Program at Johns Hopkins (*www.jhu.edu/gifted/*).

  Davidson Institute Young Scholars Program (*www.davidson-institute.org*).

  EPGY Programs at Stanford (*www-epgy.stanford.edu/epgy/*).

  Gifted Development Center (Linda Silverman's website)
  (*www.gifteddevelopment.com*).

  Gifted Resource Center of New England (*www.grcne.com*).

  GT World (*www.gtworld.org*).

  Hoagies Gifted Education Page (*www.hoagiesgifted.org*).

  The National Research Center on Gifted and Talented (*www.gifted.uconn.edu*).

  Uniquely Gifted (*www.uniquelygifted.org*).

Attention Deficit/Hyperactivity Disorder

  ADHD Canada (*www.adhdcanada.ca*) (adults).

  ADHD United Kingdom (*www.adders.org/*) (adults).

  ADHD UK (*www.adhdalliance.org.uk*).

  ADHD New Zealand (*www.ADHD.org.nz*).

  Learning Differences Coalition of New South Wales (*www.add.org.au*).

  One ADD Place (*www.oneaddplace.com*).

Asperger Syndrome

ASPEN (*www.aspennj.org*).

Asperger Syndrome Coalition of the US (*www.asperger.org*).

Cloud 9 Children's Foundation New Zealand
(*www.withyoueverystepoftheway.com*).

Families of Adults Afflicted with AS (*www.faaas.org*).

Future Horizons (*www.futurehorizons-autism.com/*).

OASIS (*www.udel.edu/bkirby/asperger*).

Tony Attwood's website (*www.tonyattwood.com*).

Yale Child Study Center (*http://info.med.yale.edu/chldstdy/autism/index.html*).

Other

Canadian Learning Disabilities Association (*www.ldac-taac.ca/*).

Learning Disabilities Association of America (*www.ldanatl.org*).

Nonverbal Learning Disability (*www.NLDline.com*).

(*www.NLDontheWEB.org*).

(*www.tsa-usa.org*).

The Bipolar Child (the Papolos's website) (*www.bipolarchild.com*).

Tourette Syndrome Association (*www.tsa-usa.org*).

(*www.tourette.ca*).

Appendix A

Diagnostic Criteria

Diagnostic criteria for AD/HD DSM-IV

A. EITHER 1 OR 2:

(1) six (or more) of the following symptoms of *inattention* have persisted for at least 6 months to a degree that is maladaptive and inconsistent with developmental level:

Inattention:

(a) often fails to give close attention to details or makes careless mistakes in school work, work, or other activities

(b) often has difficulty sustaining attention in tasks or play activities

(c) often does not seem to listen when spoken to directly

(d) often does not follow through on instructions and fails to finish school work, chores, or duties in the workplace (not due to oppositional behavior or failure to understand instructions)

(e) often has difficulty organizing tasks and activities

(f) often avoids, dislikes, or is reluctant to engage in tasks that require sustained mental effort (such as school work or homework)

(g) often loses things necessary for tasks or activities (e.g., toys, school assignments, pencils, books, or tools)

(h) is often easily distracted by extraneous stimuli

(i) is often forgetful in daily activities.

(2) six (or more) of the following symptoms of *hyperactivity/impulsivity* have persisted for at least 6 months to a degree that is maladaptive and inconsistent with developmental level:

Hyperactivity:

(a) often fidgets with hands or feet or squirms in seat

(b) often leaves seat in classroom or other situations in which remaining seated is expected

(c) often runs about or climbs excessively in situations in which it is inappropriate (in adolescents or adults, may be limited to subjective feelings of restlessness)

(d) often has trouble playing or engaging in leisure activities quietly

(e) is often "on the go" or acts as if "driven by a motor"

(f) often talks excessively

Impulsivity

(g) often blurts out answers before questions have been completed

(h) often has difficulty waiting turn

(i) often interrupts or intrudes on others (e.g., butts into conversations or games).

B. Some hyperactive/impulsive or inattentive symptoms that caused impairment were present before age seven years.

C. Some impairment from these symptoms is present in two or more settings (e.g., school [work] and at home).

D. There must be clear evidence of clinically significant impairment in social, academic, or occupational functioning.

E. The symptoms do not occur exclusively during the course of a Pervasive Developmental Disorder, Schizophrenia, or other Psychotic Disorder and are not better accounted for by another mental disorder (e.g., Mood Disorder, Anxiety Disorder, Dissociative Disorder, or a Personality Disorder).

Code based on type:

314.01 Attention Deficit/Hyperactivity Disorder, Combined Type: if both A1 and A2 are met for the past six months.

314.00 Attention Deficit/Hyperactivity Disorder, Predominately Inattentive Type: if A1 but not A2 has been met for the past six months.

314.01 Attention Deficit/Hyperactivity Disorder, Predominately Hyperactive/Impulsive Type: if A2 but not A1 has been met for the past six months.

Coding Note: For individuals (especially adolescents or adults) who currently have symptoms but no longer meet full criteria, "In Partial Remission" should be specified.

Source: American Psychiatric Association (2000) *Diagnostic and Statistical Manual of Mental Disorders, Fourth Edition, Text Revision.* Washington, DC: American Psychiatric Association. Copyright 2000 by the American Psychiatric Association. Reprinted by permission.

Diagnostic criteria for AS DSM-IV

A. Qualitative impairment in social interaction, as manifested by at least two of the following:

  (1) marked impairment in the use of multiple nonverbal behaviors such as eye-to-eye gaze, facial expression, body postures, and gestures to regulate social interaction

  (2) failure to develop peer relationships appropriate to developmental level

  (3) a lack of spontaneous seeking to share enjoyment, interests, or achievements with other people (e.g., by a lack of showing, bringing, or pointing out objects of interest to other people)

  (4) lack of social or emotional reciprocity.

B. Restrictive repetitive and stereotyped patterns of behavior, interests, and activities, as manifested by at least one of the following:

  (1) encompassing preoccupation with one or more stereotyped and restricted patterns of interest that is abnormal either in intensity or focus

  (2) apparently inflexible adherence to specific, nonfunctional routines or rituals

  (3) stereotyped and repetitive motor mannerisms (e.g., hand or finger flapping or twisting, or complex whole-body movements)

  (4) persistent preoccupation with parts of objects.

C. The disturbance causes clinically significant impairment in social, occupational, or other important areas of functioning.

D. There is no clinically significant general delay in language (e.g., single words used by age two years, communicative phrases used by age three years).

E. There is no clinically significant delay in cognitive development or in the development of age-appropriate self-help skills, adaptive behavior (other than in social interaction), and curiosity about the environment in childhood.

F. Criteria are not met for another specific Pervasive Developmental Disorder or Schizophrenia.

Source: American Psychiatric Association (2000) *Diagnostic and Statistical Manual of Mental Disorders, Fourth Edition, Text Revision.* Washington, DC: American Psychiatric Association. Copyright 2000 by the American Psychiatric Association. Reprinted by permission.

Diagnostic criteria for AS (Gillberg and Gillberg)

1. Social impairment (extreme egocentricity) (at least two of the following):

(a) difficulties interacting with peers

(b) indifference to peer contacts

(c) difficulties interpreting social cues

(d) socially and emotionally inappropriate behavior.

2. Narrow interest (at least one of the following):

(a) exclusion of other activities

(b) repetitive adherence

(c) more rote than meaning.

3. Compulsive need for introducing routines and interests (at least one of the following):

(a) which affect the individual's every aspect of everyday life

(b) which affect others.

4. Speech and language peculiarities (at least three of the following):

(a) delayed speech development

(b) superficially perfect expressive language

(c) formal pedantic language

(d) odd prosody, peculiar voice characteristics

(e) impairment of comprehension including misinterpretations of literal/implied meanings.

5. *Non verbal communication problems (at least one of the following)*:

    (a) limited use of gestures

    (b) clumsy/gauche body language

    (c) limited facial expression

    (d) inappropriate facial expression

    (e) peculiar stiff gaze.

6. *Motor clumsiness:*

    poor performance in neurodevelopmental test.

Source: Gillberg and Gillberg (1989). Reprinted with permission of Christopher Gillberg.

List of Test Distributors for Professionals

These sources are not meant to be a comprehensive listing of assessment instruments, but are the instruments most often used at the Gifted Resource Center of New England or are commonly used in schools and clinics. These instruments cannot be purchased by parents or teachers, as they require training and experience to administer properly. In fact, test companies will only sell them to people with the proper professional credentials. They are listed here though as a service to professionals reading this book. Several companies often offer the same instrument; it is good to check several as prices can vary widely.

The Psychological Corporation
 19500 Boulevard Road
 San Antonio, TX 78259-3701
 800-872-1726
 (*www.PsychCorp.com*)

 The Wechsler Intelligence Scales

 Test of Nonverbal Intelligence – 3

 Detroit Tests of Learning Aptitude

 Wechsler Individual Achievement Tests

 Wide Range Achievement Tests

 California Verbal Learning Test – Children's

 Children's Memory Scale

 Wide Range Assessment of Memory and Learning

 Continuous Performance Tests (Conners', Vigil, Auditory)

 NEPSY (Tower of London)

 Wisconsin Card Sorting Test

 Beck Scales (Depression, Anxiety, Youth Inventory)

Reynolds Scales

Rorschach

Thematic Apperception Test

Brown ADD Scales

Conners Rating Scales.

Riverside Publishing

425 Spring Lake Drive
Itasca, IL60143-2079
800-323-9540
(*www.riversidepublishing.com*)

The Stanford-Binet Intelligence Scales

Woodcock-Johnson-III Tests of Cognitive Abilities

Test of Nonverbal Intelligence – 3

Detroit Tests of Learning Aptitude

Woodcock-Johnson-III Tests of Achievement

Test of Early Reading Ability – 3

Test of Reading Comprehension-3

Gray Oral Reading Tests

Wide Range Achievement Tests

Test of Written Language

Wide Range Assessment of Memory and Learning

Test of Memory and Learning

Test of Language Development

Token Test for Children

Boston Naming Test (Part of Boston Diagnostic Aphasia Examination)

Expressive One-Word Picture Vocabulary Test

Receptive One-Word Picture Vocabulary Test

Beery-Buktenica Developmental Test of Visual-Motor Integration (VMI)

Purdue Pegboard

Stroop Color and Word Test

Rorschach

Thematic Apperception Test

Achenbach Child Behavior Checklists

ADD-H: Comprehensive Teacher's Rating Scale (ACTeRS).

Psychological Assessment Resources (PAR)
16204 N. Florida Avenue
Lutz, FL 33549
800-331-8378
(*www.parinc.com*)

Kaufman Intelligence Scales

Slosson Intelligence Scales

Leiter International Performance Scale

Test of Nonverbal Intelligence – 3

Detroit Tests of Learning Aptitude

Wide Range Achievement Tests

Test of Written Language – 3

Gray Oral Reading Tests

Children's Memory Scale

Test of Memory and Learning

Wide Range Assessment of Memory and Learning

Children's Auditory-Verbal Learning Test – 2

Token Test for Children

Expressive One-Word Picture Vocabulary Test

Receptive One-Word Picture Vocabulary Test

OWLS: Listening Comprehension and Oral Expression Scales

Beery Developmental Test of Visual-Motor Integration (VMI)

Developmental Test of Visual Perception – Adolescent and Adult

Benton Laboratory of Neuropsychology: Left-Right Orientation; Judgment of Line Orientation; Facial Recognition; Finger Localization

Wisconsin Card Sorting Test

Tower of London Drexel University

Developmental Scoring System for the Rey-Osterrieth Complex Figure

Comprehensive Trail Making Test

Stroop Color and Word Test

Portable Tactual Performance Test

d2 Test of Attention

Continuous Performance Tests (Conners; TOVA)

Reynolds Scales

Rorschach

Thematic Apperception Test

Conners Rating Scales

ACTeRS Teacher/Parent Forms

Brown ADD Scales

Asperger Syndrome Diagnostic Scale

Self-Esteem Inventory (also Piers-Harris; Tennessee, and Culture Free Self-Esteem).

Slosson Educational Publications

PO Box 544
East Aurora, NY 14052-0544
888-756-7766
(*www.slosson.com*)

Slosson Intelligence Scales

Kaufman Intelligence Tests

Test of Nonverbal Intelligence – 3

Detroit Tests of Learning Aptitude

Wide Range Achievement Tests

Gray Oral Reading Tests

Test of Reading Comprehension – 3

Test of Written Language – 3

Slosson Oral Reading Test

Wide Range Assessment of Memory and Learning

Test of Memory and Learning

Expressive One-Word Picture Vocabulary Test

Receptive One-Word Picture Vocabulary Test

Test of Auditory Reasoning and Processing Skills

Test of Language Development

Test of Pragmatic Language

Token Test for Children

Developmental Test of Visual-Motor Integration (VMI)

Developmental Test of Visual Perception – 2

Conners Continuous Performance Test

Conners Rating Scales

Reynolds Scales

Gilliam Asperger Disorder Scale

Asperger Syndrome Diagnostic Scale

ACTeRS.

AGS
4201 Woodland Road
Circle Pines, MN 55014-1796
800-328-2560
(*www.agsnet.com*)

Kaufman Intelligence Tests

Test of Nonverbal Intelligence – 3

Detroit Tests of Learning Aptitude

Kaufman Test of Educational Achievement – Normative Update

Peabody Individual Achievement Test – Revised Normative Update

Woodcock Reading Mastery Tests Normative Update

Key Math Normative Update

Test of Reading Comprehension – 3

Test of Early Reading Ability

Test of Written Language – 3

Test of Memory and Learning

Peabody Picture Vocabulary Test – 3

OWLS

Test of Language Development

Vineland Adaptive Behavior Scales

Asperger Syndrome Diagnostic Scale.

Pro-Ed

8700 Shoal Creek Boulevard
Austin, TX 78757-6897
800-897-3202
(*www.proedinc.com*)

Slosson Intelligence Tests

Test of Nonverbal Intelligence – 3

Detroit Tests of Learning Aptitude

Wide Range Achievement Test

Test of Written Language – 3

Gray Oral Reading Tests

Test of Reading Comprehension – 3

Wide Range Assessment of Memory and Learning

OWLS

Test of Language Development

Expressive One-Word Picture Vocabulary Test

Receptive One-Word Picture Vocabulary Test

Developmental Test of Visual Perception – Adolescent and Adult

Developmental Test of Visual Perception – 2

Developmental Test of Visual-Motor Integration

Wisconsin Card Sorting Test

Asperger Syndrome Diagnostic Scale

Gilliam Asperger Disorder Scale

Conners Rating Scales

Culture Free Self-Esteem Inventories (Self-Esteem Index; Piers-Harris also)

Reynolds Scales.

Western Psychological Services

12031 Wilshire Boulevard
Los Angeles, CA 90025-1251
800-648-8857
(*www.wpspublish.com*)

Kaufman Intelligence Tests

Slosson Intelligence Tests

Detroit Tests of Learning Aptitude

Test of Nonverbal Intelligence – 3

Wide Range Achievement Tests

Test of Written Language – 3

Gray Oral Reading Tests

Wide Range Assessment of Memory and Learning

Test of Memory and Learning

Test of Auditory Reasoning and Processing Skills

Token Test for Children

Test of Language Development

OWLS

Expressive One-Word Picture Vocabulary Test

Receptive One-Word Picture Vocabulary Test

Test of Pragmatic Language

Developmental Test of Visual-Motor Integration (VMI)

Developmental Test of Visual Perception – 2

Developmental Test of Visual Perception – Adolescent and Adult

Hooper Visual Organization Test

Comprehensive Trail Making Test

Wisconsin Card Sorting Test

d2 Test of Attention

Stroop Color and Word Test

Continuous Performance Test (TOVA)

Rorschach

Thematic Apperception Test

Piers-Harris Self-Concept Scale

Asperger Syndrome Diagnostic Scale

Conners Rating Scales

ACTeRS

The New Social Story Book (Carol Gray).

Bibliography

AAUW Education Foundation (1992) *The AAUW Report: How Schools Shortchange Girls. Executive Summary.* Washington, DC: American Association of University Women Educational Foundation.

Abroms, K.J. (1985) 'Social Giftedness and its Relationship with Intellectual Giftedness.' In J. Freeman (ed) *The Psychology of Gifted Children: Perspectives on Development and Education* (pp.201–218). New York: Wiley.

Achenbach, T.M. (1991a) *Manual for the Child Behavior Checklist/4-18 and 1991 Profile.* Burlington, VT: University of Vermont Department of Psychiatry.

Achenbach, T.M. (1991b) *Manual for the Teacher's Report Form and 1991 Profile.* Burlington, VT: University of Vermont Department of Psychiatry.

Ainsworth, M. D. S. (1964) 'Patterns of Attachment Behavior Shown by the Infant in Interaction with his Mother.' *Merrill Palmer Quarterly 10,* 51–58.

Alexander, J.M., Noyes, C.R., MacBrayer, E.K., Schwanenflugel, P.J., and Fabricius, W.V. (1998) 'Concepts of Mental Activities and Verbs in Children of High and Average Verbal Intelligence.' *Gifted Child Quarterly 42,* 16–28.

Alessandri, S.M. (1992) 'Attention, Play, and Social Behavior in ADHD Preschoolers.' *Journal of Abnormal Child Psychology 20,* 289–302.

Amabile, T.M. (1983) *The Social Psychology of Creativity.* New York: Springer-Verlag.

American Psychiatric Association (2000) *Diagnostic and Statistical Manual of Mental Disorders, Fourth Edition, Text Revision (DSM-IV-TR).* Washington, DC: American Psychiatric Association.

Anthony, E.J. (1987) 'Risk, Vulnerability and Resilience: An Overview.' In E.J. Anthony and B.J. Cohler (eds) *The Invulnerable Child* (pp.3–48). New York: Guilford.

Arbuthnot, J. (1973) 'Relationship Between Maturity of Moral Judgment and Measures of Cognitive Abilities.' *Psychological Reports 33,* 945–946.

Asperger, H. (1991) '"Autistic psychopathy" in Childhood.' In U. Frith (ed) *Autism and Asperger Syndrome* (pp.37–92). Translated by Uta Frith. Cambridge: Cambridge University Press.

Attwood, T. (1998) *Asperger's Syndrome: A Guide for Parents and Professionals.* London: Jessica Kingsley Publishers.

Attwood, T. and Grandin, T. (2000) 'Tony and Temple: Face to Face.' *Autism/Asperger's Digest Magazine* (Future Horizons), January/February, 8–12.

Attwood, T. and Gray, C. (1999) *Understanding and Teaching Friendship Skills.* Available from Tony Attwood's website (*www.tonyattwood.com*).

Aylward, G.P., Gordon, M., and Verhulst, S.J. (1997) 'Relationship Between Continuous Performance Task Scores and Other Cognitive Measures: Causality or Commonality?' *Assessment 4,* 313–324.

Baker, D.B., Taylor, C.J., and Leyva, C. (1995) 'Continuous Performance Test: A Comparison of Modalities.' *Journal of Child Psychology 51*, 548–551.

Barkley, R.A. (ed) (1990) *Attention-Deficit Hyperactivity Disorder.* New York: Guilford.

Barkley, R.A. (1995) *Taking Charge of ADHD: The Complete, Authoritative Guide for Parents.* New York: Guilford.

Barkley, R.A. (1997) *ADHD and the Nature of Self-Control.* New York: Guilford.

Barkley, R.A. (ed) (1998) *Attention Deficit Hyperactivity Disorder (Second Edition).* New York: Guilford.

Barkley, R. A., Grodzinsky, G. and DuPaul, G. (1992) 'Frontal Lobe Functions in Attention Deficit Disorder With and Without Hyperactivity: A Review and Research Report.' *Journal of Abnormal Child Psychology 20*, 163–188.

Baron-Cohen, S. (1995) *Mindblindness: An Essay on Autism and Theory of Mind.* Cambridge, MA: MIT Press.

Baron-Cohen, S. (2000) 'Theory of Mind and Autism: A Fifteen Year Review.' In S. Baron-Cohen, H. Tager-Flusberg, and D. J. Cohen (eds) *Understanding Other Minds, Second Edition.* (pp.3–20). New York: Oxford University Press.

Baron-Cohen, S., Jolliffe, T., Mortimore, C., and Robertson, M. (1997a) 'Another Advanced Test of Theory of Mind: Evidence from Very High Functioning Adults with Autism or Asperger Syndrome.' *Journal of Child Psychology and Psychiatry 38*, 813–822.

Baron-Cohen, S., Wheelwright, S. and Jolliffe, T. (1997b) 'Is There a "Language of the Eyes"? Evidence from Normal Adults and Adults with Autism or Asperger Syndrome.' *Visual Cognition 4*, 311–331.

Baron-Cohen, S., Bolton, P., Wheelwright, S., *et al.* (1998) 'Autism Occurs More in Families of Physicists, Engineers, and Mathematicians.' *Autism 2*, 296–301.

Baron-Cohen, S., Ring, H., Wheelwright, S., *et al.* (1999) 'Social Intelligence in the Normal and Autistic Brain: An fMRI Study.' *European Journal of Neurosciences 11*, 1891–1898.

Baum, S.M., Olenchak, F.R., and Owen, S.V. (1998) 'Gifted Students with Attention Deficits: Fact or Fiction? Or, Can We See the Forest for the Trees.' *Gifted Child Quarterly 42*, 96–104.

Bear, G.G. and Rys, G.S. (1994) 'Moral Reasoning, Classroom Behavior and Sociometric Status Among Elementary School Children.' *Developmental Psychology 30*, 633–638.

Bell, L.A. (1989) 'Something's Wrong Here and It's Not Me: Challenging the Dilemmas that Block Girls' Success.' *Journal for the Education of the Gifted 12*, 118–130.

Benbow, C.P. and Minor, L.L. (1990) 'Cognitive Profiles of Verbally and Mathematically Precocious Students: Implications for Identification of the Gifted.' *Gifted Child Quarterly 34*, 21–26.

Berry, C.A., Shaywitz, S.E., and Shaywitz, B.A. (1985) 'Girls with Attention Deficit Disorder: A Silent Minority? A Report on Behavioral and Cognitive Characteristics.' *Pediatrics 76*, 801–809.

Berthier, M. (1995) 'Hypomania Following Bereavement in Asperger's Syndrome: A Case Study.' *Neuropsychiatry, Neuropsychology, and Behavioral Neurology 8*, 222–228.

Biederman, J., Newcorn, J., and Sprich, S. (1991a) 'Comorbidity of Attention Deficit Hyperactivity Disorder with Conduct, Depressive, Anxiety and Other Disorders.' *American Journal of Psychiatry 148*, 564–577.

Biederman, J., Faraone, S.V., Keenan, K., *et al.* (1998b) 'Evidence of Familial Association between Attention Deficit Disorder and Major Affective Disorders.' *Archives of General Psychiatry 148*, 633–642.

Biederman, J., Faraone, S.V. and Lapey, K. (1992a) 'Cormorbidity of Diagnosis in Attention-Deficit Hyperactivity Disorder.' *Child and Adolescent Psychiatric Clinics of North America 1*, 335–360.

Biederman, J., Faraone, S.V., Keenan, K. *et al.* (1992b) 'Further Evidence for Family-Genetic Risk Factors in Attention Deficit Hyperactivity Disorder (ADHD): Patterns of Comorbidity in Probands and Relatives in Psychiatrically and Pediatrically Referred Samples.' *Archives of General Psychiatry 49*, 728–738.

Biederman, J., Faraone, S.V., Mick, E., *et al.* (1995) 'Psychiatric Comorbidity Among Referred Juveniles with Major Depression: Fact or Artifact?' *Journal of the American Academy of Child and Adolescent Psychiatry 34*, 579–590.

Biederman, J., Faraone, S.V., Mick, E., *et al.* (1996) 'Attention Deficit Hyperactivity in Juvenile Mania: An Overlooked Comorbidity?' *Journal of the American Academy of Child and Adolescent Psychiatry 35*, 997–1008.

Biederman, J., Faraone, S., Mick, E., *et al.* (1999) 'Clinical Correlates of ADHD in Females: Findings from a Large Group of Girls Ascertained from Pediatric and Psychiatric Referral Services.' *Journal of the American Academy of Child and Adolescent Psychiatry 38*, 966–975.

Bird, H.R. (1998) 'The Prevalence and Cross-Cultural Validity of ADHD.' In *Diagnosis and Treatment of Attention Deficit Hyperactivity Disorder. Program and Abstracts* (pp.53–55). NIH Consensus Development Conference, Bethesda, MD, November 16–18.

Blachman, D. R. and Hinshaw, S. P. (2002) 'Patterns of Friendship among Girls with and without Attention-Deficit/Hyperactivity Disorder.' *Journal of Abnormal Child Psychology 30*, 625–640.

Blakemore-Brown, L. (2002) *Reweaving the Autistic Tapestry.* London: Jessica Kingsley Publishers.

Bland, L.C., Sowa, C.J., and Callahan, C.M. (1994) 'An Overview of Resilience in Gifted Children.' *Roeper Review 17*, 77–80.

Bolick, T. (2001) *Asperger Syndrome and Adolescence.* Gloucester, MA: Fair Winds Press.

Borland J.H. (1986) 'A Note on the Existence of Certain Divergent-Production Abilities.' *Journal for the Education of the Gifted 9*, 239–251.

Borland, J.H., Schnur, R., and Wright, L. (2000) 'Economically Disadvantaged Students in a School for the Academically Gifted: A Postpositivist Inquiry into Individual and Family Adjustment.' *Gifted Child Quarterly 44*, 113–132.

Borland, J.H. and Wright, L. (1994) 'Identifying Young, Potentially Gifted, Economically Disadvantaged Students.' *Gifted Child Quarterly 38*, 164–171.

Bowler, D.D. (1992) 'Theory of Mind in Asperger Syndrome.' *Journal of Child Psychology and Psychiatry 33*, 877–895.

Braaten, E.B. and Rosen, L.A. (2000) 'Self-Regulation of Affect in ADHD and Non-ADHD Boys: Differences in Empathic Responding.' *Journal of Consulting and Clinical Psychology 68*, 313–321.

Brown R., Madau-Swain, A., and Baldwin, K. (1991) 'Gender Differences in a Clinic-Referred Sample of Attention Deficit Disordered Children.' *Child Psychiatry and Human Development 22*, 111–128.

Brown, T.E. (1995) 'Differential Diagnosis of ADD and ADHD in Adults.' In K.G. Nadeau (ed) *A Comprehensive Guide to Attention Deficit Disorder in Adults* (pp.93–108). New York: Bruner-Mazel.

Brown, T.E. (1996) *Brown Attention Deficit Disorder Scales*. San Antonio, TX: Psychological Corporation.

Brown, T.E. (1998) 'ADHD in Persons with Superior IQs: Unique Risks.' Presented at the 10th Annual CHADD International Conference, October 15–17, New York, NY.

Brown, T.E. (2000a) 'Attention-Deficit Disorder with Obsessive-Compulsive Disorder.' In T.E. Brown (ed) *Attention-Deficit Disorders and Comorbidities in Children, Adolescents and Adults* (pp.209–230). Washington, DC: American Psychiatric Press.

Brown, T.E. (2000b) 'Emerging Understandings of Attention-Deficit Disorders and Comorbidities.' In T.E. Brown (ed) *Attention-Deficit Disorders and Comorbidities in Children, Adolescents and Adults* (pp.3–55). Washington, DC: American Psychiatric Press.

Brown, T.E. (2001) *Brown Attention Deficit Disorder Scales for Children*. San Antonio, TX: Psychological Corporation.

Brown, T.E. (2002) 'ADHD Impairments in Learning.' Retreat Healthcare Continuing Education. Presented April 5, Providence RI.

Cadesky, E.B., Mota, V.L., and Schachar, R.J. (2000) 'Beyond Words: How Do Children with ADHD and/or Conduct Problems Process Nonverbal Information about Affect?' *Journal of the American Academy of Child and Adolescent Psychiatry 39*, 1160–1167.

Callahan, C. (1991) 'An Update on Gifted Females.' *Journal for the Education of the Gifted 14*, 284–311.

Carr, M., Alexander, J., and Schwanenflugel, P. (1996) 'Where Gifted Children Do and Do Not Excel on Metacognitive Tasks. *Roeper Review 18*, 212–217.

Carte, E.T., Nigg, J.T., and Hinshaw, S.P. (1996) 'Neuropsychological Functioning, Motor Speed, and Language Processing in Boys With and Without ADHD.' *Journal of Abnormal Child Psychology 24*, 481–498.

Cash, A.B. (1999) 'A Profile of Gifted Individuals with Autism: The Twice Exceptional Learner.' *Roeper Review 22*, 22–27.

Chae, P. K., Kim, J. and Noh, K. (2003) 'Diagnosis of ADHD Among Gifted Children in Relation to KEDI-WISC and TOVA Performance.' *Gifted Child Quarterly 47*, 192–201.

Chiron, C., Leboyer, M., Leon, F., Jambaqué, I., Nuttin, C., and Syrota, A. (1995) 'SPECT of the Brain in Childhood Autism: Evidence for a Lack of Normal Hemispheric Asymmetry.' *Developmental Medicine and Child Neurology 37*, 849–860.

Columbus Group (1991, July) Unpublished transcript of the meeting of the Columbus Group. Columbus: OH.

Comings, D.E. (2000) 'Attention-Deficit/Hyperactivity Disorder with Tourette Syndrome.' In T.E. Brown (ed) *Attention-Deficit Disorders and Comorbidities in Children, Adolescents and Adults* (pp.363–391). Washington, DC: American Psychiatric Press.

Conners, C.K. (1995) *The Conners Continuous Performance Test*. North Tonawanda, NY: Multi-Health Systems.

Conners, C.K. (1997) 'Is ADHD a Disease?' *Journal of Attention Disorders 2*, 3–17.

Conners, C.K. (2001) *Conners' Rating Scales – Revised*. North Tonawanda, NY: Multi-Health Systems.

Cornell, D.G., Delcourt, M.A.B., Bland, L.C., Goldberg, M.D., and Oram, G. (1994) 'Low Incidence of Behavior Problems among Elementary School Students in Gifted Programs.' *Journal for the Education of the Gifted 18*, 4–19.

Cramer, R.H. (1989) 'Attitudes of Gifted Boys and Girls towards Math: A Qualitative Study.' *Roeper Review 11*, 128–130.

Cramond, B. (1994) 'Attention-Deficit Hyperactivity Disorder and Creativity: What's the Connection?' *Journal of Creative Behavior 28*, 193–210.

Cropley, A.J. (2000) 'Defining and Measuring Creativity: Are Creativity Tests Worth Using?' *Roeper Review 23*, 72–79.

Cross, T.L., Coleman, L.J., and Stewart, R.A. (1993) 'The Social Cognition of Gifted Adolescents: An Exploration of the Stigma of Giftedness Paradigm.' *Roeper Review 16*, 37–40.

Csikszentmihalyi, M. (1996) *Creativity: Flow and the Psychology of Discovery and Invention.* New York: HarperCollins

Csikszentmihalyi, M., Rathunde, K., and Whalen, S. (1993) *Talented Teenagers.* New York: Cambridge University Press.

Culbertson W.C. and Zillmer, E.A. (1998) 'The Construct Validity of the Tower of London DX as a Measure of the Executive Functioning of ADHD Children.' *Archives of Neuropsychology 13*, 285–301.

Cytowic, R.E. (1993) *The Man Who Tasted Shapes.* Cambridge, MA: MIT Press.

Dahlberg, W. (1992) 'Brilliance: The Childhood Dilemma of Unusual Intellect.' *Roeper Review 15*, 7–10.

Dark, V.J. and Benbow, C.P. (1991) 'Differential Enhancement of Working Memory with Mathematical versus Verbal Precocity.' *Journal of Educational Psychology 83*, 48–60.

Dauber, S.L. and Benbow, C.P. (1990) 'Aspects of Personality and Peer Relations of Extremely Talented Adolescents.' *Gifted Child Quarterly 34*, 10–15.

Daugherty, M., White, C.S., and Manning, B.H. (1994) 'Relationships among Private Speech and Creativity Measurements of Young Children.' *Gifted Child Quarterly 38*, 21–26.

Davidson, J.E. (1986) 'The Role of Insight in Giftedness.' In R.J. Sternberg and J.E. Davidson (eds) *Conceptions of Giftedness* (pp.201–222). New York: Cambridge University Press.

Dawson, G., Warrenberg, S., and Fuller, P. (1982) 'Cerebral Lateralization in Individuals Diagnosed as Autistic in Early Childhood.' *Brain and Language 15*, 353–368.

DeGangi, G.A. (1991) 'Assessment of Sensory, Emotional, and Attentional Problems in Regulatory Disordered Infants: Part 1.' *Infants and Young Children 3*, 1–8.

DeGangi, G.A., Porges, S.W., Sickel, R.Z., and Greenspan, S.I. (1993) 'Four-year Follow-Up of a Sample of Regulatory Disordered Infants.' *Infant Mental Health Journal 4*, 330–343.

Denckla, M.B. (1991) 'Academic and Extracurricular Aspects of Nonverbal Learning Disabilities.' *Psychiatric Annals 21*, 717–724.

Denckla, M.B. (1994) 'Measurement of Executive Function.' In G.R. Lyon (ed) *Frames of Reference for the Assessment of Learning Disabilities: New Views on Measurement Issues* (pp.117–142). Baltimore, MD: Paul H. Brooks Publishing.

Denckla, M.B. (1996) 'A Theory and Model of Executive Function: A Neuropsychological Perspective.' In G.R. Lyon and N.A. Krasnegor (eds) *Attention, Memory, and Executive Function* (pp.263–278). Baltimore, MD: Paul H. Brooks Publishing.

Denckla, M.B. (2000) 'Learning Disabilities and Attention-Deficit/Hyperactivity Disorder in Adults: Overlap with Executive Dysfunction.' In T.E. Brown (ed) *Attention-Deficit Disorders and Comorbidities in Children, Adolescents and Adults* (pp.297–318). Washington, DC: American Psychiatric Press.

Dewey, M. (1991) 'Living with Asperger's Syndrome.' In U. Frith (ed) *Autism and Asperger Syndrome* (pp.184–206). Cambridge: Cambridge University Press.

Donnelly, J.A. and Altman, R. (1994) 'The Autistic Savant: Recognizing and Serving the Gifted Student.' *Roeper Review 16*, 252–256.

Dover, A. and Shore, B. M. (1992) 'Giftedness and Flexibility on a Mathematical Set-Breaking Task.' *Gifted Child Quarterly 35*, 99–105.

Dunn, J. (1987) 'The Beginnings of Moral Understanding: Development in the Second Year.' In J. Kagan and S. Lamb (eds) *The Emergence of Morality in Young Children* (pp.91–112). Chicago: The University of Chicago Press.

Ehlers, S. and Gillberg, C. (1993) 'The Epidemiology of Asperger Syndrome. A Total Population Study.' *Journal of Child Psychology and Psychiatry 34*, 1327–1350.

Ehlers, S., Nyden, A., Gillberg, C., Dahlgren Sandberg, A. *et al.* (1997) 'Asperger Syndrome, Autism, and Attention Disorder: A Comparative Study of the Cognitive Profiles of 120 Children.' *Journal of Child Psychology, Psychiatry, and Allied Disciplines 38*, 207–217

Eisenmajer, R., Prior, M., Leekam, S., *et al.* (1996) 'Comparison of Clinical Symptoms in Autism and Asperger Disorder.' *Journal of the American Academy of Child and Adolescent Psychiatry 35*, 1523–1531.

Epstein, J.N., Goldberg, N.A., Conners, C.K. and March, J.S. (1997) 'The Effects of Anxiety on Continuous Performance Test Functioning in an ADHD Clinic Sample.' *Journal of Attention Disorders 2*, 45–52.

Faraone, S.V., Biederman, J., Mennin, D., Wozniak, J., and Spencer, T. (1997) 'Attention-Deficit Hyperactivity Disorder with Bipolar Disorder: A Familial Subtype?' *Journal of the American Academy of Child and Adolescent Psychiatry 36*, 1378–1387.

Faraone, S.V., Biederman, J, and Monuteaux, M.C. (2000) 'ADHD and Conduct Disorder in Girls: Evidence for a Familial Subtype.' *Biological Psychiatry 48*, 21–29.

Feldman, D.H. and Goldsmith, L.T. (1986) *Nature's Gambit: Child Prodigies and the Development of Human Potential*. New York: Basic Books.

Fern, T.L. (1991) 'Identifying the Gifted Humorist.' *Roeper Review 24*, 30–34.

Fine, J., Bartolucci, P.T., Szatmari, P. and Ginsberg, G. (1994) 'Cohesive Discourse in Pervasive Developmental Disorders.' *Journal of Autism and Developmental Disorders 24*, 315–329.

Fishkin A.S. and Johnson, A.S. (1998) 'Who is Creative? Identifying Children's Creative Abilities.' *Roeper Review 21*, 40–46.

Fishkin, A.S., Kampsnider, J.J. and Pack, L. (1996) 'Exploring the WISC-III as a Measure of Giftedness.' *Roeper Review 18*, 226–231.

Folstein, S.E. and Santangelo, S.L. (2000) 'Does Asperger Syndrome Aggregate in Families?' In A. Klin, F.R. Volkmar, and S.S. Sparrow (eds) *Asperger Syndrome* (pp.159–171). New York: Guilford.

Forbes, G.B. (2001) 'A Comparison of the Conners' Parent and Teacher Rating Scales, the ADD-H Comprehensive Rating Scale and the Child Behavior Checklist in the Clinical Diagnosis of ADHD.' *Journal of Attention Disorders 5*, 25–40.

Ford, D.Y. (1994/5) 'Underachievement among Gifted and Non-Gifted Black Females: A Study in Perceptions.' *Journal of Secondary Gifted Education 6*, 165–175.

Frazier, J.A., Biederman, J., Bellordre, C.A., Garfield, S.B., Geller, D.A., Coffee, B.J. and Faraone, S.V. (2001) 'Should the Diagnosis of Attention-Deficit Hyperactivity Disorder be Considered in Children with Pervasive Developmental Disorder?' *Journal of Attention Disorders 4*, 203–211.

Freed, J. and Parsons, L. (1997) *Right-Brain Children in a Left-Brain World.* New York: Fireside Books.

Freeman, J. (1994) 'Gifted School Performance and Creativity.' *Roeper Review 17*, 15–19.

Frith, U. (1989) *Autism: Explaining the Enigma.* Cambridge: Blackwell.

Funk, J.B., Chessare, J.B., Weaver, M.T. and Exley, A.R. (1993) 'Attention Deficit Hyperactivity Disorder, Creativity and the Effects of Methylphenidate.' *Pediatrics 91*, 816–819.

Future Horizons (2002) *The Temple Grandin Award.* Arlington, TX: Future Horizons.

Galbraith, J. (1985) 'The Eight Great Gripes of Gifted Kids: Responding to Special Needs.' *Roeper Review 8*, 15–18.

Gallagher, J.J. and Crowder, T. (1957) 'The Adjustment of Gifted Children in the Classroom.' *Exceptional Children 23*, 306–319.

Gallagher, S.A. and Johnson, E.S. (1992) 'The Effect of Time Limits on Performance of Mental Rotations by Gifted Adolescents.' *Gifted Child Quarterly 36*, 19–22.

Gallucci, N.T. (1988) 'Child Behavior Checklist Scores for Gifted Children.' *Gifted Child Quarterly 32*, 273–276.

Gallucci, N., Middleton, G. and Kline, A. (1999) 'Intellectually Superior Children and Behavioral Problems and Competences.' *Roeper Review 22*, 18–21.

Gardner, H. (1983) *Frames of Mind: The Theory of Multiple Intelligences.* New York: Basic Books.

Gaub, M. and Carlson, C. (1997) 'Gender Differences in ADHD: A Meta-Analysis and Critical Review.' *Journal of the American Academy of Child and Adolescent Psychiatry 36*, 1036–1045.

Gershon, J. (2002) 'A Meta-Analytic Review of Gender Differences in ADHD.' *Journal of Attention Disorders 5*, 143–154.

Getzels, J.W. (1964) 'Creative Thinking, Problem-Solving, and Instruction.' In E.R. Hilgard (ed) *Theories of Learning and Instruction* (pp.240–267). Chicago: University of Chicago Press.

Getzels, J. (1987) 'Creativity, Intelligence and Problem Finding: Retrospect and Prospect.' In S. Isaksen (ed) *Frontiers of Creativity Research* (pp.88–102). Buffalo, NY: Bearly

Getzels, J.W. and Csikszentmihalyi, M. (1976) *The Creative Vision.* New York: Wiley.

Giedd, J.N. (2000) 'Is Brain Imaging Useful in the Diagnosis of Attention-Deficit/Hyperactivity Disorder?' *Attention 6,* (4), 19.

Gillberg, C. (1989) 'Asperger's Syndrome in 23 Swedish Children.' *Developmental Medicine and Child Neurology 31*, 520–31.

Gillberg, C. (1991) 'Clinical and Neurobiological Aspects of Asperger Syndrome in Six Family Studies.' In U. Frith (ed) *Autism and Asperger Syndrome* (pp.122–146). Cambridge: Cambridge University Press.

Gillberg, C. (2002) *A Guide to Asperger Syndrome.* Cambridge: Cambridge University Press.

Gillberg, C. and Gillberg, I.C. (1989) 'Asperger Syndrome – Some Epidemiological Considerations: A Research Note,' *Journal of Child Psychology and Psychiatry 30*, 631–638.

Gillberg, C., Gillberg, I.C. , Rastam, M. and Wentz, E. (2001) 'The Asperger Syndrome Diagnostic Interview (ASDI): A New Structured Interview for Use in Clinical Practice.' *Autism 5*, 57–66.

Gilligan, C. (1982) *In a Different Voice.* Cambridge, MA: Harvard University Press.

Gilligan, C., Lyons, N.P., and Hanmer, T.J. (eds) (1989) *Making Connections: The Relational Worlds of Adolescent Girls at Emma Williard School.* Troy, NY: Emma Williard School.

Gilligan, C. and Wiggins, G. (1987) 'The Origins of Morality in Early Childhood Relationships.' In J. Kagan and S. Lamb (eds) *The Emergence of Morality in Young Children* (pp.277–305). Chicago: University of Chicago Press.

Gogel, E.M., McCumsey, J. and Hewett, G. (1985 November/December) 'What Parents are Saying.' *G/C/T 41*, 7–9.

Goldstein, S. and Goldstein, M. (1990) *Managing Attention Disorders in Children: A Guide for Practitioners.* New York: Wiley.

Goldstein, S. and Goldstein, M. (1998) *Managing Attention Deficit Hyperactivity Disorder in Children, Second Edition.* New York: Wiley.

Gopnik, A., Capps, L., and Meltzoff, A.N. (2000) 'Early Theories of Mind: What the Theory Theory Can Tell Us about Autism.' In S. Baron-Cohen, H. Tager-Flusberg, and D.J. Cohen (eds) *Understanding Other Minds. Second Edition,* (pp.50–72). New York: Oxford University Press.

Gordon, M. and Barkley, R. A. (1998) 'Tests and Observational Measures.' In R. A. Barkley (ed) *Attention-Deficit Hyperactivity Disorder: A Handbook for Diagnosis and Treatment* (pp 295–311). New York: Guilford.

Gottfried, A.W., Gottfried, A.E., Bathhurst, K., and Guerin, D.W. (1994) *Gifted IQ: Early Developmental Aspects (The Fullerton Longitudinal Study).* New York: Plenum.

Gottlieb, S. (1973) 'Modeling Effects upon Fantasy.' In J.L. Singer (ed) *The Child's World of Make-Believe* (pp.155–182). New York: Academic Press.

Grandin, T. (1995) *Thinking in Pictures.* New York: Doubleday.

Gray, C. (1994) *Comic Strip Conversations.* Arlington, TX: Future Horizons.

Gray, C. A. (1998) 'Social Stories and Comic Strip Conversations with Students with Asperger Syndrome and High-Functioning Autism.' In E. Schopler, G. Mesibov and L. J. Kunce (eds) *Asperger Syndrome or High-Functioning Autism?* (pp 167–198). New York: Plenum.

Gray, C. and Attwood, T. (1999) 'The Discovery of "Aspie."' *The Morning News, Fall, 11,* 3.

Greene, R. (1998) *The Explosive Child.* New York: HarperCollins.

Greene, R.W., Biederman, J., Faraone, S.V., Monuteaux, M.C. *et al.* (2001) 'Social Impairment in Girls with ADHD. Patterns, Gender Comparisons and Correlates.' *Journal of the American Academy of Child and Adolescent Psychiatry 40,* 704–710.

Gross, M.U.M. (1993) *Exceptionally Gifted Children.* New York: Routledge.

Gross, M.U.M. (1998) 'The "Me" Behind the Mask: Intellectually Gifted Students and the Search for Identity.' *Roeper Review 20,* 167–174.

Gross, M.U.M. (1999) 'Small Poppies: Highly Gifted Children in the Early Years.' *Roeper Review 21,* 207–214.

Gruber, R., Sadeh, A. and Raviv, A. (2000) 'Instability of Sleep Patterns in Children with Attention-Deficit/Hyperactivity Disorder.' *Journal of the American Academy of Child and Adolescent Psychiatry 39,* 495–501.

Guevremont, D. (1990) 'Social Skills and Peer Relationship Training.' In R. Barkley (ed) *Attention-Deficit Hyperactivity Disorder* (pp.540–572). New York: Guilford.

Guilford, J.P. (1967) *The Nature of Human Intelligence.* New York: McGraw-Hill.

Hall, K. (2001) *Asperger Syndrome, the Universe and Everything.* London: Jessica Kingsley Publishers.

Hallett, M., Lebiedowska, M.K., Thomas, S.L., Stanhope, S.J., Denckla, M.B., and Rumsey, J. (1993) 'Locomotion of Autistic Adults.' *Archives of Neurology 50,* 1304–1308.

Hallowell, E.M. and Ratey, J.J. (1994a) *Answers to Distraction.* New York: Pantheon.

Hallowell, E.M. and Ratey, J.J. (1994b) *Driven to Distraction.* New York: Pantheon.

Happé, F. (1994) 'An Advanced Test of Theory of Mind: Understanding of Story Characters' Thoughts and Feelings by Able Autistic, Mentally Handicapped, and Normal Children and Adults.' *Journal of Autism and Developmental Disorders 24,* 129–154.

Happé, F. (2000) 'Parts and Wholes, Meaning and Minds: Central Coherence and its Relation to Theory of Mind.' In S. Baron-Cohen, H. Tager-Flusberg, and D.J. Cohen (eds) *Understanding Other Minds, Second Edition* (pp.203–221). New York: Oxford University Press.

Harris, C.R. (1992) 'The Fruits of Early Intervention: The Hollingworth Group Today.' *Advanced Development 4,* 91–104.

Harris, P.L. and Leevers, H.J. (2000) 'Pretending, Imagery and Self-Awareness in Autism.' In S. Baron-Cohen, H. Tager-Flusberg, and D.J. Cohen (eds) *Understanding Other Minds, Second Edition* (pp.182–202). New York: Oxford University Press.

Hart, E.L., Lahey, B.B., Loeber, R., Applegate, B., and Frick, P.J. (1995) 'Developmental Changes in Attention-Deficit Hyperactivity Disorder in boys: A Four Year Longitudinal Study.' *Journal of Abnormal Child Psychology 23,* 729–749.

Hartmann, T. (1993, 1997) *Attention Deficit Disorder: A Different Perception.* Grass Valley, CA: Underwood Books.

Hartmann, T. (1996) *Beyond ADD: Hunting for Reasons in the Past and Present.* Grass Valley, CA: Underwood Books.

Hayes, S.C., Gifford, E. V., and Ruckstuhl, L.E. Jr. (1996) 'Relational Frame Theory and Executive Function. A Behavioral Approach.' In G.R. Lyon and N.A. Krasnegor (eds) *Attention, Memory, and Executive Function* (pp.279–305). Baltimore, MD: Paul H. Brooks Publishing.

Hermelin, B. (2001) *Bright Splinters of the Mind.* London: Jessica Kingsley Publishers.

Hewitt, J.K., Silberg, J.L., Rutter, M., *et al.* (1997) 'Genetics and Developmental Psychopathology, I: Phenotypic Assessment in the Virginia Twin Study of Adolescent Behavioral Development.' *Journal of Child Psychology and Psychiatry 38,* 943–963.

Hocevar, D. (1980) 'Intelligence, Divergent Thinking, and Creativity.' *Intelligence 4,* 25–40.

Hoffman, M.L. (1994) 'Empathy, Role Taking, Guilt, and Development of Altruistic Motives.' In B. Puka (ed) *Reaching Out: Caring, Altruism, and Prosocial Behavior* (pp. 196–218). New York: Garland Publishing.

Hollingworth, L.S. (1926) *Gifted Children: Their Nature and Nurture.* New York: Macmillan.

Hollingworth, L.S. (1931) 'The Child of Very Superior Intelligence as a Special Problem in Social Adjustment.' *Mental Hygiene 15,* (1), 1–16.

Hollingworth, L.S. (1942) *Children Above 180 IQ Stanford-Binet: Origin and Development.* Yonkers-on-Hudson, NY: World Book.

Howard-Hamilton, M. F. (1994) 'An Assessment of Moral Development in Gifted Adolescents.' *Roeper Review 17,* 57–59.

Hoza, B., Waschbusch, D.A., Pelham, W.E., Molina, B.S.G.*et al.* (2000) 'Attention-Deficit/ Hyperactivity Disordered and Control Boys' Responses to Social Success and Failure.' *Child Development 71,* 432–446.

Jackson, L. (2002) *Freaks, Geeks and Asperger Syndrome: A User Guide to Adolescence.* London: Jessica Kingsley Publishers.

Janos, P.M. and Robinson, N.M. (1985) 'Psychosocial Development in Intellectually Gifted Children.' In F.D. Horowitz and M. O'Brien (eds) *The Gifted and Talented: Developmental Perspectives* (pp.149–195). Washington, DC: American Psychological Association.

Jenkins, M., Cohen, R., Malloy, P., *et al.* (1998) 'Neuropsychological Measures which Discriminate among Adults with Residual Symptoms of ADHD and Other Attentional Complaints.' *The Clinical Neurologist 12*, 74–83.

Jensen, P.S., Martin, D., and Cantwell, D.P. (1997) 'Comorbidity in ADHD: Implication for Research Practice and DSM-V.' *Journal of the American Academy of Child Psychology and Psychiatry 36*, 1065–1079.

Kagan, J. (1981) *The Second Year.* Cambridge, MA: Harvard University Press.

Kaplan, B.J., Dewey, D.M., Crawford, S.G., and Wilson, B.N. (2001) 'The Term Comorbidity as a Questionable Value in Reference to Developmental Disorders: Data and Theory.' *Journal of Learning Disabilities 34*, 555–565.

Kaufmann F., Kalbfleisch, M.L., and Castellanos, F.X. (2000, November) 'Attention Deficit Disorders and Gifted Students: What Do We Really Know?' RM00146. *The National Research Center on the Gifted and Talented.* Storrs, CT: University of Connecticut.

Kavanaugh, R.D. and Harris, P.L. (1994) 'Imagining the Outcome of Pretend Transformations: Assessing the Competence of Normal Children and Children with Autism.' *Developmental Psychology 30*, 847–854.

Kearney, K. and LeBlanc, J. (1993) 'Forgotten Pioneers in the Study of Gifted African-Americans.' *Roeper Review 15*, 192–199.

Keller, E.F. (1983) *A Feeling for the Organism: The Life and Work of Barbara McClintock.* San Francisco: W.H. Freeman.

Kempton, S., Vance, A., Maruff, P., Luk, E. Costin, J., and Pantelis, C. (1999) 'Executive Function and Attention Deficit Hyperactivity Disorder: Stimulant Medication and Better Executive Function Performance in Children.' *Psychological Medicine 29*, 527–538.

Kerr, B.A. (1985) *Smart Girls, Gifted Women.* Columbus, OH: Ohio Psychology Publishing.

Kerr, B.A. (1991) 'Educating Gifted Girls.' In N. Colangelo and G.A. Davis (eds) *Handbook of Gifted Education* (pp.402–415). Needham Heights, MA: Allyn and Bacon.

Kimball, J.G. (2000) 'When Individuals with High IQ Experience Sensory Integration or Sensory Systems Modulation Problems.' In K. Kay (ed) *Uniquely Gifted: Identifying and Meeting the Needs of the Twice-Exceptional Student* (pp.227–243). Gilsum, NH: Avocus Publishing.

Kitano, M.K. (1994/5) 'Lessons from Gifted Women of Color.' *Journal of Secondary Gifted Education 6*, 176–187.

Kitano, M.K. and De Leon, J. (1988) 'Use of the Stanford-Binet Fourth Edition in Identifying Young Gifted Children.' *Roeper Review 10*, 156–159.

Klin, A., Schultz, R., and Cohen, D.J. (2000a) 'Theory of Mind in Action: Developmental Perspectives on Social Neuroscience.' In S. Baron-Cohen, H. Tager-Flusberg, and D. J. Cohen (eds) *Understanding Other Minds, Second Edition* (pp.357–388). New York: Oxford University Press.

Klin, A., Volkmar, F.R., and Sparrow, S.S. (eds) (2000b) *Asperger Syndrome.* New York: Guilford.

Klin, A., Volkmar, F.R., Sparrow, S.S., Cicchetti, D.V., and Rourke, B.P. (1995) 'Validity and Neuropsychological Characterization of Asperger Syndrome: Convergence with Nonverbal Learning Disabilities Syndrome.' *Journal of Child Psychology and Psychiatry 36*, 1127–1140.

Kohen-Raz, R., Volkmar, F.D., and Cohen, D.J. (1992) 'Postural Control in Children with Autism.' *Journal of Autism and Developmental Disorders 22*, 419–432.

Kohlberg, L. (1964) 'The Development of Moral Character and Moral Ideology.' In M. Hoffman and L. Hoffman (eds) *Review of Child Development Research, Vol. 1* (pp.383–431). New York: Russell Sage Foundation.

Kohlberg, L. (1984) *The Psychology of Moral Development: Essays on Moral Development. Vol. 2.* San Francisco: Harper and Row.

Kopp, C.B. (1982) 'Antecedents of Self-Regulation. A Developmental Perspective.' *Developmental Psychology 18*, 199–214.

Kutner, D.R. (1999) 'Blurred Brilliance: What ADD Looks Like in Gifted Adults.' *Advanced Development 8*, 87–96.

Landa, R. (2000) 'Social Language Use in Asperger Syndrome and High-Functioning Autism.' In A. Klin, F.R. Volkmar and S.S. Sparrow (eds) *Asperger Syndrome* (pp.125–155). New York: Guilford.

Lazarus, R.S. (1993) 'From Psychological Stress to the Emotions: A History of Changing Outlooks.' *Annual Review of Psychology 44*, 1–21.

Leevers, H. and Harris, P. (1998) 'Drawing Impossible Entities: A Measure of the Imagination in Children with Autism, Children with Learning Disabilities, and Normal 4-year-olds.' *Journal of Child Psychology and Psychiatry 39*, 399–410.

Leroux, J.A. and Levitt-Perlman, M. (2000) 'The Gifted Child with Attention Deficit Disorder: An Identification and Intervention Challenge.' *Roeper Review 22*, 171–176.

Levy, F., Hay, D.A., McStephen, M., Wood, C., and Waldman, I. (1997) 'Attention-Deficit Hyperactivity Disorder: A Category or a Continuum? Genetic Analysis of a Large Scale Twin Study.' *Journal of the American Academy of Child and Adolescent Psychiatry 36*, 737–744.

Lewis, M. and Michalson, L. (1985) 'The Gifted Infant.' In J. Freeman (ed) *The Psychology of Gifted Children: Perspectives on Development and Education* (pp.35–57). New York: Wiley.

Lincoln, A.J., Courchesne, E., Allen, M., Hanson, E., and Ene, M. (1998) 'Neurobiology of Asperger Syndrome: Seven Case Studies and Quantitative Magnetic Resonance Imaging Findings.' In E. Schopler, G. Mesibov, and L.J. Kunce (eds) *Asperger Syndrome or High-Functioning Autism?* (pp.145–166). New York: Plenum.

Lovecky, D.V. (1991) 'The Divergently Thinking Child.' *Understanding Our Gifted 3*, (3), 1, 7–9.

Lovecky, D.V. (1992a) 'The Exceptionally Gifted Child (Part II).' *Understanding Our Gifted 4*, (5), 3.

Lovecky, D.V. (1992b) 'Exploring Social and Emotional Aspects of Giftedness in Children.' *Roeper Review 15*, 18–25.

Lovecky, D.V. (1993) 'The Quest for Meaning: Counseling Issues with Gifted Children and Adolescents.' In L.K. Silverman (ed) *Counseling the Gifted and Talented* (pp.29–50). Denver: Love.

Lovecky, D.V. (1994a) 'Exceptionally Gifted Children: Different Minds.' *Roeper Review 17*, 116–120.

Lovecky, D.V. (1994b) 'Gifted Children with Attention Deficit Disorder.' *Understanding Our Gifted 6*, (5), 1, 7–10.

Lovecky, D.V. (1994c) 'The Moral Gifted Child in a Violent World.' *Understanding Our Gifted 6*, 1, 3.

Lovecky, D.V. (1994/5) 'Ramifications of Giftedness for Girls.' *Journal of Secondary Gifted Education 6*, 157–164.

Lovecky, D.V. (1995) 'Highly Gifted Children and Peer Relationships.' *Counseling and Guidance Division Newsletter 5* (3), 2, 6–7.

Lovecky, D.V. (1997) 'Identity Development in Gifted Children: Moral Sensitivity.' *Roeper Review 20,* 90–94.

Lovecky, D.V. (1999) 'Gifted Children with AD/HD.' Presented at the 11th Annual CHADD International Conference. October 8.

Lovecky, D.V. and Silverman, L.K. (1998) 'Gifted Children with AD/HD.' Submitted to the National Institute of Health Consensus Development Conference on Attention Deficit Hyperactivity Disorder on November 16–18.

Luftig, R.L. and Nichols, M.L. (1991) 'An Assessment of the Social Status and Perceived Personality and School Traits of Gifted Students by Non-Gifted Peers.' *Roeper Review 13,* 148–153.

MacKinnon, D.W. (1962) 'The Nature and Nurture of Creative Talent.' *American Psychologist 17,* 484–495.

Mandal, R. L., Olmi, D. J. and Wilczynski, S. M. (1999) 'Behavior Rating Scales: Concordance between Multiple Informants in the Diagnosis of Attention-Deficit/Hyperactivity Disorder.' *Journal of Attention Disorders, 3,* 97–103.

Manjiviona, J. and Prior, M. (1995) 'Comparison of Asperger's Syndrome and High-Functioning Autistic Children on a Test of Motor Impairment.' *Journal of Autism and Developmental Disorders 25,* 23–39.

Mariani, M.A. and Barkley, R.A. (1997) 'Neuropsychological and Academic Functioning in Preschool Boys with Attention Deficit Hyperactivity Disorder.' *Developmental Neuropsychology 13,* 111–129.

Markham, E.M. (1979) 'Realizing That You Don't Understand: Elementary School Children's Awareness of Inconsistencies.' *Child Development 50,* 643–655.

Matthews, G.B. (1980) *Philosophy and the Young Child.* Cambridge, MA: Harvard University Press.

Matthews, G.B. (1994) *The Philosophy of Childhood.* Cambridge, MA: Harvard University Press.

Mayer, J.D., DiPaolo, M.T., and Salovey, P. (1990) 'Perceiving Affective Content in Ambiguous Visual Stimuli: A Component of Emotional Intelligence.' *Journal of Personality Assessment 54,* 772–781.

Mayer, J.D. and Geher, G. (1996) 'Emotional Intelligence and the Identification of Intelligence.' *Intelligence 22,* 89–113.

Mayer, J.D., Perkins, D.M., Caruso, D.R., and Salovey, P. (2001) 'Emotional Intelligence and Giftedness.' *Roeper Review 23,* 131–137.

Mayer, J.D. and Salovey, P. (1997) 'What is Emotional Intelligence?' In P. Salovey and D.J. Sluyter (ed) *Emotional Development and Emotional Intelligence* (pp.3–31). New York: Basic Books.

Mayes, S.D., Calhoun, S.L., and Crowell, E.W. (1998) 'WISC-III Freedom From Distractibility as a Measure of Attention in Children With and Without Attention Deficit Hyperactivity Disorder.' *Journal of Attention Disorders 2,* 217–227.

McCallister, C., Nash, W.R., and Meckstroth, E. (1996) 'The Social Competence of Gifted Children: Experiments and Experience.' *Roeper Review 18,* 273–276.

McGuffog, C., Feiring, C., and Lewis, M. (1987) 'The Diverse Profile of the Extremely Gifted Child.' *Roeper Review 10,* 82–89.

Mckinna, K.D. (1999) 'The Social Perspective-Taking Knowledge and Performance of Children with Attention Deficit/Hyperactivity Disorder.' *Dissertation Abstracts International Section A: Humanities and Social Sciences March 59 (9-A),* 3352.

Mealer, C., Morgan, S. and Luscomb, R. (1996) 'Cognitive Functioning of ADHD and non-ADHD Boys on the WISC-III and WRAML: An Analysis Within a Memory Model.' *Journal of Attention Disorders 1*, 133–145.

Melnick, S.M. and Hinshaw, S.P. (1996) 'What They Want and What They Get: The Social Goals of Boys with ADHD and Comparison Boys.' *Journal of Abnormal Child Psychology 24*, 169–185.

Mendaglio, S. (1995) 'Sensitivity Among Gifted Persons: A Multi-Faceted Perspective.' *Roeper Review 17*, 169–176.

Mika, E. and Meckstroth, E. (2001) '…To Suffer Fools Gladly.' *Highly Gifted Children 13*, (4), 5–8.

Mikami, A. Y. and Hinshaw, S. P. (2003) 'Buffers of Peer Rejection among Girls with and without ADHD: The Role of Popularity with Adults and Goal-Directed Solitary Play.' *Journal of Abnormal Child Psychology 31*, 381–397.

Miller, A.I. (1984) *Imagery in Scientific Thought.* Boston: Birkhauser.

Molina, J.L., Ruata, J.M., and Soler, E.P. (1986) 'Is There a Right Hemisphere Dysfunction in Asperger's Syndrome?' *British Journal of Psychiatry 148*, 745–746.

Moon, S.M., Zentall, S.S., Grskovic, J.A., Hall, A., and Stormont, M. (2001) 'Emotional and Social Characteristics of Boys with AD/HD and Giftedness: A Comparative Case Study.' *Journal for the Education of the Gifted 24*, 207–247.

Moran, J.D., Milgram, R.M., Sawyers, J.K., and Fu, V.R. (1983a) 'Original Thinking in Preschool Children.' *Child Development 54*, 921–926.

Moran, J.D., Milgram, R.M., Sawyers, J.K., and Fu, V.R (1983b) 'Stimulus Specificity in the Measurement of Original Thinking in Preschool Children.' *Journal of Psychology 114*, 99–105.

Moran, J.D., Sawyers, J.K., Fu, V.R., and Milgram, R.M. (1984) 'Predicting Imaginative Play in Preschool Children.' *Gifted Child Quarterly 28*, 92–94.

Morelock, M.J. (1996) 'On the Nature of Giftedness and Talent: Imposing Order on Chaos.' *Roeper Review 19*, 4–12.

Morelock, M.J. (1997) 'Imagination, Logic, and the Exceptionally Gifted.' Gifted Education Supplement Number 3: Meeting the Needs of the Highly Gifted. *Roeper Review 19*, A-1–A-4.

Morelock, M.J. and Feldman, D.H. (1992) 'The Assessment of Giftedness in Preschool Children.' In E.V. Nuttall, I. Romero, and J. Kalesnik (eds) *Assessing and Screening Preschoolers* (pp.301–309). Needham Heights, MA: Allyn and Bacon.

Mumford, M., Connelly, M.S., Baughman, W. and Marks, M.A. (1994) 'Creativity and Problem-Solving: Cognition, Adaptability and Wisdom.' *Roeper Review 16*, 241–246.

Myles, B.S., Bock, S.J. and Simpson, R.L. (2001) *Asperger Syndrome Diagnostic Scale Examiner's Manual.* Austin, TX: Pro-Ed.

Nadeau, K.G., Littman, E.B., Quinn, P.O. (1999) *Understanding Girls with AD/HD.* Silver Spring, MD: Advantage Books.

Nail, J.M. and Evans, J.G. (1997) 'The Emotional Adjustment of Gifted Adolescents: A View of Global Functioning.' *Roeper Review 20*, 18–21.

National Association of Gifted Children (2001) *Nicholas Greene Awards.* Washington, DC.

National Institutes of Health (1998) *NIH Consensus Development Conference Statement: Diagnosis and Treatment of ADHD. Bethesda, MD, November 16–18.*

Neihart, M. (2000) 'Gifted Children with Asperger's Syndrome.' *Gifted Child Quarterly 44*, 222–230.

Norvilitis, J.M., Casey, R.J., Brooklier, K.M., and Bonello, P.J. (2000) 'Emotion Appraisal in Children with Attention-Deficit/Hyperactivity Disorder and their parents.' *Journal of Attention Disorders 4*, 15–26.

Nucci, L.P. and Herman, S. (1982) 'Behavioral Disordered Children's Conceptions of Moral, Conventional, and Personal Issues.' *Journal of Abnormal Child Psychology 10*, 411–426.

O'Boyle, M.W. and Benbow, C.P. (1990) 'Enhanced Right Hemisphere Involvement During Cognitive Processing May Relate to Intellectual Precocity.' *Neuropsychologia 28*, 211–216.

O'Leary, Q. (2001) 'On Being Highly Gifted in High School.' *Highly Gifted Children 13*, (4), 1, 4.

Osborn, A.F. (1963) *Applied Imagination, Third Edition.* New York: Scribner's.

Osborn, J. (1995) 'Using Traditional Assessment Tools for Non-Traditional Assessment.' Presentation for Ninth Annual Hollingworth Conference for Highly Gifted Children, Boston, MA, May 6–7.

Osborn, J. (1998) 'Assessing Gifted Children.' *Understanding Our Gifted*, Winter, 9–12.

Osborn, J. (1999) 'Best Practices in Assessing the Gifted: A Psychologist's Perspective.' In S. Cline and K. Hegeman (eds) *Gifted Education in the 21st Century: Issues and Concerns.* New York: Winslow Press.

Ozonoff, S., Dawson, G. and McPartland, J. (2002) *A Parent's Guide to Asperger Syndrome and High-Functioning Autism.* New York: Guilford.

Ozonoff, S. and Griffith, E.M. (2000) 'Neuropsychological function and the External Validity of Asperger Syndrome.' In A. Klin, F.R. Volkmar, and S.S. Sparrow (eds) *Asperger Syndrome* (pp.72–96). New York: Guilford.

Ozonoff, S. Pennington, B.F., and Rogers, S.J. (1991) 'Executive Function Deficits in High-Functioning Autistic Individuals: Relationship to Theory of Mind.' *Journal of Child Psychology and Psychiatry 32*, 1081–1105.

Ozonoff, S., Rogers, S.J. and Pennington, B.F. (1991) 'Asperger's Syndrome: Evidence of an Empirical Distinction from High Functioning Autism.' *Journal of Child Psychology and Psychiatry 32*, 1107–1122.

Papolos, D. and Papolos, J. (1999) *The Bipolar Child.* New York: Broadway Books.

Parnes, S. J. (1962) 'Can Creativity be Increased?' In S. J. Parnes and H. F. Harding (eds) *A Source Book of Creative Thinking* (pp 185–193). New York: Charles Scribner's Sons.

Pearson, D.A., Yaffee, L.S., Loveland, K. and Norton, A.M. (1995) 'Covert Visual Attention in Children with Attention Deficit Hyperactivity Disorder: Evidence for Developmental Immaturity?' *Development and Psychopathology 7*, 351–367.

Pelham, W.E. and Millich, R. (1984) 'Peer Relations of Children with Hyperactivity/Attention Deficit Disorder.' *Journal of Learning Disabilities 17*, 560–568.

Piaget, J. and Inhelder, B. (1969) *The Psychology of the Child.* New York: Basic Books.

Piechowski, M.M. (1986) 'The Concept of Developmental Potential.' *Roeper Review 8*, 190–197.

Piechowski M.M. (1991) 'Emotional Development and Emotional Giftedness.' In N. Colangelo and G.A. Davis (eds) *Handbook of Gifted Education* (pp.285–306). Needham Heights, MA: Allyn and Bacon.

Piirto, J. (1992) *Understanding Those Who Create.* Dayton, OH: Ohio Psychology Publishing.

Powell. P.M. and Hayden, T. (1984) 'The Intellectual and Psychosocial Nature of Extreme Giftedness.' *Roeper Review 6*, 131–133.

Quinn P.O. (1997) *Attention Deficit Disorder: Diagnosis and Treatment from Infancy to Adulthood.* New York: Bruner/Mazel.

Ratey, J.J. (2001) *A User's Guide to the Brain.* New York: Pantheon.

Ratey, J.J. and Johnson, C. (1997) *Shadow Syndromes.* New York: Random House.

Reilly, J.M. and Welch, D.B. (1994/5) 'Mentoring Gifted Young Women: A Call to Action.' *Journal of Secondary Gifted Education 6*, 120–128.

Rest, J. (1979) *Development in Judging Moral Issues.* Minneapolis, MN: University of Minnesota.

Rietschel, L. (2000) 'How Did We Get Here?' In A. Klin, F.R. Volkmar and S.S. Sparrow (eds) *Asperger Syndrome* (pp.448–453). New York: Guilford.

Risemberg, R. and Zimmerman, B.J. (1992) 'Self-Regulated Learning in Gifted Students.' *Roeper Review 15*, 98–101.

Robinson, N.M. and Noble, K.D. (1991) 'Social-Emotional Development and Adjustment of Gifted Children.' In M.C. Wang, M.C. Reynolds, and H.J. Walberg (eds) *Handbook of Special Education. Research and Practice: Vol. 4. Emerging Programs* (pp.57–76). New York: Pergamon Press.

Roedell, W.C. (1984) 'Vulnerabilities of Highly Gifted Children.' *Roeper Review 6*, 127–130.

Roedell, W.C. (1989) 'Early Development of Gifted Children.' In J. VanTassel-Baska and P. Olszewski-Kubilius (eds) *Patterns of Influence on Gifted Learners: The Home, the Self, and the School* (pp.13–28). New York: Teachers College Press.

Roeper, A. (1982) 'How the Gifted Cope With Their Emotions.' *Roeper Review 5*, (2), 21–24.

Roeper, A. (1989) 'Empathy, Ethics, and Global Education.' *Understanding Our Gifted 1*, (6), 1, 7–10.

Roeper, A. (1995a) 'Global Awareness and the Young Child.' In *Annemarie Roeper: Selected Writings and Speeches* (pp.179–182). Minneapolis, MN: Free Spirit Publishing.

Roeper, A. (1995b) 'Should Educators of the Gifted and Talented Be More Concerned with World Issues?' In *Annemarie Roeper: Selected Writings and Speeches.* (pp.168–171). Minneapolis, MN: Free Spirit Publishing.

Roeper, A. (1995c) 'The Young Gifted Girl: A Contemporary View.' In *Annemarie Roeper: Selected Writings and Speeches* (pp.58–64). Minneapolis, MN: Free Spirit Publishing.

Rogers, M.T. and Silverman, L.K. (1988) 'Recognizing Giftedness in Young Children.' *Understanding Our Gifted 1*, (2), 5, 16, 17, 20.

Root-Bernstein, R.S. (1987) 'Tools for Thought: Designing an Integrated Curriculum for Lifelong Learners.' *Roeper Review 10*, 17–21.

Rosenn, D. (2002) 'Is it Asperger's or ADHD?' *AANE News 10*, Spring, 3–5.

Ross, D.M. and Ross, S.A. (1982) *Hyperactivity: Current Issues, Research and Theory, Second Edition.* New York: Wiley.

Rourke, B.P. and Tsatsanis, K.D. (2000) 'Nonverbal Learning Disabilities and Asperger Syndrome.' In A. Klin, F.R. Volkmar and S.S. Sparrow (eds) *Asperger Syndrome* (pp.231–253). New York: Guilford.

Rucklidge, J.J. and Tannock, R. (2001) 'Psychiatric, Psychosocial and Cognitive Functioning of Female Adolescents with ADHD.' *Journal of the American Academy of Child and Adolescent Psychiatry 40*, 530–540.

Runco, M.A. (ed) (1991) *Divergent Thinking*. Norwood, NJ: Ablex.

Runco, M.A. (1993) 'Divergent Thinking, Creativity, and Giftedness.' *Gifted Child Quarterly 37*, 16–22.

Runco, M.A. and Nemiro, J. (1994) 'Problem Finding, Creativity and Giftedness.' *Roeper Review 16*, 235–241.

Sadker, M. and Sadker, D. (1994) *Failing at Fairness: How America's Schools Cheat Girls*. New York: Charles Scribner's Sons.

Schultz, R.T., Gauthier, I., and Klin, A., *et al.* (2000) 'Abnormal Ventral Temporal Cortical Activity During Face Discrimination Among Individuals with Autism and Asperger Disorder.' *Archives of General Psychiatry 57*, 331–340.

Scott, F. and Baron-Cohen, S. (1996) 'Imagining Real and Unreal Objects: An Investigation of Imagination in Autism.' *Journal of Cognitive Neuroscience 8*, 400–411.

Seidman, L.J., Biederman, J., Faraone, S., Weber, W., Mennin, D., and Jones, J. (1997) 'A Pilot Study of Neuropsychological Function in Girls with ADHD.' *Journal of the American Academy of Child and Adolescent Psychiatry 36*, 366–373.

Shah, A. and Frith, U. (1993) 'Why Do Autistic Individuals Show Superior Performance on the Block Design Task?' *Journal of Child Psychology and Psychiatry 34*, 1351–1364.

Shaw, G.A. (1992) 'Hyperactivity and Creativity: The Tacit Dimension.' *Bulletin of the Psychonomic Society 30*, 157–160.

Shaw, G.A. and Brown, G. (1990) 'Laterality and Creativity Concomitants of Attention Problems.' *Developmental Neuropsychology 6*, 39–57.

Shery, L.S. (2000) 'A View from Inside.' In A. Klin, F.R. Volkmar and S.S. Sparrow (eds) *Asperger Syndrome* (pp.443–447). New York: Guilford.

Shmukler, D. (1985) 'Foundations of Creativity: The Facilitating Environment.' In J. Freeman (ed) *The Psychology of Gifted Children: Perspectives on Development and Education.* (pp.75–91). New York: Wiley.

Shore, B.M. and Dover, A.C. (1987) 'Metacognition, Intelligence, and Giftedness.' *Gifted Child Quarterly 31*, 37–39.

Siegle, D. and Reis, S.M. (1994/5) 'Gender Differences in Teacher and Student Perceptions of Student Ability and Effort.' *Journal of Secondary Gifted Education 6*, 86–92.

Silver, S.J. and Clampit, M.K. (1990) 'WISC-R Profiles of High Ability Children: Interpretation of Verbal-Performance Discrepancies.' *Gifted Child Quarterly 34*, 76–79.

Silverman, L.K. (1986) 'What Happens to the Gifted Girl?' In C.J. Maker (ed) *Critical Issues in Gifted Education, Vol. 1: Defensible Programs for the Gifted* (pp.43–89). Rockville, MD: Aspen.

Silverman, L.K. (1991) 'Helping Gifted Girls Reach Their Potential.' *Roeper Review 13*, 122–123.

Silverman, L.K. (1993a) 'A Developmental Model for Counseling the Gifted.' In L.K. Silverman (ed) *Counseling the Gifted and Talented* (pp.51–78). Denver: Love.

Silverman, L.K. (1993b) 'Counseling Families.' In L.K. Silverman (ed) *Counseling the Gifted and Talented* (pp.151–178). Denver: Love.

Silverman, L.K. (1993c) 'Social Development, Leadership and Gender Issues.' In L.K. Silverman (ed) *Counseling the Gifted and Talented* (pp.291–327). Denver: Love.

Silverman, L.K. (1993d) 'The Gifted Individual.' In L.K. Silverman (ed) *Counseling the Gifted and Talented* (pp.3–28). Denver: Love.

Silverman, L.K. (1994) 'The Moral Sensitivity of Gifted Children and the Evolution of Society.' *Roeper Review 17*, 110–116.

Silverman, L.K. (1994/5) 'To Be Gifted or Feminine: The Forced Choice of Adolescence.' *Journal of Secondary Gifted Education 6*, 141–156.

Silverman, L.K. (1998) 'Developmental Stages of Giftedness: Infancy Through Adulthood.' In J. VanTassel-Baska (ed) *Excellence in Educating Gifted and Talented Learners, Third Edition* (pp.145–166). Denver, CO: Love.

Silverman, L.K. (2002) *Upside-Down Brilliance: The Visual-Spatial Learner.* Denver, CO: DeLeon Publishing.

Silverman, L.K. and Kearney, K. (1992) 'The Case for the Stanford-Binet L-M as a Supplemental Test.' *Roeper Review 15*, 34–37.

Simonton, D.K. (1994) *Greatness: Who Makes History and Why.* New York: Guilford.

Smalley, S.L. (1997) 'Behavioral Genetics 1997: Genetic Influences in Childhood-Onset Psychiatric Disorders: Autism and Attention Deficit/Hyperactivity Disorder.' *American Journal of Human Genetics 60,*1276–1282.

Smith, I.M. (2000) 'Motor Functioning in Asperger Syndrome.' In A. Klin, F.R. Volkmar, and S.S. Sparrow (eds) *Asperger Syndrome* (pp.97–124). New York: Guilford.

Smith, I.M. and Bryson, S.E. (1994) 'Imitation and Action in Autism: A Critical Review.' *Psychological Bulletin 116,* 259–273.

Smith, I. M. and Bryson, S. E. (1998) 'Gesture Imitation in Autism I: Nonsymbolic Postures and Sequences.' *Cognitive Neuropsychology 15,* 747– 770.

Smith, S. (1985) *Journey to the Soviet Union.* Boston: Little, Brown and Company.

Sowa, C.J., McIntire, J., May, K.M. and Bland, L. (1994) 'Social and Emotional Adjustment Themes Across Gifted Children.' *Roeper Review 17,* 95–98.

Spencer, T., Wilens, T., Biederman, J., Wozniak, J., and Harding-Crawford, M. (2000) 'Attention Deficit/Hyperactivity Disorder with Mood Disorders.' In T.E. Brown (ed) *Attention Deficit Disorders and Comorbidities in Children, Adolescents and Adults* (pp.79–124). Washington, DC: American Psychiatric Press.

Spreen, O. and Strauss, E. (1998) *A Compendium of Neuropsychological Tests, Second Edition.* New York: Oxford University Press.

Stanley, J.C., Keating, D., and Fox, L. (1974) *Mathematical Talent: Discovery, Description and Development.* Baltimore, MD: Johns Hopkins Press.

Stern, D.N. (1974) 'Mother and Infant at Play: The Dyadic Interaction Involving Facial, Vocal and Gaze Behaviours.' In M. Lewis and L.A. Rosenblum (eds) *The Effect of the Infant on its Caregiver* (pp.187–213). New York: Wiley.

Stern, D. (1985) *The Interpersonal World of the Infant: A View from Psychoanalysis and Developmental Psychology.* New York: Basic Books.

Sternberg, R.J. (1991) 'Giftedness According to the Triarchic Theory of Human Intelligence.' In N. Colangelo and G.A. Davis (eds) *Handbook of Gifted Education* (pp.45–54). Needham Heights, MA: Allyn and Bacon.

Sternberg, R.J. and Lubart, T.I. (1993) 'Creative Giftedness: A Multivariate Investment Approach.' *Gifted Child Quarterly 37,* 7–15.

Stewart, K. (2002) *Helping a Child with Nonverbal Learning Disorder or Asperger's Syndrome.* Oakland, CA: New Harbinger Publications.

Stormont, M. (2001) 'Social Outcomes of Children with ADHD: Contributing Factors and Implications for Practice.' *Psychology in the Schools 38,* 521–531.

Subotnik, R.F. and Strauss, S.M. (1994/5) 'Gender Differences in Classroom Participation and Achievement.' *Journal of Secondary Gifted Education 6,* 77–85.

Szatmari, P., Archer, L., Fisman, S., Streiner, D.L., and Wilson, F. (1995) 'Asperger's Syndrome and Autism: Differences in Behavior, Cognition, and Adaptive Functioning.' *Journal of the American Academy of Child and Adolescent Psychiatry 34,* 1662–1671.

Szatmari, P., Tuff, L., Finlayson, M., and Bartolucci, G. (1990) 'Asperger's Syndrome and Autism: Neurocognitive Aspects.' *Journal of the American Academy of Child and Adolescent Psychiatry 29,* 130–136.

Szatmari, P. Offord, D. R. and Boyle, M. H. (1989) 'Ontario Child Health Study: Prevalence of Attention Deficit Disorder with Hyperactivity.' *Journal of Child Psychology and Psychiatry 30*, 219–230.

Tannock, R. (2000) 'Attention-Deficit Disorder with Anxiety Disorders.' In T.E. Brown (ed) *Attention-Deficit Disorders and Comorbidities in Children, Adolescents and Adults* (pp.125–170). Washington, DC: American Psychiatric Press.

Tannock, R., and Brown, T.E., (2000) 'Attention-Deficit Disorders with Learning Disorders in Children and Adolescents.' In T.E. Brown (ed) *Attention-Deficit Disorders and Comorbidities in Children, Adolescents and Adults* (pp. 231–295). Washington, DC: American Psychiatric Press.

Tantam, D. (1991) 'Asperger Syndrome in Adulthood.' In U. Frith (ed) *Autism and Asperger Syndrome (pp 147–183)*. New York: Cambridge University Press.

Tantam D. (2000) 'Adolescence and Adulthood of Individual with Asperger Syndrome.' In A. Klin, F.R. Volkmar, and S.S. Sparrow (eds) *Asperger Syndrome* (pp.367–397). New York: Guilford.

Taylor, M. and Carlson, S.M. (1997) 'The Relationship Between Individual Differences in Fantasy and Theory of Mind.' *Child Development 68*, 436–455.

Terman, L.M. (1925) 'Mental and Physical Traits of a Thousand Gifted Children.' *Genetic Studies of Genius (Vol. 1)*. Stanford, CA: Stanford University Press.

Terman, L.M. (1931) 'The Gifted Child.' In C. Murchison (ed) *A Handbook of Child Psychology* (pp.568–584). Worcester, MA: Clark University Press.

Thomas, A., Chess, S., and Birch, S.G. (1968) *Temperament and Behavior Disorders in Children*. New York: New York University Press.

Thompson, L.A., and Plomin, R. (1993) 'Genetic Influence on Cognitive Ability.' In K.A. Heller, F.J. Monks, and A.H. Passow (eds) *International Handbook of Research and Development of Giftedness and Talent* (pp.103–114). Oxford: Pergamon Press.

Thompson, S. (1997) *The Source for Nonverbal Learning Disorders*. East Moline, IL: LinguiSystems.

Thorndike, R.M. and Lohman, D.H. (1990) *A Century of Ability Testing*. Chicago: The Riverside Publishing Company.

Tirosh, E. and Cohen, A. (1998) 'Language Deficit with Attention-Deficit Disorder: A Prevalent Comorbidity.' *Journal of Child Neurology 13*, 493–497.

Tolan, S.S. (1985, November/December) 'The Exceptionally Gifted Child in School.' *G/C/T 41*, 22–26.

Tolan, S.S. (1987) 'Parents and "Professionals," A Question of Priorities.' *Roeper Review 9*, 184–187.

Torrance, E.P. (1966) *Torrance Tests of Creative Thinking*. Princeton, NJ: Personnel Press.

Torrance, E.P. and Safter, H.T. (1989) 'The Long Range Predictive Validity of the Just Suppose Test.' *Journal of Creative Behavior 23*, 219–223.

Ulmann, R.K., Sleator, E.K., and Sprague, R.L. (1997) *ACTeRS Manual Teacher and Parent Forms*. Champaign, IL: MetriTech.

Vilensky, J.A., Damasio, A.R., and Maurer, R.G. (1981) 'Gait Disturbances in Patients with Autistic Behavior: A Preliminary Study.' *Archives of Neurology 38*, 646–649.

Volkmar, F.R. and Klin, A. (2000) 'Diagnostic Issues in Asperger Syndrome.' In A. Klin, F.R. Volkmar, and S.S. Sparrow (eds) *Asperger Syndrome* (pp.25–71). New York: Guilford.

Volkmar, F.R., Klin, A., and Pauls, D. (1998) 'Nosological and Genetic Aspects of Asperger Syndrome.' *Journal of Autism and Developmental Disorders 28*, 457–463.

Wallace, J. (2000) 'Walter.' In A. Klin, F.R. Volkmar, and S.S. Sparrow (eds) *Asperger Syndrome* (pp.434–442). New York: Guilford.

Webb, J.T. and Dyer, S.P. (1993) 'Unusual WISC-R Patterns among Gifted Children.' Presented at the National Association of Gifted Children Annual Conference, November 5.

Webb, J.T. and Latimer, D. (1993, July) 'ADHD and Children Who Are Gifted.' (*ERIC Document No. EDO-EC-93-5.*) Reston, VA: The Council for Exceptional Children.

Webb, J.T., Meckstroth, E.A., and Tolan, S.S. (1982) *Guiding the Gifted Child: A Practical Source for Parents and Teachers.* Columbus, OH: Ohio Psychology Publishing.

Weiss, G. and Hechtman, L.T. (1993) *Hyperactive Children Grown Up, Second Edition.* New York: Guilford.

Wender, P.H. (1987) *The Hyperactive Child, Adolescent, and Adult.* New York: Oxford University Press.

Werner, E.E. (1984) 'Resilient Children.' *Young Children 40* (1), 68–72.

West, T.G. (1997) *In The Mind's Eye, Updated Edition.* Amherst, NY: Prometheus Books.

Wheeler, J. and Carlson, C. (1994) 'The Social Functioning of Children With ADD With and Without Hyperactivity: A Comparison of their Peer Relations and Social Deficits.' *Journal of Emotional and Behavioral Disorders 2*, 2–12.

White, B. (1985) 'Competence and Giftedness.' In J. Freeman (ed) *The Psychology of Gifted Children: Perspectives on Development and Education* (pp.59–73). New York: Wiley.

Whitmore, J.R. (1980) *Giftedness, Conflict and Underachievement.* Needham Heights, MA: Allyn and Bacon.

WHO (1993) *The ICD-10 Classification of Mental and Behavioral Disorders: Diagnostic Criteria for Research.* Geneva: World Health Organisation.

Willey, L.H. (1999) *Pretending to Be Normal: Living with Asperger's Syndrome.* London: Jessica Kingsley Publishers.

Williams, D. (1992) *Nobody Nowhere.* London: Transworld Publishers.

Wing, L. (1981) 'Asperger's Syndrome: A Clinical Account.' *Psychological Medicine 11*, 115–130.

Winner, E. (1996) *Gifted Children: Myths and Realities.* New York: Basic Books.

Wright, L. (1990) 'The Social and Nonsocial Behavior of Precocious Preschoolers During Free Play.' *Roeper Review 12*, 268–274.

Wright, L. and Borland, J.H. (1993) 'Using Early Childhood Developmental Portfolios in the Identification and Education of Young, Economically Disadvantaged, Potentially Gifted Students.' *Roeper Review 15*, 205–210.

Zentall, S.S., Cassady, J.C., and Javorsky, J. (2001a) 'Social Comprehension of Children with Hyperactivity.' *Journal of Attention Disorders 5*, 11–24.

Zentall, S.S., Moon, S.M., Hall, A.M. and Grskovic, J.A. (2001b) 'Learning and Motivational Characteristics of Boys with AD/HD and/or Giftedness.' *Exceptional Children 67*, 499–519.

Zimmerman, B.J. and Martinez-Pons, M.M. (1986) 'Development of a Structural Interview for Assessing Student Use of Self-Regulated Learning Strategies.' *American Educational Research Journal 23*, 614–628.

Subject index

Name index

Different Minds